CHRISTIANITY AND THE WORLD RELIGIONS

Hans Küng was born in Sursee, Switzerland, in 1928, and grew up to become one of the most brilliant, controversial and outspoken priests in the Roman Catholic Church this century.

He is highly regarded for his theological knowledge and insights, not only among Catholics but by theologians of all religious persuasions, and is also able to communicate his ideas clearly to non-theologians as well.

In December 1979 his disagreements with the Roman hierarchy came to a head when he was condemned by the Congregation for the Doctrine of Faith, mainly for his views on papal infallibility, and had his right to teach as a Catholic theologian withdrawn. He has, however, continued to teach independently at the University of Tübingen, in Germany.

Professor Küng is the author of many books, including *On Being A Christian*; *The Council: Reform and Reunion*; *The Church* – which was dedicated to the then Archbishop of Canterbury, Michael Ramsey; *Infallible?*; *Why Priests?*; *What Must Remain in the Church*; *Does God Exist?* and *Eternal Life*.

Professors U. van Ess, H. von Strietencron and H. Bechert are also on the staff of the University of Tübingen.

Books by the same author
available from both Collins
and Fount Paperbacks

DOES GOD EXIST?
ETERNAL LIFE?
ON BEING A CHRISTIAN

available only as a
Fount Paperback

INFALLIBLE?

Hans Küng

Josef van Ess
Heinrich von Stietencron
Heinz Bechert

CHRISTIANITY AND THE WORLD RELIGIONS

*Paths of Dialogue with Islam,
Hinduism, and Buddhism*

Translated by Peter Heinegg

Collins
FOUNT PAPERBACKS

The original German edition of this book was first published
under the title *Christentum und Weltreligionen* in 1985 by
R. Piper Verlag, München

First published in English in 1986 by Doubleday & Company, Inc.,
New York, and in 1987 by Collins Publishers, London
This edition published by Fount Paperbacks, London in 1987

Made and printed in Great Britain by
William Collins Sons & Co. Ltd, Glasgow

Contents

Hans Küng: Toward Dialogue

There are now 4.8 billion people living on this earth. Of these, 1.4 billion are nominally Christian—almost one third of the world's population. That compares with 723 million Muslims, 583 million Hindus, and 274 million Buddhists. We can already see from these figures, calculated over many years of painstaking research by the staff of the World Christian Encyclopedia (Oxford, 1982), just how much is at stake here.

Whether I am a Christian or a non-Christian, what is my attitude toward these other religions? That question is getting continually more urgent, since not only the geographical horizon of our religious world (thanks to the great voyages of discovery) but its historical horizon as well (thanks to modern history of religions) have expanded enormously. In a world so closely knit together, the old religious boundaries are becoming increasingly blurred; and we find large numbers of people with different faiths even in our own country, in our home town, in our factories and schools, often on our own block. What indeed is my attitude toward these other religions?

En Route to a Global Ecumenical Consciousness

Apart from a few specialists, the knowledge we have of the other religions is still very limited. If we compare interreligious dialogue (between the world religions) with interconfessional dialogue (between the various Christian churches), we have to admit we are now roughly at the same stage in interreligious dialogue that we were about fifty years ago in interconfessional dialogue.

It is surely a slow process, but we are overcoming our isolation and learning to grasp the reality of the others. That means that after a period of hot and then cold wars, and finally a time of polite truce, rather than peaceful coexistence, we may be standing today on the verge of a new, fourth epoch, one of *"pro-existence."* Despite all the obvious obstacles and difficulties, we seem to be witnessing the slow *awakening of global ecumenical consciousness* and the beginning of a serious religious dialogue between both leading experts and broad-based representatives. This is possibly one of the most important phenomena of the twentieth century, though its consequences will likely not make themselves felt until the twenty-first century—should humanity live to see it. And so we have less reason than ever today for understanding ecumenism in a narrow, constricted, ecclesiocentric fashion: Ecumenism should not be limited to the *community of the Christian churches;* it must include the *community of the great religions,* if ecumenism—in accordance with the original meaning of *oikumene*—is to refer to the whole "inhabited world."

A *dialogue* will be presented here between Christianity and those world religions that carry a special weight because of their vitality, their broad distribution, and their large membership. From any perspective, *Islam, Hinduism,* and *Buddhism* would have to qualify as world religions alongside *Christianity.* Neither Judaism nor the religions of China can be given the attention they deserve, primarily because of time and space limitations. Furthermore, the religions of *China*—Confucianism and Taoism particularly, as well as Buddhism—are scarcely able to find expression nowadays, since in the People's Republic, freedom of religion is granted only in theory. On the other hand, *Judaism,* which is a spiritual world power despite its mere .4 percent share of the world's population, would have to be treated separately, since Jewish-Christian dialogue, because of Christianity's Jewish origins, raises some quite specific problems (I myself have taken a position on these issues in various publications). Still, many concerns (belief in one God) and problems (legal piety) of Judaism will come up in connection with Islam. Beyond that, an effort will be made to frame the response to the great religions coming out of India—Hinduism and Buddhism—as far as possible in terms of the common Jewish-Christian-Islamic tradition.

Conversation between Christianity and Islam, Christianity and Hinduism, and Christianity and Buddhism had not been going on in earnest until this century. This book will attempt to draw up something like an *interim balance sheet* of the twentieth-century conversation, in order to stimulate further discussion.

This dialogue is the transcript of an actual dialogue that took place in the summer semester of 1982 at the University of Tübingen within the framework of its General Studies program. It took the form of twelve lecture-dialogues before a large audience. These lectures were thoroughly revised and in parts expanded for publication wherever we took into account the discussions that followed the double-lectures, but the character of the live, face-to-face lecture-dialogues was by and large maintained. My fellow author Heinz Bechert, because of an imminent journey to Southeast Asia, was not able to agree with me on the definitive and greatly expanded form of my "Christian Responses" to his contributions on Buddhism. As we didn't want to miss the schedule publication deadline, Alois Payer, Lic. Phil., kindly took over as my technical adviser on Buddhism at that stage.

These lecture-dialogues, delivered one after the other by two professors from different disciplines, were and are didactic and practical, a bold *experiment*. For both intrinsic and technical reasons, it seemed best to begin the dialogue with specialized academic representatives of Islamic, Hindu, and Buddhist studies and a spokesman for Christian theology. Later on it will surely be possible to plan for lecture-dialogues at universities engaging Christian theologians and believing adherents of the religions in question, not just scholarly experts on foreign cultures and religions. But the first step has to come before the second. During our work, we saw clearly that each of the religions had to be presented not just objectively but also sympathetically. Such an effort at dialogue makes sense only if the individual religions recognize themselves in their portraits. But does this dialogue make any sense for Christian theology as well?

WHAT IS RELIGION?

More and more theologians nowadays consider it a disaster that as a result of the theological revolution after World War II and of the influence of Karl Barth, Christian theology on one side and the history of religion, the phenomenology of religion, and religious studies in general have gone their separate and often mutually hostile ways. Theology can go along with Barth's legitimate grand design without closing its door on the scientific study of religion or encapsulating itself within the prickly defenses of Christian "faith"—as opposed to mere "religions." Splendid isolation is no longer possible for any religion. The religious, moral, and aesthetic values of billions of men and women outside Christianity cannot and should not be ignored any longer. Conversely, however, more and more scholars of religion, with the Americans in the lead, are acknowledging that in the long run they mustn't dodge the normative questions of truth and values.

Religion is as hard to define as art. "I knew what it was until you asked me to explain it," we might answer, as Augustine did (to the question

"What is time?"). Often enough we find completely different material lumped together under a single heading. The term "religion" is a problematic one in many respects, and has been subjected by both scholars of religion and theologians to critical study. This is not the place to enter into this debate, with its many broad ramifications. It's enough to recognize that "religion" is an analogous, although not a wholly equivocal, term that encompasses similar and dissimilar elements. The dissimilarity can be seen above all in the fact that the term has to cover practically every option, from belief in many gods, through belief in one God, all the way to rejection of belief in God (in early Buddhism). Likewise these lecture-dialogues between scholars of religion and a theologian presuppose no normative concept of religion. And yet it's important for the Christian theologian to give an account of his use of the term "religion" —in the form, so to speak, of a working hypothesis. This is possible because, with all the dissimilarities, some similarities may also be observed, though I can only outline them here.

Religion always deals with an experiential *"encounter with the holy"* (R. Otto, F. Heiler, M. Eliade, G. Mensching), whether this "sacred reality" be understood as power, as forces (spirits, demons, angels), as (a personal) God, as (an impersonal) Divine, or an ultimate reality *(nirvāna)*. Hence "religion" can be paraphrased, for the purposes of our dialogue, as follows: Religion is a *social and individual relationship, vitally realized in a tradition and community* (through doctrine, ethos, and generally ritual as well), *with something that transcends or encompasses man and his world:* with something always to be understood as the utterly final, true reality (the Absolute, God, nirvāna). In contrast to philosophy, religion is concerned at once with a *message of salvation* and the *way to salvation.*

For this is precisely what the scientific studies of religion have made clear: Religion is more than a purely theoretical affair, a simple matter of the past, a problem for researchers in archives and specialists in ancient texts. No, religion, as sketched out here, is always far more than this, a *lived life,* inscribed in the hearts of men and women, and hence for all religious persons something that is supremely contemporary, pulsing through every fiber of their everyday existence. Religion can be lived traditionally, superficially, passively, or in a profoundly sensitive, committed, dynamic way. Religion is a *believing view of life, approach to life, way of life,* and therefore a *fundamental pattern* embracing the individual and society, man and the world, through which a person (though only partially conscious of this) sees and experiences, thinks and feels, acts and suffers, everything. It is a transcendentally grounded and immanently operative *system of coordinates,* by which man orients himself intellectually, emotionally, and existentially. Religion provides a comprehensive meaning for life, guarantees supreme values and unconditional norms, creates a spiritual community and home.

Beyond Absolutism and Relativism

The lecture-dialogues at Tübingen between colleagues otherwise separated by the strict boundaries of separate departments unquestionably have their own peculiar charms and strains. For the theologian especially they are an intellectual adventure, since he doesn't know in advance where the dynamics of the discussion will take him. And even though both sides are presumably threatened by a certain role conflict, the theologian must get the worse of the bargain: He has a different sort of existential involvement, since he belongs to a specific tradition and community of belief. In this sort of conversation the scholar of religion can speak in a primarily narrative, descriptive, and comparative fashion. He can depict the great colorful, dramatic history of Islam, Hinduism, and Buddhism; he can elaborate and compare their eternal themes in the vicissitudes of time, while voicing (at most) some mild, marginal criticism. But it would undoubtedly not help the dialogue if the theologian followed a similar line by giving an account of the familiar history of Christianity and its traditional teaching, without professing any commitment to Christian faith and life. And a rather onerous feature of this arrangement is that the Christian theologian has to justify a position which a Christian audience thinks it knows, whereas, for many people, foreign religions still have the charm of novelty.

Despite all such difficulties, the Christian theologian must try to *build arguments,* rather than simply narrate and describe. He must painstakingly develop areas where Christianity clearly agrees or disagrees with other religions. Misunderstandings are practically unavoidable here. If, for example, you point out the merits of Muhammad and his prophetic work, you will surely be asked afterward whether you actually wish to become a Muslim. If you try to elaborate your understanding of God's sonship and the Trinity on a solid New Testament foundation in such a way that they might not strike a Jew or a Muslim from the outset as totally absurd, you will surely be reproached for departing from the usual teaching on the Trinity. Conversely, if you speak critically as a Christian theologian (always ready for self-criticism), for instance, on the problem of the law in Islam or mythology in Hinduism or monasticism in Buddhism, then you easily incur the suspicion of engaging in theological apologetics, Christian propaganda, or even arrogant condemnation.

As a theologian, I am already well aware of these problems, and hence in my "Christian Responses" I have sought to provide two things:

1. Christian self-criticism in the light of the other religions
2. Christian criticism of the other religions in the light of the Gospel,

which will naturally mean comparing like with like, not one random item with another.

Thus I have tried to walk the difficult *via media* between two extremes. On the one hand I wanted to avoid a narrow-minded, conceited *absolutism* (of Christian or Islamic provenience), which sees its own truth as "ab-solute," that is, detached from the truth of the others. I have aimed to defend neither a *standpoint of exclusivity*, which issues a blanket condemnation of the non-Christian religions and their truth, nor a *standpoint of superiority*, which rates my own religion as a priori better (in doctrine, ethics, or system). That sort of standpoint leads only to comfortable apologetics, to a closed and opinionated mind, in short to the dogmatism which thinks it already possesses the whole truth and, for precisely that reason, doesn't find it.

But at the same time neither will anyone expect me as a Christian theologian to maintain a superficial and irresponsible *relativism* (of Christian, Hindu, or Buddhist provenience) that relativizes all truth and nonchalantly equates all values and standards. I consider an *arbitrary pluralism* untenable, the view that approves and endorses without differentiation both one's own and the other religions, without calling attention to the presence in both groups of the untruth despite all the truth. I find equally untenable the *indifferentism* that exempts certain religious positions and decisions from criticism. Such an attitude leads only to cheap tolerance, to "anything goes," to a falsely understood liberalism in which one trivializes the question of truth or no longer even dares to ask it.

This, then, must be the point of departure: The boundary between true and false today, even as Christians see it, no longer runs simply *between* Christianity and the other religions, but at least in part *within* each of the religions. The principle here is that nothing of value in the other religions is to be denied, but neither is anything of no value to be uncritically accepted. On this score a consensus should be possible among representatives of the various religions. We need a dialogue with give and take, into which the deepest intentions of the religions must be introduced. Thus it must be a critical dialogue, in which all religions are challenged not simply to justify everything, but to deliver their best and most profound message. In short we need a dialogue in *mutual* responsibility and in the awareness that none of us possesses the truth "readymade," but are all on the way to the "ever greater" truth.

It is only to be expected that this will change us, change not merely our answers but our questions, too, not merely our understanding of ourselves and the world, but also our understanding of God. We should have no anxiety over this; it will make us not poorer but richer. The truth cannot be different in the different religions, but only one: through all the contradictions, we have to seek what is complementary; through all the exclusions, what is inclusive.

In this process we must concentrate in the first instance on ideas, teachings, doctrines; we have to take texts, dates, and events into cognizance, without mistaking the fact that religion is more than ideas. And yet, religious practices are often not the factor that divides religions (we shall note many refreshing and also horrifying parallels), but the ideas, teachings, dogmas, and everything that follows from them. And so we cannot know enough about one another. But no less important than knowledge are empathy and sympathy with the men and women of the various religions, who, even though in a very different way, are our fellows in this world.

What are we doing, then, in these lecture-dialogues? At a time when world peace and humanity's life together in freedom and justice are so often threatened precisely by religious tensions, the primary aim must be to broaden our *horizon of understanding and information*. For the reader with a close eye on what is going on in the world today, this book aims to offer the absolutely necessary knowledge about the great religions of the world: Islam, Hinduism, and Buddhism. It will present the findings of current research, but in the form of a broad, popular survey. Doing this, we know, is often harder for the specialist than going into a lot of technical details. (As far as possible, footnotes have been dispensed with. Instead a chronological table is provided for each religion along with a brief, select bibliography for further reading.)

The secondary aim of the book is to link the information with *discussion*. The "Christian Response" of the theologian should make clear where dialogue can be sought today—and often only sought, not necessarily found—and where the sore spots lie. Hence the goal is less to answer all specific questions and formulate every rebuttal than to create something like a *presentation of Christianity in the light of the world religions*.

Reciprocal information, reciprocal discussion, and reciprocal transformation. Thus we can slowly arrive not at an uncritical mishmash, but at a *mutual critical enlightenment, stimulation, penetration, and enrichment* of the various religious traditions, as has already been seen, in theory and practice, for some time now, between the various confessional traditions in Christianity itself. Indeed this should be the way leading to the sort of understanding between religions that doesn't give rise to a unified world religion, but that, after so many hot and cold wars, with their countless casualties, seeks to bring about a genuine state of peace.

A.
Islam and Christianity

Chronology

Ca. 570 Birth of Muhammad

Ca. 613 Beginning of Muhammad's mission

622 Muhammad's emigration to Me·lina (Hegira); marks the start of the Muslim Era

630 Conquest of Mecca

632 Death of Muhammad

632–61 The four "rightly guided" caliphs (Abū Bakr, 'Umar, 'Uthmān, and 'Alī)

635 Conquest of Damascus

638 Conquest of Jerusalem

639–42 Conquest of Egypt and Persia; beginning of the conquest of North Africa

661–750 The Umayyad caliphate

711–14 Conquest of Spain; crossing of the Jaxartes (modern Syr Darya); invasion of the Indus Valley

732 Battle of Poitiers

750–1258 The Abbasid caliphate

756 Beginnings of the Umayyad dynasty in Spain

762 Foundation of Bagdad

Ca. 850 First evidence of the spread of Islam to Indonesia and China

873 Disappearance of the last (twelfth) Shī'ite imam

970 Construction of the Al Azhar mosque, in Cairo

1096–99 The First Crusade

1099 The Crusaders take Jerusalem

1058–1111 al-Ghazzālī (Algazel)

1187 Reconquest of Jerusalem by Saladin

1212 Battle of Las Navas de Tolosa; beginning of the decline of Islamic domination in the Iberian Peninsula

1258 Conquest of Bagdad by the Mongols; end of the Abbasid caliphate from the thirteenth century onward; spread of mystical orders

1453 The Ottomans capture Constantinople; end of the Byzantine Empire

1492 Fall of the kingdom of Granada; end of Islamic rule in Spain; expulsion of the Jews and Muslims from Spain

1501–1732 Rule of the Safavids in Iran, which becomes definitively Shī'ite

1798 ●Bonaparte in Egypt; first contacts of the Islamic world with European science

Second half of the nineteenth century   Weakening of the Ottoman Empire; establishment of European colonies and protectorates on Islamic territory (India, Egypt, North Africa)

1817–92   Bahā' ullah, founder of Bahaism

Ca. 1840–1908   Mīrzā Ghulām Ahmad, founder of Ahmadīya

1917   Balfour Declaration: England promises a "national home" for people of the Jewish faith in Palestine

1923–38   Secularization of Turkey under Atatürk

Post World War II   Black Muslims in the U.S.A.

I.
Muhammad and the Qur'an: Prophecy and Revelation

1. *Josef van Ess:* Islamic Perspectives

A BAD IMAGE AND ITS CONSEQUENCES

Interest in Islam goes way back, but it hasn't been supported by reliable information. The things one hears or reads in the media about Islam, like the things intellectuals generally have to say about it, are alarming. Alarming in a double sense: first, because of the bias and prejudices that these judgments betray, and second because of the demonizing accent with which they are rendered. Nobody is afraid of Buddhism or Hinduism; vis-à-vis Islam, however, fear is the normal attitude. And this doesn't date just from the oil crisis and the Islamic Revolution. Even in the Middle Ages and the early modern period, broad public interest in Islam thrived particularly when there was something to fear: when the wave of conquest from the Crusades was subsiding, and later during the Turkish wars. In this sort of climate, stereotypes flourish; the desire for information is all too quickly satisfied by generalizations and hasty conclusions. Around the beginning of the twelfth century, when Guibert of Nogent came to speak briefly about Muhammad in his *Gesta Dei per Francos,* he may have garbled his name and pushed him a few centuries forward in time, but he was not to be denied the chance to reproduce the usual hostile image. He knew that he hadn't verified his assertions. His only source, as he admits, was the *plebeia opinio,* the opinion of the man on the street. But, he thought, "it doesn't make any difference if we speak ill of someone whose wickedness exceeds all measure anyway."

Now we know that this sort of thing no longer appears in the media, and we know too that all of us, with the theologians leading the way, have come to think ecumenically. The Second Vatican Council, in fact, issued a declaration on the Muslims, and one can be sure that wherever Catholic Christians and Muslims meet for dialogue, it will be quoted in the introductory speeches. But, for all that, the *plebeia opinio* has yet to be eradicated; its anti-Islamic clichés lie deep in the subconscious and often meet with unanimous approval, for example in newspaper cartoons. This is because Islam doesn't form part of our cultural heritage. Until recently there was practically never any mention of it in the schools, whether in history, social studies, or religion classes. Teachers were— and still are—hardly prepared to handle the subject. Of course, the situation is much the same with the other world religions as well. But Islam does not enjoy the aura of transfiguring distance and exotic magic that surrounds the image of Indian religions in the mind of the general public—it has always been too close to us. It shares this fate with Judaism. Judaism, Christianity, and Islam have lived since time immemorial at close quarters; and they are likewise so closely related in a structural sense as religions of revelation, that tensions and petty rivalries have been common. In recent days, to be sure, it has become customary to stress the legacy of Abraham shared by all three religions, but each of them in its own way finds it hard to abandon its claims to a transcendent status; and it strikes me as still far from certain that they are at all capable of abandoning them. As for Christianity, we can say that it has most notably changed its relation to Judaism. This change, though, was initiated not by theology but by historical and political events, and in any case it has affected only Western thinking; if one wishes to hear Islam and Judaism still lumped together as diabolical forces, one need only talk to Middle Eastern Christians.

POSITION IN TIME AS A STANDARD OF VALUE

One important factor in the relations between the three religions is their temporal sequence. The two later religions view themselves as, respectively, abolishing and superseding their predecessor(s). By contrast, the oldest, Judaism, proceeds on the assumption that God has spoken only once, to a definite partner, whom he thereby chose forever. This approach creates a ticklish problem especially for the middle religion, Christianity. The well-known formulas by which it defines itself over against Judaism (the "new covenant," etc.) and rejects the Torah are applied in turn by Islam to Christianity.

Islam, too, interprets God's plan for humanity in a linear fashion: There is no question of its arriving late on the scene, only of forward progress. Earlier religions are preliminary stages, not useless, but imperfect. For a long time Islam felt that this view was confirmed by its history. It had occupied the heartland of Judaism and broad stretches of the world empire that Christianity saw at the time as its primary representative, namely Byzantium. This "imperialistic" vision is familiar to us from Christianity; only, there it is focused analogously on the Jews: They were, it was said, punished with a worldwide diaspora and political impotence for having murdered Christ. But of course both these historical images have fallen apart as a result of developments since the nineteenth century: The Islamic world won its independence from Europe, and Europe, in the wake of its self-destruction in the Second World War, has grown strong again. By retaking and settling Palestine, Jews were able, in the region they controlled, to cast Christians and Muslims in the role of tolerated and subject minorities. The Christian world, once weak vis-à-vis Islam and strong vis-à-vis the Jews, has switched those positions.

But these are late and perhaps ephemeral developments. A religion's sense of itself is largely determined by its past, a rule that holds especially true for Islam. The past with which it identifies, and which it is always reliving afresh, essentially coincides with the fate of the earliest Islamic community and the events of the first century after the Hegira. That was when it realized its greatest achievements and experienced its chosenness. I shall therefore limit myself to this epoch in the brief historical exposition preceding my systematic presentation of Islam.

MUHAMMAD, AN "ARABIAN PROPHET"

Muhammad's life followed a quite different course from Jesus'. Jesus came to grief in his earthly existence; Muhammad was a success. The disappointments Muhammad knew came at the beginning of his career; at the end came the conquest of Mecca and the unification of the Arabian Peninsula beneath his leadership. His background was not as humble as Jesus': his father was a merchant, although he died before the birth of his son, and Muhammad's mother was dependent upon the clan for support. In this environment he got his first commercial experience. Since his situation didn't allow him to set up in business on his own, he entered the service of a merchant's widow, whose confidence he soon won. Without him she could scarcely have run her operation; he went on business trips for her, reportedly to Syria. It comes as no surprise that she eventually offered to marry him. At this point he was around twenty-five, she was about forty, a somewhat unusual combination under the circumstances then. Nonetheless he had many children from her, four daughters and two or three sons. All the sons, however, died early, a highly important fact in the development of Islam. Muhammad's world, then, was not that of a nomad, but of a sedentary burgher. Islam came into existence not in the wilderness but in the city—a city, moreover, at the intersection of several caravan routes. Mecca lay in the path of the incense trade, a decidedly luxurious line of business, in which the profits piled up, from Yemen to the Mediterranean Basin, where the pleasant fragrance was appreciated in temples, churches, and private dwellings.

With trade, therefore, came riches, and with riches, social discontent. For although the Meccans were by no means Bedouin, they were incorporated into the tribal structure of the world around them. The hierarchy of this world and the solidarity that went along with it were now becoming undermined by the spread of an egoism based on personal possessions. The solution to this tension clothed itself in the language people used then to speak of values and existential predicaments: the language of religion.

Old Arabian polytheism couldn't cope with the problem, because it was bound up with the tribal system through the local cults. Above all, however, it was too thoroughly oriented to the here and now. "The unbelievers say," according to the Qur'an, "there is only our life in this world. We die and live, and only time works our destruction." (Sura 45, 24) For quite some time there had been men and women who felt the inadequacy of this attitude and of the religion that supported it. Still, the majority of them saw no reason to give up the old faith, for the tribal shrines and the pilgrimages people made to them afforded a certain sense of identity and—in connection with the fairs held at pilgrimage time—many economic benefits. But the way was being paved for the idea of a judgment in the Beyond, a day of reckoning outside this world, in which everyone would be called to account for his transgressions.

This was the message of Judaism and Christianity, which had spread all over the fringes of the Arabian Peninsula and had even managed to form isolated communities in Arabia itself. Judaism was centered in Palestine and Iraq, but since the destruction of Jerusalem by Titus and the collapse of the Bar Kochba uprising under Hadrian, it had also gained a firm footing in various oases of northwestern Arabia. Christianity, which was the predominant religion in Syria and Ethiopia, had been able to found an episcopal see farther toward the south, in the oasis of Najrān. There, in the territory of the old kingdom of Saba (modern-day Yemen), the two religions had long been in hostile competition. They were tools in the power politics of the two superpowers of the day: Byzantium and the Sassanid dynasty. The Byzantines used Christian Ethiopia as a base for expansion into Yemen; the Persians came down to the Gulf or from Oman and allied themselves with the Jews. Both had a stake in the incense traffic; the Byzantines were also interested in trade through the Red Sea, by which, once mariners learned how to handle the monsoon, connections could be made to the markets in India, thereby avoiding the land route by way of Iran, which was bristling with toll stations.

These circumstances suggest what it meant for an Arab when he converted to either of the two religions: he linked up with one of the great civilizations in the world around him. But he was also submitting to a foreign power. He was taking sides in a political contest, and in a certain sense he was losing his independence. But people wanted their independence in the Arabian Peninsula, especially in Mecca. The welfare of the city rested on its autonomy, which was another version of the Bedouin ideal of freedom.

FORM AND CONTENT OF THE NEW REVELATION

Thus, while some features of Jewish or Christian thought may have gained ground, there were only a limited number of conversions. And when Muhammad took up the idea of judgment beyond the grave, though he did so with the awareness that he was copying a Jewish and Christian model, he was also convinced that he had given it a new formulation, because he presented it in Arabic. For the first time, revelation was couched in an immediately comprehensible idiom. There was as yet no Arabic translation of the Bible. Christian monks read their sacred texts in Aramaic (Syriac), the Jews in Hebrew. For a long time, Muhammad thought the originality of his message was in its language. He was an Arabian prophet, his book of revelation was an "Arabic Qur'an."

To his polytheistic contemporaries in Mecca, of course, he also brought something substantially new: monotheism, and linked to it eschatology. With that, he took aim at the social abuses I mentioned before: He pointed out to the merchants of Mecca that they would someday have to open their books for the great inspection. He complained that men boasted of their possessions and in their greed wished to have still more, that they robbed widows and orphans of the little they had left. He knew what it meant to be poor, for, as he had been told in an early revelation, "Didn't [God] find you as an orphan and shelter [you], find you gone astray and lead you on the right way, find you in need and make you rich? Therefore you shall not do violence to the orphan, nor shall you assault the beggar." (Sura 93, 6–9) Apocalypses got a good reception then, as they do today, and for similar reasons.

Still we must resist the modern obsession with reducing everything to the social question. Muhammad was no revolutionary, but a prophet. He had no wish to alter possessory interests. "He didn't preach against wealth in itself but against the mentality of those who think they are entirely on their own and have no higher power to answer to." (Paret, *Muhammad und der Koran*, 5th ed., 1980, p. 42) And although he gathered the weak about him, many young people, and even slaves, he also knew that he couldn't do without the powerful, and he considered slavery to be a natural institution. Whenever and wherever there is injustice on earth, God is involved, but he will not bestow justice until the next world. From the very beginning, expectation of a Last Judgment was bound up with faith in a kindly Creator. For a while there was some controversy over which of these theological notions came first, but it wasn't worth the trouble: They are correlative parts of one and the same religious experience. Muhammad's message cannot be derived wholly and simply from either social conditions or the systematic context of the older revelatory religions. And no one who wants to keep the avenues open to conversation with Muslims should even try to make such an inference.

Muhammad didn't become aware of his vocation until rather late in life. Tradition says he was already about forty years old, an age that Jesus never lived to see. The prophetic type that he represents is difficult to identify. The Qur'an speaks of visions, but we don't know whether they were present at the beginning of his career. There are reports of ecstatic experiences. During these, Muhammad apparently covered himself with a veil, as other visionaries are known to have done. But the Qur'an gives only hints about all this, and later exegesis has often obscured the situation still further. One vexing difficulty here is that the Qur'an, in contrast to the Gospels, doesn't follow any chronological order.

The single reliable criterion we have is diction: short, even elliptically abbreviated statements, reminiscent of loud cries and introduced by mysterious oaths, held together by striking prose rhymes, gripping images in rapid succession—this is the style of the prophets as the Arabs knew them. When he first appeared, Muhammad's closest kinship was probably with such men; he knew nothing at all about prophecy in the Old Testament sense. Such figures as Jeremiah and Amos, who make so strong an impression on us, never played any role in his thinking; for that matter, they had a quite marginal position in Judaism at this time. His contemporaries generally compared him with soothsayers or possessed persons—or with the poets, whom people thought of as likewise possessed or inspired by a jinni. Muhammad himself indignantly rejected this idea, no doubt precisely because he was conscious of how depressingly close he was to these false prototypes. Naturally he was right when he stressed the differences between himself and them: What he was presenting had nothing to do with divination, and above all he accepted no payment for his visions. He was acting under a holy compulsion.

The community in Mecca remained small; and the resistance of influential groups stiffened. Muhammad began to speak of his precursors: of Moses and Jesus, but also of Noah, Abraham, Lot, and even the prophetic figures of the mythic Arabian past. And he shaped them all to fit his archetypal model: They had all brought their contemporaries a message from God, and yet they had all been rebuffed; but in the end their opponents had been overtaken by divine vengeance. A prophet's life is hard, but God is on his side and ultimately He would prove it. This was the origin of the legends of punishment that are so characteristic of the Qur'an. The Christian reader often finds them disturbing; he thinks he has a different and clearer notion of the context from what he has read in the Old Testament. But we are not dealing with historical representation. These accounts were already in existence, and Muhammad could probably assume that his audience was familiar with some of them. The model for his procedure was a typological understanding of sacred history, which was also common in Judaism and Christianity at the time. Only certain isolated points—and in this case always the same ones—are accentuated; others recede into the background or become distorted.

The Departure to Medina

Unfortunately, the divine vengeance on the pagans of Mecca was taking its time. Muhammad would have been forgotten like many other nameless prophets before and after him, or like his competitors, who appeared among the Arabian tribes not far from him and around the same time, men whom Islamic tradition recorded in malicious commentaries—he would have gone under as they did if he hadn't changed his base of operations.

This step is known as the Hegira, and it was so decisive that to this day Muslims—apart from the Libyans, who in a recent and no doubt only temporary move have tried another date—begin their chronology with it. Hegira is sometimes rendered as "flight," but this is a false translation and misses the facts of the matter. What is meant is an emigration. Hegira had all along been the method by which a dissident group renounced its membership in the tribal federation and went off to settle elsewhere. This also meant that both communities no longer felt bound, in their relations with each other, to the intratribal norms and decencies. They could count on war.

This consequence was clear to everyone as Muhammad gradually sent his followers on the road to Medina, some 350 kilometers away, and then himself followed after. The Meccans didn't simply let this exodus take place, relieved that they no longer had to listen to unpleasant talk about a judgment in the hereafter. Rather, they tried with all their might to stop it. But first Muhammad had to come to terms with his new allies. He had chosen his destination cleverly. The two important Arabian tribes of Medina were at enmity with each other; they saw him as an arbitrator who kept the peace between them and to whom they were both indebted.

But along with the Arabs there was another element in the population: three Jewish tribes that had resided there from ancient times and practiced agriculture. They constituted a test that Muhammad's self-concept would have to pass. For previously in Mecca he had had to deal only with polytheists; the idea that monotheists, too, might not agree with him had never entered his mind. But that is exactly what happened. The Jews met him with icy reserve and ironic hauteur. And so the battle against Mecca was accompanied by increasingly bitter arguments with his halfhearted Jewish allies. Ultimately Muhammad triumphed on both fronts: after many ups and ·lowns, he conquered Mecca toward the end of his life by means of a highly adroit policy of isolation; the Jews were driven out of Mecca, and some of them, in keeping with the customary martial law, were sold into slavery or executed.

These events will not be recounted in detail, since that isn't our concern. The important thing for our purposes is, *first,* that in the end Muhammad actually got the success he had believed in from the start even in moments of desperate loneliness. When he died, not only had the cities of Mecca and Medina accepted Islam, but so had the tribes in the wilderness and the inhabitants of southern Arabia; and the first skirmishes had begun with Byzantine border troops in East Jordan; the *second* important point is the consequences that Muhammad's relationship to the Jews of Medina and the Meccan aristocracy would have for his teaching. His disappointment over the Jews led to a change in the direction of prayer: Whereas Muslims had hitherto bowed toward Jerusalem, Muhammad now chose Mecca instead.

Here we can already see that even after breaking with it, he couldn't do without his old home town and its cult, which was the religious and political center of the peninsula. The pilgrimage to the Ka'ba became, along with most of its pagan customs, a constituent part of Islamic ritual. The other shrines were destroyed, but after the occupation of Mecca the Ka'ba was only purified. Even the historical was adjusted to include the Ka'ba, with the help of a cult legend that picture had most likely been long associated with it. The Ka'ba, says the Qur'an, was founded by Abraham, who had stayed in Mecca with his son Ishmael in remote antiquity. With Ishmael, not with Isaac—the son of Hagar, whom she bore in the wilderness, had already been incorporated into the tribal genealogy by pre-Islamic Arabs. This doubtless reflects a power shift in favor of the ruling family in Mecca, the Quraish.

But Abraham, the father, was now no longer just another prophet— and still less just a patriarch, which was never Muhammad's view of him —but the first monotheist, even before Moses and Jesus proclaimed the two great monotheistic religions. Muhammad established both geographical and theological ties with Abraham. Islam had thus ceased to be the latecomer in the family of revelatory religions, the one that accepted and agreed with the ideas of the others; now it was the primeval revelation that had been accepted by Moses and Jesus and, logically speaking, could only be falsified by their followers—unless they converted to Islam.

MUHAMMAD'S PROPHETIC IDENTITY

Thus there can be no doubt: Muhammad never thought he had brought anything *fundamentally* new; he had merely brought something new *to his people*—and that was only because the first proclamation had fallen into oblivion. Islam is a religion of reform. What is new is at the same time the oldest thing of all, a primeval truth that God had written down in a heavenly book and that is, as it were, forever being recopied. In this process the prophets are only messengers, mouthpieces through whom God himself speaks. They may be chosen, but they remain human beings, with all their weaknesses. Revelation doesn't transform them; rather, it passes through them. "I am only a mortal, as you are," says Muhammad in the Qur'an at God's command. "To me it has been revealed that your God is One God." (Sura 41, 5) The revelation granted him came only as an undeserved, inexplicable grace: "If We willed, We could take away that / We have revealed to thee, then thou / wouldst find none . . . to guard / thee against Us, / excepting by some mercy of thy Lord." (Sura 17, 86 f.)

Hence he has no knowledge of hidden things that lie outside the scope of revelation: "Say," God bids him, "I am not an innovation among / the Messengers, and I know not what / shall be done with me or with you. / I only follow what is revealed to me; / I am only a clear warner." (Sura 46, 9) He runs the danger of falling into error and sin. When he was making no headway at all in Mecca, he is supposed to have given in one time to the temptation to compromise with the polytheistic pantheon; after which, God himself upbraided him in a revelation that strikes us as rather cryptic. (See Sura 17, 73 f.) He cannot work miracles: "They [the unbelieving Meccans] say, 'We will not believe thee till / thou makest a spring to gush forth from / the earth for us, / or till thou possessest a garden / of palms and vines, and thou makest / rivers to gush forth abundantly / all amongst it, / or till thou makest heaven to fall, / as thou assertest, on us in fragments, / or thou bringest God and the angels / as a surety . . . Say: 'Glory be / to my Lord! Am I aught but a mortal, / a Messenger?' " (Sura 17, 90–93)

Muhammad's testimony about himself speaks clearly. The lesson all Muslims gather from it is that one must distinguish between the messenger and his message. Here, they will argue, lies the mistake committed by Christian theology: It has allowed the message to be injected into the messenger, so that the word of God transformed Jesus himself into the divine Word, the Logos. This doesn't prevent Muslims from conceding that Jesus performed miracles (the Qur'an makes explicit reference to them). But they are only signs that God worked in Jesus and on his behalf, miracles to confirm his mission; they do not attest his superhuman nature. A prophet must not be a miracle worker; revelation itself is the miracle. "They [the unbelievers] say, 'Why have signs not been sent / down upon him [Muhammad] from his Lord?' Say: / 'The signs are only from God, and I am only a plain warner.' / What, is it not sufficient for them that / We have sent down upon thee the Book / that is recited to them?" (Sura 29, 50 f.)

THE NOTION OF INSPIRATION

Scripture is the essential thing: God reveals himself in a book. And that is how Islam views the religions that precede it: Judaism and Christianity are "religions of the Book," their adherents are "possessors of Scripture," literally "people of the Book." This lends them nobility; they partake in the eternal, unchanging, revealed truth, which is likewise contained in a Book, the primeval heavenly Scripture. But it also deprives them of their historical concreteness. The Old Testament dwindles to the Pentateuch and the Psalms (which were sent down as a revelation to David, just as if he were a prophet in the Islamic fashion). In addition, all historical evolution stops short, leaving only a series of edifying examples. Jesus' life and activity fade away before his preaching, and he preaches what all prophets preach: monotheism.

Of course, this scripturalization of religion was nothing new; Judaism and Christianity had displayed the same tendency ever since the establishment of the biblical canon, if not before. Once again, Islam was only following a model whose consequences it pursued, as it did with monotheism, to the radical limit. Nowhere else, if we are to believe Muslim tradition, did the process of canon formation move more swiftly than in Islam. A generation after the death of the Prophet—under the third caliph, 'Uthmān, and at his prompting—the text of the Qur'an, at least in its consonantal skeleton, had been fixed in the form we know today. Versions that differed from it, venerable copies that were sometimes less complete (we would very much like to know whether they contained unwelcome heterodox material), were reportedly all burned.

Since then, God has ceased to speak to man. There is no Holy Spirit—not, at least, in the Christian sense—continuing to work in the life of the community. Muhammad was, the Qur'an tells us, the "seal of the prophets," which was early understood to mean that none other would come after him. But the Muslims are not cut off from the Word of God, for the Qur'an not only interprets what God has said but contains God's *ipsissima verba*. Each and every denomination of Islam believes in Muhammad's verbal inspiration. This was a logical result of the Islamic notion of prophecy, and we have already seen it taken for granted at every point when God turns to Muhammad with the imperative "Say." Islamic theology is thus spared the trouble of searching the Qur'an for the authentic sayings of Muhammad; and only an unbelieving student of Islamics could claim that the utterances of the Qur'an reflect the faith of the earliest Muslim community.

So God has actually *not* stopped talking to man; it's just that he doesn't say anything new any more. In his Word, the Qur'an, the Muslim comes closer to God than anywhere else. For the Christian, the most intimate experience of God takes place in the Eucharist, because Christ is the Word made flesh. The Muslim experiences God in the recitation of the Qur'an, because the Qur'an is the Word made book. Muslims, therefore, devote themselves to the Word with much greater passion than we are accustomed to doing. We have gotten used, at least since the days of the liturgical reform, to the idea that religious texts can be manipulated. People always want to hear something new—and not only in the Gregorian melodies of the Kyrie or in the intercessory prayers, but sometimes in the canon itself. Muslims, by contrast, are absorbed in listening to a message that is always the same, continually meditating on it afresh as they hear it recited.

For ages, Christians have known Scripture only in translation. The Church used the Old Testament only in the form of the Vulgate, and even Protestantism did not return to the original text, creating instead only a new translation. The Gospels, or part of them, have not even been preserved in their original versions. Muslims, on the contrary, maintain that the Qur'an is fundamentally untranslatable. Though in recent years translations—into Turkish, say—have been prepared, they are considered only aids to understanding the Arabic text. This translation first made its way into the liturgy during the time of Kemal Atatürk; in the meantime, that step has been undone. I do not wish to slide over the fact that a number of translations have acquired a sacrosanct character for Christians, like that of the Qur'an for Muslims. Two notable examples would be the King James Bible and the Luther Bible. But, as history has shown, these versions are not irreplaceable; they can be—in fact they positively demand to be—adapted to the mentality of a later period.

To overstate the point, Christians feel closer to various interpretations of the Bible than to the text itself. And it is certainly no accident that Catholic liturgical reform has brought back the homily. Islam, of course, is familiar with preaching, but as an element of the liturgy it plays a different role. In the early years, it had a political function; it was the prerogative of the ruler or governor, who invoked religious formulas to secure the obedience of his subjects before God and man. Nowadays the sermon is at times an instrument of religious revolution, but that is only the other side of the same coin. Preaching in Islam has hardly ever had an exegetical function, just as with prayer the idea is not to interpret Scripture but to recall it to mind with familiar phrases. Christians are hardly surprised to hear the names of Nietzsche, Sartre, and other dubious saints invoked from liberal pulpits, but for Muslims that would be an unpardonable breach of settled limits.

THE MIRACULOUSNESS OF THE QUR'AN

Actually exegesis *can* be found in Islam, precisely as in Christianity; and in many fringe groups, which have claimed legitimacy for themselves through allegorical interpretations of the Qur'an, it has at certain times infiltrated the preaching. As everywhere else, the opportunity arose to give Scripture a contemporary point or to turn it into the vehicle of new ideas; and scholars made the most of such opportunities. On the other hand, however, the tendency spread to remove the Qur'an from time altogether and to treat it as an unchangeable, for-all-intents-and-purposes perfect record of God's utterances.

Muslims pondered what God might have meant when he bade Scripture be called the only miracle. At first this was taken to refer to its content, to the miraculous predictions, prophecies in the vulgar sense of the word. And indeed the beginning of Sura 30 reads: "The Greeks [Byzantines] have been vanquished / in the nearer part of the land [i.e., Syria or Palestine]; / and, after their vanquishing, / they shall be the victors / in a few years." That was what had happened: The Persians had made broad advances into Byzantine territory, had even conquered Jerusalem, and stolen Christ's cross there. But shortly thereafter, in a grand triumphant sweep, the emperor Heraclius overthrew them and brought back the holy relic. For the Arabs, who until then had been partly dependent on both the Persians and the Byzantines, these were moving events and pointed to the future: The exhaustion of the two major powers made Islam's lightning expansion possible, to begin with.

But however striking the accuracy of this prediction, as a miracle it was not enough. In the long run it was not the contents of the Qur'an, but its linguistic form, that Muslims came to look upon as supernatural and therefore completely inimitable. God speaks Arabic, and God never makes a mistake. The consequences of this belief were incalculable: Grammar, rhetoric, and poetics were oriented to the Qur'an. What had once been the language of an ecstatic [who later had to legislate for his community], a text that had been thoroughly rearranged in the 'Uthmān edition and in many cases joined together with nothing more than fragments and remnants, now became the supreme stylistic norm. Now that language had been fixed from all eternity, it couldn't change except for the worse. Even today the Arabs are still struggling with this dilemma: They revere a language that many of them have not perfectly mastered and some of them not at all; and they speak dialects, which they can view only as the result of decadence, not of natural growth. But, for the very same reason, classical Arabic has been preserved till this day. The Qur'an is "a Book confirming, *in the Arabic tongue,* / to warn the evildoers, and good tidings / to the good-doers." (Sura 46, 12)

By contrast with Arabic, Latin developed into a number of separate languages· and as early as Pentecost, "each one heard them [the Apostles] speaking in his own language." (Acts 2:6)

THE EXALTATION OF THE PROPHET

Over the course of the centuries, the image of the Prophet has, like his language, undergone changes. But in this case the evolution has not been so straightforward. For some time the equation seems to have been accepted that however much prestige was added to the Qur'an was subtracted from the Prophet. In order to exclude any possibility that Muhammad's own ideas may have had some influence on revelation, Muslims imagined that he was illiterate. This notion was derived from a somewhat problematic term in the Qur'an that probably just means that Muhammad came from a group of people to whom no Scripture of their own had been revealed. But it was thought that the Prophet could neither read nor write, and so he could also never have picked up any knowledge of earlier scriptural revelations, of the Old or the New Testament. If, despite this, numerous parallels with the Bible can be found in the Qur'an, Muhammad can only have been inspired by God to put them there. And that, from the Muslim point of view, closed the door on any suggestion that the message of the Qur'an might be traced back through the history of religion.

This line of thought, however, was not pressed further. We might have expected that, since not only the contents but the verbal form of the Qur'an was raised above and beyond the level of human achievement, everything about the Prophet, including his natural mastery of language, would be depreciated. By this logic, just as God speaks classical Arabic, Muhammad would have had to speak a dialect. But that ran counter to the notion people had about the development of Arabic. Arabs, especially those from the Arabian Peninsula, speak good Arabic. The mistakes had crept into the language on account of the many foreigners: Aramaeans, Persians, Turks, Berbers. And the Prophet had been, it was stressed, an "Arab prophet."

In later years, Muslims were no longer so consistent in denying Muhammad's miraculous powers as he himself had been. One of the reasons for this, it seems, was Christian polemics. Christians kept insisting that by his miracles Jesus had given much better proof of his chosenness than Muhammad, and Muslim theologians responded to this challenge, forgetting that in the process they were contravening a basic tenet of the Qur'an. In augmenting the stature of Muhammad, the theologians were helped by popular tradition, which filled out the gaps in the Qur'an with all sorts of miracle stories. That the Prophet had been a mere human being was not, in the end, enough. That he had been a pagan himself for forty years was completely hushed up; that he was capable of sinning was no longer believed. Islamic mysticism then made the greatest contribution to exalting Muhammad. At times it went so far as to consider him the "perfect human being," the *"ánthropos téleios,"* whom God created before all creation and in whom the entire creation found its microcosmic pattern. But I want to put off speaking of mysticism until later. The important point here is that, even when most idealized, Muhammad always remains a creature. Anyone who would liken him to, or identify him with, God, would have thereby crossed a threshold at which the Muslim sense of identity stopped short. Incarnation, "indwelling," as it was called *(hulūl,* probably a loan translation from the Greek *enoíkesis),* has always been an abomination to Islam.

2. *Hans Küng:* A Christian Response

The success story we have heard is a truly impressive one, an account of Muhammad's ambitions and his teachings, his battles and his victories, and at the center of all that, the Qur'an—the beginnings of a world religion. We must try to understand this story from within, from the standpoint of a believing Muslim, and not only from without. Over the course of history, Islam has often been a disturbing, threatening, alarming reality for Christendom; and in fact for most Christians it still remains—almost two thousand years after Christ and fourteen hundred years after Muhammad—a sinister phenomenon, despite (and because of) our geographical nearness to it. With their finger on the pulse of contemporary life, recent popular writers have treated the resurgence of Islam once again as an ominous turning point in the history of the West.

Let's admit the fact: Islam continues to strike us as essentially foreign, as more threatening politically and economically, than either Hinduism or Buddhism, a phenomenon, in any case, that we have a hard time understanding. It surely doesn't take an expert to realize that a dense informative presentation like Professor van Ess's can be made so readily comprehensible only after a scholar has worked his way through a body of tremendously difficult material. And yet, despite all our inevitable difficulties in absorbing such information, this is precisely the task of ecumenical Christian theology: to face the challenge of Islam and work for mutual understanding.

From Ignorance Through Arrogance to Tolerance

That is a rather schematized formula to describe the attitude of Western Christendom, over the centuries, toward Islam. More than four hundred years after the appearance of Muhammad, Western Europeans still had no reliable knowledge about Islam. It was not until 1142 that the eminent abbot of Cluny, Peter the Venerable, visited Spain, which was occupied by the Arabs, and farsightedly recognizing the need for authentic textual sources, laid the foundations for serious study of Islam. He commissioned the first *translation of the Qur'an* (into Latin). But, for another five hundred years—until 1650, when the Scottish scholar Alexander Ross published his pioneering work *Pansebeia*, on the history of religion—people had a completely distorted picture of Islam, as Norman Daniel's *Islam and the West: The Making of an Image* (1960) amply demonstrates. Such a religion, Europeans thought, could only be heretical, a deliberate falsification, a blend of violence and sensuality. And Muhammad? He was an impostor, possessed by the devil, the Antichrist pure and simple. Over against this caricature of Islam it was easy to set an idealized picture of Christianity as a religion of truth, peace, love, and abstinence. The way to immunize Christians against competing belief systems was to slander the competition.

In the high Middle Ages, it is true, Europeans had felt great admiration for the superior state of Arab culture, philosophy, science, and medicine, as well as for the economic and military power of Islam. And much theological writing, such as that of Thomas Aquinas, is inconceivable without the Arabs. The Renaissance, however, saw the rise of a tendency to disparage and reject everything Arabian, including the language. This was despite the efforts of such distinguished scholars and statesmen as Juan de Segovia, Nicholas of Cusa, and Enea Silvio Piccolomini (later Pius II), who in a "moment of vision" between 1450 and 1460 (R. W. Southern, *Western Views of Islam in the Middle Ages,* 1962) had taken a new, irenic approach to the problem of Islam. Around a hundred years later, in the face of the increasing military threat to Christendom from the Turks (who were besieging Vienna in 1529) and in the same year that the Lutheran Augsburg Confession appeared, the *Pope* ordered the burning of the Arabic text of the Qur'an immediately after its publication in Venice, which was known at the time as "the whore of the Turks." For his part, Luther had spoken out in favor of translating and publishing the Qur'an, but only so that everyone could see what an accursed, shameful, desperate book it was, full of lies, fabrications, and all sorts of horrors. Adrian Reland's *De religione mohammedica* (1705), the first reasonably objective work on Islam after Ross's *Pansebeia*, was promptly placed on the Roman Index of prohibited books; but it later won the support of George Sale in his translation of the Qur'an, with its famous "Preliminary Treatise" (1734).

By now, the *Enlightenment* had won a place of honor for the idea of tolerance, which was graphically presented in Germany by Lessing's play *Nathan the Wise* (1783), with the famous parable of the three rings or religions, none of which could be positively identified as the genuine original, and the figure of the Muslim Saladin as the ideal image of the wise ruler. Few Europeans, of course, did as much to raise the popular estimation of Islam (which Voltaire had mocked) as Goethe did in his *Westöstlicher Diwan* (1819), followed in England by Thomas Carlyle's lecture "The Hero as Prophet" which caused a sensation by treating Muhammad as a sincere and honest prophet.

The nineteenth century—the century of history and of European colonial expansion—finally witnessed a tremendous upsurge in Orientalism and hence in scientific studies of Islam, which set the scene for a less polemical view of Islam on the part of Christian theologians and the Church. In the *nineteenth and twentieth centuries,* decisive progress was made on four fronts:

- A historicocritical assessment of Muhammad by scholars such as Gustav Weil, Aloys Sprenger, William Muir, Leone Caetani, Tor Andrae, Régis Blachère, and W. Montgomery Watt;
- A history of the Qur'an, still considered fundamental today, by Theodor Nöldeke, along with critical editions of the Qur'an and adequate modern translations, the work of such Islamicists as Gustav Flügel, Richard Bell, and Rudi Paret;
- Comprehensive research on Islamic culture, from liturgy and mysticism through law and customs to literature and art, conducted by such eminent scholars as Ignaz Goldziher, C. Snouck Hurgronje, and especially the great Orientalist Louis Massignon, who demanded from Christians a "spiritual Copernican revolution" and pressed for a reconciliation between the religion of hope (Judaism), the religion of love (Christianity), and the religion of faith (Islam).
- A historicocritical evaluation of the image of Jesus in the Qur'an was set in motion 150 years ago by G. F. Gerock and continued by various explorations into the history of Islamic tradition. With the wideranging, more recent studies of Henri Michaud, Geoffrey Parrinder, Heikki Räisänen and Claus Schedl (in addition to the work of Olaf H. Schumann on later Arabic-Islamic literature), this process of fairminded evaluation has once and for all replaced the old apologeticmissionary approach.

The evolution of Islamics, increasingly a joint effort by Western and Muslim scholars, is a development whose fruitfulness even outsiders can recognize. Together with the greater political and economic respect accorded the Islamic nations and the immigration of Muslims into Western Europe and America, this was the prerequisite for the *epoch-making reorientation of the Catholic Church* that is documented in the Declaration on Religion by the Second Vatican Council (1965) and that found expression after the Council in various official and unofficial Islamic-Christian conferences.

There will be no returning, then, to the old "Christian" polemics, to the policy of immunizing through slander. For more and more people, the centuries-old isolation and ignorance are becoming an impossible anachronism: Books, mass media, travel, the presence of millions of Muslim "guest workers" in Western Europe, a hundred thousand immigrants in America, have all had their effect. Contempt for the "foreign" religion is slowly giving way to understanding, ignorance is being replaced by study, and missionary campaigns by dialogue.

But this is only a beginning. All too often, Christians (and not a few Muslims) still look upon Islam as a vast monolith, a closed religious system, rather than as a living religion, a religious movement that has experienced constant change over the centuries and has acquired a high degree of inner diversity, a faith shared by concrete men and women with a broad spectrum of attitudes and feelings. The task for today is slowly to understand from within why Muslims look upon God and the world, the worship of God and the service of man, politics, law, and art through different eyes and a different sensibility than do, for example, Christians. And the first thing which must be understood is that for Muslims, even today, Islam as a religion is not just another compartment of life, or what secular-minded people like to call "the religious factor," alongside other "cultural factors." On the contrary, here we find life and religion, religion and culture woven into a living web. Islam wishes to be an all-embracing view of life, an all-involving attitude toward life, an all-determining way of life—and thus in the midst of this temporal life a way to eternal life: a *way of salvation.* Salvation? What can a Christian theologian respond to this claim?

ISLAM: A WAY OF SALVATION?

I am asking this question so directly for a number of reasons, not the least of which is the ambiguous stance taken on it by the World Council of Churches. Neither in its "Guidelines for Dialogue for Men and Women of Different Religions and Ideologies" (1977/79), nor at the most recent plenary gathering in Vancouver (1983) did the WCC manage to answer the extremely urgent question of salvation outside the Christian churches. There was no answer because its member churches are divided on the issue. But what sort of "dialogue" can one have with people who are—unless they convert—all headed for hell?

The *traditional Catholic position*, prepared in the early Christian centuries by Origen, Cyprian, and Augustine, is widely known: *Extra Ecclesiam nulla salus*—there is no salvation outside the Church, which also means that there are no prophets outside the Church. The Ecumenical *Council of Florence* (1442) had spoken unmistakably: "The holy Roman Church . . . firmly believes, confesses, and proclaims that outside the Catholic Church no one, neither heathen nor Jew nor unbeliever nor schismatic, will have a share in eternal life, but will, rather, be subject to the everlasting fire which has been prepared for the Devil and his angels, unless he attaches himself to her (the Catholic Church) before his death" (Denz 1351). That, it seemed, settled the claims of Islam, as far as Catholics were concerned, for more than twelve hundred years.

In the past few decades, of course, Catholic theology has tried to "reach a new understanding" of that uncompromising *Extra Ecclesiam* dogma, meaning, for the most part, to reinterpret it or, in fact, turn it upside down. Because of its "infallible" status, the teaching was never openly repudiated. As early as the seventeenth century, to be sure, Rome had been forced to condemn the harsh Jansenist proposition *Extra Ecclesiam nulla gratia* (There is no grace outside the Church, Denz 1295, 1379). But if there *is gratia, charis, charisma*, outside the Church, might we not also find prophecy—plainly called a "charisma" in the New Testament—outside it as well?

In any case, the traditional Catholic position is nowadays *no longer the official Catholic position*. Back in 1952 the Congregation of the Faith, in a rather paradoxical move, *excommunicated* the Catholic chaplain at Harvard, Father Leonard Feeney, S.J., for asserting, along with the old Church Fathers and the Council of Florence, that everyone outside the visible Catholic Church was damned. Finally the *Second Vatican Council*, in its Constitution on the Church (1965) declared unequivocally: "Men and women who through no fault of their own do not know the Gospel of Christ and of his Church, but who sincerely search for God and who strive to do his will, as revealed by the dictates of conscience, in deeds performed under the influence on his grace, can win eternal salvation." (Art. 16)

And here the declaration expressly mentions those who by their very origins have the most in common with Jews and Christians because of their faith in one God and the doing of his will: the Muslims.

> God's saving will also embraces those who acknowledge the Creator, and among them especially the Muslims, who profess the faith of Abraham and together with us adore the one God, the Merciful One, who will judge men on the Last Day. (Art. 16)

And so, according to Vatican II, Muslims need no longer "be subject to the everlasting fire which has been prepared for the Devil and his angels"; they "can win eternal salvation." This means that Islam, too, can be a way of salvation; perhaps not the normal, the "ordinary" way, so to speak, but perhaps a historically "extraordinary" one.

In fact, thanks to this about-face, contemporary Catholic theologians distinguish between the *"ordinary" (Christian) way of salvation* and the *extraordinary (non-Christian) ways of salvation* (sometimes, in a similar vein, between "the way" and the various "paths"). But then shouldn't we also —as a condition of possibility, as it were—be able to distinguish between "ordinary" (Christian) and "extraordinary" (or whatever) *prophets?* And on that basis would Muhammad no longer be dismissed in advance as a false, lying pseudoprophet, a fortune-teller, magician, faker, or at best just another Arabian poet—as Christians claimed for centuries—but treated as a genuine, possibly even a true prophet? But was Muhammad really a genuine or a true prophet?

MUHAMMAD: A PROPHET?

The figure of Muhammad and his message have to be seen in their historical context, a current amid the tremendous stream of the religious history of all humanity. This is the point of departure for modern-day scholarship. And the eminent expert on Islam Wilfred Cantwell Smith bids us understand this tremendous stream as a *historical continuum* in which we can observe at all points a pattern of crossovers and overlaps, interdependence and interaction, give-and-take between religions that are unquestionably different but by no means disparate. Muhammad stands at an intersection in world history where the ancient Arabian tribal religion encountered Judaism and Christianity. In this way there was from the outset a confluence of certain elements of a common religious heritage (from the idea of God to forms of piety).

And yet the case of Muhammad makes it clear that this historical continuum of the religious history of humanity must be understood— dialectically—as a continuum *in discontinuity.* Naturally a "Big Bang theory," to use Smith's ironic term, is not what we want for interpreting the history of religion: Neither for Muhammad and Islam nor for Buddha and Buddhism nor, finally, for Jesus and Christianity was there in the beginning any *creatio ex nihilo,* a sudden creation out of nothing, but a quite specific historical context that frames everything spoken and done and that guarantees a connection with all of the past and contemporary life.

On the other hand, neither would it seem right, as Smith argues, to talk about a continual creation, a single mighty stream of religion. Organic images, such as a river or a tree, tend to make us overlook the fact that the religious history of the human race is not a natural "flow" or organic "growth." That history simply cannot be explained if we reject outright "dialectics" (Hegel) or "the category Novum (novelty)" (Ernst Bloch) and "leading individuals" (Karl Jaspers). History is always a process of unfolding and entangling, with not just quantitative but qualitative leaps, with changes and breaks, extinction and new life. And Muhammad—to be more precise, the Qur'an—obviously constitutes an epochal turning point in the history of the Arab peoples: Muhammad is discontinuity in person, an ultimately irreducible figure, who cannot be simply derived from what preceded him, but stands radically apart from it as he, with the Qur'an, establishes permanent new standards. In that respect, Muhammad and the Qur'an represent a decisive break, a departure from the past, a shift toward a new future. It was fitting to make the Hegira the start of a new era: Without Muhammad as a source, there would be no stream; without this sprig, there would be no tree.

Hence we can't say that in the religious history of mankind everything runs in cycles, as, for example, with the custom of saying the rosary, which was originally Hindu-Buddhist, then Islamic, and finally Christian; or the legend of the Christian saint "Josaphat," who proves to be none other than the "Bodhisattva," the Buddha. At certain specific moments in time, the figure of the prophet emerges and breaks clear from the continual flow or, better, the prophet wades into the sluggish stream of religious history and tries with all his might to change its course. If he succeeds, he joins the company of those "leading individuals" who have set the standard for their religion by which the centuries to come will all be measured. Karl Jaspers, of course, pays no attention to Muhammad, ostensibly because the Prophet lacked originality, but this is a serious misunderstanding. Muhammad has functioned as a religious archetype for a large part of the human race; down through the ages, people have repeatedly, consciously fallen back on him, on the earliest Islamic community, on the Qur'an.

Many religions, as we know, are unacquainted with prophets in the strict sense: The Hindus have their gurus and sadhus, the Chinese their sages, the Buddhists their masters; unlike *Jews, Christians, and Muslims,* none of these groups have prophets. Meanwhile, when the history of religion speaks of "*the* Prophet," *tout court,* of a man who claimed to be *that* but absolutely nothing *more,* then there can be no doubt that this is Muhammad. But was he one? Even orthodox Christians (or Jews), provided they confront the facts with an open mind, cannot deny certain parallels:

- Like the *prophets of Israel,* Muhammad based his work not on any office given him by the community (or its authorities) but on a special, personal relationship with God.
- Like the prophets of Israel, Muhammad was a strong-willed character, who saw himself as wholly penetrated by his divine vocation,

totally taken up by God's claim on him, exclusively absorbed by his mission.

● Like the prophets of Israel, Muhammad spoke out amid a religious and social crisis. With his passionate piety and his revolutionary preaching, he stood up against the wealthy ruling class and the tradition of which it was the guardian.

● Like the prophets of Israel, Muhammad, who usually calls himself a "warner," wished to be nothing but God's mouthpiece and to proclaim God's word, not his own.

● Like the prophets of Israel, Muhammad tirelessly glorified the one God, who tolerates no other gods before him and who is, at the same time, the kindly Creator and merciful Judge.

● Like the prophets of Israel, Muhammad insisted upon unconditional obedience, devotion, and "submission" (the literal meaning of "Islam") to this one God. He called for every kind of gratitude toward God and of generosity toward human beings.

● Like the prophets of Israel, Muhammad linked his monotheism to a humanism, connecting faith in the one God and his judgment to the demand for social justice: judgment and redemption, threats against the unjust, who go to hell, and promises to the just, who are gathered into God's Paradise.

Anyone who places the Bible, especially the Old Testament, alongside the Qur'an, and reads both together, inevitably wonders: Don't the three Semitic *religions of revelation*—Judaism, Christianity, and Islam—have *the same basis*? And isn't this particularly true of the Old Testament and the Qur'an? Doesn't one and the same God speak loudly and clearly in both? Doesn't the Old Testament's "Thus says the Lord" correspond to the Qur'an's "Say," as the Old Testament's "Go and tell" matches the Qur'an's "Take your stand and warn"? As a matter of fact, the millions of Arabic-speaking Christians have only one word for God: "Allah."

Perhaps, therefore, it is only dogmatic prejudice when we recognize Amos and Hosea, Isaiah and Jeremiah, as prophets, but not Muhammad. Whatever objections one may have against Muhammad from the standpoint of Western-Christian morality (armed violence, polygamy, sensuality), there is no way to deny the following facts:

● To this day nearly 800 million men and women living in the vast expanses from Morocco in the West to Bangladesh in the East, from the steppes of Central Asia in the North to the islands of Indonesia in the South, are all marked by the exacting power of a faith that, more than practically any other, has shaped its followers into a uniform type.

● All these people are bound together by a simple confession of faith

("There is no God but God, and Muhammad is his prophet"), by five basic duties (professing the faith, prayer, almsgiving, a month of fasting, pilgrimage to Mecca), by an all-pervasive resignation to the will of God (suffering, too, is to be accepted as an immutable, divine decision).

- Among all these peoples there continues to be a live feeling for the fundamental equality of all human beings before God, and an international brotherhood that has managed to overcome barriers between the races (Arabs and non-Arabs).

In the Christian world today the conviction is surely growing that, faced with the world-historical reality of Muhammad, we have no choice but to make some corrections. The "plague of exclusivity" stemming from dogmatic intolerance, which Arnold Toynbee so castigated, must be abandoned; and with regard to the Prophet the following points must be conceded:

- The people of seventh-century Arabia were justified in listening to Muhammad's voice.
- They were lifted to the heights of monotheism from the very this-worldly polytheism of the old Arabian tribal religion.
- Taken as a whole, they received from Muhammad, or rather from the Qur'an, a boundless supply of inspiration, courage, and strength to make a new departure in religion, toward greater truth and deeper knowledge, a breakthrough that vitalized and renewed their traditional religion. Islam, in short, was a great help in their life.

For the men and women of Arabia and, in the end, far beyond, Muhammad truly was and is *the* religious reformer, lawgiver, and leader: *the* prophet, pure and simple. Actually, Muhammad, who always insisted he was only a human being, is more than a prophet in our sense for those who follow in his footsteps *(Imitatio Mahumetis):* He is the model for the kind of life that Islam wishes to be. And if, according to Vatican II's Declaration on the Non-Christian Religions, the Catholic Church "also looks upon the Muslims with great respect: They worship the one true God . . . , who has spoken to man." Then, in my opinion, that Church—and all the Christian Churches—must also "look with great respect" upon the man whose name is omitted from the declaration out of embarrassment, although he alone led the Muslims to the worship of the one God, who spoke *through* him: Muhammad, the Prophet.

The fact is often overlooked that even in Old Testament times there were very different sorts of prophets, not all of whom were necessarily great saints. And according to the New Testament there were also authentic prophets who came *after* Jesus: men and women who attested to him and his message, who interpreted and translated it for a new age and a new situation. Thus, as we see in I Corinthians, the "prophets" occupied the second rank in Pauline communities after the apostles. Nevertheless prophecy, whose origins were primarily Judeo-Christian, disappeared soon after the end of the Pauline mission as Jewish Christianity faded from the picture of most Christian communities. After the Montanist crisis, in the second and third centuries (the teachings of Montanus, inspired by the primitive Church and apocalyptic visions, were presented as "the new prophecy"), prophets largely fell into discredit. But the New Testament doesn't bid us reject in advance Muhammad's claim to be a true prophet *after* Jesus and in basic agreement with him. Naturally, the relationship between Jesus the Messiah and Muhammad the Prophet has yet to be explained in detail. Still, the simple recognition of Muhammad's title of "prophet" would have momentous consequences, especially for the message he proclaimed, which is written down in the Qur'an.

THE QUR'AN: GOD'S WORD?

The Qur'an is more than an orally transmitted—and therefore easily altered—text; it is the *written word* laid down once and for all—and therefore inalterable. In this sense it is like the Bible. By being fixed in writing, the Qur'an has been an astonishing stabilizing force in the complex, varied history of Islam from century to century, country to country, generation to generation, person to person. What is written remains. For all the different interpretations and commentaries, for all the elaborate structures of Islamic law *(shari'a)*, the Qur'an remains the common denominator, the recurrent pattern woven into the fabric of all Islamic forms, rites, and institutions. If we wish to know *normative Islam*, and not just Islam in its historical development, we have no choice but to go back, even today, to the seventh-century Qur'an. For Islam and its whole legislative corpus, the Qur'an is something like the constitution, the fundamental law that cannot be read arbitrarily, even though it has given rise to a broad spectrum of interpretation by different people at different times in different places.

To be sure, the Qur'an has in no way predetermined the evolution of Islam, but it *has* inspired it. It has penetrated the entire *shari'a*, molding not just law, but mysticism, art, and the whole Islamic mentality. Commentators have come and gone, but the Qur'an remains. Despite the countless variables, it is the great *constant* in Islam. It has provided Islam with its notion of moral obligation, its external dynamic, its religious depth, but it has also supplied quite specific, lasting doctrines and moral principles: human responsibility before God, social justice, and Muslim solidarity. Thus the Qur'an is the holy book of Islam, and it is such precisely because Muslims understand it as the word that has been written down, the word not of man but of *God*. But—Christians ask—is this book really God's word?

For centuries it was forbidden even to ask that question seriously: Excommunication, with all its consequences, threatened those who did, both Muslims and Christians. And who could deny that from the time of the first Islamic conquests, the Crusades, and the fall of Constantinople, all the way till the Iranian revolution under Khomeini, this question has deeply divided the world? For, just as Muslims from West Africa to Central Asia and Indonesia automatically answered yes, and oriented their living and dying to the Qur'an, so believing Christians everywhere in the world automatically said no, and not just Christians, but, later on, the secular-minded Western religious scholars, who have automatically read the Qur'an not as God's word, but Muhammad's.

The Canadian scholar Wilfrid Cantwell Smith was the first one to pose this question, which many believers on both sides still find threatening, with real clarity and a trenchant analysis of its implications (see *On Understanding Islam*, 1963, Chapter 16). Smith argues—and we can only agree with him—that these conflicting answers, which have been given, remarkably enough, by intelligent, critical, and thoroughly honest persons, are ultimately based on an unexamined, dogmatic "pre-conviction." This assumption equates one's opponent's view with either unbelief (the Christian "no," as Muslims see it) or superstition (the Muslim "yes," as Christians see it).

Does this mean that Smith's colleague Willard Oxtoby is right to propose (in *The Meaning of Other Faiths*, 1983) the formula "You get out what you put in" as a rule of thumb in the study of religion? That is, whoever takes the Qur'an a priori to be the word of God will find this belief confirmed every time he reads it—and the reverse will be true of the nonbeliever.

And yet we may wonder if there is no way beyond this impasse, which in the long run can never be an intellectually satisfying solution. Aren't there an increasing number of Christians and perhaps of Muslims as well who have become better informed about their own position and the faith of the others and so can ask self-critical questions? I shall attempt, first of all, to sketch out some critical issues for Christians, and then move on to others equally critical for Muslims.

REVELATION OUTSIDE THE BIBLE

The better Christians and Muslims get to know each other and give up trying simply to "convert" each other (the Christian mission to the Muslims failed completely, and the Muslim mission to Christianity will likewise fail), the more Christians will come to doubt whether their negative attitude toward the Qur'an was right. For our theological purposes, the key problem is not *how* Muhammad received his revelation, but *whether* he got it from God.

Yet, as Christians, may we even ask this question? Aren't we obliged by both the Old and New Testaments to reject this idea in advance? Don't the Hebrew Bible and the New Testament contain a host of negative statements on the errors, darkness, and guilt of the non-Jewish or non-Christian world? In point of fact, these judgments are aimed at people who culpably reject the biblical message; they are, of course, not so much definitive condemnations as outspoken calls to conversion. And it should not be overlooked that alongside such passages there are also more than a few *positive* statements about the non-Christian world, according to which God originally manifests himself to all of humanity. Non-Christians, too, the Bible says, can come to know the true God; they can recognize what the biblical texts themselves understand to be God's revelation through creation.

Even Karl Barth was compelled to admit in the last complete volume (IV/3) of his monumental *Church Dogmatics* (1958) that alongside the one "light" of Jesus Christ (which he had laid so much stress on all his life) there were other "lights" deserving of honor, that alongside the one word of God there were other true words: "profane" words from non-Christians, who also spoke, in their own way, of God's grace, forgiveness, reconciliation, and human faith; lights and truth of the created world ("the revelation of creation"), though, to be sure, in Barth's view they serve merely as a sort of backlighting for biblical revelation. In saying this, however, Barth neglects the fact that 1) from Genesis to wisdom literature, from Romans to the prologue of John's Gospel, the Bible opens up universal perspectives; 2) according to the Old Testament, God is the creator and preserver of all men and women, his power reaches everywhere, and he has entered into an alliance (the Noachian covenant) with all of humanity; 3) according to the New Testament, God is no respecter of persons, but seeks the salvation of all people; and 4) non-Christians, too, can be justified as doers of the Law.

Hence the basically positive (though negatively framed) statements of Scripture about non-Christians (such as Romans 1–2) should be translated to fit the contemporary situation (we no longer live in *imminent* expectation of the end of the world) and the billions of people to whom the Gospel has been proclaimed either badly or not at all. And Paul's remarks should be completed by the much more positive approach found in the Acts of the Apostles, one generation later. Acts says that God has not left the pagans without witnesses to himself, that he is close to every person. We also need to refer to the still later prologue of the Gospel according to John, which declares that the Word of God is the true light which enlightens every man who comes into this world. These texts manifestly distinguish between, on the one hand, the enlightenment made possible at every time and in every place by the Word who is with God and, on the other hand, the calling of the community to God by Jesus of Nazareth, God's incarnate Word.

This notion of the Word, working like a seed *(logos spermatikós)* everywhere in the world from the very beginning, was applied early on by Christian theologians (Justin Martyr in the second century, Clement of Alexandria and Origen in the third) to the pagan world, so that for them even Plato, Aristotle, and Plotinus were considered "pedagogues," guiding their readers to Christ. And the Reformers, too—though they never took up abstract "natural theology" in the neo-Scholastic sense— affirmed a theology of creation in the great Catholic tradition.

Against this biblical background, then, can we rule out the possibility that, on the strength of God's revelation through creation, countless individuals in times past and present experienced and continue to experience the mystery of God? Or that certain of these individuals may have been granted a special kind of knowledge, a special responsibility, a special charisma? And mightn't this be the case precisely for Muhammad, the prophet from pagan Arabia? *Extra Ecclesiam gratia,* outside the Church there *is* grace. In any case, if we acknowledge Muhammad as a post-Christian prophet, then to be consistent we shall also have to admit the point most important to Muslims: that Muhammad didn't simply get his message from himself, that his message is not simply Muhammad's word, but *God's word.*

But what does "God's word" mean? What does revelation mean? Are we to take revelation as something that has fallen straight down from heaven, *inspired or dictated verbatim by God*? That belief, of course, is held not only by Muslims but by a good many Christians, too—with regard to the Bible. We have reached a decisive stage in the argument.

INSPIRED VERBATIM?

The Qur'an itself repeatedly stresses that Jews and Christians are, as well as Muslims, "people of the book," "possessors of scripture," and this common feature of the three monotheistic, prophetic religions of revelation should not be slighted. But are Judaism and Christianity really *"religions of the book"* in the sense peculiar to Islam? Do their scriptures contain God's *ipsissima verba*, is each and every word inspired, and is the Bible therefore from every standpoint—linguistic, stylistic, logical, historical, scientific—a miraculous, absolutely perfect, holy book, which must be accepted down to the last letter? That, as everyone knows, is how many Christian fundamentalists have interpreted and still do interpret the *verbal inspiration of the Bible.*

This might exemplify a developmental law of religion that seems to hold equally for Christianity and Islam: Later generations subscribing to a very human religion try to escape a crisis of legitimacy that threatens their faith and its claims with the help of extreme theological measures, usually a direct shift of emphasis back onto divine origins. In this way one immunizes oneself against competition, legitimates one's claim to truth, strengthens one's power of persuasion, and binds one's group together. To be sure, we must immediately concede to Muslims that there is a major difference here: Unlike the Qur'an, the *Bible* was never credited with having been written by a heavenly Author, but by altogether different authors *on earth*, as the Letters of Paul and the beginning of Luke, in particular, quite unabashedly reveal. It follows from this that the Bible is not without faults and errors, murky and muddled sections, limitations and mistakes. It is, at all events, a highly complex collection of *religious documents* that cannot be simply *equated* with God's revelation and his word, but, rather, *attest to* that revelation and word in human form: In the many human words, we find the one Word of God.

If believers hadn't strayed from this biblical approach to the Bible, they would have been spared *many conflicts* with science (from the days of Copernicus and Darwin) and history (since the Enlightenment). Two hundred years of historicocritical research on the Bible have shown that the authors' supposed infallibility and impeccability do not guarantee the truth, that the truth of the contents, of the testimony given, must stand, like the biblical message as a whole, on its own feet. The Bible needs no "external" divine legitimation; it creates its own legitimacy on the strength of the testimony "from within"; it is at once inspired and inspiring.

There should be no doubt that the Qur'an, too, has been and is an effectively inspired and inspiring book. It is not simply a piece of evidence from the seventh century, to be analyzed by scholars of religion, but, for countless men and women, a twentieth-century document; it is no dead letter, but the most vital of texts, a source both literary and religious—a book not for study and analysis, but for life and action, and that not only in matters of faith, but of law and morals as well.

But even, and especially, if we as Christians do not dispute the *transcendent religious character* of the Qur'an, we may be allowed to pose the question of its *historically contingent qualities,* despite the fact that traditional Muslims feel as threatened by this problem as traditional Christians feel threatened by parallel issues concerning the Bible. Admittedly, Western students of religion have not taken the Qur'an seriously enough as a living, contemporary religious document, but that is no reason for discrediting all their insights into the historical genesis, literary structure, and social context of the Qur'an as "imperialistic" undermining of the Muslim faith or for dismissing such scholarly work as totally irrelevant for believing Muslims.

The names of some famous "heretics" may serve as a warning: In the cases of Judaism (Spinoza), Catholicism (Richard Simon), and Protestantism (Reimarus, Lessing), the authorities tried, but in the long run failed, to suppress historical criticism of the Bible. It hardly seems possible that in the long run historical criticism of the Qur'an can be suppressed either. Such studies are being carried out not just by Western scholars, but by many Hindus and Buddhists, too—something that thousands of intelligent, critical young Muslims studying at foreign universities are quite aware of. Ever since Western books on Islam began showing more empathy and sympathy for their subject, aren't they finding more Muslim readers? And aren't the doubts about the heaven-sent book much more widespread among Muslim intellectuals than official Islam acknowledges or tolerates? Unless appearances are completely deceiving, faith in the verbal inspiration of the Qur'an faces a long-term danger from the breakdown of what sociologists call its "plausibility structure": the presuppositions undergirding the faith of the masses.

FROM BIBLICAL CRITICISM TO QUR'ANIC CRITICISM

Islam maintains that Muhammad received the Qur'an directly from God: The Qur'an is God's Word, and the question of any Jewish or Christian influence on it is not and may not be raised. This conviction must be taken seriously if for no other reason than that numberless generations of Muslims have drawn strength, courage, and comfort from it in their public and private lives. And it has at least one historical reality behind it, on which Muslim scholars lay the greatest stress: the fact that Muhammad, although hardly illiterate, neither read the Bible himself nor had it read to him. In his time, as we have heard, there was no Arabic translation of the Bible in existence; if there had been, the passages in the Qur'an relating to the Bible would have been clearer, more precise, and less fragmentary.

In his magisterial *Islam* (1980), W. M. Watt shows that Muhammad held a deep religious conviction of his ability to distinguish between the revelations of Allah and his own ideas. Nevertheless, many questions in this regard (including, perhaps, the most basic ones) remain unanswered. Over a century ago, the Jewish scholars Abraham Geiger (*What Did Muhammad Borrow from Judaism?* 1833) and Hartwig Hirschfeld (*Jewish Elements in the Qur'an,* 1878) attempted to demonstrate the Prophet's dependency upon Judaism. But only in very recent years have the highly refined instruments and techniques of biblical criticism been employed to do a form-critical analysis of the Qur'an. According to the revolutionary *Qur'anic Studies* (1977) by the British Arabist John Wansbrough, the Qur'an was shaped by the community, which interpreted certain sayings of the Prophet, fusing various traditions, as in the Bible. The process of forming the canon, says Wansbrough, lasted almost two hundred years (see *The Sectarian Milieu,* 1978). The research of another British Arabist, John Burton *(The Collection of the Qur'an,* 1977), has the modern text of the Qur'an going back to the Prophet himself. Günter Lüling, in *The Rediscovery of the Prophet Muhammad* (1981), which is based on his earlier thesis *On the Primitive Version of the Qur'an* (1974), even claims to have found pre-Islamic Christian strophic hymns in the Qur'an, which enable him to distinguish between a Christian-Arabian primitive Qur'an, a Qur'an composed by the Prophet, and the (present standard) post-Prophetic Qur'an. Hypotheses piled upon hypotheses in a discussion that seems, as biblical scholarship sometimes does, to swing from one extreme to the other . . . An apparently more solid and careful work than all the foregoing is Angelika Neuwirth's *Studies on the Composition of the Meccan Suras* (1981). With her training in the form-critical approach to the Old Testament, Neuwirth can prove that, whatever the case with the rest of the Qur'an, the Meccan suras were put together by the Prophet himself for liturgical recitation, and that behind the text as we have it stands a single creative force, so that we are not reduced to postulating a mere editor who assembled variant readings with scissors and paste.

This discussion is likely to go on for a long while. Muhammad's role in the genesis of the Qur'an can scarcely be swept aside; but neither can the early influence of *oral tradition* from Judaism and Christianity be denied. Well-informed Muslims will not deny that:

1. In Muhammad's day there were ties between the nascent Islamic community and not just Christian Byzantium, but Jews and Christians in neighboring territories, the Arabian Peninsula, and even in Mecca and Medina.

2. The Qur'an itself continually refers to biblical figures: aside from Abraham (and two ancient Arabian prophets), it makes special mention of the three great "prophets" Noah, Moses, and Jesus, but also of David, Solomon, Jonah, John the Baptist, and the Virgin Mary. Might not all this have been known to Muhammad *before* his revelatory experience, and been important to him?

Consequently, it can only prove helpful to the faith of Islam when Islamic intellectuals begin to address the challenge posed by these problems. As early as 1958, the Pakistani Fazlur Rahman had clearly shown that even in classical Islam opinions about the Qur'an were not as monolithic as is often asserted. In his latest book, *Major Themes of the Qur'an* (1980), Rahman, now a professor at the University of Chicago, presents the origins of the Qur'an as follows:

According to the oldest accounts, when Muhammad was about forty years of age, he had one or more genuine ecstatic experiences, for which he had been prepared by a long process of development. The most crucial of these experiences concerned his vocation, one that he, like the prophets of the Old Testament, had not aspired to. This was followed by further moments of revelation, which Muhammad experienced through the agency of the "Spirit" or "spiritual Messenger" (sometimes identified with the angel Gabriel) in his "heart," or innermost being. It was only later Islamic orthodoxy that objectified this inner spiritual experience, which may have been accompanied by somatic phenomena, in the form of a publicly visible angel (or audible voice). Muhammad undoubtedly elaborated his insights during the course of further activities in Mecca and Medina (regular community prayers and alms collecting, however, surely contributed just as much as Muhammad's preaching to the solidarity so typical of the Muslim community). In this way, the revelation of the Qur'an lasted twenty-three years. Rahman concludes that:

> There can be no doubt that while on the one hand revelation came from God, on the other hand it was intimately connected with his [Muhammad's] underlying personality. [p. 100]

However we may answer the question of the origins of the Qur'an, the important thing is that nowadays the *divine word of the Qur'an* must be understood at the same time, from the standpoint of a reflective, educated Muslim, as the *human word of the Prophet*. The problems with the Qur'an resemble those affecting the Bible; i.e., the uncomfortable but unavoidable question arises: If we already have historical criticism of the Bible (which has favored contemporary biblical faith), why not also have historical *criticism of the Qur'an* (which would benefit a Muslim faith suited to our times)?

Christians and Muslims today need to continue their conversation about this difficult but fundamental point of how to understand revelation (to do this we shall need not only Christian experts on Islam, but, something rarely seen till now, Muslim experts on Christianity). We shall make no real progress in Christian-Muslim dialogue unless we come to terms on the notion of truth required for the use of historicocritical instruments. Everyone knows that in various Islamic countries right now there are powerful movements for Islamic renewal at work; these will be dealt with later. Perhaps over the long haul, in a more self-conscious Islamic world that is trying in many ways to catch up with Western science and culture, historicocritical study of the holy book will eventually be allowed to become a reality. What does such a critical reading of the Qur'an entail?

● Neither understanding the Qur'an as a collection of cut-and-dried formulae, rigid doctrines, unchangeable legal principles, as if the Qur'an could be handed down in some unhistorical fashion, with no regard to time, place, and individual persons. There is no dispensing with history! That would be an *uncritical, dogmatic* approach to the Qur'an, whether it be of Muslim or Christian provenience.

- Nor understanding the Qur'an as a flux of constantly varying (with time, place, and individual persons) interpretations, as if the Qur'an were nothing more than the history of its meanings. There is no dispensing with criticism! That would be an *uncritical, phenomenological* approach, whether it be of Muslim or Christian provenience.

- Rather, understanding the Qur'an as a *living message,* continually heard anew in liturgical recitation, as the great *prophetic* testimony to the one and only mighty and merciful God, the creator and completer, his judgment and his promises. A consistent testimony that may and should be handed down in a variable form, always freshly adapted to the time, place, and individuals in question, so as to provide an unambiguous, constructive solution for the present-day conflicts with science and history, as well as the modern ethos and sense of law. That would be a historicocritical approach, whether of Muslim or Christian provenience, which need in no way contradict a believer's positive basic attitude toward either religion.

I realize that the distance between the modern approach to the Bible and the traditional approach to the Qur'an is at present enormous. But it is not, I would hope, unalterable and unbridgeable for all time and eternity. Convergence between the two strikes me as necessary—for the renewal of Islam, for understanding between Muslims and Christians, and for world peace—and a real possibility.

Each of the great Middle Eastern religions, says Islamic theologian Riffat Hassan, has a specific sore point that it considers "nonnegotiable," while the other two consider it unacceptable. For Judaism, this is the unique, chosen status of Israel as *God's people* (with its promised homeland); for Christianity, the teaching of Christ as the *Son of God;* for Islam, the Qur'an as the *word of God.* But, the Pakistani theologian (now at the University of Kentucky) continues, we must be able to talk about these issues. And this attempt at a first Christian response has, perhaps, made one thing clear: how overdue theological dialogue is precisely with regard to the "sore points."

II.
Sunnites and Shi'ites:
The State, Law, and Religion

1. *Josef van Ess:* Islamic Perspectives

A WORLD-HISTORICAL SUCCESS—AND ITS SHORTCOMINGS

It's hard to say how far beyond the Arabian Peninsula Muhammad himself had intended to carry Islam. After his death, however, when the unity he had forged among the tribes of Arabia threatened to disintegrate, the idea of armed proselytism was the best way to divert their disruptive energies. Arab nomads had long been used to launching raids on the civilized areas of Syria and Iraq; but now they were favored by an opportune moment: Byzantium and Iran had exhausted each other in a series of murderous wars. In addition, Byzantium, which had won the most recent struggle, had little support among the indigenous, mostly "heretical" population of the Near East, on account of its unfortunate religious policy. Another surely important factor was that this time the Arabs had more on their mind than just plunder: they were bearing a message. And so they stayed—in many countries they have yet to leave. This grand expansion was accomplished in several waves; by and large, the whole process was over in less than a century.

Setbacks were paid little heed. The fact that Charles Martel stopped an Arab assault at Tours and Poitiers is noted with satisfaction only in European schoolbooks; Arab sources say nothing at all about it, and contemporary Arabs have long since lost sight of the whole episode. Similarly, the Crusades were for Muslims local events in a region that was being harassed and torn by petty princes anyway. The atmosphere of a religious war was late in developing; and the Crusades never became a symbol until the twentieth century, when the Arabs discovered parallels between the Crusades and both European colonialism and

Israeli expansionism. The *Reconquista* brought real losses, but Spain had always played a somewhat marginal role in the Islamic sense of identity. Only the fire storm of the Mongol hordes had a traumatic effect. In 1258, Bagdad was destroyed and the last caliph murdered. Broad regions of what had been considered the Islamic heartland fell for around two generations under non-Islamic rule—the Mongols were shamanists or Buddhists, though some, especially women of the court, were Nestorian Christians. But around the late-thirteenth and early-fourteenth centuries, the Mongols, too (or at least the dynasty they had founded in Iran) converted to Islam, and science and theology blossomed as seldom before. Then, once again, the Ottoman Empire thrust its boundaries outward, primarily at the expense of Christendom. From that time until into the nineteenth century, Muslims, like the Chinese, had little reason not to think themselves the center of the world.

Nonetheless, right from the start there was a cloud on this bright horizon. It was not so much the fact that three of the first four caliphs, who had all been among the Prophet's closest followers, were assassinated by their own fellow believers. That was no doubt too normal, in an environment that took blood vengeance for granted, to be thought ominous. More important was the fact that Muslims could never agree on the legitimacy of these caliphs; a significant and very stubborn minority had the impression that, from the very beginning, at the moment of Muhammad's death, something had "gone wrong."

This situation had arisen in part because the Prophet himself had left no successor. His sons had died in childhood, and for reasons that aren't clear he had been reluctant, or felt it was unnecessary, to appoint a deputy. The election of the first caliph took place rather abruptly. Some important people were absent or outmaneuvered. But the actual, underlying grounds of contention did not emerge until later. It was not so much a clash between immediate political interests as a conflict between divergent images of history. Such images tend to become ideological, and in those days ideology meant religion. And so that divergence led to the most far-reaching split in Islam: I refer to Sunna and Shi'a.

DIFFERING IMAGES OF HISTORY

Sunnites and Shi'ites, as everyone knows, are still with us today. The Shi'ites make up about 7 percent of the total Muslim population, with most of them living in Iran. This geographical separation, however, is relatively recent. It was not until the rise of the Safavid dynasty, in the early-sixteenth century, that the clusters of Shi'ites, which had always existed in Persia and elsewhere, grew together, under pressure from the Safavids, into a compact whole. A much less-well-known fact is that in Iraq more than half the population is Shi'ite. What is highlighted in Iran as a symbol of unity and identity is hushed up in Iraq as a symbol of division.

Actually the two "confessions" can get along quite well with each other, and over the centuries they have often done so. They can be recognized, as is so often the case, by little details: variations in the call to prayer or in religious ablutions, the way Catholics and Protestants could be distinguished, until recently, by their use of the rosary or a different text of the Our Father. They can also be recognized, of course, by their names. Just as we know that anyone named Margaret Mary or Francis Xavier is most likely Catholic, we can be almost certain that anyone who calls himself Abū Bakr or 'Umar or 'Uthmān is a Sunnite.

We are now no longer dealing with shibboleths, but with the heart of the matter: history. Because Abū Bakr, 'Umar, and 'Uthmān were the first three of those four caliphs with whom Islamic history begins. In the Sunnite view they were all, as the saying goes, "rightly guided," together with the fourth, 'Alī, who closes out this epoch of ideal rulers, which was, despite all its ups and downs, considered a true Golden Age. All four were, the Sunnites claim, lawfully elected; and in theory election has remained over the centuries the only, or at least the most honorable, method of regulating the succession, from the Sunnite standpoint. For the Shi'ites, on the other hand, only the fourth caliph, 'Alī, had the right to rule: He had been named beforehand as the Prophet's successor and was excluded from power only through political intrigue. He was not the lawful successor, however, because of election (which was at first denied him), but because he belonged to Muhammad's intimate family. He had married Muhammad's daughter Fātima; and the two sons she bore to him, Hasan and Husain, are supposed to have been especially dear to the Prophet.

Thus there is more at stake here than a few individuals; there is above all the problem of legitimacy. The manifest blood ties between the house of the Prophet and his grandsons and their successors meant more to the Shi'ites than the electoral assent given by the majority of the primitive community. Shi'a means "party," i.e., the party of 'Alī.

We have to wonder why this difference of opinion has worked its way so deeply into the fabric of Islam. Certainly the problem was an important one, but, after all, the historical moment when it had that importance lies almost fourteen hundred years behind us. This moment, however, came during a time when everything still had a paradigmatic character; and it concerned a decision reached by men who had known the Prophet's intentions. Dealings with power in those days were not "value-free": anyone who misused it was committing a sin. This was connected with the fact that, right from the start, Muslims were able to make decisions in the realm of power politics. Back in Medina, the Prophet had had the opportunity of founding a community based on his own ideas or, rather, based on God's ideas, because its organizing principles had been set down as revelations in the Qur'an. The Qur'an does not speak in parables, as the Gospels do; it gives concrete orders. Islam is a religion of law; it does not merely orient men and women to the next life, but reaches a shaping hand into the here and now. It is very much a part of this world too. It knows of no separation between the secular and the spiritual; it is, we might say, totalitarian. Christianity was born into a world empire, where one could, and pretty much had to, render to Caesar what was Caesar's. Islam managed to build such a world empire for itself, and its followers are responsible to God for the way they run it.

According to the Shi'ites, this mandate was disregarded by the earliest Muslim community at a critical point. True, the situation was briefly straightened out when 'Alī took over the caliphate. But he was soon murdered, and his descendants (at least those from the line important to Shi'ite Iran) never succeeded in winning back power. Their supporters did carry on a permanent resistance to the authorities. Ideally speaking, they had their own supreme ruler, whom they looked up to, the imām. But, though they believed at first that the imām was bound to make his presence felt in their rebellion, the majority soon became inclined to dispense him—and themselves—from such dangerous experiments. The only important thing was that each generation had a representative from Muhammad's family, a man who had been appointed by his father (and for that reason could come only from a specific line) and who carried on the legacy. In the middle of the third century of the Hegira (mid-ninth century), this succession, too, was broken off. The twelfth imām is reported to have disappeared in a cellar in Samarra, the Abbasid residence near Bagdad. But the Shi'ites believe that he did not die; he is still alive, though in hiding, and he will return at the end of time—as the Mahdī, the Messiah, who will set up the kingdom of justice that the majority of Muslims let slip away as soon as the Prophet died.

Thus Utopia grew out of initial failure. For long ages history has been for the Shi'ites not a confirmation of their faith, but only disappointment and frustration. That is why they are the Muslims with the most keenly developed sense of suffering. The Sunnites, for whom everything has gone as it should, find it hard to get an unobstructed view of the darker side of life. For the Shi'ites, power carries with it the odium of usurpation; they live by going around it, and wait for better times. There had always been others, however, activists and revolutionaries, whose patience was exhausted by this passivity and who formulated their programs in apocalyptic terms. They tried to force the Messiah to come.

This state of affairs changed somewhat when Shi'a became the state religion of Iran. But the Mahdī had still not yet come. In the constitution in effect under the late Shah, there was an article providing for the abdication of the ruler, should the hidden imām return. In his stead came Khomeinī, and the Shah had to go just the same. But Khomeinī was not the hidden imām. Our picture is not yet complete: We have to speak of the role played by the religious scholars.

LAW AND THE ADMINISTRATION OF POWER

This brings us back again to the Sunnites. Although history *did* after all go their way, and they do consider power legitimate and God-given, even for them the caliph does not embody both secular and spiritual authority. He is no divine king, nor is he pope and emperor in one. It is true that, literally translated, caliph means "successor" or "deputy" of the Prophet; but in the long run the caliphs have kept only the Prophet's role of sovereign, not that of legislator, and most certainly not that of recipient or interpreter of revelation.

The ruler has, at least in theory, no juridical power. There has never been anything in Islam like the Codex Justinianus or the Code Napoléon.

The purpose of the caliph was to make the law respected, but how to apply the law was something that, once again theoretically, he learned from others. These others were the 'ulamā', the experts in religious law, who could be called "clergy" but are quite different from our kind of clergy. They are laymen, not ordained or specially consecrated. They do not constitute a separate caste, although they frequently behave as if they did. In the Middle Ages these religious scholars often had a respectable profession; they were merchants or craftsmen, and in principle this is still possible today. If they were fortunate and not averse to depending upon the state, they could become judges. Once Islamic religious academies came into existence (the renowned Azhar, in Cairo, was founded back in the tenth century, long before the European universities), the scholars increasingly took over teaching posts, with salaries paid by the state or religious foundations.

The Prophet's real successors, one could argue, were the professors of canon law. They were indispensable; because the law, as is its wont, had grown complicated, both among the Sunnites and the Shi'ites. The 'ulamā' of Sunni have their counterpart in the mullahs or, more recently, the ayatollahs of Shi'a. They can be viewed as "clergymen," but they are in any case clergymen without a church, and generally without a permanent and clearly delineated hierarchy. Islam is a religion without a magisterium.

Law became complicated because its Qur'anic base was inadequate. The Qur'an does contain a large number of commandments and prohibitions, but it is not a statute book. It rests on the legal system of the society in which the revelation was first given. It corrects some details of that system, with respect, for example, to the laws of marriage and inheritance, and it adds some wholly new areas, such as cult and ritual, but it presupposes many things as self-evident. It did not take long before some of these things ceased to be so obvious. The rapid expansion of Islam, the transition to sedentary life, the close contact with advanced civilizations, and above all the enormous increase in wealth and luxury, created entirely new social circumstances and problems. Help was needed to explain this situation, and Muslims got it from tradition.

Tradition was also perceived to be not secular, but religious, and was traced back to the Prophet. The model of Muhammad and his most excellent supporters would serve to fill the gaps left by the Qur'an. Over the course of time, thousands of sayings and stories were collected to cover, and provide an exemplary ruling for, every individual case of daily life, from politics to hygiene, from business to table manners. Now, "tradition" in Arabic is *sunna*, and the Sunnites greatly pride themselves on being the only ones who hold to the tradition of the Prophet. But this is not so: The Shi'ites also believe in tradition, although they define it somewhat differently.

TRADITION AND LEGAL METHOD

With these thousands and thousands of sayings piling up, the question arose as to their authenticity and to the criterion for determining which of them were true. But here the Muslims—Sunnites and Shi'ites alike—came to a very characteristic decision: The truth of a dictum was to be recognized not by its content, inner logic, or agreement with the "system," but by the credibility of the person who was its source. This is truth by handshake, so to speak, neither derived discursively nor preached rhetorically, but granted as an "advance," with the trust characteristic of tradespeople in a society where everything is out in the open. But then everything was pinned on those *boni homines*, the good men one trusted, the bearers of tradition, on their moral and religious integrity, which was how trustworthiness was primarily understood.

On this point, Sunnites and Shi'ites had a fundamental difference of opinion. For the Shi'ites started out from the assumption that the primitive community had gone wrong. Most of the Prophet's companions had decided against his one true successor and thereby committed a grave sin. Thus the majority of those who had been able to hear the Prophet's sayings and pass them on were no longer irreproachable. Tradition had to be limited to the Prophet's family, or, rather, to those family members who had stood up for 'Alī. In fact this group was narrowed down to the imāms. But, as we have heard, the line of the imāms broke off; and so, for the Shi'ites, living tradition was also cut short. For the Sunnites, by contrast, it grew more widely diffused from generation to generation.

But I have not yet gotten back to Khomeinī. Islamic law is, materially speaking, a divine law, completed by the Prophetic tradition. The religious scholars no more create laws out of the plenitude of their power than the caliph does; they merely interpret and combine them. But here they have, or had, considerable leeway; and they are responsible for the "system." Hence, Islamic law is also, and very much, a jurists' law, but these jurists were guided less by practical needs than by religious and moral ideas. And so, along with the legal matter, the legal method is important for our purposes; and there, too, Sunna and Shi'a disagree. The jurists have developed two instruments to adapt the matter so as to meet continually changing demands: consensus and analogism. Consensus established that a certain custom had been practiced or approved by the jurists of one generation or another, and made it binding for the future. Analogism allowed parallel treatment of cases that had not been explained in the Qur'an and Sunna, and thereby opened the way to the passing of new law. Each method contradicted the other to some extent. Once a practice had been consolidated by consensus, it could not be disintegrated by the free creation of new law.

Here once more the Sunnites and Shi'ites took different approaches. The Shi'ites did not rate consensus very highly: The behavior of the first Islamic community had already shown that the truth might just as likely be on the side of a small minority. With the Sunnites, on the other hand, the continual formation of patterns of consensus (which varied slightly from region to region) led to the founding of schools of law, which increasingly limited the formation of new law, in favor of official academic opinion, and ultimately did away with it altogether.

For this reason, Sunnite jurists, loyal to government authorities, were less innovative. The Shi'ite jurists, by contrast, abided by the principle of free legislation, and so were more flexible. Since they rejected the state, they could live undisturbed in the belief that with their juridical theory they were administering the legacy of the hidden imām and paving the way for his return. For a long time, they drew quietistic conclusions from this faith: the imām had not yet come, and so ideal conditions could not be brought about in any event. Two generations ago in Iran, however, an activist, revolutionary interpretation grew up alongside the passive one: When the mullahs themselves assume power, the imām will have yet to come, but at least the people will have moved somewhat closer to his intentions. In that case, secular and spiritual power would be united in a single ruler, more than they ever were in the hands of a Sunnite caliph. And then we find ourselves right back with Khomeinī.

THEONOMOUS LAW, THE SECULAR STATE, AND THE INDIVIDUAL
CONSCIENCE

This excursus to Khomeinī has admittedly taken a good deal of time.
But legal matters are quite central to Islam. Religious law is to the
Muslim what theology is to the Christian—by which I mean to suggest
more than a mere exchange of one discipline for another. For, however
such legal thinking may occasionally display a speculative vein akin to
that of Christian theology, its governing assumption is that reality must
be fashioned in accordance with its conceptions. Hence Muslims place a
higher value than contemporary Christians would on the presence of
political authorities that help to implement their religion (which also
means their law). Muslims have a hard time adjusting to life in the
diaspora. The state is supposed to be more than a neutral institution
that guarantees freedom of religion.

That is why in almost all Muslim countries, Islam is the state religion.
Some, Pakistan for example and most recently Iran, have a constitution
based, as far as possible, on the Qur'an and Islamic law. The historian
may be able to show that as far back as the Middle Ages a number of
Muslim rulers freed themselves from the clasp of their religion and,
precisely in the matter of establishing jurisdiction and administering
justice, went their own separate—though not necessarily better—ways.
And in the contemporary Islamic world the state has taken over many
areas originally regulated by religious law and its representatives.

But only a man like Atatürk, consistent secularist that he was, dared
simply to adapt the Swiss statute book. In the other Islamic countries
(each in its own way), modern legislation has built upon the foundations
of the old canon law. This does not exclude open-mindedness or accommodation to changes in sensibility (e.g., in marriage law), but such
things are justified, down to the fine details, by appeal to religious
tradition and by means of religious arguments. A large majority continues to think that God's glory forbids the existence of any free zones of
secularity.

This runs very much against the grain of modern Western thinking, as
we most readily sense in those areas of our liberal, capitalistic world
where secular freedom meets the least resistance: in the economic
sphere and the realm of the autonomous individual. We are amused and
highly skeptical when we read about attempts, as reported from Pakistan, say, to create an interest-free banking system. We are untroubled
by that sort of scruple: Since the Middle Ages, no one in the Western
world still believes that charging interest is *per se* usury; and a little
aggressive salesmanship is what makes the businessman tick. A Muslim,
on the other hand, knows that in the Qur'an "increase" (to translate

literally; "surplus value," if you will) is forbidden (cf. Sura 2, 275); which leaves him face to face with the problem whether he should understand the word to mean usury in our sense of the word or any kind of interest-taking at all. By contrast, nowhere is it written that he should adhere to a specific price; if a customer insists on paying more, why not? "O believers," the Qur'an says, "consume not your goods / between you and vanity [through usury, etc.], except there be / trading, by your agreeing together" (Sura 4, 29). Purchasing is a sacred thing in itself; and over the centuries Islamic canon law has sharpened people's feeling for what is permissible in the marketplace and what is not.

In the domain of the individual, the differences between the basic axioms of Western and Muslim culture can be seen with especial clarity in the argument over human rights. Outside pressure, notably from President Carter, led to the drawing up of a *Universal Islamic Declaration of Human Rights,* based, as it says at the very beginning of the document, "on the Holy Qur'an and the Sunna." It was passed on September 19, 1981, in Paris by the "Islamic Council of Europe." But we can understand why Muslims had thitherto considered such a declaration superfluous: Basically, it does no more than make explicit what is already laid down in religious law. Human rights are nothing new, they have always been there, God's gift to us. Indeed for that very reason they can be justified only on the strength of God's law. They cannot be conceived as natural rights, because a natural right has scarcely any standing in a system where everything is attributed to God, and not just in principle but in every concrete instance. But if human rights have been defined by God, this has some serious consequences. For one cannot maintain one's innocence over against God, so the only adequate stance to take is one of obedience. More than Westerners, then, Muslims conceive of human *rights* as the complement to human *duties.* From the outset, Islamic law has been an ethics of duty.

Unused as they were to working with the idea of natural rights, Muslims were equally unfamiliar with autonomous morality. From time immemorial, questions of ethics were settled not by recourse to conscience, but by referral to tradition, the word of God, and the model of the Prophet. Only the Islamic philosophers—al-Farabi, Avicenna, Averroës—deviated slightly from this approach. They tried to naturalize the ideas of the *Nicomachean Ethics* and Plato's *Republic* on Arab territory. But their works were forgotten, and restored to the Islamic world only through the medium of Western Islamicists. Only in Iran has their thought been continually kept alive, down to the present day, although in something of a theosophical disguise. Naturally, Muslims have never doubted, nor do they doubt now, that there is such a thing as a conscience. But it is nonetheless significant that classical Arabic has no exact term for it. Only in the mystics do we find the beginnings of some such term, like Meister Eckhart's "little spark of the soul." What does not exist for Muslims is conscience as an autonomous authority, because conscience can only appeal to God or be touched by him. But God is also the originator of those laws that one would refuse to obey for reasons of conscience. Muslims follow not their conscience but the will of God.

Which of these two ethical paths is the better cannot be easily decided. For the high value accorded conscience in the Western world also points up the Christian retreat into subjectivity, long since an accomplished fact. We have gotten used to the idea that religion is a private affair; one communes best with God in a quiet little room. There one has him to oneself and, above all, one doesn't attract attention, one avoids "practicing your piety before men." Christianity is a religion in a secularized world, and it has also, it seems, become the religion of a minority. That is an experience Islam has so far never had. No one leaves Islam—and not because there is no Islamic church. Islam is a way of life; to leave Islam would mean to withdraw from a society. There have practically never been conversions from Islam to another religion, save perhaps in a pluralistic country like Lebanon—as it once was. Anyone who converts has no choice but to emigrate; until not so long ago, apostasy was punished with death. Muslims have often preferred emigration to conversion or isolation, as in Spain, when, together with the Jews, they fled before the Catholic kings into the Maghreb, or on the Indian subcontinent when, after the Second World War, India and Pakistan split apart amid great torment. Christians carry their faith within them, Muslims want to have it all around them as well. In the Western world, religion (from *religio,* bond) has become a more or less personal bond of commitment. In the Islamic world the corresponding Arabic word, *dīn,* still means an all-encompassing way of life, which is upheld by external controls.

THE BASIC COMMANDMENTS OF ISLAM

That difference would probably shrivel away at once, were we to compare Islam, not with the rather anemic Western notions of religion, but with Eastern Christianity. One difference, however, would still remain: A Muslim comes to know his religious identity not through creedal formulas, but through certain actions that he carries out the same way that his neighbor does, and usually together with him. There is nothing in Islam comparable to the Christian creeds. In their stead, Muslims acknowledge five universally binding fundamental obligations, the so-called "pillars" of Islam. At least four of these (but actually the fifth, too) must be put into practice: daily prayer, fasting in the month of Ramadān, pilgrimage to Mecca, almsgiving, and finally a brief and very broadly phrased profession of faith. It is highly characteristic of Islam that these "pillars," including a supplement in the profession of faith, are recognized equally by both Shi'ites and Sunnites. The goal here is not orthodoxy, but orthopraxy, which is demonstrated in public in the experience of communal worship with other believers.

The difference between Christianity and Islam can be seen quite clearly in the very first of the "pillars," *prayer.* Neither the form nor the time of prayer is left to the believer's free choice. He is supposed to perform it five times a day, within certain intervals determined by the position of the sun. The prayer consists not just of words, but of movements, which are regulated down to the smallest detail. The words are fixed and unvarying. Prayer is "celebrated"; it is liturgy, worship of God, not conversation with God. Even when Muslims pray at home on days other than Friday, they are generally not alone. One often sees men unfold their prayer rugs and perform their devotions right on the street, amid enormous, milling crowds. There are, of course, individual prayers not connected to the public ritual; but these are not prescribed by law and can therefore only complement ritual prayer, never replace it.

The difference between the two religions is still more striking in the case of the second "pillar," *fasting.* Among Christians, fasting has gone almost completely out of style; even the Catholic Church, in the course of making some recent reforms, dropped this medieval symbol. But even when the days of fast and abstinence were still observed, Catholics merely reduced the amount of food they ate. During Ramadān, by contrast, Muslims abstain entirely from food—and from drinking, smoking, and sexual intercourse—from dawn to sundown for a whole month. Since the Islamic calendar follows the lunar year, Ramadān always comes eleven days earlier than the year before; thus, when it occurs during high summer, especially in the heartlands of Islam, fasting is a tour de force that only the most hardened Christian ascetics could match. Modern Europeans have little understanding of this sort of pious exercise; and even Christians criticize it not on religious, but economic, grounds: exhausted people, drained by fasting, produce nothing; and so religion stands in the way of economic development. Muslims are not much impressed by this argument, which sounds purely materialistic to them. The Ramadān fast gives them the experience of Muslim solidarity. Precisely because of its rigor, it is subjected to unusually strict public control; and even among intellectuals there are not many who openly ignore it.

This experience of Muslim solidarity is raised to worldwide dimensions with the third "pillar," the *pilgrimage* to Mecca, which every believer is supposed to complete at least once in his life. The rites of the pilgrimage derive from pre-Islamic times, but no Muslim would think of them as pagan—the Ka'bah, after all, was built by Abraham. During the *hajj*, Muslims enter a state of exceptional purity, manifested by various external signs: special dress, no washing or cutting of hair, etc. In Mecca itself the pilgrims walk in a sacred procession seven times around the Ka'bah and finally march out through the outskirts of the city to 'Arafa, where they remain from noon to sunset, "standing before the face of God"—not alone, as this Protestant-sounding formula might lead us to believe, but in an unimaginable crush, surrounded by other Muslims.

The fourth "pillar," *almsgiving*, also grounded in the Qur'an, regulates the Muslim's charitable obligations. Every believer is bound to give away between 2½ and 10 percent of all his assets for the benefit of the poor and needy. Beneficence here has nothing to do with conscience; it is the law. Each individual is free, of course, to give alms voluntarily over and above the required amount; and this is often done, sometimes in the form of religious foundations; but the danger of providing a sop for the conscience of the rich with a paltry sum is obviated by the law. Islam will never have difficulties with the church tax (which Germans have to pay): it is levied, so to speak, by the Good Lord himself. Interestingly enough, the Qur'an is also the basis for including slaves (whose freedom this tax is theoretically supposed to help purchase) among the ranks of the needy. Beyond that, the manumission of a slave has always counted as a meritorious deed and is prescribed for expiating a number of offenses, such as manslaughter or perjury.

Only one of the "pillars," although it is generally the first one mentioned, is concerned with faith and not works: the so-called *shahāda*. This is not a spiritualized affair, however, but the mere *profession* of a single, two-part sentence: "I testify that there is no God but *the* God, and that Muhammad is the messenger of God [i.e., his Prophet]." In Islam, faith has an essentially testimonial character; it means consent to two fundamental truths, which have nothing mysterious about them. The first, monotheism, is looked upon as rationally deducible; the second, Muhammad's prophecy, as historically verifiable.

Faith, then, is not directed to truths that transcend human reason; and hence it also presupposes no special act of the will for surpassing reason's limits. To Muslim ears, *Credo quia absurdum* is blasphemous. Faith comes from God, but it requires no particular illumination by grace. Sincerity in professing one's faith is taken for granted; no one can (or wishes to) check up on this. Testimony has a higher significance in the Islamic world than it does with us: Only someone who is irreproachable can give it. But it is not, like baptism, a sacrament.

THE MEANING OF THE COMMANDMENTS

At this point we probably cannot help asking the typically Christian question: What is behind all this? Where do Muslims see the meaning of the "pillars"? For Christians, ritual and liturgy, insofar as they still exist, are always symbolic, and so always accompanied by texts that explain what is going on. Islam has scarcely anything to correspond to this; here, as elsewhere, it strikes us as being rationalistic and arid. The Muslim does postulate an intention for every action. He tells himself why he is doing it, and he often accompanies it with a religious formula. But what he expresses by it is always one and the same thing: his obedience to God. Ritual and cult are meaningful because God has willed them to be so. The Muslim finds further justification, if need be, from rules placed in a social context, such as the prohibition against drinking wine, but not from worship.

This is quite conspicuous in the case of the *hajj*. Although various ritual elements juxtaposed here take up a goodly amount of time, and although the cult legend connected with Abraham can be found in the Qur'an, no cultic "drama" has developed, and no mythic paradigm is relived by the pilgrims. Not a single text refers to the idea that the Muslim in this situation is *like* Abraham or *like* Hagar. When he kisses the Black Stone, he does so only to follow the custom of Abraham and the Prophet, in other words because that was how Abraham accomplished the will of God. His behavior is a matter of commemoration, not identification. Much the same can be said of the animal sacrifices offered at the great festivals. They are absolutely unmagical, with no accompanying text. Nor is there a need for sacramental efficacy. Any symbolism that may be read into them remains diffuse and conceptual. Such actions, the texts say, serve to manifest God's "right guidance" or the recognition of God's uniqueness. This, presumably, gives us the explanatory key: Islamic monotheism, as I said, is reformist. Every trace of idolatry is obliterated; nothing has self-contained meaning. The next chapter will have to focus more sharply on this point.

2. *Hans Küng:* A Christian Response

An ancient religion in modern times: Does it adapt or resist, secularize or resacralize? In addressing the legal and social problems that arise here, I shall slowly circle the issue in order to close in on the decisive point in the controversy.

AN ANCIENT RELIGION IN MODERN TIMES

As we have seen, law, the state, politics, and religion are a unit for Islam. Accordingly, a separation between the spiritual and the secular, religion and law, religion and the state, or religion and politics would be thoroughly un-Islamic. And it should be noted that this linkage supplies Islam with a critical argument against Christianity that must be taken quite seriously. Aren't all the vices of the West, especially the sexual vices (promiscuity, prostitution, abortion, nudism), the result of the depoliticization of religion and the desacralization of politics—in short, the result of *secularization?*

Criticism of civilization, criticism of secularization, and that means disillusionment with the forces of modernity (science, technology, industry, progress)—all this is spreading from the West to (among other places) Islamic countries. There, as almost everywhere else these days, we see the secularized, Western-educated elites turning away from European and American culture with a sense of manifold disappointment. Back to the native culture—which is largely identical with the old religion—is their watchword, uttered in the hope that this old religion can be reactivated and revitalized so as to enable the people and the nation to have an identity of their own once more, instead of borrowing one from the West. Only if we are aware of these connections can we understand today's widespread current of resacralization and re-Islamization. In this regard, Iran is only a particularly drastic example (though a highly attractive one for many Muslims around the world), as powerful forces try to stop and, where possible, reverse the earlier secularization (adaptation, Westernization, acculturation) with the help of "counteracculturation." Although there is no definite general rule in the Qur'an about the veiling of women, the readoption of the veil in Iran has sent a strong symbolic signal to other Islamic countries. The *shari'a*, Islamic law, which regulates every facet of life, is once again to be fully enforced!

Islamic apologists maintain that Islam has nothing to fear from secularization, because, unlike Christianity, it has never gone through a process of clericalization. Islam, they say, has neither an autonomous church, separate from the state, nor an ordained clergy. Of course, we have learned just how wishful such thinking is, at least as far as the clergy goes. Because the legal or religious scholars—the Sunnite *'ulamā'* ("knowers") and the (Shi'ite) mullahs (ayatollahs)—although laymen, actually function as clerics in Islamic society. And no one could miss the fact that this clerical body in no way limits itself to the religious leadership of the people, but exercises considerable political power.

In orthodox Sunnite Islam, within an organic religious system where there may be no independent church but where religion and state are integrally united, the *'ulamā'* not only legitimate the power of the political rulers, but increasingly exert practical influence on the legislature, executive, and judiciary. In Shi'ite Iran, after the fall of the Shah's secularist regime, the mullahs straightforwardly assumed political power and are now trying to set up an Islamic theocracy (not unlike an ecclesiastical state, with an inquisition and an ayatollah as infallible pope) by means of the "Islamic republic." This Islamic restoration, known as "revolutionary popular Islam" (akin to the Sunnite Muslim Brotherhood), is actualizing the Qur'an's social critique ("Justice!") and threatening, far more effectively than Marxism, to become the instrument of protest for the impoverished, oppressed masses from Pakistan to Morocco.

A MEDIEVAL PARADIGM OF RELIGION?

So, is there to be sacralization instead of secularization? Not necessarily, the question is still very much open. *In the long run*, we may well ask, will Islam, whether Sunnite or Shi'ite, be able to avoid secularization? In discussing secularization or re-Islamification with Muslims, it has often been pointed out to me that Islam is the only religion which has developed a comprehensive "system" embracing all of private and public life. In reply I like to call attention to the fact that Christianity, too, once had such a comprehensive system, in which law, the state, politics, and religion pretty much formed a unit. It was primarily embodied in the *medieval paradigm** of Christianity, which in its specifically Roman Catholic configuration superseded the crisis-ridden orthodox Hellenistic/Byzantine model of the Church in the eleventh century. As everyone knows, this medieval Latin paradigm of Christianity was itself overtaken by a thoroughgoing crisis in the fifteenth and sixteenth centuries, which led to its replacement in another "paradigm change." Roman Catholic authorities, to be sure, thought they could withstand Luther's Reformation as well as the later, seventeenth-century paradigm change to modernity and the Enlightenment (new philosophy, science, and conceptions of the state and society with the American and French revolutions and the Declaration of Human Rights as a political consequence). The carefully preserved medieval Roman-Catholic paradigm grew more and more inflexible in its opposition to Protestantism and modernity. As late as the nineteenth century, Rome believed it could cope with both the Protestant and the Enlightenment paradigms by a forced resacralization and romantic Catholic restoration, which reached its acme in Pius IX's *Syllabus,* the condemnation of all "modern errors" (1864) and in the First Vatican Council (1870), with its edict promoted by the Pope himself, conferring absolute primacy of jurisdiction as well as infallibility upon the Church's spiritual leader.

Still, as Muslims can see for themselves, in the end *even Catholicism could not avoid absorbing both paradigm changes of modern times.* A century later, at a new Vatican Council (which from 1962 to 1965 set its seal on a development initiated long before but continually repressed), the hierarchy had to affirm what it had once officially condemned: The paradigm change of the Reformation was belatedly carried out by the revaluation of the Bible and preaching, the use of the vernacular in the liturgy, the active participation of lay people, and the adaptation of the Church to the various nations. The Council fathers explicitly approved the modern science (Copernican world picture, Darwinian evolutionary thinking) that had earlier been anathematized, along with modern history, modern biblical scholarship, modern democracy, popular sovereignty, freedom of conscience and religion, and human rights as a whole (abolition of church censorship and the Index). The Middle Ages, which had been kept alive for so long in the Catholic world with Latin as the ecclesiastical language, Scholasticism, canon law, and the Inquisition, had come to an end. Nonetheless, at present Rome is tempted to restore the medi-

---

* In Thomas S. Kuhn's sense of an entire constellation of beliefs, values, techniques, and so on, shared by a given community.

eval/Counter-Reformation/antimodern paradigm to the Church (while applying a veneer of modernity), on the model of Catholic Poland, which has known neither the Reformation nor the Enlightenment.

The result of this encounter with the Reformation and secularization has suggestive implications for Islam. Though we can readily understand disillusionment with scientific and technological advances, many observers of the whole development in *Islamic countries* are wondering: With greater exposure, voluntary or not, to the modern world, won't Islam ultimately have to go through these paradigm changes? The spread of Islam in the early Middle Ages, when it became a great cultural as well as political power, is unquestionably impressive (consider the adoption of Persian administrative methods, Hellenistic philosophy, and Indian medicine). Yet in modern times, to the regret of Muslims in all countries, Islam has increasingly slipped into a defensive posture with regard to *scientific, technological, economic, and political* developments in the West. But this Western superiority—and here we have the crucial point—is based on the functional differentiation of modern society, which was accomplished in the Reformation and the Enlightenment. Based, that is to say, on a process of *secularization,* an utterly un-Islamic affair (as things now stand), where religion, the clergy, theology, and sacred law no longer determine everything as in the medieval paradigm; where, instead, science, technology, the economy, and culture have acquired independence, autonomy—in a word, *secularity.* And whether people in Islamic countries like it or not, thanks to the introduction of modern science and technology, industrialization, urbanization, and mass media, secularization is now threatening Islam, too. This threat comes not only from outside, from the West, but also from within: from the structural alterations in the values and ideals, norms and patterns of action peculiar to religious and moral thinking.

THE DILEMMA OF RELEVANCE AND IDENTITY

The *dilemma facing all of Islam* can be seen right in the Islamic heartland of Saudi Arabia, which is currently undergoing a hectic transformation from an almost medieval desert kingdom to a modern industrial state: Will it be possible in the long run for the same state to be completely open to technological progress and at the same time to act as the strict guardian of a puritanical Islamic outlook on life? The development going on in the various Islamic countries seems to be coming down to an either-or situation.

Either the attempt is made to emerge from a preindustrial culture through industrialization. But in that case one is forced willy-nilly to make the *scientific/technological* culture *one's own.* And the longer this appropriation goes on, the more that simply appealing to the Qur'an and Sunna or *sharī'a* will fall short of solving the complex problems of an industrial society. Thus one would have to make allowances for a functional differentiation of society. This was, after all, the path followed in the Turkey of Mustafa Kemal and in Tunisia, the path that was all too imperiously dictated from on high in the Shah's Iran, the path that has been favored by Egypt, Syria, and Malaysia, and that even the officially Islamic states of Saudi Arabia and Pakistan have to tolerate. The many Muslim students who have studied in the West are playing a part in this process, as are the increased numbers of foreign workers (over two million in Saudi Arabia alone). Only with time will the effects of this development become fully visible.

Or else the Islamic states will try, following the example of the Iranian restoration, to resist secularization and so, for ultimately religious motives, to *block the further advance of Western scientific and technological culture.* This is the "great refusal"—but in actuality we don't see it carried out consistently. A standstill in the field of industrial and technological development would of course be tantamount to permanently fixing the sharp gradient between the countries of the North and South, and preprogramming North-South conflict. But in that case the Third World would never, even in the longest term imaginable, enjoy equal rights with the industrialized countries. What, then, is to be done in this dilemma?

There is no mistaking the fact that Islam—like Christianity long before it—has been caught in a double crisis typical of modern times: *a crisis of relevance and identity.* These are connected in a complementary fashion. Because the more a traditional religion tries to become relevant in a largely secular period shaped by this-worldly values, norms, and behavior models, the more deeply will it be drawn into an identity crisis. And, vice versa, the more a religion tries to assert its identity in traditional rites, dogmatic beliefs, and moral ideas, the more irrelevant it becomes for a secular society. American sociologists of religion have characterized this as the "identity involvement dilemma." Hence we can understand that informed Muslims, too, are facing this difficult question: Doesn't secularization ultimately mean the dissolution of their very substance, the disintegration of Islam itself? Politically speaking, that would mean the loss of historical continuity and cultural identity for the Islamic states. If one finds that unacceptable, what might the alternative be?

THE THIRD WAY: RELIGION IN SECULAR SOCIETY

This is, in fact, a fateful question for Islam. Is there a thinkable, practicable way between religious re-Islamization and anti- or non-religious secularization?

For a long time, many Westerners believed that secularization leads to *the end of religion*. For this reason many Muslims, with the example of Christianity before their eyes, are skeptical. And nobody would deny that this was precisely what was feared in Shi'ite Iran: The Shah's regime had no religious legitimacy, and could therefore be toppled. Nor could anyone fail to see that the same fear is present even in conservative religious countries like Saudi Arabia, where the regime, just because it has religious legitimacy, has so far managed to stay in power, despite all the opposition.

But does this thesis about the end of religion hold up? From the Muslim standpoint, there is no ignoring the fact that, regardless of all the secularization in the West, the prophecies by Feuerbach, Nietzsche, and Freud about the "death of God" and the end of religion have in no way come true—not for Western Europe and America, nor for Eastern Europe and the Soviet Union. Secularization, in other words, doesn't necessarily mean sliding into godless secularism, as propagated by Marxist-Leninists or Western "freethinkers." For the modern paradigm holds that secular humanism cannot be equated with secular atheism. Worldliness is not identical to godlessness.

Building on the work of Max Weber, Talcott Parsons elaborated the notion that secularization was less a process of the general decline, or even downfall, of religion than of its *changing function*. In a society becoming increasingly more complex and differentiated, the original identification of religion and society had to be abandoned in favor of a separation, at least in principle, of religion from other structures and institutions. There was no avoiding an evolutionary *differentiation* (division of labor) between various institutions. Thanks to this separation, religion, like the family, was freed from secondary tasks and could concentrate on its primary responsibilities. Religion thus acquires a different social significance as well as a new, independent position. And this means that religion, whether Christianity or Islam, is confronting not its downfall, but a new chance.

For man's eternal questions about the meaning of life, suffering, and death, about the highest values and ultimate norms for the individual and society, about where humanity and the cosmos have come from and where they are going, are not simply still with us, but have grown far more urgent in the face of political catastrophes and disenchantment with blind faith in progress. Unless I am completely deceived, for the past few decades we have been engaged in an epochal paradigm change: from modernity to "postmodernity." Though we can distinguish only its outlines (at best), in postmodernity the absolutized forces of the modern period (science, technology, industry) will be increasingly relativized for the sake of human welfare. Many people are longing for genuine transcendence in theory and practice: an authentic qualitative step beyond one-dimensional modern thought, speech, and action into a real *alternative domain*, where the relations of men and women to nature, to their fellows, to society (in justice, freedom, and peace), and finally to ultimate reality will materialize in a new and more hopeful way.

In a postmodern paradigm, religion is *not* in need of a *restoration* (which would, in the final analysis, be doomed), but of a *transformation*, pregnant with hope for the future. Call it piety in a secular context. Believing Christians will agree with believing Muslims: If one wishes to prevent some false god (be it führer, political party, nation, or even science) from being made into humanity's ground of meaning, supreme value, and ultimate norm, then *faith in the one true God must replace faith in the false gods of modernity*. And so, these days especially, one must affirm, together with the Qur'an and the Bible: "There is no god but God." "You shall have no other gods before me." Which means that faith, whether Qur'anic or biblical, in the one true God is capable of demystifying the powers of this world and, insofar as they are idols, of dethroning them.

Hence we can conceive of a "third way," which many Muslims happen to be seeking too. I should like to make a case here for a *new ecumenical paradigm of secularity viewed against a religious background*, as a *via media* between a religious re-Islamization, which has little future promise, and an anti- or non-religious secularization, which is equally unpromising, given the "dialectic of the Enlightenment." Thus I am not proposing a hopeless, anachronistic struggle against science, technology, industrialization, and progress. But science, technology, and industry must not become the ultimate meaning, the supreme value, and absolute norm; progress must not be turned into a false god and pseudoreligion. To be sure, this sort of paradigm will not preserve all the functions once exercised by traditional religion, but its (critical and constructive) essential functions will be kept. These are to supply meaning, to establish norms, and to shape the community. In short, the substance will be protected, including *the substance of Islam*, especially its belief in the one God, along with (perhaps in modified form) its five basic duties or pillars and its advocacy of social justice. Why shouldn't Islam and postmodern secularity be fundamentally compatible?

Lest there be any misunderstanding, I am not recommending to Islam the modern technological/technocratic "success story," which has long since become problematic for Westerners and which has so often perverted instrumental reason into unreason, technological mastery of nature into devastation of nature, and enlightenment into human enslavement (to science, technology, the economy). The constant menace of atomic war and possible self-destruction have opened many eyes. Nor am I urging Islam to adopt the pseudovalues of a self-indulgent Western culture as "progress." Instead, Islam and Christianity should jointly (so far as possible) maintain a critical distance from technological and scientific developments, so as to disenchant those agents of (Weberian) disenchantment, in the name of the one true God; not to reject them, but to rediscover their potential for making life more peaceful and humane, and to integrate them into a radically different understanding of religion *and* technology. "Postmodernity," whose consequences are by no means clear for Christianity, either, would then constitute a common challenge for both Christian and Islamic theology.

EFFORTS AT INTERNAL ISLAMIC REFORM

Critical Muslim observers place the operative paradigm of contemporary Islam somewhere between the Middle Ages and Reformation/modernity. Islam is "in transition," as J. J. Donahue and J. L. Esposito impressively demonstrate in their study (1982), "from Muslim perspectives." The nineteenth century, as we all know, was not only an age of enormous European expansion, but also (and in reaction to it) of Islamic efforts at reform, which often ran counter to despotic Oriental rulers such as the archconservative *'ulamā'*. Even before this, in the eighteenth century, there was the Wahhābi reform movement in Arabia, which later led to the founding of the kingdom of Saudi Arabia. Though conservative in social and political matters, it attacked the superstition and obscurantism of popular religion and called for the return to an authentic form of Islam, to the Qur'an and Sunna (interpreted in a puritanical, traditionalist sense, to be sure), and thus paved the way for the liberal "modernist" reform movements of the nineteenth century.

In India, which had been colonized much earlier, Sayyid Ahmad Khān (1817–98) was the first to advance modern ideas of reform, which he expressed in a programmatic and highly rational fashion. An admirer of the British, Khān argued for the adoption by Islam of the modern Western paradigm. The Muslim political and intellectual elite on the subcontinent still invokes him and the man who followed in his footsteps, the poet-philosopher Muhammad Iqbāl (1873–1938), the spiritual father of Pakistan. Another very significant figure even today, although, like the other two, never fully accepted, is Jamāl-ad-dīn al-Afghānī (1838–97), the charismatic father of a modern, reform-oriented Islam in the Near East. Altogether different from Khān in his anticolonial and anti-British feelings, al-Afghānī nonetheless resembled him in advocating "true Islam" within the framework of a modern paradigm. He denied that there was any conflict between reason and Islamic faith; he insisted on the need for a broad, general, secular education and formation; he spoke up for populism and Islamic humanism. His student and comrade-in-arms Muhammad 'Abduh (1849–1905) was primarily a theologian; and, unlike al-Afghānī, strove not for a political, but for a spiritual and social revolution. As he saw it, "true Islam" demands the integration and cooperation of faith and reason in education and science ('Abduh explicitly acknowledges "the laws of nature" and not just "God's habits"). As supreme mufti of Egypt, he worked tirelessly for liberalization and especially for the reform of theological training and the religious courts.

Interestingly enough, Afghānī appealed to Luther's Reformation by way of justifying his own reform of medieval Islam. He did so, admittedly, without raising historicocritical questions about the dogmatic-theological foundations of Islam; "modernist" though he was, he still understood and applied the Qur'an and Sunna in a largely unhistorical manner. As Rotraud Wielandt has shown in detail in her survey of *Revelation and History in Modern Muslim Thought* (1971), even Islamic reformers have for the most part refused to face the central issue of whether God is the sole author of the Qur'an, which would then be literally inspired and infallible. Such men as Rashīd Ridā, al-'Aqqād, and Mālik Bennabī were no more prepared than their master 'Abduh to consider the Qur'an from a historicocritical standpoint, as the Bible had been. Hence they were also incapable of recognizing that some of the ethical and legal norms in the Qur'an were the product of their times and possibly antiquated.

Nowadays, however, we have a generation of younger Muslim scholars, for whom *the earlier "modernist" interpretation of Islam,* which aimed to reconcile with the demands of modern life, *did not go far enough.* These thinkers are in no sense part of the group of Western or westernized secularists, whether liberal or Marxist, who dissolve Islam, so to speak, into modern thought. Of course, their criticism of the old reform movement for its failure to reflect on the sociohistorical implications and theological foundations of Islam could be aired only at Western universities. There they can freely express and publish their opinions unmolested by censorship, repression, and serious dangers to their careers —even their very lives. Thus, for example, after the case of the Egyptian scholar, 'Alī 'Abdarrāziq (who as early as 1925 called for the separation of politics and religion and thereby lost his teaching position and his judgeship), one could cite the Pakistani Fazlur Rahman in Chicago, the Algerian Muhammad Arkoun in Paris, and the two Syrians philosopher Sādiq Jalāl al-'Azm (who was put on trial in Lebanon) and political scientist Bassam Tibi, now teaching in Göttingen. The latter, in his recent book *The Crisis of Modern Islam: A Pre-industrial Culture in the Age of Science and Technology* (1981) makes the following programmatic demand of Islam: It must give up its aggressive defensive attitude toward Western modernity and, as a prerequisite for that, it must undergo *a partial secularization.* In that way, the essence of Islam (which Tibi characterizes as "religious ethics" and apparently apolitical "inwardness") could be kept intact. In connection with this, autonomous institutions would have to be set up to defend human dignity, which is often neglected in Islam, to protect human rights, and to ensure tolerance toward dissidents.

Lest I be misunderstood here, I am not citing Muslim critics out of a sense of Christian or Western superiority. And I firmly reject the temptation to play the various critics and reformers of Islam against one another or to maintain that only critics and reformers are "true" Muslims. But in any case the question will arise, Aren't Islamic reformers fighting for a lost cause, in view of the newly reawakened and spreading Islamic traditionalism, which has been rightly labeled Islamic "fundamentalism," on account of its scriptural piety and its refusal to accept any criticism of the Qur'an?

CAN ISLAMIC FUNDAMENTALISM SURVIVE?

Islamic fundamentalism has a conservative "right" wing, with Saudi Arabia (and its Islamic World League), and a revolutionary "left" wing, Khomeinī's Iran. In both cases, however, its goal is to preserve and strengthen the entire historical structure of Islam as it has accumulated over the centuries. This means not only the substance of Islam, the essentials of the faith, but all the (more or less Islamic) accidentals, the whole Islamic "system," together with the "Islamic state." Theological authority shapes the conviction that Sunna, tradition, belongs on the same level with the Qur'an as divine revelation. Naturally it then becomes possible to quote one of the *hadīth* (sayings attributed to, or stories concerning, the Prophet) in any situation whatsoever so as to justify the status quo.

This kind of traditionalism is propelled by the fear that a critical examination of the authenticity of the *hadīth* and of their function in society, past and present, might lead to the collapse of the whole Sunna, and ultimately, along with it, of the Qur'an itself. But present-day traditionalists often forget that, back in the Middle Ages, brilliant Islamic scholars saw this problem and subjected the *hadīth* to critical scrutiny (if not quite "critical" in our sense). If we also bear in mind that many *seemingly primitive Islamic traditions* (such as the veiling of women, the separation of the sexes in the mosques, or the contemporary form of the five daily prayers) are *not even found in the Qur'an*, we shall see clearly why Islamic fundamentalism finds the critical demand "Back to the Qur'an" just as revolutionary as Roman Catholicism once found Luther's cry "Back to the Gospel." And once again, every political means is being used to silence the voices of those urging the change to a new paradigm.

Certainly there is no disputing that the Islamic restoration is *justified insofar* as it is swinging the pendulum back from a nonreligious Enlightenment and secularization in a religious direction, insofar as the movement is fueled, on the one hand, by the quest for a lost Islamic identity and, on the other (especially with the Iranian "left") by the demand for social justice. Still, for the ruling classes (the government authorities, the army, the *'ulamā'*), both those motives are often more a question of solemn rhetoric and political calculation than concrete reality. When criticism comes from without, and even more when it comes from within, the reaction is swift and severe. On that score, "progressive" states like Libya and Algeria hardly differ from "conservative" states like Saudi Arabia, Pakistan, Kuwait, or the United Arab Emirates. But restorations—and the Metternich era is only one reminder of this—always make the mistake of assuming that new ideas can be *permanently contained* by suppressing and repressing them. This will no doubt prove true for Islam as well, for a number of reasons:

1. Through a thousand channels—from new management and legal practices, the army, the mass media, etc.—"Western" secular ideas are trickling into Islamic states and "contaminating" social institutions (from marriage and the family to the government bureaucracy) not yet adapted to them. Hence the effort to keep out the West by means of traditionally Islamic ideas—the renewed isolation of women, say, or an interest-free banking system—has little likelihood of success. Nor have we seen any alternative "Islamic order," with a specifically Islamic economic and social policy, emerge, not even in Iran.

2. Like traditional Christian religious instruction, Islamic religious education is not in the least oriented to current problems, but to the memorization of traditional formulas (the Qur'an, *hadīth*, Islamic law, Arabic grammar). It pounds into the student's head largely outdated notions that prove quite inadequate when the educational level of the masses is lifted. The universities in Islamic countries—apart from the theological academies—have, to a great extent, been secularized already.

3. Anyone who reads what Muslims are writing about Islam nowadays will be surprised to note that the Islamic and Western standpoints have tacitly drawn closer on many basic principles and individual issues (such as the role of Muhammad). Although these writers invoke the Qur'an and Sunna, in fact they have integrated Western thought into their work.

4. The complete identification of religion and politics—the Islamization of politics and the politicization of Islam—will exact a high price from religion. A politicized "totalitarian" religion loses religious substance, and can all too easily be replaced by a quasi religion, like nationalism. Not to mention the fact that rigid conservative systems always have to fear the backlash of political radicalism. Religion as a spiritual orientation should no doubt penetrate all of human life, personal and social; but all of human life is not religion.

5. The greatest long-term threat to traditional Islam is liable to arise (in connection with oil revenues and a higher standard of living) from secularist materialism ("car, sex, and career") that scarcely bothers with religion any more and mostly ignores morality. This is the sort of thing that up till now some Muslims, from their apparently impregnable base in Islamic spirituality, confidently thought they could criticize as a typical product of the West.

6. Almost a third of all Muslims live as a minority in a diaspora situation (in the Soviet Union, the Balkans, Western Europe, and America), where the complete observance of Islamic law is an illusion. In the pluralistic society of the West, especially, everyone is expected to display a high degree of openness to other people's outlooks on life and of adaptation to modern conditions.

7. In Islamic states such as Egypt and Tunisia, Morocco and Somalia, Turkey, India, and Indonesia, an exchange between traditionalist and liberal forces is in full swing, at least on the subliminal level. This dialectic has by no means already been resolved in favor of those traditionalists who understand Islam as a total system of life that answers all questions. Some liberal Muslims, admittedly, are of the opinion that individual countries will have to go through a phase of re-Islamization, in order to learn firsthand the practical impossibility of restoring medieval conditions (including the prohibition against charging interest, and the death penalty for adultery). In any event, it has been noted that in the congested industrialized districts of Islamic cities it is impossible, all the loudspeakers notwithstanding, to observe the prescribed times for prayer.

Meanwhile, as a Christian I wonder what the spokesmen for Muslim missionary endeavors would say if Christian churches in Europe and America responded to their efforts with a re-Christianization campaign (at the expense of Muslims)? In any case, one can scarcely preach Islam in free Western society with any credibility if one construes all religious activities of non-Muslims (the Bahā'īs, for example) as anti-Islamic acts.

What might the alternative be? Instead of a restoration looking back to the past, I have argued for a transformation of religion rich in future possibilities: religion in a secular context, secularity against a religious background. The Iranian writer Bahman Nirumand, one of the Shah's most vehement critics, who contributed to the fall of his regime, now says: "In the dreadful fate that has befallen the Iranian people under Khomeinī isn't there at the same time a chance to harmonize a positive, future-oriented nationalism with an Islam both reformed and adapted to the modern situation? Any alternative to the Khomeinī regime would undoubtedly have to be built on the two pillars of Iranian culture and history. And anyone who disregards tradition and culture or thinks that after all the negative experiences with the Islamic Republic it's possible to bypass Islam will simply come to grief." *(Die Zeit,* November 19, 1982)

". . . an Islam both reformed and adapted to the modern situation"? Or, as the (Sunnite) Egyptian Hamdī Mahmūd 'Azzām puts it, in *Islam: A Muslim Makes His Case* (1981): a "rational model that can yoke basic Islamic values and the demands of the modern technological age"? (p. 47) But *can* divine law, the *sharī'a,* which is rooted in the Qur'an and tradition, and therefore is understood as the explanation of God's will— can such a law be reformed at all, and made compatible with the de- mands of contemporary life?

THE PROBLEM OF A RELIGION OF LAW

The *sharī'a,* Islamic law, the complete corpus of dogmatic teachings and legal prescriptions, is an integral part of Islam. It is at the same time a constituent of the *umma,* Islamic society: an organic religious "system" that makes no distinction between what is Caesar's and what is God's. According to Islamic apologetic literature, *sharī'a,* the ancient holy law, as collected and formed by legal scholars from the seventh to the tenth centuries, continues to be fully binding. It remains, they say, thoroughly up to date and capable of regulating all of today's social problems. When contradictions arise, the best that can be done is to admit that God himself allows "abrogation" of individual stipulations of Qur'anic law. A number of Islamic jurists admit that there are gaps in the *sharī'a,* but these may be closed by means of *ijtihād* ("exertion"): independent interpretation of the law. But can this work by medieval jurists, which was designed for totally different social circumstances, still claim validity today on every point? Many Muslims are asking this question, which echoes the ideas of the nineteenth- and early-twentieth-century Islamic reformers. Such questions should be explored in depth and exposed to fresh insights in Islamic-Christian dialogue, so we can finally study the problem of the connection between law and religion in a thorough, thematic fashion.

As with Judaism and Christianity, the central difficulty facing Islam is *literal faith,* or legal piety, the fundamentalist approach to scriptural law. In Old Testament law we find 613 regulations, in Rome's Codex Iuris Canonici (1918) 2,414 canons, and in the most famous traditional Is- lamic collection, by al-Bukhārī (d. 870)—which is the basis for rendering juridical decisions—7,300 *hadīth* (along with some nonlegal material as well). All questions, whether about the call to prayer, buying and selling, or dental care, are settled here by religious law. The spiritual/secular rulers who make and apply the laws always find them easy, but in prac- tice they are often a terrible burden.

While dealing with the subject of literal belief in dogma, morality, and law, I had occasion earlier to speak about the necessity of Qur'anic criticism (analogous to biblical criticism), which would naturally include scholarly examination of the *shari'a*. We have seen that al-Afghānī himself invoked the memory of the Protestant Reformation, which subjected the literal faith of the medieval clergy to a sharp critique. But don't we need to press our questions still further?

What about the law and piety based on it? What attitude should Christians assume—for themselves, in the first instance, but in dialogue as well? If we speak frankly and to the point, then however greatly we may esteem Muhammad the prophet and politician, the idealist and realist who founded a *religion of law*, as Christians we cannot side-step the *criticism of the law* uttered by that other "prophet" (recognized as such by the Qur'an) Jesus of Nazareth. From Jesus comes the admonition: "Woe to you lawyers also! for you load men with burdens hard to bear, and you yourselves do not touch the burdens with one of your fingers." (Lk 11:46) Later on we shall have to deal more extensively with the image of Jesus in the Qur'an. But here let me address, this once, the problematic nature of the law in Jesus' preaching. This is a topic that the Qur'an, for all the (extremely positive) things it has to say about Jesus, blots out of the picture, and probably not by accident. A simple reading of the gospel can make it clear to a Muslim that the Qur'an's treatment of Jesus is inadequate: It fails to appreciate the very point that all the original sources containing Jesus' message tell us was the most crucial one, and that after Jesus' death Paul made into the pivot of his theology of "justification for the Gentiles": "freedom from the Law."

GOD'S COMMANDMENTS—FOR HUMANITY'S SAKE

First we must keep clearly in mind the fact that Jesus had the same central concern as Judaism before him and Muhammad after him: with *God*, with *unconditional obedience* to God. There is unquestionably a fundamental common bond linking Judaism, Christianity, and Islam. "Islam" means "submission" or "surrender" to God (understood not as passive resignation, but as active commitment). This can be paraphrased perfectly well by Jesus' prayer "Thy will be done." What God wishes in heaven, should be done on earth (which Christians may not take to mean resigned "submission to God"). The English word "will" is only an approximate rendering of the Hebrew *rāsōn* or Aramaic *re'ūthā,* which actually mean "favor, satisfaction": what God in his favor, in his satisfaction with us, has decided for our well-being. Thus Jesus means God's saving will: May this will be fulfilled! As we shall later see in greater detail, there is no contradiction between the Islamic "It is God's will" and Jesus' "God's will be done."

In Jesus' day, a great many pious individuals (but not "the Jews" as a whole) had completely identified obedience to the will of God with obedience to *the written law* of Moses and the tradition that interpreted this law. Now, no one would deny that a law can give people security. Isn't it often easier simply to cling rigidly to the generally accepted law, instead of deciding from the standpoint of the person involved? And yet, no law can take into account all the vicissitudes of life, stop all the gaps, or consider all the concrete interests of the individual. Naturally, efforts were made in first-century Judaism, as they would be later in Christianity and Islam, to straighten out, in a lawyerly fashion, the provisions of the law that had become meaningless, or artificially to derive something from them to fit the altered situation and thereby to refine the rules. This really seems to be the only option if one equates the letter of the law with the will of God: to accumulate laws by continually interpreting and explaining them. But the finer the net, the more holes it has. And the more one bids and forbids, the more one obscures what is most crucial.

It was precisely this attitude toward the law that Jesus of Nazareth gave the deathblow to. His attack is aimed not at God's holy law itself, but at the human *self-righteousness that corrupts it,* and at the "traditions" and "things handed down by our fathers," which, like weeds, have overrun God's commandments. "And why do you transgress the commandment of God for the sake of your traditions?" (Mt 15:3) *Jesus measures the letter of the law against God's will itself,* thereby liberating and blessing men and women, placing them immediately in God's presence. This is *a new kind of obedience to God,* not according to the letter, but (as Paul will say) in the "spirit." Jesus neither asks for recommitment to the old law nor does he proclaim a new law embracing every aspect of life. He issues neither moral nor ritual regulations spelling out how a person should pray, fast, observe the holy times, and act in the holy places, or even how to live hygienically.

Jesus is concerned with inculcating a new, all-pervasive outlook. Taking a wholly concrete approach, far from all casuistry, pedantic dogmatism, and literal-minded credulity, the Jesus of the Sermon on the Mount and the parables calls for a new attitude of faith and active love. He calls for the fulfillment of the will of God, who has no other goal but the salvation, the comprehensive *well-being, of humanity.* That is the reason for *submission* ("islām") *to God,* an act, of course, that is supposed to encompass *our whole life and all people,* even our enemies. In this sense, Jesus proposes a *"new righteousness"* as the foundation of human life. Rather than promulgate law upon law, he issues simple, transparent, liberating appeals, which dispense with arguments from authority or tradition and instead offer examples, signs, and symptoms of the changed life spent loving God and man. The Sermon on the Mount testifies eloquently to this life, for which there is no equivalent in Islam.

I say this not because I believe that in this area and in every case Christianity is "superior" to Islam. I say it because we have arrived at the crux in the theological controversy about the law: What should a person follow as his guide? What should he base his life on? How is God to be understood? How do I recognize him? What is his will, and how do I carry it out? And I say this fully aware that laws are a part of every political structure; that rules, regulations, and "pillars" are an inalienable property of every religion; and that a number of superficial, muddle-headed Christians could learn a great deal today from the elementary core of orthopraxy in Islam: from the spiritual ideal of daily prayer, from the ascetical ideal of fasting, from the social ideal of almsgiving, and finally from the meaning of the public profession of faith.

But I wonder whether it might not have a positive effect on the Qur'an and the *shari'a* if, instead of medieval scholasticism and casuistry, one applied to them the hermeneutic principle that the will of God is carried out through service to human beings. This would mean that the *serving our fellow men and women takes priority over complying with the law.* Humanity instead of legalism. This is not a retreat into inwardness, just an insistence that norms and institutions must not be set up as absolutes. It is God's will (look at Jesus' message) that human beings never be sacrificed to a norm or institution that poses as absolute. God's commandments exist for man's sake, and not the other way around. That is not to say that norms and institutions should be simply repealed or abolished. But all rules and regulations, all laws and commandments, norms and institutions, all analogy and consensus, all legal compilations and schools of law, are subject, by God's will, to the criterion of service to humanity. Perhaps, then, Muslims might not find it misleading if we say: by God's will even the *shari'a exists for the sake of man,* and not man for the sake of the *shari'a.* Man is therefore the measure of the law. And so might it not be the function of *conscience* here and now to distinguish which parts of a religious system are just and unjust, what is essential or dispensable, constructive or destructive, good law or bad?

This would allow the creation of the *religious elbow room* needed to eliminate—without exegetical tricks—the scandalous shortcomings of Islamic law (the repudiation of women; violations of human rights, including the right to dissent; the prohibition against charging interest) and in particular of penal law (mutilation, flogging, public executions, the death penalty for apostasy from Islam). As far back as the ninth century, Islamic scholars vehemently argued the question of whether the Qur'an was the created or uncreated word of God. Some maintained that the Qur'an was created in time (and therefore modifiable?). And the doctrine of *ijtihād* (independent determination), despite the supposed "closing of the gate of *ijtihād* around the year 900, was never abandoned, even after the *sharī'a* administrative system was given political support under the Ottoman sultans in the sixteenth century.

From the eighteenth century onward, colonial status, in Algeria, say, or India, led to the altering of Islamic law. And beginning in the nineteenth century, as a result of increased contact with Europe and America, legal changes were made even in the Ottoman Empire and Egypt. Finally, in 1926, the Turkish Republic dropped the *sharī'a* altogether and did away with the religious courts. And for all practical purposes, the other Islamic countries (except for Saudi Arabia, Yemen, and recently Iran) abandoned the *sharī'a* in civil and criminal law. Its sphere of influence was further narrowed by the introduction of other codices and specific laws—apart, that is, from the vital areas of law governing marriage, the family, and inheritance. One wonders if this whole process can be reversed, as Pakistan and the Sudan are currently trying to do.

EFFORTS AT AN INTRA-ISLAMIC CRITIQUE OF THE LAW

History, then, has largely gone in the direction of the reformers. Yet if we take the long-term view, a fundamental theological solution suggests itself, which can be reached only (to echo the end of my first response) with a *historical reading of the Qur'an.* Apropos of this, Fazlur Rahman correctly observes in the epilogue (1979) to his book *Islam* (1966), on understanding the Qur'an:

> It should be studied in chronological order, so as to assess the development of its themes and ideas (otherwise one can be easily misled at certain important points). It should be studied against its sociohistorical background. This is true not only of individual passages, for which there is what the commentators call "occasions for revelations," but also for the Qur'an as a whole, for which there was a background in pagan Mecca, which was the "occasion for the Qur'an." Unless one understands this macro- and micro-background adequately, one will probably make serious mistakes in judging the fundamental impetus of the Qur'an and the effectiveness of the Prophet. (p. 261)

Islam in Transition, mentioned previously, is full of stimulating ideas advanced by Muslim intellectuals concerning a basic change in the Islamic understanding of law. As a representative case, we may cite the Egyptian Arabist Muhammad Nuwaihī, who calls for a thorough transformation of Islamic law—as opposed to piecemeal reforms—prompted by a spirit of religious renewal. In *Call from the Minaret* (1979), a "self-presentation" of Islam compiled from the original sources, the Yugoslavian Muslim Smail Balić makes an equally clear demand and forceful argument for distinguishing between the time-bound and the permanent: "The Qur'ān ('a.s.) is the unshakable foundation and point of orientation *(habl matīn)* for Muslim religious life. No believer can doubt that. Still, it seems that there has not been enough in-depth progress in studying the *esbāb enuzūl,* the concrete occasions for individual Qur'ānic revelations and the legal philosophy that resulted from them, so as to separate the time-bound element from what is lasting. The realization that the Qur'ān is in part a collection of period documents from the early history of Islam has thus far not managed to pass beyond the status of pure theory." (p. 90)

In India a whole group of Muslim scholars has explicitly moved away from the notion of the literal inspiration of the Qur'an and endorsed a historical interpretation that should, at the same time, make it possible to translate the Qur'an into the idiom of the present. "I am sure," says Asaf A. A. Fyzee, a prominent spokesman for Indian Islam, "that we cannot go 'back' to the Qur'an; we must instead go 'forward' with it. I wish to *understand* the Qur'an as the Arabs in the days of the Prophet understood it, but only in order to *reinterpret* it, to apply it to the conditions of my life, and to believe in it to the extent that it addresses me as a 20th-century person." (quoted by R. Wielandt, p. 159)

We hear these words echoed in the position of Muslim scholar living in Europe Muhammad M. Arkoun, professor of Arabic language and Islamic culture at the University of Paris. During an Islamic-Christian colloquium in Bonn in 1981 he decisively opposed the kind of Christian-Muslim encounter in which only the integralist and fundamentalist forces on both sides merely affirm their own viewpoints. In lieu of that, Arkoun insisted that each group take seriously the radical changes that have occurred in the natural sciences and modern culture as a whole, and turn them to account in shaping a fresh understanding of religion: "Rather than pursuing its urgent responsibility of raising new questions about the function of religion in human existence, the philosophy underlying Islamic-Christian dialogue continues to propagate the fiction of an eternally unchanging Reason, which is illuminated by revelation, rooted in the ontology of the holy scriptures, and consequently infallible in its dealings and statements. —For this reason I, for one, call for a new critical reading of the scriptures (Bible, Gospels, Qur'an) and a philosophical critique of exegetical and theological reason." (quoted from *Religion in Culture, Law, and Politics,* ed. M. S. Abdullah, 1982, pp. 141 f.)

In concluding this response from both the Islamic and the Christian sides, we may ask, To what degree can the Qur'an or the Bible still be revelation and the word of God after a "critical reading"? As I indicated at the end of my first response—and the Islamic scholars quoted here, along with the majority of Christian exegetes, would agree—the alternatives, a) either purely God's word and therefore binding revelation or b) purely man's word and therefore nonbinding human experience, is outdated. For the Qur'an, as for the Bible, *God's word* can be heard only in *human words;* divine revelation is imparted only through human experience and interpretation.

As social circumstances change, religion will not disappear, but (and to this extent Karl Marx was right) it will *change.* In the contemporary situation—externally stable, internally labile—that many Islamic countries find themselves in, the more promising strategy for the future ought to be as follows: Instead of trying (in the traditionalist style) to preserve everything, both the *"achievements" of the West* and their *own traditional positions* should be subjected to a *discriminating, constructive Islamic critique,* so as to distinguish in Islam between the permanent and the transitory, between what is essentially Islamic, the great Islamic tradition (based on the Qur'an), and the *idées reçues,* every conceivable customary notion, and so as to be able to draw a clear distinction between morality and legality, between unchangeable ethical constants and changeable legal stipulations. Many Muslims, too, are looking for an Islamic ethic and vision of the world, distinct from the law actually in effect (but serving as its basis, in a nonsimplistic sense), and, generally speaking, in view of their improved educational system, they are hoping for a newly creative literature and intellectual life, as in the centuries when Islamic science and culture were flourishing.

In conclusion I shall quote once again from Fazlur Rahman, who presses for an understanding of the Qur'an that is both historical and synthetic-systematic and that, above all, as Rahman says in *Islam and Modernity* (1982), must include "a clear distinction between Qur'anic ethics and Qur'anic law." (p. 154) He continues:

> The sole possibility of creating genuine Islamic law consists in illuminating the public conscience, especially that of the educated classes, with the light of Islamic values. This, in fact, underlines the necessity of systematically elaborating Islamic ethics from the Qur'an, and of making such work accessible to the general public. This sort of creation of Islamic law cannot be done overnight. Hence, there is no doubt that a broad study of the earlier work done in the field of Islamic jurisprudence and Islamic law will be helpful. If first-class works on the history of Islamic law and Islamic are written—and they must be—then they should be assigned in the schools of law as part of the normal curriculum. In this way central concepts of Islamic law and morality could gradually find their way into the legal profession. In many Islamic countries the lawyers themselves are eager to learn more about Islamic law. Perhaps an international committee of Muslim jurists should be formed with first-class traditionalist scholars of law and jurisprudence from various medieval schools, in order to undertake larger studies in this area. For the present, al-Azhar would be the most promising center for such a development. (pp. 156–57)

For the sake of Islam, of Christianity, and of world peace, it is of the utmost importance that the newly awakened Islamic self-awareness and the feeling of worldwide Muslim solidarity should not in the end move in the direction of fundamentalist legalism, but lead to a self-critical Muslim reform. Speaking as a Christian, perhaps I may be permitted to join with many Muslims in saying this on behalf of Islam: Like Christianity, what Islam needs (once its struggles against Western colonialism have been fought through) is neither an exclusively inner reorientation without social consequences nor an exclusively outer adaptation to a Zeitgeist made in the West, and not just socioeconomic improvement. Like Christianity, Islam needs a *comprehensive spiritual renewal* in which a religiously and theologically grounded ethos could serve as the foundation for a better political, social, and legal order. In this way the substance of Islam would be transfigured in a truly contemporary ecumenical paradigm.

III.
The Image of God and Islamic Mysticism, the Image of Man and Society

1. *Josef van Ess:* Islamic Perspectives

THE PRIMACY OF MONOTHEISM

Pascal distinguished between the "God of Abraham, Isaac, and Jacob" and the "God of the philosophers." When we contemplate the Islamic image of God, we may easily get the impression that we are dealing with the "God of the philosophers," so clear and rational does everything seem. Monotheism typically strikes Christians as a mere idea, but for Muslims it is an experiential reality; and as a matter of fact their God *is* in a special way, as we have seen, the God of Abraham. Pascal's distinction really doesn't apply to Islam; it presupposes a conflict between faith and knowledge that isn't there.

Compared with the triune God of the Christians, the God of the Muslims is indeed a God without mystery; or, rather, his mystery lies not in his nature, but in his actions, in the unfathomable way by which he directs humanity or has made certain things obligatory through his law. He has spoken about his nature in revelation. There one learns that he has attributes, and those attributes may cause problems if they turn out to be too human. But Muslim theology has often let things rest with a *non liquet;* it has a noticeable aversion toward going too far beyond revelation. That doesn't mean that we won't meet with some interesting speculative thinking, particularly in the fertile early history of Islam. But Muslims never formulated new truths of faith, as in the church councils, that were understood as the unfolding of revealed axioms. There was, after all, no magisterium that could have done this. The consensus of the religious scholars, which might most readily be compared to the councils, has always limited itself to legal findings, precedent-making decisions, as it were.

The classic formula expressing the unity and uniqueness of God is found in a short sura (no. 112) that is always quoted by Muslims as a kind of credo: "Say: 'He is God, One, / God, the Everlasting Refuge, / who has not begotten, and has not been begotten, / and equal to Him is not any one.' " This sounds like a polemic against the "begotten, not made" of the Nicene Creed, but it may not be meant that way at all. Perhaps the sura originated in Mecca, in which case it would be aimed against heathen polytheism. When he was still the supreme god of the Meccan pantheon, Allah had several daughters. Nonetheless, nowadays every Muslim will insist that with this sura the Trinity, too, is rejected. Even if he doesn't interpret it as tritheism, which often happens in the heat of controversy, he will consider it utterly superfluous. Muslims see in the Trinity a triumph of theology over scripture. But theology is a human enterprise; only Christians bother to invoke the Holy Spirit while engaged in it. This conclusion is all the easier for Muslims to reach when trinitarian theology is presented to them—as it is to us, for that matter—in a foreign language; the terms they hear it expounded in come from the Aramaic (Syriac), which sounds at least as amusing to Arabs as sociologese does to us. Also important is the fact that the Trinity implies the Incarnation, and that, Muslims will say, is certainly a misguided notion: the boundaries between God and man cannot be blurred.

GOD AS THE MERCIFUL LORD

Islam, in fact, has no idea of a mediator. Muhammad is the bringer of salvation only in the sense of information. Otherwise every bridge between heaven and earth is deliberately torn down: There are no sacraments, no cult images, no church music. God is transcendent. But that sounds to us as if he were far away or impersonal; because for us God manifests himself in various persons, and monotheism is above all a philosophical idea. For Muslims, by contrast, God is not simply the One, but the Only One, to whom all things are oriented, and who cares for all things. He is the Lord, and he is the Merciful One.

This is expressed in the two names of God, which play a central role in the Qur'an, both of them names with a long pre-Islamic tradition, and both more than mere attributes: Allah, translated as "the God [pure and simple]", and ar-Rahmān, the "Merciful"—the "Gracious," to put it in a somewhat more Christian fashion. Thus God in Islam is no despot; he can do with man as he sees fit, but he does this in the sense of caring for man. He directs men and women, but they do not feel helplessly passive as a result. To be sure, the Muslim speaks of himself as the "slave of

God," the "servant." But we are so allergic to such expressions mainly because we operate on the assumption of individual autonomy. We call ourselves "your obedient servant" only in old-fashioned or ironic epistolary style. Islam stresses, far more than Christianity, the creaturely status of man.

But, it will be objected, a person is not a "slave" of God for another reason. We describe human beings as God's children, and God is not just the Lord, but the Father, too. This sort of language is just not heard in Islam, but we must consider the reason for that: A child for the Arabs is always a son, and God has no son; he does not "beget." That formula is impossible, because it has trinitarian associations. In point of fact, God's mercifulness contains a good deal of the fatherliness that we look upon as typically Christian. And while Muslims consider obedience the cardinal virtue, in view of man's servant nature, they speak in the same breath about trust and gratitude; the word for "unbelief" means the same thing as "ingratitude."

It is a similarly complex situation with another term, one that Christians are so proud of, namely love. The Qur'an continually says that God loves the people who follow his commandments, the "righteous," the "repentant," the "God-fearing" (cf. sura 2, 195; 2, 222; 3, 76, etc.) But theologians in general have not concluded from these passages that God *has* love, and still less that God *is* love. This was in some small part due to the ambiguity of the word: "Love" could also mean amorousness, as in the poets, or even a sickness of the soul, or madness, a usage familiar from Aristotle and the physicians of antiquity. Still, it is characteristic of Muslim theologians that they did not create their own definition of God. They were certain that God does not disclose himself beyond the limits of revelation; he does not give himself away. And when man surrenders himself to God—for *islam* means just that, surrender—it is to God's will, not to God as a person.

THE CONCEPT OF LOVE IN ISLAMIC MYSTICISM

But theologians and jurists are not, of course, the sole representatives of Islam. Alongside the "religion of the law"—and by no means necessarily at odds with it—there was from the very beginning the world of the personal search for God and of mysticism. Here love, in the reciprocal sense of God's love for man and man's love for God, was centrally important, as the highest stage of the ascent to him, equivalent to dissolving into him. At this point, contact with God deepened until he became the Thou into which the I is completely absorbed. Among the oldest texts informing us about this phenomenon are the poems and sayings of a woman who lived in the Iraqi city of Basra in the eighth century (A.D.). The following verses from her pen were well known:

> I love You in a twofold way: in selfish surrender
> or because You deserve it.
> Selfish surrender means that I am consumed
> with thoughts of You, far from all that is not You.
> But [love] that is worthy of you means
> that You lift the veil so that I look upon You.
> I deserve neither the one nor the other;
> all praise is Yours for both!

This also shed a new light on "works." Not that they were absolutely depreciated, as happened with the jurists. But tradition has the same woman mystic saying, "I have served God not in fear of hell, for I would be only a wretched hireling, if I did it out of fear. Nor did I do it out of love of paradise; for I would be a bad servant if I served for what is given to me. I have served him only for love of him and longing for him."

We must wonder, naturally, how influential such thinking was on Islamic culture as a whole. In this context it is important to know that mysticism did not remain, as it did in the West, an individual concern; but over the course of the centuries it circulated among the people. Communities arose, orders, to which varied groups of the population belonged (in the late Ottoman period, especially the nineteenth century), including artisans and legal scholars and powerful military men. The movement had sprung up as a reaction against the pronounced legalization and intellectualization of Islam, against the pharisaical element, as we would—too harshly—label it. But in the end it turned out that the two parties *were* compatible: Heart and mind, immediate experience of God and the most scrupulous observance of his commandments were not contrary to each other. This inevitably brought with it a certain shallowness: In the orders, mysticism offered people the amenities of a club. But it also meant that concepts like love or fusion with God made their way into the consciousness of the general public.

Since we are chiefly concerned here with present-day Islam's understanding of itself, it is equally important to know that for some time now these mystical brotherhoods have been losing a lot of ground in the heartland of Islam. They are a thorn in the side of the nationalists, because they look for the experience of community outside the nation. They are repugnant to the fundamentalists, because they have deviated too far from the paradigmatic sobriety of primitive Islam. Only in the borderlands, in Africa, for example, or in India, do they continue to play a major role. This means that nowadays mystical values are often heatedly rejected, above all by intellectuals and ideologues.

And there is a second point that must be considered: Though love as a religious category may take a very prominent place in mysticism, still this is not, on the whole, a love between equal partners, but a love in which one of the partners, namely God, gradually takes the place of the other. For the human being this means not integration, but disintegration, fulfillment, but rather in the sense of depersonalization. It is true, the mystics sometimes speak of a "staying on" after the "annihilation," a condition in which the person rediscovers himself in God; but they can tell us very little about this. In the final analysis the element of submission resonates through this kind of love too. In mystical poetry, God always plays the part of the one who receives love, the beloved. But the beloved, as the mystics knew, has the lover in the palm of his hand.

NATURE AS THE MIRROR OF DIVINE POWER

Thus God remains the Lord, however subtly understood. And such subtleties apply only to God's relation to man. In his relation to inanimate creation, his controlling power is nakedly clear. Just as God cares for humanity at every moment, so at every moment he holds nature in his hand, and not only in the manner of the artificer, the *technités*, as antiquity and modern deism imagined. The world is no clockwork, nor does it run according to its own intrinsic laws. God himself determines everything that happens at every moment, without "second causes," i.e., without what we from our perspective would view as the immediate, and the only valid, causal connection. The world does have its system, but this is not the system of a cosmos. The system is not binding for the one who has put it in place, namely God. God can, of course, work miracles. We call this occasionalism. Malebranche thought along these lines, and so did the medieval philosopher Nicholas of Autrecourt. Thus causality is, in the strict sense, only an optical illusion. What we interpret as *propter hoc* is in reality only a *post hoc*, as the theologian al-Ghazzālī said—in a work, by the way, that was translated into Latin and in which he anticipated the epistemology of David Hume. Even natural laws have only a limited validity—insofar as God, out of habit, always makes the same decisions, the *coutumes de Dieu*, as Leibniz called them. God is free, though not necessarily capricious.

The last sentence implicitly answers a question that immediately suggests itself here to every enterprising Westerner: Where do these theological teachings leave science and technology? As a matter of fact, neither of them is especially impaired; because, while God's ways may be beyond human calculation, he is not always doing something different from one minute to the next. He has his customs, and basically these customs can be relied on. He doesn't work miracles simply when he has a mind to, because a miracle, according to the definition elaborated by Islamic theology, is always an act of confirmation designed to help a prophet move the public more effectively. After Muhammad, however, no other prophet will appear; he was, after all, the "seal" of the prophets. This sort of convention is enough for the scientist. He knows anyway that natural laws are merely inductive conclusions which we accept as given until further notice.

On the other hand, we have to take into account the fact that, primarily through the influence of the mystical orders, the faith of the simple people in miracles was increasingly free to develop over time. The head of such an order, the sheikh in Arab territory, the pir in Iran, the marabout in the Maghreb and elsewhere in Africa, were all credited with preternatural powers: telekinesis, clairvoyance, bilocation; and just like a prophet, each of them had to win legitimacy with powers of this sort. In addition, the devaluation of second causes, however theoretical, is ill suited for stimulating interest in them. One finds it easier than it might be otherwise to retreat into the inscrutability of God's decrees. At the least, therefore, religion offers no incentive for pursuing science. But it doesn't offer that incentive anywhere else, either. That's not its purpose. As a rule, interest in the natural sciences grows out of different roots.

We can say, however, that for a Muslim, God does not speak from within nature, but past it. Nature, to exaggerate a little, is theologically just not there. It is thus not a force to which man might entrust himself; it has no emotional value. "Mother Nature" cannot be translated into Arabic, and the Muslim is no protector of the environment. Now, we need not lay the burden of explanation for all this at the door of theology. Islam is at home in regions of the earth where nature generally confronts humanity in a hostile guise. Here man must defy it; he cannot merge with it. His ideal is the artificially fashioned world: the city, the irrigation system, the garden (which he brings into the house in the form of the carpet). And the poetry of Islamic urban culture, when it speaks of nature, does not describe untouched wild landscapes, but garden flowers, which it usually compares to something dead, with jewelry or precious stones. The thought that other things, the desert, mountains, the forest, are creation too, and so might have a meaning in themselves, simply does not occur to Muslims. Creation has its meaning either with a view toward human beings, insofar as they make use of it and can thank God for it, or with a view toward God, insofar as he manifests his power in it.

God and man are the coordinates of this system; *tertium non datur*. Islamic theologians do not take cosmogony as their point of departure, as did the Greeks and, in a certain sense, the medieval Scholastics. They do not search for the first principle of nature; and they write no commentaries on Genesis. The proofs of God's existence that they use are in general neither cosmological nor teleological. These theologians were mostly jurists by profession, and their world picture was a juridical one: entirely oriented to action, and indeed to responsible action, such as can be found only among human beings.

DIVINE POWER AND HUMAN FREEDOM

The key question, then, is how responsible action can come about when God holds firmly in his hand the events caused by humans. In other words, the question is, To what extent do we have freedom of the will? At this point we need to clear away the prejudice that Muslims are fatalists and believe in "kismet." "Kismet" is a Turkish word (borrowed from Arabic) that does not appear at all in theology and is doubtless familiar to Germans only because of Karl May's novels, and to Americans only because of the musical of the same name. Muslims, however, are *not* fatalists, because they believe in a personal, caring God. If they believe themselves at the mercy of fate, this conviction comes—as it does for us—in times of powerlessness, in the experience of absolute helplessness.

On the other hand, one often encounters a notion of predestination in which the unbelievers are struck blind by God and earmarked for hell, while the Muslims, in the end, all go off to paradise. Muslims sometimes appear astonished at people who remain obdurate and refuse to acknowledge the truth—a usual point of departure for predestinarian thinking. This is still a long way off from the predetermining of actions, and only when we get to that stage are we really denying the freedom of the will, because both Muslims and pagans continue to do good *and* evil together, and at least Muslims can establish the proportion of reward to punishment through their decisions. The fact that Westerners pride themselves so much on their faith in free will is probably connected with their no longer seeing the theological problem. Christians pass judgment on this matter not at all as Christians; they are, instead, committed to the imaginative world of modernity. In dealing with free will, they know that it faces obstacles, but they prefer to speak about historical necessities or compulsions or social constraints, not about God.

As with nature, so with man, Muslims explain God's behavior as a balance between the theoretical extremes of constant intervention and the normal "hands off" policy. God helps with the doing of good and lets evil take place. Both correspond to his eternal plan, which he knows in advance. But knowing things in advance is not the same as determining them in advance. True, they will not happen any differently, but man must still decide for good or evil; and he will rightly be rewarded or punished. God, not man, sets up all the preconditions for what human beings do with the objects of their actions in the realm of nature, for example. But this, as we have seen, is at most of philosophical, not theological, interest. In theology all considerations focus on how human action takes place.

The language used here is quite interesting. Theologians habitually speak not of free will, but of "choice." This means that the framework within which freedom is exercised is already given. The individual chooses between obedience and disobedience. He can disregard a commandment, but he can't place himself outside the system. "Freedom" is liberty to make decisions from among the alternatives created by divine law; it is not spontaneity or radical openness, and still less is it the negation of authority and obligation. There *is* a word in classical Arabic for "freedom," but it refers to something given and irrevocable: to the legal status of the free man as opposed to the slave. Thus the slave has no "freedom," but he does have a "choice" in the eyes of God. The Muslims first encountered freedom in the sense of the rights of a citizen when Napoleon, who was still General Bonaparte at the time, appeared in Egypt. But it comes as no surprise that at first they viewed the *liberté* thus displayed to them as libertinism and anarchy. It was an abrupt invasion of secularity into their traditional frame of reference.

Islamic theologians, thus, do not speak directly of freedom; and the same is true of the will. What interests them is, rather, the extent to which a person is actually capable of willing and acting. The important thing here, however, is that they think of this capacity of action, like events in nature, as connected to God, in principle, at every moment. Capacity is only capacity for a single action, and not a permanent quality. The individual does not *have* a will, but receives it anew every time he is faced with a choice, because a choice is always something singular, a momentary decision—only freedom would be permanent. Hence we are also guaranteed that God immediately perceives every single action of a person. As Islamic theology maintained against the philosophers, such as Avicenna, God has not only a general knowledge of the development of a person, he is aware of all the "particulars" of his or her behavior. The problem with this is that logically it makes action discontinuous.

In analyzing the Islamic concept of nature, we have already seen that this has hardly any *practical* effect, but it does have further *systematic* consequences. Evil, too, is actualized only in an atomistic fashion. There are sins, but there is no Sin that has come into the world. There is no "mystery of iniquity"; there are just wrong decisions. Only Islamic mysticism took a deeper view of this situation, when it meditated on Satan's fall. According to the Qur'an, Satan sinned by refusing to bow down before Adam, God's privileged creature, when God bade him. Thus he disregarded a command from God (cf. sura 15, 28–35). And yet, the mystics said, he was actually right to do so. For such a prostration was due to God alone, not to his creature. Satan, as it were, realizes the ideal of monotheism against God's explicit bidding. He ignores a *command* of God, but at the same time he fulfills God's *will.* And God has damned him, but he loves him still. The thinking here is not at all atomistic, but cosmic in the sense of a great universal drama. But even in this case

Satan's rebellion has no metaphysical consequences. Humanity remains untouched by it. Much the same is true of Adam's fall. It was really not a fall but a blunder, and Adam himself made reparation for it. Reparation takes place through penance, which in turn applies only to specific individual transgressions. There is no redemption in this system, and Muhammad does not intercede for anyone.

THE UNITY OF SOUL AND BODY IN MAN

All this has interesting consequences for the image of man. Since action is at every moment directed to God,* there is no need of a special agency to give these individual acts coherence. Islamic theology has scarcely any notion of the person. For a long time, the immortality of the soul was not generally recognized, and it has been a serious issue only on the fringes of Islam. For many theologians, the soul was a "part" of man, like his appearance or height—the breath of life, and no more. Here Islam is very much in the Semitic tradition; Plato has had almost no influence. Conversely, this means that body and soul do not separate from each other; both die together, and both will be restored to life together. This concept of man may be discontinuous, but it is also monistic. The resurrection of the body creates no philosophical problems at all here. It is, besides, once again a Semitic idea, and not Greek.

Furthermore, we can now see why the Qur'an describes the joys of paradise as both physical and spiritual. Muslims, as everyone knows, can look forward to more than just the beatific vision in the next world; eating and drinking (wine, which is forbidden on earth) play an important role there, along with the houris, who were sometimes thought to be identical to the earthly wives of the faithful. The vision of God is undoubtedly, for Muslims as for Christians, the ultimate reach of happiness. But one small difference should be noted: Muslims think of it not as permanent but intermittent; God reveals himself on a stage, in front of which the curtain rises from time to time—a spectacular but not quite transforming experience. The whole thing is reminiscent of a banquet at the palace of a caliph (when Abbasid caliphs gave an audience, they were concealed behind a curtain).

Someone who need not change his habits in paradise will take a more relaxed view of his own bodily nature in the here and now as well. One notices this in the way Muslims speak. They use fewer euphemisms than we do (or did until recently). Sexuality is not decried, not even by ascetics. Christian polemicists have always sensed a talking point here, as early as John Damascene and the Byzantines, and then, with a vengeance, the nineteenth-century Anglo-Saxon missionaries, they imme-

---

* Rather than forging ahead into the future.

diately raised the subject of polygamy and conjured up a licentious harem atmosphere.

But this presents a distorted picture. In Islam, sexuality is legitimate only within the law. Adultery and other sexual offenses incur harsh punishment. Muslims do not experience sex as the privilege of adults living on their own; hence they are, nowadays, more prudish than Europeans. Yet this prudery does not grow out of guilt feelings. It signifies, instead, that one may not aggrandize one's God-given share of the world. The ideal is not the monk, but the married man. A religious dignitary who is unmarried would create a considerable stir. There is no demand in Islam as yet for the single life. Even the ascetics generally have families.

Islamic asceticism was also different from its Western counterpart. It often found expression in scrupulous observation of the rules governing religious purity. Ascetics kept away from everything that had been acquired in a forbidden manner or had come into contact with what was forbidden. This led to criticism of ill-gotten gain, and sometimes of any sort of possessions. But poverty never actually became the ideal. The Qur'an accepts private property as a fact of life, and almsgiving (one of the five "pillars" of Islam) is possible only if one already has something to give. Since, this way, wealth necessarily promotes the common good, attacks on possessions had a much smaller target area than was the case with Christianity. Most wealthy people, once they had deducted the required amount for charity, felt hardly any compunction. Riches were ordained by God. Muslims enjoyed them without embarrassment, without creeping into a posture of this-worldly asceticism. Precisely because *caritas* was never lost sight of, it never developed a special explosive power. On the other hand, Muslims were never so perverse as to understand wealth as a sign of election.

The Community of Believers

In speaking of Islam, we cannot limit ourselves to the individual; we must view him as a member of Islamic society. Here is where the "election" just mentioned comes in. Over the course of time, Muslims have become increasingly convinced that the individual, however much he may have sinned, at the very end will go to paradise on the strength of his membership in Islam. Note the "very end": First there will have to be some purgation. But his faith will help him. He is, we might say, justified by his profession of belief, by the *shahāda*. God refuses forgiveness to only *one* sin: polytheism, which also means renunciation of Islam.

In this certainty, we see manifested once again the unusual feeling of solidarity that we already saw as a characteristic feature of the performance of cultic duties. The ecumene, the *umma* as it is called, has remained for Muslims a lofty and unchallenged value. Christianity, with its dogmatic structure, has been much more sharply rent by schism than Islam. We saw that even Sunna and Shi'a, at least as far as the "pillars" are concerned, scarcely differ from each other. Not until the present day was the ideal of the ecumene challenged by a counterforce—by nationalism, which the Islamic world, like Judaism, borrowed somewhat belatedly from Europe. It is significant that Arab nationalism, especially in its beginning stages, was promoted not at all by Muslims, but by Arab Christians. And even today some extremist groups within the PLO still have Christian leadership.

Until this turn toward nationalism, however, the ideal of the community of believers helped to smooth some of the rough edges that create social pain and tension. Racial differences, for example, have never played the sort of role in Islam that they have in Christianity. Islam spread much too quickly and much too far for initial Arab feelings of superiority (which have, of course, never quite disappeared) to have any chance of winning out. In addition, the Arabs were culturally inferior to the newly converted peoples. There were blacks in the primitive community. It is easy enough to find evidence for the fact that racial differences were noted and minor forms of discrimination were incorporated from time to time into the system. But Islam has never known deliberate racism. This is one of the reasons why it has had an easier time proselytizing in Africa than has Christianity.

In the same way, other privileges, though very much a part of the social world were less frequently undergirded by ideology or religion than in Europe. Remarkably, Islamic countries have never had classes or a nobility in the Western sense. In contrast to Roman and medieval law, Islamic law has no category of persons (apart from slaves) for whom separate regulations were in force. To be sure, there were great landowners, as well as economic arrangements quite similar to medieval fiefs. But, before the law, all men and women were, at least theoretically, equal. Medieval Islamic society was relatively fluid. Proof of this might be seen in the fact, say, that children born of concubinage with a female slave were considered free. The ideal of *limpieza de sangre,* so familiar to us from *Don Quixote,* did not survive the first century of Islamic history. Islam is basically egalitarian.

ISLAMIC EQUALITY AND ITS LIMITS

It is just as true, of course, that in social matters Islam has by no means fomented revolution. It has, admittedly, prevented certain conditions from arising to begin with; but often it has simply accepted the conditions it found in place. This is the case, for example, with slavery. No Muslim jurist has ever doubted, on religious grounds, that this institu-

tion made sense. Even radical religious groups, whose ideology is sometimes thought nowadays to harbor a communism *avant la lettre,* made no
objection to slavery. In the ninth century, a group of slaves in Iraq
managed to stage an insurrection and win their independence for a time
from their masters and the central government—but they, too, kept
slaves. The jurists, however, have always treated slavery as an exception;
the normal state is freedom. On that score, the abolition of slavery,
under pressure from the Europeans, brought on no great change in the
law. A Muslim could not be enslaved anyhow. But this didn't mean that a
slave who converted to Islam had thereby won his freedom. The equaliz-
ing force of the *umma* did not extend that far.

On certain points, women, too, were—and still are, to some extent—
discriminated against by the law. In the Near East, as in the Mediterranean Basin as a whole, the family traditionally has a patriarchal structure. The line of descent is for the most part determined agnatically, that
is, through the male descendants. The Qur'an did introduce certain
corrections and do away with the worst injustices, for example in marriage law. But it did not touch the principle of male supremacy, and the
later jurists were not great innovators.

Thus it happened that with the growing European influence in the
twentieth century, a number of problematic areas, particularly in marriage law, were revised. According to the old religious law, divorce was
unilaterally declared by the husband, without any court's troubling itself
about the question. Actually it was a repudiation, rather than a divorce.
Today the state has jurisdiction over such cases in all Islamic countries.
In some of them, the rights of women in divorce are as well protected as
they are in the West—and the whole business is equally expensive.
Polygamy, which was always an exclusively masculine privilege, has now
generally become quite difficult and is no longer very popular. In Turkey and Tunisia it is forbidden by law.

This point also illustrates, however, the limits of adaptation. The
verse in the Qur'an that allows men to marry more than one wife at the
same time (sura 4, 3) is quite unambiguous. It actually even permits
believers to exceed the maximum of four wives permitted by canon law.
The only way to cut down the number is by taking very seriously the
condition mentioned in the following verse: ". . . but if you fear you
will not be equitable, / then [marry] only one." Tunisian jurists have
taken this to heart and declared that monogamy is the only form of
marriage humanly possible, especially since the same warning is found
still more clearly expressed elsewhere in the Qur'an (sura 4, 129). But
the original meaning of the text cannot have been so restrictive; otherwise the preceding permission ("marry such women / as seem good to
you, two, three, four") would make no sense. The only way to make any
progress here is to consider the verse in its historical context. But, for

many Muslims, historical exegesis still bears the stigma of relativizing the word of God.

Nevertheless, Tunisia may be leading the way into the future (more so, in any case, than Turkey, where polygamy was prohibited by executive fiat in 1925). A great deal depends upon the development of the social situation as a whole, which is, for the time being, quite different in different areas of the Islamic world. The position of women varies from the nomads to the sedentary population, from a traditional agricultural to an urban-bourgeois or even industrial environment. In Egypt or Turkey the percentage of women on university faculties is probably higher than in Europe. In Southeast Asia the veil is unknown—and in Indonesia, Malaysia, etc., live more than three times as many Muslims as in the entire Arabic-speaking world (which contains over 100 million). Emancipation in our sense is a phenomenon of the urban nuclear family and industrial society. In the traditional Eastern milieu, a woman is liberated not from her husband, but from her mother-in-law.

As everywhere else, in Islam religion and society are dialectically related. Islam would never have survived without the capacity to adapt to social change. Like Christianity, it does this by means of exegesis. At the same time, of course, it influences society; religion is itself a social force. There is no mistaking the fact that Islam exerts a stronger influence than we are used to seeing from Christianity (contemporary or otherwise). Certain social conditions are firmly enshrined in the Qur'an and religious law. True, one can always interpret the texts as if they meant other than what they say. But the danger of a reversion to the past is very great—and what is more important, this reversion can claim with some justice to be a return to the truth. The danger is removed only when religion acknowledges the historical relativity of religious statements. I shall have to return to this problem later on.

2. *Hans Küng:* A Christian Response

An almost overwhelming throng of highly complex problems has now been raised, from the mystery of the Trinity to the treatment of slaves and women. I have the unenviable task of trying to respond briefly but convincingly to all this; and I can only single out a few points here. As the Christian interlocutor in this dialogue, I am tempted to begin at the end and—in the wholly unpedagogical fashion of so many Christian apologists—to zero in on one of the obvious weak points of Islam: its discrimination against women.

WOMEN IN ISLAM

This is unquestionably an important topic, one that shows to what a great extent reforms in Islam are the concern not just of individual intellectuals, but of a broad section of the population, especially—in this case—of women. Far too few Westerners are aware that, since the end of the nineteenth century, Islam has had its share of writers urging the emancipation of women, and that after the First World War, women's movements were organized in many Islamic countries. On the other hand, the new German *Lexicon of the Islamic World* (1974) devotes less than twenty lines to the article on "Women," which is roughly the same size as the entry for Karl May, the author of *Wild Kurdistan* and many novels of adventure for boys. The article on "Women," it is true, also contains references to related issues such as marriage, the law of inheritance, harem, veil, and Muhammad, which I have already partially dealt with in my last response. Here I wish to address only one point, which, crucial as it is, I cannot pass over in silence.

There can be no doubt that for men and women raised in a culture influenced by Christianity the practice of *polygamy* (along with the possibility of unilateral repudiation of the wife without a court judgment) creates the worst sort of problem. Yet it was permitted by Muhammad, who first lived monogamously but in the end had something like three times the number of wives that the Qur'an allows to ordinary mortals. We can, to be sure, make Islamic polygamy more intelligible by noting that:

1. Polygamy or, more precisely, polygyny and, according to many Islamists, polyandry as well were to be found in pre-Islamic tribal culture.

2. The patriarchs of Israel—Abraham, Isaac, and Jacob—also had more than one wife each.

3. Muhammad introduced certain reforms, particularly with respect to the law of inheritance.

4. Any given ethos and its laws have to be judged by the standards of their own day and not by ours.

Thus our argument should not proceed anachronistically. Still, there is no denying that, even measured against seventh-century Christian ideas, the Qur'anic arrangement—four legitimate wives and any number of concubines—hardly does justice to the *dignity of women.* From the Christian standpoint, therefore, all legislative steps taken by Islamic countries in the twentieth century to raise the public estimation of women and guarantee them equal rights must be considered very much overdue. (Not to mention the fact that the practical implementation of these efforts is still a long way off.)

On the other side of the coin, Christianity has scarcely any reason for pride in its historical record in liberating women. But instead of going over this classic theme of Islamic-Christian polemics, let me make just two more basic observations—critical of both sides:

For *Muslims,* the concrete, supremely momentous issue of feminism shows how important a historicocritical interpretation of the Qur'an is. Without it, exegesis, when it runs into difficulties, degenerates into sleight-of-hand hermeneutics or stiffens into traditional-minded literalism. Critical exegesis, by contrast, makes the necessary, intellectually honest translation of the Islamic religious-ethical message from its original social and cultural situation into the present time—all the while observing the historical relativity of religious statements.

Much the same is true of the discrimination against women in the law of inheritance and the rules of evidence. In the past few decades, the emancipation of women has made powerful advances in some countries, such as Egypt (at least for the women of the upper and middle classes): the right to vote, a relatively high percentage of women in the universities (students and faculty members), growing numbers of women doctors, lawyers, politicians, and diplomats. Of course, lower-class women have been barely touched by this development. And the practical impediments afflicting even upper-class women in the social life of many Islamic countries still astonish the European.

For *Christians*, this means that they ought not boast too much of their moral superiority here. Because scholars have by no means fully explored the question of the extent to which Christianity helped or hindered the emancipation of women, whether in the first Christian centuries or in the twentieth. Research on this issue—conducted primarily by women—is still in full swing.

This controversial subject ought not to obstruct our view of the fundamental theological agreement that exists with regard to the notions of God and humanity. And it is now time to emphasize this consensus between Islam and Christianity (Judaism, too, can be included here).

COMMON FEATURES OF THE BELIEF IN ONE GOD

First of all, I am not proposing a simply philological-historical comparison of two great religious documents, the Bible and the Qur'an. What is at stake is the primeval message based on these texts, the *living faith* of Jews, Christians, and Muslims in the one God and his activity in the world.

What is this "living faith"? Is it a matter of understanding? An act of the will? An emotion? For Christians, Jews, and Muslims, faith is surely not just a matter of the understanding alone. Faith for them is neither a mere acceptance of biblical or Qur'anic texts as true nor even the assent to more or less improbable assertions. This would be a thoroughly intellectualist misunderstanding of faith. On the other hand, neither is faith for Jews, Christians, and Muslims simply the product of an exertion by the will, a blind risk, a gratuitous leap, or a *credo quia absurdum*. That would be a voluntarist misunderstanding of faith. Finally, faith is also not a mere subjective emotion, an act of believing (*fides qua creditur*) without any content (*fides quae creditur*); it is not a kind of feeling where having a credo matters more than what is in it. This would be an emotionalist misunderstanding of faith.

On the contrary, for Jews and Christians as well as for Muslims, faith means an *unconditionally trusting commitment to and reliance on God and his word by the whole person here and now* with all his mental powers. Such faith is thus at once an act of knowing, willing, and feeling: a kind of *trust* that includes an affirmation of truth. We are dealing here with a personal, experiential, trustful basic attitude, whether simple or highly complex: a believing outlook on life and way of living, on the strength of which people live and think, act and suffer.

Neither the Bible nor the Qur'an tries to "prove" God; rather, they constantly "point toward him." Like Judaism and Christianity, Islam stresses that belief in God is not irrational, that faith is a matter of reasonable trust, not rational proof. In other words, *because* the Qur'an is so utterly taken up with human beings and their life, it is centrally concerned with God. The name "Allah" is mentioned in the Qur'an more than twenty-five hundred times. Where, then, are the common features of belief concretely to be found?

- The fundamental common feature shared by Jews, Christians, and Muslims consists in belief in the *one and only* God, who gives life and meaning to all things. This faith in one God is a primeval truth that was already given with Adam. The unity of the human race and the equality of all men before God is grounded in the one God. And whatever may be said about the Christian doctrine of the Trinity, its purpose is to explain and not challenge faith in that one God. This means that in confronting pagan polytheism, Judaism, Christianity, and Islam are just as united as they are against modern gods of every sort that threaten to enslave humanity. Long before Islam, in fact, Judaism and then Christianity overthrew the old gods of the pantheon.

- Jews, Christians, and Muslims are at one in their faith in the *God of history*, in the God who is not only the Greek-style *arché*, the first principle of nature, the original source, but the creator of the world and man who takes an active part in history: the one God of Abraham who speaks through the prophets and reveals himself to his people, although his actions continually present a new and impenetrable mystery. God certainly transcends history, but he is nonetheless immanent in it. He is nearer to us than our own carotid artery, as the Qur'an graphically puts it.

- Jews, Christians, and Muslims are at one in their faith in the one God who, though he embraces and governs all things, is for them *a partner they can speak to*. He can be "reached" in prayer and meditation, praised in joy and gratitude, accused in distress and despair. He is a God before whom man can "genuflect in awe," "pray and sacrifice," "make music and dance," to borrow a famous remark by Martin Heidegger.

- Finally, Jews, Christians, and Muslims are also at one in their faith in a *gracious, merciful God*, in a God who takes care of human beings. In the Qur'an, as in the Bible, men and women are called "God's servants." This expresses not enslavement to a despot, but elementary human creatureliness face to face with the one Lord. The Arabic *al-Rahmān* ("the merciful one") is etymologically connected with the Hebrew *rahamim,* which, together with *hen* and *hesed,* constitutes the semantic field for the New Testament term *charis* and our word "grace." God may seem high-handed in this or that passage of the Bible or the Qur'an, but the Bible and the Qur'an as a whole attest decisively to a God of mercy and grace.

Hence Judaism, Christianity, and Islam are the joint representatives before the world of faith in the one God; they share in a single grand world movement of monotheism. This common faith has implications for world politics that should not be underestimated and that people should be made aware of. Just as this faith played a role, for example, in the Camp David Accords, it might be significant for the next stages of the peace process in the Middle East.

If, then, all three religions are convinced that God is at work in history, how is this working to be understood theologically?

GOD'S ACTIVITY AND HUMAN FREEDOM

Not just "God's will be done"; God's will, says Islam, *is* done. When Islam traces everything that happens back to God and his will, and sees *all events as determined, at every instant, by God,* this would seem to constitute a distinctive feature that separates it from Judaism and Christianity. Now, there is no doubt that late-medieval Islamic theology in particular had a strongly predeterminative bias, whose influence continues to make itself felt. But in our time Muslims are rethinking the nature of Islam: It does not mean mere resignation and passive acceptance, submission to God's will and no more; it means active devotion, the readiness to become involved with God's will. Human beings are *by no means the helpless tools of an arbitrary God,* because the Qur'an also

1. Clearly stresses man's responsibility for his actions.
2. Tells us that man himself determines the measure of reward and punishment by his decisions.
3. And so there can be no question of human actions being determined.
4. And the so-called Muslim "fatalism" must therefore be regarded as a Western prejudice.

As in the Old Testament (where "freedom," the catchword of the Greek world, occurs only once), in the Qur'an the word "freedom" does not mean "freedom of choice," but the social condition of a free man as opposed to a slave. But as in the Old Testament, in the Qur'an, too, man is very much *the active force, the decision maker.*

I would like to add some further clarification on this point for readers interested in philosophy and theology. As far as Islam is concerned, I think we should not speak of "occasionalism" with regard either to human beings or to inanimate nature. "Occasionalism" is the name given to the Augustinian-Cartesian theory developed by the Oratorian Father Nicolas de Malebranche concerning God's activity in the world. It holds that the effect things have on each other is a mere appearance, since in reality God is the only agent: as if human beings were only the "occasion" for divine action. Leibnitz modified this idea and argued for a continuous correspondence, a preestablished harmony produced by God.

Like Judaism and Christianity, Islam rests upon the basic assumption that all things are contingent and always dependent upon God. The Qur'an never stops stressing that God has "taken the measure" of all things. Islamic theology joins its Jewish and Christian counterparts in denying that nature is either the "clockwork" of Enlightenment deists (originally made by God but now running on its own) or the passionately adored "Mother Nature" of tender-minded Romantics. Rather, nature is God's creation, to be used, but also to be cared for, preserved, and protected, after the archetypal model of the Garden of Eden. For all its laws, it has no autarky, but an autonomy founded on theonomy, the rule of God. It necessarily functions in accordance with certain laws, but these are God-given.

Does this mean that with regard to Islam it would be better to speak of a *concursus divinus (generalis)*—that is, of a continually necessary, universal "divine cooperation" in all creaturely activity? This is a classical theory of Christian theology; it holds that God not only created all things in the beginning *(creatio)*, and not only constantly maintains all things in existence *(conservatio)*, but also takes part, as the first cause, in all creaturely activity *(concursus)*. In support of this position, Isaiah 26:12 is cited ("thou hast wrought for us all our works"), along with the statement from Acts of the Apostles 17:28 (" 'In him we live and move and have our being' ")—a quotation from Greek sources. This notion would differ from occasionalism in that it attributes to both God and man a complete causality all their own. On this issue, the Thomistic school of the Dominicans has always placed a greater emphasis on God's omni-causality, while the more recent, Molinist school of the Jesuits put more stress on human freedom. But each of these schools agrees, and so, I believe, could Judeo-Christian and Islamic theology, on two major points:

- The world is governed not by blind chance or obscure destiny, but by the gracious and merciful God. Creation and conservation, presence and judgment, are expressions of his freely granted compassion.
- God's absolute freedom does not threaten man's relative freedom, but makes it possible and powerful. In this sense, the Infinite represents not the far limit of the finite, but its enablement and fulfillment.

ETERNAL PREDESTINATION AND ETERNAL LIFE

In spite of all their partisan pronouncements and differences in detail, I think it likely that a *similarly basic agreement* between Islam and Christianity could be noted *on other doctrinal matters* as well. Since I cannot go into all the fine points here, let me just mention two especially important topics:

a. Eternal *predestination* of human beings to salvation or perdition. There is no mistaking the fact that the general tenor of Islamic theology runs roughly along the same lines as that of such great Christian theologians as Augustine, Luther, and Calvin. All three men repeatedly and forcefully emphasized the influence of God's grace (with Calvin's double predestination being the extreme instance), without, however, fully excluding responsibility—and, consequently, freedom—from the picture of human weal and woe. And for Christianity, too, God's foreknowledge cannot be simply equated with predestination or pure determinism. In the final analysis, man's freedom is not Promethean pride and arrogance, something wrested away from God; it is humanity's great prospect, which God has willed, affirmed, and made possible to begin with.

Like the axiom *Extra Ecclesiam nulla salus*, its obverse, *Extra "Ummam" nulla salus* ("No salvation outside Islam") needs to be corrected; Muslims are still too ready to consign all non-Muslims to hell. And, in this context, another idea, not only un-Qur'anic but unbiblical, requires correction: that *"original sin"* is transmitted through the sexual act. This notion goes back to Augustine and not to the Old or New Testament. The Bible and the Qur'an agree that, for all its entanglement in collective life, sin comes into existence only with the full responsibility of the individual. God does not will sin; of course, neither does he will it away, but (this is the answer that has become classic in both Judeo-Christian and Islamic tradition) he permits it, he lets it, as a human act, take place. Why? Evil is a dark mystery, hidden only in God's grace and not to be unlocked by man.

b. *The immortality of the soul* is neither an Islamic nor a specifically Jewish or Christian idea, although it had already found its way into Islamic orthodoxy before the time of the medieval Arab philosopher al-

Ghazzālī. It derived, as everyone knows, from Plato and the Platonists, who believed in a mind/soul independent of our bodily functions—noncomposite, immaterial, and hence indestructible. In death this soul is liberated from the prison of the body. The New Testament (along with several later Greek writings in the Old Testament canon) takes a different approach: Here, as in the Qur'an, there is no belief in a cleavage of the body from the soul in death. The New Testament does not believe in a redemption of man *from* his corporeal nature, but *in* and *with* it. In other words, there is a new creation, the transformation of the entire individual, together with his whole life history—not the same molecules, but the same person—by God, by God's life-creating spirit (which we shall have to discuss later).

As Christianity sees things, therefore, the consummation of our existence involves a transformed, transfigured, *spiritualized corporeity* in an altogether different, divine dimension beyond time and space. And so naturally the Qur'an's descriptions of the joys of paradise—all sorts of food and wine, and the big-eyed, broad-bosomed houris—always strike Christians as highly terrestrial, as an all too crude projection of all too obvious sensual pleasures, on the model of the Land of Cockaigne. Needless to say, this does nothing to improve the bloodless Christian accounts of heaven, such as the one we find in the *Supplementum* to the *Summa theologica* of Thomas Aquinas, where human beings supposedly neither eat nor drink, in an environment with no flora, fauna, or even metals, content with only the vision of God and their own halos. Which brings us to the subject of eros and agape, so rich in misunderstandings between Christianity and Islam.

EROS AND AGAPE

The God of the Qur'an, the All-Merciful One, is certainly not loveless. But the Qur'an, as we have learned, does not use the word "love," insofar as it means *eros*, with reference to God: Love is not a divine predicate; God is not love. Here we see a parallel with the Bible, at least in the sense that the word *eros* is nowhere to be found in the New Testament and only twice (with negative connotations) in the Septuagint version of the Book of Proverbs (7:18; 30:16). The word, evidently, had become compromised by its association, in Greek culture, with morbid eroticism and purely carnal sexuality, which pervaded even religious cults.

In contrast to Muslims, it is fair to say, *Christians began by fashioning their own word for love*, one that could be applied to God without causing any problems. The main word, *agape* (love), scarcely appears in profane Greek literature, and the verb *agapān* (to love) occurs only marginally.

Several Christian theologians—in particular the Swedish Lutheran Anders Nygren—concluded from this that one could not overestimate the difference between the lustful eros of the Greeks and self-sacrificial agape, modeled on Jesus. But in the face of Muslim criticism of the hostility toward the body and sex shown by patristic Christianity (which has many sources—gnosticism, Manichaeism, Augustine's repressions and sublimations, etc.), we must be allowed to counter with a question: Is Christianity so very different from Islam in that, right from the start, it was based on a kind of love (agape) removed from and even hostile to eros?

One more thing we ought to consider about Islam—and not only the Islam of *shari'a*, but the mysticism of the brotherhoods and orders: the difference between *love as desire*, which seeks its own and nothing else, and *love as gift*, which seeks what is the other's, the difference, in other words, between a possessive love and an authentic love as seen shining forth in Jesus. Yet, wouldn't it be misunderstanding Jesus to make the difference between egoistic and genuine love the same as the difference between eros and agape?

Because it is by no means the case that only agape and not *eros can be authentic love.* Why shouldn't someone who desires another person be able at the same time to give himself to that person? And conversely, why shouldn't the one to whom the other gives himself be allowed to desire him? So far as that goes, in the Old Testament and in Jesus' native Aramaic, there is only *one* word for love. And the God of the Old Testament has a passionate, "jealous" desire for his people Israel, like the love of a husband, in Hosea's image, for his faithless wife. God's covenant with his people is illustrated throughout the Bible by the erotic symbol of marriage, while the nation's apostasy is presented as adultery. And then we find in the Old Testament, astonishingly, the Song of Solomon, a collection of highly sensuous love songs that were not allegorized and spiritualized until the Christian Era. In the New Testament too, God's love has a very human face: the love of a father who longs for the return of his prodigal son, a love that is meant (otherwise than in the Qur'an) less for the "upright" (the self-righteous son who stayed home) than for the "lost" (sinners of every kind).

Once again, I must refer to the question of language: The Old Testament speaks as a matter of course about a man's loving *(agapān)* his wife, and parents' loving their children. In the Greek New Testament, Jesus himself uses the same word for the love of God as he does for the love of a friend or an enemy. And Jesus never demands celibacy of his disciples; he is no monk and no ascetic. Rather, he is reproached for being a glutton and a drunkard, because he has no qualms about taking part in banquets. Jesus appears totally authentic in his humanity, embracing children, letting himself be anointed by women, joined together in "love" particularly with Lazarus and his sisters, which obviously doesn't preclude eros. Jesus calls his disciples "friends," and the women who (contrary to all custom) accompany and look after him are the only ones not to flee at the end; they remain with him beneath the cross.

All this means that the New Testament speaks of the love of God and man in warmly human terms, and elementary human love is in no sense treated as evil. But whenever later Christian theologians not only distinguished between eros and agape but found them *mutually exclusive, both eros and agape paid the price.* Eros was devalued and demonized: Passionate love, which desires the other for oneself, was limited to sex, thereby lowering the status of eroticism and sexuality. But, at the same time, agape was exalted and dehumanized by a process of desensualization and spiritualization: Christian *caritas* was often not very convincing, because it was not very human.

And yet with all this we have not yet looked into the crux of this issue. The really challenging feature of love in Jesus' sense, as compared with Muhammad's, emerges only when that love, which aims to preserve everything human, is seen in all its radicalness. Unlike radical ideologies, it is marked by sobriety, realism, and an eye for everyday life. Nonetheless it is of the greatest importance not only for individuals but for society.

THE RADICALNESS OF CHRISTIAN LOVE

I cannot judge to what extent the Qur'an or individual Islamic theologians may have made efforts in this direction, but one fact is incontestable: By contrast with Muhammad, the decisive thing that interested *Jesus* was quite different from, say, the rules for ritual purity or the prohibition of wine. At the same time, to point out what is most characteristic of Jesus is to criticize radically a pattern of Christian living (individual and social) that has time and again betrayed the message of its Master.

1. Above all, the *unbounded readiness to forgive:* not seven times, but seventy times seven—in other words, continually, ad infinitum. And not only is there to be no blood revenge and no "eye for an eye," but no blood money and no ransom, which is what the word "forgiveness" occasionally means in the Qur'an. Naturally, Jesus' call for forgiveness should not, in turn, be interpreted legalistically. Jesus was not thinking of a law to the effect that one should forgive 490 times, but not the 491st. Rather, Jesus is pointing to something that defies legal categorization; he appeals to human love to forgive in advance, over and over again.

2. Unselfish *"democratic" service.* This is not merely the sort of obedience to authority so strongly emphasized in early Islamic tradition, but the reciprocal service of all people. And again, this should not be understood as a law that there oughtn't to be any hierarchical order, but instead as a crucial appeal for service, even on the part of superiors to their subordinates.

3. Finally, voluntary *renunciation without getting anything in return.* As opposed to every kind of glorification of power in public and private life, Jesus calls for renunciation of one's *rights* in favor of the other (going two miles with the person who has forced me to go one), renunciation of *power* at one's own expense (giving my cloak to someone who has already taken my coat), renunciation of *counterviolence* (turning my left cheek toward someone who has already struck me on the right). Once more, all this is not to be understood legalistically, as if we were bidden to perform just these actions, and only these, in every instance. Renunciation of counterviolence does not mean giving up in advance any use of force in self-defense. Jesus himself, the gospels tell us, did *not* turn the other cheek when he was struck in the face at his trial; instead, he protested. Renunciation should not be confused with weakness. Jesus' demands are not a matter of ethical or even ascetic achievements done for their own sake. Rather, they are drastic appeals, on a case-by-case basis, for the radical fulfillment of God's will in favor of one's fellow man. All renunciation is only the negative side of a new, positive praxis. As Augustine says in a famous hyperbole, *"Ama, et fac quod vis"* ("Love, and do what you want").

Needless to say, down through history Christians have played fast and loose with the message of the crucified Nazarene—we need only think of the oft-cited treatment of women and slaves. But I cannot ignore the fact that in the history of Christianity this Jesus of Nazareth has *also* played the part of a critical corrective, of a believable appellate authority, precisely on the issues of violence/nonviolence, mercy/mercilessness, peace / no peace.

The question, then, that I would ask Muslims in a religious dialogue is, Can we say the same thing about Muhammad? Can he become in the same way a critical corrective, a court of appeals on these matters? Isn't it true that a Muslim who wishes to use violence in reaching his political/ religious goals can invoke Muhammad in general and in particular, even as Marxist-Leninists can invoke Marx and Lenin in staging violent and bloody revolutions? On this point, at least, Friedrich Dürrenmatt is surely right when he notes in his worthwhile essay on the relations between Judaism, Christianity, and Islam: "Muhammad, of course, has nothing in common with Jesus . . . but Muhammad can well be compared to Paul and to Karl Marx." *(Collected Works,* Vol. 29, pp. 54 f.) An important problem arises here, which needs to be discussed: Christians can never honestly invoke Jesus of Nazareth to bless violence, hatred, killing, and war—even though this implies and creates a burden of pain for the peacemakers. The reason for this has to be sought on a deeper, theological level. It has to do with Jesus himself and his understanding of God.

THE POSSIBILITY OF MEANING IN MEANINGLESS SUFFERING

Both Muhammad and Jesus faced the problem of suffering in their work. Each of them met with stiff resistance, life-and-death situations, in preaching his message; each showed an unusual endurance and an admirable ability to overcome suffering. But, in all this, Jesus opened up a different and more profound dimension of experience; for, quite unlike Muhammad, Jesus lived a life of *exemplary suffering:* the suffering of the *innocent,* of the *person abandoned by God and man.* Thus Jesus entered history as the archetype of *meaningless* human suffering, as the *sufferer pure and simple,* the Man of Sorrows.

That is why Christian theology felt compelled from the outset to make the suffering of this innocent person the focus of theological reflection, to be a *theologia crucis:* Is there a hidden "meaning" in this pain of an innocent man, is the suffering of the God-forsaken Jesus borne by God in an ultimate act of solidarity? As far as I can see, one scarcely finds a point of departure for such thinking in Muhammad. No doubt, Christian theology has over and over again switched its identity from a *theologia crucis* to a *theologia gloriae.* But, with Muhammad, such a theology of triumph was present from the very start, since God will not only liberate his chosen ones from all dishonor, but he has in fact already liberated them in the figure of Muhammad, the successful prophet, general, and statesman (indeed, according to the Qur'an and against all historical evidence, God did not, in the end, let Jesus die on the cross).

This means that we find a new attitude toward suffering, toward failure, toward everything negative delineated in Jesus' work and suffering, in his whole destiny. I can hardly see a parallel to this at least in Sunnite Islam (and in Shi'a, suffering is often the occasion for proclaiming a campaign of revenge). The basic question is, What sort of an *incomprehensible, transcendent* God is it that, for all his compassionate concern, is *exalted beyond all suffering,* that leaves human beings to suffer, lets them fight, protest, or simply resign themselves, and finally die in immeasurable misery and, often enough, meaningless, endless pain? And is this basic question answered, as Muslims themselves now rightly demand it to be, by saying that we must trust in God and fall silent before his inscrutable plan, which remains a mystery we can never fathom? Or perhaps the question can be reversed: Is God really so exalted, so purely the Lord and Ruler, above all meaningless suffering,

as we in our human fashion imagine and presume despite all our protests?

Christians believe that, although God may be incomprehensible (as
the Qur'an so strongly emphasizes and as the Book of Job with its
exemplary hero so painfully shows), *Jesus' meaningless suffering and death*
reveals a *definitive redemption from suffering* by the God who cannot be made
the instrument of human will. God transforms suffering and death into
eternal life and fulfillment of all our longing. To be sure, even faith in
Jesus cannot reverse the fact of suffering; and it will always be possible
to doubt. But there is something vital we can say as a result of the life
and pain of this one person, to people living and suffering for no
apparent reason: Even patently absurd human life and pain *can* have a
meaning, can *take on* a meaning.

This meaning is a *hidden* one, not an automatic gift, but a *permanently
open offer* of meaning that challenges me to choose it. Obviously I can
reject this hidden meaning out of defiance, cynicism, or despair. But I
can also accept it out of faith and trust in the one who has given meaning
to the meaningless suffering and death of Jesus.

THE GOD OF LOVE

Has Christianity set its sights too high? Is Islam more realistic: does it
make things easier for people? The message of the one whose yoke is
easy and whose burden is light is realistic all the way to failure and
collapse. It aims to offer meaning to men and women. That is, not only
in light and in joy, but also in darkness, in mourning, in pain, depres-
sion, and meaningless, I *can* encounter Him, I can find love and not just
hatred and revenge. What Leibnitz merely claimed and Dostoyevsky
obscurely sensed is announced to Job and Muhammad, and now, thanks
to the Crucified (the true victor), becomes manifest and certain: My life
and death are encompassed by *God;* my life and death, for all their
godforsakenness, *become* the site of an encounter with God. Christians
remain realists: They know there is no way around suffering and death,
but they know there is a way through: in active indifference, ultimately
facing suffering and in the same way ready to fight against pain and its
causes, until death.

Quite unlike the life and message of Muhammad, it seems to me,
Jesus' life and work make it clear that this God is a phil-anthropic (loving
humanity) and sym-pathetic (co-suffering) God, "down here with us."
The God who manifests himself in Jesus is not the all too masculine,
often arbitrary God we can still find in the Old Testament and the
Qur'an as well. Rather, this is a God who not only demands love, but
gives it (even to failures); and who thus may be called "father" (and
surely "mother," too). That is why Christians share with the New Testa-

ment (which differs here with the Qur'an) the conviction that God *has* love, still more that God *is* all love. As the First Letter of John says: "God is love. In this the love of God was made manifest among us, that God sent his only Son into the world, so that we might live through him." (1 Jn 4:8–9)

We shall have more to say about God's "only Son." But the idea of God as the source of love has played a significant role not in law-oriented, but in mystical Islam. As one fine testimony among many—an echo of the eighth-century woman poet from Basra mentioned by Professor van Ess—let me quote a few words by the mystic Abū Yazīd al-Bistāmī: "At first I imagined that I was the one who thought of God, who knew Him and loved Him. When I came to the end, I saw that He had thought of me before I thought of Him, that He had known me before I had known Him, that His love for me preceded my love for Him, that he sought me to begin with, so that I could seek him." (Tor Andrae, *Islamic Mystics,* p. 130)

Could there be some material here for further discussion between Muslims and Christians? Perhaps, because a polarity between mysticism and law, experience and order, inner and outer life, creates the same sort of basic tension in Christianity that it does in Islam. *Christianity,* too, has room for mysticism if that means not pantheistic unity with the godhead, but the divine love that envelops and penetrates all things. In *Islam,* also—as was recognized from the time of al-Ghazzālī (twelfth century), the great reconciler of orthodoxy and mysticism—the rational, orderly, social qualities of *law-oriented Islam* (the religious scholars, or mullahs) and the emotional, experiential, personal qualities of *inward-oriented Islam* (the mystics, or Sufis) are in no way mutually exclusive. As many Muslims today are convinced, they can contribute to a mutual enrichment.

God as the source of love: This would be the point of departure for raising questions about Christology. In my next presentation, I would like to outline my position on this issue as well as respond to Islamic objections to the Christian doctrine of the Trinity.

IV.
Islam and the Other Religions: Jesus in the Qur'an

1. *Josef van Ess:* Islamic Perspectives

Are Muslims Ready for Dialogue?

So long as Christianity was a great political force and Europe felt sure of its superiority, Christians hardly doubted that their religion was better than others, more advanced, the only true faith. They wanted to proselytize. Now that these assumptions no longer hold, they are more inclined to dialogue. Each of these attitudes is the child of its time and is neatly displayed in the scholarly writing by Westerners on the Qur'an. Up until the 1930s, Islamists were primarily interested in what Muhammad had borrowed from Judaism or Christianity. When Christian theologians addressed the subject, they generally talked about the "Christian truths" to be found in Islam. Both historians and theologians overlooked or denied outright the Prophet's originality. They interpreted the Qur'an as an *omnium gatherum* of theological utterances, among which there were, admittedly, some gems; but all of these drew their value from their source alone.

Nowadays this notion has lost ground among Islamists and even among theologians. Wilfred Cantwell Smith, a scholar who spent many years as a Protestant missionary in Pakistan, has laid down the axiom that "no statement about religion [probably meaning, about a religion's conception of itself] is valid until it is recognized by the adherents of this religion itself." It must be noted that in the case of Islamists, at least those of the younger generation, this has led to a marked decline of interest in the Qur'an. It is not at all easy to meet Smith's demand; and treating the Qur'an as a historical document greatly increases the dangers of clashing with Muslims. Because Muslims, as of yet, are not too keen on dialogue. They still feel that they belong to a *religio triumphans.* This should be kept in mind as we now address the subject of the way Christian theology is presented in the Qur'an. I shall limit myself to the central points: the statements about Jesus and the Holy Spirit.

JESUS IN THE QUR'AN

The information we are given about Jesus fits together quite well into a coherent picture. Muhammad spoke repeatedly about Jesus, whom he saw as an interesting case parallel to himself. What we want to look at are the shifts of emphasis involved in this. The Qur'an leaves no doubt about the fact that Jesus preached the truth; but the language that it has him speak is altogether different from that of the Gospels; and it makes Jesus insist that he is only a human being: "And when Jesus came [to the Jews] / with the clear signs he said, 'I have / come to you with wisdom, and / that I may make clear to you / some of that whereon you are / at variance; so fear you God / and obey you me. Assuredly *God is my Lord and your Lord;* therefore serve him; this is / a straight path.' " (sura 43, 63–64) In one of such sermons, the Qur'an maintains, Jesus also announced the coming of Muhammad. (sura 61, 6)

Jesus' miracles are explicitly acknowledged; but he works them not as God's Son, but "with God's permission." (sura 3, 49; sura 5, 110) He was one of the righteous, one of God's intimates. (3, 45 f.) At God's command he says his prayers and gives alms, just as Muslims do, and behaves respectfully toward his mother. (19, 30) Nevertheless, his message is rejected by his contemporaries as "manifest sorcery" (61, 6; 5, 110); only his disciples stand by him. (61, 114) The Jews try to kill Jesus and boast that they have actually done so; but "they did not [really] slay him, neither crucified him, / only a likeness of that was shown to them." Their efforts failed, and God "raised him up to Him" in heaven. (4, 157)

This last passage contains the real surprise for Christian readers: Jesus is so closely modeled on Muhammad that the crucifixion is denied. "A likeness of that was shown to them," as the Qur'anic text says rather obscurely: The Jews took the wrong person and instead of Jesus executed someone else, Judas perhaps, as later exegesis proposed. This is docetism, which we also find among the Gnostics, in Basilides for instance; and it fits in quite logically here: All prophets are successful, as Muhammad was. They are persecuted, their message is denounced as "sorcery" (Muhammad, too, was always afraid of being lumped together with magicians and soothsayers), but they may not come to grief. The Passion, in fact, makes sense theologically only if it is understood as redemption, but that is a category Islam doesn't understand. Unless it is redemptive, the Passion becomes tragic; but this is a way of thinking that only the Greeks mastered properly. In place of the tragic, the Muslim puts the absurd; and what would be more absurd than that the truth, which like monotheism can be rationally inferred, should not prevail?

We may reproach the Qur'an for fashioning an image of Jesus so far out of line with the Gospels. We should not forget, however, that the Gospels took a similar approach in typifying a man whom they viewed as a precursor of Jesus: John the Baptist. They, too, omitted most of the historical reality and, still worse, of the self-concept of this messenger from God (who, Muslims think, was just as much a prophet as Jesus).

As for the Qur'anic Jesus, Christian analysis, or polemics, has sometimes claimed to discover two points where the foreshortening in his portrait is evident, and the original "truth" still glimmers through: In spite of its "reduced" vision of Jesus, the Qur'an accepts the Virgin Birth and speaks of Jesus as God's "word." But this is a mistake; the Christian observer has detected meanings that were never intended. The Virgin Birth is no proof for Christ's divinity, but a mere sign of God's omnipotence (sura 19, 21); and if Jesus is characterized as the "word," this usage undoubtedly goes back, historically speaking, to the Logos; but it had lost for Muhammad the implications it once had for the Greeks and still has for Christians today. Neither of these two things played any role in later Islamic theology or in Islam's conception of itself. Hence they should *not* be taken as a point of departure for dialogue, and missionary endeavors based on them would be greeted with incomprehension.

Jesus, says the Qur'an, predicted the coming of Muhammad; here, too, we have a pattern of thinking that can be found in the Gospels and that early-Christian theology got a great deal of mileage out of (with reference, of course, to the Old Testament prophets). The verse in the Qur'an reads: ". . . Jesus son of / Mary said, 'Children of / Israel, I am indeed the / Messenger of God to you, / confirming the Torah / that is before me, and / giving good tidings of / a Messenger who shall / come after me . . ." (sura 61, 6) At this point the text says, "with a most praiseworthy name," but the interpretation of this phrase is still disputed; it can also be translated, "whose name is Ahmad," which is how Muslims understand it. Because Ahmad, which later became a widespread proper name, is formed from the same root as Muhammad. Ever since Marracci's translation of the Qur'an, at the end of the seventeenth century, Arabists have uncovered the Greek *períklytos* (famous) beneath "most praiseworthy" (the meaning of the name "Ahmad"). This *períklytos*, they argue, was in turn erroneously derived from *parákletos*, the Paraclete of Jn 14:16 and 14:26. This would mean that the Paraclete, who Christians believe descended upon the apostles at Pentecost, is thought by Muslims to have appeared in the figure of Muhammad.

The (Holy) Spirit

But this explanation remains purely speculative. The only thing that can be proved is that, later on, when Muslim apologists were asked about the connections between this passage in the Qur'an and the Gospels, they often referred to the Paraclete. They were not disturbed by the fact that, as far as the Christians were concerned, the Paraclete (or Counselor) had already been sent. This hadn't disturbed Mani (third century A.D.) either; he had interpreted the Paraclete to mean himself. So we may toy with the idea that Muhammad simply adopted a Manichaean model. After all, like Muhammad 350 years later, Mani had considered himself to be the "seal of the prophets." In that case, the apologists would not have been so misled. But then the texture of historical links becomes even more complicated. One thing for certain is that Muhammad did not see himself as the Holy Spirit, with whom the Paraclete is identified in Jn 14:26.

It is clearly difficult to say what to make of the Spirit in the Qur'an. On this issue, Muhammad's preaching takes certain associations for granted which we can hardly reconstruct today and which even the early exegetes were no longer familiar with. Sometimes the Spirit functions as the breath of life—for example, at Mary's conception (sura 21, 91)—sometimes as an angelic messenger. It seems that Muhammad equated the Spirit with Gabriel; in some especially enigmatic passages (cf. sura 17, 85), it may also be related to a Logos/hypostasis. There is no question that it is understood exclusively as God's instrument. Even Islamic mysticism and philosophy (influenced by Neo-Platonism) have occasionally invoked these passages, but have never drawn the faintest trinitarian conclusion from them.

Judaism and Christianity in Islamic Salvation History

Muslims have hardly shown any interest in whether the contents of the Qur'an are confirmed by earlier Scriptures. Their relation to the Gospels and the Torah is altogether different from the Christians' to the Old Testament. This brings me back to something I stressed at the outset in discussing Muhammad's spiritual development: From the Christian standpoint, the New Covenant presupposes and builds upon the Old; in the Islamic view, the Qur'an goes back beyond the Gospel and the Torah; it reestablishes the religion of Abraham, a point subsequently enlarged on by the exegetes. According to sura 7, 172, God asked Adam's descendants, even before they were born, "Am I not your Lord?" By answering yes, they accepted Islam from all eternity. Thus even Abraham was not the first Muslim; rather, Islam was the first profession of faith made by humanity before time began; and when the Muslim recites his credo, the *shahada,* he is actually simply repeating the "testimony" that he has already given in a preexistent state.

There is a famous and undoubtedly very old saying by the Prophet, that everyone is born in the primeval Islamic religion. Only afterward do his parents—we would say, his environment—make him into a Jew, a Christian, or a Zoroastrian. He has, to paraphrase Tertullian, an *anima naturaliter moslemica.* The action performed on behalf of all humanity before creation is thus repeated at the birth of each individual: The *shahada* is whispered into the newborn's ear. Jews and Christians, therefore, are unbelievers not because they don't know any better but because they don't want to be anything else. And if they claim that the things Muslims tell them are treated differently in their own scriptures, then they must have distorted these texts or suppressed the true evidence. This is the argument Muhammad used against the Jews of Medina and still used by Muslim theologians—although they noticed that in so doing they were also discarding positive testimony to Islam, such as the "Paraclete."

JEWS AND CHRISTIANS IN THE QUR'AN AND IN ISLAMIC LAW

That was the opinion of the theologians. But we now have to address the practical treatment of non-Muslims in the Islamic world. From the Christian standpoint, we are leaving behind the subject of religion and turning to social and political issues; but, as we have seen, this distinction does not obtain in Islam: Religious law had to take a stance on the problem, and the Qur'an has done just that.

The statements by the Qur'an, to be sure, are not fully consistent. They reflect in this, as in other matters, the various situations that Muhammad found himself in. He got a different reception from Jews and Christians. The Jews, as a closed group, were his political opponents, whereas for a long time he knew Christians only as individuals. That is why "the Jews are [censured and] *morally* condemned on account of their refractoriness and other reasons," while the Christians "[are reproached] more on account of certain *dogmatic* assertions and errors" (Rudi Paret, *Muhammad and the Qur'an,* p. 141). There is hardly any dogmatic criticism of Judaism, and by comparison with the Jews, the actual behavior of Christians comes close to being praised: "Thou wilt surely find," God says to Muhammad, "the most hostile / of men to the believers are the Jews / and the idolaters; and thou wilt surely find / the nearest of them in love to the believers / are those who say, 'We are *nasara* [Christians]' that, / because some of them are priests and monks, and they wax not proud." (sura 5, 85)

Muhammad, then, is not at all anticlerical; and to this day Muslims show respect for Christian clergymen, although they themselves have a totally different ideal in life. When, toward the end of his career, Muhammad concluded treaties with partly Christianized tribes, only the pagans had to accept Islam, while the Christians were allowed to keep their churches and priests. Contractual arrangements, by the way, had also been made with the Jews, even though, as we recall, at the high point of the crisis, one tribe from Medina was nearly exterminated. But after a number of armed conflicts with the Jews, Muhammad neither killed them nor forced them to emigrate or abjure their religion. They had to agree only to make permanent payments in kind (i.e., a tribute).

These stipulations, in part, were recorded in the Qur'an—but so were the calls for waging war against the "possessors of scripture" and all non-Muslims in general: "Fight those who believe not in God and the Last Day / and do not forbid what God and His Messenger / have forbidden—such men as practice not the / religion of truth, being of those who have been given / the Book—until they pay the tribute out of hand [?] . . ." And, shortly afterward, "That is the utterance of their mouths, conforming / with the unbelievers before them. God assail them! / How they are perverted! / They have taken their rabbis and their monks as lords / apart from God, and the Messiah, Mary's son— / and they were commanded to serve but One God; / there is no god but He." (suras 29–31) Thus it becomes clear at the end whom the passage (probably something of a composite text) is aimed at, and even the monks do not come out unscathed.

Islamic law has taken these declarations, which are bound up with a specific historical context, and combined them into a *system*. This creates, on the one hand, the obligation to take part in the *jihād*, which we usually call the holy war but which we might do better to translate as holy combat, since it's a matter of individual duty. The purpose of *jihād* is not, as Westerners often assume, to spread Islam, but to spread Muslim rule. It is involved with missionary activity only insofar as out-and-out pagans (all those who are not "possessors of scripture"), once their territory has been conquered, can only choose between death and conversion. By contrast, Christians and Jews—the Zoroastrians were soon made "People of the Book" as well, out of political necessity— need but pay tribute. When all such arrangements were properly organized, this tribute was collected in the form of a head tax, something the Arabs were long familiar with from the Sassanid dynasty. It was justified, all the way into the late-Ottoman period, by the fact that non-Muslims were exempt from military service.

In this sense, the *jihād* was considered the permanent duty of Muslims so long as any part of the earth was still not subject to Muslim sovereignty. A formal peace with non-Muslim states was therefore fundamentally impossible, although an Islamic government might always see its way to a temporary armistice. At any rate, not all Muslims were obliged to serve under arms; there simply had to be a sufficient number in the field.

All Muslims have to take up arms only when Islamic territory is attacked by a non-Muslim power. As late as the beginning of the First World War, Sheikh al-Islām, in Istanbul, issued such a proclamation, but it met with only a limited response. The western colonial powers affected by it, England in particular but Holland too (which had to keep a vast population of Muslims under control in Indonesia), became quite unnecessarily excited. A similar situation arises nowadays whenever Muslim leaders use the word *jihād;* only journalists sit up and take notice.

In the meantime, many prescriptions of Islamic martial law, especially those not directly based on the Qur'an, have been repealed by Islamic governments themselves. Some jurists go so far as to give *jihād* an interpretation altogether different from its basic meaning, because the word means only "to strive, to labor," with the usual addition of "on God's way." But this must not be connected with the business of war; early on, in fact, it was applied to the struggle with oneself, to asceticism. Nowadays this sense of *jihād* is often given prominence in order to stress Islam's readiness for peace. Actually this serves merely to show once again that exegesis can do anything. In this case it adapts itself to modern constitutional law. There are, of course, peace treaties and peaceful relations between Islamic and non-Islamic nations, even those that have common borders with Muslims. The classical theory, on the other hand, took as its point of departure the concept of the Islamic ecumene, which, as the abode of the definitive truth, positively demanded further expansion.

Practical Treatment of the "People of the Book"

Accordingly, the positions of Christians and Jews differed, depending on whether they were inside or outside the ecumene. Beyond its frontiers, they were enemies such as, for example, the Byzantines, with whom Islam was occupied until the fall of Constantinople in 1453, or the Khazars, who were neighbors of the Muslims in the Caucasus region and converted to Judaism in the time of Hārūn al-Rashīd. Within the ecumene, however, they were tolerated; better yet, they had clearly defined rights, derived from the very same treaties that the Prophet had made with Jews and Christians.

Here it seems that in systematizing these precedents, Muslims relied on a model of religious autonomy that took shape in the later Sassanid kingdom. Because autonomy *was* granted to a certain extent: the "people of the Book" were not only, as Muslims said, "charges" or "wards";

Islamic authorities were committed not just to keep them from harm and to protect their life, property, and the exercise of their religion. They also allowed them jurisdiction over their fellow believers in matters of civil and inheritance law. The leader of these independent communities and their representative before the Islamic authorities was in each case the highest religious dignitary: the patriarch or *katholikos* for the Christians, the exilarch or *gaon* for the Jews, and the supreme *mobad* for the Zoroastrians (until they ceased to play any significant role).

In this situation, autonomy did not mean segregation; there were no ghettos in the Islamic world, all the way down to modern times. Members of the same religious community often lived in the same quarter for reasons of family solidarity; but they were not kept apart from Muslims deliberately and on principle. In particular, they were not unclean; they could be invited to dinner. On this point, Islam is more broad-minded than Judaism. Christians and Jews were not strangers in the Islamic world; after all, historically speaking they were old, established residents who had lived in those regions much longer than the Muslims. They spoke the same language as the Muslims and shared the same culture with them.

The possibilities for advancement were great; we meet Christians and Jews holding the post of vizier. In medieval Egypt, the bureaucracy was totally controlled by the Copts; most physicians were likewise Christians or Jews. Non-Muslims were especially suitable for occupations involving contact with the non-Muslim world: foreign trade, banking, espionage. They maintained their autonomous status by observing certain regulations: by paying a special tribute (the head tax), treating Muslims with deference, and not marrying Muslim women. This system played an important role in the Ottoman Empire, and in some respects it still survives. Lebanon, for example, which until its destruction was the classical land of religious pluralism, has no civil marriage. A Christian who wants a divorce often cannot get one except by converting to another faith. In this matter he is entirely subject to the jurisdiction of his religious community. The state doesn't interfere.

"Tolerance" Outwards and Inwards

That is what Muslims today, with justifiable pride, call the "tolerance" of Islam. In the medieval Islamic world, Christians and Jews could actually practice their religions more freely than in many present-day totalitarian states. And the contrast with the Christian Middle Ages is striking. Pogroms were relatively rare, and Muslims could scarcely feel within their rights taking part in them: They were not only morally reprehensible, but violations of the law; and since the law was divine, they were also a sin.

Of course, we must realize that, in the language of contemporary Islam, "tolerance" does not mean freedom of religion in the usual modern sense. All the privileges mentioned were available only to the "people of the Book." Manichaeans, Buddhists, or Hindus did not qualify for them, nor did—and this is far more important for Islam today—members of religions that grew out of Islam itself: the Bahā'is, for example, and to a certain extent the Ahmadiyya. These individuals may consider their faith an independent religion (somewhat as the Mormons view theirs, in relation to Christianity); but, for the Muslims, they are simply heretics. That is because they have, as it were, committed the sin against the Holy Spirit, by believing that a new prophet—i.e., their founder—has arisen within the Muslim ecumene after Muhammad. These prophets are Mīrzā Ghulām Ahmad, the founder of Ahmadiyya (d. 1908), in India, and Bahā' ullāh, the originator of Bahā'i (d. 1892), in Iran. Significantly, both men are figures from a period during which Islam had to a large extent lost its political power.

That is why, since the new Iranian constitution is falling back upon Islamic law as its all-sufficient source, the position of the Bahā'ism is much more precarious than that of the Jews and the Christians. They are not helped by a verse in the Qur'an that modern-day Muslims are forever quoting and that they generally translate as "No compulsion is there in religion." (sura 2, 256) But this statement can be interpreted to mean not only that no one *ought* to be compelled in religious matters, but also that no one *can* be compelled, because people are much too obstinate to recognize the truth. In fact, this was probably the original meaning.

We must also make another qualification. This "tolerance" does not include the civil liberties that we generally associate with it. In the West, the concept of "tolerance" has secular roots. In Islam, by contrast, it was a matter of a religious concession, which did not affect Muslims' sense of their own superiority. Non-Muslims had, as it were, the right to hospitality. They were, in an obvious way, part of the scene; society could hardly be imagined without them. But, for a long time, that did not entitle them to equal rights, as it had not done for slaves and women, who were just as omnipresent. Islam, as we have seen, was more egalitarian than other religions. Yet, like every revelatory religion, it was convinced that it owned the absolute truth—and absolute truth becomes tolerant only when people no longer believe in it. Equal rights might be granted under favorable circumstances, and circumstances were generally more favorable to adherents of alien religions than they were in the Christian world. But equal rights was never the ideal, nor was it meritorious to win them for others. Islamic tolerance prevented persecutions, but it did not prevent discrimination.

Such discrimination was not permanent. One gets the impression from the sources that, for decades at a time, for centuries in some places, it was not put into practice; it had to be implemented afresh on each occasion. But, like the special privileges, it was legally protected. A ruler or jurist who distinguished himself by making use of it could be sure that he was fulfilling God's will. Its character was essentially symbolic, but it touched on matters of everyday life and was therefore especially painful: Non-Muslims were not allowed to build their houses as high as Muslims could; they had to ride donkeys instead of horses, wear a certain kind of clothing, or identify themselves with insignia.

This last item sounds all too familiar. Nevertheless, we must beware of anachronistic thinking. The Middle Ages took it for granted that one sort of person could be distinguished from another by his clothing; only since the nineteenth century have men and women begun wearing nondescript suits, dresses, or jeans. At first, "discrimination" in Islamic countries worked the other way around: We are told that Muslims, too, once had to wear distinctive clothing, for reasons of security; during the first centuries, they were, in many places, a minority of the population. Security reasons may also have had some importance later on, but the main thing these symbols expressed was a factor that we always see prominently displayed when feelings of superiority create second-class citizens: disdain.

CONVERSION AND MISSIONARY ACTIVITY

In any case, contempt is not as bad as the hatred with which Christians treated Jews in the Middle Ages. And as we have seen, Muslims were often prevented by circumstances, and perhaps sometimes by their own convictions, from openly showing such disdain. They needed their "wards," and besides, in some regions, the non-Muslims, especially the Christians, were by no means a minority, although we can now see why they *became* one over the course of time. It is interesting to note that the Jews have made out much better than the Christians: Jews still live in the Maghreb, the homeland of St. Augustine—those that haven't emigrated to Israel—whereas there is hardly a trace left of the Christians. For centuries, the Jews had been accustomed to the Christians' despising them. With the rise of the Muslims, their situation only improved. The Christians, on the other hand, had thitherto governed themselves, and they couldn't get over their sudden demotion.

Thus, Islam did not prevail by missionary activity in our sense; as a system, it is simply not designed for that sort of thing. On the contrary, a good number of rulers directly forbade conversions of Christians and Jews, because, as "wards," they paid more taxes than Muslims, and one doesn't kill the goose that lays golden eggs, not even for a reward in the hereafter. But, perhaps without always realizing it, Islam exerted social pressure on unbelievers, and that, in the long run, is stronger than religious conviction. Islam did not convert Christians through "fire and sword"; rather, they turned Muslim in a centuries-long process of attrition through their own altogether human weakness.

It was a different story, of course, in places where Islamic expansion encountered "pagans"—in India, for example, where around the year 1000 Mahmud of Ghazni directed massacres of the Hindus and plundered and destroyed temples. To a certain extent, the same thing happened in Africa. But even there the great missionary successes were achieved through peaceful infiltration instead of violence. The missionaries were the merchants, who also preached their faith, and sometimes, too, the mystical brotherhoods, in Indonesia, China, and to this day in black Africa. The merchant—or modern businessman—makes particularly effective use of his social prestige; he is richer than most people, and he represents a higher level of culture. And a businessman never demands the impossible. Islam is spread by lay apostles, which most likely gives it an advantage over Christianity, which has a hard time explaining the discrepancy between the message presented by its missionaries and the behavior of its lay people—not to mention the enormous burden of colonialism.

SUMMARY: ISLAM'S STRENGTH AND WEAKNESS

This brings me, by way of conclusion, to a general, rather than a particular, comparison between the two religions. If one asks a Muslim about the advantages enjoyed by Islam, he will presumably stress two things: the absolute rationality of its teaching, and a certain flexibility in its practice, which he may call something like the golden mean. Both points may be contested, but we would surely never define Christianity in such a way. This leads to differences of opinion on specific issues: The Trinity is a mystery for the Christian; for the Muslim, it is logical nonsense. Celibacy for some Christians means freedom from the world; for the Muslim, asceticism carried too far. Christians view the regulations imposed by a religion of law as too constricting, and immediately think of the Pharisees. For a Muslim, these rules are a perfectly sensible way to order his life; through them he translates his obedience to God into reality.

Where, on the other hand, do we find the weakness of Islam? Muslims, of course, will seldom reply to this question; but our answer may likewise prove too subjective. It seems to me that Islam's weakness lies just where its strength lies: in its success. For that reason, the awareness Muslims have of their own orthodoxy is tied in with expectations of worldly glory. "The Church beneath the Cross" is barely conceivable in Muslim categories. Only Shi'a has made room in its thought for suffering and failure. But, as we see today, the Shi'ites, too, feel quite comfortable amid success. The crucial factor here is that the first Islamic community met with success, which thereby became part of the basic model. The more reality diverges from this expectation, however, the more believers turn back to this model. It is precisely in times of crisis and insecurity that people look for salvation in the past. This attitude is doubtless characteristic of human beings everywhere, but the typically Islamic feature is that the "good old days" were shaped by God down to the last detail. This view gives rise to what we nowadays call fundamentalism. Such a revival of the idealized primitive period is only self-deception, and the present historical moment is utterly unlike the distant past, but the protagonists of this movement do not realize that. To do so, they would first have to acknowledge the fact of historical change, something they deny in the name of the eternal truth of revelation. Thus far, scarcely anyone in the Islamic world has done a historicocritical analysis of the Qur'an or of the life of the Prophet; and there is little interest in doing one, at least right now.

To balance things out, we should discuss the weakness of Christianity. But I leave that to my Christian readers. Perhaps Islam can be of help in recognizing the weak point(s) of their faith. In that sense it may be a real alternative.

2. *Hans Küng:* A Christian Response

As far as the subject of *tolerance* and the *relation to other religions* is concerned, I have already (in my first response) called for a thoroughgoing revision of the image that Christians have had of Islam for well over a thousand years. I have argued not simply for tolerance, but for a whole new attitude toward Islam. Following the guidelines of Vatican II, the old exclusivism should be avoided, and a complete, consistent reevaluation made of Islam as a way of salvation, of Muhammad as a prophet, and of the Qur'an as God's word. By the same token, however (and this is connected with the problem of secularization, which I addressed in my second response), we must now demand from Islam a universal tolerance and freedom of religion, including full civil rights (even for those who are not "people of the Book" and for Islamic "heretics," such as the Ahmadiyya and the cruelly persecuted Bahā'is). In short, we must call for the Islamic states to respect the UN Human Rights Declaration with regard to non-Muslims. The "Universal Islamic Human Rights Declaration" of 1981 uses the term "human being" in the French and English version where the Arabic original has "Muslim." As we have heard, according to the *sharī'a*, only Muslims have civil rights; Christians and Jews merely have the status of "tolerated guest" *(dhimmī)*. Finally, in my third response I tried, wherever possible, to elaborate some points of theological agreement, without either old-fashioned polemics or superficial irenics. The path leading to the central question has been a long one; that question must now be dealt with.

THE QUR'AN'S PORTRAIT OF JESUS

The Qur'an, as we have seen, speaks often, and always sympathetically, about Jesus of Nazareth. If one looks into the "Qur'anic texts relevant to Christians," edited and published under the title *Muhammad and Jesus* (1978), by the Catholic exegete Claus Schedl, who translates and explains them in an all too "Christian" fashion, this much is evident: All the material in the Qur'an concerning Jesus has been *fully and coherently integrated into the Qur'an's overall theological vision.* From whatever source the information about Jesus may derive, all the texts have been unmistakably stamped by Muhammad's intensive prophetic experience of the one God. Thus Muhammad had no need to contradict Jesus: Jesus' preaching was his, too, and he had no qualms about admitting the Virgin Birth and the miracles. Except for one: Jesus might not be made into God, might not be placed alongside the one God as a second god— from the Qur'an's point of view, an abomination pure and simple.

The place of Jesus in the Qur'an is so clear-cut that it does not promote dialogue when well-meaning Christians find more theological implications in the Qur'an than it actually yields. For example, in the Qur'an, Jesus is the "word" of God—but *not* in the sense of the prologue to John, where the preexistent divine Logos becomes flesh. As for Jesus' *Virgin Birth,* the Qur'an views it as a sign of God's omnipotence, not of Jesus' divinity. Nor does it help much when writers psychologize theology and, disregarding the historical context of the Qur'an, interpret its statements about Mary and the child Jesus as a Jungian archetype. That is the approach Paul Schwarzenau takes, with the best of intentions, in his book *The Qur'an for Christians* (1982): "The Virgin's son . . . represents the undisturbed happiness of the mother-son bond, with no father to interrupt or interfere, the utopia of a wish-fulfillment paradise, which continually lavishes and nourishes without toil or struggle." (p. 100)

Reflecting on and speculating about the Qur'an is one thing, interpreting it another. Ex-egesis, reading-out, must never become eisegesis, reading into. The Qur'an should be interpreted *from the standpoint of the Qur'an,* not from that of the New Testament or the Council of Nicaea or Jungian psychology. For the Qur'an, Jesus is a prophet, a great prophet, like Abraham, Noah, and Moses—but nothing more. And just as in the New Testament John the Baptist is Jesus' precursor, so in the Qur'an Jesus is the precursor—and highly encouraging example—for Muhammad. To be sure, the Qur'an says that Jesus (in contrast to the Prophet) was directly fashioned by God, but this means that he is God's creature *par excellence.*

We Christians should not try to co-opt either Muhammad or the Muslims as "anonymous Christians," the way some well-intentioned

Christian theologians repeatedly do—against the grain of every self-conception Muslims have. Of course, this raises the parallel question of whether Muslims have the right to turn Jesus into an "anonymous Muslim." If we on the Christian side make an effort to reevaluate Muhammad on the basis of Islamic sources, especially the Qur'an, we also hope that for their part the Muslims will eventually be prepared to move toward *a reevaluation of Jesus of Nazareth on the basis of historical sources* (namely the Gospels) as many Jews have already been doing. The portrait of Jesus in the Qur'an is all too one-dimensional, ill-defined, and devoid of substance—apart from the features of monotheism, the call for conversion in view of the judgment to come, and a few miracle stories. The historical Jesus was quite different. Despite what the Qur'an says, he did not uphold the Law. Rather (as the evidence in the Gospels has compelled us to argue), he opposed every kind of legalism with his radical love (which embraces even the enemy), and for this reason was executed. But this is precisely what the Qur'an, flying in the face of history, will not admit.

"Why then, it must be asked, does the Qur'an deny the crucifixion of Jesus in the face of apparently overwhelming evidence?" asks the Islamic scholar Mahmoud M. Ayoub *(The Muslim World, LXX, 1980, p. 116)*, after subjecting all the tortured Muslim interpretations of sura 4, 157 (see p. 186) to critical scrutiny. He himself seems to consider Jesus' death on the cross a reality, and he tries to understand the statements in the Qur'an theologically, rather than historically: "Muslim commentators have not been able convincingly to disprove the crucifixion . . . Commentators have generally taken the verse to be an historical statement. This statement, like all the other statements concerning Jesus in the Qur'ān, belongs not to history but to theology in the broadest sense." What, then, is the theological meaning of this verse from the Qur'an, which Ayoub wants to promote, within the framework of an "authentic Islamic understanding of Christ," an "Islamic Christology"? The answer given by Ayoub (who did an important study in 1978 on "Redemptive Suffering in Islam") can be understood in the context of the elevation of Christ to a new life with God, which is affirmed in the same passage of the Qur'an. "Thus the denial of the death of Jesus is the denial of the power of men to control and destroy the word of God, which is always victorious." (p. 117) It would be interesting to pursue further the discussion about the interpretation of this verse in the context of a more historicocritical reading of the Qur'an.

I have already argued, in my third "Christian Response," that Islam faces a challenge raised by the man from Nazareth with regard to violence and nonviolence, hatred and love of one's enemies, success and failure. But this is not where the crucial theological difficulty for Muslim-Christian understanding really lies.

THE TRINITY—AN INSURMOUNTABLE OBSTACLE?

For Jesus himself, the central problem was this: In the face of the coming Kingdom of God, how to overcome legalism by fulfilling God's will in love? For the Christian Church, however, the central issue shifted, over the course of time, to the person of Jesus and his relation to God. And the controversy between Christianity and Islam remains wholly concentrated on this question. Up till now, the decisive Christian objection was that Islam denied the two basic, interconnected dogmas of Christianity; the *Trinity* and the *Incarnation.* As a matter of fact, the Qur'an addresses Christians as follows: "People of the Book, go not beyond the bounds / in your religion, and say not as to God / but the truth. The Messiah, Jesus son of Mary, / was only the Messenger of God, and His Word / that He committed to Mary, and a Spirit from / Him. So believe in God and His Messengers, / and say not, 'Three.' Refrain; better is it / for you. God is only One God. Glory be / to Him—that He should have a son!" (sura 4, 169)

It might seem that for all the points of agreement in the Muslim and Christian understanding of God and man, we have finally come to a *dead end.* The situation resembles that of the most recent declaration of the German Catholic bishops "On the Church's Relations with Judaism" (1980). The statement does acknowledge that the Christian belief in the "Son of God, equal in essence to Him" strikes "many Jews as absolutely contradictory . . . to strict monotheism, if not as downright blasphemous." But instead of offering an answer to this central difficulty, which is just as disturbing to Muslims, the bishops make only a gesture of easy resignation: "The Christian must be understanding about this matter, even if he himself sees no contradiction to monotheism in the doctrine of Jesus' divine sonship." (pp. 21 f.) But we may wonder what good it will do Jews and Muslims if Christians are "understanding," if they are not at the same time ready to have their own Christian self-concept seriously questioned. The same is true of the otherwise very helpful "Orientations pour un dialogue entre Chrétiens et Musulmans," by the Roman Secretariat for Non-Believers (1969). For this reason it was sharply criticized by the Catholic side. (See Y. Moubarac, "L'Islam et le dialogue islamo-chrétien," Beirut 1972–73; unfortunately the revised edition of "Orientations" [1981] does not take cognizance of this criticism.)

It is by no means the case, as Christian apologists often claim, that all Muslim theologians without exception have mistaken the Christian doctrine of the Trinity for tritheism. Admittedly, the Qur'an labors under the misapprehension, possibly based on certain apocalyptic traditions, that the Trinity consists of God the Father, Mary the Mother of God, and

Jesus the Son of God. But even well-informed Muslims simply cannot follow, as the Jews thus far have likewise failed to grasp, the idea of the Trinity. They do not see why faith in one God, the faith of Abraham, which both Moses and Jesus and, finally, Muhammad, clung so firmly to, is not abandoned when, along with the one godhead, the one divine nature, Christians simultaneously accept three persons in God. Why, after all, should one differentiate between nature and person in God?

It is well known that the *distinctions* made by the doctrine of the Trinity between one God and three hypostases do not satisfy Muslims, who are confused, rather than enlightened, by theological terms derived from Syriac, Greek, and Latin. Muslims find it all a word game. What are they to make of the conglomerate of hypostases, persons, *prosopa*, two processions, and four relations—in the one and only God? What are all the dialectical artifices for? Isn't God absolutely simple, rather than composite in this way or that? What is the meaning of a real difference in God between the Father, Son, and Holy Spirit that nonetheless does not do away with the real unity of God? What, on the other hand, is a logical difference between the Father and the nature of God that still has a foundation in reality? Why should anyone want to add anything to the notion of God's oneness and uniqueness that can only dilute or nullify that oneness and uniqueness?

The Qur'an says, "They are unbelievers / who say, 'God is the Third of Three' [or threefold in trinity]." This position, which Muhammad takes to be quite out of the question, is flatly rejected: "No god there is but / One God." (sura 5, 78)

MUSLIM CRITICISM OF THE TRINITY

A literature of controversy between Islam and Christianity was quick to appear on the scene. We see it in the tenth century, for example, which for Rome (then a dilapidated provincial city) and Christianity was a *saeculum obscurum*, but for Islam was a century of brilliant culture and science, with the Abbasids in Iraq and the Fātimids in the Maghreb and Egypt. In this period a man named Hasan ibn Aiyūb wrote a long letter to his brother to explain why he, who had once been a Christian, after twenty years of doubts, especially about the Trinity and the Incarnation, had finally become a Muslim—even though conversion brought a break in family ties and all sorts of insecurity into his life. We find such a step less surprising when we listen to all the various arguments employed, then and now, to defend the dogma of the Trinity. Hasan pointedly remarks apropos of the Matthean baptismal formula ("in the name of the Father and of the Son and of the Holy Spirit") that the mention of the three names in no way implies that the bearers of these names are alike in quality and rank. How, he wondered, could anyone say that in speaking of the Son and the Spirit Jesus had meant two other persons both of whom were God?

The Christians attacked by shrewd Muslim critics presumably got little help from the sort of arguments we hear, for example, from Paulus ar-Rāhib, "the monk," bishop of Sidon in the thirteenth century. In his "Exposition of Christian Doctrine," he speaks first about faith in the one God in a way Muslims would find perfectly understandable. But then he notes, rather abruptly, that all these statements hold true for the one God, who is a single substance in three persons. In his "Letter to a Muslim," Paulus then tries to substantiate this with seemingly plausible arguments. He maintains that God is one being (the Father), who also possesses reason (the Son) and has life (the Spirit). Thus there are three persons and still only one God, who was, is, and will be ever alive and rational. The Son, he says, proceeds from the father and was begotten— not through some sort of corporeal procreation, but through a different, more subtle form of generation, so that we may not suppose that the Father came before the Son or the Son after the Father. Just as the sun is differently perceived as a disk in the sky, as light, and as warmth, but is one and the same, so with God. And the bishop of Sidon thought he could make out all this not just in the New Testament, but in the Old Testament too, and even in the Qur'an.

A line-by-line refutation promptly arrived from the pen of the learned Muslim al-Qarāfī (d. 1285) in his "Excellent Answers to Shameful Questions." This piece became the standard Islamic rebuttal to Christianity and was continually referred to in the following centuries. Al-Qarāfī had no great difficulty in showing that reason *(logos)* and life are undoubtedly predicates of God, but that there is not the slightest justification for turning these divine qualities into divine persons. With the help of this hypostatization, one might just as well declare every other quality of God to be a person, and thus arrive at four, five, or still more persons in God. Christians had attempted to support their doctrine of the Trinity by citing the formula that introduces the suras in the Qur'an: "In the Name of God, the Merciful, the Compassionate." But these words would be perverted from their true sense should one, like the bishop, make the two predicates two persons. It was impossible to find any such thing in the Qur'an, which constantly stresses God's oneness. The Christian Scriptures, namely the Gospels, had a priori falsified God's revelation. This counterargument by al-Qarāfī was, of course, oversimplifying things. But before we give our answer to the question of the relation among Father, Son, and Spirit, we must first consider an important issue governing the connection between Islam and Christianity.

THE RAGE FOR DEFINING

Historians always note with surprise how little power of resistance Christianity has shown (even compared with Judaism, so much weaker numerically) in competition with Islam. Aside from Islam's great military, political, and organizational strength, a major cause of this shortfall seems to have been the *inadequate rationale of the "central" Christian dogma* (the Trinity and, along with it, the Incarnation). Catholic theologian Hermann Stieglecker, who in his book *The Teachings of Islam* (1960), gives a fine report on the theological controversies between Christians and Muslims, rightly treats this inadequacy as one of the main reasons leading to the collapse of Christendom in the very regions where it had first sprung up, the Near East and North Africa. Naturally, there were other factors at work here, such as the lamentable turmoil rending the Christian world and the waves of fear and shock unleashed everywhere by the Muslim battalions as they stormed ahead.

But this *"inner turmoil* rending Christendom" was very much linked to the "central dogma" of Christianity. Internal conflict was obviously a second theological element, together with the inadequate case for the Trinity, behind the Christian world's inability to withstand pressure from Islam. Both Rome and Byzantium displayed a hunger for dogmatic supremacy and a spirit of intolerance, especially toward the churches of the Middle East and North Africa. As we have heard, Islam (and Judaism, too, for that matter) never felt the unfortunate *compulsion to define and spell out its religious thought with the utmost exactitude.* After we have looked into the other two great world religions, Hinduism and Buddhism, this point should be still clearer. The rage to "dogmatize" (i.e., to lay down the law) on questions of faith is a Christian, or more precisely a Greco-Roman, specialty. The taste for philosophy and aesthetics, for polished language and harmonious articulation of doctrine, is *Greek.* Greek, too, is the intellectualization of belief through dogmatizing, high-flown speculation, and sterile, abstract mysticism. The taste for form, law, and organization, for tradition and unity, usefulness and practicality, is *Roman,* as are the emphasis on efficiency, power politics, authoritarian methods of leadership even in religion, and the traditionalism, legalism, and triumphalism continually revealed in definitions. As late as the Second Vatican Council, bishops protested against all this, and while the Council was being prepared, John XXIII forbade the Council to declare any new dogmas. This was an altogether different line from that of his predecessor, Pius XII, who had viewed the definition of Mary's assumption as the high point of his pontificate.

Islam considers this sort of theology as a rather peripheral, otiose philosophy of religion. It has limited dogma and definitions to the sphere of law. Instead of orthodoxy, it has concentrated on *orthopraxy*, though, needless to say, the predominance of law in Islam has created nearly as many problems as the predominance of theology in Christianity. In any case, Islam did a much better job of preserving its unity (despite the division into Sunnites and Shi'ites, which arose from different causes). The Christian world extols its great Christological-trinitarian councils, but it usually forgets that the names of Nicaea, Ephesus, Chalcedon, and Constantinople were bound up not only with the controversies that continued afterward, but with great schisms that to this day have not healed, despite the mortal danger posed by Islam in Egypt and the Middle East.

The fact is that until the Enlightenment (which all the forces of orthodoxy in every denomination fought against, and still do), official Christianity seldom showed much *tolerance.* And yet Jesus, the ultimate authority for Christians, was no fanatic for the law or a zealot given to defining the tenets of faith. We can make no progress in dialogue unless we trace our way back through the Qur'an to the New Testament. (A number of Islamic theologians have already tried to do this, though naturally their objectives were polemical.)

WHAT DOES IT MEAN TO SAY GOD HAS A SON?

Like Judaism as a whole, Jesus of Nazareth was not committed to formulas and dogmas. He engaged neither in profound speculation, after the fashion of Greek philosophers and mystics, nor in learned legal casuistry, such as that of the rabbis or the *'ulamā'*. He made use of readily graspable proverbs, stories, and parables from the unprettified everyday world familiar to all his listeners. At the center of his preaching he placed not his own person, role, or dignity, but *God: God's* kingdom, *God's* name, *God's* will, which man is to fulfill through service to his fellow men and women. No secret revelations, no complex allegorisms with a cast of unknown characters. Jesus questions no one about the true faith, he asks no one to profess his or her orthodoxy. He expects no theoretical reflection, but an urgent practical decision: orthopraxy.

This sort of preaching would certainly not be unacceptable in principle to Muslims. But then there is the idea that this herald of God's kingdom must be called not just the *Son of God,* but *God.* How can such a thought (which will receive considerable stress) be made somewhat plausible to Muslims? Under the circumstances, it is no wonder that Jesus never proclaimed (as theologians would later) as a great "mystery": "God is one nature but in three persons; and I am one person but in two natures." Only one passage of the New Testament clearly affirms that the Father, Son (Word), and Spirit are "one" (see 1 John 5:7–8), but these particular verses are not found in the old manuscripts of the New

Testament. Although their authenticity was defended by the Roman Congregation of the Faith (Sanctum Officium Sanctissimae Inquisitionis) as late as the turn of the century, they are nowadays commonly recognized as an interpolation from third- or fourth-century North Africa or Spain. How, then, should we look upon Jesus' relationship to God? This is the original Christological (and, *in germine*, the Trinitarian) question.

In discussing it, people continually forget that *Jesus himself was a Jew* and phenotypically much closer to a present-day Palestinian Arab than to all our Byzantine, Italian, Spanish, or German images of Jesus. This Jewish Jesus had no more notion than a Muslim in our time would of weakening faith in the one God (breaking the First Commandment). "Why do you call me good? No one is good but God alone" (Mk 10:18) was his reaction when addressed as "Good Teacher."

Jesus undoubtedly spoke, prayed, struggled, and suffered from the standpoint of an ultimately inexplicable experience of God, presence of God, certainty of God, indeed on the strength of a oneness with God as his Father. Modern historicocritical exegetes are agreed that Jesus did not apply the title "Son of God" to himself. *Nevertheless his claims went beyond those of a prophet,* in that he assumed God's authority (especially with respect to the Law and the forgiveness of sins). Here, in Jesus, something "more than Moses," more than the prophets, made its appearance. He not only talked about forgiving sin, about challenging every hallowed tradition and rule, about tearing down all the boundaries separating clean and unclean, just and unjust—he did all these things. And he proclaimed them not for "one day" and "the future," but —amid eschatological portents—for "today" and "now." No wonder he was accused of blaspheming God, condemned, and *executed* (on this last point, as we have seen, the Qur'an's image of Jesus is particularly in need of correction).

Only *after* his death, on the basis of their Easter experiences, were Christians entitled to believe that Jesus had transcended suffering and death, had been taken up into God's eternal life, had been "lifted up" to God, his Father. It was only then that the *believing community began to use the title "Son" or "Son of God" for him.* Why? There was an inner logic and solid reasoning in giving the name "Son" to someone who called God his "Father." I am aware, of course, that calling God Father causes problems nowadays, but I cannot go into that now. In order to explain the Christological issues, I have to stick to the language used by the Bible.

The Bible speaks as follows: Just as Israel's king was appointed the *"son of Yahweh"* through his accession to the throne (Ps 2:7; 89:26–27; cf. 2 Sam 7:12–16), the *crucified* Jesus was made God's son through his resurrection and exaltation. There is no trace of physical/sexual (or even metaphysical) procreation akin to that of the Old Arabian "daughters of God."

In one of the oldest pre-Pauline professions of faith, cited in the introduction to Romans, it says: "designated Son of God in power . . . by his resurrection from the dead." (Rom 1:4) Elsewhere, in an echo of a royal psalm, Jesus is "begotten" as God's Son: "He [God] said to me [to the king, to the Messiah, and now to Jesus]: 'Thou art my Son, today I have begotten thee.' " (Ps 2:7; Acts 13:33). "Begotten" as king, "begotten" as the Anointed One (Messiah, Christ), as deputy and Son. By "today," the Acts of the Apostles unequivocally means not Christmas, but Easter, not the feast of the Incarnation, but that of Jesus' resurrection and exaltation, about which the Qur'an, too, speaks quite clearly.

And so what was the original New Testament position on Jesus' sonship? What the New Testament unquestionably has in mind is not a relation of parentage, but an appointment, in the *Old Testament sense*, conferring legal status and power. Not a physical divine sonship, as Islam always assumed and rightly rejected (because it awakened associations of intercourse between a god and a mortal woman), but God's *choosing Jesus and granting him full authority*. As far as Jewish monotheism goes, there were scarcely any fundamental objections to be raised against this interpretation of divine sonship; the primitive Christian community, made up entirely of Jews, would have no difficulty holding this view. Nor would Islam. But the faith of the Jewish Christians was to develop into something else again.

THE SPECIFICALLY CHRISTIAN ELEMENT

With the spread of Christianity to the world of Hellenistic thought, there was an increasing tendency *to put Jesus, as the Son of God, on the same level of being as the Father*. This inevitably led to a growing series of problems, because the more theologians tried to define the relation between Father and Son with Hellenistic categories of nature over the course of an unimaginably complex doctrinal history, the harder it got to harmonize conceptually belief in one God and Jesus' divine sonship, while distinguishing the Son of God from God and at the same time stressing their unity. The relationship of Father, Son, and Spirit became more and more of a *mysterium logicum*, in which the contradiction between unity and trinity seemed to have been overcome only by means of technical verbal distinctions (nature/person). So it was hardly surprising that in later times it became ever more impossible to make a credible presentation to the Jews and, later still, to the Muslims, concerning this God (of Israel) and his (Jewish) Jesus as the Anointed One, the Messiah, the Christ. The complete failure of the Christian "mission," first to the Jews and then to the Muslims, all of whom absolutely refused to give up their old faith in one God, provides eloquent evidence of this, as does the conversion of countless Christians (not Jews) to Islam.

But the New Testament does not have to face the question that necessarily arises when one tries to think in Hellenistic categories of nature: How are God's three persons in one nature or Christ's two natures in one person related to one another? In the language of the New Testament, the question runs this way: How is one to think about and confess the unity of God and Jesus—the Father and the Son (and then the Spirit) —so that both God's oneness and uniqueness and the identity of person of Jesus Christ are kept intact?

What are we to understand by the scriptural statement (see Gal 4:4; 2 Cor 8:9; Rom 8:3; John 1) that God's Son (i.e., not God the Father) has been "sent," or that the Word of God has been "made flesh"? Even in the late, fourth Gospel we find the innocuous formula: "And this is eternal life, that they know thee the only true God, and Jesus Christ whom thou hast sent." (John 17:3) Or: "I am ascending to my Father and your Father, to my God and your God." (John 20:17) On no account should the "incarnation" of the Son be connected exclusively to the "mathematical" or "mystical" point when Jesus was conceived or born; it must, rather, be linked up *with his entire life, death, and new life:* In everything he said, in his preaching, his conduct, his fate, in his entire person, the man Jesus proclaimed, manifested, and revealed God's word and will. In other words, God's word and will took on human form in him. Only in this fashion will it be unequivocally understood that Jesus, in whom word and deed, doctrine and life, being and acting, perfectly coincide, *is* God's "word," God's "will," God's "Son" in human form. According to the New Testament, then, what we have here is a unity of knowledge, will, action, and revelation between God and Jesus.

Statements such as this must be protected against widespread Islamic (and, often enough, Christian) *misunderstandings.* The New Testament also tells us that in no case should the terms "Father" and "Son" be turned into bitheism and then tritheism. For Jesus, God always remained the "one and only," and the same has been true for Christians in every age. In the Bible, too, there is no god but God. Regardless of all the speculations by theologians, the New Testament holds that there is no third choice between monotheism and polytheism. The New Testament also holds that God and Jesus cannot be simply identified, as was done in the heterodox movements (Monarchianism, modalism) of the first centuries of the Christian Era: The Son is not God the Father, and God the Father is not the Son. "Son" is not simply a name *(modus)* of God; and so comparisons of the Trinity with the ninety-nine names (qualities) of God in Islam are misleading.

For twenty centuries, Christianity and all the churches have agreed that the foundation and core of faith is *not a holy book* or law, but the historical *person of Jesus Christ,* who represents God, manifests God, and definitively reveals him. What, then, marks off Christians from Muslims? It is this trusting commitment to *Jesus* as the ultimate standard of the Christian concept of God and man. The part that the Qur'an plays for Muslims is played for Christians not by the Bible, but by Christ—God's word made manifest in human form.

But the conversation should not stop here. The message of the Qur'an could be substantially enriched by taking the Bible seriously. On the other hand, the message of the Bible could be freed from later overlays and exaggerations by taking seriously the warnings of the Qur'an. This one point, in any event, must be conceded to both Islam and Judaism: According to the New Testament, *the principle of unity* is not a single divine nature common to several entities, but *the one God (ho theós = the* God = the Father), from whom all things come and toward whom all things are oriented. Thus the New Testament is not concerned with metaphysical/ontological statements about God in himself and his innermost nature, about the static, serenely self-contained essence of a triune God. Rather, the New Testament is concerned with soteriological-Christological statements about the manner in which God reveals himself: about his dynamic activity in history, about his relation to human beings and their relation to him. In keeping with this, how should we understand the doctrine of the Trinity for the purposes of dialogue with Judaism and Islam (a test case for every Christian theology)? Here, in summary fashion, is my answer:

- In the New Testament, believing in God the Father means believing in the one God, a belief that Judaism, Christianity, and Islam all share. "Father" is often misunderstood, not only by Muslims but also by Christians: "Father" should not be understood literally, as opposed to "mother," but symbolically (or analogously). "Father" is a patriarchal symbol (with maternal features) for a primordial, ultimate reality that transcends humanity and sexuality. That means—and the Qur'an has a great deal to say about this—power and at the same time compassion, care as well as protection, dependency and security. Understandably, however, the Qur'an, while it has ninety-nine names for Allah, avoids the name "Father," which from Muhammad's standpoint was hopelessly compromised by the tribal religions of Arabia, with their belief in the children of the gods.

- Believing in the Son of God means believing in the revelation of the one God in the man Jesus of Nazareth. In the New Testament, Jesus Christ is primarily viewed not as an eternal, intradivine hypostasis, but as a human, historical person concretely related to God: the ambassador, Messiah, word of the eternal God in human form.

- Believing in the Holy Spirit means believing in God's power and might at work among human beings in this world.

Islam, too, sees God as the ruler (leader) and helper of humanity. God is closely present to the believer and the believing community: invisible yet powerful, intangible yet as necessary to life as air, wind, respiration, the breath of life, called *ruah* in Hebrew, *rūh* (or *rīh*) in Arabic, *Geist* in German, and "spirit" in English. It follows, I think, that Muslims as well as Christians will find meaning in the statement that the transcendent God is close to human ("closer than his carotid artery") and present in the Spirit, through the Spirit, as Spirit.

In the Bible, God's Spirit is called *the Holy Spirit* to distinguish it from the unholy spirit of man. But God's Holy Spirit is not distinguished from God himself, nor is the Spirit a third being between God and man. From the biblical standpoint, the Holy Spirit is God himself insofar as he is active among human beings as the power that grasps but is not graspable. Paul says that, through the resurrection and exaltation of Jesus, the Spirit of God became the Spirit of Christ as well. Indeed, Christ became "a life-giving spirit." (1 Cor 15:45) The Qur'an is by no means simply mistaken on this point. That is, the one who was lifted up to God now is the Spirit's mode of existence and activity; he presently acts through the Spirit, in the Spirit, as Spirit. As Paul writes: "The Lord is the Spirit." (2 Cor 3:17) Therefore the encounter with God, with Jesus Christ, and with the Spirit ultimately come down to one and the same encounter, as Paul says in the salutation: "The grace of the Lord Jesus Christ and the love of God and the fellowship of the Holy Spirit be with you all." (2 Cor 13:14)

And so *the criterion for being a Christian* is not the doctrine of the Trinity, gradually elaborated by the Church, but belief in the one and only God, the practical imitation of Christ, trusting the power of God's Spirit, that Spirit who in dialogue with non-Christians, as in other matters, works *wherever* he wishes, and will lead us wherever *he* sees fit.

This much should serve to provide an unambiguous account of what is *the specifically Christian element* in Christianity—God's revelation in Jesus Christ through the Spirit—and to separate it clearly from Islam, which recognizes Jesus as one of the prophets, but no more. The reader may wonder, though, whether this attempt to redefine Christianity (on the basis of the New Testament) will really help promote dialogue with Islam, or whether we don't find ourselves as much as ever at an impasse over the crucial issue. I don't believe we are at an impasse and I would like to clarify my position further by suggesting *some ideas* that might prove helpful in getting *future dialogue* with Islam over the central theological difference it has with Christianity.

JESUS AS THE SERVANT OF GOD

The rule that holds for the doctrine of the Trinity also holds for Christology: If contemporary Christians and Muslims want to understand each other better, they have to go *back to their origins* (and apply a discriminating critique to later developments). At our origins, all of us—Jews, Christians, and Muslims—are closer to one another. New Testament scholarship has recognized how great the distance is between the original statements about the Father, Son, and Spirit, and the Church's subsequent dogmatic teaching on the Trinity. It has also shown how different are the Christologies one finds even in the New Testament. Heikki Räisänen, one of the few New Testament scholars to have seriously studied the Qur'an, writes in his brilliant essay "The Portrait of Jesus in the Qur'an":

> Today it is clear to New Testament scholarship that there is hardly anything in the New Testament even remotely like the doctrine of the Trinity. This realization may in itself be a fresh starting point for a dialogue. But perhaps still more interesting is the fact that some passages of the New Testament show a striking similarity to the Qur'an's portrait of Jesus. (p. 127)

The late, fourth Gospel, which shows signs of Hellenistic influence, has Jesus speak of the glory he had with God before the world was made (John 17:3), a passage that even conservative exegetes do not accept as spoken by the historical Jesus. The first three Gospels, on the other hand, know nothing of Jesus' preexistence (the first, Mark, doesn't even know about the Virgin Birth). Right through the Passion, the fourth Gospel presents Jesus in a highly glorified fashion as a near god (but still clearly distinguished from God) walking the earth. According to the Synoptics, however, he is wholly the suffering Son of Man, through whom God acts. Räisänen points in particular to the speeches in the Acts of the Apostles where Luke uses old, traditional material that completely subordinates Jesus to God. These passages plainly speak of Jesus as *God's* servant, *God's* Christ, *God's* chosen one: God acts through him, God was with him; he was killed in accordance with God's plan, but God raised him from the dead, made him Lord and Christ and—I have already cited the key passage here—appointed him the Son of God. Don't all these Lucan statements (with their "adoptionist" coloring) still very much fit into the framework of a strict Jewish or Islamic monotheism? And yet this was the faith of Christians—of Jewish Christians. And, perhaps, of Muslims, too?

It was an unparalleled calamity for the developing Church, especially after the total destruction of Jerusalem under Hadrian in 132 and the flight of all Jewish Christians eastward, to be almost completely cut off from its native Jewish soil: The Church, once made up of *Jews,* which had become a Church of Jews *and* Gentiles, now turned into a Church of (Hellenistic) Gentiles. The few *Jewish Christians* who did not go along with the development of the Hellenistic Church and its increasingly exaggerated Christology, were *labeled as heretics.* Such, for example, were the Ebionites, who, the church historian Eusebius tells us, accepted the Virgin Birth of Jesus but rejected his eternal preexistence. Exactly like . . . the Qur'an.

Time and time again, Islam has been shown to "derive" from Judaism or Christianity; and ever since the days of John Damascene it has been written off as a "Christian heresy." My purpose here is not to repeat any of that, but to take a fresh, serious view of Islam in a way that poses a challenge to Christians: Islam as a reminder of their own past. Here, it seems to me, we have an extremely important example of the interdependence and interaction between the religions of mankind that have been stressed by a number of scholars, especially Wilfred Cantwell Smith. Paul Schwarzenau, too, has the right idea when he says, "It is the Jewish element of the Christian message which the Qur'an decisively accentuates. The once rejected Jewish Christians emerge again from the shadows." (p. 124) Schwarzenau cites a perceptive analysis by the great Protestant exegete Adolf Schlatter, who explored the connections between Gentile Christianity, Jewish Christianity, and Islam in his *History of the Early Christian World:* "The Jewish church, however, had died out only in Palestine west of the Jordan. Christian communities following Jewish customs still survived in the eastern regions, in Decapolis, Batanaea, among the Nabataeans, on the edge of the Syrian wilderness, and over towards Arabia, completely severed from the rest of the Christian world and having no fellowship with it . . . For the Christians the Jews were simply enemies, and the Church came to share the Greek feeling that the slaughter unleashed by the generals of Trajan and Hadrian was something to be ignored, that the fate of the mischievous, contemptible Jews was richly deserved. Even the leading figures in the Church who lived and taught in Caesarea, men like Origen and Eusebius, remained surprisingly ignorant about the end of Jerusalem and its church. Their accounts of the surviving Jewish Christians are similarly inadequate. Because they had not submitted to the law in force among Christians elsewhere, such people were heretics and no longer part of Christendom. None of the leaders of the imperial Church ever dreamed that a day would come when this group of Christians, whom they so despised, would once again shake the world and shatter the ecclesiastical system they had built up. That day came when Mohammed took over the legacy of the Jewish Christians, their consciousness of God, their eschatological prophecies of the coming Judgment, their customs and legends, and, as the one sent by God, set up a new apostolate." (p. 367)

According to Schlatter, then, Muhammad was something like a "Jewish Christian Apostle" in Arab clothing. This is a remarkable insight, which Schlatter had argued in detail as far back as 1918 in an essay on "The Evolution of Jewish Christianity into Islam," *Evangelisches Missionsmagazin*, pp. 251–64. But not many people know that, forty years before Schlatter, Adolf von Harnack maintained that one could see in Islam the aftereffects of Jewish Christianity. Harnack was speaking more particularly about gnostic Jewish Christianity and, above all, in this context, of the sect known as the Elkesaites, who advocated, among other things, a strict monotheism and disapproved of church doctrines about divine hypostases and the Son of God. In his monumental *History of Dogma*, Harnack incorporated an earlier study of his into his summary conclusion that "Islam is a transformation of Jewish Christianity, which was in turn a transformed version of Judaism, that took place on Arabian soil at the hands of a great prophet . . . Because of its strict emphasis on the oneness of God and its rejection of image worship, and, generally, because of its simplicity, which let spiritual religion once again shine through, Islam had a decided advantage over Christianity, with its doctrine of the Trinity, which only lofty scholars could understand as monotheism, and its magical rites, with all their appurtenances. Along with Islam's liberating reduction of monotheism to a few crucial factors not a few Christians were willing to accept the new prophet, especially since they were allowed to go on venerating Abraham, Moses, and Christ." (4th ed. [1909], p. 537)

Admittedly, current research would indicate that any direct dependency of Islam upon Jewish Christianity (of whatever sort) will continue to be disputed for a while. We simply know too little about the Arabian Peninsula in those centuries before Muhammad. But the analogies are as astonishing as ever. Even if we could never scientifically verify a genetic connection, the traditional-historical parallels are inescapable. And how can we explain why Muhammad—although he rejected orthodox (or Monophysite) Christology—nonetheless always spoke sympathetically of Jesus as the great "messenger" (*rasūl*), indeed as the "Messiah" (*masīh*), who brought the gospel? In his *Theology and History of Jewish Christianity* (Tübingen, 1949) Hans-Joachim Schoeps, taking up the research of Harnack and Schlatter, and completing it with studies by C. Clemen, T. Andrae, and H. H. Schaeder, comes to the following broadly substantiated conclusion: "Though it may not be possible to establish exact proof of the connection, the indirect dependence of Mohammed on sectarian Jewish Christianity is beyond any doubt. This leaves us with a paradox of truly world-historical dimensions: the fact that while Jewish Christianity in the Church came to grief, it was preserved in Islam and, with regard to some of its driving impulses at least, it has lasted till our own time." (p. 342)

Surprisingly, Christian theologians have hitherto scarcely known of these historical insights, much less taken them seriously. There is a lot of territory that remains to be investigated here, such as the story of Waraqa, Muhammad's Hebrew-speaking cousin by marriage. He was a Christian (surely not from a Hellenistic background) who alerted the Prophet, at an early stage of his career, to the affinity between his revelatory experience and that of Moses. Whatever the facts in the matter, no one could fail to notice the previously unsuspected openings here for trilateral dialogue ("trialogue" among Jews, Christians, and Muslims). And however the question of genetic dependency may be decided, in *Muhammad's* conception of Jesus, we see traditions of the *Jewish Christian world,* which had been superseded, despised, and forgotten in the Hellenistic church, again coming to the light of history. And this Jewish Christianity, in turn, had kept central Jewish concerns alive in the young Christian Church.

It should not be forgotten that in his campaign against the polytheism of old Arabia (which worshipped any number of Allah's children), Muhammad really had no choice but to condemn the term "Son of God" because of its pagan associations. But, at the same time, Muhammad adopted the story of Jesus in the form then current among the Arabs, and interpreted it in his own fashion. The process so often observed in the Bible was now at work in the Qur'an: An older tradition is not simply taken over, but reinterpreted and updated in the light of contemporary experiences. And just as Christians applied to Jesus many Old Testament passages (the "prophecies") whose original meaning had been quite different, so Muhammad related to his own situation much of what he had heard about Jesus. For Muhammad, Jesus' greatness consisted in the fact that through him and in him, as God's servant and ambassador, God himself had been at work. Thus Muhammad's "Christology" may not have been all that different from the Christology of the Jewish Christian church.

On this point, Claus Schedl's analysis of the Qur'anic texts referring to Christ would seem to be on target:

> It is true that the Hellenistic church of the West did not develop further the outline of a Servant-of-God Christology, of which we find fragments in the Acts of the Apostles. But for the Syrian-Semitic Christians of the East calling Jesus the Servant (*'abd*) of God seems to have been the prevalent Christological creedal formula. Thus when Muhammad placed the title of Servant in the center of his preaching about 'Īsā (Jesus), he was adopting an early-Christian model, purifying it of contemporary misinterpretations, but avoiding precise ontological definitions (the sort of thing one would expect from a Hellenistic or Western thinker).

Despite this lack of hard and fast formulas the Qur'an makes it quite clear that God's servant 'Īsā has a special place among God's other servants. At the beginning and the end of his life the effective power of Allah becomes manifest. 'Īsā came into existence only through Allah's creative word, and on the cross he was spirited away and swept up to Allah. Not only did he perform miracles in his life, but he himself was established as God's exemplary miracle amidst all of humanity.

Hence we should stop saying that Muhammad had only a faulty knowledge of Christianity. In the Qur'an, to be sure, he does not address the doctrinal decisions promulgated by the councils of the western Church. But from what we have seen so far it would appear that he was quite familiar with the basic structure of Syrian-Semitic Christology and developed it further on his own. If Muslim-Christian dialogue is to be fruitful, it will have to start out from these fundamental facts. (pp. 565 f.)

WHAT WE SHOULD TALK ABOUT

What is the upshot of all these new findings? We are faced with a momentous problem, whose consequences cannot yet be reckoned. If the exegetical findings presented here are correct and can be further clarified, that will challenge both sides to move beyond the old alternative, Jesus *or* Muhammad, and—assuming all the necessary distinctions and limitations—to think more forcefully of a synthesis between Jesus *and* Muhammad. The point here is that Muhammad himself can to a certain extent be viewed as a witness for Jesus—a Jesus who could have been understood not by Hellenistic Gentile Christians, but by Jesus' first disciples, who were Jews, because, with his Jesus tradition, Muhammad reminds the Jews that Jesus fits into the continuity of *Jewish salvation history.*

Muhammad conspicuously refrains from passing over Jesus in silence, the way the rabbis did during the first centuries of the Christian Era, as a result of the curse laid on Jesus in the synagogue. Muhammad's valuation of Jesus against a Jewish background, therefore, was in all probability due not to Jewish but to Jewish Christian influences. Not Jews, but Jewish Christians would have advocated the replacement of the old law by a new one, the spiritualization of the law into a law of faith, and would have stressed the last judgment and the importance of the bearer of revelation himself (Jesus is named in the Christian profession of faith, as Muhammad is invoked by Muslims, but Moses is not by Jews)—all these traits Christianity has in common with Islam, rather than with Judaism. Another aspect of this connection is the fact that later tradition shaped the image of Muhammad so as to make it a counterpart to the image of Jesus: Muhammad, too, is said to have had a supernatural birth, to have worked miracles, to have been without sin, to have gone up into heaven.

Still, do we have to compare Jesus and Muhammad at all? Essentially, from the standpoint of our own faith, we don't have to, but we can. And given the times we live in, as well as for the sake of peace between the two religions, we should do it. We have nothing to fear from the comparison, but, as we have seen, a lot to learn.

Meanwhile, lest I be misunderstood as I deal with a question that both Muslims and Christians find so delicate, let me say this much: As a European Gentile Christian, I can thoroughly understand the Hellenistic development of Christology. I can accept the truth of the great Christological councils from Nicaea to Chalcedon. The broad outline of their purposes and contents can be roundly affirmed. And so I do not mean to say that, as a Christian, one can naively start out from zero all over again, that one should, as it were, become a Jewish Christian.

But, in the *ecumenical* context (with reference to Muslims and Jews), I cannot help wondering: How can I make a Muslim (or Jew) understand why Christians believe in Jesus as the Christ, the revelation of God? And with this intention in mind, I am perfectly entitled to call attention to what is an altogether legitimate, in fact the original, Christological option, though it has been driven to the fringes of theology and buried there. This option was the point of departure for Jesus' disciples and the oldest Jewish Christian community; for centuries it was handed down by the scattered Jewish Christian communities living east of the Jordan, who probably spread it all the way into Arabia, where Muhammad finally encountered it. Might it not provide us with ready-made categories for making the idea of Jesus as God's revelation more comprehensible to Jews and Muslims than the Hellenistic doctrine of Jesus' two natures does?

MUHAMMAD—"NO MORE THAN A CLEAR WARNER"

How, then, from this ecumenical perspective, might a Muslim try to view Jesus—and Christians, Muhammad? Since dialogue is at such an early stage right now, I can only venture a few suggestions, with three working assumptions:

1. Christians and Muslims believe in a single God and thus in a single salvation history. Just as Christians, for this reason, look upon Adam, Noah, Abraham, and all the patriarchs of Israel as "Christians" before Christ, so Muslims regard these same figures (whatever the historical facts may be about the nonverifiable line of Ishmael) and Jesus, too, as "Muslims" before Muhammad.

2. Muhammad (who bore witness to Jesus) is not a person whom Christians may dismiss as indifferent; nor can he be written off as a false prophet, as though there were by definition no prophets after Christ.

3. Jesus (to whom Muhammad bore witness) has a message of lasting importance for Muslims.

Thus Christianity and Islam cannot be set off against each other as totally separate religions. Rather, they are—like Judaism and Christianity—interwoven religious movements. How, therefore, might Muslims regard Jesus, and Christians, Muhammad?

How might *Muslims* look upon Jesus? They already consider him the greatest prophet and messenger of the one God, a man who was particularly distinguished by God as the Servant of God, from his birth until he was lifted up to God, and who, together with the message he preached, always played an important part in Muhammad's thought.

Obviously, Muslims will continue to see in Muhammad and the Qur'an, which he brought, the crucial guidelines for believing and acting, living and dying. Hence, for the sake of avoiding all conceptual confusion, Muslims should not be characterized as "Christians," even in the broad sense, as Wilfred Cantwell Smith, for example, does.

Nevertheless, since the Qur'an calls Jesus the "word" of God and the bearer of the "gospel," it would seem that Muslims have to try to get a more comprehensive understanding of this gospel. They should take seriously such insights as these:

That the preaching and practice of Jesus have relativized the often oppressive Islamic law, in the name of both God and man; that man has been set free, not from law, but from legalism (much as happened with the Jewish Christians).

That Jesus' life, death, and new life gives us a new and deeper understanding of God as one who loves and has compassion for humanity.

That Jesus' death offers us a fresh source of meaning, in the name of this God, however meaningless our suffering and failure may appear to be.

The Muslim theologian Mahmoud M. Ayoub, now living in America, has made some bold and broad-minded ecumenical statements apropos of an "Islamic Christology." His approach toward this goal is a promising one, and must be pressed further: "Thus we see that the Christ of faith and hope, the Jesus of the Qur'ān and later Muslim piety is much more than a mere human being, or even simply the messenger of a Book. While the Jesus of Islam is not the Christ of Christianity, the Christ of the Gospel often speaks through the austere, human Jesus of Muslim piety. Indeed, the free spirits of Islamic mysticism found in the man Jesus not only the example of piety, love, and asceticism, which they sought to emulate, but also the Christ, who exemplifies fulfilled humanity, a humanity illumined by the light of God. This reflection of the divine light in the human heart and soul is known in the language of Islamic mysticism as *tajallī,* the manifestation of divine beauty and majesty in and through man. In this concept of divine manifestation, the Christian and Muslim images of Jesus converge at many points." ("Toward an Islamic Christology: An Image of Jesus in Early Shī'ī Muslim Literature," *The Muslim World*, LXVI, 1976, 187)

How might *Christians* look upon *Muhammad?* Many Christians already consider him an important prophet for many nations in the world, a man who even in his lifetime was blessed with immense success.

Obviously, Christians will continue to see in Jesus Christ and the gospel he proclaimed the *crucial standard* for believing and acting, living and dying—the definitive word of God. (Heb 1:1 f.) Conversely, therefore, Christians should not be styled "Muslims" in the broad sense, as Smith once again suggests. Christ is and remains the Christian's decisive norm, for both God's and man's sakes.

Nevertheless, shouldn't Christians (who know from the New Testament about prophets after Jesus) take Muhammad more seriously? And shouldn't they take the admonitions of the Qur'an more seriously— when it says, for example:

That the one incomparable God has to stand in the absolute center of faith;

That associating with him any other gods or goddesses is out of the question;

That faith and life, orthodoxy and orthopraxy, belong together everywhere, including politics?

In this way, Muhammad would once again be a *prophetic corrective* for Christians in the name of the one and only God; he would be a "prophetic warner": " 'I only follow what has been revealed to me; / I am only a clear warner.' " (sura 46, 9)

May we, despite all this, demand that a Muslim or a Jew accept the Hellenistic councils from Nicaea to Chalcedon? What would the Jew Jesus of Nazareth have done? The question is not a trivial one, not for Arabs who would be Christians, or for Africans, Indians, Indonesians, or even Chinese and Japanese in the same position.

Finally, in both Islam and Christianity we are dealing with a *faith decision* for which one must render a reasonable account to oneself and others. In making it, I can as a Christian be convinced that if I have chosen this Jesus as the Christ for my life and death, then along with him I have chosen his follower Muhammad, insofar as he appeals to one and the same God and to Jesus.

· The helpful contribution "Christians and Muslims in Dialogue," put out on behalf of the Evangelical Church in Germany (and edited by J. Micksch and M. Mildenberger, 1982), briefly calling attention to the possible connection between Islam and Jewish Christianity, rightly observes, "Christians and Muslims have to live and keep their faith amidst the same world. They will not always react in the same way to the challenges of that world. Yet for all their differences both are bound by their faith to a responsible life before God and to service for the human community. While fully respecting each other, they cannot deny each other the testimony of their faith." (p. 12)

What is needed today is *not missionary activity in the colonialistic style* (Christians converting Muslims, and now vice versa), *but this testimony of their own faith* (Muslims witnessing to Christians, and vice versa), with the goal of a mutual exchange of information, a mutual challenge, and so, ultimately, a mutual transformation.

But the last word in this attempt at a "Christian Response," which aims to be not the end, but the beginning of a conversation, belongs to a believing Muslim scholar whom I have already quoted, Mahmoud Ayoub: "The final stage in the long history of Muslim-Christian relations is still in its beginnings. When it is fully realized, it will, we hope, lead to true ecumenism, an ecumenism that will accommodate Islam not as a heresy of true Christianity, but as an authentic expression of the divine and immutable truth. In this spirit of mutual recognition and appreciation, Islam may have something to teach Christians that would strengthen their own faith in the Truth, the Truth which is greater than the expression of any one religious tradition or the understanding of any single individual or community. In order to realize this ideal, Muslims must likewise rethink their own understanding of the true meaning of Islam as the living up to the primordial covenant between God and all human beings and the divine reaffirmation of this covenant in a variety of expressions to a religiously pluralistic world." ("Toward an Islamic Christology," 165)

Basic Readings on Islam

(Titles with an asterisk were more specifically consulted in preparing this section)

GENERAL
1. Pierre Rondot. *L'Islam et les Musulmans d'aujourd'hui.* Paris, 1958.
2. Kenneth Cragg. *The Call of the Minaret.* New York, 1964.
3. Fazlur Rahman. *Islam.* Chicago/London, 1966; 2nd ed., 1979.
4. *Louis Gardet. *L'Islam, religion et communauté.* Paris, 1967.
5. W. Montgomery Watt. *What Is Islam?* London/Beirut, 1968.
6. Claude Cahen and G. E. von Grunebaum. *Der Islam,* I–II. Frankfurt am Main, 1968–71. (Fischer Weltgeschichte, Vols. 14–15)
7. J. Schacht and C. E. Bosworth, eds. *The Legacy of Islam.* London, 1974.
8. *Emma Brunner-Traut. *Die fünf grossen Weltreligionen.* Freiburg, 1974; 11th ed., 1984.
9. Adel-Theodor Khoury. *Einführung in die Grundlagen des Islam.* Graz, 1978.
10. *Maxime Rodinson. *La fascination de l'Islam.* Paris, 1980.
11. Wilfred Cantwell Smith. *On Understanding Islam.* The Hague, 1981.
12. Peter Antes. *Die Botschaft fremder Religionen: Buddhismus, Hinduismus, Islam.* Topos Taschenbücher, 1981.
13. Gerhard Endress. *Einführung in die islamische Geschichte.* Munich, 1982.
14. Werner Ende and Udo Steinbach, eds. *Der Islam in der Gegenwart.* Munich, 1984.

FOR PART I
1. *Rudi Paret. *Mohammed und der Koran,* 5th ed. Stuttgart, 1980.
2. Rudi Paret. *Der Koran. Übersetzung.* Stuttgart, 1966.
3. Rudi Paret. *Der Koran. Kommentar und Konkordanz.* Stuttgart, 1971.
4. *Arthur J. Arberry. *The Koran Interpreted.* Oxford, 1982.
5. Fazlur Rahman. *Major Themes of the Qur'an.* Chicago, 1980.
6. Annemarie Schimmel. *Und Muhammed ist sein Prophet.* Düsseldorf/Cologne, 1981.

FOR PART II
1. Tilman Nagel. *Staat und Glaubensgemeinschaft im Islam. Geschichte der politischen Ordnungsvorstellungen der Muslime.* 2 vols. Zurich/Munich, 1981.
2. W. Montgomery Watt and Alford T. Welch. *Der Islam,* I. Stuttgart, 1980.

3. Constance E. Padwick. *Muslim Devotions. A Study of Prayer-Manuals in Common Use.* London, 1961.

FOR PART III

1. Louis Gardet and Georges Anawati. *Introduction à la théologie musulmane.* Paris, 1948.
2. Louis Gardet. *Dieu et la destinée de l'homme.* Paris, 1967.
3. W. Montgomery Watt. *The Formative Period of Islamic Thought.* Edinburgh, 1973.
4. Annemarie Schimmel. *Mystical Dimensions of Islam.* Chapel Hill, 1975.
5. Wiebke Walter. *Die Frau im Islam.* Stuttgart, 1980.

FOR PART IV

1. Josef Henninger. *Spuren christlicher Glaubenswahrheiten im Koran.* Schönebeck/Beckenried, 1951.
2. Geoffrey Parrinder. *Jesus in the Qur'ān.* London, 1965.
3. Heikki Räisänen. "The Portrait of Jesus in the Qur'an: Reflections of a Biblical Scholar," *The Muslim World* (Hartford Seminary Foundation), 70, 1980, 122–33.
4. *Heikki Räisänen. *Das koranische Jesusbild. Ein Beitrag zur Theologie des Islam.* Helsinki, 1971.
5. Thomas O'Shaughnessy. *The Development of the Meaning of the Spirit in the Qur'ān.* Rome, 1953.
6. *Rudi Paret. "Toleranz und Intoleranz im Islam," *Saeculum* 21, 1970, 344–65.
7. Adel-Theodor Khoury. *Toleranz im Islam.* Munich, 1980.
8. *Bernard Lewis. "L'Islam et les non-musulmans," *Annales* 1980, 784–800.
9. Norman Stillman. *The Jews of Arab Lands.* Philadelphia, 1979.
10. Alain Ducellier. *Le miroir de l'Islam. Musulmans et chrétiens d'Orient au Moyen Âge.* Paris, 1971.

B.
Hinduism and Christianity

Chronology

7th to 4th millenniums B.C. Forerunners of Indus Valley Culture

3rd to 2nd millenniums Height of Indus Valley Culture

ca. 1750 Downfall of Indus Valley Culture

ca. 1700–1200 Immigration of the Aryans into the Punjab, composition of Books 2–9 of the Rig-Veda

ca. 1000 Canon of the Rig-Veda complete; the Sāma-Veda and Yajur-Veda follow soon afterward; the Atharva-Veda remains open to further additions

ca. 1000–850 Aryans penetrate into the upper Ganges Valley; heyday of religious scholarship dealing with sacrifices (older Brāhmana texts)

ca. 850–500 Aryans in the lower Ganges Valley as well; early philosophy (older Upanishads); Brahman and Ātman; doctrine of reincarnation, theory of karma; redemption through knowledge

ca. 600–300 Period of radical change; attempts at reform; founding of the monastic orders (Buddhism, Jainism); middle Upanishads; beginning of the *bhakti* movement and increasing importance of popular religion

266–233 Emperor Ashoka Maurya promotes Buddhism

3rd century B.C. to 3rd century A.D. Vishnuism, Shivaism, and other Hindu religions come to the fore; composition of the great Hindu epics, the *Mahābhārata* and the *Rāmāyana;* formation of the six philosophical systems (first Sāmkhya, Yoga, Pūrva Mīmāmsā, and Vaisheshika, then Nyāya, and finally Vedānta; Brahmasutras not composed until the 4th century [?]); Lakulin (ca. 2nd century), founder of Pāshupata-Shivaism; Buddhism and Shivaism move toward Central Asia; Shivaism and Vishnuism advance into Indochina and Indonesia; in northwestern India foreign domination by the Indo-Greeks, Parthians, Shakas, and Kushānas

320–500 Gupta dynasty in northern India; golden age of the Hindu religions

ca. 600–900 Advance of Shāktism and Tantrism; heyday of Pāñcarātra-Vishnuism; Kashmirian Shivaism flourishes from the 9th century onward; decline of Buddhism in India (ultimately driven out by Islam in the early-13th century)

Between 650 and 820 Shankara, leading exponent of Advaita (traditional dates, 788–820)

712 Arabs in Sind

1000–1027 Islamic raids on India

ca. 1056–1137 Rāmānuja, advocate of qualified monism (traditional dates, 1017–1137)

1206 Founding of the sultanate of Delhi

ca. 1199–1278 Madhva, chief spokesman for the dualistic Vedānta

12th to 13th centuries Formation of the Shaiva-Siddhānta by Shrīkantha and Meykanda

1498 Vasco da Gama in India

15th to 17th centuries Intensification of the Vishnu-bhakti to Rādhā-Krishna (Vallabha, 1479–1531; Caitanya, 1486–1533) and to Rāma (Rāmānanda, ca. 1400–70, traditional dates ca. 1299–1410; Tulsīdāsa, 1532–1623); efforts at mediation between Islam and Vishnu-bhakti: Kabīr (1440–1518); Guru Nānak (1469–1539), founder of the Sikh movement; Dādū (1544–1603)

1526 Founding of the Mughal Empire

1556–1606 Emperor Akbar, attempt at religious compromise in the year 1582

1600 Founding of the East India Company

1858 India becomes part of the British Empire

19th and 20th centuries Neo-Hindu reform movements: Brahmo Samāj (1828), Rāmakrishna (1836–86) and the Rāmakrishna Mission (1897), Prārthana Samāj (1867), Ārya Samāj (1875), Theosophical Society (1875), Mahātmā Gāndhi (1869–1948), Srī Aurobindo (1872–1950); Srī Ramana Maharishi (1879–1950)

1947 Division of the subcontinent, independence for India and Pakistan— India becoming a secular state, Pakistan an Islamic republic

Post 1947 Appearance of a series of gurus, some of whom also enjoy great success in the West: Krishnamūrti, Cinmayānanda, Maharishi Mahesh Yogī (Transcendental Meditation), Satya Sai Baba, Bhaktivedānta Swāmī Prabhupāda (Krishna Consciousness), Bālyogeshvar (Divine Light Mission), Bhagavān Rajneesh, et al.

I.
What Is Hinduism?
On the History
of a Religious Tradition

1. *Heinrich von Stietencron:* Hindu Perspectives

With Islam, which has been our subject thus far, everything seemed quite simple. The history of Islam is clear, its teachings are readily graspable; and despite all the differences, it is at bottom rather familiar to us, because it has such close ties to Christianity. We can't miss the fact that the two religions have common structures and a common legacy.

With Hinduism, I am afraid, things get more complex and involved. Not only does it have no church, but it also lacks any universally binding doctrines. It offers instead many possible varieties of religious thought, belief, and action; and as we shall see, it largely defies our concept of religion.

By contrast with Islam, Hinduism has not (until recently) been in serious competition with Christianity, and so has not been burdened with a hostile image. It may even be that in its encounter with Western cultures Hinduism has profited from a certain exotic enchantment and the transfiguring glow of distance. But in this distance it has also remained vague and nebulous. Europe had no need to fear Hinduism, as it did Islam, and so it paid less attention to it. There were more points of contact with it in philological research, in literature and philosophy, than in the realm of everyday life. For a long time there was no significant influx of Indians into Europe. This changed with the mass expulsion of Indians from Uganda by Idi Amin, which forced Britain to accept large numbers of refugees who had British citizenship. Elsewhere in

Europe there was little direct contact with Hinduism; and it was completely ignored by popular writers. Thus Westerners respected it but knew next to nothing about it.

It is only within the past few years that the situation has changed. Young people from Europe and America have discovered the religions of India. They seek in the East what they miss in the West: religion that speaks to both the intellect and the senses, religion full of warmth, diversity, and imagination. They sense a different attitude toward the creatures and objects in the environment, as well as a different view of human beings and their needs. Some are seriously turning to yoga and meditation; but they are not, like Westerners of a previous generation, treating them as a fashionable appendage to health-food-store culture, which took up yoga merely as fitness training or a technique to fight stress. Rather, they are trying, with the help of yoga and meditation, to open up a path for a new experience of self, for another way of being human.

They have probably also sensed something of the magic of endless chanting and the special power that grows out of inner serenity. In short, it could be that lately Hinduism in the West is appealing not just to the intellectualism of Western scholars or the utilitarianism of the apostles of health, but to many others by sending down roots in the domain of the emotions.

The churches seem not altogether pleased by all this. With skepticism and sometimes justified concern, they observe the impact of gurus on the West. Their distress is all the greater because they lack criteria for distinguishing a charlatan from a saint—never a simple task, since the guru passes on his knowledge without having any supervisory authority behind him. As I said, Hinduism has neither churches nor binding dogmas. There is only the background of religious tradition, which provides (or at least is supposed to provide) the guru with guidelines. This is a powerful feature of religious life in India, though with us it doesn't come clearly into play. It is time to begin a dialogue, before a new polemical image is fashioned. We shall need understanding, and we shall have to discard a few errors: for example, the idea that Hinduism is a polytheistic religion and, above all, the idea that Hinduism is one and only one religion.

"Hinduism": A European Term

European scholars have been studying Hinduism for almost two hundred years, but defining just what Hinduism is still presents the greatest difficulties.

This is primarily because of its multiform nature and inner contradictoriness. Even within Hinduism, one person's sacred scripture is by no means necessarily someone else's. This individual may assign a minor role to a god whom another individual worships with deep devotion as the supreme divinity and Lord of the world. One man teaches that living creatures should never be harmed, while another man's altar drips with the blood of sacrificed goats and buffalos. One believer's Tantric practices are an abomination to others. Even the doctrine of reincarnation, which we think of as being so closely linked with Hinduism, is *not* a universally accepted part of Hindu teaching and faith.

Hence we are facing a hard job in our effort to integrate the varied phenomena of Hindu religion into a clearly perceivable pattern. And no wonder: after all, we are dealing with expressions of religion that cover an immense spectrum, from the use of magical powers in fertility rites and sacrificial cults, across every nuance of polytheistic, dualistic, and monotheistic modes of faith, all the way to the concept of a nonanthropomorphic, impersonal Absolute which transcends the human imagination.

Perhaps no one would have tried so hard to bring all these things under a single heading if confusion had not already crept in during the very formation of the term "Hinduism." No Indian religion ever called itself "Hinduism," a word invented by Europeans. It was supposed to designate the religion of the Hindus, but unfortunately not enough was known about the Hindus when the term was coined. Westerners had not yet realized that Hindus had a number of different religions. Since then it has become customary to speak and write about Hinduism as one of the great world religions. And for some time people believed that there really was such a thing. Nowadays they know, without admitting the fact, that Hinduism is nothing but an orchid cultivated by European scholarship. It is much too beautiful to uproot, but it's a test-tube plant and not found in nature.

No doubt, this is a rather shocking assertion. What's the point of the many books about Hinduism? Why does the term appear in all works about the religions of the world? And don't all the religious statistics offer impressive proof that Hinduism is one of the greatest, numerically speaking, religions in the world, the third-largest, after Christianity and Islam? But such statistics disguise more than they reveal. As government officials see it, every Indian is automatically a Hindu unless he or she specifically claims adherence to another religion. Recent Indian jurisprudence goes even further than this, in some ways, by expressly subsuming Buddhists, Jains, and Sikhs as well under the umbrella term "Hindu." Thus the Orissa Religious Endowments Act, 1969 (Orissa Act 2 of 1970), among the preliminary observations on page 1, declares: "The expression 'Hindu religion' shall include Jain, Buddhist, and Sikh religions and the expressions 'Hindu' and 'Hindu public religiou institutions and endowments' shall be construed accordingly." *(Cuttack Law Times,* 1970, p. 1)

To deal properly with the terms "Hindu" and "Hinduism" we must first know what they really mean—and for that purpose it is useful to recall how these terms arose.

Ultimately it all goes back to the names of the great Indus River (which flows from Tibet through Pakistan into the Arabian Sea). From its old Sanskrit name *Sindhu* comes the name of the Pakistani province of Sind. We owe our words "India" and "Indians" to the Greek name of this river, *Indos.* The same river is called *Hindu* in Persian, and, as in Sanskrit, this word also indicated the land through which the river flows: in the first instance, the province, conquered by the Persians, on the river itself, and then the rest of the country beyond that, India. The plural of this geographical name stood for the people who lived there, the Hindus, the "people of the Indus" or the "people of India," the Indians.

As far back as the Old Persian cuneiform inscriptions and in the Avesta, the word "Hindu" appears as a geographic term; and once the Persian king Darius I, in the year 517 B.C., had extended his empire to the banks of the Indus, Hindus (inhabitants of the land of the Indus, i.e., the Indians) were incorporated into the multination Persian state and its army. From then on, for more than a thousand years, the Persians and other Persian-speaking peoples lumped all Indians together as "Hindus." The Arabs, too, later called India "Al Hind." The meaning shift in this word began relatively late, took place quite gradually, and was fully completed only by the Europeans. Ever since the year 712, when Arab Muslims began penetrating into the Indus Valley and settled there permanently, there was a large group of people in India who were reckoned by Arab and Persian authors as not belonging to the Hindus. And the Hindu converts to Islam, too, were now looked upon as Muslims, and no longer as Hindus. In addition, having known them from Central Asia, the Muslims were familiar with the Buddhists, whom they called "Shamaniyya" or "Sumaniyya," a word derived from the Sanskrit *shramana* or Middle Indic *samana,* both of which mean "monk." Thus they could distinguish in India between the Buddhists and the Brahmans (Arabic *barāhima).*

When Persian-speaking Muslims from Afghanistan and Central Asia invaded India, first around the year 1000, as plunderers but later, after 1200, also as empire builders, they did subjugate large parts of India, but they managed to convert only a fraction of the people to the religion of the prophet Muhammad. The Muslims then used the word "Hindu" to characterize the Indians who would not convert to Islam and who were also not Buddhists, in other words the majority of India's "infidels." And so in this Islamic context the word "Hindu" contained a distinct religious element, not as the label for a religion, but as a mark of separation from Islam and Buddhism. Muslim travelers and scholars, such as abū-al-Qāsim, al-Masʿūdī, al-Bīrūnī, al-Idrīsī, and especially Shahrastānī were very much aware of the manifold Indian religions and cults, as Bruce B. Lawrence has amply demonstrated in his work on "Shahrastānī on the Indian Religions" (1976). They also knew different names of these indigenous forms of faiths, although they also used "Hindu" as a generic term for all adherents of alien religions in India.

In the sixteenth century, merchants and missionaries from Europe came to know this expression for the majority of non-Muslims in India; and it was Europeans who for the first time separated the terms "Indian" and "Hindu," applying the first to the secular sphere, the second to religion, and ultimately deriving from it the word "Hinduism."

"Hinduism" a Collection of Religions

This created confusion. Even when Westerners subtracted from the non-Muslim Indians not just the Buddhists but other important religious groups such as the Sikhs, the Jains, the Parsees, Jews, native Christians, and the followers of tribal religions, they still tried to describe all the others (the great majority of the population) as Hindus and their religion as Hinduism. That led writers on the subject into difficulties. In surveys of Hinduism they were practically forced to elaborate points of agreement; differences were played down. Indian religions, as it happens, readily lend themselves to such synoptic presentation. In almost all cases they accept and recognize each other; and they postulate not that all religions are one, but that the ultimate goal of all religions is one and the same.

Furthermore, in the opinion of orthodox (i.e., based on Vedic tradition) Brahmanism, there is only one *dharma*, a single normative principle that determines religious, ethical, and practical human behavior.

Even if this principle prescribes partially different norms of behavior to the various strata of society (the warrior's code, for example, is not the same as the Brahman's), that does not impair the universal validity of *dharma*. Rather, *dharma* controls and structures behavior at every level of society and assigns to each creature its own *dharma (svadharma)*, its particular rules, tasks, and duties. *Dharma* is thus both a universal ethical norm—and as such only approaches realization in a society founded on Vedic tradition—but also a prescription for individuals and groups, regarding tasks, morality, and the rules for social behavior or religious practice. In the latter sense, it affects all forms of religion—from the various Hindu religions through the heretics (such as the Buddhists and Jains) to the heterodox barbarians (such as the European Christians or the Muslims, who none but extremely conservative Brahmans would say act altogether without *dharma*).

Each group has its own peculiar form of *dharma*, and if the group is powerful and literate enough, it can claim this form as the highest or best. That is what the different Hindu religions did when they classified the other Hindu religions on a scale of increasing distance from realizing pure *dharma*. That is what the Brahmans did when in their capacity as bearers and transmitters of sacred knowledge they claimed for themselves a place at the summit of the social hierarchy.

The Brahmans' claim to superiority as experts on *dharma* resembles, perhaps, the claim put forth by Christian clergymen as experts in the "true" religion. But *dharma*, although sometimes translated as "religion," embraces a considerably wider domain than our term "religion," since it also includes the general conditions of individual existence and all worldly action, and even operates in the plant and animal kingdom. As a result of the breadth of the concept of *dharma*, the Hindu—in contrast to the often antagonistic relationship between Christians and pagans—can view the many attempts at, and forms of, realizing *dharma* as meaningful, because they correspond to the hierarchical structure of spirituality and to the multiplicity of the possible earthly forms of existence.

Hence there is a great difference between the Hindu understanding of religion, which is guided by the concept of *dharma*, and the Christian or Islamic notion. What a Christian or Muslim should believe and how he or she should act are defined in a more standardized manner and with far more precision than what a Hindu, who can belong to quite different religious systems, is supposed to believe and do. But anyone who wishes to engage in a meaningful religious dialogue must know more exactly whom he is dealing with. The issue here is not simply one of religion in general, but of the specific contents of faith. Therefore we must know what our dialogue partner believes and what his ideals of religious behavior concretely demand of him.

For this reason we must, as a precondition for dialogue, revise our idea of Hinduism. We may have gotten used to looking upon Hinduism as a single religion, but that was never quite correct. In the sense that Westerners understand religion, the Hindus have not one, but various religions. They themselves do not claim to have just one religion; this, as I have said, was a European invention.

Words are seductive, they shape our thinking; and it is not easy to break away from them. When a term like "Hinduism" has become a fixture not only in the education of German or English speakers, but of the entire world, then it is especially hard. Any attempt to get rid of it would probably be fruitless. It is more important to give the word a new and more accurate content, that is, by understanding it not as a religion but as a collection of religions. Though actually different, they are nonetheless bound together by geography and history, as well as by the socioeconomic conditions and cultural frames of reference that developed in their common space. These are religions containing elements of shared traditions, and religions that have continually influenced each other down through the ages, and that have jointly contributed to forming the culture of India.

The boundary between tribal religion and "Hinduism" is blurry and, once again, the result of habitually jumping to conclusions. Some authors speak about a "Hinduization process," thanks to which whole tribes or parts of tribes have gradually been integrated into Hinduism. What they really mean is a form of social mobility that includes adopting a number of brahmanical rites, laws of religious purity, and pieces of transregional mythic traditions. The further question of whether the Untouchables actually belong to the Hindus or not, has recently, with the conversion of some Harijan groups to Islam, been the subject of spirited discussion and has been widely answered in the affirmative.

Nowadays Vishnuism (worship of the god Vishnu) and Shivaism (worship of the god Shiva) are by far the most important Hindu religions. The next-largest is Shaktism (or the cults devoted to a female divinity). Many smaller cults are loosely associated with these great religions.

Of course, practically all the books on Hinduism say that the cults of Vishnu, Shiva, and the other gods and goddesses are Hindu sects. But we cannot apply the term "sect" to religious bodies that, despite their adherence to a common cultural tradition, have obviously different founders, holy scriptures, seers, theologians, and liturgies, and that, above all, do not worship the same highest god. To do so would be comparable to labeling Judaism, Christianity, Manichaeism, and Islam different sects of the same religion. They are, in fact, rooted in the same religious tradition and have important elements in common, despite their different founders, scriptures, and names for the highest divinity. This would set up a parallel with "Hinduism," but the members of such a Procrustean unit would presumably give a cry of outrage.

TOLERANCE, TRUTH, AND TRADITION

Modern Indians characteristically do *not* utter indignant cries when we lump their religions together as "Hinduism." There were times when they might have, but not today. There are differences, to be sure; but, as Indians see it, stressing what separates them, insisting on the rightness of my religion and the wrongness of yours, is rather petty. This sort of attitude overlooks the fact that there has to be a variety of religions to offer approaches to the divine to a variety of people with differing needs and at differing stages of development, to enable everyone to pursue his own access to the divinity. Besides, all this variety stops at the surface. Beneath it, Hindus think, lies a broad intentional unity, insofar as all religions are trying to open up a path for human beings to God (or to the ultimate reality, to the Absolute) and to salvation, however defined. This holds true not merely for Hindu religions but, in the eyes of the Hindus, for all the religions of humanity.

Compared with the other revealed religions, this is an extraordinarily liberal position. It makes possible the productive coexistence, the reciprocal respect, recognition, and equal social status of the great Hindu religions, which suggested to Western observers that they were looking at a single religion. Christians, by contrast, like Muslims and Jews, live in a tradition of religious confrontation, or at least of religious differentiation, where in the most favorable situation alien religion is tolerated, although one never gives up one's claim to absolute religious truth.

Anyone acquainted with Islam who refuses to accept it is considered obdurate and deserves to go to hell. And when someone who knows the gospel does not become a Christian, while mitigating circumstances may be invoked, some believers still mourn him or her as a lost soul.

Such contemporary views still are far removed from the liberal outlook that Vishnuism developed already about two thousand years ago. For according to the teaching of the Vishnuites, if a person turns to another god, through his own fault or otherwise, the grace of the highest God will not be taken from him.

Thus, for example, in the *Bhagavad-Gita*, one of the Vishnuites' fundamental texts, Krishna says that he himself is the one who fulfills the requests that a person makes out of deep faith in another god. (VII, 22) And in another passage he gives a theological justification for his generosity to the worshippers of other gods:

> "Those devotees of other gods
> Who worship them, endowed with faithe,
> They even worship me alone,
> If not quite in the proper way." (IX, 23)

The highest God does not see the other gods as His rivals. They all exist only through Him, have the fullness of their power from Him, are manifestations of parts of His reality. Why should He be jealous of them?

This doesn't mean that it's all the same what god one worships. Here is where the particular Hindu religions show how different they can be. Their unity consists in a common goal, but the ways to it are not the same, and not all have the same value. Some lead to the goal more quickly than others, some prove to be detours that one takes out of ignorance or is forced to take by one's karma. Krishna addresses this matter when he says, just after the first passage mentioned above, that in worshipping other gods the faithful believer will gain only temporary results. And he continues:

> "Celestials reach who worship them,
> My devotees proceed to Me!" (VII, 23)

Going to the celestials means a great deal. It is the fulfillment of one of the highest wishes man can have. He himself becomes a celestial being, enjoying divine joys and divine power in heaven for thousands of years. The only drawback is that one remains bound up in the cycle of becoming and decaying. One might sink back into lower forms of existence, and the struggle for salvation will have to go on. It will not end until one reaches the highest divinity. To get there, Vishnuite theology points out a shorter, more reliable way, the promise made by the highest God Vishnu, incarnate as Krishna: "My devotees proceed to Me!"

Similar positions may be found in the sacred scriptures of the Shivaites or the worshippers of the Great Goddess, with the roles reversed in each case, so that one's own religion integrates and at the same time surpasses other people's religion.

There is no need to disguise the fact that India, too, has occasionally known interreligious conflict, for example when triumphant Muslim zealots destroyed the images of Hindu gods and desecrated their temples. In contemporary religious documents the Hindus sometimes describe the Muslims as demons, and to this day Hindus and Muslims continue to be at odds. From time to time there were also conflicts with the Buddhists, who played a key role in India for several centuries before they were partly absorbed and partly driven out by an increasingly powerful wave of emotional piety. And finally, there were also occasionally violent quarrels between different groups of Hindus, especially in southern India. But these episodes are the exception, because the protection of all religious communities has been one of the traditional duties of Indian princes since at least the middle of the first millennium B.C. Since then the rule has been not conflict but competition, and Hindu theologians have been more inclined toward integration than confrontation. Naturally this attitude cannot neutralize all social tensions, but when conflicts flare up it is rarely owing to religious affiliations only, but rather due to economic or political interests and sometimes also owing to friction and rivalry within the caste system, which cuts across most Hindu religions.

Nowadays many educated Hindus carry their individual tolerance still further by dropping any insistence that their religion is superior to the others. "This is the right way for me," they will say; "yours is the right one for you. We shall meet at the goal, in final salvation."

But it would doubtless be a mistake to think that such tolerance arises from a lack of self-confidence and so from a weakness of faith. On the contrary, Hindus are at ease with their religious convictions and their habits (which are structured and stamped by countless ritual elements) in a way that many a Christian pastor would envy.

This is not the case, to be sure, with some members of the small political ruling class, people trained in Oxford, Cambridge, Yale, and Moscow. But it does hold true for the overwhelming majority of Indians. And this majority gives the lie to most of our clichés about Hindus. They are not, in the main, unworldly, passive, emaciated, and miserable. Nor are they all gurus, yogis, and ash-smeared ascetics. They are men and women like us, human beings with troubles big and little. But unlike too many of us, they are not driven by the inexorable hands of an internalized clock measuring time's forward rush. They are not pressured by the anxious thought that at any moment they may be missing something. They don't feel thrust into a brief, now-or-never life, which all too quickly passes away, in which one must prove oneself, and which may decide one's eternal salvation or damnation. The possibility of rebirth gives a wider horizon to life and a different sense of time.

A characteristic feature of the great Hindu religions is that they never start out by assuming an irreconcilable opposition between two postulated truths. Any claim to absoluteness is alien to them. They see it as narrowing the range of potential human consciousness. Wherever they find unavoidable contradictions, they view them as lodged within the framework of complementary oppositions, and they try to integrate them into some comprehensive connection.

In practice, this attitude has led the Hindus to develop an unusual capacity for assimilating foreign influences and other religions, while maintaining their own traditions.

This preserving of tradition has in itself a religious quality. One does not throw old truths overboard for the sake of new discoveries; one adds on the new to the old, because truth is eternal and unchangeable. By contrast, the world is in a state of constant change, and our understanding is limited. Hence, when in the course of time any group of Hindus can no longer quite comprehend or accept the teachings of olden days, such sacred lore is brought up to date by means of commentaries and glosses, shifts of accent and supplements, but not by abandoning tradition. In this regard the Hindu attitude has similarities with Islam. Both start from the supposition that at the very beginning—or at the instant of revelation—the sacred knowledge imparted by the gods was pure and unadulterated. That is why one focuses on the origins. The watchword is not progress but preventing decline, and it is precisely in order to prevent decline that one has to adapt to changing conditions and needs or even to make innovations.

In this way Hindu religions have preserved and kept alive substantial portions of the legacy of various and sometimes very old traditions. A glance at the past, which follows, should make this clear.

INDUS VALLEY CULTURE AND THE ARYAN IMMIGRATION

Up until the 1920s it was believed that Vedic Aryans had given rise to the first great culture on Indian soil. Then a report by John Marshall in the *Illustrated London News* of September 20, 1924, alerted Western experts to the existence and importance of an older culture in the Indus Valley. Actually, as early as 1856 the British had stumbled upon an abandoned city belonging to that culture, at Harappa, while they were building the railroad line from Karachi to Lahore. But the significance of the find was not appreciated at the time. In fact, the engineers, John and William Brunton, used both the ruins at Harappa and those of the medieval city of Brahminabad, to the south, as a quarry for the roadbed. The extent of the damage done to archaeological studies in the Harappa region can best be illustrated by Stuart Piggott's bitter remark that even today the trains rumble over a hundred miles of line laid on a secure foundation of third-millennium brickbats. *(Prehistoric India,* Harmondsworth, 1950, p. 14) Numerous other settlements and cities of this culture were discovered later; these fortunately escaped the fate of Harappa.

Indus Valley culture was a very highly developed, centrally organized urban culture. It was first believed to be a direct descendant of Mesopotamian culture (there was proof of commercial ties with Mesopotamia). Today, however, we know that in the Indus Valley and particularly in Baluchistan, which borders it on the west, there was from the seventh millennium B.C. onward a continual autonomous development, which ultimately led to the formation of the culture of the Indus Valley. At its point of greatest expansion it covered a territory nearly five and a half times larger than West Germany. It had a uniform policy of colonization, standardized weights and measures, a centralized food supply, even a largely uniform kind of pottery. The capital of this vast kingdom seems to have been Mohenjo-Daro, on the Lower Indus.

Sadly, its writing, contained on more than two thousand five hundred steatite seals, has yet to be reliably deciphered, although intensive efforts to do so are being made, both inside and outside of India. Thus we lack an important key to the religion of the people. There are wonderful depictions of animals on the seals, but they don't carry our speculations about religion very far. As to the question whether the Hindu religions have inherited anything from the Indus Valley culture, they do at least provide some crucial clues. The typical sitting position of the Indian yogi, which was unknown to other cultures of this time, can be seen represented here. There are also portrayals of episodes found in later

Indian literature. Finally, some scholars believe they can make out on one of the seals a prototype of the Hindu god Shiva. I am not fully convinced that this assumption is correct. But even without this detail, and even though we don't have the historical connecting links, it seems clear today that one of the strands of tradition preserved in Hinduism runs all the way back to the culture of the Indus Valley.

This culture perished probably in the eighteenth century B.C. While it used to be assumed that the Aryan invasion had brought about its collapse, scholars now think that its downfall was due not to war but to climatic changes, and that this had occurred before the arrival of the Aryans.

The Aryans penetrated through what is now Afghanistan into north-western India. We don't know exactly when the immigration took place, but a growing number of archaeological finds, as well as the Vedic texts, offer us some leads. The Aryans probably invaded northwestern India in several migratory waves between 1700 and 1200 B.C., until, gradually advancing toward the east, they arrived in the upper Ganges Basin around 1000 B.C.

There is no doubt that the mainstream of tradition feeding all the great Hindu religions has its source in the Aryans. From them, to begin with, comes Sanskrit, the sacred language of India. It is an Indo-European language, related to ours, a language that, compared with others, has changed little over the past three thousand years, because it was the language of holy tradition and believed to be the language of the gods. Muslims believe that God speaks Arabic, but he has been doing so only since about A.D. 600. In India the gods have been speaking Sanskrit for more than three thousand years.

THE VEDAS: THE OLDEST INDIAN SCRIPTURES

From the Aryans come the oldest sacred texts of the Hindus, the Vedas. The names of the poets and visionaries who supposedly "saw" the individual Vedic hymns have been handed down to us; but at the same time the notion was also kept that the Vedas were eternal revelations, with no beginning, not even fashioned by the gods, and only passed along by the seers. In accordance with the medium used in their transmission, these authoritative texts are called *shruti* by the Indians, or "hearing," i.e., the formulation of eternal truths passed on through the ear.

All the great Hindu religions, including those that came into existence later, are revealed religions and are connected more or less clearly to a Vedic tradition. The content of the revealed texts considered valid today may have little to do with the content of the Vedas, but that is quite immaterial. The gods keep on talking to human beings. When times change, they reveal new ways to salvation to their believers. This becomes necessary whenever the decline of a tradition has distorted the old revelations. It was just the same in Islam, except that in Islam the prophets don't say anything new, they only repeat the same original message. Vishnuites and Shivaites are more willing to acknowledge historical change, but they, too, have no hesitation in speaking about the "eternal truth" that lies beneath the changes in the external form of its transmission. But, as in Islam, they are concerned strictly with the message of the divinity, not with the person who hears it or recognizes it and passes it on to posterity. The founder of the religion is almost always a god (perhaps in a human incarnation, as, for example, Lakulin and Basava with the Shivaites, Shankara with the Smārtas, and Rāmānuja, Madhva, Vallabha and Caitanya with the Vishnuites). The process of transmitting a new teaching to the first disciple and from him in succession to generations of further disciples was also preserved in myth and in the carefully handed-down lists of teachers, but the sacred knowledge itself is eternal. It would be foolish to pin it down to a specific date.

Another characteristic feature of the Hindu religions that comes from the Vedic tradition is the belief in the immediate effectiveness of the holy word. It is good to understand it, but its power works even if one doesn't. According to Hindu belief, mantras, sayings helpful for thought and meditation that are sometimes only syllables with no immediately recognizable meaning, possess a peculiar creative power on account of their superhuman origin and their inherent potential for promoting spiritual development.

That is the reason why, for instance, the more than ten thousand verses of the Rig-Veda, the oldest of the four Vedas, were preserved even when people no longer really knew what to make of their contents. With unbelievable precision they were passed on, syllable by syllable, including acoustic values, accents, and intonations—passed on orally, from teacher to disciple, from mouth to ear, to this day. Long after writing was invented, Hindus were reluctant to entrust their sacred knowledge to it. Contact with the holy word is like contact with the gods: a blessing, but also dangerous. Not just anyone may have access to it; the disciple is closely scrutinized before being entrusted with the highest knowledge.

The Vedic texts are remarkable in many ways. It is amazing that around 1000 B.C. at the latest, the Rig-Veda's collection of hymns to various gods was closed, thereby creating a canonical text that from then on was transmitted largely without alteration. It appears that even back then the ancient Hindus wanted to safeguard religious knowledge which threatened to disappear. Thereafter, additional materials continued to be collected. They were handed down in independent supplements but were no longer integrated into the body of the sacred text.

But the hymns to the gods and the songs from the Rig-Veda were not the only texts preserved. There were three further collections, one in which these hymns and their intonations were put to ritual use (Sāma-Veda), another recording all the sayings to be used while performing sacrifices (Yajur-Veda), and a third, grouping together apotropaic and other magical formulas aimed at averting evil influences and strengthening positive forces (Atharva-Veda). In these four great collections, each of which was closely connected with a particular priestly function, religious knowledge of an early period was codified once and for all. The word Veda, indeed, means knowledge.

Today the Veda is still held in the highest regard, but only a very small body of Vedic scholars really know the texts. The Vedas have little to do with the religion of the people; indeed some Hindu religions have arisen in outspoken opposition to the orthodox Vedic priestly tradition, and the most important gods of the Vedic period have lost their importance and now play only a quite subordinate role.

SPIRITUAL AWAKENING AND SOCIAL RESTRICTIONS: PHILOSOPHY AND THE CASTE SYSTEM

The basis for this development, which led to the decline of the ancient Vedic gods, was laid as early as the beginning of the first millennium B.C. Around that time, the Vedic priests launched an impressive attempt, with the help of esoteric sacrificial rites, to harmonize man with his environment, the microcosm with the macrocosm. In the process they developed a new kind of thought, using symbols and abstractions. The importance of the gods in offering sacrifices sharply diminished, and the prerequisites became available for an early form of philosophy. Starting in the ninth or the opening years of the eighth century this fresh approach was articulated in the Brāhmana texts and the Upanishads. It was tentative at first, but it eventually influenced almost all later religious thinking in India, including Buddhism and Jainism.

The quest for unity behind the outward multiplicity of worldly phenomena, the transformation of polytheism by monistic thought, the abstract conception of an absolute consciousness, the doctrine of reincarnation and of salvation through knowledge—all this was developed *in germine* between the tenth and sixth centuries B.C. in the latest Vedic hymns, in the Brāhmanas, and above all in the Upanishads.

But, at the same time, the caste system began to take shape, and this, too, is a legacy of the Aryans to present-day India. We have the Portuguese to thank for the word "caste." They were the first Europeans to settle permanently in India after Vasco da Gama discovered the sea route to India in 1498. "Caste" is not an Indian word; it comes from the Latin *castus* ("pure," "chaste") and designates social groups separated from each other by strict rules of purity. "Purity" refers to everything that one comes into intimate contact with, especially food and one's spouse.

Today in India there are an immense number of castes (Sanskrit *jāti* = birth), which theoretically break down into four social strata (Sanskrit *varna* = color); and these strata or classes provide a rough hierarchical structure for the caste system. Three of the classes used to correspond to the most important functions within Aryan society, namely 1) the priests (*brāhmana*), 2) the nobles and warriors (*kshatriya*), and 3) the people who look after house, livestock, and fields (*vaishya*). After the Aryan immigration into India, the fourth class was made up of their non-Aryan subjects (*shūdra*). Nowadays this is still the largest stratum, containing most of the service-rendering castes.

One has to imagine the situation of the Aryan tribes in order to grasp what purity meant for them. The more deeply some of them penetrated the Ganges plain and went east and south, the more distinctly they found themselves in the minority vis-à-vis the original population. If they wished to hold on to their special position, they had to maintain their racial and cultural identity. They had to avoid blending into subject peoples. This was possible only through isolation—an interesting example of apartheid in antiquity. (It led, by the way, to continually increasing tensions, even back then.) To the Aryans, "purity" applied to race and, even more strictly, to religion. For this reason, non-Aryans were excluded from both active and passive participation in the Vedic religion. Simultaneously, their special religious position consolidated the Aryan upper classes.

REFORMATION AND INTEGRATION: SELF-LIBERATION THROUGH KNOWLEDGE

By the middle of the first millennium B.C., maintaining religious purity had proved to be, in the long run, impossible. Outer pressure and inner evolution led to an opening for the religious needs and traditions of the non-Aryan low-class population. The importance of once powerful gods had faded. Instead, questions about man's soul and consciousness, and about definitive salvation from the cycle of existence, had caught the attention of philosophers and the cultured upper classes.

At the same time, the development of scientific thinking in the late Vedic period had introduced the first experiments and a new skepticism. Thinkers appeared who advocated pure materialism, wholly denying the existence of the soul and a divine world beyond this one.

Finally, the development of the science of sacrifice into a highly specialized esoteric doctrine had the usual effect of such restrictive elitism. It made it very hard for outsiders to see what was going on inside; and while it gave the Brahmans some advantages, it simultaneously stirred up vehement opposition. And so we see a period of reformation set in between the sixth and the fourth centuries B.C.

As so often during phases of religious awakening, a number of religious reformers were at work, and they gathered disciples around them. Among these were two men who founded long-lasting monastic traditions, which later gave rise to independent religions. One was Mahāvīra, the Jina (conqueror), whose followers called themselves Jains after him, and who spoke out for a strictly ascetic life. The other was Gautama, the Buddha (Awakened One), whose teaching became the foundation of Buddhism. Both came from the *kshatriya* class, and hence were nobles. Both objected to the religious monopoly of the Brahmans. They rejected the authority of the Vedas, took up the doctrine of rebirth and karma already developed in the Brāhmanas and Upanishads, and systematically expanded it. Several other teachers, whose followers did not eventually leave the mainstream of Hindu traditions, delivered a similar message. An ideal of nonviolence *(ahimsā)* came to the fore. And one of the most vital elements of the Upanishads, the doctrine of self-liberation through knowledge, became a central way of salvation.

Self-liberation through knowledge—a bold, self-confident undertaking. It presupposes that our normal, earthbound condition is based on ignorance, an essential theme of the Hindu religions as well as Buddhism and Jainism, all of which later developed and went their own, separate ways from that common ground. It is founded both on the immediate experience of meditative vision and practice and on the consistency of the theoretical findings that result from such experiences and that were initially presented in the Upanishads. Knowledge, which grows out of this combination of experience or vision and reflection, brings not only additional information but—and this is the main point— it effects a change in consciousness, opening up new dimensions of perception and understanding. In meditation the everyday experience of the split between subject and object can be overcome, man is seen to be capable of experiencing a state of unity that suppresses the distance separating him not just from worldly appearances but from divinity itself. Shortly before the middle of the first millennium B.C., the doctrine, derived from late Vedic tradition, of the essential unity of individual and absolute being was linked up with the personal experience of such unity, to be gained from the practice of meditation, thus becoming one of the essential elements of Indian religion.

Such extremists as, say, the older Buddhist community, consistently followed the path of self-redemption and rejected everything else as meaningless. But not everybody was so rigorous. I have already said that the ancient Indians—perhaps I should add, the Brahmans above all— didn't like to give up time-tested beliefs. They kept their confidence in the truth and effectiveness of sacred tradition, which taught that the Vedic Aryans had called upon their gods in time of need. With the gods' help they had looked forward to prosperity and happiness on earth, they had implored the gods to forgive their sins, and they knew that man is dependent on the aid of the gods.

INCORPORATION OF LOWER-CLASS RELIGIOUS FORMS

This knowledge survived, and in the reaction to two extreme, elitist schools of thought—on the one hand, the priestly experts on sacrifice, with their emphasis on ritual practices and speculation and, on the other, the monks and ascetics, with their renunciation of the world—strong gains were made by those who saw the heart of their religious efforts in human communication with God. At the same time, people were seeking forms of religion accessible to everyone and not just Brahmans, monks, and ascetics. Emotional commitment to one divinity became more prominent and led to the emergence of Hindu religions that were monotheistic (there is only one God, even though he may have various manifestations) or henotheistic (there are many gods, but *my* God is the highest and the only important one for me). For all that, the techniques of self-redemption were not abandoned, but used for spiritual purification. Believers focused their meditations on God, turning to Him in humility and acts of private and public worship. They visualized Him in their images, built Him temples, and made a place for Him in their hearts.

The religious movement I am speaking of was not originated by the Brahmans, but they were forced to respond to it. It criticized the exclusion of the lower classes from religion, and attacked the caste system. This created an explosive situation, which the Brahmans managed to defuse only with difficulty and in the face of opposition from their conservative colleagues. They allowed an amalgamation of thitherto strictly separated religions. They succeeded in fusing cult forms and divinities popular among the lower classes with Vedic divinities and cultic forms, thereby integrating large sections of the fourth social class into a common religious life. Wherever such fusion occurred, a connection was established between a wide spectrum of believers and the authority of Vedic tradition.

A number of religions got their start this way, and depending upon the specific thrust of their origin they developed along different lines. In most cases we don't know how old their non-Aryan components are; we can only surmise that these, too, have their roots far back in the past. We do know, however, that the changeover from the religion of an Aryan elite to a religion of the masses was not a simple one, and led to factionalism. It bypassed the chief gods of the Vedic pantheon. Vishnu and Shiva (or Rudra), the leading gods of the major Hindu religions today, did belong to Vedic tradition, but they didn't have a central position in it; and this is probably no accident, because human relations with these gods were less strictly defined by orthodox priestly practice, and therefore more open to new developments.

Vishnuism and Shivaism, then, were essentially created from the fusion of at least two and possibly three old strands of tradition. These were the religious traditions of Vedic culture, the pre-Aryan culture of the Ganges and Jumna basin, and—indirectly, I presume—the Indus Valley culture. These three traditions became linked together in the course of the first millennium B.C. and later underwent further evolution.

A fourth strand of tradition, which becomes noticeable in the first century A.D., did not become fully manifest until the sixth to seventh centuries. It was bound up with the social integration of parts of the Indian population that I have not yet mentioned. These were the native tribes that lived in the jungles of the river plains and mountainous regions apart from the societies previously described and entirely outside the caste system. The process of integrating these tribes went forward very slowly and has yet to be completed today. But in the sixth to seventh centuries it had gotten far enough to allow the integration of an important element from the religion of certain tribes. They were first incorporated into, and subdued by, the theology of Shivaism, but later gained prominence and led to the formation of Shāktism; that is, of the cults in which a goddess plays the central role.

THE SYNTHESIS WORKED OUT BY THE BRAHMANS; THE ORTHODOX SYSTEMS

In the gradual, more than thousand-year-long merging of these traditional currents, the Brahmans played a decisive role, selecting, systematizing, and establishing and maintaining norms. At the same time, they became the chief practitioners and exponents of the burgeoning sciences, in particular of grammar and philosophy, medicine, mathematics and astronomy, economics and political science and, most important for their influence in society, of secular and religious law. An abundance of sophisticated ideas about man and his environment, about time, space, and causality, about the possibilities and conditions of human knowledge, called for new efforts at a systematic interpretation of the world. Six "conceptions" (*darshana*), or philosophical-theological systems, came into being. Indian tradition organized them into three pairs: they are *Sāmkhya* and *Yoga*, *Nyāya* and *Vaisheshika*, *Pūrva Mīmāmsā* (older *Mīmāmsā*) and *Uttara Mīmāmsā* (later or higher *Mīmāmsā*), the last of which is also called Vedānta (end, i.e., crown, of the Veda). They evolved in continuous dialectic with each other and with Buddhism and Jainism.

All these systems are concerned with explaining the world and with the highest goal of humanity—salvation—and they all strive to reach this goal through cognition. The older *Mīmāmsā* seeks to establish correct understanding of the Vedas and their injunctions—scriptural interpretation, in other words—as the basis for right behavior, which alone leads to heaven *(svarga)*. For all other systems and for the later stages of the *Pūrva Mīmāmsā*, what counts is knowledge as a means of salvation from the cycle of rebirth, with the final state conceived either as a complete coming to rest of the individual soul *(Nyāya/Vaisheshika* and the later *Pūrva Mīmāmsā)* or an overcoming of the distance between individual and absolute consciousness *(Sāmkhya, Yoga,* and parts of the Vedānta).

Although their goals are similar, the theoretical approaches of the systems are different, and they all have different centers of gravity. *Sāmkhya* attempts to discern the causal principles underlying the structure of the world, to trace back the chain of evolution, and finally to achieve liberating knowledge through existential understanding of the difference between matter *(prakriti)* and spirit *(purusha). Vaisheshika,* by contrast, focuses its interest on the categories according to which we discriminate all things intelligible; it seeks to find out what are the physical components of matter and its inherent laws. In so doing it gave rise to an early form of the atomic theory.

Yoga and *Nyāya,* each of which is coordinated with one of the foregoing systems and is based on its theoretical framework, deal mostly with man and human knowledge. The aim of *Yoga* is to train the yogi in self-control and power of concentration, so as to conquer all the bodily impediments to the spirit and to raise the hidden capacities of human-divine consciousness to the heights of redemptive fulfillment. *Nyāya,* on the other hand, aims to grasp the laws of thought, to understand possibilities and pitfalls of deductive and inductive argumentation, to refine logic and the theory of categories, and to train the mind so that a person can avoid error and use reason to gain knowledge of the truth and of the (highest) self.

Pūrva Mīmāmsā and Vedānta do not, in the final analysis, rely upon systems devised by individuals, but go back to the sacred tradition of the Vedas *(shruti),* whose secret truth they try to fathom through reason and intuition. *Pūrva Mīmāmsā* seeks, on the one hand, a correct understanding of traditional religious rites and an explanation for the fact or postulate of their effectiveness. On the other hand, it also seeks a theoretical foundation and justification for the claim that the Veda is eternal, has no beginning, and is the highest authority. This presupposes the priority of concepts over appearances, of words over things, as well as a boundless continuity of Mind, even though the worlds come into existence and pass away in a continual cycle.

The *Vedānta*, by contrast, picks up the philosophical teachings of the Upanishads and carries them further. In it we find the Upanishadic question about the relation between the individual soul *(ātman)* and the Absolute *(Brahman)*, and their union, once again coming to the fore. At the same time, the Vedānta asks about the relationship of worldly appearance to pure being. For some schools of Vedānta this is where the doctrine of the illusionary and superficial character of the world *(māyā)* fits in. Finally, questions are raised about the relation between personal God and absolute Spirit—an issue that Indian theology has always been concerned with, from its beginnings in the Rig-Veda until modern times.

Along with *Yoga*, the subtle intellectual edifice of the Vedānta has acquired a special renown in the West. It belongs among the great achievements of the human mind. In particular, the monistic *(Advaita)* teaching of Shankara (whose traditional dates are 788–820, but who may have lived about a hundred years earlier according to recent Western scholarship) made an enormous stir among Indologists and philosophers. But other Vedānta schools too, such as the qualified monism *(Vishishtādvaita)* of the eminent south Indian Vishnuite Rāmānuja (?1017–1137?) or the dualistic *(dvaita)* teaching of another Vishnuite, Madhva (1199–1278) have been praised in the West. In India the various schools of the Vedānta have continued right up to the present, but the other philosophical-theological systems had no less an impact and in part still have considerable significance.

It is not possible to consider in any further detail here the ways in which these six systems influenced the different Hindu theologies. Suffice it to say for the present that *Yoga*, *Nyāya*, and *Vaisheshika* flourished most notably among the Shivaites, while *Sāmkhya* had stronger associations with Vishnuism and Shāktism. *Mīmāmsā* has retained and defended successfully a part of the Vedic tradition, and Vedānta was important to all major religions either as challenge or as a source of inspiration.

In all three religions, as well as in some other cults of the Hindus, there were from time to time vigorous social reform movements and a continual elaboration of theology and the doctrine of salvation, a subject I shall address later on.

THE ENCOUNTER WITH ISLAM AND CHRISTIANITY; NEO-HINDUISM

New impulses finally brought about an encounter with Islam (from A.D. 712 onward in the lower and middle Indus Valley, not until the beginning of the thirteenth century in the rest of India if we except the raids of the warlike Sultan Mahmūd of Ghāzna in the early-eleventh century) and with European Christianity.

Islamic mysticism was familiar with Indian thought and may even have been prompted by it. In the late Middle Ages, with religious reformers such as Kabīr (1440–1518), a disciple of the Vishnuite Rāmānanda, Guru Nānak (1469–1538), founder of the religious community of the Sikhs (meaning "Disciples"), and others, this led to an attempt at linking elements of Islam and of Indian religious tradition, particularly the Vishnuite *bhakti* piety, in a creative synthesis. Internal political tensions, however, and the predominantly hostile attitude of orthodox Muslims prevented these efforts from making any broad progress.

In Christianity, too, especially in the Sermon on the Mount, Indians rediscovered features of their own faith. The concept of God's incarnation on earth was familiar to them, and so they raised no objections to the claim of Jesus' divinity.

According to an account in the apocryphal Acts of Thomas, whose oldest version goes back to a manuscript, in Syriac, from the second or third century, the apostle Thomas is supposed to have come to India by ship as a slave. He was active in the kingdom of Gudnaphar (Gondophernes) in the Indus Valley, and later traveled to southern India, where he died as a martyr (A. F. J. Klijn, *The Acts of Thomas*, 1972). Another tradition, from Kashmir, reports that Jesus did not die on the cross, but was still alive when he was laid in the burial chamber. He escaped from it—as witnessed by the empty tomb—and traveled to the East, until he finally arrived in Kashmir, where his real grave is supposedly located.

None of these reports has thus far been verified, but the sources compiled by L. W. Brown (*The Indian Christians of St. Thomas*, 1956) and C. V. Cheriyan (*A History of Christianity in Kerala*, 1973) show that there was a Christian community in India from very early times. In the year A.D. 189, a certain Pantaenus journeyed to visit it on orders from Bishop Demetrius of Alexandria. There also seem to have been Nestorian Christians in Kerala from the fourth century at the latest. Their descendants called themselves the Thomas Christians. Scholars still argue whether this early contact with Christianity has left any trace in the Hindu scriptures.

With the establishment of European trading posts in India (Vasco da Gama landed in May 1498, Goa was captured in 1510) and colonial expansion after 1600 (founding of the East India Company), European Christians and Christian missionaries entered various regions of India. Christianity arrived on the scene with the privileges and pretensions of those in power. As was the case with Islam earlier, Christianity in India was associated for several centuries with foreign domination, social oppression, and economic exploitation. The Indian students who went to Oxford and Cambridge to acquire Western learning immediately noticed that the gap between Christian claims and Christian reality was as wide in Europe as in India. It was not love of neighbor that prevailed, but materialism and lust for power.

Nonetheless, European Christianity was capable of giving new impulses to Indian religion by condemning polytheism, by heightening awareness of social abuses, and challenging the caste system. Christian ideals such as love of one's neighbor and responsibility for one's fellow men and women were seized upon and linked to the teachings of the *Bhagavad-Gītā*. European scholarship, especially Indology and comparative linguistics, provided an impetus that led to a sharpening of Indian self-consciousness and to a reconsideration of the values that had largely been submerged during the centuries of Islamic and European domination. A series of reform movements grew up that have often been labeled Neo-Hinduism. They include, among others, the Brāhmo Samāj (founded in 1828 by Rājā Rāmmohan Roy), the *Ārya Samāj* (founded in 1875 by Swāmī Dayānanda Sarasvatī), the Rāmakrishna Mission (founded in 1897 in memory of Srī Rāmakrishna, 1836–86, by his disciples), and the school of Srī Aurobindo in Pondicherry. Some of these movements entered into temporary partnership with political Hinduism and the Indian independence movement; and men like Gandhi and his followers bore their imprint.

Finally, among the forces in Neo-Hinduism we should not forget the recent Indian movements that have been still more profoundly influenced by Western thinking and that have found broad fields of activity in some Western countries. However many points these movements may differ on, they share a universalist approach that sees the founders of foreign religions, such as Jesus and Muhammad, like Buddha and Rama, as incarnations of the *one* godhead. Many of them also share a social commitment that transcends the barriers of caste and is trying to train a new kind of human being. Finally, some of them share an effort to reach out beyond India in a mission to teach tolerance and peaceableness, which places at the heart of their work the exertions of the individual person on himself, the schooling of one's own capacities for meditation, and the expansion of consciousness. It should be noted here that, according to Indian tradition, a key criterion for the spiritual status of a guru who deserves to be taken seriously is—along with magnetic charisma—complete unselfishness and freedom from desires. Whenever the profit motive shows its head, or the guru aims for external possessions, he cannot claim the authority of Indian spiritual tradition. In these cases we see a lack of wisdom or the mark of Western influence, or both.

This has been only a brief historical survey of the most important traditional currents out of which the Indian religions have grown and through whose combined action they have changed over the course of history. A great deal of material, including some vital matters, had to be left out. But this much may serve as a provisional outline, which will be given more specific content when, in the following sections, I try to describe Hindu conceptions of the world and divinity, man and salvation, as well as the concrete practice of religion.

2. *Hans Küng:* A Christian Response

Heinrich von Stietencron's survey was not only brief, but also a very dense and complex one; it puts into historical perspective a goodly number of substantial theological problems: truth and tolerance, redemption, the meaning of scripture, the practice of mystical contemplation, the relation between God and the world . . . The presentation indirectly shows just how much, even in Hinduism, we have to deal with new developments, upheavals, re-formations, in short with "paradigm changes," where as a group of religions evolve we find both constants and variables coming to light. In my response I can neither follow the same method (by describing the genesis of the Christian religion) nor address at once all the specific problems. My first response must focus on a central issue and leave the treatment of the others to future chapters.

No one would deny the fascination of the infinite variety, complexity, color, and vitality of Indian religions, which appeal simultaneously to our intellect, imagination, and senses. No one could doubt that the ideal of tolerance, the capacity of these religions for assimilation and integration, have a seductive impact on those Christians, particularly in the West, who are disgusted with the institutional rigidity of their own form of Christianity, with the discrepancy between claims and reality. We need only glance at the diary of such an open-minded writer as Luise Rinser to find an example of the fascination with Hindu religion felt by a Christian intellectual. Apropos of the people she met in a Hindu shrine she says: "There is no commandment of Sunday worship or sabbath

observance hanging over them, no dogmatic system has taken possession of their pious thoughts, no Church threatens to expel them for
breaking the commandments. The Hindu has no need of all this: he
rests in the Divine One, which flows through him as it flows through
everything. For a Hindu it is impossible to be an atheist or a heretic. The
Divine (whether it be 'purusha,' *the One,* or appear in the likeness of a
thousand gods) is as undeniable a reality as the air he breathes. Not in
Lourdes, nor even in Assisi, have I ever felt the divine presence so
powerfully as in these little street temples." (*War Toy,* 1978, p. 72)
Nowadays even Catholic missionaries, who bear witness to the Christian
message, no longer wish to save the "heathens" from "damnation."

Nor is there any denying that in the collection of Indian religions that
we call "Hinduism" for short, primeval experiences and hopes of the
infinitely rich and infinitely poor subcontinent have been preserved and
articulated. There seems to be no limit to the religious expressiveness in
this grandly developed, ancient religious tradition of India, which was
called "eternal" because it had known no author. There seems to be no
limit, given an apparently boundless openness, to strivings for infinity
and evolutionary capacity. Alongside primitive mythological polytheism
and orgiastic rituals, we find the strictest asceticism, yoga, sublime meditation, a highly spiritual philosophy. In any event, this is an open,
growing religious system—*a living unity amid an astonishing variety* of viewpoints, forms, and rites. And it has been achieved not only without a
church, but also without any commonly binding doctrine, and yet with
unbroken continuity and seemingly indestructible vital energy. The goal
it aims at, through multifarious forms of asceticism and meditation, is
redemption from the ignorance of illusory appearances by means of
knowledge about the one true reality: liberation from the cycle of
rebirth through a putting to rest of the I or through its union with the
Absolute. Yet one cannot avoid the self-critical observation that our
attitudes toward Indian religion and piety have not always been so
unbiased.

EUROPE AND THE DISCOVERY OF INDIA

It should not be forgotten that as far back as the sixth or the fifth
century B.C., when the Persian Empire stretched from Greece to the
Indus Valley, even as far as northwestern India, there were numerous
contacts between Greeks and Indians. At the same time, although hitherto the exact historical connection has been only a matter of conjecture, astonishing similarities can be seen between the teaching of the
Upanishads on the nature of reality and the teaching of the first Greek
metaphysicians, the Eleatic school, in Lucania, Italy (Parmenides), as
well as between Indian thought and Orphism (Pythagoras).

From the time of Alexander the Great's bold thrust toward Afghanistan and into the Indus Valley, in the fourth century B.C., we have clear evidence of *cultural exchange between India and the Western world*. One permanent, precious testimony to this encounter in the Indus Valley is Greco-Indian art, with its Hellenistic statues and reliefs of Buddha (the very first such images we have), as well as the Corinthian capitals in Buddhist monasteries: an art (called Gandhāra, after the region in northern Pakistan) that unfolded from the first to the fifth centuries and carried its representations of Buddha all the way to central Asia, China, and Japan.

As far back as the second century, we have learned, there were also contacts between India and early Christianity, most notably in Hellenistic Egypt and its capital city, Alexandria (founded by Alexander, who was buried there). We have evidence that there were Indian saints or ascetics in Alexandria, but so far it has been impossible to prove anything but a direct influence on, say, Egyptian monasticism. For the third century we have evidence of Christian communities (Nestorian "heretics") in southwestern India. These people traced their lineage back to the apostle Thomas, but the tradition cannot, in fact, be vouched for historically. It was not until the Middle Ages that we note any veneration of the site where the apostle was allegedly executed and buried (at Mylapore, near Madras), along with a few insignificant missionary efforts by Roman Catholic missionaries along the trade route toward the Far East.

Only with the *modern period* did Europeans acquire any truly reliable information about India, which up till then was still largely unknown. In the sixteenth century, the Franciscans, Dominicans, and especially the Jesuits went to work in India, at first under Portuguese patronage. In the following century there was Roberto de Nobili, and after him Danish and German Protestants, as well as Anglicans. Thus until near the end of the eighteenth century almost everything known about the culture of India came from the reports by *missionaries* and a few odd travelers. The first Sanskrit grammars were composed by seventeenth- and eighteenth-century Jesuits (Heinrich Roth, J. E. Hanxleden), the first *Genealogy of the Gods of Malabar* was written by the seventeenth-century Lutheran missionary Bartholomäus Ziegenbalg; the first Tamil dictionary and Bible translation by another Lutheran missionary, J. P. Fabricius, in the eighteenth century. Around the same time, the German Carmelite Paulinus a Sancto Bartholomeo (P. Weszdin) was a prominent Sanskrit philologist in Europe.

The beginnings of *scientific Indology*, of course, cannot be dated any earlier than 1784, when Sir William Jones (in the service of the East India Company) founded the Bengal Asiatic Society, in Calcutta. Only little by little did accurate information about the British studies of Sanskrit (the classical language of India, comparable to Latin in the West) make its way to Europe. But the early-nineteenth century in Germany and France brought the first wave of an immense enthusiasm for India. In the century before, the Enlightenment had felt an affinity with the cool rationality of Confucianism; the Romantic period now discovered a deep kinship with the mysteries of Indian spirituality. In Germany the great stimulating mind Johann Gottfried von Herder was the first to call attention to Indian philosophy, religious poetry, and art as independent creations absolutely worthy of preservation, in keeping with the right of every people to their own culture and religion. The first European university chairs for Sanskrit were founded in Paris (1815) and Bonn (1817), occupied by a A. L. Chézy and August Wilhelm von Schlegel, respectively. The initiative for this development in Germany came from Schlegel's brother, Friedrich, and his foundational work, *On the Language and Wisdom of the Indians* (1808, four years after Herder's death).

The hundred years between 1820 and 1920 became the century of the great European scholars of Indian philology and antiquity. In this endeavor the British devoted themselves particularly to archaeology, ancient India, and (a topic later covered by the Americans and Russians as well) modern Indian languages. Meanwhile, the French, Germans, and Dutch explored classical Indian culture: language, religion, literature, and art. For the first time, scholars now distinguished Hinduism from Buddhism, and in the process concentrated especially on research into the Vedic texts (A. Bergaigne, A. Weber, T. Aufrecht, H. Oldenberg, H. Lüders).

We should not forget the great founders of comparative linguistics and religion, Franz Bopp and Friedrich Max Müller, and the many others who labored to translate the classic Indian scriptures into modern languages. All these efforts to shed light on Indian religion and philosophy and to compare them with Western thought were continued in our century by such eminent figures as Rudolf Otto, Albert Schweitzer, and Helmuth von Glasenapp.

The strategies of adaptation devised by the Jesuit missionaries T. Stevens and R. de Nobili in the sixteenth and seventeenth centuries were eventually suppressed by Rome. In the wake of this, it was not until the end of the nineteenth and the beginning of the twentieth centuries that serious efforts were again made (by such men as Brahmabandhab Upadhyaya, J. N. Farquhar, and the Belgian Jesuits G. Dandoy and P. Johanns) to achieve a deeper understanding of the Hindu religions. The first steps toward authentic Hindu-Christian dialogue were taken by two Christians, Jules Monchanin and Henri Le Saux (Swami Abhishiktānanda), who lived in an ashram near Tiruchirapalli and followed Upanishadic tradition. On the Protestant side the first to engage in dialogue with present-day Hinduism was P. V. Devanandan. The documents of

Vatican II along with those of the World Council of Churches (for which
S. J. Samartha in particular did the spadework) finally gave these pio-
neers their due. In November 1964 I was privileged to speak on "Christian Revelation and Non-Christian Religions" at the first national Indian
theological seminar in Bombay. (The address was published in 1967 by
one of the champions of a positive approach to Hinduism, Josef Neuner,
S.J.) Since then a great deal has been done on Christian theology in
India, both through the study of Hinduism and self-scrutiny by Christians. All this can serve as a foundation for what follows.

RELIGION AS COMPENSATION?

In the face of Indian religion—less from the standpoint of scholarly
research than of concrete life—the Western Christian still finds himself
rather overwhelmed and helpless. On the one hand, we see the exuber-
ance of Indian piety; on the other, the indescribable misery of the
masses in the large cities and villages (in 1979, 64 percent of the population was still illiterate; 40 percent was beneath the poverty level and
another 20 percent on the edge, despite a growing well-off middle
class). One is tempted to ask, Isn't India a perfect example confirming
the classic arguments put forth by European critics of religion? Doesn't
India seem to show with particular clarity that religion is nothing more
than the projection and wishful thinking of alienated individuals, as
Ludwig Feuerbach would have it, and the opium of an exploited and
wretched people, in Karl Marx's metaphor?

It is still not at all certain whether Marx got his famous/infamous
remark (from his critique of Hegel's *Philosophy of Right*) about religion as
a kind of opium, offering an illusory happiness to the masses living in
very real misery, directly from Hegel, from the Berlin Young Hegelians,
or from the German poet exiled in Paris Heinrich Heine, or from the
"red rabbi," Moses Hess. One fact which is not of merely historical
interest is that Hegel himself paved the way for Marx's celebrated
phrase in his lectures on the "Philosophy of World History," in the
context, actually, of India.

Thoroughly receptive as he was to the prevailing romantic enthusiasm for India, Hegel called that country the "land of longing," the
"empire of dreams," the "enchanted world," whose God was still to be
found "in the rapture of his dreaming." (*Jubiläumsausgabe*, Vol. 11, pp.
191 f.) Then follows the sharp critical comment that, in the religion of
India, superstition, fueled by the wild power of the imagination, bursts
through all barriers, and thus the physically and spiritually degenerate
individual "can win for himself a world of dreams and a mad happiness
only by means of opium." (p. 226)

Hegel's judgment—which was naturally shaped by the information available to him at the time—is not only harsh, but unfair. There is no way we could have an exchange of views with Islam in this fashion today. But the "opium of the people" remark—especially since it has been trumpeted by Indian, Russian, and Chinese Communists, all of whom want to see a different, nonreligious India—must still be taken very seriously. As a matter of fact, one of the most respected, though also most controversial, Indian journalists, Nirad C. Chaudhuri *(Hinduism, a Religion to Live By,* 1979), has recently laid the blame for a slackening of India's vitality at the door of the later Indian religions: Shivaism, Vishnuism, and Shaktism. Though Chaudhuri also considers other factors, such as climate and a lack of political stability and order, he argues that religion as it is actually lived is, vampire-like, sucking away the nation's energy.

Marx's charge against religion, needless to say, applies not only to India, but also to Catholic Latin America and to any other place in this world where religion is used and misused as consolation or *compensation.* (Chaudhuri, by the way, is not against all religions; he advocates the strong original Hinduism of the Vedas.)

The fundamental principles here are these:

● Religion—not only Hinduism, but Christianity, too—can be the "opium of the people," but it need not be. It can be consolation (false or authentic) for the wretched, but it can equally be (as Marx himself pointed out) a protest against their wretchedness. This has been proved true in India by the Hindu reformers who fought against social injustice on religious grounds (often under Christian influence) and challenged the caste system.

● Religion—not only Hinduism, but also Christianity—includes, as do all human faith, hope, and love, a certain amount of projection. But to say that religion is mere projection and no more is to make an unprovable assertion. It presumes that no ultimate/primeval reality exists, which is something, Immanuel Kant would insist, that pure reason can simply not show. Whether one should accept (or reject) an absolute reality is a matter for "practical reason" or, better, for reasonable (answerable to reason) trust.

A NEW LONGING FOR INDIA?

Today we are faced with a new enthusiasm for India and Indian religion. It would be wrong to dismiss these *new religious movements* in the Western world with a critical shrug, to write them off as "youth religions"—as if they were simply fleeting social phenomena, something for wild-eyed young dreamers. In fact, they lay bare a fundamental problem, they serve as a seismograph to measure the hidden shock waves running through society. As Western pilgrims from Europe and the U.S.A. flock to Indian ashrams, while Indian swamis surround themselves with large communities in Europe and America, Christian apologists and official church opponents of "cults" now evidently fear that the Christian mission to Asia is giving way to an Asian mission to Europe and America. And they have a point: Does anyone nowadays know the names of any great Christian missionaries in India, whose personal magnetism could be compared to that of men like Ramakrishna and Vivekananda, to Yogānanda, Maharishi Mahesh Yogi, and Bhagwān Rajneesh? Certainly one can argue that all the followers of these new movements (Yoga, the Divine Life Mission, Srī Aurobindo, Transcendental Meditation, Hare Krishna) have been "led astray," which gets the churches, with all their shortcomings, off the hook; but the charge is unfair. No doubt, some of the new Asiatic missionaries are not too scrupulous about their proselytizing methods, but neither were the old Christian missionaries.

Obviously, most of the new India enthusiasts have little interest in a laborious study of the classical Indian scriptures (and still less in Sanskrit and other ancient languages). Instead of revering ancient sacred writings, they turn to the great guru as their ultimate authority; and instead of seeking the truth with the help of scholarship and science, they often look to ecstatic experience. The widespread aversion (especially among the younger generation) to science, technology, and industrial progress (with its potential for destruction, its susceptibility to breakdowns, and its injustices) forms the dark background against which the new religious movements are presenting a message that attracts a large audience. In the face of an evident loss of meaning, moral norms, and community, people are looking for alternative goals, styles, and forms for their lives. Is this a sign of a postmaterialist shift in orientation?

Institutionalized Christianity and its representatives, the churches, are at once the causes and the victims of what has now become a manifest religious crisis. This doesn't mean, of course, that religion has disappeared from secular society; indeed many people who had once *repressed* their religious sensibility now find it once again awakening. But, to a frightening extent, it *has* fled from the highly bureaucratized large church institutions, which are often totally absorbed in defending their own interests; and no church festivals can disguise the seriousness of the situation. Many people are calling into question the religious monopoly of the major churches; and as a result of the prevalent freedom of religion, tolerance, and ecumenism, they are claiming the right to shape their own religious lives. We are confronted by the (ambivalent) phenomenon of a "diffusion of the religious": The substance of religion, liberated from the bonds of churches, dogmas, and institutions, and often freely floating about, has settled in a great variety of places and situations. It has now clustered around different values and is being realized in every possible form and configuration. And this in turn has led to an increasing pluralization of religious life.

What, then, are the adherents of the new, modern Eastern, and in particular Indian, religions looking for? In an analysis of the "new religious movements" *(Concilium*, 1983, Vol. 1) the editor, American sociologist John Coleman, lists the following three motives, which evidently dovetail with each other:

- A desire for intensive *experience* of the self and of the transforming power of the holy. Almost all commentators on the new religious movements strongly emphasize this theme of the quest for a palpable, experiential religion.
- Desire for a supportive *community*.
- Desire for the true *charisma* of religious leaders and hence for fellowship with other believers.

Far beyond the boundary of such organized movements, especially sensitive men and women often wonder whether they might not find a better "alter-native" ("born different") life within the framework of *Indian religion*. Might they not find a better experience of the self, the *self-realization* they are looking for, in a Hindu than in a Christian context? Might not Hinduism be a wholly new way for them to experience the self and, at the same time, the Absolute, numinous, *mystical reality*?

WHAT IS MYSTICAL EXPERIENCE?

Not only pop musicians and film stars, but crowned heads and distinguished Western intellectuals have visited Indian gurus and ashrams. The German physicist and philosopher Carl Friedrich von Weizsäcker tells us that, early in his career, ever since reading the sermons of the Buddha and the Chinese classics, he "felt more spontaneously at home in spiritual Asia than in Europe." This is how he relates his indescribable mystical experience at the grave of the Hindu saint Srī Rāmana Maharishi in Tiruvannamalai: "Once I had taken off my shoes and stepped in front of the Maharishi's grave in the ashram, I knew in a flash: 'Yes, this is it.' The truth is, all my questions were already answered. Grouped in an affable circle, we were given a tasty lunch served on large green leaves. Afterwards I sat near the grave on the stone floor. The knowledge was there, and everything had happened in half an hour. I was still aware of the world around me, the hard seat, the humming mosquitos, the light on the stone. But in those rapid moments the onionskin-like layers that words can only hint at, 'You'—'Me'—'Yes,' had been broken through. Tears of bliss. Bliss without tears.—Very gently the experience brought me back to earth. I now knew the love that is the meaning of earthly love." (*The Garden of the Human,* 1977, p. 595)

Indeed, isn't religion, above all—before it is doctrine and morality, rites and institutions—*religious experience?* Under the influence of Protestant theologian Friedrich Schleiermacher in nineteenth century Europe and philosopher-psychologist William James in early-twentieth-century America, many Westerners have come out in support of the priority of religious experience. And isn't religious experience in its highest form *mystical experience,* as in India, where it seems more at home than anywhere else? In Christianity the writings of the mystics have always been under suspicion. Great mystics like Eckhart, Teresa of Ávila, John of the Cross, and Fénelon, were persecuted by the Inquisition (and also radically rejected by the early "dialectical theology" of Karl Barth, Emil Brunner, and Friedrich Gogarten) on charges of a hybrid identification with God ("self-divinization," "pantheism," "works righteousness"), of unchurchly introspection ("subjectivism"), of disdain for creation ("Manichaeism," "quietism"). By contrast, mysticism has a recognized place in Hinduism, in the center of orthodox Hindu teaching, as a matter of fact. It is not merely, as in Christianity, an enrichment of religion, but its innermost essence. This has already been made clear, and at this point I would like to open the discussion between Hinduism and Christianity.

Respected philosophers of religion, both in India (such as Sarvepalli Rādhakrishnan, first president of the Republic of India) and in the West, have argued that spiritual experience, whether Eastern or Western, is, at bottom, everywhere the same; and thus all religions, because they have the same mystical experience, are in the final analysis equal. This view, needless to say, has been disputed, and needs careful analysis. First of all, we have to ask, what is "mystical experience," anyway?

Discussion of this matter has not quieted down since the appearance of Aldous Huxley's *The Doors of Perception* (1954), in which he reported personal *mystical experiences while taking drugs* that approached the highest levels of religious thought and perception: the Christian beatific vision, the Hindu *saccidānanda* or the Buddhist nirvana. Are all mystical experiences, then, fundamentally alike, regardless of whether one reaches them through asceticism and meditation or mescaline and LSD or sex? That is the message preached (and practiced) by the Hindu monk and expert on Indian Tantrism Āgehānanda Bhārati. In his book *The Light at the Center* (1976), Bhārati (who was born in Vienna and now teaches at Syracuse University) follows up Huxley's ideas in a programmatic manner while launching a broad polemic against the Christian churches and their thinking.

No one has criticized Huxley more vehemently (for which he was taken to task just as vehemently by Bhārati) than the Oxford professor of religion R. C. Zaehner. In *Mysticism, Sacred and Profane* (1957) Zaehner argues against Huxley from beginning to end. He denies the thesis, which has also been advanced by Arnold Toynbee, Frithjof Schuon, Huston Smith, and others, that mystical experience is basically the same, whatever religion one may belong to; that at all times and in all places mysticism appears in more or less identical forms, whether in the case of an Indian yogi, a Persian Sufi poet, a Neo-Platonic philosopher, a medieval monk, or finally a modern intellectual disgusted with Western civilization. Zaehner's counterthesis: There is a substantial difference between sacred mysticism, which is necessarily bound up with a moral life, and secular mystical states, be they induced by drugs or whatever, which are compatible with an immoral or amoral life. And there is also a difference within sacred mysticism between the monistic variety (such as the extremely nondualistic Vedānta of Shankara) and the theistic, which constitutes the mainstream not only of Christian but of Islamic mysticism (Abūl-Qāsim al-Junaid, Ghazzālī).

The question, then, is, Is there one *single* mystical experience or are there *several?* In other words, are there only variants of the same single type or are there wholly different mystical experiences? The numerous contradictory discussions by twentieth-century Anglo-Saxon scholars (of the sort collected by Richard Woods in his large volume *Understanding Mysticism* [1980]) show just how fiercely complex this problem is (as do the contributions by German Catholic and Protestant theologians assembled by Fritz-Dieter Maass under the title *Mysticism in Dialogue* [1972]). Such complexity, of course, is due in large part to the fact that "mysticism" is an extremely vague term. In popular language, "mystical" is often equated with puzzling, strange, mysterious, or just plain religious. But even students of mysticism understand it very differently; and so it is difficult to give the word a univocal definition.

Is All Mysticism Religious?

One thing, at least, is clear: "Mysticism," in the original, *literal sense,* comes from the Greek *mýein,* to close (the mouth). The "mysteries" are, therefore, "secrets," "secret teachings," "secret cults," which one does not speak about in the presence of the uninitiated. One closes one's mouth in order to seek salvation within oneself. And silence is recommended to those who wish to draw near to the mystery. Renunciation of the world, turning inward, immediate union with the Absolute—these have long been viewed as the characteristics of mysticism. But that is just where our problems today begin.

Mystical experience can be generally defined as an *immediate, intuitive experience* of unity, as an intuition of a great unity that abolishes the subject-object division. If such a general definition is adopted, we can hardly dispute the fact that experimenters with drugs also may have "mystical experiences," perhaps even schizophrenics or manic-depressives can have them too. Completely nonreligious people can likewise undergo abnormal changes and expansion of consciousness with artificial means (alcohol is often enough): a diffuse feeling of surpassing the self and becoming a nonself, as Huxley has described apropos of his taking mescaline. Naturally, this raises the question: What does this kind of experience have to do with *religion*?

Granted, the term "religion" must be understood very broadly, so as to cover the gamut of the historical religions from the polytheistic nature religions, theism, and pantheism all the way to atheistic Buddhism. But unless the limits separating religion from the quasi-religious and the irreligious are to be arbitrarily dissolved, leaving a shapeless blur, the word should not be arbitrarily extended. Religion should remain religious. Religion, as I tried to define it in the Introduction, is the many-layered realization of a relationship to something that encompasses man and his world, to an ultimate reality (however understood), an Absolute (God, Brahma, dharma, emptiness, nirvāna). Putting it another way, a person is "religious" if he recognizes and is ready to bear witness to the fact that the "world" (i.e., humanity, history, nature, the cosmos) is *not*, as it appears to be, the final word; but that the "world" points us to a comprehensive reality that embraces and determines all things, that is the very first and the very last. Conversely, whenever people have a similar relationship, not to something that encompasses the "world," not to an Absolute or Ultimate, where instead the "world," which is relative, is absolutized, then to avoid misunderstandings we should not speak of religion, but, rather, of *para-religion* (in the case of indifference to religion) or *pseudo-religion* (in the case of surrogates for religion). What does this mean, then, for the mystical experience of unity?

Not every immediate, intuitive experience of union, not every mystical experience, is automatically religious, and not all mysticism is genuinely religious. We cannot exclude a priori the possibility that there may be experiences of union which are not religious at all, which are limited to what is present and contingent, and so do not really transcend the relative. Here it would be best to speak of *para-religious mysticism:* union of myself with nature, with the cosmos, with the matter of this world, with "life" (understood in the instinctive/vitalistic or visionary/cosmic sense), behind which there is nothing. Or we might use the term *pseudo-religious mysticism,* which functions as a substitute for religion: union of myself with a force such as the people, the nation, the party, or the leader, moments when individuals are fused together in drunken mass hysteria at huge rallies (the "folkish mysticism" of fascism or Nazism).

Zaehner's distinction between sacred and profane mysticism may not be on target here. Mystical experience is equally possible in the everyday profane environment, and not only in the sacred context. And with many experiences of unity, as reported by Huxley or Bhārati, and deep moods, as given artistic expression by poets (Rilke, say), painters (Chagall, Nolde), and musicians (Scriabin, Schönberg), we are told by the individuals in question that something more than just relative, contingent here-and-now is at stake. Here things, sounds, nature—the world in its profoundest sense—opens up and reveals an ultimate reality, the "secret," the "mystery," the "light" of reality, the cosmic foundation, the Absolute. One does not necessarily make things in nature into God, but one comes to the Absolute through nature, an experience many people feel is not self-produced, but "granted," a "gift." Hence we ought not to deny the religious character of such experiences as Zaehner does (a convert to Roman Catholicism, he shows an all-too-dogmatic bias). We are dealing here with *religious mysticism*—although the monistic, not the theistic or, still less, the Christian, variety. So if someone wishes to be a mystic by invoking this sort of experience in a believable fashion, his claim should not be denied. The ecumenical spirit is not interested in monopolizing religion.

This doesn't mean, of course, that every method, every technique, every experiment leading to this experience is to be commended, or that the religious end justifies the means. Meditation grounded in abstinence and in narcotic ecstasy, sacrificial asceticism and libertine cultivation of the pleasure principle, can scarcely be placed on the same level, as Bhārati would have us do. Religion should remain religious not only so that God may remain God (the Absolute); but religion should also not be disengaged from morality, so that man may remain human.

On the other hand, to allow religious experiences only to those living a moral life in the bourgeois-Christian sense would be unfairly to absolutize a specific historical version of morality. And the notion proposed by Zaehner, that nature or the cosmos is excluded in advance from genuine mystical experiences, seems utterly unacceptable. Even Thomas Aquinas would agree that the Absolute is present in every flower and grain of sand, and there is a great deal of truth in Einstein's notion, inspired by Spinoza, of "cosmic piety." Nature mysticism open to the Absolute should by no means be dogmatically declared the highest form of mysticism, but neither should it be equated with para-mysticism (uninterested in the true Absolute) or pseudo-mysticism (which replaces the Absolute with a surrogate). We have to look for answers to the questions raised here about religious criteria; but with everything said thus far the issue of whether there is one kind of mystical experience or many has not yet been settled. How does the argument look?

A SINGLE MYSTICAL EXPERIENCE?

Some writers maintain that all mystical experience is all essentially the same (although ineffable). In this reading, the *differences* would be found simply in the *interpretations* of this experience, all of which could be traced back to the different religious traditions and social contexts (India, the Middle East, Greece, Latin America, etc.). Obviously this approach sharply relativizes the differences in mysticism in the various religions.

Others maintain that mystical experiences are *multiform* and basically different. They see the differences as rooted in the *experience itself* and thus capable of being at least partly independent of their sociocultural context. The differences between the mysticism practiced by the different religious logically provide an occasion, then, for distinguishing the various types of mystical religions.

Which side to choose? I consider the whole question badly framed— as if religious experience and interpretation could ever be separated! One will search in vain through the history of religion for a "naked" experience, untrammeled by interpretation. A mystical experience could always be defined a priori in some way and postulated as a universal, but it would never be empirically verifiable. My own position, therefore, simply echoes what has increasingly become the consensus in discussions of hermeneutics: Religious experience doesn't wait until after the fact to be interpreted; it never occurs at all without being *shaped in advance by some interpretation* (though not necessarily a conscious one). Thomas Aquinas gave voice to this in principle when he wrote, *"Quidquid recipitur, ad modum recipientis recipitur."* (Whatever is received, is received in the manner of the receiver.)

The rule holds for both Hinduism and Christianity: Every religious experience brings along with it its own interpretation, which is at the same time enriched by further interpretive touches and finally given linguistic expression (though perhaps only of a very sketchy sort). This is done by means of certain conceptual or pictorial interpretive articulations, which can in turn react on the original experience, deepening it or flattening it. And beyond all concepts and representations, each experience always has its own (more or less conscious) general interpretive framework, its "paradigm," the theoretical/practical model of understanding, the total constellation of convictions, values, and behavior patterns of a given community, which serves to grasp, organize, and synthesize the experiences.

Thus there is no religious or mystical experience without an interpretive context, a conceptual model, a paradigm. Even in sacred texts and altogether personal religious testimony we find only *interpreted experiences* of the Absolute, which have been taken from a quite specific cultural context, a definite tradition, and translated into language. Would Huxley, Bhārati, and others have had precisely the sort of experience of unity they did if they hadn't already intensively familiarized themselves with Indian wisdom? I believe that my view on this question has been fully confirmed by the recently published collection by S. T. Katz, *Mysticism and Religious Traditions* (1983). Katz makes it clear that

> the interpenetration of the mystical event and the religious tradition out of which the mystic grows has emerged as a central concern requiring new and innovative study. (p. 5)

Thus experience and interpretation influence each other. Interpretive identification is not an accident, an appendage, but an intrinsic element in the mystical experience itself. To vary Kant's famous remark, experience without interpretation is blind, interpretation without experience is empty. So we can draw three conclusions about mystical experience in the various religions:

1. The mystical experiences found in different religions undoubtedly have some *common ground:* Mystics from differing religions have similar experiences. Despite all the formal variety, there are common deep structures: The goal is oneness and redemption; purification, illumination, and union are the way. Mystics of quite different religious origins often resemble, and are closer to, one another, than to the average believer in their own religion. Amazing parallels, for example, can be noted between Yogasūtra Patanjali's stages of inner contemplation and Teresa of Ávila's stages of prayer.

2. There are also, however, contradictions and apparently irreconcilable *conflicts* separating the mystical experiences found in differing religions: the conflict, for instance, between impersonal-monistic mysticism and personal-theistic mysticism. One can label them "perspectives" or "superstructures" (Frits Staal) or "doctrinal ramifications" (Ninian Smart) or whatever. One can and must reflect on them, but they cannot be simply removed, like some screen or railing superimposed on a "pure" mystical experience. There is no method for extracting "pure" mysticism from all explanatory structures, just as no "pure" crystal can be extracted without crystal structures. Even if we appeal to an individual experience to justify such a claim, it is a dogmatic, illegitimately generalizing line of argument to assume the existence of a pure, uniform, universal mystical experience, monistic or otherwise. Those who do, forget that they make this sort of assertion on the strength of their own monistic (or nonmonistic) predisposition. As Terrence Penelhum argues (in *Understanding Mysticism*) against John Hicks and Ninian Smart, an aversion to doctrinal differences, however reasonable that may be, is

no reason for criticizing such differences in advance as obstacles to the understanding of mystical experience.

3. What we see, then, in the mystical experiences of the various religions is a *common bond linking contrasts. Not* an exclusive antagonism, as some theologians apparently assume, nor wholly irreducible differences in forms of mystical experience, of which only one's own is authentic. *Nor* an undifferentiated unity, as some academics appear to think. To quote Hegel's taunt at Schelling, there is no mystical "night in which all cows are black." There is no one single form of mystical experience, identical in all structures and functions.

Instead, there is a *differentiated commonness* between mystical experiences which show an internal variety, but uniform features. This makes communication possible even between very dissimilar religions, a point I shall pursue in the following section.

MYSTICAL AND PROPHETIC RELIGION

And so "mysticism," in the religious sense, proves to be a term neither equivocal (lumping together completely dissimilar things) nor univocal (labeling wholly dissimilar things), but *analogous* (comprehending things that are at once like and unlike). As we shall see, in real life mystical religion can in no way be cleanly separated from the nonmystical sort; there are too many transitional and mixed forms. But that makes it all the more important, for dialogue between Christianity and Hinduism, that we begin by working out the fundamental difference between mystical and nonmystical religion.

In *The Varieties of Religious Experience* (1902), William James draws the psychological distinction between the cheerful, optimistic religion of the "healthy soul" (the "once born") and the gloomy, pessimistic religion of the "sick soul" (the "born again"). Writing from the standpoint of comparative religious history, Friedrich Heiler alters this distinction. In his fully documented, perceptive studies (*Prayer*, 1918; *Buddhist Contemplation*, 1918; *The Forms and Essence of Religion*, 1961), which look to earlier research by Nathan Söderblom, Reinhold Seeberg, and Rudolf Otto, Heiler contrasts *mystical and prophetic religion.* (Otto similarly opposes mysticism to orthodox piety.)

I do not wish to support any oversimplified classifications or false alternatives. But it is extremely important for the whole discussion among Christians, Muslims, Hindus, and Buddhists to focus on the two (or three) great independent lines of development among the early world religions (I am disregarding primitive religion here). Both of them, unlike the religions of Egypt or China, have won a significant place for themselves far beyond the land they came from: I mean the religions of Indian and of Semitic origin.

On the one hand, *mystical religion* arose in India as a reaction to the already developed, indeed overdeveloped, cultic religion of the late-Vedic sacrificial priesthood. The theory of unity elaborated in the Upanishads, as well as the experience of unity gained from immediate meditative practice, became the basis not only for the Hindu religions, but also for Buddhism and Jainism. Perhaps (thus far, as I noted in the beginning, we have had to rely on conjecture), India was also the source of the other broad stream of mysticism (from Asia Minor, Greece, and the Hellenistic ecumene): from the early metaphysicians of Ionia, Orphism, and the Pythagoreans, through Plato and the late Hellenistic mystery cults to Plotinus. Plotinus was the teacher of that fifth- or sixth-century mystical philosopher who, concealed behind the mask of Paul's disciple Dionysius the Areopagite, wrote his *Mýstike theologia* (the source of our word "mysticism"). Eventually translated into Latin, this treatise largely shaped mystical piety in the West.

On the other hand, *prophetic religion,* which grew out of the primitive religion of nomadic tribes, arose in the Semitic cultural complex: Around 1200 B.C., when the Aryan immigration into the Punjab had ended, the Mosaic religion of Yahweh came into being in the Middle East. "Like the so-called patriarchs, Moses was first of all a receiver of revelation, the founder of a cult, and the inspired leader of a nomadic (or seminomadic) group, which united around its new religion and tried to realize the promise given to it of possessing its own land. The flight from Egypt also took place under the auspices of the new religion. The success of that effort, which was attributed to Yahweh, was a major reason why the Mosaic religion of Yahweh did not remain a variety of tribal religion. The rescue from Egypt always played a decisive role when later generations spoke of Yahweh and his relationship to Israel. In that escape, the Hebrews sensed the irrational element which enabled faith in Yahweh to make the transition from the religion of a group of nomads to a religion for the world." (G. Fohrer, *History of the Israelite Religion,* pp. 59 f.) The monotheistic religion of Yahweh was embodied twice, in the prophets of Israel and then, in a unique fashion, in Jesus the Christ; finally, for a third time, in Muhammad the Prophet.

These two lines of religious tradition have branched out again and again; they have often mingled with primitive popular piety and folk cults, and to some extent have even flowed into one another. In the case of Christianity, biblical/prophetic religion merged with Hellenistic/mystical elements. A rudimentary form of this combination can be seen as early as Paul and John; then it occurs in Clement of Alexandria and Origen (contemporaries of Plotinus) and in Augustine of Hippo. A parallel process appears in Arabian/Persian Sufism. By the same token, in India the mystical religion of the Upanishads and the Vedanta fused, as we have learned, with yoga techniques and the personally oriented cults of Vishnu, Bhagavān, Krishna, and Rāma. An emotional bond with the one God is at the center of the monotheistic Hindu religions.

With respect to the theological debate over the relation between mystical and prophetic religion, this means:

- Neither should mystical religion be looked upon as a mere preparatory or aberrant form of prophetic religion, as Christian dogmatic theologians are continually inclined to do.
- Nor should prophetic religion be reduced to mystical religion, as if the latter were the only "real" kind, as philosophers and psychologists of religion in particular have sometimes done.

I cannot, therefore, agree with Leszek Kolakowski, who usually argues against technical theology, when he writes: "The experience of mystical union is a rare phenomenon, but nonetheless one may say that it constitutes the essence of religious life." But why should a "rare phenomenon" constitute the "essence" of a thing? If the mystical and the prophetic element, if Hindu religions and Christianity, are to have justice done them, we must examine this issue precisely, as Friedrich Heiler does (though one can quarrel with him over details). Following up on the distinctions he draws (cf. *Das Gebet*, 5th ed. [1923], pp. 255–58), I would like to try to sketch a generic profile of mystical and prophetic religion and so of Hinduism and Christianity.

The basic experience of *mystical piety* is the denial of the vital instincts, a renunciation and dissolution of the human, a dedication to infinity, which climaxes in ecstasy or nirvana. Mystical piety is thus primarily turned inward; it strives to be free from desire, to extinguish affective and volitional life. It is a process of self-transformation, in which the mystic appears as one who goes without but, in the end, as one who knows. The high point of a life of mystical piety is reached in extraordinary experiences beyond normal consciousness: new dimensions of perception and discernment, ecstasies and ecstasy-like visions and hearing of voices, in which sensory excitement blends with purely spiritual experience, and the everyday subject/object split is abolished. Yet it is equally important to observe that mystical experience, as manifested in Hinduism, is never simply naive, but generally comes linked to a high degree of reflection, regardless of whether this may be elaborate philosophical speculation, as in the Upanishads, or precise psychological analysis, as in yoga. Mystical piety is familiar with the most sophisticated methods of asceticism and meditation so as to induce mystical states and thus find the way to redemption.

The basic experience of *prophetic piety*, by contrast, is characterized by a strong will to live: an instinct for affirmation, a condition in which one is gripped by values and responsibilities, a passionate striving for the realization of certain goals and ideals. Prophetic piety is thus primarily turned outward, stands up to confront the world, and aims to prevail in it. Emotions are not suppressed, but awakened: The will to live asserts itself and seeks to triumph even amid external defeat. In this respect the prophetically oriented person is a fighter who struggles through from doubt to the certainty of faith, from insecurity to trust, from the consciousness of being a sinner to the attaining of salvation with the gift of grace. True enough, the life of prophetic religion includes experiences of receiving a "call" or revelation from God; but they come less often, they have essentially less to do with ecstatic raptures, and in any event they do not abolish the subject/object split. Concerning Jesus himself (often falsely termed a mystic), tradition reports only two mystical states, neither of which is definitely historical. Neither extraordinary ecstatic experiences nor meditative speculation on God's nature nor psychological self-dissection has any substantial importance for actual religious life or for the relationship with God, which is realized in prayer, faith, and moral conduct. The highest charisma, according to Paul, is not ecstatic speaking in tongues, but faith, hope, and love. Prophetic piety, as embodied in Judaism, Islam, and even Christianity stands out most emphatically by a kind of spontaneity that cares little for systems and methods, psychological techniques and training. All those things, needless to say, came to play a significant role (under the influence of Eastern mysticism) in the later history of Christianity.

ARE ALL RELIGIONS EQUAL?

Having made this broad distinction, we can now go about giving an answer to the question: Are all religions really *equal*? Aren't all religions equally true? Don't they teach the same things? That is the point made by both a number of modern swamis now traveling through the Western world (and preaching their own religion as the best) and many Western secularists (who belong to no religion).

Once in the history of India an attempt was launched to turn to political advantage the idea that all religions are ultimately one, in hopes of uniting this enormous country: That occurred under the Mogul emperor Akbar (a Muslim), called "the Great," who lived from 1542 to 1605. One is constantly running into Islam in India, where the memory of the Mogul emperors is kept fresh not only by their outrages, which to this day have not been forgotten, but also, happily, by what are perhaps the most beautiful monuments of Islamic art: the Pearl Mosque in the Red Fort at Delhi, the Taj Mahal in Agra, and finally Fatehpur Sikri. This was the residence of Akbar, which had to be abandoned after only a decade and a half for lack of water and is still in a fine state of preservation. The emperor conquered and thoroughly organized a kingdom that stretched from Baluchistan and Afghanistan almost to the center of the giant subcontinent (about as far south in latitude as Bombay).

Akbar was the most important of the Mogul emperors who ruled India until it was incorporated into the British Empire (1857). He not only married wives of different religions (including, an unverified tradition claims, a Portuguese Christian named Miriam or Maria). He also, cosmopolitan, skeptical thinker, and mystical seeker for God that he was, *tried to fuse religions into unity* partly for reasons of state, partly out of Sufi mystical convictions. He joined together—and expressed this in various ways—the Jewish-Christian-Islamic belief in one God, Hindu elements, and the Persian cult of the sun, to form a religion of "universal toleration," which Akbar himself called *Dīn Ilāhi* (= divine faith). And so, two hundred years before Lessing's parable of the rings (Gotthold Ephraim Lessing, *Nathan the Wise*), the emperor put that Enlightenment wisdom into practice in his own way: Knowing the three rings, he believed in none of them, and molded himself a new one out of all three.

Needless to say, his success did not last long. The universal religion he had fashioned, which had had its own rites and initiation ceremonies, fell apart after his death. Along with Pharaoh Akhenaton's introduction of the monotheistic sun cult into Egypt three thousand years before, it remains the best-known example of the fact that an old religion can be replaced by a revolution from the top only with difficulty, and that the attempt to found a new religion of unity is an illusion.

There is no way to equate all religions. The basic distinction between mystical and prophetic religion, if nothing else, would prevent it. And not only the prophetic religions, but, as we have seen, even the Hindu religions, which in principle recognize each other (but whose cults are often mutually exclusive) in no sense postulate that all religions are one —only their goal. And having one goal does not mean there is only one way to it, nor does it preclude detours. Remarkably, the scholar who more than any other stresses the unity of mankind's religious history, Wilfred Cantwell Smith, also makes the lapidary remark:

> It is not the case that all religions are the same. The historian notes that not even one religion is the same, century after century, or from one country to another, or from village to city. [*Towards a World Theology* (1981), p. 4.]

And nothing shows this more clearly than the history of "Hinduism," of whose manifold epochs and trends Professor von Stietencron has given us a bird's-eye view: a history not of a single religion but of a *whole collection* of them.

In the religious history of mankind, which is characterized by immeasurable variety, all things may hang together, but they don't all come down to the same thing. There is no undifferentiated identity, but an *interdependence, with every possible kind of convergence and divergence*. This becomes most obvious when we sharply contrast the two basic types of "higher" religion, the mystical and the prophetic.

MIXED FORMS

Yet these two types have cross-bred with each other and with primitive/popular religions, producing the most varied kinds of mixed forms. How, one may ask, was this possible? Aren't they by definition essentially foreign to each other? In any event, these hybrid forms exist; and, having contrasted the ideal types, we now have to glance at the concrete varieties.

In doing so, of course, we want to avoid *harmonizing* different traditions. Thus, it is not very helpful to misread the deeply prophetic character of both Old Testament and New Testament piety and to locate the essence of Christianity in some mystical core. Jesus of Nazareth was no more a mystic than the Old Testament prophets were, and the continually cited verse "I and the Father are one" is not from Jesus himself, but an interpretation by the fourth Evangelist, who wished to point out the unity, in will, action, and revelation, of the man Jesus with God, of the Son with the Father. And it is equally unfair to label as "mystics" such typical Christian figures as Luther, Kierkegaard, and many others who invoked the preaching of Jesus and the theology of Paul. Mysticism is not *originally* Christian.

But *exclusivist views* are also misleading. It is by no means the case that India has only one kind of mysticism, which denies personality, while Christianity likewise has only one kind, which affirms it. There are both kinds on both sides, which means that we are not dealing here simply with *conflicts between* Christianity and Hinduism. Conflicts can also be found *within* Christianity and *within* Hinduism.

No one could overlook the fact that personalist/theistic piety can be found not only in Christianity, but, as we have heard and shall discuss in greater detail, in the monotheistic Hindu religions as well (the Bhakti movement). Conversely, we can find an impersonal/monistic piety not only in India but also in Christianity (derived from Plotinus and especially notable in the works of the Areopagite, Eckhart, and Angelus Silesius). Furthermore not only Christians but many Hindus, too, speak with God in the simple dialogue of prayer. On the other hand, not only Indian mystics, but individual Christians, too (Tauler, Angelus Silesius), practice a pure contemplative mysticism without any of the dramatic structures of conversation, and so we find a manifold mysticism on *both* sides: an intensely emotional kind and a cool, unemotional kind; an ardently erotic and a detached, intellectual kind; cult-oriented and noncult-oriented, nonsensuous mysticism; naive-imaginative-poetic and reflective-rational-theoretical mysticism.

Thus we have cross-breeding, exchange, *interpenetration* both between the two basic types of religion and between them and primitive/popular religion. Theologians should not simply write off all these historical processes as "syncretism"—a mingling of religions and therefore a polluting of faith. Such critics fail to notice that not only in India but also in the West there is not a single nonsyncretistic religion, in the strict sense of the word. How many different elements have merged in the Old Testament, in the New Testament, too, and still more in the Qur'an! And to that extent there is, in fact, as Wilfred Cantwell Smith never tires of stressing, one "religious history of mankind." We can trace it through the millennia in the enormous diversity of religions on all the continents, with every possible phenomenological similarity and historical connection.

It is generally a sign of weakness and anxiety when a religion goes into a shell and becomes isolated; and conversely a sign of strength when it can learn from another while maintaining a critical perspective. Anyone who wishes to may take the late-Greek term *syn-kretismós* in the more positive, original sense. Whether one agrees with Plutarch in relating it to the alliance of the cities of Crete, most of which had been at odds with the rest; or with Erasmus of Rotterdam in tracing it back to *syn-kerranýnai* (= mix together, but meaning the efforts at peaceful behavior on the part of religious adversaries), in either case the word points to the crucial thing: understanding, reconciliation, peace.

In the meantime one would do better to speak of the attempt at a tension-rich *synthesis:* the goal is not a compounding of various features from various religions, nor a mingling of gods (theocracy), nor a fusing of religions, but, rather, a dialectical "transcending" *(Aufheben)* of conflicts through inner mediation, which at once includes affirming, denying, and overcoming antagonistic positions. Shouldn't religions that have so much in common be able to have still more in common in the future? The key is not a political decision on the part of secular or spiritual authorities, but a slow evolution from below.

Naturally, such a dialectical mediation presupposes that each religion recognizes the others as *dialogue partners of equal value and with equal rights.* As Martin Kämpchen, a Catholic theologian living in India, has phrased it: "Up till now theology has taken as its point of departure a *mock* pluralism. It says that everything good and true found in other religions is actually to be ascribed to Christianity; in other words, that a Hindu, insofar as he lives a morally pure life and truly seeks God is an 'anonymous Christian' (K. Rahner). Or theology shifts the accent slightly by claiming that all other world religions are a 'preparation' for Christianity, which leads them all to fulfillment. —*Genuine* pluralism, however, recognizes not only the existence of other religions, but their intrinsic *equal value.* The Indian theologian Ignatius Puthiadam, S.J., formulates the problem concisely: 'It is a matter of doing the impossible, of removing the contradiction between a religion's totalitarian claim to uniqueness and an affirmation of pluralism.' " *(Publik-Forum,* 22, 1983, pp. 20–21) These reflections from a Christian standpoint were designed to point out a path in that direction.

II.
World and Deity: Conceptions of the Hindus

1. *Heinrich von Stietencron:* Hindu Perspectives

COSMIC ORDER

The religions of the Hindus may draw their life from a tradition several millennia old, which still serves, to some degree, to orient them; but over that long time they have been continuously changing and have, in part, gone their separate ways. We need not wonder, then, to see them making different attempts to grasp the nature of God and the world, and to define the relations between these two.

These conceptions do not follow in simple temporal sequence so that one definitively takes the place of another. Rather, the Hindu tends to hold on to the beliefs of his fathers even when he himself puts the accent elsewhere or sees things differently. In this way there arises a juxtaposition of differing interpretations—a juxtaposition that many educated Indians feel does not meaninglessly preserve outdated traditions, but deals fairly with the various levels of human experience. Hence they generally don't think that, of two differing descriptions of reality, if one is true, the other must be false; but, rather, that each of them is appropriate to the perceptual capacity and understanding of certain individuals or certain stages in the evolution of consciousness.

The experience of the world that was characteristic for Indians of the Vedic period still holds true for many Indians today—particularly, but not only, for lower-class Indians. They see the world as governed, but not by man; they sense in it the presence of a great number of powers, which order and preserve or disturb and destroy and in so doing can influence our lives.

These are the powers with whom humanity has most immediately to deal. Hence they occupy a relatively large place in mythology and the religion of the people. There are gods of heaven *(deva)* and of the underworld *(asura)*, forces of light and forces of darkness, forces of order and forces of movement and vitality. Both groups oppose each other; and human beings live and act amid the field of tension created by this opposition. But beyond their domain, ever since the post-Vedic period, lies the sphere of the gods Brahmā, Vishnu, and Shiva, each one of whom formed the center of a particular religion (that of Brahmā has died out). Later each of the great Hindu religions integrated these three great gods in their functions as Creator of the world (Brahmā), Preserver of the world (Vishnu), and Destroyer of the world (Shiva). This triad of gods is, once again, seen only as a functional differentiation of the highest divinity—be it Vishnu, Shiva, or the Great Goddess—which towers over, includes, and wraps around all these forms. The highest deity itself has many names and is called upon by Shivaites as "Lord" *(Tshvara)*, by the Vishnuites as "Exalted One" *(bhagavān)*, and by the Shāktas as "Goddess" *(devī)*.

Anyone who speaks of Hindu polytheism is referring to the sphere of the heavenly gods, which is still important in the Veda but was later considered lowly. At the head of these gods, the devas, is Indra. One turns to the devas for help, and one fears the asuras. But in general the heavenly gods are not classified as good or the gods of the underworld as evil. Both have their assigned tasks. Both also have the tendency on occasion to neglect their responsibilities or overstep their competency. In a way, the gods, too, are only human. They have similar joys and similar adventures. That is exactly what makes them so accessible to humans with troubles and wishes.

Strictly speaking, the devas and asuras are substantially the same as men and women. They are souls on different levels in the cycle of rebirth, but with greater capacities and powers. And if one cannot quite consort with them as equals, dealing with the gods is somewhat like dealing with benevolent, friendly kings; while the asuras are something like enemies with whom one now and then has a skirmish, but who can sometimes be induced to declare an armistice, and even form an alliance.

Only someone who has experienced the intensity of the environmental influences to which Indians see themselves exposed can understand why a crude polarity of good and evil has never developed in India. There is only good and less good. The notion of the devil has never played any appreciable role in India. Even Māra, the Buddhist tempter, and Mahāmoha, the great deceiver in medieval allegorical dramas, can be compared to the devil only in a very limited sense. The Indians learned early on that good and evil, pleasure and pain, can flow from the same source. The forces and drives in man, as well as the powers at work in nature and the cosmos, are ambivalent and can affect human life positively or negatively.

The sun god, for example, is a protector and friend of man. He brings light and life, chases away the darkness and the dangers that lurk invisibly in it. He reveals good and evil, divides day from night, and measures time.

Nevertheless, the sun is not simply kind. In the months of April, May, and June it torments the land with scorching rays. Its heat becomes unbearable. The plants wither, men and animals are parched with thirst. The sun steals the water from the last brackish water holes, and even today in many parts of India it becomes an immediate threat to life.

Finally the monsoon rains come bursting forth and redeem the languishing earth; the land turns green and blooms within a few days. But if the rains fail to appear, or arrive only a few weeks late, thousands of beasts and human beings will die.

Yet the monsoon, too, has its treacherous side. As longingly awaited and lifesaving as the rains are, they are also dangerous. Every year, newspaper and TV reports tell of their devastating consequences. In some regions the water pours in a positive deluge from the sky. It sweeps away the dried-up, cracked-open soil, gathers itself into raging torrents, wipes out the burgeoning crops, carries off huts and entire villages. Nowadays people are often rescued with helicopters, leaving behind the corpses of drowned domestic animals, devastated fields, and destroyed bridges. Man discovers that in this climate the giving of life and its annihilation go hand in hand, two sides of the same coin.

Many of the myths of India have to be seen against this ecological background: the stories of the battles between the devas and the asuras, of the threatened breakdown of the divinely established order, and of its restoration. Order is not something static. It is a balance of forces that complement each other but wreak destruction when one of them gets the upper hand over the others and rules all alone. The cosmic order was not set up with dictators in mind, not even a divine dictator.

Cosmic Time

Order is cyclical; it divides the goings-on in this world into a temporal course that regularly repeats itself. Experience teaches that there is no beginning and no end, that every destruction is followed by a new beginning. But it also teaches that the cycles are essentially asymmetrical and subject to deterioration. This asymmetry can be clearly seen in the pattern of the year. The rainy season starts in June, and the first great harvest is completed in November. This is a time of prosperity and religious feasts. There follows a period of pleasant living, the second planting and the second, less productive harvest, which ends in March. The part of the cycle when the vegetation dies off is limited to the last two and a half months.

Similarly, the cosmic process too is marked by a succession of asymmetric cycles, which in turn are caught up into ever larger ones. We can just about survey the universal cycles, which begin with a creation by the god Brahmā and end with a destruction by the god Shiva. These periods are divided, as with the Greeks, into four ages.

In the first age, when the world has come forth fresh from the creator Brahmā, and sacred knowledge has been imparted to men, the cosmic order is perfect, and the moral law stands firm and solid, like a cow on four legs. Caste differences have not yet come into being. Humans live a long time, and food is abundant. Truthfulness, kindness, humility, and generosity are prized; everyone is satisfied, gentle, and amiable. But as the origin and its purity recede into the distance, signs of decadence begin to appear. Not only do the aeons grow shorter and shorter, morality, too, continually decays, leading to social distinctions. Quarrelsomeness and viciousness become widespread. The gods fail to uphold the world order, and the asuras temporarily get the upper hand.

In such moments of danger, say the Vishnuites, the highest god, Vishnu himself, intervenes. The cyclical cosmic process is abruptly broken and dramatically altered by a unique divine intervention in history. Some of these earthly manifestations (*prādurbhāva*) or "descents" (*avatāra*) of Vishnu (and, *mutatis mutandis,* of Shiva, too) have a mythic-cosmogonic nature or celebrate a culture hero. The god embodies a part of himself in the world so as to restore the cosmic order, at least for the time being; or, as in the case of Krishna, he takes on human form without curtailing his divinity. Thus Vishnu returned the Veda to man when the gods of the underworld had robbed it, and rescued Manu, the ancestor of humanity, with a ship during the great flood. He helped the gods to whisk out the treasures hidden in the Sea of Milk, which included the Potion of Immortality, the Goddess of Luck, the Heavenly Physician, and other precious things. He was also the one who saved the earth when the princes of the underworld had seized it and were dragging it down into the depths of the ocean.

He intervened more than once when the lords of the underworld, who had become unconquerable through the power of their ascetical practices and through an act of grace by Brahmā or Shiva, were driving the gods from heaven and robbing the sacrifices offered them. For while Vishnu may be willing to grant salvation to the believing asura, he does not allow him to violate the order of the world.

The final incarnations, however—and these are the most important ones for Vishnuite *bhakti* piety—take place against a concrete historical background. This is especially true of his incarnation as Krishna, who for many Vishnuites is the only form of God at once completely accessible to man and absolutely transcendent. Krishna is a *pūrna-avatāra*, a full incarnation of the Highest in human shape.

Vishnu has become incarnate in the world nine times in the 3,893,086 years that have passed since the beginning of the present world cycle to 1984. But this served only to avert premature disaster; the cosmic degeneration has merely been slowed down. There is no way to stop it.

For present-day Vishnuites, Vishnu's appearance as Rāma and as Krishna were the most important. The one, Rāma, embodied the ideal of a ruler and left his mark, still visible today, on many aspects of Indian social ethics. *Rām Rāj*, bringing back a just rule, like that of Rāma, was the great goal of the Indian independence movement, which in the year 1947, however, brought only a divided country amid terrible bloodshed. The other manifestation of Vishnu, Krishna, became incarnate at the end of the third age, in order to kill Kamsa, a god-hating ruler, and to give men and women guidelines for the coming dark age, or rather, to provide them with a new approach to the deity.

Neither the life of Jesus nor that of Muhammad has come down to us in such detail or with so many embellishments as the life of Krishna. The circumstances of his birth, the miracles of the divine child, his youth, his tricks, his heroic deeds, and his teachings, set forth in the *Bhagavad-Gītā* as revelation, are the object of contemplation by countless Vishnuite believers. For them, Krishna is at once an authentic historical personality and a god, the time and place of whose earthly activities can be precisely indicated. And although historians do not always accept the traditional dates, and think they can recognize the features of several personalities in the traditional image of Krishna, nobody doubts that a historical Krishna did exist.

The Vishnuites, as it happens, are not alone in postulating the historicity of certain incarnations of God, although the idea of the earthly embodiment of God plays the largest role in their theology and may have also first come to full flower in Vishnuism. The Shivaites as well have recognized manifestations of their supreme god, Shiva, in historical personalities. Thus, for example, Lakulin is regarded as an incarnation of Shiva (and as such respectfully called Lakulīsha). He lived in Broach, in Gujarat, and the dissemination of his teaching by a long series of disciples is unusually well documented. Later bearers of Shivaite revelation are also considered manifestations of Shiva.

But let us return to the incarnations of Vishnu. According to Indian tradition, Krishna died shortly before the coronation of the king Parīkshit in the year 3102 B.C., with which the last of the four ages of the present world cycle began. After this, Vishnu appeared once more, as

Buddha in fact, in order (the Vishnuites claim) to confuse and weaken the demons with a false teaching. He was evidently successful, at least from the Vishnuite point of view, because the followers of Buddha actually became weaker and weaker. When Islam invaded India, they had no inner strength left to oppose it with, so that, since then, Buddhism, once so powerful in India, no longer plays any role.

Nowadays we are in the sixth millennium of the Kali Yuga, the final age. One still finds calendars in India that give the date in Kali Yuga years. This age will last another 426,914 years (counting from 1984), until the present world cycle comes to a definitive end and the earth is cleansed once more with fire, wind, and water.

Then there will be a new creation, order will be restored, and this cycle will be repeated countless times, as it has been before. Gods will come into being and pass away. Their life is relatively short, though calculated to last at least 36,000 or 38,880 years (i.e., 100 or 108 divine years). For Indra, the king of the gods, the figure is at most 306,720,000 years, assuming that his life comprises 71 great world cycles, as specified in the Brahmavaivartta-Purāna (4, 47, 100–60). But this, as the Vishnuites reckon, is no more than 48 minutes in the life of Brahmā or Shiva. When one of Brahmā's days has past, there occurs a temporary disintegration of the world and a new creation the next morning. And so it continues until Brahmā's lifetime, too, comes to an end. Brahmā is then 120 years old and reenters the cycle of births, while simultaneously a day of Vishnu ends and a night of Vishnu begins. As we measure time, more than 795 billion years have then gone by—and there are texts that say this is only the twinkling of an eye for the eternal Vishnu.

Such are the numbers that Hindu scholars juggle effortlessly. For us, of course, they have little meaning. The significant point here is the sense of time that lies behind them.

The individual person lives through this dimension of time in unending repetition until he ascends to the highest deity. The space at his disposal is also infinite; for he knows that the Creator brings forth not only our earth, sun, moon, and stars, in short our world, but countless parallel worlds as well. Like lotus flowers, they float on the endless waters on which the god Vishnu rests. Like lotus flowers, they open and close, come to be and pass away.

How did this world, or more precisely this plurality of worlds, come into existence?

THE GENESIS OF THE WORLD

The Vedic poet used various images to describe the genesis of the world. He saw the world as emanation, as procreation, and as sacrifice. He also saw it as the work of a great Arranger, who pressed apart the heavens and the earth, stretched out the sky between the trees, and fastened the stars in place. Or he saw it as the work of a craftsman, somewhat like the Bible's account of how God fashioned man from the earth. But this raises the question—as it did in India also—of where the arranger or craftsman got the material for his work. Was it already there at his side, without beginning or source? Was there some sort of primeval stuff out of which the world could have been made? Or is the Veda right to say that in the beginning there was only the One, and nothing else? (Rig-Veda X, 129, 2)

Both these rudimentary notions were followed up on and have been important factors in the debate over what the world actually is. The first idea leads to dualism of God (or souls) and the world, of consciousness and matter. The philosophical system of Sāmkhya provided the groundwork for such dualistic approaches. The second idea leads either to an identity of God and the world or to a participation by the world and all creatures in God's essence. For in that case the world has not been created by the One, but the One has brought forth the multiplicity of things through an unfolding of itself; and there is nothing in the world, no animal, plant, or stone, that is not still related in this way to its origin and hence does not participate in the one absolute Being.

Before the emergence of monotheistic and henotheistic religion, dualism was not a problematic doctrine. Only when the believer wishes to think of the Creator as the first and unique Cause and as the fullness of power, to which everything must submit, is it relevant to ask whether there can be any material for creation outside of God. The answer must be no. As far back as the creation hymn of the Rig-Veda we read that apart from the One there was nothing else in existence. If God is really unique there can be no second primordial substance "alongside" him.

One may now propose the thesis that God must have created the world out of nothing. But that in no way gets rid of the difficulty. The question now runs: Can there be alongside the absolute One a Nothing, that is, a realm not penetrated by the all-encompassing fullness of the One? That would be to restrict and limit God, and hence an argument against his claim to absoluteness.

Christians had to wrestle with this problem. But Hindus could avoid it, because with the rise of monotheism they referred back, with perfect consistency, to the passages in the Veda where the genesis of the world is ultimately thought of not as creation but as an evolutionary unfolding, and because they therefore accepted in advance the essential identity of the world and a fragment of God. God is the Other, but not the totally Other. The identity of individual and absolute consciousness is merely concealed, obscured by ignorance, and clouded by human desires, which make us cling to the appearances of the world.

BRAHMAN AND ĀTMAN

This was the great message of the Upanishads, that the individual self, called *ātman*, is identical to universal consciousness, to *brahman*, the primordial absolute One. The only thing was, the believer had to recognize this unity, had to understand that every individual being is part of the Absolute, draws his life force from it, and bears the Absolute invisibly within him. Awareness of this was supposed to lead to the fusion of *ātman* and *brahman* and overcome the division between the individual and his eternal source.

This is, historically speaking, the most abstract idea of God that has ever been conceived. It is completely unencumbered by anthropomorphic images and functional ties. *Brahman* is neuter, neither god nor goddess, without attributes, without form, without task—omnipresent and yet imperceivable. It is a transcendent being that penetrates, vivifies, and supports the world. An immortal principle within and beyond a transitory world.

It was not easy for the masters of the Upanishads to speak about the Absolute at a time when people were used to very down-to-earth gods. One could, above all, make negative statements, could say what the Absolute was not, could deny every concrete connection to worldly existence. In this respect we can see similarities between *brahman* and the Buddhist *nirvāna*, about which one can affirm nothing.

But the seers of the Upanishads were less rigorous in their caution than the Buddhists. They made, first, the positive statement that *ātman = brahman*. Second, they tried to illustrate *brahman's* effective power and omnipresence by means of similes.

Thus, for example, Uddālaka Āruni had his studious son Shvetaketu go fetch a fig and open it. Inside were many seeds. He then told him to open one of these, and to see what he could find there. But there was nothing there. Then the father said to him: "My dear, that minute essence which you cannot perceive—because of that minute essence yonder fig tree has grown so big. Believe me, my dear, this minute essence—the whole universe has it as its self *(ātman)*. That is the truth, that is the [individual] self, that art thou, Shvetaketu." (Chāndogya Upanishad 6, 12, 2–3)

Thus, the invisible but effective reality is the vital element, the essence, the self. And it joins man, in this case Shvetaketu, both with the self of the universe and with the self of all other beings, for example that of the fig tree. Part of this idea has certain parallels in Taoist teachings, but it appeared later in China than in India.

Shvetaketu did not quite get the point, and so Uddālaka Āruni tried a second comparison. He said to his son: " 'Put this piece of salt in the

water. Then come tomorrow morning and sit at my feet [for a lesson].'
He did so. Then he said to him: 'The salt that you put in the water
yesterday evening, please bring it here.' Then he grasped for it but did
not find it. It seemed to have disappeared.

" 'Please sip from the edge of this water. How is it?' 'Salty.' 'Sip from
the middle. How is it?' 'Salty.' 'Sip from the other edge. How is it?'
'Salty.' 'Now eat something, and sit at my feet again.'

"He did so, and said: 'This salty taste keeps coming back.' Then he
said to him: 'In this [experiment] indeed, my dear, you cannot see the
real, and yet it is there. This minute essence—the whole universe has it
as its self *(ātman)*. That is the truth. That is the [individual] self. That art
thou, Shvetaketu.'" (Chāndogya Upanishad 6, 13, 1–3)

Once again, we hear the famous "That art thou," which binds together individual and absolute being. To this day it shapes an important
part of Indian teachings on salvation. But we shall discuss them later.

The statements about *brahman,* it should be noted, are not limited to
comparisons. Philosophical conclusions can already be seen on the horizon in the Upanishads, and in later Vedānta doctrine they become explicit: *brahman* (as in the Upanishad text just cited) is an existing being
(sat), or as we would possibly say, pure being. For from nothingness will
come nothing. Only from actual being can existence proceed. (Chāndogya Upanishad 6, 2, 1–2)

Secondly, *brahman* is consciousness *(cit),* because consciousness is the
prerequisite for any sort of knowing, willing, and creating. *Ātman* too,
the individual self, is consciousness, and as a result, consciousness in
man establishes the connection with the deity or the Absolute. But no
consciousness could emerge from anything unconscious. The materialists quickly raised loud protests over this thesis, but they were not
heeded.

Thirdly, we can say of *brahman* that it enjoys bliss *(ānanda)* or rather *is*
bliss. Bliss is understood as the fulfillment of all wishes, since there is
nothing the Absolute does not contain in itself. We have here no dull
absence of desire, no apathy, but radiant joy, just as absolute consciousness is the glowing light of awareness.

Being, consciousness, and bliss—in Sanskrit *sat, cit,* and *ānanda*—are
brahman's three modes of existence. They are also the three modes of
existence of Vishnu and Shiva in later, monotheistic theology.

One might think that if *brahman* is the highest of all beings, then the
part of the Creator god is finished, and he must step down from the
platform. But such is not the case. Rather, with the change in perspective the question takes on a new form, and knowledge extends further. It
goes beyond the arguing back from creation to a creator, and turns to
the essence of the supreme One, the Absolute. This cannot be determined by the function of creator, but quite obviously points past it. For

the absolute One existed *before* creation, *before* the world, and must have already been perfect then. The creator aspect is, accordingly, a partial aspect that does not come to light until the One unfolds itself and becomes many. Hence the personification of the creator aspect as "the Creator" also belongs to this stage. We may now recognize this god's peculiar place in the hierarchy of existence without belittling his function and its importance.

And so the idea of a Creator is assigned to a specific stage of the process through which the Absolute unfolds itself. Here there are gods who act, who create and then destroy what they had first created. But the primordial reality, the final ground of all existence, the absolute Being does not act, does not make anything, has no "opposite number" of any sort. There is nothing in existence outside it, not even nothingness.

The One and the Many

But, then, how did the world come about? The impulse for the creation—and here Indian thinkers agree with those in the West—must have come from the will of the Absolute. The One wished to become many. But such a voluntary impetus toward creation presupposes reflection, and in the case of absolute consciousness, outside of which there is nothing, reflection can only be self-reflection.

Hence the real mystery is this first reflection. Absolute consciousness is directed toward itself, it objectifies itself, and thereby at once becomes a subject for the first time. Thus it divides itself into two parts. Then it confronts this second entity, which has emerged within itself, as a partner.

We are dealing, in other words, with a kind of self-alienation; and this self-alienation marks the starting point of creation. Once the first division and objectification has been accomplished, then it will be possible for further division, differentiation, and reflection—or union, penetration, fertilization, and reproduction—to occur.

It is not, of course, a great leap of the imagination from the primeval division and the beginning of the concretization process to a split into a male and a female half; and that is what actually happened. From this notion emerged all the myths that begin with an androgynous being which divides itself up into man and woman, thereby creating a duality. Scarcely have these two halves been separated, than they reunite. This time, however, they do not become, as before, an undifferentiated whole, but they maintain their polarity and their new disjunctive individuality. In this way, what emerges from union is not unity, but fertilization, reproduction, and multiplicity.

This conception of masculine-feminine polarity plays a decisive role with the Shivaites—their whole later theology is built upon it. That is why they placed so strong an emphasis on the teaching of the motive force of the feminine principle and hence on the importance of the mother goddess. The religion of the Shāktas has gone even further along these lines.

The Vishnuites have always viewed this interpretation as a weakness of Shivaism. For the image of man and woman may be appropriate for explaining the origin of creatures that are born into life, but it fails as soon as the question of the origin of matter arises. In addition, it obstructs the believer's vision of the unity of the Absolute, which does not really divide itself. The Absolute simply fixes its consciousness upon itself and in so doing creates an inner distance from itself, the distance that in consciousness separates subject and object, although the two continue to form a unit.

THE POWERS OF GOD AND THE WORLD AS PLAY

It is typical of the course of Indian religious history that the abstract conception of *brahman* was not only preserved in the Vedic tradition of the Vedānta, but also entered the monotheistic religions of Vishnuism, Shivaism, and Shāktism. This lends these religions their peculiar appeal: they can conceive of the highest deity as both personal and abstract. The abstract form takes priority when the divine nature is seen from the standpoint of ontology, while in the process of individual salvation the personal aspect comes to the fore.

The highest deity is basically none other than *brahman*. But by aiming the light of consciousness at itself, out of the wish to unfold itself, *brahman* becomes a subject; and from then on, all God's further unfolding of Himself is shot through with a personal quality.

It is here that God's powers—the capacity to will, know, and act—take on special importance. All three are unlimited, so that the deity is characterized by boundless free will, omnipotence, and omniscience.

Power in Sanskrit is *shakti*, a feminine noun, so that the sum of all God's capacities for unfolding Himself is interpreted in the myths of the Shivaites as a great goddess, as Shiva's female partner. But that might lead us to think that without his powers (i.e., without the Goddess) Shiva would be unable to act. That is not the way the Shivaites would have it, because Shiva and Shakti are from the outset interrelated and ultimately One. There is nonetheless a polemical pun that without Shakti Shiva is nothing but a corpse *(shava)*. And that is, in fact, one of the most momentous theses of Shāktism (related to Shivaism but clearly divergent from it), in which the Goddess stands at the center because she alone is the acting and effective principle.

With the Vishnuites, God's powers have not been given an independent status, as they have been by the followers of Shiva or the Goddess.

They still remain part of Vishnu, whose omnipotence can in no way be restricted. Vishnu has one special power, the ability to transform, to disguise, to enchant. This is part of his omnipotence, and its name is *Māyā*, illusion. Vishnu has imagination, he is a divine player, and Māyā is his partner in this game.

The term Māyā has already become naturalized in Western languages. It is often translated as "(illusory) appearance." The whole world is only appearance, say the thinkers of the Vedānta, whose monism was further elaborated out of the philosophy of the Upanishads, having its supreme flowering in the second half of the first millennium A.D.

The world is illusory appearance, insofar as it conceals the reality of *brahman*. Instead of recognizing *brahman*, man sees only a multitude of objects to which he clings. Like a mirage, Māyā deludes him with the image of a reality that he chases after but never gets to, or that, just when he thinks he has it, he cannot hold onto, because it is transitory. Just as he seems to have it in his grasp, it speeds off again, vanished, gone, melted away like a dream. Man stands alone, what he loved has slipped away from him. He has failed to find the mainstay he wanted. He has been left with nothing but grief, which he tries to forget by once more clinging to another product of Māyā, to another illusion. But only *brahman* is everlasting; only there does one find eternal rest and support, only there is ultimate reality.

The Vishnuites see things somewhat differently. To be sure, only *brahman* is eternal, which means that only Vishnu is eternal. But Vishnu is also the Only One, and Māyā, as a part of him, naturally shares in his reality. Vishnu plays by means of Māyā, and his play—be it comedy or tragedy—is what happens in the world. We may call it illusion, but this illusion has a divine origin, and its transitoriness is grounded in Vishnu's immortality.

The world made by Vishnu's Māyā contains gods and spirits, beasts and men, along with plants and things of every kind. The god Brahmā appears in it as the creator and Shiva as the destroyer, while Vishnu himself sees to its preservation. Nevertheless the cosmic and moral order staggers, and divine and human efforts to maintain it are vain. Crises are built into the system, so as to generate tensions, and the inventiveness of Vishnu and his Māyā knows no bounds.

In this game all worldly reality, physical and psychic, comes into being, out of different combinations of three qualities of Māyā, which are simultaneously three qualities of primal matter, since Māyā *is* primal matter. But the individual mind gets ensnared in the game. Human beings identify themselves with the events of their lives, and wander from birth to birth. Not until a person realizes at last that he is only attending a spectacle, that he is not in the least affected by all the doings, sufferings, and rejoicings of the creatures of this earth, will he liberate himself from the limitations imposed by illusion. He will then merge with the unclouded consciousness of the highest God, who was watching all along from outside, as a witness, so to speak, watching the actress (Māyā) and the spectators, following the action without being moved by it.

THE NATURE OF GOD

I have tried to depict the relation between God and the world with the image of a play. The same metaphor can also be found, with a few variations, in Shivaism. Still there are sharp differences between Vishnuism and Shivaism.

Vishnu is interested in the play. He plays along, he joins in. In his omnipotence he breaks the rules of the game if he feels like it, or he changes its direction. Vishnu is always present, his face turned toward the world, which is at his disposal everywhere, at all times, down to the smallest details. So he is likewise always on hand when the play of Māyā leads to seemingly hopeless situations. His incarnations are spontaneous interventions in the world of Māyā. And one more thing: Vishnu loves his creatures. He approaches them; he is a kind, occasionally roguish, but generally equable god.

Not so Shiva. He is a god of extremes, a god whose polarities move this world. On one hand, he is a god of ascetics, and an ascetic himself. Absorbed in yoga, he abides for millennia in complete self-sufficiency. He switches off. He forgets the world, trifle that it is. Only in the greatest distress, and at the risk of one's life, is it possible to jolt Shiva out of his meditation. Yet anyone who dares to do this, as Kāma, the god of love, once did, runs the danger of being immediately burned to ashes by the angry glance of the great ascetic.

But once Shiva is awake—and it must be understood, of course, that this is not a matter of temporal succession but of Shiva's power acting on a different level—he bristles with energy. His potency is as boundless as his ascetical restraint. His pulsating dance forms the world and keeps it in motion, until he finally crushes it again in even wilder, more pounding rhythms. His rage is deadly to his enemies.

In this respect, Shiva is much closer to the God of the Old Testament than is the eternally serene or mischievous Vishnu. Shiva demands recognition, demands submission, and hounds with hatred and destruction anyone who disdains him. The fear of God's wrath, which plays such a noteworthy role in Judaism, Christianity, and Islam, can also be found in Shivaism and Shaktism, but only rarely in Vishnuism.

The concept of an avenging and jealous God derives from the early history of certain religions and the social conditions under which they developed. They were all religions that had to win their independence and recognition in the face of strong resistance. But there is more to it than that. Shiva's temperament is altogether different, a priori, from Vishnu's.

Both unite in themselves and embrace all opposites, the one in the form of reconciliation and order, the other in the form of tension and synthesis.

Vishnu is a cosmic god. Countless worlds proceed from him and sink back again into him. His incarnations are always for the good of the entire world, the salvation of its cosmic and moral order, and the redemption of all humanity.

It is a different story with Shiva. He, too, is involved in cosmic activity, but not that prominently. If he destroys demons, then they are *in* human beings: lust, spiritual blindness, or ignorance. As an ecstatic and a great yogi, he shows humanity the way to overcome the world, paying no heed to cosmic or social or moral order. He shatters all three.

Shiva is radical in many ways. He shocks established society, laughs at all norms, and leaves not a value standing, with the exception of a single predominant value, namely individual salvation.

For most Shivaites, salvation means becoming one with Shiva. This can be achieved in meditation or in ecstasy—conditions that are very clearly illustrated in the myths about Shiva. In both conditions, as far as individual consciousness is concerned, the world is extinguished, consumed, destroyed. Thus Shivaites focus not on the creation but on the destruction of the world, which is Shiva's most important salvific activity. For destruction is salvation. Destruction is liberation of the soul from the chains of existence. And destruction is always merely destruction of the transitory. What is imperishable passes into Shiva.

Shivaism is consequently a radically individualistic religion of salvation. Yet, at the point where this religion of ascetics, "drop-outs," and exiles from the world joins with Vedic tradition—and that had already taken place before the Christian Era—it undergoes a peculiar transformation, because Vedic tradition has associated salvation with the word, with knowledge, and the Veda itself. Thus Shiva as Lord of the Redeemed also became the Lord of Knowledge—not only of the highest wisdom, but of logic, the arts and sciences as well. Shiva is the one who presented humanity with dance, music, the fine arts, and poetry. He, of all the gods, to whom external things mean nothing, the naked, ash-smeared despiser of the world's vanity—is the patron of aesthetics and master of the arts.

Historians would like to know the origin of Shiva's distinctive relation to the arts. The Shivaites, however, take the contradictions in Shiva's nature for granted. The moon, which he wears, in the form of a crescent, as an ornament in his hair, symbolizes death *and* life. His trident is at once a weapon of destruction and a sign of knowledge.

Given the conception of God and the world that I have described, it is no surprise that the supreme deity, the absolute *brahman*, is not called Father. Man is a part of the Absolute, not its son or daughter. Nor is Krishna the Son of God, but God himself. In the process of evolution from the deity to the world, man has, in some ways at least, left his beginnings so far behind that he doesn't feel like a son. He feels like a protégé, like a yearning lover, or like a devoted slave. Thus, if Vishnu and Shiva are occasionally invoked as Father, that refers not to a relationship with human beings based on generation or creation, but to their role as protectors and teachers of man—two functions that in Indian tradition are bound up with the father. In the genealogical sense only, Brahmā the Creator is lovingly characterized as Grandfather, because his spiritually begotten sons brought forth all living creatures at the beginning of the present world.

Only in Shāktism is the situation different. There the Great Goddess is emotionally revered as a loving, life-giving Mother. This is true even though she sometimes, in fact as a rule, turns into a furious, chastising mother. It is precisely in this that the ambivalent nature of mothers consists, as is most clearly reflected in the case of Mother Earth: She gives birth to her creatures and swallows them up again. Man is completely in her hands, and dependent on her kindness and mercy.

The god to whom Vishnuites or Shivaites turn in loving devotion is also not a judge. This is probably the most glaring difference between those faiths and Judaism, Christianity, and Islam. India, too, had the idea of the righteous ruler of the kingdom of the dead, who assigns various penalties to the sinners in hell, while the good enjoy the paradisiacal life in the palaces of his city. But this notion survived only in popular religious tradition as an incentive to ethical behavior, whereas the theology of the great theistic religions no longer had any need for the figure of the judge of the dead. From the standpoint of monistic theology, a judgment would be nonsensical; because if man is part of the Absolute, i.e., part of God, and if, secondly, the world is a game God plays; and if, besides, God is almighty, then such a judgment could only end with God's condemning himself, unless he wished to unload his own mistakes on scapegoats.

But a judgment is not only absurd, it is also superfluous—a point even the nonmonistic theologians agree on. The deity has laid down norms of behavior for man; and it knows that these norms are often violated. But it has at the same time seen to it that violating the norms brings on its own punishment. This is manifested, on a lower level, through rebirth, which can lead one into hell or the body of a worm, and which follows the law of karma, to be treated more fully in the next chapter. But even rebirth does not really constitute a punishment; it is only experience of the self in the condition that one has gotten oneself into through earlier deeds. The supreme god has nothing to do with the unsatisfactory duties of a judge.

And what about the love of God? It stands in the center of *bhakti* piety, which plays a paramount role as a way of salvation in the great Hindu religions. This, too, is a subject I shall discuss later on in more detail.

2. *Hans Küng:* A Christian Response

"Myth" literally means "story." Strictly speaking, "myths" are "sacred stories," "tales of the gods." The educated Westerner, trained to think in accord with the natural sciences and critical historiography, has immense difficulties in understanding the importance of myth for Indian society. And with reason: *mythological thought,* which is concerned with the continual intervention of supernatural powers, of gods and demigods, heroes and demons, in the course of nature and history, is basically different from *scientific thought* (whose foundations were laid in classical Greece), which takes no account of such intervention and views the course of nature and history as a continuous whole that follows its own set of laws.

For a long time, Western scholars had a hard time with myth, especially because they limited themselves, for the most part, to studying the texts of myths (particularly from Greece) out of context, as if they were mummified remains, neglecting their "Sitz im Leben" and their deeper meaning. I cannot offer here even a roughly adequate discussion of all the different theories of myth in ethnology, sociology, psychoanalysis, structuralism, literary criticism, and theology. In his detailed treatment of "The Concept of Myth from Early Christianity to the Present" *(Archiv für Begriffsgeschichte,* XXIII, 1979, 5-54, 197–245), Axel Hortmann has exploded the hopes anyone might have cherished of finding "commonly accepted definitions and theories" of the term. The problem of myth and mythology (in the sense of the totality of myths handed down by a group, a nation, or a society) will occupy us throughout the entire section on Hinduism.

THE ROLE OF MYTH IN LIFE

It is important to note, *first of all*, that contemporary Christian theology has widely recognized a structural connection between myth and its own discourse about the "reality of God." No longer does it play mythos and logos, mythology and revelation, off against each other as the lie versus the truth; nor does it necessarily subscribe to Rudolf Bultmann's program of demythologization. Nowadays we must endorse Ernst Troeltsch's remark, made in 1913, that "a great religious body [can] no more live without Logos . . . than without Mythos" (*Collected Works*, 1962, II, 817). And we readily subscribe to Karl Jaspers' effort to correct an imbalance in the debate over demythologizing the Bible: "The grandeur and the wonders of the mythological world view must be purified, but not done away with," he said in 1954, for the task with regard to the "coded language of the mythical" was precisely "to extract the pure substance of mythical thought for the apprehension of reality, to appropriate the wonderful mythic content in this mode of thought that deepens our morality, broadens our humanity, and indirectly brings us closer to the sublimity of the image-less transcendence of the divine thought which the myths never matched, which transcended them all." (*Keryga and Myth*, 1954, III, 19–20)

A *second* important consideration is that Christian theology, thanks to the work of ethnologists such as James Frazer, psychologists such as Wilhelm Wundt, and sociologists such as Émile Durkheim, can recognize the close link between myth and ritual on one hand and social structures on the other. The truth of this has been brought into sharp focus by the intensive field work among primitive peoples, often lasting many years, by such anthropologists as Bronislaw Malinowski, who analyzed the original role of myth in the concrete life of the people.

Today we know that the myths (which, as "sacred stories," whose protagonists are the gods, must be distinguished from both fairy tales, on the one hand, and historical accounts, legends, and sagas, on the other) vouch for the antiquity, wisdom, and holiness of certain rites and ceremonies, as well as for moral and social rules. In this way, within the context of living faith, they are extremely effective in shaping and regulating moral and social behavior. That is how, according to Malinowski, the function and power of myth is to be understood: "Studied alive, myth . . . is not symbolic, but a direct expression of its subject matter; it is not an explanation in satisfaction of scientific interest, but a narrative resurrection of a primeval reality, told in satisfaction of deep religious wants, moral cravings, social submissions, assertions, even practical requirements. Myth fulfills in primitive culture an indispensable function: it expresses, enhances, and codifies belief; it safeguards and enforces reality; it vouches for the efficiency of ritual and contains practical rules for the guidance of man. Myth is thus a vital ingredient of human civilization; it is not an idle tale, but a hard-worked active force; it is not an intellectual explanation or an artistic imagery, but a pragmatic charter of primitive faith and moral wisdom." ("Myth in Primitive Psychology," in *Magic, Science, and Religion* [New York, 1954], p. 101)

Regardless of whether these "sacred stories" tell about the genesis of the gods or the world, about the salvation of man or the world, or about its end—i.e., whether we are dealing with theological or cosmogonic, soteriological or eschatological myths—myth does not try to entertain, as a fairy tale does. It does not try to inform, the way a historical report does. The gods of the Hindu pantheon, therefore, should not be made light of, as if they were fantastic figures out of the Grimm brothers; nor should they be objectified as historical personalities. Myth aims to express an older, greater, more original reality, which determines the entire life, work, and destiny of the human race. Yet myth does not seek to provide either a conclusive explanation or mere poetic interpretation of that reality. And psychological or psychoanalytic readings that look upon myths as individual and collective experiences of the religious consciousness, generally set their sights too low. Rather, myth tries—in a nonhistorical, nonconceptual, graphic, personalizing fashion—to open up this greater reality existentially, and so impart a *direction in life*, and—through ritual performance—to offer a share in the reality's *saving power*.

Myths are enormously important for the understanding of Indian literature, sculpture, painting, music, and, of course, personal piety. They are not, however, "prescribed" articles of faith, as faith in God and his messenger is in Christianity and Islam. That is significant: They can preserve the contents of belief, but they are not a creed for Hindus. The numerous powers of the gods, combined with the vivid imaginativeness of the stories, and the motley qualities of the lower cults—all this began to raise questions early on, in India as well as Greece.

MONISM OR DUALISM?

In ancient Greece, myths penetrated deeply into human life, in ritual, customs, and social structures—a bewildering, contradictory variety of narratives about the gods. As far back as the Pre-Socratics, thinkers took offense at these human, all-too-human divine figures. Should gods be like human beings, at once good and evil? Isn't God good, *the* Good? Isn't there a single Entity at the origin of all things?

Around the year 500 B.C., the comic poet and satirist Xenophanes, as is well known, first charged Homer's gods with being projections and exposed them to ridicule. More than a century later, Plato demythologized the capricious, good-natured/bad-natured Homeric gods and discerned behind them all the one, unique, eternal, divine idea of the Good as the primordial principle, the spiritual sun. Finally, in the 3rd century A.D., the great Alexandrian philosopher Plotinus carried Plato's ideas further in the direction of religious/mystical experience. He believed that the sole highest reality was "the One," which transcends all concepts—the eternal sun that released from within itself the world of ideas, the world soul, and last of all the sensory world. The souls confined in the sensory world should liberate themselves from it through asceticism and knowledge, so as to be reunited with the divine One.

The divine One: On this subject it seems that European/Greek and Asiatic/Indian thought display amazing parallels. As in Greece, so in India, mythology is only one aspect of religion. There is at the same time immersion in the depths of philosophical and religious meditation, experience of the one divine Being. As early as the Vedas, Professor von Stietencron has told us, we hear about the One, aside from which, in the beginning, there existed nothing at all; the One that the Upanishads see as the divine primordial foundation, the source and goal of all beings: Brahmā.

The relation of Brahmā to the world can be conceived of in three ways. All three are based on the Vedic "revelation" (*shruti*, in Sanskrit) of the early "seers" and, because of their revealed character, are not considered simply "natural theology." Although their broad thrust had already developed beforehand, they became and have remained associated with three great names and schools from the religious history of India. As opposed to Buddhism and Jainism, they have held fast to the authority of the Vedas and could be called classic positions. They are not philosophical speculation or metaphysics, but theology, doctrines of salvation, religion.

FIRST POSITION: *Brahmā and the world are wholly one.* In the latter part of the eighth and the early part of the ninth centuries, the most famous of all Indian thinkers was active in the service of the Brahmanic restoration. Shankara (supposedly 788–820) was not simply a philosopher, but a profound religious mystic, reformer, founder of a religious order, and champion of Hindu unity. (Although strongly influenced by Buddhism, he was anti-Buddhist.) To this day, Shankara has a large following, especially among Indian intellectuals. His simple, comprehensive system is often falsely presented in the West as the one and only Indian theology. At the heart of Shankara's thought are the possibility and reality of redemption of ignorant man through knowledge—redemption through discovery of the One, of the unity of the human soul (ātman) with Brahmā. A mystic par excellence, Shankara interpreted the Upanishads, the Bhagavad-Gītā, and the Brahmā Sutras (in other words, the fundamental Hindu texts) to contain a "pure," consistent, absolute "doctrine of oneness" (*a-dvaitam* = non-duality).

According to Shankara, the prerequisite for true knowledge is the distinguishing of two levels of truth. On the level of ordinary empirical truth there are, of course, many things and many separate selves. But this naive kind of knowledge is deceptive. On the level of the higher, metaphysical truth, all the various selves are one with the absolute Self: "That art thou." Only the One really exists, the truly real, outside of which there is no true reality, the eternal, infinite Brahmā, which is at once pure Being (*sat*), cognitive consciousness (*cit*), and overflowing bliss (*ānanda*), but which can be known only through holistic mystical experience. In the mystical experience of unity, our individual self, the ātman, is known for what it is: only another aspect of the absolute Self, Brahmā. And we see through the world, realizing that it is pseudo reality, a great cosmic illusion, Māyā, which only a person in the unredeemed state of ignorance and greed mistakes as real. In this illusory world (and only here) Brahmā reveals itself as a personal God with distinct qualities: as the "Lord" (*īshvara*), who as pure light amid the darkness periodically sends forth the world from within himself, preserves and rules it, and finally takes it back. Since all multiplicity is only appearance anyway, this God can be worshipped under various names, as Vishnu, Shiva, etc. And so Shankara also wrote religious hymns. There are indeed differing degrees of truth, but only through higher knowledge of the All-One (not through ritual or ethical activity) does man reach redemption.

SECOND POSITION: *Brahmā and the world are wholly separate.* Shankara had a fanatical opponent, a sharp-witted interpreter of the basic texts (who found quite contrary—and often arbitrary—meanings in them) and, like himself, a good organizer. This was Madhva (1199–1278), who originated the Madhvas, a religious movement that still exists. For Madhva the world is completely real. It is created, preserved, ruled, and then destroyed by Vishnu, who is the one and only God, who is also being, consciousness, and ecstasy in one. God is thus the architect of the universe, an efficient cause, and no more. He has not, as Shankara maintains, transformed himself into this faulty, imperfect world (as if he were its material cause as well). Instead, the difference between God and the world is utterly real, like the difference between God and the individual soul, one soul and another, animate and inanimate beings. Madhva, therefore, proposes a radical dualism (*dvaita*) as against Shankara's monism (*a-dvaita*).

But there are obvious objections to both dualism and monism. Is there no way of avoiding the difficulties of these extreme positions? Isn't there a third possibility?

UNITY IN DIFFERENCE—FROM AN INDIAN STANDPOINT

There is, in fact, a THIRD POSITION: *Brahmā and the world are one amid their diversity.* Shankara's antagonist and equal, Rāmānuja (ca. 1056–1137), influenced all of India's spiritual life more than Madhva or any other Vishnuite theologian. Unlike Madhva, he did not disown the Vedānta or the doctrine of unity developed from the philosophy of the Upanishads. But he understood them differently from Shankara, in whose system he had been raised. Rāmānuja, too, was a brilliant mystical thinker and reformer, a founder of monasteries, temples, and an order for Untouchables that still exists. He, too, was primarily concerned with redemption. But he interpreted the Upanishads, the *Bhagavad-Gītā,* and the Brahmā Sutras as a philosophical realist, refuting Shankara's idealism right down the line. All human perception, he argued, cannot simply be declared an illusion because of occasional errors. The whole world and everything in ordinary life that we take to be real cannot be illusory. As a matter of fact, such a view finds no support in the older Upanishads.

It is true that, like Shankara, Rāmānuja believes that Brahmā is "without second" ("no secondness = *a-dvaitam*"); but not that it is without characteristics, attributes, or personality. Rāmānuja's crucial insight is that *Brahmā is identical with the personal God.* As against Shankara, for whom all good works, adoration, and divine services are part of the illusory world of appearances, Rāmānuja finds worship of a personal God and mystical union with him clearly expressed as far back as the Upanishads. On the strength of that, he reinstates *bhakti,* the trusting, loving, worshipping devotion to God. Brahmā is none other than the personal God who from eternity releases the world from within himself, upholds it, directs it internally, and takes it back again.

But precisely for this reason, Brahmā (God) is essentially distinct from matter and the individual soul: Brahmā and ātman, Brahmā and the world, contrary to what Shankara says, must be distinguished. Statements of identity from the Upanishads ("That art thou"; Brahmā = ātman; Brahmā = the world) are to be given an altered interpretation: as unity in diversity. God and the world are in fact one, but as soul and body are one. And this God, possessed as he is of all good qualities, stands in unconditional opposition to everything wicked: not only to finitude and pain, but to evil. He is decidedly not beyond good and evil, but is himself the supreme good and highest goal of human piety. In comparison with Shankara's pantheism, his absolute "pure" monism, Rāmānuja advocates an equally comprehensive but theistic monism, so that his school is also called *vishishtadvaita* = "qualified no-secondness."

CREATION FROM NOTHING?

There are, as we know, certain parallels in the West to these three possible relations between the Absolute and the world. Western thinkers, too, have presented *monistic views* of God and the world. First came the Ionian philosophers of nature, who tried to explain the origin of the world from a single principle (primal matter). Parmenides, like Shankara, thought there was only a single, unchangeable Being, in contrast with which all coming into being and passing away of individual beings is pure semblance. Since that time, the striving for unity, which seems to be an intrinsic part of the human mind, has again and again produced monistic systems. Some of them (from ancient atomic theory to modern materialism) are materialistic, but the majority, as in India, have been spiritualistic; e.g., in the Christian Middle Ages the teachings of Amalric of Bena and David of Dinant, in the modern period the much more influential current represented by Giordano Bruno and Spinoza, all the way down to German idealism and beyond. This is a monism whose religious mode was pantheism and whose piety was mysticism.

While the climate of mystical religion in the West generally favored monistic tendencies, that of prophetic religions fostered *dualism.* Even though early Jews and Christians never sought, as in Persian Mazdaism or Manichaeism, to explain the existence of good and evil by postulating two primordial principles, one good, the other evil, there were trends (closely connected to belief in demons) toward placing an extraordinary stress on opposition between God and Satan, God and the world. Along with this usually went the conflict between spirit and matter, soul and body, good and evil, light and darkness. In early Judaism this dualism grew out of Persian influences; in early Christianity the sources were Jewish and Greek.

Greek philosophy as a whole was clearly inclined toward dualism, and its impact was felt well into the modern period (affecting Descartes, Kant, not to mention Kierkegaard and the young Karl Barth). The same cannot be said about *Christianity* as a whole. On the contrary, under the influence of both the Old and the New Testaments, Christian theology from the beginning reacted *against the dualism of classical Greek metaphysics.* As the Fathers of the Church saw it, Greek philosophy had rightly carried the day against the anthropomorphic pantheon of the Homeric myths, but in so doing it had overemphasized the difference between God and the world, the divine and the human. For this reason, Christian thought had to criticize both Plato's momentous dualistic separation of the false, material world of becoming from the true, spiritual world of being, and, still more, Aristotle's God, who as the first, unmoved Mover lives alongside the world without any real relation to it, merely thinks himself, and so neither knows nor loves the world. Finally, Christian theologians also had to correct the idea of the divine One advanced by the Neo-Platonist Plotinus. The One was wholly removed from a world (and here there must have been Eastern, perhaps even Indian, influences at work in Alexandria) that has overflowed and poured out from the fullness of the Primal One. The world here is understood as a fall from the heights of God; matter, the body, is seen as bad, something from which the spiritual soul of man must free itself.

Mainstream Christian theologians, guided by both the idea of creation ("and behold, it was very good") and by Christology and soteriology (in Christ, God has become radically committed to this world), have always managed to rebuff a dualistic interpretation of the world. The very notion of *God's creation of the world* did not permit an a priori depreciation of the world, matter, or the body. Needless to say, Genesis 1:1 and the Vedas agree that the world was created from a kind of primordial matter and not from nothing. In the Bible, creation "from nothing" (*ex nihilo*) is a relatively late notion, the result of intense Christian theological reflection. On this point, classical Christian theology is in complete agreement with Indian thinkers: Outside of God there was no second primal being, no "domain" that God had to penetrate, no "space" that confined God, as the creation hymn of the Rig-Veda rightly says.

"Nothing" should not be thought of as something actually existent. Nothingness is not a "domain," like that of darkness, for example. Nor is it "something" that might be able to limit the Absolute. Creation *ex nihilo*, therefore, does not mean an independent status for nothingness or a competing principle ranged alongside God. It is a theological formula for the belief that the world and humanity, space and time, have no other cause but God for their existence. And since God is the origin of each and every thing, he faces no competition from an evil or demonic counterprinciple (as he would in Mazdaism or Manichaeism): According to the biblical account of creation, the world in general and in particular, including matter, the human body, and sexuality—is fundamentally good.

Like all three classical Indian schools, Christian theology accepts a first and single cause of everything that is. This would put it in a middle position between the monism of Shankara and the dualism of Madhva, that is, in the same place as Rāmānuja, who, together with Shankara, is India's most important theologian. This middle position can be summarized in thesis form, as follows:

- The world should not be understood as God's *emanation* (as the product of an evolving deity) in such a way that we must speak of the *identity* of God and the world, as in Shankara's monism and Western pantheism. Rāmānuja's criticism of Shankara must be taken seriously.

- The world should also not be understood as God's *creature* in such a way that we must assume a strict *duality* of the world and man (spirit and matter), as in the teaching of Madhva (and Western dualism).
- Instead, Christian theology ascribes to God a basic relationship with the world, and to the world a basic *participation in the divine Being,* in the dynamic Being that is God. God is immanent in the world precisely because he transcends the world. The reality of the world is not autonomous, and neither is it only apparent, but relative. This is identity in duality (as Rāmānuja would have it).

In Christianity, too, time and again, negative dualistic tendencies have met with some success, prompted by anxiety (widespread in both East and West) over defilement through matter, the body, and the senses. Nevertheless, Christians have always regarded the world, in principle, as God's good creation: the world and man, which can only exist as real beings insofar as they share in the Being Itself *(ipsum esse)* that is God. This was the teaching of *Scholasticism,* which took up the Platonic-Neo-Platonic-Augustinian line of argument and adjusted it.

UNFOLDING CREATION

Other Christian thinkers went still further and came much closer to Indian beliefs. According to Meister Eckhart, for instance, God creates the world and humanity *in himself,* and God's own being spreads itself out into all things so that in the "depths of the soul" the mystic can experience the underlying unity of everything in existence with God. As Nicholas of Cusa sees it, God's superabundance contains *all opposites in itself,* so that God is at once the greatest and the least, center and periphery, past and future, light and darkness, even Being and non-Being. But opposites that are one in God go their separate ways in the world, which is to be understood as the *explicatio Dei,* the *unfolding of God,* who is himself the Many without multiplicity and difference in identity. This idea led straight to German idealism and to Hegel, as well as to Whitehead and Teilhard de Chardin.

The Christian theologian will not be prepared to travel so far down the road of mysticism and will have justified misgivings, especially toward Hegel's identification of God and the world, faith and knowledge. But nowadays even he, or she, can start out from an *"holistic"* understanding of reality and affirm the following:

Even though God is not the world, nor the world God, yet God is *in* this world, and this world is *in* God.

God must not in any event be considered only a part of reality, as a finite being (howsoever exalted) alongside other finite beings.

Rather, God is the One in the many, the Infinite in the finite, Transcendence in immanence, the Absolute in the relative.

There is no way to talk about God here except in paradoxes, in a *coincidentia oppositorum*. As Bonhoeffer said, "God is the Beyond amidst our lives." This strikes me as an understanding of the God for modern times and the world at large. Not only does it tally with the contemporary scientific world picture, but it also seems appropriate to the still more uniform pattern of Indian thinking: a *God both immanent in and superior to the world*, a God who as the bearer, maintainer, and companion of the world is simultaneously the depth, the center, and the height (images all) of the world and man. Precisely because God is this way, he can justly be called the creator, conserver, and completer of the world. That is why Christian thinkers have understood God's creative nature as his vitality and the power of his being, as the fullness of his self-giving to the other, the world. Christians see this process, in the deepest sense, as love.

In this way, I believe, we can come to an understanding of the relation between God and the world that (a) is neither mythological and anthropomorphic nor abstract and overintellectual, that (b) unites religion and philosophy (which in both India and the West are threatening to come permanently apart), and that (c) *avoids a monism* which rates the world as nothing but illusion and fleeting appearances, as well as a *dualism* which views the world as all too autonomous and detached from God. Positively speaking,

- The *world* should be thought of as *God's creation* in such a way that the creator does not remain outside his work. Instead, creation can be understood as *God's unfolding* in the world, without the world dissolving into God or God into the world, without the world surrendering its autonomy or God vanishing into the world. Thus we would have creation as a process of unfolding, or unfolding through creation. No being would be made into God, but neither would it exist outside God and be added to him.

- *God* is to be thought of as the omnipresent, ineffable *mystery of this world*, a mystery that embraces the origin of its being, its becoming, its order, and its goal, such that man and the world are neither independent of God nor a mere illusion, but a relative reality. Neither undifferentiated identity of God and the individual soul, nor a permanent distinction between them, but the difference dialectically "sublated" in identity.

I wonder whether on this basis we might not have a dialogue with Hindus about the nature of God. The above position seems to correspond closely to the classic Indian *via media* of Rāmānuja, which is probably the main current in Vishnuism today. My point can be elucidated by looking into an especially difficult question:

IS GOD PERSONAL OR IMPERSONAL?

We must not overlook the fundamental difference between mystical and prophetic religion. Both in Hinduism and Christianity there is a tension between the personal and the impersonal modes of understanding God.

However much *the Hindu religions*, ever since the time of the Upanishads, have taken the one, all-encompassing Brahmā to be the final reality to which man has access only through mystical absorption, this belief has nonetheless remained bound up with an abundance of anthropomorphic, personalistic myths. And however much Brahmā is the key to ontological reflection on the nature of God even in the monotheistic religions of Vishnuism, Shivaism, and Shaktism, these very faiths have stressed God's personal relation to humanity in the work of redemption.

By the same token, Christian theology does not limit its discourse to anthropomorphisms, of which we find such a rich assortment in the Bible. It also speaks of God as the hidden One *(latens deitas),* as the elusive deity *(divinitas),* the highest good *(summum bonum),* Being Itself *(ipsum esse),* truth, goodness, and beauty itself *(veritas, bonitas, pulchritudo ipsa).* And it knows of the Ineffable, the Mystery, which it attempts to grasp symbolically with the use of comparisons, metaphors, and images such as sea, ocean, wilderness, or sun, light, and fire. Christian theology likewise gives a thoroughly dialectical answer to the question of God's personality, so as to avoid crude objectification. The following three points might well win the approval of Hindus:

1. The one God is *not masculine or feminine;* he is *not a person* the way a human being is. The all-encompassing and all-penetrating One is not an object, "about" which a man might make statements from a superior distance. There is no standpoint "beyond" God, from which a person could pass judgment on the One that embraces all things. What we call the primal Ground, Support, and Goal of all reality cannot be represented as "a god" or "a goddess" beneath (or above) others. He can in no way be an individual person among other persons, nor a Super-man nor a Super-ego. Even the term "person," like the name "Father" or "Mother," is a mere encoded approximation to the highest/deepest reality, which is in fact a nonduality.

2. But can we think of the one God, who is the source of personality, as himself wholly *impersonal?* Evidently not. God is *not neuter,* either. Precisely because God as the ground and purpose of all reality is not a "thing," and cannot be seen through, disposed of, or manipulated, *neither* can God be *impersonal* or, still less, *subpersonal.* This means that he shatters the concept of the nonpersonal, because he is also not less than a person. In the Hindu view the primordial One, or Brahmā, is at the same time, universal consciousness, to which real powers are ascribed: an unlimited capacity to know (omniscience), to will (absolute freedom), and to act (omnipotence).

3. God as the primal reality, therefore, *comprises* the masculine, feminine, and neuter, the personal and the impersonal. In him *all the contradictions* of the created human world are "sublated" *(aufgehoben)* in the triple Hegelian sense: affirmed (conserved), denied (relativized), and overcome (transcended). Thus God is in fact *the Other,* and *not the totally Other,* as Karl Barth increasingly recognized in his later theology, when he began to speak more about the "humanity of God."

Hinduism and the tradition of Christian negative theology seem to me to agree that this primordial/ultimate reality must first of all be described negatively, but by no means only negatively. We are dealing, it must be remembered, with the all-penetrating, all-vivifying divine reality, hence the *realest reality (satyasya satyam* = "the real of the real" = *ens realissimum),* which Indian thinkers rightly conceive of as pure being *(sat)* cognitive consciousness *(cit),* and radiant bliss *(ānanda)*—three essential predicates, not three persons, as in the postbiblical doctrine of the Trinity. This is, in short, the pure Self, which inhabits our individual selves and, in the final analysis, constitutes all other beings. If the reader insists on a special term, Paul Tillich's "transpersonal" would be preferable to personal or impersonal, and his "transsexual" to sexual or nonsexual. God is, as it were, the "personification" of the divine.

THE WORLD AS GOD'S PLAY?

But that does not settle the issue of myth and demythologizing. We shall have to return to it after, having discussed the problems surrounding the world and the deity, we give due attention to those surrounding man and redemption. Yet, since we have heard so much, in the language of mythology, about Vishnu's playing with world as *Māyā,* I would like to point out, by way of conclusion, that one can also speak quite nonmythologically about God's playing with the world. I am referring to a contemporary paradigm of Christian (and possibly Hindu) theology that takes seriously the findings of modernity and the natural sciences, and yet goes beyond them in a postmodern "second naïveté" (Paul Ricoeur).

It has already been noted that *demythologizing can in no way mean removing all images from the language,* be it of Christianity or of Hinduism. There is no reason why images, allegories, symbols, or metaphors for God's activity in the world have to be myths. I can use an image in a basically mythological or nonmythological fashion. I take the image or metaphor of God's playing with the world *in a mythic sense* when I use it to assert an objectively observable "intervention" ("coming between") by God, which takes place miraculously *between* worldly events. I take the same image *nonmythologically* when I apply it to God's real but hidden activity, which takes place in a marvelous manner *in* worldly events, so that it can be perceived only by the believer, while it remains concealed from the objective observer. It is in this second sense that I would have the reader understand the image or metaphor of God's playing with the world.

We must first realize that an interpretation of the world and its laws as a "game" is not at all foreign to present-day *scientific thought*. The Nobel Prize winner for biology Manfred Eigen and Ruthild Winkler in their book *The Game* (1975) point to the variables, in all their possible permutations, that govern the course of natural and human history, as they show that man did not invent play. Play is a phenomenon of nature that has guided the evolution of the world from the very beginning, from the formation of matter and, still more, its organization into living structures, all the way to human social behavior. The basic elements of play, "chance and necessity" (Jacques Monod), determine everything that happens in the universe, without the need of a God to intervene in the natural course of things at any point of the process. Equilibrium, growth, and evolution are the result of law and accident: "Everything that occurs in our world is like a great game, in which there is nothing laid down in advance except the rules." (Eigen and Winkler, *The Game: Natural Laws Directed by Chance*, p. 11)

Scientists today, however, will also admit that scientific knowledge does not get past a certain level of reality in the world and man. In and of itself, it can neither affirm nor deny the reality of God. But anyone (even a scientist) who commits himself to faith or confidence in this reality can recognize the fact that in the interplay of the forces of nature and history, God's reality is playing along. *Christian theology*, too, is familiar with the category of play as a symbol for the world. In his book *Man at Play* (1952), which was prompted by Thomas Aquinas and the pioneering work *Homo Ludens* (1938), by the Dutch cultural historian Johan Huizinga, patrologist Hugo Rahner devotes a brief but impressive chapter to the idea of a "God at play," *deus ludens*. This notion is quite in the spirit of the Greeks and the Fathers of the Church (Plato called man a *paígnion theou*, a "toy of God." In recent times, Protestant theologian Jürgen Moltmann has once again taken up this theme. Working from a theological vision of the world as God's creation and of God's inalienable freedom vis-à-vis the world, he qualifies God's relationship to his creation as a game played out of "delight" (not necessity or whim): "For this reason creation is a game of God's, the play of his bottomless, unfathomable wisdom. It provides free play for the unfolding of God's magnificence." *(The First Freedmen of the Creation,* 1971, p. 24)

If we consider these fundamental scientific and theological ideas together, the following theological maxim must hold: The whole great game is *God's playing with and for the world,* with and for man. God himself started the game off, determining nothing in advance except the rules: The world, though it does not play games with God, is to be maintained and governed by him; its own game of chance and necessity may proceed. Man, however, is to be not God's toy, but his free partner in the game.

Would it be possible for Hindu theology to think of God's play in such nonmythological terms? If so, the image of the god Vishnu playing with the world would then exemplify an impressive pictorial-symbolic statement about the way God deals with a world—untrammeled yet intensely involved, cheerful, earnest, and active. In any case, a nonmythological Christian reading of the world as play presupposes a God who does not use man and creation as material for his game, but accepts them as partners. God can also reach his goal without any miracle that breaks the chain of causality. He can likewise "address" (analogously speaking) and, in that (not "supernatural" but "intranatural") sense, he can "intervene."

At the same time, the Christian vision of the world as play further assumes a creation that is not mere illusion and a human race that has not fallen prey to gross deception and will not have to wait till the end to be freed from the bonds of illusion. To be sure, Christian thought is also aware that man has often enough been not simply a free partner in the game but an unwilling victim of it. He has often enough not been a player himself, but has been played with—vilely. And the basic law of evolution—natural selection of the strong, who survive, at the cost of the weak, who go under—is a cruel game that can teach us to wonder and shudder simultaneously. Its pitilessness has turned people of deep Christian faith, like Reinhold Schneider *(Winter in Vienna,* 1958) into doubters of God's goodness. But Christian faith is rooted in the certainty afforded by Jesus of Nazareth that God is not a capricious player "up in heaven," playing games with man and the world, but a sympathetic lover of humanity, who has affirmed man and the world and so bound himself to laws on which all things are founded and which in turn are founded on him. Still, the question of human suffering and divine justice, the problem of theodicy, will be left open here. We shall have to come back to it later.

III.
Man and Salvation in Hindu Religions

1. *Heinrich von Stietencron:* Hindu Perspectives

WHERE DOES HUMAN INEQUALITY COME FROM?

People have different opinions about what the essence of man is, what makes him different from other creatures. The oldest Indian definition of the human being that I know of derives from the late-Vedic period of the Brahmanas and says, "Man is the only animal that offers sacrifices."

An interesting statement. The crucial difference between human beings and other earthly creatures is taken to be not man's upright gait, the formation of the jawbones, not even superior intelligence or the possession of instruments of power like weapons and fire, but a specific kind of behavior, namely the active partnership and communication with God or gods. This viewpoint has remained substantially unchanged in India. Man is different from other living beings not in his nature, but in his relation to God.

I spoke earlier of the development of the One into the many, and of the ultimate identity of individual and absolute consciousness. This identity applies to all conscious life, not only in humans but also in animals and plants. But then, how explain the limitations of individual consciousness? What hampers it so that it normally does not recognize the unity of all being?

In order to answer this question, one must first realize how human perception operates. And in so doing we immediately come up against the next problem: Why are people so different, anyway? There can be no doubt that they are born with different makeups. They have different physical and intellectual abilities, different interests, different characters, different appearance, degrees of health, sociability, responsiveness, etc. And even where they seem to be of a similar predisposition, they are born into different conditions of life, castes, and families. They do not have the same chances or get the same education. They are rich or poor, meet good fortune or bad.

Indian thinkers did not simply accept unquestioningly the idea that these differences are created and willed by God. They wanted to understand why man is the way he is. For if all beings have the same absolute consciousness in them, if the one universal brahman is present in all beings as ātman, and all share in the same way in the divine Being, then one has to explain where the differences come from. And these questions carry still more weight if animals and plants are included with humanity.

Neither the environment nor genetics offers a satisfactory explanation for the phenomenon of individual differences. Because even if one assumes that they correctly describe the causes and effects, they do not answer the question of meaning at all.

Why does it befall one man that he is blind, deaf, or crippled from birth, or that he must be shunned by his fellows and agonize in a leprous body? Why do others enjoy life in health and prosperity? What principle determines how happiness or suffering, talent or stupidity, birth into a rich or a poor family, into a human or animal existence is allotted to individual beings? Is Providence, or blind destiny, in control here?

An attempt was made to think both possibilities through. But, given an all-encompassing consciousness, given the omnipotence and omniscience of a supreme god, there was in the long run no room for blind destiny. And if this deity is conceived as pure being *(sat)*, as unlimited awareness *(cit)*, and as bliss *(ānanda)*, then it becomes difficult to deduce from it a Providence that cruelly and cynically forces creatures into a tormented existence.

That is why the educated upper classes in all great Hindu religions are sure that the qualitative differences in the fate of individual persons (with all the pain, the injustice, the physical, psychic, and social inequality this implies) cannot be blamed on the deity: It could not contain such wickedness. The qualitative differences must have been acquired by the creatures themselves.

Yet it is also clear that they do not emerge only after birth, as a result, say, of external influences. Rather, they are already present, most of them, at the child's conception, in the form both of hereditary traits and of the social milieu into which it will be born. Thus if the individual soul exercises an influence on its own destiny, this can only have happened in a previous existence. What it experienced and suffered there, but also what it did there and did unto others, makes itself felt in the new life.

And what it now does or neglects to do will determine the quality of its next existence.

The Hindus speak in this connection of *karma*. Karma that has accrued from earlier lives, they say, decides both the physical and the psychic qualities of the individual creature and the environmental conditions to which it is exposed in the new birth. The word "karma" is derived from a verb root meaning "do, act." In general it designates what results from doing something: the act, the work, in particular the work of offering sacrifice, but also the inner psychic consequences of an act that are as yet invisible and will appear only in the future.

Various stages in the evolution of this concept might be shown, but I can mention only one of them here. The law of karma decrees that every act and every omission—insofar as it is due to ignorance, self-centeredness, sensual appetite, or laziness—has an internal as well as an external effect. It leaves behind a psychic change or an impression that programs future experience. Opinions differ to some extent on how this happens, because of the different notions Hindus have of the human soul.

THE SOUL AND REBIRTH

Educated Hindus believe in the existence of a subtle substance, called *jīva* or *jīvātman*, that migrates from life to life. If we should translate this word as "soul," we must remember that it is not spiritual but a finespun bodily entity. Only ātman can be considered spiritual, the individual consciousness, which does, however, unite with the *jīva*, so long as it lingers in the cycle of births.

Buddhists and materialists have doubted that this *jīva* survives the death of the body. In the major Hindu religions, though, the existence of the *jīva* is held to be proved, for several reasons:

● First, it can be perceived in contemplative vision.
● Second, a very advanced yogi can remember his earlier births, so there must be something in him that preserves the experiences of earlier lives.
● Third, the doctrine of reincarnation, as the basis for human differences, makes moral sense, confirming divine norms and enabling divine justice, only if there is a continuity and so, too, a possibility for individual development in a number of lives.

The *jīva* contains (here I cite as an example a Shivaite conception based on ideas of Sāmkhya) among other things a subtle aggregate of conditions of perception, the so-called "inner instrument" *(antahkarana)*. This instrument stores up all perceptions and sensations, conscious and unconscious. It accumulates not only sense impressions and the record of thoughts, but also the imprints left by one's own actions—in a word, karma.

In addition, the structural conditions of the "inner instrument" limit and alter our perception in a decisive fashion.

First, they cause all perceptions to be punctually registered and to be opposed, as objects of sense, to consciousness as the knowing subject. In this way, the same thing takes place on the individual level that I have already described as the fundamental principle in the unfolding of the One, namely the separation of subject and object.

Secondly, they arrange the objects according to the categories of time (*kāla*) and causality (*niyati*), so that, instead of a comprehensive intuition, the impression arises in consciousness of one thing succeeding another, and the unity of existence is reduced to a sequence of causal dependencies. The series of objects, of course, is passed on to the knowing subject's capacity to understand and to act. Instead of comprehensive knowledge, it records only moments of partial cognition (*vidyā*), and instead of an unlimited capacity for action it has only limited spheres of action (*kalā*).

Thirdly and lastly, the objects are colored by being assigned emotional qualities (rāga), so that bonding or rejection, love or hate, arises.

The conditions of perception just described are responsible for the ego experience of human beings, and hence they are usually gathered together under the heading of *ahamkāra*, "the I-maker." They lead us to distinguish between ourselves and our environment, between "I" and "you" and all the beings and things that surround us. Because we make these distinctions and overlay things with emotional qualities, we see them as beautiful and ugly, desirable and repulsive. We lust to possess what is beautiful and pleasant, and to unite ourselves with it. We feel horror, disgust, and hatred toward what displeases us. The awareness of mine and thine leads to greed and envy. We desire what we don't have; we cling to what we do have; we act so as to obtain what we lack. We suffer when we don't get what we want; we fight to win or defend a possession; and we suffer once more when we can't hold on to what we have, because all possessions prove to be transitory and run through our fingers.

Egoism develops out of ego. If there were no *ahamkāra*, no "I-maker" in our psychic instrument, there would be no separation of subject and object and so no objects "out there" at all. If there were no objects seen at a distance from us, there would be no desires. If there were no desires, we would not cling to things or strive for power or tie ourselves up emotionally and intellectually in the world of material appearances. *Ahamkāra* is thus responsible for the fact that we coordinate people and things around ourselves, so that we say, "my" child, "my" wife, "my" friends; or "my" horse, "my" money, "my" role in society.

If we believe, as most Indian thinkers do, in the existence of a finespun "soul substance," which wanders from birth to birth till it finally dissolves, then we can imagine the psychic effect of karma as a factor that alters the quality of this subtle substance and of the psychic organs built into it. According to the teaching of Sāmkhya, which on this point has won broad acceptance, matter has three qualities *(guna)*: fine or light *(sattva)*, restless or moved *(rajas)*, and coarse or dark *(tamas)*. Karma changes the proportion of these qualities in the psychic organs. They can become finer and more subtle through good deeds, coarser and more undifferentiated through bad ones. They can become more mobile or immobile, responsive or sluggish. Karma alters the "inner instrument," which is so essential for our conscious faculties. That is why the psychic quality created over the course of a life by one's own acts determines the form of existence in which one will become incarnate in the next life.

For this incarnation, one has available not only human existence but the whole variety of living beings bound up in the cycle of becoming and passing away—from the denizens of the underworlds through the animals and man up to the heavenly gods. There are even groups that view plants as capable of experience and hence ensouled, so that rebirth can also reach into the vegetable kingdom. The finer and lighter the substance of the psychic organ becomes, the greater will be the capacity for understanding, and the higher one will climb in the hierarchy of the living. The coarser and darker it becomes, the deeper one will sink down.

But the karmic factor determines more than the general condition of the psychic organ. It also brings it about that—insofar as the karma has not been blotted out by asceticism, knowledge, or God's grace—one must experience what one has caused by one's actions but not tasted to the full. Consequently, in the course of rebirths, one inevitably gets caught up in external circumstances that enable one to know and live through such experience. Each individual, then, is guaranteed to enjoy the fruits of his own actions, if not in this life, then in one of the future lives. All individual and social differences have been self-acquired and self-chosen in this way. But karma is canceled by experiencing its effect. Thus someone whose good works get him all the way to the heaven of the gods will enjoy the reward for these works only until his good karma is used up. But someone who expiates the consequences of evil deeds in a lower or more painful existence thereby destroys his bad karma.

Whether subject to good or bad karma, the soul remains in both cases temporarily caught up in the cycle of births. The creatures with bad karma will be freed from rebirth at the latest of these births when the highest deity mercifully takes back into himself all creatures without exception in a periodic act of universal salvation. According to the

Vishnu-Purāna and related texts, this always happens at the end of one of the god Brahmā's lives.

The creatures with good karma, who are in the atmosphere *(bhuvarloka)* and in heaven—the wise *(munis)*, the perfect *(siddhas)*, the gods, and other heavenly inhabitants—have, by contrast, an opportunity, whenever a day of Brahmā ends, to leave the cycle of births and ascend to higher regions that no longer have to submit to rebirth.

Bad karma, then, leads to a deeper entanglement in the world and matter, while the accumulation of good karma leads to ever higher positions in the world. And every creature, without exception, will one day share in redemption. But anyone who does not wish to wait for the distant evening of a Brahmā day and the still more remote end of a Brahmā life can attempt here and now definitively to opt out of the cycle of becoming and passing away. To do so, one needs to stop accumulating karma and to destroy the karma that already exists. That way, one breaks all ties to the world.

If one is aware of these connections—and can muster the necessary willpower—then one can escape the cycle of births all by oneself, by using ascetic discipline and meditation to undo existing karmic bonds, and by avoiding new bonds. The same goal can also be attained through divine grace, which may intervene on the individual level at any time, "burning up" karma and releasing the believer from the cycle of births.

The doctrine of reincarnation has many advantages. It gives a rational explanation for the de facto inequality of human beings and the conditions of their existence. As we have seen, at the beginning of the present age or cycle, men and women were created by Brahmā without any flaws and, according to one source, without caste differences. He did not create them to be unchanging automata, but as beings endowed with freedom and the ability to learn and to forget. Thus the differences between one person and another gradually emerged during the course of countless rebirths as a result of the various sorts of karma that developed.

Reincarnation frees the deity from immediate responsibility for all the misery in the world, without requiring a devil and without glossing over that misery. At the same time, it gives man hope for a better future in a life to come, as well as a strong motive for working on himself to make such improvement possible. Thus it provides the point of departure for all important South Asian theories of salvation. We may now deal with some aspects of these in greater detail.

WAYS TO SALVATION

When adherents of Indian religions speak of salvation, they sometimes name two ways, sometimes four, but most often three: the way of action *(karma-mārga),* the way of knowledge *(jñāna-mārga),* and the way of the love of God *(bhakti-mārga).* But these ways are not so strictly separate from one another as they seem. Along with them, various techniques for gaining access to salvation have been developed, which can be, and often have been, combined.

Indians further distinguish between two basic human attitudes in the struggle for salvation: the way of the monkey and the way of the cat. They differ as follows: The baby monkey is active from the start. It hangs on to its mother's fur all by itself and so finds safety. By contrast the kitten is passive. It meows and whimpers pitifully, but it doesn't move. The mother cat has to carry it away if she wishes to save it from danger.

The same difference is found among human beings. Some try to reach salvation by their own efforts, others merely cry out and hope for deliverance.

For Hindus, the way of the monkey comprises asceticism, the way of action (above all the fulfillment of one's duties, sacrifices to ancestors and gods, and helping others through gifts and "good works"), and the way of knowledge, which also includes yoga. The love of God belongs to the way of the cat—only, with time even kittens become active, and so the love of God does not remain passive.

One of the oldest active forms of seeking self-perfection consists in what the Indians call *tapas,* which we usually translate as ascetic practices. These aim to generate creative ardor by schooling the will. The will is trained by means of physical privation and spiritual exertion in such a way that the ascetic can ultimately transcend the normal limits of bodily existence and can develop superhuman powers of perception and action. If he manages to burn away the fetters of his body in the fire of his will, then that will is transformed into power—power to do various miracles, to heal and to curse, and also the power to know. But power is a temptation; and so ascetics often try to reach worldly goals. They undergo discipline in order to get a son, to become invincible, to win the rank of king or world ruler or even of a king among the gods.

All that may be worth striving for. Yet with the emergence of the doctrine of reincarnation these goals lost a little of their attractiveness. They can be realized and enjoyed only in the world; they do not lead one out of the cycle of rebirths. The ascetic's power leads to salvation only when it is oriented toward spiritual awareness or causes a god to grant redemptive knowledge. Only in Shivaism, which finds the great ascetical model in Shiva himself, did this archaic type of self-perfection maintain its full importance as a way to knowledge and salvation. By contrast, Vishnuism and Shaktism have in general turned away from strict asceticism *(tapas),* with Vishnuism mostly preaching moderate abstinence, while Shāktism is inclined to make use even of radically differing modes of human life for self-perfection.

A second, but also very old, way is that of ritual action, the way of the deed. In Vedic tradition, sacrifice was the most important activity, because with its help man established contact with the heavenly gods. Sacrifice gave him the possibility of making his contribution to the order of the cosmos, of showing his gratitude for aid received, and of expressing his petition for more assistance. Over time, the manner of offering sacrifice has changed in some Hindu religions, but its significance as an approach to the deity is as great as ever.

Not only do priests sacrifice, but all householders in the three upper classes as well. Even the feeding of the hungry and unexpected guests counts as a sacrifice to the deity. But sacrifice, which was once an independent way for reaching the heavenly world, is today largely embedded in a more complex system that unites the way of divine love with the way of knowledge.

Of these two, the way of knowledge is the older. It came to the fore after the introduction of the theory of reincarnation, when it became important to discover the causes of the sorrow-filled cycle of existence and to look for a way out of it.

THE WAY OF KNOWLEDGE (JÑĀNA-MĀRGA)

It is easy to say that *ātman* and *brahman* are identical. But it is hard to become existentially aware of this, to experience unity with the Absolute; because this first requires overcoming ignorance, overcoming the factors that make the world appear to be manifold, and overcoming the ties binding us to this multiplicity. There are several possible ways of doing this. One of the best known requires us to see through the whole process by which the world unfolds, and to trace it back step by step until the multiplicity is again dissolved in one's own consciousness. Thus one returns to unity.

But knowledge is no intellectual game; it presupposes a transformation of human consciousness. It demands, as we have seen, an overcoming of the structures of our "inner instrument." And so, he who wishes to take the path of knowledge has recourse to asceticism and yoga. The ascetical practices are moderate. The point is no longer to attain unlimited power, but only as much purification as needed to let thought and meditation proceed unhampered by bodily functions. And the techniques of yoga are employed in the service of knowledge. For knowledge that leads one back to pure consciousness or can experience the Absolute as it unfolds is realized not through discursive thinking but, in the final analysis, through meditation or vision.

The goal of the way of knowledge can also be expressed in another image taken from Vedic tradition. A hymn from the Rig-Veda says that the world came into existence from a sacrifice. The one cosmic man *(purusha)* was sacrificed, and from the parts of his body the world emerged.

This image conveys two ideas in particular. First, the profusion of appearances is nothing else than the One in altered form. Second, multiplicity means that unity has been sacrificed. Both these ideas pervade the theology and techniques of salvation taught by the way of knowledge. The One is to be found *in* the Many. Anyone can find it in himself. And if the self-sacrifice of unity has led to multiplicity, this process can also be reversed. By leaving behind every last bit of multiplicity in the depths of meditation, unity can be reexperienced. Each individual is part of the multiplicity. By sacrificing himself, as it were, renouncing his autonomy as an individual and at the same time blotting out the multiplicity of other things and beings from his consciousness, he comes back into the One.

The way of knowledge or of awareness enjoys the highest prestige of all the ways of salvation in India, but it has two disadvantages. Following it on one's own strength is hard. It presupposes a degree of inner purity and spiritual training, which not everyone can readily obtain. Countless incarnations are necessary to reach the condition from which the way of knowledge leads to definitive enlightenment.

The second disadvantage is social. How would it be if everybody devoted himself to knowledge and meditation? Not only Jains and Buddhists, but many adherents of the Hindu religions also were fascinated by this way. They were ready to turn their back on the world and dedicate themselves exclusively to the quest for perfection. We know that it was primarily Brahmans, warriors and citizens from the prosperous middle class, who espoused this way. But they did not do so, as was intended in the earlier time, only *after* meeting their social obligations and caring for their families, when their children had been raised and provision had been made for the grandchildren. Instead of waiting, some people shirked their duties; they abandoned father and mother, wife and child. The hope of overcoming the cycle of births drove them from their responsibilities to society.

The Way of Action (karma-mārga)

In this situation, renouncing the world was challenged by a different ideal, which is clearly presented, for example, in the *Bhagavad-Gītā*. This text offers an alternative to a break with the world. Here, too, the acquisition of wisdom remains the highest goal, but as a prerequisite for that, the *Gītā* refers back to the way of action, which had been known from ancient times as a way of sacrifice and ritual acts. It gives this way a new dimension by adding social responsibilities to ritual as an essential element. Fulfill your duty *in* the world, the *Gītā* would say, but don't tie yourself down *to* the world. Do what you have to do without eager desire. For it is only selfishness, craving, clutching things, that engenders karma when you perform an act, and thereby leaves behind a psychic impression that makes rebirth necessary. The selfless deed, on the other hand, has no negative repercussions. And it is activity in the world, activity in accord with one's proper duties and norms, that is man's assigned task. Moreover, the individual overestimates himself if he thinks that he is the one who acts, that he is the doer of his deed. Because, in reality, as we have seen, the deity alone is the origin of all activity.

The *Bhagavad-Gītā* declares an end to denial of the world. Man can work in the world so as to free himself from it. He can free himself by surmounting and stripping away desire and longing and everything that result from them, such as lust and passion, hatred and rage, anxiety and carelessness.

That, too, is easier said than done. Christians can sympathize, because they, too, are called to selflessness and generally fail to keep this straightforward commandment. To be selfless to the degree that no more ties of any sort are created—and that also means that no more karma is generated, not even good karma—is a radical demand. To be strictly logical, this kind of unselfishness would require giving up the wish for one's own salvation. But only the Buddhists, with their ideal of compassion, have taken an explicit step in this direction. For the people, for the simple man on the street, the way of selfless activity is still too hard.

THE WAY OF DIVINE LOVE (BHAKTI-MĀRGA)

There remains the way of redemption based on the love of God (*bhakti*), which promises to be truly accessible to everyone, the wise and the foolish, high-caste people and those who live on the lowest margin of human society. Bhakti—devotion to God, love for God, and being loved by God—stands in the center of this way to salvation.

The word itself comes from the verb root *bhaj*. This verb conveys two meanings: "to divide, apportion" and "to serve lovingly." Accordingly, the noun *bhakti* has also double meaning. It is the act of apportioning as well as the loving service (to God). If we translate *bhakti* as "love of God," this has to be understood as equivalent to the Latin *amor dei*, which conveys both the human being's love for God as expressed in his or her devoted service to God, and God's love for the human being. Man partakes in God's grace through unconditional devotion to him and through a love for him that overcomes all the distance separating them. But it is not entirely by their own strength that human beings translate this love into reality. To the extent that they exert themselves God comes to them and apportions them, grants them what they seek to realize, namely *bhakti,* the love of God, participation in God that brings salvation.

Thus, in the literature of bhakti the first and most important wish of the believer, and his central prayer to the deity, is that the latter may give him bhakti or that the believer may become capable of realizing bhakti.

Bhakti, therefore, is a reciprocal movement, the mutual approach of God and man. It is another attempt to overcome the separation of the individual self and the absolute Self, of *ātman* and *brahman,* not in the fire of knowledge this time, but in the flames of love, which presupposes a personal relationship.

This in fact is easier than the way of knowledge, which demands so much renunciation. Here human emotional forces are put to use, the same forces that cause attachments to the world, for the believer's pursuit of salvation.

Three things, say the Pāshupata Shivaites, characterize the relation between man and God: *pashu* (= the beast), *pati* (= the Lord), and *pāsha* (= the fetter). The beast is a sacrificial animal, the fetter binds it to the stake, and it is to be offered to the Lord. Only the sacrifice will free it from this situation.

It is the same with human beings. The individual person is the sacrificial animal; his attachments to the cycle of existence are the fetters. Only someone who devoutly sacrifices himself as it were, by completely surrendering to the Lord Shiva achieves salvation.

But how is this sacrifice, this offering of oneself to God actually performed? Only pure sacrificial animals are worthy to be sacrificed. Hence the first prerequisite is a pure life *(caryā).* Further purification consists in God-related activity *(kriyā),* which includes, most notably, the giving of gifts, prayer and ritual in the home and in the temple, as well as study with a spiritual teacher. After long practice in this kind of self-purification, there follow meditation (yoga) and finally liberating knowledge *(jñāna).*

The deity reveals itself to the person who praises it. It helps him, shows itself to him in images, in mental visions, and in all beings. Love for God prompts service of God, which should find expression in every thought and deed. The other ways to salvation are also partly integrated into this process. Sacrifice is taken up and incorporated into divine worship. The study of sacred texts and the endeavor to gain wisdom become part of the devoted concentration on the deity. Asceticism and meditation serve to cleanse the self, make it worthy of God's grace, and transform it into a pure site for the presence of God. The fulfillment of social duties or, as with Gandhi and others, concern for the poor and oppressed, likewise become component parts of the service rendered to God.

In all this, the ideal of salvation is essentially the fusion of the individual with the Absolute, with the deity. Entrance into the supreme consciousness, which means canceling the distance between self and God, and at the same time abandoning one's individuality, remains the leading goal.

We need mention only two characteristic sectarian deviations from this goal:

One of these was an intense love mysticism, which developed especially in the Krishna cult of Bengal and in South Indian Shivaism. The deity is thought of as the bridegroom, the human soul as the bride, who pines away, longing for the beloved and finds fulfillment only when it is united with him. Rich, erotic-mystical poetry, whose sensuality might amaze Christian theologians, has grown out of this love mysticism. But the major change here was the intention of believers: The great object was no longer identity with the deity, but union with it while keeping one's individuality.

The second tendency derived from an old tradition of the bhakti movement. With the increasing intensity of their love for God, both the Vishnuite and the Shivaite feel their inadequacy and unworthiness with ever greater force. They know that they are incapable of praising their God as he should be praised. They regard themselves as slaves *(dāsa)* and God as the Exalted One *(bhagavān)* or the Lord *(Īshvara)*. Just to adore God's feet strikes them as the loftiest goal.

This attitude results, first with Shivaite groups, then with Vishnuites as well, in a new orientation, which likewise diverges from unification with God. Believers strive not to merge into Shiva, but to win a gracious glance from him. Consequently, theologians of the Shaiva-Siddhānta, for example, have come to the conclusion that the soul of man is divine, but not because it is identical to God; rather, because it is continually linked to God's grace.

This movement spread to a number of Vishnuites and led the theologian Rāmānuja, for instance, to his teaching of qualified monism. According to him, God works as the "inner ruler" *(antaryāmin)* in numberless individual souls *(ātman)* and in matter *(prakriti)*. Both constitute, as it were, a body of God, making together with him a unit *(advaita)*, which is differentiated *(vishishta)* in itself. God is closely bound up with souls and matter, but he is not identical to them and not dependent upon them. According to this doctrine, salvation of the soul takes place through knowledge of the difference between *ātman* (soul) and *prakriti* (matter) and leads to exclusive attention to God and the most intimate union with him.

Finally, the fundamental difference between God and human souls was given a systematically dualist treatment by Madhva (thirteenth century) and his school. That school insists upon a complete separation between the individual self and the highest deity. At the same time, it rates the goal of coming near to God and seeing Him face to face as higher than the goal of becoming one with Him.

If I go after sugar, Madhva argues, I do this mainly to taste and enjoy its sweetness, not to become sugar myself. It is the same with God. I want to see and praise God, not become God myself.

The upshot of this is a permanent distinction between the soul and the deity and so, too, the existence of a limitless number of individual souls in the sense of independent, conscious units. Such a plurality of individual souls could be found as far back as Sāmkhya, but there they had a dualistic relation to primordial matter. With Madhva the dualism consists in the ultimate opposition between individual souls and God.

But Madhva and his school overlooked or paid too little heed to the idea that the highest deity is unlimited being, unlimited consciousness, and unlimited bliss. Compared with entering this condition, the mere view of God seems clearly inferior, because it sets a partial joy in the place of an infinite and all-encompassing one. For this reason, the ideal of the "beatific vision" won acceptance only in parts of Vishnuism and Shivaism.

2. *Hans Küng:* A Christian Response

Reincarnation and redemption were the two key issues in the foregoing section, which challenges the Christian theologian to come up with an equally concise, substantial statement on these broad themes. I shall now continue the line of argument I pursued earlier and consider both the extremes (monism and dualism, mythological anthropomorphism and abstract nonpersonalism) and the classic via media in Hinduism and Christianity. We have found surprising similarities in the Christian and Hindu understanding of God and the world; others can be shown in their understanding of man and salvation, without suppressing real differences. We turn first to the problem of redemption.

THE LONGING FOR REDEMPTION

One thing is clear: Both Christianity and the Hindu religions are not satisfied with being a merely *theoretical answer* to the great eternal questions of where man and the world come from and whither they are going, the questions about a reality "behind"—or rather "in"—the visible, palpable universe, about what comes after—and before—our own life span. Above and beyond interpreting the world and humanity, both faiths seek to build a *practical* path leading out of the distress and torment of existence to salvation, however conceived. In other words, redemption—from what and for what? Despite the many particular differences here, we can make out, for the time being, a basic agreement on two points:

- Christianity *and* Hindu religions have a sense of the world as alienated, fallen, and *in need of redemption.* In one way or another, both know about man's ignorance and blindness, his lonely, fleeting life, his compulsive carnality, his laziness and anxiety—in a word, his immense self-centeredness. Both are troubled by the unspeakable *suffering* that grows out of individual human actions and their effects, as well as by the misery of this whole broken world.

- Christianity *and* Hindu religions look forward to redemption through an *Absolute:*

Both long for knowledge, transformation, enlightenment, liberation—the redemption of man and his world.

Both hope to achieve this by entering into an ultimate, unconditioned, supreme Being, the realest reality, whatever it may be called and however understood.

Both know that this most real reality, as close as it may be to us, is hidden, that the Ultimate is not a priori objectifiable, accessible, or disposable; that the Absolute itself must grant enlightenment, revelation, release from suffering.

Thus, having noted parallels in both sides' predispositions and goals, upon closer inspection we also see parallels in the ways to salvation.

PARALLEL WAYS

As in the Hindu religions, so too in Christianity (if we look at the whole spectrum of Christian theology and piety) there are *different ways* of salvation. They are not utterly and unalterably separate, but variously accentuated. Crudely oversimplifying, one could even point to certain resemblances—no more than that—between the *three Hindu ways of salvation* and the three great Christian confessions:

Karma-mārga: the way of actions, deeds, works—whether ascetical or cultic—might be called the Roman Catholic way.

Jñāna-mārga: the way of knowledge, awareness, gnosis—in an altogether existential, experiential sense—might be more comparable to the Greek Orthodox, or Alexandrian, way.

Bhakti-mārga: the way of unconditional devotion (bhakti = distribution and participation), of trust, faith, and love might prove analogous, in spite of all the differences, to the Augustinian-Lutheran-Protestant way, which is committed to neither works nor knowledge.

But this schema, while it illustrates the theological spectrum, is of course too mechanically oriented toward the far ends. In reality, the Roman Catholic way is not identical to pious works righteousness (that would be sheer legalism). Nor is the Protestant way equivalent to trusting devotion (which would be pure quietism). And the Greek Orthodox way is not the same as a mere striving for knowledge (which would simply be gnosticism).

Just as, in India, these three ways are bound up with each other in a complex system, so we find a similar pattern in Christianity, where in each of these Christian confessions the believer can (though with different emphases) draw upon a complex combination of knowledge, activity, and devotion. And so the intellectual, practical, and emotional factors are in continual interplay.

This becomes even clearer if we consider the *two basic attitudes* toward the quest for redemption, or what the Indians so plausibly call the way of the monkey and the way of the cat. It would seem that all Christian confessions are characterized, theoretically and practically, by concurrent principles of *passivity and activity*. It is a fundamental Christian conviction that in defining the relationship between God and man, passivity and activity have to be affirmed simultaneously:

1. As the kitten lets itself be carried by its mother, so a person should let himself be borne by unconditional trust in his God. For Christians, justification is based not on pious accomplishments but on trusting faith alone. Thus passivity comes before activity.

2. And as the baby monkey actively brings its own forces into play, the justified Christian should attest his faith by works of love. Thus activity grows out of passivity.

Here it becomes clear that, unlike Buddhism, Christianity and the Hindu religions are not monkish and averse to the world. Nowhere is this clearer than in the "Song of the Exalted One" (= of Krishna, the incarnation of the one God, Vishnu), composed around 300 B.C. (the text as we now have it can be traced back to around A.D. 800), which recommends a thoroughly secular piety—the *Bhagavad-Gītā*.

WORLDLY PIETY

We should no doubt bear in mind the point stressed by Helmuth von Glasenapp: that this great didactic poem from the Mahābhārata, perhaps the most widely read piece of classical Indian literature, presents a comprehensive view of the world and life but also embraces conflicting approaches: sometimes its understanding of God is theistic, sometimes panentheistic; sometimes it proposes independently acquired knowledge, sometimes pious devotion (bhakti), as a way of salvation. The question, however, is precisely whether these opposites might not, in a deeper sense, include each other.

In any case, the idea that suggests itself as the basic motto of the *Gītā*, Do your *duty in the world*, but *don't become attached* to it, is perfectly amenable to a Christian reading. The following of Christ did not originally mean turning away from and renouncing the world (as will become still more evident in the context of Buddhism, Jesus was no ascetic), but doing the will of God here and now in faith and love. Following Christ meant working in the world without becoming attached to things or getting lost in one's job or seeking oneself. Or, as Paul said, "Be not conformed to this world." Detachment from the world not as an excuse for doing nothing, but as freedom for action without self-seeking, freedom for selfless acts. Needless to say, both Hinduism and Christianity have learned over the course of their history how hard it is to live this life of selfless freedom. But they have also had the time-tested experience that man can free himself and undo his attachments to the world only if he relies on the "pure Self," on God, on the Absolute.

This way, therefore, is possible for human beings only if it is opened up, given as a gift by God himself—made possible by his bhakti, as Hindus say, by his *charis*, as Christians put it, his grace. This is a reciprocal activity and passivity, but in a movement that goes from the Absolute Self to the individual self, from Brahmā to ātman. What is expected of man is unconditional self-donation as the *basic attitude* governing his life. This devout love of God is, once more, called bhakti in Hinduism. In Christianity, as in Judaism, it is known as faith (unconditional trust) and love (unreserved giving of self). In Islam (to close the circle) it is just . . . *islam*. This means that the "knowledge" (in the Hindu sense) gained in personal experience is in no way incompatible with the "certainty of salvation" based on historical revelation and the preaching of a divine message.

Ever since the *Gītā*, bhakti has been at the center at least of Vishnuite theology; and one of the great spokesmen of the bhakti religion, as we have heard, was none other than Shankara's great opponent, Rāmānuja, to whom, back in 1930, Rudolf Otto dedicated a monograph entitled "Christianity and India's Religion of Grace."

A RELIGION OF GRACE

To understand Rāmānuja, one has to appreciate the fact that he was a *scriptural theologian.* As he sees it, human reason is incapable of the knowledge of salvation. The source of theological knowledge has to be the scriptures, which Rāmānuja (reading between the lines for long stretches) interprets in an existential fashion, exclusively from the standpoint of his own hermeneutical assumptions, with an eye to his system of "qualified non-duality." Thus he manages, in an original way, to link traditional mystical thought about oneness to personally oriented bhakti piety. In the process, he claims many passages from the Upanishads that other theologians neglected or did violence to, and appropriates them for his teaching. He does, on the whole, more justice to the *Gītā* and the Brahmā Sutras than either the monists or the dualists. And so it is easy for him to pin the hope of redemption not on self-acquired knowledge, in Shankara's sense, but on trust in God's (= Vishnu's) saving grace. Rāmānuja subordinates knowledge to bhakti (loving devotion), but he by no means sacrifices it to a cheap "devotionalism."

Man's faith is awakened by the word of revelation, as set down in the holy scriptures. Through the *grace (prasāda)* of God, the Lord, the spirit/ soul is granted the knowledge of salvation. Though darkened by ignorance and snared, through the body, the senses, and desires, in the deceptive (but real) world of Māyā, the soul is enabled to find the way of salvation, leading to the goal, redemption. This goal is not, as Shankara assumes, the extinguishing of the "I," whether in this life or after death. It is personal service rendered to the Lord, both here on earth and eternally in heaven. The individual, who is completely imbued and controlled by God—and separate from him—strives not for identity, but *union* with God.

The means of salvation is *knowledge,* which is at the same time *bhakti.* This believing, trusting, and loving adherence to the Lord marks Rāmānuja off from both the passionately erotic cults of Tantrism and the cool intellectual mysticism of Shankara. What interests Rāmānuja is a knowledge from the heart and an intimate personal relationship with the saving and loving God, who calls the believer to a personal communion with him. Here is where *good works,* ritual, and the lofty ethos demanded by the *Gītā* come in, along with *contemplation,* which is to be practiced regularly under the direction of a yogi: By abstraction from the world of the senses, one can now come to the vision of the Lord and become conscious of *advaita,* that "undividedness," which consists not in simple identity with God (Shankara), but in an affectionate essential communion with God through the indwelling of the "inner ruler." In other words, unity with God and at the same time independence from God.

In this way, Rāmānuja created a great synthesis of *karma-mārga, jñāna-mārga,* and *bhakti-mārga.* Unlike his disciples later on, Rāmānuja himself refused to decide for either the way of the cat or the way of the monkey. Which raises the question, Doesn't a brief description of this synthesis make it evident how close is the affinity between such a "religion of grace" and Christianity? Yet caution is advisable here, because this religion comes from a different, and quite specifically Indian, context, where, along with all the common features, we also find many alien ones. For Rāmānuja, as for all of Indian tradition, man is burdened by grim fate: The spirit/soul, ātman, trapped in the misery of *samsara,* the continual *cycle of existence,* must submit to the law of karma by migrating again and again from birth to birth, from life to life, a hundred times, perhaps a thousand.

This is a clear-cut *difference*. In the Jewish-Christian-Islamic tradition, man has only a *single life*, which decides everything for all eternity. Hindu tradition, by contrast, speaks of *a number of lives*, in which man can purify and perfect himself over and over again.

One Life or Many?

Christian theologians are scarcely inclined to take such a question seriously. The idea of living more than once—reincarnation, rebirth, metempsychosis, the transmigration of souls—strikes most of them as curious, as grotesque, as nothing but superstition. In taking this position, however, they overlook two facts:

1. Not only the Hindus, but *a large part of humanity*, have, for millennia, believed in reincarnation or rebirth. This belief is held by many primitive peoples, among whom it is closely connected with animism and totemism, by 600 million Hindus, and by around 300 million Buddhists in China, Japan, and all of Southeast Asia. Indian influence on early Greek thinkers in Asia Minor and mainland Greece has not been proved, but is altogether likely. It is certain, in any case, that Pherecydes of Syros (sixth century B.C.) was the first Westerner to advance this theory, which had been clearly formulated long before him in India. He was followed by the Orphics, Pythagoras, and Empedocles, then Plato, Plotinus, and the Neo-Platonists (as well as by Roman poets such as Virgil in the *Aeneid*). The doctrine of reincarnation had an impact on Christian gnosticism and on Manichaeism, an influence that extended as far as such medieval sects like the Cathars.

2. Even in present-day *Europe* and *America*, there are countless men and women who find the Indian teaching on reincarnation quite convincing. Among these are not only every conceivable group of spiritualists, many believers in various modern revelations, theosophy (as expounded by Elena Petrovna Blavatsky and Annie Besant), and in recent days especially the adherents of Rudolf Steiner's anthroposophy. Important German thinkers, classic and romantic; poets; and philosophers such as Kant, Lessing, Lichtenberg, Lavater, Herder, Goethe, and Schopenhauer, accepted the doctrine of reincarnation, at least for a while. Even as critical a mind as Lessing, who launched a scientific investigation of the life of Jesus with the startling fragments by Reimarus on Jesus and his resurrection, could write in his *Education of the Human Race* (1780): "Why should I not come back as often as I am sent to acquire new knowledge and new skills? Do I bring back so much from one trip that it might not be worth the trouble to return? . . . Recalling my earlier states would only enable me to make ill use of the present one. And have I forgotten for all eternity what I *have to* forget for now?" (pp. 98–99)

One can't help noticing that for many people in the West the theory of reincarnation fills up an intellectual and religious vacuum and answers questions they would otherwise find unanswerable. Instead of dismissing this idea on the spot as superstition, we must consider the issue objectively and weigh the arguments pro and con. Indian religions, of course, largely take reincarnation for granted, without much critical reflection on it. As Ninian Smart points out in his excellent book *Doctrine and Argument in Indian Philosophy* (1964), Indian tradition witnessed a long debate over the existence of God, since nontheistic opinions were widespread, but serious discussion of reincarnation barely got off the ground. The doctrine was accepted by all schools except for the materialists, who had practically disappeared since the Middle Ages anyway. On the other hand, Heinrich von Stietencron's "Hindu perspectives" have made it emphatically clear that behind the doctrine of reincarnation lies concealed the religious-philosophical search for a meaningful, moral, just world order—the question of where to find justice in a world in which human destinies have been so unequally and unfairly allotted.

I am attempting here to introduce trains of thought rather Western in character. But so as to avoid unnecessary discussion, I should like to settle one point with regard to the anthropological part of the previous chapter: Just because Christianity and Hinduism start out from different anthropological presuppositions, there need not be conflict between them. One may think what one likes about the concept of *jīva* and all related explanatory models, but in the final analysis such theorems and models are not crucially important. Ever since antiquity, Christian theology has also coupled its discourse about flesh and spirit, body and soul, with various highly complex psychological/anthropological models, depending upon whether the Aristotelean/Thomistic dichotomy (man consists of soul and body, form and matter) or a trichotomy (man consists of body, soul, and spirit) happened to prevail. In Plato's image of the charioteer, the soul is guided by a supreme rational principle, which has to control the two lower principles as if they were two horses. The first principle is located in the head and is intent on truth and knowledge; the second lies in the breast, contains all the emotions and passions, and strives for honor and prestige. The third is located in the belly and includes sensuous desire, sexual drives, and the pursuit of material wealth.

Here, too, we find an effort to capture the many-layered essence of humanity. But there is no reason why the relation of man to the Absolute cannot be expressed by means of a two- or three- or four- or five-part system; with all the cultural differences, we need not invoke religious ones to explain such variety. The Christian message is not tied down to any specific Greek psychology or anthropology. But whether we presuppose a Greek *or* Indian, ancient *or* modern psychology and anthropology, in either case the question arises: Could there be a life, perhaps a thousand lives, before this one? Could there be a life, perhaps a thousand lives, afterward? What we need is a retrospective and prospective scrutiny of the arguments.

A LIFE BEFORE THIS ONE?

The first, "backward-looking" thesis maintains that a truly moral world order necessarily requires the idea of a life before this one. For how could we come up with a satisfactory explanation of the unequal chances people have, of the bewildering differences in their moral dispositions and individual fates, unless we assume that they brought about their present destiny through good or evil deeds in an earlier life on earth? Otherwise, I would have to attribute all this to blind chance or to an unjust God, who let the world become what it now is. The notion of rebirth, therefore, serves to enlighten man about himself, his origin and future, *and* to justify God. The problem of theodicy would now be solved, because we could explain why the good so often do badly (on account of earlier guilt), and why the evil so often do well (on account of earlier good deeds). This is the doctrine of reincarnation, based on karma, on the "repercussion" of both good and evil actions that determine every human destiny in this present life and in future births. Good conduct leads to rebirth in a better existence (as a Brahman, a king, or in heaven), bad conduct leads to rebirth in a worse existence (in a lower caste, as an animal, or in hell—though not, of course, an eternal hell).

As plausible as this might seem at first glance, I would also like to air the *counterarguments:*

1. In both the Hindu and the Christian views, man was originally created good, but endowed with freedom to behave either well or badly. This capacity for evil, this human freedom to fall away from the moral order, remains a question directed at God, the Creator, regardless of whether this fall takes place in this life or in an earlier one. By referring back to an earlier life—even if one follows the chain of life all the way back to the Creation in paradise—the question of theodicy is not really answered, just postponed. Is God exonerated by tracing present evil to guilt from earlier lives? Why was man, from the beginning, free to do evil?

2. Doesn't belief in reincarnation at least give human beings (and all other creatures) an equal chance by pointing to the totality of possible

lives? Equality, it might be said, proves its worth by holding good even when one person's life may last only a few days and another's many years. Here we must counter by asking: What is the price of such equality if it has to be bought with a long, long chain of lives filled mostly with grief? Can't there be an equality of human beings before God, created not by their actions but by the merciful justice of God, which embraces both good and evil deeds? That would be God's definitive justice, realized not through countless lives in time but through one eternal life.

3. The doctrine of karma and rebirth might explain why the moral makeup, the hereditary gifts, and circumstances of different people can be so different without calling God's justice into question. Yet it seems that such a belief falls into an ahistorical individualism. It seems to underestimate the effect of all that is imparted to us quite concretely through the genes, through the shaping of our conscious and unconscious minds in early childhood, through the men and women in our lives, and finally through the whole social situation. Furthermore, here, too, the idea of reincarnation, by referring to earlier lives, only shifts the question about God's justice, without giving it a better answer.

4. Within the framework of reincarnation, Professor von Stietencron has told us, there is no need for God as a judge. But, in its own way, Hinduism is familiar with judgment. "The history of the world is the judgment of the world," as Schiller said. A Hindu who believes in the law of karma might say that a person's history is his own tribunal. From a Christian standpoint, however, we may ask whether this sort of judge isn't somewhat merciless, since karma automatically condemns human beings to a new, sorrowful life. The Hindu, of course, will observe that the law of karma offers man enough time for self-purification, and that not only can the deity spontaneously free the individual from the cycle of births, but in the end it graciously takes *all* creatures back into itself. This in turn raises a question for Christians, at least those who frighten people with the threat of (literally) eternal punishment in Hell. But that brings us to the prospective part of the case:

A LIFE AFTER THIS ONE?

The second, "forward-looking" thesis maintains that a truly moral world order also necessarily requires the idea of a life *after* this one. For how could the expiatory compensation for actions (think of murderers and their victims), which so many people rightly look forward to, ever take place, how could a person develop the necessary ethical perfection in his life, if there is no opportunity for another life? Hence reincarnation provides an appropriate requital for all deeds, good and bad, as well as serving for the moral purification of man. Or, in more Indian terms, only when one no longer accumulates karma, and destroys what karma is still left over, can one get out of the cycle of coming to be and passing away, of *samsara.* The doctrine of karma and rebirth thus allows a person to undo the disturbance caused in the world order by his acts or his failure to act, and at long last to step out of the eternal cycle of rebirths. At this point, incidentally, we may ask whether the Christian teaching on purgatory isn't motivated by a similar notion of a second life, which would then be followed by a sort of third life ("eternal life"), although these lives have been placed in superterrestrial regions.

But here, too, we should listen to the *counterarguments:*

1. Doesn't the demand for an expiatory compensation in many additional historical lives fail to appreciate the seriousness of history, which is by nature singular and unrepeatable, so that an opportunity once missed can never return? To be sure, a Hindu, with his cyclical notion of history, would deny that there is any such thing as uniqueness or nonrecurrency. He would ascribe belief in such an idea to the narrow horizon of men and women who think events happen once and only once because they falsely absolutize their egos and feel themselves to be unique. Nonrecurrency would apply at most to the history of individuals who meet in any given historical situation. They are always different, the way the drops of water flowing in a river are always different. Whether we stress the uniqueness of each momentary collocation of drops in the river, or the river's continuous flow, depends upon our perspective. The Judeo-Christian approach to history would emphasize that God has given man this portion of time and history as a task for which he must in the end give an "account." In this way, and only in this way, unrepeatable history gets its seriousness, as the place where the individual person is put to the test in the presence of God, his merciful judge. Even if Hindus, with their basic concept of the world, can experience both the uniqueness and the continuity of history, we can scarcely exaggerate how far removed their view is from the biblical tradition.

2. The Hindu on the way to self-perfection (as an ascetic, a monk, or a *bhakta)* may be able to work for a positive transformation of the world and his own future. But, even so, doesn't the expectation of further lives carry with it a very great danger of feeding people with promises while legitimizing and stabilizing the social status quo, so that there is little incentive to make changes here and now—in the caste system, for example?

3. Aren't there disturbances in the world order that cannot be undone by any human action—debts, say, that cannot be paid back but only forgiven? Hindus are familiar with the notion that, in his love, God intervenes and blots out human guilt, that he can "extinguish" karma. Still, Christian tradition puts it in an altogether different manner by saying that God, as he has manifested himself in Jesus of Nazareth,

"forgives" guilt. This thought, too, is by no means foreign to Hindus, who have given it expression in bhakti piety.

4. According to Indian tradition, it is possible to recall earlier lives. Nowadays some authors attempt to find support for this by referring to the unconscious, which is, after all, not constantly accessible to the conscious mind. But even in the case of the unconscious, one may not presume what must first be proved (an earlier life). The unconscious, as Freud showed, can be explained without going beyond this present life. Individual claims to the contrary pose the problem of verification.

CAN REINCARNATION BE VERIFIED?

Whatever may be said retrospectively or prospectively about the doctrine of reincarnation, we are told that empirical evidence confirms the fact of repeated life on earth. There are many detailed accounts of people who are able—on the strength of yoga exercises, perhaps—to remember their earlier life. How can this be explained except through reincarnation? In addition, numerous studies by modern parapsychologists have supposedly provided scientific confirmation of the theory of incarnation, especially through research into the effective powers of dead people. For this reason it would seem that so-called spiritualistic experiences with the spirits of the dead ought to be reevaluated and really taken seriously. Aren't there at least allusions to this teaching in the Old and New Testaments, when the text speaks, for instance, of the return of the prophet Elijah in the form of John the Baptist? Shouldn't the anathemas heaped upon reincarnation by the Church and its councils be read in the context of their day and so relativized? In that case, a genuine reconciliation might be possible between Christianity and reincarnation. It might be removed from its Indian setting, whose ideology is so different from ours, and integrated into a Christian context, just as, during the course of church history, other once novel doctrines, from Greece or the Hellenistic world, were taken over and fully incorporated into Christian theology.

In fact, such an integration of new teachings into Christian tradition can by no means be ruled out, sight unseen. But here, too, I must make an objective presentation of the *counterarguments* to be considered:

From the Christian standpoint, one finds oneself already viewing the Hindu idea of reincarnation with a skeptical eye. Should the human soul be understood as a rarefied substance, independent of the body, outlasting its downfall, and wandering from life to life? And as far as the New Testament is concerned, passages such as the one about the return of Elijah are at best popular traditions marginal to the gospel. But even so, what they have in mind is not the rebirth of the dead Elijah in another body, but the return of Elijah in his own body, after being carried off into heaven. And this much is historically certain: all the fathers of the Church, beginning with Hippolytus and Irenaeus in the second century —including Origen, who is often misquoted in this connection—just like the later Councils, criticized the doctrine of reincarnation as advanced by the Pythagoreans and Platonists.

This same skeptical attitude also applies to the contention that, even as the soul exists *after* the body, it also exists *before* it. The assumption of either sort of existence for a separate soul-substance, independent of its bodily substrate, corresponds neither to our experience nor to the findings of modern medicine, physiology, and psychology, which in general work from the supposition that human beings are a psychosomatic unit. The Bible, too, unlike Platonic dualism, takes a holistic view of man.

But the decisive fact is this: Despite the numberless reports of reincarnation or transmigration of souls, there are no scientifically undisputed, generally recognized, data to back them up. This is something that even someone like the English philosopher John Hick is forced to concede, although he has tried to mediate between the Indian belief in reincarnation and the Judeo-Christian belief in the resurrection *(Death and Eternal Life,* 1976). The reports come mostly from India (or England); many of them are from children. But none of these accounts of memories of one or more earlier lives, even those submitted by yogis, has won broad acceptance. And needless to say, the obviously legendary narrative, written many centuries after Buddha's death, about Buddha's recollection of a hundred thousand previous lives cannot be verified.

It would be unwarranted to dismiss all the phenomena that parapsychology deals with (telepathy, clairvoyance, etc.) as a priori nonsense. But scientifically serious parapsychologists are themselves extremely reticent about theories of reincarnation. Even when they personally believe in reincarnation, they usually admit that in the cases they have studied, one cannot speak of a truly convincing proof for repeated life on earth. Similarly, many anthroposophists look upon reincarnation less as an empirically proven theory than as an unprovable conviction rooted in faith. And I have no intention of taking away such a conviction from anyone.

Thus, surveying all the arguments pro and con, we can on no account say that the doctrine of reincarnation is proven. Rather, there is no ignoring the very weighty reasons against it, for all its attractiveness. And indeed, among educated Indians, Chinese, and Japanese, one encounters a good deal of skepticism on the subject. In any case, with a view toward making a responsible decision, it ought to be worthwhile to turn to the alternative solution offered by the Jewish-Christian-Islamic tradition. On this point it is confirmed by another great but often neglected Eastern tradition, the Chinese tradition, which has also made itself felt in Korea, Japan, and Vietnam. Before the introduction of Buddhism, the Chinese did not believe in reincarnation, and even afterward, Confucian scholars continued to reject reincarnation, since they found it beneath human dignity to respect all sensate beings as equal and to imagine their highly revered ancestors as beasts of burden or even as insects . . . But it would lead us too far afield to include Chinese religion in our reflections.

CIRCULAR OR GOAL-DIRECTED HISTORY?

Hindus believe, as we have been told, not only in the continuity of the individual through many lives, but also in a cyclical course of history, in which worlds arise, gradually move toward their downfall, and are created anew. This rotation through ever new forms of existence, however, is not an infinite one for the individual. Rather, he or she has the possibility of a final exit from the cycle, from *samsara*, and of entrance into the Absolute. And this entrance into the divine Source is certain to occur no later than at the end of a world cycle. This kind of thought, in other words, may move in circles, but ultimately it is headed toward a definitive goal. We can catch sight here of an important area of agreement between mystical and prophetic mystical traditions. Whether it travels in circles or in a dialectic movement through crises and ruptures, the history of mankind (and perhaps of the cosmos, too) is aimed at what in the final analysis constitutes the fulfillment of human life: liberation through entrance into "nirvana" or the "Kingdom of God."

For Christian thinking about history, the idea that time is irrevocable plays an essential role. Admittedly, the notion that *time and historical events follow a cyclical course* has a certain suggestive power, particularly since we find in nature itself a universal periodicity, by which rhythmic patterns such as star movements, seasons, day and night, are continually repeated. All this serves, as Indians see it, not least of all for a warning sign that the great will not remain great forever, nor will the small remain small.

On the other hand, we cannot overlook the fact that, as we now know, nature does not simply go through cycles. Everything in it, from the nuclei of atoms to the constellations, has a history—with a direction. Ever since the Big Bang, that *history* has been in motion, for billions of years; and it is also presumably headed toward an end. Of course, Indian mythology, too, proceeds on the assumption that the world will end, but only to begin a new cycle. Jewish-Christian-Islamic tradition, by contrast, assumes there will be not simply an *end* to human life and the history of man and the world, but also a true *consummation*, the completion of something radically new: "the new man," "the new earth," "the new heaven"; in short, eternal fulfillment through the Absolute itself, which will judge and separate humanity while simultaneously saving and transfiguring it.

Consequently, the alternative to cyclical thinking is the Jewish-Christian-Islamic notion of *history* as a *meaningful,* coherent, continuous, *goal-directed process* that is completed by God himself. This does not mean a simple, "linear" interpretation of history in which everything goes onward and upward in a constant state of progress. It is, rather, a "dialectical" reading of history, which takes quite seriously the nonstop crises and disruptions, the wars and catastrophes, mentioned so often in the epics of India. It is not a theory of "decline and fall," full of nostalgia for an ideal primordial, exemplary period. Instead, it honestly confronts every moment and history as a whole, it is aware of the individual's inalienable responsibility and of the meaning of what he does—with the final consummation in sight.

The Christian theologian asserts the goal-directedness of history, trusting that, despite all the crises, catastrophes, and disruptions, it can be affirmed as a meaningful whole. But precisely because he makes this claim, he cannot dodge the question of the connection between the meaningfulness of the whole and the personal experience of meaninglessness. In a word, he must face what philosophy has known, ever since the days of the great Gottfried Wilhelm von Leibniz, as the problem of theodicy: how to justify God in the face of the evil in the world.

Christian theology in no way claims to have solved this problem. To do so would be to claim that the mystery of God himself had been unraveled. But theology can propose some "simpler" answers that aim to dispense with speculative hypotheses. Three of these can be presented here, though only in very abbreviated form:

1. Christian theology has never denied suffering, but has seen it as a test case for basic trust in God, who is challenging human beings to make decisions. Experiences of suffering, in fact, are often ambivalent: on the one hand, the breakdown of structures of meaning, on the other a new, resolute hope.

2. Given the overwhelming reality of suffering in the history of mankind and in individual human life, Christian theology has taken from its fundamental text, the Bible, a counterimage of hope, which it holds out to suffering, doubting, despairing men and women, a figure opposed to resignation and the easy consolation of the life to come, as well as to revolt or rebellion in this life. Instead of the defiant anger of a Prometheus or Camus's Sisyphus, Christianity points to the attitude of Job. That means, displaying an unconditional, unshaken, and yet not unreasonable trust in an incomprehensible God, despite all the suffering that racks this world. For Job, this had nothing to do with resignation or

passivity, nor does it now. Christian faith lives on the tried and tested hope that a hand is stretched to man across the dark abyss of pain and evil.

3. In the light of the experience of Jesus' death and elevation into eternal life, Christian theology has learned to rethink and reexperience God as a God of sympathy, concern, and solidarity. A new vision of God, a qualitatively different experience of God, comes to light here; and it has given a new depth of focus, theologically speaking, to the problem of suffering.

From the Christian standpoint, therefore, the experience of suffering has always been bound up with hope for ending pain once and for all in the Kingdom of God. For Christian theology, the irrevocable responsibility of the individual before God is the prerequisite not for accepting suffering quietistically, but for transforming it through acts of hope— out of trust in God's transforming power. This hopeful trust can no more be suspected of being projection than of being a pacifier for adults. The believer in the God who creates and who brings to completion knows what he expected to do: fight a battle for justice, freedom, and peace against the forces of evil, injustice, unfreedom, misery, and death. To believe in God who completes the world and man, means to affirm in trust (not blind but enlightened) that the ultimate destinations of man and the world are forever inexplicable; that the world and man are not flung meaninglessly out of nothing into nothing, but are meaningful and valuable as a whole—they are not chaos, but a cosmos; that they have their first and last security and permanent home in God, their creator and finisher.

FAITH IN PROGRESS?

I cannot judge to what extent cyclical thinking has influenced the social situation in India, has encouraged people to reconcile themselves to often inhuman living conditions, or has prevented active efforts to reform the caste system, etc. This much is certain, that *a different sense of time prevails in India* than in the highly urbanized, highly industrialized West. But no one can deny the connections between this sense of time and belief in reincarnation as well, with the still largely preindustrial structure of Indian society. To be sure, one must add at once that the Jewish-Christian-Islamic idea of progress, translated into the secular terms of science, technology, and industry, has presented us with enormous *problems*. Hence the thoroughly understandable caution shown by the present Indian Government toward Western imports of all kinds, whether industrial or cultural.

Back in our discussion with conservative Islam, we had to admit that in the last two centuries many Westerners have turned scientific-technical-industrial progress into a god. For this reason, many Indians have rightly joined Gandhi in lashing out at European-American materialism, in which the standard of living has often been used as a substitute for the meaning of life. As a matter of fact, haven't many of us become idolaters of this god, who literally dissolves into nothingness when the Enlightenment self-destructs and the history of progress threatens to change abruptly into a history of disaster?

Today we realize that everything depends not on negating progress, but on relativizing it, controlling it, taming it for the sake of humanity, so that man may remain human and the world inhabitable. And mightn't this be done in a new way—in a postmodern paradigm of society *and* religion—on the basis of that true faith which worships not the false god of progress, but the one true God? And might not such a faith be common to Jews, Christians, Muslims, *and* Hindus? Because all these religions share the same fundamental experience: Only the people whose faith in the true God has swept away their illusions about themselves and their world will be truly free from this world and from themselves and will also be able to transform this world into a more humane one. All these religions are convinced that without God man remains a torso, a fragment, a *homo in se curvatus,* a creature warped in upon itself, as Augustine and Luther keep stressing.

IV.
Religious Practice: Rite, Myth, and Meditation

1. *Heinrich von Stietencron:* Hindu Perspectives

THE TOURIST'S FIRST IMPRESSIONS

To conclude this brief introduction to the religions of the Hindus we now turn to religious practice, a living, many-sided, diversified force that embraces nearly every aspect of life. At the same time, practice also reveals essential differences between the individual religions classified as Hinduism. These differences are found above all in ritual and theology (altogether different core texts used by various religious groups), but also in behavior, in dress, food, festivals, and other details of daily life. I cannot deal specifically with such differences here. Instead I shall present the most important presuppositions and basic attitudes in the area of religious practice that, expressed in various ways, shape the life in more than one religion.

Just as we can say that Islam basically comes down to orthopraxy, so in these religions, too, we find that praxis is tremendously important. But since people are de facto different in many ways, and the Hindu religions want to do justice to this variety, there is not, even in religious practice, any overall conformity. The most significant approximate framework where the same behavior pattern holds is the caste as an endogamous group (the group within which one looks for a marriage partner), but even within the boundary of the caste there are differences, and in the final analysis there is hardly any limit placed on individual variations.

The tourist who witnesses the practice of religion in India sees a colorful kaleidoscope of possibilities. Every bus, every truck, and almost every taxi traveling the roads of India has a little picture of a deity mounted somewhere in the driver's field of vision. Often it is decorated with fresh flowers. The driver will stop somewhere on a mountain pass or in the jungle to say some brief prayers and make a donation of a couple of coins or perhaps a coconut at a temple or little wayside shrine. The Constitution of India is secularized, but so far its traffic is not. People know that with the dangers of the road they need the help of a god, not only to survive but also not injure anyone else—man or animal. In view of the bustling swarms on the streets of India, that cannot be taken for granted.

Both in the country and in the city, one often notes a tree in the middle of the line of traffic, usually with an image of one of the gods set up in it. The road divides and goes around the tree on both sides. In the West, the tree would have long since fallen victim to the ax, but in India it lives and thrives. The tree can stay, but the road has to change its course. In the same way, Indians patiently drive around cattle sleeping on a shady spot in the road, even when they have to go off the asphalt pavement and risk breaking an axle of their usually overloaded car. The irritated European calls this inefficiency. He fails completely to understand—because he is so unused to it—that in India respect for the life and the needs of other creatures is an obvious part of everyday reality. The doctrine of reincarnation, it is true, rarely brings people to take tender care of animals and plants, but it protects them from needless violence by placing them in immediate kinship with man. There is no reason to deny animals their right to live: After all, in the next incarnation one might be cast in the part of an animal oneself.

In the lanes of villages or the back streets of cities, religion is everywhere, although the tourist will miss its presence. It can be found in the plants whose blossoms or leaves are dear to Shiva and used for his worship, other plants and flowers that will be offered to Vishnu or to a goddess. These are sometimes as humble as the little *tulsī* shrub, which shows that one is entering the house of a Vishnuite.

The tourist sees other things, for example the coming and going in the temples; the old and the sick lining the way to famous sanctuaries, waiting for alms; the busy Brahmans who guide pilgrims into the temples and demand a contribution for their trouble. In the cities, he meets an indifference to the suffering and distress of other people that strikes him as strange and appalling; and at the same time he witnesses scenes of self-sacrificing helpfulness within the caste and touching examples of solicitude and respect for the elderly within the family. He sees the faithful bathe in the Ganges, submerging in its brown waters, where they hope to find purification for body and soul. He sees corpses burning on the ghāts by the sacred river. And if he gets up early enough, he will likely also see the prayers at sunrise, in which Hindus offer water to the rising sun and beg for enlightenment. This is the sole prayer that binds all members of the three upper classes together. It is at the same time the sole verse of the Rig-Veda that every Hindu from these classes is supposed to know and use.

If he is lucky, the tourist may also witness one or other of the numerous religious festivals that divide up the year and accentuate it in various ways, depending upon the region. Such festivals are celebrated in the home, as well as on the street and in the temples. They often have fairs connected with them, and some are so famous and promise so great a store of religious merit that they draw hundreds of thousands, sometimes millions, of pilgrims, like the feast of Kumbh Melā in Allahabad, which takes place every twelve years.

Not only for Hindus, but for Christian observers, these festivals leave behind an enduring memory. One can feel the intensity, for example, with which the followers of Shiva, on the so-called "night of the great Shiva" (*mahāshivarātrī*) praise their God, listen to his myths, and fight off sleep, because staying awake on this night is specially meritorious. One finds oneself riveted by the daylong performances of episodes from the life of Rāma, fascinated by the round dances on Krishna's birthday (both Rāma and Krishna are incarnations of the god Vishnu). One notes with admiration the loving care with which countless plaster images of the goddess Durgā are made and painted, only to be gaily sunk in the river after the feast of the Great Goddess, which lasts for nine nights. And one enjoys Dīvālī, the feast of lights, which is as rich in charm as the smile of Lakshmī, the goddess of luck, who is venerated on this day.

There are many festivals in honor of regional and supraregional gods, and besides that, festivals on the occasion of celestial conjunctions and ritual festivals in centers of pilgrimage. Indians like to celebrate; their feasts are brightly colored and last until late into the night, often for several days and nights.

The relaxed, peaceful atmosphere that prevails in these festivals is striking. Also conspicuous is the individualistic style of life in the temples. The people are not wrapped in solemn silence; each one prays or meditates when he sees fit, undisturbed by the coming and going around him.

DOMESTIC RITUAL

Impressed by these and many other forms of public religious activity, the short-term visitor usually doesn't notice that most of religious life takes place in the home. In this setting, Indians perform rites that perhaps have no parallel in Christianity, that are neither the religion of the simple people nor the religion of priests and theologians alone, but serious religious practices of the three upper classes, the Brahmans in particular. The center of gravity of Hindu religious life is found not in the temple, but in one's own house. All the "sacraments" are celebrated not in the temple, but at home. Not the community, but the individual, is the vehicle of religious activity.

This is a characteristic feature that separates Hindu religion from Christianity, a difference caused not only by the caste structure, but by the much deeper individuality of the Indian ways to salvation. As I tried to show earlier, each person is at a different stage of the way to self-perfection, and so it is only logical that his relations to the deity should undergo their most intense development in the private sphere.

There is also a difference in the attitude of the individual toward God. Like Westerners, Indians have many ways of relating to God. But if we were to attempt to pick an especially characteristic attitude, we could say that in his dealings with God, the Christian is perhaps above all a repentant sinner and the Muslim an obedient slave, while the Hindu encounters his god primarily as a host.

This is something characteristically different from anything Westerners are familiar with, and it goes all the way back to the Vedic period. The god is called upon, as Christians often invoke their God in prayer. He comes, however, not only as a helper and savior, but first and foremost as a guest. One greets him, entertains him, gives him gifts, and praises him. Man appears here as the giver, the god as the receiver. The critic of religion will label this *do ut des* (I give in order to get). The person offering a sacrifice gives a small present and asks for a big one. Indeed, why not? After all, one gives as much as one can, and God can give more. But much more important than that is the psychological effect of this daily practice of receiving God as guest, preparing oneself for this reception, and delighting the guest with the sixteen little services or rituals, the sixteen *upacāras*, as the Hindu calls them.

The inner preparation is of great importance for understanding the relation of man to the deity, and it follows a pattern in the home similar to that of the temple. Hence I shall discuss it at some length in connection with the temple ritual. For the moment, I shall simply describe the visible course of divine worship in the home.

The object venerated with the sixteen rituals is a little bronze statue of a god, found in practically every house (or, if one cannot afford bronze, at least a cheap print of the deity). That is enough to bring the god to mind and to enter into a dialogue with him.

The sixteen rituals have regional variants, but in essence they are as follows: (1) The deity is led in, (2) offered a seat; and since the guest has traveled far, he is (3) offered water to wash his feet, (4) face and hands, as well as (5) water to rinse his mouth. Each of these actions is naturally accompanied by pertinent ritual sayings and gestures. If now one should happen to offer the deity (5a) a little sweet refreshment, then he is also given (5b) some more water to rinse his mouth. Then the deity is (6) bathed, (7) dressed, (8) furnished with the sacred cord carefully decorated, and (9) rubbed with aromatic ointments—usually sandalwood paste, camphor, and saffron. The god receives (10) blossoms from his favorite flowers and trees, (11) incense, and (12) light from a lamp burning sesame oil or melted butter. Then a sacrificial meal (13) is set before the god and after that some betel nuts (14). Only when the guest has dined is he given a present (15), and the ritual ends (16) with a reverential circumambulation of the deity.

This ritual can be extended to as many as ninety-four little services, or *upacāras.* Anyone who can't perform the usual sixteen services should at least bring sandalwood, a light, and flowers. If even that much is impossible, he can simply offer water to the god; and if he has no water, a prayer will be enough to win the god's grace. Along with the god, by the way, one also venerates the guru, the teacher to whom one owes one's religious knowledge.

THE FOUR LIFE STAGES (ĀSHRAMA) OF THE TWICE-BORN

Such domestic worship of God as a guest begins with the marriage ceremony and is a religious responsibility common to man and wife. That is why, for a Hindu, entrance into wedlock is more than just a license for procreation. It is at the same time an entrance into the phase of ritual actions and the beginning of the second and most important of the four stages of life, that of the householder *(grihastha).* Hindus feel bound not only to do the specific jobs of the social class *(varna)* into which they have been born—whether they be Brahmans, Kshatriyas, Vaishyas, or Shūdras—but also to fulfill the religious duties connected to the various stages of their way through life *(āshrama).*

With marriage, i.e., with the second life stage, one begins to do one's inherited duties toward one's parents, one's ancestors, and the gods—duties for which one has been carefully prepared in the first stage *(brahmacarin),* which is reserved for acquiring religious knowledge and familiarity with the rituals.

All three duties of the young married couple aim to assure the continuity of the family: Only this will guarantee care for the aged, the carrying on of sacrifices to the ancestors, and the survival of ritual tradition. (For large parts of India, the continuation of the family refers to the masculine line. For this reason, the passing on of duties from father to son is among the most important elements of tradition.)

Accordingly, the child is accompanied by domestic ritual even as a fetus in its mother's womb, then at birth, upon being given a name, when it eats its first solid food, has its first haircut, etc.: It is at all steps ritually purified and prepared for entrance into a society whose essential distinctive feature is the fact that it communicates with the gods.

One enters this society by crossing two important thresholds. The first is initiation by the spiritual teacher (guru), which occurs between the ages of seven and fourteen, depending upon one's caste, and makes the members of the three upper social classes "twice-born." Through their first birth, they were born into the social framework of family and caste. Through the second, they enter into their religious tradition. They have to learn this tradition, study the sacred texts, and practice performing the rituals. In earlier days, Brahmans began an apprenticeship of at least twelve years with a guru. Nowadays compulsory schooling has cut out a great deal of this religious education and contributed to a decline in the vigor of tradition.

The second important threshold is, once again, marriage, which in the Vedic rite is solemnized in front of the fire and renders the couple responsible for the fire, that is, for the ritual; because in the Vedic period fire was the mediator between men and gods. Only with marriage is the ritual integration of a person complete. He is now in regular, ritualized communication with his ancestors and with the gods. With the help of the prescribed sacraments, he will also be able to prepare his children for this "vertical connection."

Traditionally, parents choose a marriage partner for their son or daughter. In modern times, with industrialization and the influx of the rural population into the cities looking for work and with the increasing number of university-educated men and women, this has changed a little and will go on changing. But this sort of arranged marriage is still the predominant one.

Love is not a prerequisite for getting married. It will develop of itself if the partners have been chosen correctly by the parents. In many cases, the bride and groom have not even been introduced before the wedding. The criterion for marriage is, in the first stance, the caste, and secondly the education and economic situation, of the families in question. A marriage based on similar family backgrounds is then given additional stability by the ritual tasks shared by the couple.

Later, when the children have grown up and been integrated into the ritual and religious tradition, and when, finally, the grandchildren become independent adults, the husband and wife, now grandparents, enter the third stage of life *(vānaprasthya)*. Earlier they would have withdrawn into the silence of the forest, feeding only on fruits and roots, practicing asceticism and studying sacred texts. Today such old people usually stay at home, but there is still a tendency to involve themselves more intensely in religious affairs.

There is no obligation to enter into the fourth and last life stage. But if one so decides, one becomes a *sannyāsin,* that is, a person who casts off everything, including his rights and duties in society. A sannyāsin no longer belongs to any caste. He travels around without a roof over his head or any property, training himself to break attachments to possessions, to persons he loves, and to bodily needs. Women, too, can become sannyāsins, but it is not for everybody. It is hard to give up the security of family life, deliberately to put oneself at the mercy of sickness and old age. Those who do are highly respected, though in the eyes of the tourist they may look like ragged beggars. The sannyāsin is fulfilling a religious ideal, taking an important step on the road to perfection and salvation. As a householder, he once fed sannyāsins who passed his way; now he, too, receives food wherever he asks for it. He wanders from one holy place to the next, learns to master his senses and to concentrate wholly on salvation. His contemplation of God is supposed to become so intense, his thought so constantly fixed on God that it never fails him, not even in the moment when he is overtaken by death.

. A person who dies this way, with his mind fastened on God even in the agony of death, a person who does not forget, even in death, that his self is identical to the highest Self, can find salvation. But there are places where it is easier to die this way, holy places, for example, where the presence of God is felt more strongly than elsewhere. Thus it is said that on the Manikarnikā Ghat, of Benares, Shiva himself in his mercy whispers the liberating knowledge once more into the ear of the dying person, in case he forgets it in his death agony.

IS THE CASTE SYSTEM ABOUT TO BREAK UP?

Only in the last of the four stages of life is the connection with one's caste broken. Until that point, the caste structure shapes the life of the individual, even today, in a variety of ways. I discussed the origin of the caste system and the distinction between social class (*varna*) and caste (*jāti*) in my account of the Aryan invasion of India. No Indian social institution has been criticized so often as the caste system, none is thought to be so rigid—though it has proved, over the course of history, to be quite flexible. The most comprehensive treatment of the nature of the caste system is Louis Dumont's *Homo Hierarchicus* (1966), but we still lack a solid work on the historical transformation of this institution.

Each of the castes has its own separate rights and duties. It seems obvious to us—and this is partly justified—to fit these differences into categories like "privilege," "exploitation," "oppression," but that is only half of the truth. We should not overlook the fact that the higher one climbs in the caste hierarchy, one's rights may increase considerably, but so do the spiritual and moral demands. And the possibilities of failure are correspondingly greater, which would cause one to drop down in the hierarchy of society, if indeed one remains in the realm of human existence.

The standard for evaluating the castes is their relative purity and—subordinate to that—their economic position. "Purity" refers to fitness for ritual and to religious knowledge. This does not necessarily mean that only a Brahman can win salvation. He has simply gotten himself (from his last life) a substantially better initial chance. Whether he makes use of it remains to be seen. And it is quite conceivable for a Brahman, after long efforts, to be quite close to the goal of self-perfection, but still bearing within himself a remnant of karma that will force him to enter a lower form of existence once again. As soon as this leftover karma is consumed, he can become a saint and perhaps find salvation. That is the reason why saints may come from any level of society, even from among the Shūdras or the Untouchables. But, as with the sannyāsin, a fortiori with a saint, all caste distinctions entirely cease.

Nowadays the caste structure has been officially abolished by law, but, for lack of equivalent state agencies, it still continues in many ways to support and define social life: Education; trades and professions; marriage; politics; and provisions for the unemployed, the sick, and the aged, are still largely dependent upon the old institutions of the family and the caste.

But there is no overlooking the fact that industrialization, urbanization, and the modern educational system bring with them pronounced demographic shifts, including a horizontal mobility based on occupation that is beginning gradually to break up the cohesion of the castes and the extended family.

As a matter of fact, the caste is an institution that for more than two thousand years has been repeatedly called into question and sometimes vehemently attacked by reformers from all the major Hindu religions (and Buddhism). It has survived to this day only because, so far, no one has succeeded in fashioning another nonpartisan institution for providing a social identity, mediating disputes, and protecting the unemployed, the sick, and the aged—should the family fail to do so—as effectively and reliably as the caste.

But the caste has a crucial role to play (even in religion) only so long as, first, its social-welfare functions are not attended to by other agencies and, second, individual and collective purity cannot be determined from distinctive features other than those of caste. Such features might be, for example, level of education, love of truth, character traits—but all these criteria are harder to objectify.

Ever since the middle of the first millennium B.C., there have been loud and repeated demands that people should be judged not by their social origin, but by their qualities. This ideal was tried out by a number of religious communities, but over the course of time, most of them went back to acknowledging the caste or caste-like structures. Every other principle of evaluation immediately runs up against the problem of how to justify the standards chosen, how to give them binding force, and how to apply them impartially. Any such principle also weakens the consciousness of a deep-rooted, supportive identity and of economic security, since it dissolves family ties and regroups individuals in accordance with their capabilities and qualifications. Besides, we may well doubt whether India should copy the system prevailing among middle- and upper-class Westerners, whereby one's bank account or family property or title often determines, in a manner reminiscent of a caste, the social class one belongs to.

In summary, we can say that India has long been engaged in the search for a just society. But it is still by no means sure that the caste and extended family structures will have to be completely abandoned, especially since a lasting society without social stratification has never yet been realized in any large state on this earth. It would make more sense to have a carefully planned process of adaptation to the demands and possibilities of the present that could dismantle the harsher parts of the caste system while preserving its advantages.

TEMPLES AND IMAGES OF THE GODS

The great majority of India's countless temples are dedicated to one or another of the many manifestations of Vishnu or Shiva, but other deities are also invoked. An extremely popular god, for example, is the elephant-headed Ganesha, the lord—and when properly venerated, the remover—of obstacles of every sort. Clerks, printers, and bookkeepers, in particular, frequently turn to him in hopes of avoiding serious mistakes in their records and calculations. In southern India, people deeply revere Kārttikeya, once an important god, who, like Ganesha, was integrated, as the son of Shiva, into the circle of Shivaite divinities. And in the Deccan, believers pray and sacrifice to the demigod in the shape of a monkey, Hanumān, the friend and worshipper of Vishnu in his incarnation as Rāma. The cult of the sun god Sūrya was once very important, but nowadays it has died out as an independent religion. As late as the thirteenth century, the famous temple of Konārak was built in honor of Sūrya.

Some of the temples of goddesses are dedicated to various forms of the Great Goddess, Durgā, the wife of Shiva, but a greater part of these temples serve autonomous regional deities, whose individuality has not yet succumbed to the progressive integration of local cult figures into Shāktism. Apart from Durgā, other widely venerated deities include Lakshmī, the goddess of luck and wife of Vishnu, and Sarasvatī, the goddess of learning and guardian of the Vedas.

Many of these gods play an important role in everyday life, yet they have only a subordinate position in theology. In that sense they resemble the patron saints in Roman Catholicism. Hence, in discussing temples and images of the gods, I can limit myself to the major Hindu deities.

When the Muslims came to India, they felt the worship of divine images was the worst thing about the Hindus. The Christians also took offense and called the Hindus idolaters. They might have known better, since they have had essentially the same sort of thing with their crucifixes, madonnas, and saints as the Hindus with their "idols." For Hindus, as for Christians, God is everywhere, of course, but he has certain places where his presence is especially powerful. Yet while a church is primarily an assembly room for common prayer, a Hindu temple symbolizes God's activity in the world and man's way to God.

The whole temple precinct is sacred space. One takes one's shoes off upon entering it. One takes a purifying bath in the temple pond, then one approaches the temple itself. It has the form of the world mountain, and if it is a richly decorated temple, its outer walls will display all sorts of ornaments, plants, animals, men and women, heavenly spirits, the guardians of the eight points of the compass, and other objects. There are fertility and tenderness, music and dance in the world depicted on temple walls.

The deity is within, in the center, invisible from outside and yet equally near to all creatures. It manifests itself in the main recesses of the temple in some of its particularly important forms, so that the believer can visualize it. The myths, too, come to life in the imagination as one walks clockwise around the temple. While doing so, he turns his right side to the deity as a sign of respect. (Not so the *vāmacārins*, or "left-hand-goers," members of Shivaite or Shāktist sects who vary considerably from the orthodox majority of either group.) Upon returning to the entrance door, one gazes at and touches the doorframe, where the holy, purifying Ganges and Yamunā rivers are often portrayed, as well as gatekeepers and luxuriant shoots of vegetation, while above the door the planets and the god who resides in the temple come into view.

In front of the entrance to the sanctuary, one usually finds the god's mount: in the case of Shiva, the bull Nandi; in the case of Vishnu, the bird Garuda. Each is always by its master's side and continually worships him. They are models for the believer, and in many cases, their images have been worn smooth by the reverential contact of thousands of people. At the entrance hangs a bell, which one can sound to announce one's arrival to the god and at the same time drive away, with its loud ring, any demons that might be present.

The cella is dark. The only light comes through the doorway, shining on the likeness of Vishnu or the lingam (symbolizing Shiva). The lingam is phallic in origin, but its shape is highly abstract. Anyone who looks closely can see that in the temples it is usually together with the yoni: Shiva and Shākti, the masculine and feminine principle combined, and thus the creative and undivided essence of all being.

The believer, unless he is a Brahman, generally goes no farther than the threshold of the sanctuary. There he obtains what he has come for: *darshana*, the epiphany of God. He has now seen the outer multiplicity and the inner unity. He makes an offering—a few flowers, a couple of coins. In return he receives a present from the priest—a handful of water consecrated by touching the body of the god, a blossom, or a leaf from the god's decoration; or else a dab of sandalwood paste on the forehead, or some *prasād*, that is, some of the food God has blessed by accepting.

If the believer gives a coconut, it is opened and presented to the deity, who accepts its milk as a drink offering. The priest then gives the nut back to the donor, transformed and ennobled because the god has accepted it.

Giving and taking become symbolic here. The gifts are usually small, but as far as possible one does not come before God with empty hands. A handful of water is enough, or a leaf. The gift is, after all, only a sign. Behind it stands the real offering, a devoted heart.

Then the worshipper leaves the cella of the temple, which is not meant for long visits, but for invocation, gifts, and vision. Afterward, one lingers in the temple courtyard, sitting in the shadow of the sculpture-covered walls or of a great tree, reading, meditating, letting the peace of the courtyard sink in. Here is where one listens when, in the temple porch, musicians play for the god, and when a *pandit* reads the myths aloud.

The Temple Ritual and the Inner Preparation of the Brahman

In the temple, God is treated as if he were a king. He is wakened in the morning, bathed, anointed with sandalwood paste, dressed, and richly adorned. He is venerated with the sixteen *upacāras*, and what is left over from his meal is given to the temple servants, the poor, and petitioners. Then the god grants an audience to all those who wish to come to him. Toward evening he is entertained with dancing and music; and finally, care is taken that his nightly rest is undisturbed.

For the believer, God shows himself in the temple ritual and at the great feasts as a sovereign in all the splendor and luxury of worldly power. But anyone who thinks of all this as merely a superficial spectacle with divinized puppets is mistaken.

A glance at the ritual reveals what actually goes on during the *pūjā*, or adoration, both in the temple and in the home. The ritual services which

I have described in connection with the domestic ritual and which are basically similar in the temple, have an important and telling preparatory part. There are different versions of this, longer or shorter depending upon the occasion. The example I have chosen to describe is a briefer rite used by the Vaikhānasa school.

The believer wishes to communicate with God. That is not possible unless he raises himself to God. He therefore metamorphoses and divinizes himself, in order to be fit for God's presence. The medium needed to achieve this is meditation and ritual transformation.

The Brahman's upper body is unclothed except for the sacred thread, which he never takes off. It passes over his left shoulder and under the right arm and the back across to the left shoulder. The thread is laid over the right shoulder only at rites that have to do with death and impurity. He sits in the lotus position facing the image of the god. On the ground within his reach are arranged all the utensils required for his worship. The Brahman, whether in the temple or at home, now begins, with his mind fully concentrated, to prepare himself for dialogue with the deity.

First he deliberately imagines abandoning his worldly body and his sins. He identifies his self with the deity, and in his thoughts he fashions a new, ritually pure body for the god. He controls his breath and makes the creative forces enter his new body in the form of the letters of the alphabet (because the alphabet contains every word and therefore every thought, all definable knowledge and all the things in this world). Then he mentally has the different forms of the deity take their place in all his limbs. The Vishnuite chooses forms of Vishnu, the Shivaite forms of Shiva. He invites these forms of God into his eyes, ears, mouth, and nose, into his shoulders, breast, and all his members, until the body is completely filled with the deity.

Once the body has been prepared as a residence for the deity, the next step is meditative concentration on the aspect of the deity that the Brahman wishes to venerate. For God has many aspects, many shapes, and the divine image shows only one of them. In order to worship him the believer, too, takes on only this one form of God.

He contemplates his body as a temple or platform *(pītha)* and his heart as a sacred space for the deity. There he prepares for it a lotus throne, whose leaves are covered with the mantra of the god, that is, with the syllables of the formula for invoking him, while the center of the lotus contains the sacred syllable Om. Here is where the deity is supposed to alight. Hence he pictures the god to himself as sitting on the lotus throne in his own heart. He concentrates on the deity's *dhyāna,* its meditation verse, and clearly visualizes its form, ornaments, and attributes in all their details.

When this is achieved, the individual is entirely filled with God. Then the same process of meditative divinization is also applied to the image of the god, until the deity residing in the heart of the believer can also inhabit and animate the statue. This procedure is not a mere transfer from the man to the image, but it effects the simultaneous presence of God in the person and in the statue—somewhat as one takes a burning lamp and lights another with it.

Now, with the possibility to communicate with God on the same (divine) level, the necessary precondition is fulfilled for the adoration of the god's image with external rituals. At this point, e.g., the Brahman can start with the sixteen ritual services described before.

The observer sees only this external worship. But if one knows the language of the ritual, then it turns out that the worshipper and the worshipped are identical as *ātman* and *brahman,* that the believer venerates the god in the human person and the god in the statue. In the ritual dialogue between Brahman and divine image, what is really taking place is a dialogue between two manifestations of the same God.

We might wonder what the point of all this is: God has no need of worshipping himself. But anyone who asks such a question forgets that for many Hindus there is nothing outside and independent from God. If worship occurs at all, then it is always, so to speak, God worshipping himself. This is denied only by the purely dualistic Hindu systems, but it is true for all monists and even for the "qualified" monism of Rāmānuja, who says that the deity operates as the "inner ruler" in the individual soul. Only, not everyone is aware of God's constant presence or of man's unity with him. And this is the crucial point, because ultimately knowledge alone brings salvation.

The external sacrifice accomplished in the ritual has many forms. The believer, as I said, offers however much he can. But the offering fulfills its purpose only if it is pleasing to the deity. Here we find considerable differences among the individual cults, which have undergone significant changes over the course of time. Thus, for the Vedic Indra, the most important gift was the intoxicating drink *soma,* but today even substitutes for soma are used no more except in Tantric cults.

Nowadays the rites of Vishnu employ, apart from jewelry, garments, minerals, and water, only plants and plant products (which includes certain flowers, leaves, seeds, ointments, incense, and oil) and milk products. Animal sacrifices are normally an abomination to Vishnuites, but Shivaites still offer them to some of the frightening manifestations of their god. And the Shāktas prefer to offer buffaloes, goats, cocks, and fish to various aspects of their goddess.

As a consequence, in some regions of southern India, for example, Vishnuites never enter the temples of Shiva or Shākti, and in fact they are afraid of polluting themselves merely by looking at them, so they pass them by with averted eyes. Conversely, the Vishnu temples are not visited and are sometimes even avoided by Shivaites, because they detect impurity in the communal services of worship *(bhajana)* and praise *(kīrtana)* of the god, which are often attended by Shūdras and Untouchables.

Only in the great pilgrimage centers, where the presence of numerous gods promises manifold graces, and the priests of all religions are busy trying to profit from the gifts of the pilgrims, are ordinary believers brought by the guides to the sanctuaries of the most diverse gods. Otherwise the different religious communities do not normally mingle in worship, even when they live side by side in perfect peace. The only exception to this happens when cults are deliberately fused, as with the Smārta-Brahmans or the Shāktist Vishnuites in Orissa or Bengal.

Myth—a Multilayered Phenomenon

Among the forms of religious expression and the media of religious instruction, myths play an important role in all the Hindu religions. They are retold or read aloud, presented through dance and theater; they inspire the poets, artists, and philosophers.

The myths tell of the origins of the world, of the nature and activities of the gods and demons, of the experiences of seers and saints, and of the origin of holy places. Their language is simple, but their images are striking, rich in details, and filled with complex symbolism.

Westerners sometimes have the impression that myth constitutes a lower form of knowledge about God. They think it disguises more of the truth than it reveals, and hence religion must be demythologized. For the Hindu, by contrast, the myth veils the truth only when an ignorant person hears it, because he doesn't understand the language of the symbols. For the person with knowledge, it reveals more about God's nature and actions than mere abstract discourse can grasp, because it brings an element of dynamism into play. For this reason, myth is also a significant object of meditation, like the painted or sculpted figure and the meditation verse (which describes the deity in words).

For ignorant people, myth, in fact, does hide a great deal, but by no means everything. An orange is beautiful on the outside, even if one doesn't know that it contains delicious juice. Myth likewise has layers of meaning. If one of these is hidden, the myth can still be understood on another, lower level. Here the myth provides an externalized image of the god, of the cosmogonic process, and many other things in which the god's power or love or even unpredictability can manifest itself.

Thus the myth conveys something of God's being even to the ignorant. Because it can be interpreted on several layers, it is a form of expression that has something for everybody and that no one can dispense with. For God speaks to man at every level.

To be sure, we also find demythologizing in the Hindu religions. But not by universally binding decree—there is neither authority nor necessity for that—but by means of karma, and consequently through degrees of religious knowledge or experience of God. At the highest level of such knowledge or experience, we also reach the highest level of abstraction. But this does not make the lower levels inconsequential. Without them, the ascent that leads in the end to salvation would never have begun.

YOGA AS MEDITATIVE TRAINING

Meditation, too, is a complex phenomenon. I have mentioned it a number of times without being able to go into the question of how it is done. But since there are many forms and techniques of meditation, it makes more sense to limit ourselves here to yoga, as an example of the preconditions under which meditation is generally engaged in. Continual practice, of course, is absolutely required.

Yoga is an ambiguous word. It means the harnessing, the bringing under control, of bodily functions, the senses, and thought. This is akin to yoking unruly oxen or harnessing horses to a chariot (in Plato's famous analogy), so that one can unite their forces and drive them to one's destination. But along with the beginning of this process (the harnessing and taming of the senses), yoga also refers to the outcome of the whole effort, namely the binding of the individual self and the absolute Self, the definitive union of *ātman* and *brahman*.

This union is a goal that can be reached only under certain conditions. The first of these is a blameless moral life. Except for a few religious groups, the basic moral rules of the community provide a general framework, which is obligatory until one reaches the high level of self-realization where all traces of egotism and carnal desire in one's thoughts and actions have been extinguished. Not to steal; not to harm anyone in deed, word, or thought; to live moderately, be truthful, and free oneself from greed: these are the most important of the ethical rules.

The second condition is self-discipline. This consists in outer and inner purity, contentment (achieved by giving up one's desires), abstinence, intensive study of the traditional teachings, and—in theistic systems—humility before God, or worship of him.

The third and last condition is the control of bodily functions through certain postures.

When these conditions have been met, and one has practiced long enough, the vital forces of the body can be directed by means of breath control. Then the senses withdraw from the external world, so that the yogi no longer notices what is going on around him. Such sensory turning off creates the rest situation that is needed for complete absorption. We can see how hard it is to pull a yogi out of this state, once he has turned away from the outside world and entirely concentrated his awareness on a single object, from the graphic myths of Shiva, the great yogi. Of the Buddha, too, it is reported that he was absorbed so deeply in contemplation that he never noticed a thunderstorm which killed two farmers and four oxen right near him.

After the withdrawal of the senses from the outer world, a parallel process begins with regard to the inner world. Here, too, the goal is gradually to shut off the multiplicity of ideas and to direct one's consciousness toward a single object of contemplation. If the effort succeeds, the state of absorption finally leads to a total view of the chosen object, encompassing every dimension of its reality.

In the ultimate stage, the mind's penetration and experience of what it meditates on is so profound that the distance between subject and object is overcome, and at some point the separation breaks down. What happens then is usually described as a lightning-like comprehensive flash of awareness, which for the most part cannot be reproduced in speech. It is an experience in which all being telescopes into a single point. At the same time, the yogi has the overwhelming sense of radiant light.

That was a very condensed account of the yoga process, which naturally had to leave out many details. Not everyone manages to reach the high point of absorption and experience of unity (samādhi). Even those who do, cannot at first remain there—further practice is needed. Only the consummate yogi has the ability to bring on the state of unity at will or for good. He can also determine the moment of his own death.

The believing Brahman who performs his daily ritual is only in the rarest of cases a consummate yogi; but he has been practicing for many years. Day in, day out, he concentrates on the god whom he worships and on the sacred scriptures of his tradition. Meanwhile he still lives in the stage of the householder, who has to provide for his family. Meditation is a normal component of his life, and in old age it will take up an even larger part of it. But the earlier one practices it, the more one can learn and live in a state of mental concentration. For this reason, in some families even children are given preparatory training in meditation.

THE LEVELS OF THOUGHT AND THE TRUTH

By way of conclusion, I would like to try to address a phenomenon that may be the hardest of all for a Westerner to understand. I mean the thinking on several superimposed hierarchical levels which characterizes many Indian texts.

These levels are not neatly separate from each other, like a row of labeled drawers in a pharmacy, each containing different drugs. That is the sort of organizing principle we would feel at home with: Here is

Shiva, there is Vishnu. Here is abstract knowledge, there is myth. Here is salvation through knowledge; there is salvation through the love of God. Here is the Brahman, there the earthworm.

But that is not how it is. Rather, just as the earthworm can become a Brahman, and a Brahman an earthworm, so in the next life, or perhaps even in this one, the Shivaite can recognize the greatness of Vishnu and adore him, the Vishnuite, Shiva. Everything depends on the individual's karma; that is, on his state of inner purity. *Here* there is better and worse. But what is better for one person may prove useless for another if he is not ready for it.

There is, no doubt, a highest and unique truth. Whoever has it, is ipso facto liberated. But so long as he doesn't have it or doesn't have it completely, he at least knows that truth manifests itself differently on all the levels of existence.

Furthermore, each person can consciously move on several levels at the same time. He can conceive of the Divine in a wholly abstract form as primeval *brahman,* and nonetheless bathe, dress, and decorate the statue of a god with deep devotion. He can visualize the deity in his heart, when he meditates, with all the details from the image created by artists and poets and with all the god's mythic deeds—although he knows that this is all mere semblance, the merely worldly appearance of a transcendent, ineffable being.

Along with this capacity for thinking on different levels of reality goes a different sense of time. Human beings live at the same time and in the same space, but they nonetheless belong to different levels of time and space, as measured by their inner maturity and their distances from liberating knowledge.

Thus, if the adherents of Hindu religions are more tolerant than those of other religions, this is not due to an ethical imperative, which is always hard to obey (especially when one gives one's own truth an absolute status). Rather, this tolerance arises from a knowledge of the inner structure of the world and of all the creatures in it, as well as from a consciousness of time that is foreign to our one-dimensional thinking.

This awareness is the source from which forbearance and equanimity and inner peace spring up as if by themselves. These things are precisely what Westerners, for the most part, lack. That is why India's religions offer us something new: an alternative way of thinking, which is at the least worth knowing about.

2. *Hans Küng:* A Christian Response

What can a Christian theologian say in response to this profusion of information about religious practices in India? If I were to sketch a similar picture, I would have to look, as Heinrich von Stietencron has, to *popular religion,* because in the Christian world we find related forms of piety among Catholics in Italy, Spain, Latin America, southern Germany, Ireland, and Poland, insofar as these communities have kept the *medieval/Counter-Reformation paradigm of Christianity.* No one would dispute the fact that the Christian religion in these places is extraordinarily alive—colorful, many-sided, varied. It encompasses every area of life and emphasizes orthopraxy, above all in the sense of ritual performances. (It would be interesting to investigate the parallels and differences between the more private priestly religion of the Brahmans and its more public Catholic counterpart.)

POPULAR HINDUISM AND POPULAR CATHOLICISM

Despite all the differences, almost every religious feature of popular Hinduism could be matched with an *analogue from Catholicism.* In both cases, we find religion practically omnipresent; and in both, the specially delimited holy places. Consider medieval–Baroque popular Catholicism, which has survived to the present day, often on something like religious reservations, with its many churches and chapels, roadside shrines and ways of the cross, all its countless pictures and statues (sometimes decorated), all its candles, flowers, aromatic incense, holy water, and music. Christian Europe, too, has its patron saints, votive tablets, dashboard amulets, and every sort of religious sign. In the West also there are sacred seasons and holy days; great popular festivals celebrated at home, in church, and on the streets; processions, parades, "missions," novenas, etc., day and night, all year long. Christianity has its great pilgrimages, with millions of pilgrims, many of them old and sick, with countless priests and beggars, brightly painted plaster statues, scapulars, medals, religious objets d'art and souvenirs, art and kitsch in every shape and size. Everyone can be a joyful participant in the feast and feel bound up with the great community of the faithful when the saint, in the form of a picture or statue, is received and greeted like a god, carried through the streets, and accompanied back home.

I pass over the myriad patterns of *devotion to Mary*, which became and has remained so popular that older and more recent places of pilgrimage seriously compete with each other (Altötting versus Einsiedeln, Lourdes versus Fátima). Everywhere in the Catholic world, masses are celebrated in honor of the Virgin or of other saints, with at least sixteen *upacāras*, or ritual actions, gestures, and sayings. (The pre-Vatican II solemn papal mass easily matched the total of ninety-four "services" in the Hindu rite.) At such ceremonies, numerous honors are paid not just to God or the saints, but also to God's deputies on earth. Here, too, only a small offering is expected of the simple believer in order to be plugged in to the sacred process of give-and-take, the *do ut des*. And such activity is also tied in with legends, myths, and new revelations (Lourdes: "I am the Immaculate Conception"), as well as miracles (primarily cures, but Fátima has its sun miracle). Thus, we can see all these features in Christianity, especially the late-medieval–Baroque kind, which also has a heavy share of the nineteenth-century restoration of conservative European monarchs and governments, and Romanticism, most notably in the veneration accorded Mary and the Pope (previously there had been no emotionally tinged cult of the papacy).

But is this sort of comparison justified? Some readers will protest: Aren't we putting the saints or the angels as the Catholic Church sees them on the same level as the gods of India? Yet the Church has always clearly *distinguished* between *adoration (latría)*, which is due only to God, and *veneration (dulía)*, which may be given to the saints and angels. Thus God alone is adored, while the saints are only venerated.

I do not wish to dispute this, but anyone familiar with Catholic piety from the inside knows how often *borderlines* that are so clear to theologians are *blurred* in popular piety. A flagrant example of this, once again from Catholicism, is the veneration of the female principle of the "deity," as represented by the "Mother of God." Ever since Thomas Aquinas, Mary has been allowed to receive not just veneration but hyperveneration *(hyperdulia)* by the Western Church. This has taken forms that suggest pagan models (it is well known that, in 431, Mary's divine motherhood—thanks to a "bold stroke" by Cyril, the bishop of Alexandria—was defined in Ephesus, the cult center of the Magna Mater), and the Second Vatican Council had to take a stand against Marian excesses.

In Hindu-Christian dialogue, therefore, it would be silly to play the purist, theoretically ignoring and denying practices that have been accumulating for centuries, that have blended into the fabric of Christianity, have been lived by millions of Christians and so, in any event—whether one deplores it or not—now belong to the phenotype of Christianity. In a phenomenology of religion equally applicable to Hinduism and Christianity, all this would have to be critically analyzed.

MONOTHEISM OR POLYTHEISM?

If we work from the standpoint of life as it is actually lived, and not so much from that of abstract doctrine, we as Christians will be more careful about accusing Hinduism of polytheism, as has so often been done. Or should there be a double standard for Christianity and Hinduism—for Christianity only the high ideal, for Hinduism the sobering reality? No doubt, as a Christian one feels extraordinary impressions on the holy Ganges at Benares or in the Hindu sanctuaries of Nepal or Bali, but one is scarcely tempted to become a member of such religions. By the same token, would the Vishnuite or Shivaite Hindu visiting a Baroque church in Naples or Bavaria, or even St. Peter's in Rome, be able to discover in Christianity a "monotheistic revolution" (J. Ratzinger) overthrowing all the pagan gods? One would get a stronger sense of monotheism in the smallest mosque on the edge of the Sahara; or in the Indus Valley, between the Himalayas and the Arabian Sea. But what should we say to all this? Following our reflections on the Hindu and Christian notions of God, we can make a long story short by noting two points apropos of the parallels between Christian and Hindu popular religion:

● If we understand "God" to be the highest and deepest principle of all, the very first and very last reality in the world, in human beings, and in things, then most of the *Hindus* are *monotheists.* In this sense, Hindus, too, believe in only *one God:* in the one primordial Brahma, which is identical with Vishnu or Shiva or Shākti, and so simultaneously impersonal and personal ("transpersonal").

● But if we understand "God" to be all those beings who are venerated through invocation, prayer, hymns, or the offering of gifts, then a great many *Christians* are *polytheists.* In this sense, the way they practice their religion shows that they actually believe in *several "gods,"* however these may be called in Christianity (Indians call them "devas," to distinguish them from the one "Brahma" or "Īshvara," Lord).

Perhaps both Hindu and Christian popular religion are really less a matter of monotheism or polytheism than of *henotheism:* The believer venerates the one God and also renders quasi-divine veneration to other figures. It is true that in Christianity veneration is accorded less to mythical figures (apart from St. George the dragon-slayer or St. Christopher the Christ-bearer) than to *dead historical personalities* (along with angels and archangels, "powers and principalities"), who have distinguished themselves in their lives through some sort of holiness. But in any case, next to the "Holy One" *(tu solus sanctus),* there are many other "holy ones" *(sancti).*

In the late Middle Ages, the cult of the saints had reached such a degree of crude materialism and exaggeration (trafficking in relics, worship of images, votive gifts and vows made to saints) that the Protestants · rejected the cult of the saints outright for their "new" (oriented to Christian origins) *reformed paradigm* of the Church and theology. The Reformers invoked the First and Second Commandments: "You shall have no other gods before me" and "You shall not make for yourself a graven image"—although the prohibition of images was consistently observed only in Calvinism. Yet in our overview of Christianity and Hinduism, we should not make things too easy for ourselves. In comparing Christian and Hindu practices we cannot dodge the question:

WHAT LIES BEHIND POPULAR PIETY?

How, in fact, are we to judge this bewildering proliferation of popular piety, so widespread, so hardy, so stubborn? How should it be rated by a Christian or Hindu who may have grown up with such forms of piety but now can no longer unreservedly join in them? What needs to be done here is not so much an intellectual devaluation as a theological evaluation, since such modes of religious expression cannot be accepted today simply because they belong to the "phenotype" of a religion or of a people. What, then, lies behind the resistant strain of de facto polytheism or henotheism that we find even in monotheistic religions? What lies behind the Hindu pantheon or the Christian All Saints?

I have already pointed out that *antireligious* categories (Marxist, say) fall short of the whole truth, although they do address important aspects of the situation. Popular religion (especially in the underdeveloped countries) has surely functioned—and still does function—often enough as the "imaginary flowers on the chains" of oppressed people, as the "soul of a heartless world," the "mind of mindless conditions": *"Religious* misery," accordingly, has been the *"expression* of real misery"

(Karl Marx). The economically and intellectually dominant classes have used and abused popular religion, Hindu and Christian, to keep the lower classes in a state of dependency and passivity, superstition and fatalism. But, on the other hand, as we saw, religion can simply not be reduced to these ideas or conjured away by them. Religiously motivated people in particular can free themselves from alienating religious forms and commit themselves publicly to fight poverty, social oppression, and injustice; and there are numerous examples of this not just in Christianity but in Hinduism also.

Despite all the exploitation of popular religion in the interests of politics, the economy, and tourism, one thing has become increasingly obvious to us from all the lectures delivered on the history of religion: Over the course of the many thousand years of human history, for all the bizarre forms they take, the "fulfillment of the oldest, strongest, and most urgent wishes" (Sigmund Freud, *The Future of an Illusion*, 1927, Studienausgabe, IX, 164) has everywhere been the linchpin of life. Yet (even after Freud) it is by no means clear that these wishes are illusionary. In the elementary desires of helpless man for protection from the dangers of life, for justice in an unjust society, for a life *after* this one, for ultimate meaning, for knowledge of the world's origin and destination —and the strength of these wishes, according to Freud, constitutes the strength of religion—what do we find everywhere expressed, despite the perplexing, contradictory variety of religion? *A trust*, not rationally provable but still thoroughly *reasonable*, that behind, above, *in* the visible–palpable–controllable world, is hidden an invisible–impalpable–uncontrollable world. In the final analysis, this is—whatever names or disguises it may be concealed beneath—the One that undergirds all worldly reality, penetrates it, and explains it and *manifests* itself in it. Needless to say, just *how* this One manifests itself in the many is disputed by the various religions: whether through the word alone or in nature as well, whether in man alone or in animals and plants as well, in every single thing. In any event, Hindu and Christian popular belief are agreed that the one Divine Being, or God, comes to meet us in ascetical, saintly men and women, and that it (he) discloses its (his) identity by means of marvelous powers.

Why not? Is all this necessarily sheer superstition? Some of it may be, and we certainly have to separate genuine charismas from bogus piety. But aren't there straightforward *religious needs* that no one has to be ashamed of? Even in the monotheistic religions, don't innumerable men and women feel the need to be close to God or the Divine and to be able to localize their religion at familiar holy places, where they find understanding for all their daily concerns: comfort, help, healing? Wherever a monotheistic religion has ultimately become a *religion of the masses*—and this holds true for Islam as well—a highly spiritualized belief in the one divine Being has proved inadequate. Hence the polytheistic tendencies of nature religions have left their mark even on the "advanced" monotheistic religions. Saints are revered even in Islam. What, then, are we to make of this whole phenomenon? Instead of declaring popular religions intellectually obsolete or to conjure them away with ideology, it seems to me that we ought to ask some counterquestions of the religious "establishments" of Hinduism, Catholicism, and Protestantism.

CRITICAL COUNTERQUESTIONS

The *first* question is directed at Protestant, especially European Protestant, theology: Isn't the *disappearance of the popular element,* isn't the withering away of the sacraments, the *hypo*trophy of the sacramental principle, the aversion to everything sensuous, pictorial, symbolic, or emotional in Protestantism, part of the reason why the Church has been intellectualized and *congregations have dwindled?* Yet God's revelation can take place through actions, gestures, configurations (doubtless often ambivalent in themselves), through expressive forms employing art, music, and dance, through visible symbols, and thus "sacraments" in the broadest sense of the term—all things of the greatest importance for Asian and particularly Indian sensibility.

A *second* question is directed at *Catholic* (and possibly Hindu) theology: Isn't the *exaggerated strength of the popular element;* isn't the *hyper*trophy of the sacramental principle, the proliferation of the sacraments; isn't the aversion to the prophetic spirit, to rational criticism and demystification, part of the reason why countless critical-minded Catholics have left the Church (intellectuals, industrial workers, and, increasingly, dissatisfied women and young people)?

A *third* question, of a different sort, is directed at *popular Hinduism:* Road traffic in India may still be religiously inspired, but the Constitution and the state of India, unlike those of Islamic Pakistan, have been secularized. Should we not, then, expect that all of Indian life will be more and more subject to a slow but irresistible *process of secularization?* Don't the Hindu religions, like Islam, find themselves in the middle of a paradigm change from the "middle ages" (however defined) to modernity, a change that, if it is to succeed, may have to build on something like a religious reformation?

Sobharani Basu, a professor at the Hindu University in Benares and author of a three-volume history of *Modern Indian Mysticism* (1974), writes toward the end of her presentation how attitudes toward mysticism and mystics have changed in contemporary India: "The general attitude of the world toward mystical experience is, as a rule, one of indifference, if not of antipathy." Why? Because the present generation views mystical experience "from an exclusively positivist and utilitarian standpoint" and looks upon it as utterly useless for society: Even should the mystic reach enlightenment, his success would "have no moral effect on the thinking of the individuals who constitute society." (III, 93–94)

Basu opposes this notion, referring instead to the social impact of Shankara, Rāmānuja, and Madhva, along with the more recent mystics and reformers whom she treats, from Ramakrishna to Aurobindo and Mother Ānandamayī, who all served in many ways as social models. Liberation of the individual, she argues, must be viewed in the context of universal liberation (she makes the same point in *Some Mystics of Modern India,* 1979). But Basu concedes that modern scientific–technological society has created new problems for India too. In fact, our earlier reflections on the paradigm change and the issue of secularism in Islam are equally relevant here. Let me make just a few observations on the *ambivalence* of the present transitional situation for Hinduism.

THE TRANSFORMATION OF RELIGION

India continues to be an impressive example to confute the thesis that religion is dying out. The Hindu religions, which already have so many paradigm changes behind them, are changing once again but not dying. First of all, consider these three brief points on the *survival* of religion:

1. Despite enormous upheavals, especially since the nineteenth century (colonialism, religious and social reform movements, national independence, linkup with world communications, industrialization, modernization of life), religion in India still plays a *leading role,* both in the private, family sphere and in public, political domain. Atheism or agnosticism is relatively rare, even among intellectuals.

2. Even with regard to European-American modernity, the Hindu religions have shown an extraordinary *power to adapt, assimilate, and integrate,* a power that is almost the only thing holding the giant subcontinent together. Old articles of faith and religious practices are adapted to the present, and new ones absorbed. Mythic material is reinterpreted, obsolete material is reworked, and material that has outlived its usefulness is quietly dropped. India, it has been noted, has an unlimited capacity for faith.

3. Even more than Catholicism, Hinduism seems to be a *mixtum compositum* or a "religion of contraries": a combination of often heterogeneous elements. Old and new, tradition and adaptation, naïveté and enlightenment, are frequently found side by side unconnected, or seem to have been harmonized only in a makeshift fashion. So many things are possible, not least because common worship is basically foreign to traditional Hinduism, and religious rites, as we have seen, are perfomed primarily within the family.

But unless I am deceived, we can also detect symptoms of an *epochal paradigm change* in India. A transformation of religion on the grand scale seems to be underway:

1. The process of *secularization,* brought on by industrialization, urbanization, modernization of life, and the widespread development of communications technologies, is moving unstoppably ahead. The secular attitudes already adopted by a very small, Western-educated upper class and a large number of students are spreading to the well-off middle class and the industrial workers (who have largely broken away from the caste system) in the large cities. These attitudes are slowly beginning to reach villages that have been isolated for centuries and to unsettle their deeply rooted Hinduism. This process is unlikely to be reversed, and a return to premodern conditions is by now out of the question: radio, TV, and increasingly these days videocassettes have taken care of that.

2. With the arrival of modernity, many *religious customs* are likewise apt to disappear. I mean, not just the many ascetics in the forests and the sacred cows on the streets, but many more things that the ever controversial N. C. Chaudhuri castigates as superstition, incapacitating fear, and wretched obedience, indeed as charlatanry and hocus-pocus, so different from the loftiness of Indian metaphysics. It is not just religious negligence, but, above all, the demands of modern life, with its strict apportionment of the hours of the day, that have led many Hindus, especially in the cities, to abandon the time-consuming home ceremonies. Religious festivals have in many instances degenerated into popular diversions. Technology, mass media, and a materialistic outlook are moving out into the villages (three fourths of all Indians live in the countryside). Interest in politics—unfortunately threatened by a frightening decline in political morality—is for many people taking the place of interest in religion, which has so often been misused to win political power.

3. Although many analogies have been drawn between the religiously based *caste system* and the segregation of social groups in European or American or African societies, the caste system is typical of Hinduism and has always been the main obstacle to its expansion beyond India. But it is now, at least in the cities, giving indications of breaking up similar to those given earlier by the European Estates of the Realm. The Indian Government did away with "untouchability" in 1947, and the caste system has long been fought by both religious reformers and leftist politicians.

As we have heard, the introduction of compulsory education (campaign against illiteracy) and a modern school system has sharply curtailed religious initiation by gurus (exclusively designed to make members of the three upper classes "twice-born"). Thus we may presume that the "decline in the vigor of tradition" mentioned by Professor von Stietencron will affect all four traditional stages of life. Then parents will scarcely be able to choose a marriage partner for their child, without his or her say-so, on the grounds of caste membership. Then the ideas of ritual purity linked to the caste system and the taboos that forbid certain "lower" tasks to the upper castes, while enjoining them on others (particularly the "Untouchables," who are still, at best, tolerated, but not accepted), will gradually become outdated. Then the social and economic discrimination against the roughly 110 million "Untouchables" (whom Gandhi called *harijan,* "children of God") will have to stop. These people live, now as ever, amid inhuman misery. In southern India, they are still prohibited from setting foot in the temples. They are not allowed access to wells or hotels. They are denied services such as barbers. Their protests against caste oppression, even in overpopulated northern India, have repeatedly led to bloody reprisals from the middle and upper classes; and so, in recent days, they have again been converting to Islam in massive numbers. Then, in the long run, the social privileges of the Brahmans will be stripped from them, as were the prerogatives of the medieval European nobility and clergy in the modern period.

The only thing left to be said is that in the face of religiously inspired terrorism in Northern Ireland, apartheid in South Africa, and colossal poverty in Latin America and Africa, Christians, while they are free to challenge Hinduism, have no reason to feel superior. There are, unfortunately, all too many poor, oppressed, and exploited people in "Christendom."

MYSTICISM AND ACTION

In this transitional situation, the pivotal question for the future is whether religion, either Christianity or Hinduism, will prove to be *a force for social as well as spiritual change.* It would, despite everything, be a crude oversimplification if we were to argue that Hinduism, owing to its basically mystical character, is once and for all a backward-looking religion, which simply wishes to maintain an ancient body of tradition, and which seeks to avert harm only through myth, ritual, meditation, and yoga. Nor could we reasonably claim that Christianity, on the strength of its fundamentally prophetic character, is by definition a forward-looking religion, which is oriented to the radical renewal of all the circumstances that turn human beings into despised creatures. That would be to underestimate Hinduism's religious power and to overestimate Christianity's.

We must avoid pseudo dilemmas here: There need not be a contradiction between integration and emancipation, between meditation and action, the requirements of order and the thirst for justice, the sheltering/preserving function of religion and its critical/liberating function. Why should Indian religion, which has already changed so much, not be able to show itself to be not merely *a source of meaning, stability, and security,* but at the same time a *generator of enlightenment, emancipation, and liberation?* Neither the Christian nor the Hindu has to decide between renouncing the world and commitment to the world, between concentrating on the inner depths of the person and solidarity with one's fellow men and women. *Mystical experience* and *social action* need not exclude one another.

The Hindu religions traditionally concentrate on liberation in the absolute sense: deliverance from this sorrowful life and union with the Absolute. But in India, too, many people understood, early on, a fact to which Latin American *liberation theology* has rightly attached the greatest importance: that redemption *and* changing the world go together, as do liberation of man by God *and* liberation of man by man—popular religion has a sociopolitical potential for liberation. Like Christians, the majority of Hindus have simply accepted suffering and oppression (as the "will of God," as "karma") and have been content to put off liberation till the Beyond or nirvana. Today, however, human beings are expected to liberate themselves—from the constraints of nature, of society, of themselves. They should be free from patronizing control, from second-class status, from oppression.

Many Hindus, especially educated people, students, and the young, were not alienated from traditional religion, or were won back to it because they came into contact with the *neo-Hindu reform movements.* Such men as Gandhi, Ramakrishna, Vivekānanda and Aurobindo, the philosopher Radhakrishnan and the poet Tagore are the fathers of a renewed form of Hinduism. Largely under Christian influence, they and their followers were quick to point out specific religious and social abuses and outrages. They fought not only for national liberation but also for religious renewal and social reforms.

In this connection a fundamental theological question arises that also applies, of course, to Christianity (think of the Crusades, the Inquisition, witch burnings, and other horrors). In the face of things like the religiously motivated killing of children and burning of widows (practiced, in isolated cases, as late as the twentieth century), in the face of early marriages, the vestiges of temple prostitution, the ritual mass butchering of animals, the magic and superstition, in the face of all the religiously sanctioned social and economic discrimination against the "Untouchables," Hindus, too, must face the following question: For all their multileveled thinking, their ethical relativism, and their antidogmatic, mystical world view, are there no *criteria* for distinguishing true from false elements in a religion, for distinguishing religion from pseudo religion? What basis exactly is there in Hinduism for the fact that phenomena like those mentioned above can, at least today, be rejected, opposed, and abolished by many Hindus as "false" or "bad" forms of religion? What is there to guard us against projecting *whatever needs we wish?*

I would like to return on some other occasion to address this problem of the criteria for true religion in a more theoretical and thoroughgoing manner. But even the attempt to suggest such criteria would carry us far beyond the framework of these "Christian Responses." At this juncture, though, I wish to go back to a related question (already discussed in my second response on Hinduism)—the issue of myth and demythologizing.

THE TRUTH OF PICTURES AND STORIES

As with Christianity and Islam, the task facing Hinduism was and is to preserve the religious substance beneath the timely, meaningful forms of a new paradigm. But Indian mythology, so enormously rich, still growing today, with its marvelous flowering of gods and supernatural figures, poses a question, for Christians in any event but also for critical-minded Hindus: Are we to accept this whole luxuriant, tangled growth as it is? Should we let it pass as simply another, lower level of meaning, or perhaps understand it as an expression of religious vitality? Just how are we to handle the problem of mythology?

Ever since its earliest beginnings in the darkness of prehistory, the message of religion has been clothed and passed on in a garment of myth and legend. As everyone knows, both the biblical and the Hindu scriptures come from a time when people were still conversant with mythical thinking, from a world where (contrary to scientific thinking) one takes it for granted that supernatural powers continually intervene in the course of nature and history. I have already spoken, at the outset of my second "Christian Response," about the tremendous influence of myth on the whole system of life—whether the myths of the Bible, of India, or of Homer, of ancient Rome or the Middle Ages, or even the ersatz myths of modern times. The scientific study of religion, anthropology, psychology, and sociology have all demonstrated in various ways the power of myths to create meaning and integrate cultures. Myths play a great role not only in religious art and interpretations of the world, but in the individuation and socialization of human beings.

Even today, in the age of science and technology, we keep running into *the necessity of mediation through symbolic narrative.* We need it to understand the increasingly complex world, to get a picture of the increasingly unimaginable "second creation," which is ruled by a technocratic elite that uses abstract formulas, mathematical codes, and computer language. A glance at the overflowing marketplace of comic books and sci-fi fantasy shows that recourse to archetypal symbols and mythological narratives seems indispensable for the autoillumination of our origins and destination. Hence religion can calmly assume what the experts in social psychology and communications theory have demonstrated: that our contemporaries do not live on arguments alone, but also on *stories;* not only on concepts, but also on *images,* often very ancient ones. There is no end to the need for live images and stories worth retelling. We saw earlier, in the context of God's "playing" with the world, that symbols can also be understood in a thoroughly unmythological fashion, and that *demythologizing,* even for Rudolf Bultmann, does *not* mean *desymbolizing* language.

We should not overlook the fact that not only our images (such as God's "play" or even Jesus as God's sacrificial "victim"), but our most intellectual *concepts* (such as God's "activity," "concern," "grace," or "love"), can never directly grasp the ultimate reality we call God. What other choice do we have? These terms, too, are cut to the measure of man, they are and always will be "ana–logous" (that is, "upward-saying" from a human source), and for that reason like/unlike what they speak of. We can only hope that they are enough to open the way for us to the hidden One, the un-graspable, in-comprehensible, all-embracing, all-penetrating God.

Truth is not equal to facticity, nor to historical truth. What we have heard about Hinduism also holds, *mutatis mutandis,* for Christianity: Just as there are *different levels and tiers and modes of reality,* so there are different levels and strata and modes of *truth,* often in one and the same narrative. Medieval theology distinguished, somewhat schematically, the fourfold meaning of Scripture. But isn't it still valid today? A newspaper account of a man assaulted on the way from Jerusalem to Jericho might under certain circumstances leave me completely indifferent, even though it was, unfortunately, true, true as history. Conversely, the fictional story of the Good Samaritan might immediately get me going. Why? Because it contains more truth, not only a pure fact, a purely historical truth, but a truth that has meaning for me, that is relevant to my existence, an "existential," indeed a "political," truth. In confronting a story like that of the Good Samaritan or the Prodigal Son, the historian's question about "what actually happened" is inadequate. Poetry, parables, legends, sagas all have their own truth and can announce relevant truth in their own way. Along with the logic of the head, there is also the logic of the heart.

The Bible, too, is primarily interested not in historical truth, but in the truth that is relevant to our welfare and our salvation, in the "saving truth." The stories in the Bible demand more than what historicocritical theology has often exclusively concerned itself with: dissecting texts into their component traditions and examining with an eye to historically verifiable facts. Even passages that simply report, frequently aim at expressing more than *one* truth. What is at stake in these stories is not pure information, but messages bearing a promise or a threat. In the foreground of interest is not a theoretical truth, but the practical question of *what it means for us.* Here we must turn directly to the problem of myth—using the word not in the inflationary sense (the "myth" of revolution, of money, of the Kennedys), but in the strict sense (a story about the gods). The question is, quite soberly:

WHAT IS TO BE DONE WITH THE MYTHS?

Must someone who in our scientific age affirms the necessity of stories and symbols do the same for *myths or stories about the gods, which speak about the gods or God as if they were men?* I have already acknowledged, at the beginning of my second "Christian Response," that myths reveal deep structures of man and the world, space and time; that they present models for living and can provide a direction for one's life and saving power. But to construe these myths as historical facts or to impose them as binding dogmatic truths would be to misunderstand them. This has never been done in Hinduism, and it should not be done in Christianity, either. *Myths* have "double vision"; they are *ambiguous.* Thus, at a time when people think scientifically and analytically, rather than mythologically, as Indians, too, are increasingly having to recognize, we should consider the following three points:

FIRST: As in Christianity, so in Hinduism, myths are *not to be taken literally.* In the long run the result of such "medieval" conservative mystification would be, in India as in the West, ignorance and obscurantism among the masses and the spread of unbelief among the educated. Or should the lower levels of meaning be good enough for the lower levels of the population? If one simply preserves the myths in an unmythic age, this will be at the expense of the real content of religion. And when that is confused with myth, faith degenerates into *superstition.*

SECOND: Conversely, as in Christianity so in Hinduism, *not* all myths may simply be *eliminated through critical scrutiny.* This sort of rationalistic analysis would lead to spiritual impoverishment. Imagination, fantasy, emotion, spontaneity, and creativity would all dry up for the sake of intellectual clarity. A religious tradition lays hold of a person only when a notional grasp is not substituted for the state of being grasped by God, nor concepts substituted for symbols, abstract ideas for stories, proclamation for narrative. Should that happen, the religious community would be depopulated, and the spiritual vacuum it had itself created would become susceptible to remythicization. If the mythical element is simply eliminated, it will be at the expense of religious content, which thus reduces faith to a sort of *pious rationalism.*

THIRD: There is a critical middle course between traditionalism (particularly favored in India) and (Western) rationalism. Conscious of the "dialectic of the Enlightenment," it distances itself from *all* forms of superstition, one of which is modern pious rationalism. Critical theology wishes neither to preserve nor to eliminate the mythical, but, in post-Enlightenment fashion, give it a *nuanced interpretation.* Why?

However muddled, contradictory, and extravagant myth may sometimes appear, it does contain a fragment of Logos. Narrative and yet unhistorical, a guarantee of meaning yet nonconceptual, myth *can* be, in a graphic/personifying way, *an approach to the ultimate reality;* and it is just that, for countless men and women still rooted in mythical thinking. As I argued earlier from a Christian perspective: According to the Old and New Testaments, God's "revelation" can also be found in creation; according to the Acts of the Apostles, God has not left the "pagans" without witnesses to himself; according to John's Prologue, the divine Logos enlightens everyone who comes into this world; even according to Karl Barth, alongside the Light of Jesus Christ there are other lights, alongside the one Word still other true words. Thus, logically speaking, religions for the men and women outside the Church can be ways of salvation. And if all this is true, we cannot exclude the possibility that numberless human beings in olden times and the much afflicted present day have experienced and are experiencing the secret core of reality, the mystery of God. Is it heretical for Christians to say that? The Declaration of Vatican II on the non-Christian religions explicitly affirms it:

> Thus, in Hinduism men contemplate the divine mystery and express it through an inexhaustible abundance of myths and through searching philosophical inquiry. They seek freedom from the anguish of our human condition either through ascetical practices or profound meditation or a flight to God with love and trust. (*The Declaration on the Relation of the Church to Non-Christian Religions.* [Paulist Press, 1966, p. 9])

But nowadays some intellectuals, alienated from the institutionalized religions, are calling for the "return of the gods" (already conjured up in vain by German classicism, Romanticism, and Nazism). So perhaps we are again in danger not of critically interpreting the myths, but of restoring them whole, from some aesthetic, psychological, or philosophical ulterior motive. There is nothing wrong with a careful rereading and literary reworking of old myths like those of Odysseus or Antigone, Oedipus or Faust, which is actually being done in contemporary German, French, and English literature. But we do not want a neo-Romantic restoration of myth as a replacement for religion. Modern interpretation of myths should not encourage any hermeneutics designed to legitimate or justify some current taste or trend.

Whatever one may say about the different levels of meaning, there is no way, in interpreting either Christian or Hindu scriptures, to get around *criticism of the material itself.* This holds for Old Testament war stories, with their incredible cruelty, as well as for Indian myths that no longer meet the intellectual or ethical needs of our time. Around the beginning of the nineteenth century, Rājā Rāmmohan Roy, the prophet of Indian nationalism and a pioneer in the reform of Hinduism, first objected to the system of idol worship and the injury to personal and social feelings that resulted from it. Since that time, many other Hindus have opted not only for monotheism, but also for a religion based on ethics. It is fair to say, even in the light of Christian theology:

- The myths of India, at once veiling and unveiling the cosmos, cannot simply be dismissed by Christians as superstition or unbelief. They can open up a path for Hindus and possibly for Christians as well to the myths of the "Divine," to God himself.
- Nevertheless, the myths of India should not be passed on without examination by either Christians or Hindus as the sole possible expression of their faith. They have to be submitted, in a sympathetic manner, to a critique of their substance, which could be conducted from the standpoint of Hinduism itself (that of the *Gītā,* say) or of secular analysis of religion and ideology, or of the Christian message.
- The world today does not need a "new mythology" to overcome the crisis of modernity with a postmodern paradigm. (After the racial madness of Nazism, what "stories of the gods" should be invented to create new meaning and found new communities? What "myth of the twentieth century" should we come up with?) But we do need a "new religious language" that would not go back to before the Enlightenment, but forward beyond it. Such a language would wrest a new meaning from the old symbols, images, stories, and perhaps even the old myths, insofar as they weren't obviously demeaning to our intellectual and ethical standards. Instead of a "return of the gods" for those driven mad by rationalism and nihilism, we need a "homecoming to the one true God."

The question of the criteria for true and false, good and evil in the various religions (which has been wrongly neglected both by theologians and by students of religion) also arises with respect to mythology. But, however we answer it in principle, one thing has to be kept in mind here: Despite all the analogies between them, there is a considerable formal difference between the Vedic myths, the ancient stories of the gods of India, and the stories of the Bible, especially the stories about Jesus from the New Testament. Why is this?

THE QUESTION OF HISTORY

Right from the start, we should beware of the cliché that Indians think mythologically, while Jews, Christians, and Muslims think historically. In *India*, too, there is *historical thinking*. As far as political history is concerned, most of the ancient archives have been lost to fire, but enough records (such as lists of kings) have survived to establish the presence of a real historical consciousness. With regard to religious history, we can recognize an interest in matters of the continuity and hence the authority of religious tradition (the line of gurus). This shows that not everything in the religions of India is unhistorical myth. A lot of mythical material is anchored in history. The Indra myths, for instance, are linked to the Aryan immigration; the life of Krishna to the conflict of the Aryan tribes at the battle of Kurukshetra. But only a small part of this has been researched by historians.

Conversely, we can also find *mythical thinking* in the *Bible*. There are elements of mythical piety; and depending upon how broad or narrow one's concept of myth is, one can detect a larger or smaller number of myths, including a three-tiered mythical world picture (upper world / world / underworld). One need not label all the anthropomorphic touches in the Bible as myths (which is why I have sharply distinguished between mythical, pictorial, and analogical speech). But even if one does not, one can still find myths in the strict sense in the *Old Testament:* myths of creation and the end of the world, of Paradise and the Fall, of a primordial sea, a battle with a dragon, a battle of the gods, God's accession to the throne, etc. The Psalms, too, have mythical motifs, as do First and Second Isaiah.

Of course, the Old Testament shifts its originally mythic pattern in a way that has no parallel in the cosmogonic myths of the Vedas: The Hebrew Bible typically depersonalizes and disenchants the forces of nature. In the Babylonian myth, the other gods proclaim Marduk as their king and do him homage. In the Old Testament, the coming of Yahweh means a victory over the gods, over the powers of chaos, the chaotic primordial sea, the monster Leviathan, and the enemies of Israel one and all. Increasingly the tribal god Yahweh is understood as the one God of all peoples and Lord of the Universe—and not simply through "evolution" or "folk psychology," but through concrete experiences on the part of the "prophets."

In other words, the Bible typically *historicizes supertemporal myth.* The patterns of timeless conditions and events reflected in the myth are now rooted in the history of the people of Israel, historically rooted, above all, in the exodus of the host led by Moses from Egypt.

This event lays the foundation for the theological understanding of

Yahweh's accession to power and royal sovereignty, as celebrated in the Psalms and as reflected on, with a view toward both the future (eschatology) and the beginnings of the world and the human race. Thus the core of Old Testament myths (most of which were taken over from Babylonian/Canaanite or Egyptian sources) is now *history as it really happened.* That is why the myths are often only alluded to, without their contents being reproduced. That is why the Old Testament is often less concerned with myths (in which the gods play a part) than with legends and sagas, which have human actors. That is why the text often has ties with things that actually happened, as in the story of the Tower of Babel (a Babylonian step-temple) or the Exodus stories. Many times indeed, as in the Books of Samuel and of Kings, the Bible presents straight historical narrative. This process of *historicization* can also be understood as *demythologization* undertaken by the traditions and authors of the Old Testament, in the interest of purifying the community's idea of God and at the same time giving it more historical potency.

This is still more the case with the *stories of Jesus.* For all the later mythical and legendary accretions (scholars point to the Virgin Birth, the assumption into heaven, the descent into hell), they aim to tell us about unique historical events, about a history that really happened and so is in principle open to the scrutiny of historical scholarship. This may be of no consequence to people who believe in myths, but for men and women who live in a postmythological age, it means a great deal.

The Gospels do not pretend to be scholarly biographies; they are announcements of the Good News, preaching, catechesis. Nonetheless they report what is, on the whole, actual history. They tell of a real person named Jesus of Nazareth, who was born in a specific country at a specific time, who lived, worked, struggled, and suffered. For someone who believes in Jesus and makes him the concrete standard for his behavior, it is not a matter of indifference whether this Jesus was a historical figure, the hero of a much-traveled legend, or a myth; whether his profession was hierarch, monk, or revolutionary; whether he honored the privileges of birth, caste, or race; whether he sided with the rich and the powerful or with the poor and the oppressed; whether he preached violence or nonviolence, domination or service, revenge or forgiveness; whether he was rightly put to death; whether he was justified in the end or not. In short, the believer would like to know whether and to what extent his faith has the support of historical reality.

But at this point we have what looks like a clear, ecumenical contradiction: Doesn't a faith oriented to the historical person of Jesus Christ necessarily lead to alienation from Indian culture?

THE HISTORIC AND THE COSMIC DIMENSIONS

A number of Hindu thinkers who have dealt with the figure of Christ would echo the title of a work by Vivekānanda's Swami Abhedānanda, "Why a Hindu Accepts Christ and Rejects Churchianity," 1965. There are, in turn, Christian theologians who have tried to meet Indian mythological thought halfway by arguing that these theologians have largely disregarded the historical Jesus (in the sense of the Gospels) and taken as their point of departure the cosmic Christ (from the Prologue to John and the post-Pauline Letters to the Ephesians and Colossians). This is the line followed by the brilliant Raymondo Panikkar, a Catholic who has done solid, pioneering work in the field of Hindu-Christian dialogue, in his book *The Unknown Christ of Hinduism* (1964). There he attempts a rapprochement by means of a comparison: Just as in some classic Indian texts, Brahmā (the Absolute, Transcendent, Unknown) is related to Īshvara (Lord, Creator, God), so, in Christianity, God (the Father) is related to God the Son (Logos, Christus). In this way, Panikkar manages to find something like a Hindu version of the Trinity.

I have a good deal of respect for Panikkar's bold theological effort, but, though the comparison is worth considering, I doubt that he is doing justice to Indian ideas. Isn't he comparing one speculation with another, in a manner that is still too Western? On the Christian side, this sort of comparison presupposes a fully developed doctrine of the Trinity, which we do not hear about until the neo-Nicaean fathers around the end of the fourth century, and which has little to do with the Jesus of the Synoptic Gospels, who never hinted of such a "mystery." Panikkar, too, might well have had his doubts here. Are we to burden Indians with all this highly developed, Hellenistic dogma? Is this what an Indian Christian theology will be like? If so, it will be a far cry from the Jesus of the Gospels, not to mention historical criticism of the Bible and Christian tradition.

At this point, Christology feels the impact of the *structural difference* between Hinduism and Christianity that we have already seen from the perspective of the individual's life history in the issue of reincarnation. That difference must now be spelled out more specifically, this time from the viewpoint of world history:

On the basis of their ancient, great classical tradition, the Hindu religions view God, the world, and man in a *natural–cyclical context*, which, needless to say, in no way excludes a singular act of revelation within those cycles.

On the basis of their earliest, most essential traditions, the prophetic religions—Judaism, Christianity, and Islam—view God, the world, and man in a *historical process,* which, needless to say, always has a cosmic dimension as well.

This implies that the classic contrasts between Hinduism and Christianity do have to be taken seriously, but they should not be exaggerated. Different structures of thought, which used to be limits, can be made into bridges, as W. Roth maintains in A. Bürkle, ed. *Indian Contributions to Present Day Theology,* 1966. Yet, so far, this has scarcely been done with respect to mediating between the cosmic and the historical perspectives. For that reason, I would emphasize, to begin with, that cosmic piety is in no sense excluded from the prophetic tradition, even though in both Protestant and Catholic existential theology (highly influential in the first half of this century) it was very much pushed off onto the periphery. Faith in God and in Jesus Christ may not be reduced to the compass of human existence and historicity; it has, of necessity, a cosmic dimension that embraces the world of animals and plants. Only by recognizing this can we understand mystical Hindu piety, as Bede Griffiths (the head of a Christian ashram in southern India for the past quarter century) has eloquently explained in his recent book *The Cosmic Revelation: The Hindu Way to God* (1984).

Of course, for the monotheistic religions of India, God is not only constantly present in the cosmos, but at the same time dynamically active within the history of this world even as it happens. He calls upon human beings, shakes them up, helps, hinders, and finally completes their lives. The Hindu religions are not without a historical consciousness; only, for a long time it has not been as developed as in the prophetic religions. Judaism, Christianity, and Islam understand history as a whole, *world history,* not as a continually new cyclical movement, the coming to be and passing away of the cosmos, but as a meaningful, coherent, ongoing, goal-directed process. This does not occur, however, in a constant rise ("progress") or a constant decline ("decadence"), but dialectically through crises, ruptures, and catastrophes. For believing Jews, Christians, and Muslims this history has a *telos,* a goal, a definitive fulfillment, for which the Bible uses code phrases like "the kingdom of God," "a new heaven and a new earth," and "eternal life."

The *consequences* of this approach to history are of the greatest significance for the problems facing the individual and society—including the problems of exploitation and oppression. This conception gives an extra weight of emphasis

to the history of humanity in all its phases,

to the moment, to individuals, their dignity and their rights, historical events and historical personalities, but also to human work, the occupations, to everything,

even, finally, to responsibility, guilt, conscience, and forgiveness.

In fact, at the intersections of the history of humanity, that history is given something like the importance of eternity. God, who is present in all places at all times but is not simply manifest, encounters human beings in his liberating, saving word. Not that God's eternal word is timeless, but it is met with as a concrete event in the historical experience of specific men and women. For this reason, the prophetic religions have repeatedly looked upon individual historical events and personalities as crucial for their experience of God, as *God's word or revelation in history as it actually happened.* For the three religions in the prophetic tradition this means:

That the fundamental experience of revelation for Israel is the liberation of the people from bondage in Israel;

That the fundamental experience of revelation for Christianity is Jesus of Nazareth as the Christ;

That the fundamental experience of revelation for Islam is the reception of the Qur'an by Muhammad, the Prophet.

But—the Hindu will immediately object here—is there no such fundamental revelation in the Hindu religions as well?

CHRIST AND KRISHNA

Classical Indology first concentrated on the early Vedic religion in the second and first millennia B.C. and the early philosophy of the Upanishads in the first millennium A.D. This is the reason why, to this day, Westerners are too little aware that the bhakti movement (which began back in the last centuries before Christ) and especially the monotheistic religions of Vishnuism and Shivaism (which came to the fore between the second century B.C. and the third century A.D.) definitely acknowledge a theologically relevant history and a fundamental revelation ("descent," "incarnation") of God in this history. The same holds for the revelation of Shiva in Lakulin, who taught Pāshupata Shivaism and whose four disciples and far-flung legacy are rather well known, precisely because it was important and faithfully transmitted. The same is true of the revelation of Vishnu in Krishna (and Rāma), whose historicity is of the highest importance, because with him a new epoch begins and a new teaching is proclaimed. A comparison between Krishna and Christ is particularly suggestive. Westerners often do not realize what a believing Hindu takes for granted: In *Krishna* we are dealing with a historical person (Hindus go on pilgrimage to the places where he once lived and worked), with an authentic *human being (vere homo).* At the same time we see in him the *revelation of the one God (vere Deus).* This means that for Hindus, too, the one God has revealed himself at a certain time and in a certain place. And for Hindus, too, there is within a cyclical world process a decisive intervention by God, which, as in the case of Krishna, has a sort of eschatological character for this world period. The fundamental revelation for this form of Hinduism, then, is the *avatāra,* the "descent" of God in Krishna, who has brought the good news of the *Bhagavad-Gītā.* Against this background we can understand the remark often heard among tolerant Hindus: "You believe in Christ, we believe in Krishna—it's all the same." There is no denying the parallel between faith in Christ and faith in Krishna, but are they really the same?

There is no gainsaying the fact that Krishna was a historical person, even though he can be traced to the post-Vedic period only vaguely through his connection with the battle of Kurukshetra, and though various layers of tradition have left their deposits on this real figure. But even if his life were more fully documented and the historical research about it were in better shape, the *differences* between Krishna and Christ are unmistakable:

- Jesus Christ is not, like Krishna, an amalgamation of various mythic and historical figures: Krishna is already mentioned in one of the Upanishads (eighth century B.C.?), but his importance did not grow until many centuries later, when he became identified with Krishna Vāsudeva, the founder of the monotheistic religion of the Bhāgavatas, who taught loving devotion to God (bhakti) as a way of salvation as far back as the second century B.C.
- Jesus Christ is not, like Krishna, one revelation or incarnation of God among many: Krishna is thought of as a revelation of the god Vishnu, as his eighth, in fact, to be followed by the ninth (Buddha) and a last one after him (Kalkin).

Clearly, in the religion of Krishna we find manifested a less pronounced historical consciousness, which is characteristic of cyclical thinking. The figure of Krishna represents a fusion of several traditions, and so there was simply no way to avoid a problem that the Christian community, whose Lord could be assigned to a definite time and place, managed to prevent by canonizing the credible evidence: the clustering of a mass of altogether dubious myths (at least as measured against the ethical level of the Bhagavad-Gītā) around the figure of Krishna. One need only compare some of the stories of Krishna's tricks and pranks, his love affairs and adulteries, with the Gospels, which bind together history and kerygma in a peculiar literary genre, but which also present documents of extraordinary moral seriousness.

Behind Hinduism's less sharply focused historical consciousness lies concealed, once again, the pattern of cyclical thought. If the revelations of Vishnu are repeated in every age, then in fact they tower over, explode, and devalue the concrete historical person through a continuous series of new manifestations. With revelations that can in principle occur anywhere at any time, the historicity of the event obviously plays a lesser role. And for this mystical point of view, the particular earthly manifestation is not as important as the deity hidden behind or within it, the god who becomes incarnate again and again. Even for an Indian thinker like Srī Aurobindo, who is interested in history and evolution, all revelations manifest the same "Krishna or Buddha or Christ essence" in man, which one is supposed to experience as identical to the "highest Being," the Absolute.

Thus Christianity sees a *decisive difference* separating it from monotheistic Hindu thought in the matter of Christology. Its position could be summarized as follows: *Jesus*, to be sure, is not simply another great yogi, a *satguru*, but neither is he a mythical incarnation of the Divine, an avatar, in the sense that a pious Hindu would find readily comprehensible. If Jesus were simply *one of the many avatāras* ("descents," "incarnations") of God in human form (the Dwarf, Parashu-Rāma, Rāma, Krishna, Buddha), in the animal form (fish, turtle, wild boar), or in mixed form (lion-man), as the stories of Vishnu tell, then Christ could be easily absorbed into the dynamic system of Indian mythology and cultic practice. He could be psychologized out of world history into the depths of the soul. Some Hindus do this—often in a spirit of great tolerance and understanding. Yet, in the face of such interpretations, Christians can hardly feel that they have been correctly understood.

In his very informative book *Hindus Before the Universal Christ* (1970)— which, however, would have done better to rely on Rāmānuja's qualified monism than on Shankara—the Indian Protestant theologian, S. J. Samartha rightly calls attention to the consequences of interpreting Jesus as an avatar:

> If Jesus were to be understood as an *avatāra*, then, as I have already shown, He would be relegated to a secondary level of reality; if Christ's state of being is to be preserved, then He must be placed in relation to *Brahma* himself. Further, if the world is understood as *māya* in the sense of unreal or illusion, then the historical dimension of Christ's person and work would no longer have any meaning. Hence, what we propose here is this: *Brahma*, properly explained, must not be incompatible with personal values, and characterizing the world as *māya* refers not to its state of being, but to its dependence on Brahma. Thus it becomes not impossible to relate Jesus Christ both to Brahma and to the world. In this way the dimension of the personal as well as of the historical would come into play within the domain of Hindu spirituality itself. (p. 175)

Jesus is not a mythical figure, not a divine being that takes on an earthly body for a given time, not a symbol of supertemporal truth without a trace of historical singularity. The message of the New Testament fastens Christian faith (despite some mythical language) to a real person, a quite specific historical figure, Jesus of Nazareth, whose message and life are the decisive criteria for the faith and activity, living and dying, of Christians, because he is God's unique revelation.

It makes a crucial difference whether God reveals himself to human beings in a long series of changing, contradictory, and in any case ambiguous mythical figures (Shiva can legitimate both asceticism and sexual permissiveness) or whether he, the Hidden One, commits himself to an unequivocal, permanent, reliable "image" *(eikon)* or "word" *(logos)*. This revelation, according to the New Testament, has become visible, audible, and morally binding in the figure of Jesus Christ, in this one person, who is in principle as historically tangible as Mahātma Gandhi. Paul expresses this idea in First Corinthians: "We know that 'an idol has no real existence,' and that 'there is no God but one.' For although there may be so-called gods in heaven or on earth—as indeed there are many 'gods' and many 'lords'—yet for *us* there is one God, the Father, from whom are all things and for whom we exist, and one Lord, Jesus Christ, through whom are all things and through whom we exist." (1 Cor 8:4–6) And because God has revealed himself in this way and not otherwise, Christians will see themselves as forever bound to stand up unconditionally for the things that Jesus stood up for and still does: for service to one's fellow men and women, regardless of hierarchies or caste systems, for readiness to be reconciled with others, transcending the boundaries of one's nation, religion, race, class, or family; in short, for universal nonviolence, selflessness, and love.

I believe that this idea should be vigorously developed in Hindu-Christian dialogue. The point of departure would be the concrete Jesus of the Sermon on the Mount and the Way of the Cross, whom many Hindus greatly respect as a revelation of perfect inwardness and unique closeness to God.

A COMMON STARTING POINT: JESUS IN THE SERMON ON THE MOUNT

The message of Jesus Christ should certainly *not* be understood after the manner of the *"Christian" exclusivism* that rejects all truths except its own or co-opts them as a priori ("anonymously") Christian. Neither, by the same token, should it let itself be co-opted by the sort of *"Hindu"* (or neo-Hindu) *inclusiveness* that finds its own truth and only its own truth in Christianity, that does not even confront the substance of the message which is Jesus Christ himself.

Christians in dialogue must face the truth of Indian tradition as it understands itself, and by the same token, Hindus should try to read Christian scriptures in a manner compatible with the self-concept of these sources. And in particular, they ought to face the issue of *historical research.* Because, for Christians, the truth, while not the same as the findings of history, is inseparable from them. This means that questions such as whether Krishna, Buddha, Ramakrishna, or Christ really had the same thing in mind, whether Jesus really was, as some Indian thinkers claim, a mystic who advocated a doctrine of *advaita,* or, rather, was at home in Jewish piety—these and other questions are, in the first instance, topics for historical research, which should be taken seriously, and not simply be decided by religious preference.

In the encounter with Hellenistic mythology (no less exuberant than the Indian variety), the message of Jesus Christ has already proved itself a significant critical standard. It made a large contribution, at that time, to the enlightenment and liberation, the exorcism and humanization of demon-ridden human beings. Might not this same message play a purifying, enlightening, sublimating function today in dialogue with Hindus? The old high-handed attitude once common to badly informed Christians, "We own the truth and have nothing to learn," evidently needs self-critical reflection. But there should also be critical and self-critical exploration of the uncomfortable objections of Indian thinkers to Hinduism (such as, most recently, N. C. Chaudhuri's case against Hindu animism and ritualism, against the disconnecting of religion from morality), which have been received with just as much outrage as earlier criticism of religion was received by believing Christians in Europe. Don't the Indian myths need to be historicized, relativized, and socialized, as Walter Hollenweger demands of Christianity in his attempt to do "intercultural theology" *(Dealing with Myths,* 1982)?

"First of all, we must affirm the thesis—however vague its meaning and however difficult it may be to apply," writes J. C. Hindley in his survey of the "historical Jesus as seen by Indians," "that an interpretation of Christ for India must assign a major role to the encounter with the historical Jesus." (in H. Bürkle, op. cit., p. 31) As opposed to speculative theological mediation, I would like to join with all the theologians and exegetes (since the early, important efforts of V. Chakkarai, P. Chenchiah, and A. J. Appasamy) who, in sketching out an Indian Christology, have started out "from below." These thinkers have begun with *the Jesus of the Sermon on the Mount and the Way of the Cross,* who spoke up for the poor and despised, who preached nonviolent love, and who has inspired many Indians from Rāmmohan Roy to Mahātma Gandhi. Along with Samartha, another prominent Protestant theologian from India, M. M. Thomas, points this up in his book on *The Acknowledged Christ of the Indian Renaissance* (1970). He quotes a famous remark of Gandhi's:

The message of Jesus, as I understand it, is contained in his Sermon on the Mount. The spirit of the Sermon on the Mount competes with the Bhagavad-gītā, on fairly equal terms, for the mastery of my heart. It is this Sermon that endeared Jesus to me. (p. 204)

Not only Jesus' preaching, though, but also his practice of nonviolence and finally his death:

> Although I cannot claim to be a Christian in the confessional sense, still the example of Jesus' suffering is a factor in the make-up of my fundamental belief in non-violence that guides all my worldly and temporal actions. Jesus would have lived in vain and died in vain, if he did not teach us to direct our lives according to the eternal law of love. (p. 205)

The "eternal law of love": Some Indians have found the way from the Christ who proclaims the gospel to the Christ whom the Gospels proclaim. They see in Jesus not only a great ethical model (the Sermon on the Mount) but also God himself wholly revealed through him: This is the revelation of the *love of God* that goes all the way into the negativity of suffering, abandonment, dying, the Cross.

Yet most Indians would agree with Gandhi: For him, the principle was more important than the person, the eternal more important than the historical, God living here and now more important than God acting in history. Death and resurrection happen every day . . . And from that famous discussion around 1820 between Rāmmohan Roy and the Baptist missionary Joshua Marshman (the first serious Hindu-Christian encounter on the theological plane) down to the discussion between Gandhi and Kali Charan Banerjee in our century, we may wonder: Haven't Christian missionaries overburdened their Indian contemporaries (who were or are primarily interested in the ethos Jesus, not in Hindu speculative thought) with Christian speculation about Jesus' divine nature and atonement? (Roy himself held this responsible for the failures of the Christian mission; he thought of the unity of Jesus with God the Father in the New Testament sense of a unity of will, intention, and obedience, not of being.) And above all, have the Christian churches in India, often ruled by an upper "caste" of clerics, really exemplified in this poor country the message of the Jesus who spoke to the poor and the oppressed? We need comparisons of Christian and Hindu teaching *and* theological reflection in the social situation. Theory *and* practice have to go hand in hand. This, then, is what Christians of all denominations must aim for in India: to send down roots of their Christianity into their native soil.

ENCULTURATION AND CRITICAL/CONTEXTUAL THEOLOGY

Anyone who feels misgivings here should first consider this: The Christian faith, with its Jewish-Palestinian origins, from the very beginning sank down deeply into Greco-Roman culture and (though not so "radically"—not down to the roots) into German-Slavic culture. Why should it not be able to do the same with Indian culture? Why shouldn't it put aside its European garments and dress like a native Indian? This theological and practical enculturation was put into effect in India most notably by the Italian Jesuit Roberto de Nobili (1577–1656), who lived as a *sannyasi*, was tried in the seventeenth century but later condemned by the Roman Inquisition. Since the Second Vatican Council, enculturation has finally been permitted—indeed it is now required.

This sort of enculturation of highly westernized Indian Christianity (only 2.6 percent, or around 18 million, Indians are Christians, some 60 percent, or 10 million, of these are Catholics) is being practiced in numerous Christian ashrams. Given the ghetto situation of Indian Catholicism, the Catholic Bishops Conference has also striven to make it a reality. Enculturation means more than external adaptation or accommodation. It means:

1. The introduction of Indian forms of meditation, Hindu forms of song, postures, gestures, dances, decoration, and other external liturgical elements;

2. The traditional Indian incorporation of nature (flowers, light, sunrise, and sunset) into Christian worship;

3. Liturgical reading of, and personal meditation on, Indian sacred scriptures: of appropriate texts from the Vedas, which attest to the transition of humanity to the transcendental dimension, to the Absolute, and so can impart inspiration to Christian communities too. Such practice is confirmed in principle by the theological arguments in our dialogues here.

Yet not only the adoption of Hindu dance forms (cf. A. Ronald Siqueira's *Classical Indian Dance and Christian Preaching*, 1978), but also the use of traditional Hindu texts for personal Christian prayer and meditation, for the priestly Office and community worship (see Robert Antoine, S.J., *Indian Ritual*), and so the application of Hindu spirituality as a whole, has clearly shown the need for critical discrimination, as well as further studies and reflection (on Christian thought and practice). The rule here is, There can be no critically responsible enculturation without *critically responsible theology and exegesis.*

The Christian message must be continually rethought, in the Indian context as elsewhere, and in the final analysis this can be done only by Indian Christians themselves (whose work I have in part relied on). Indian Christian theologians rightly call for a theology in the context of their culture. Such a *contextual theology* aims to create not a provincial, encapsulated school of thought, but a *truly ecumenical Indian theology, a solid critical–historical foundation,* which could enter into dialogue with Hinduism and also with Islam as a partner of equal value, enjoying equal rights, testing everything, keeping what is good from East and West, using creative imagination and critical powers of distinction so as to set off the Christian message itself—the gospel—to the best advantage, in authentic Indian dress.

Basic Reading List for the Hindu Religions

I. GENERAL PRESENTATIONS
1. Pratima Bowes. *The Hindu Religious Tradition: A Philosophical Approach.* London/Henley/Boston, 1977.
2. J. N. Farquhar. *A Primer of Hinduism.* 2nd ed. Oxford, 1912.
3. Erich Frauwallner. *History of Indian Philosophy.* Tr. V. M. Bedekar. 2 vols. Atlantic Highlands, 1974.
4. Jan Gonda. *Die Religionen Indiens.* Stuttgart, 1960–. Vol. I: *Veda und älterer Hinduismus.* 2nd ed., 1978. Vol. II: *Der jüngere Hinduismus.* 1963. (Die Religionen der Menschheit. Vols. 11, 12)
5. Troy Wilson Organ. *Hinduism: Its Historical Development.* New York, 1974.
6. *Hinduism.* Ed. Louis Renou. London/New York, 1961. (Great Religions of Modern Man)

II. PARTICULAR ISSUES
1. R. G. Bhandarkar. *Vaisnavism, Śaivism and Minor Religious Systems.* Strassburg, 1913. Reprint: Varanasi, 1965. (Grundriss der Indo-Arischen Philologie III, 6)
2. Sanjukta Gupta, Dirk Jan Hoens, and Teun Goudriaan. *Hindu Tantrism.* Leiden/Köln, 1979. (Handbuch der Orientalistik 2.Abt, Bd 4, 2. Abschn.)
3. P. B. Vidyarthi. *Divine Personality and Human Life in Ramanuja.* New Delhi, 1978.
4. S. J. Woodroffe. *Śakti and Śākta: Essays and Addresses.* 6th ed. Madras, 1965.
Further material can be found in:
5. *Einführung in die Indologie: Stand, Methoden, Aufgaben.* Eds. Heinz Bechert et al. Darmstadt, 1979.

III. SELECTED TEXTS
1. *A Source Book in Indian Philosophy.* Eds. S. Radhakrishnan and Charles A. Moore. Princeton, 1957.
2. *Hindu Myths: A Sourcebook.* Tr. from the Sanskrit with an Intro. by Wendy Doniger O'Flaherty. Harmondsworth, 1975. (Penguin Classics)
3. *Sixty Upaniṣads of the Veda.* Tr. into German by Paul Deussen, tr. from German into English by V. M. Bedekar and G. B. Palsule. 2 vols. Delhi, 1980.

4. R. C. Zaehner. *The Bhagavad-gita.* With a commentary based on the original sources. Oxford, 1969.

5. *L'Īśvaragita: le chant de Śiva.* Texte extrait du Kūrma-Purāna. Trad. du Sanskrit par P. E. Dumont. Baltimore/Paris, 1933.

6. *Classical Hindu Mythology: A Reader in the Sanskrit Purāṇas.* Ed. and tr. by Cornelia Dimmitt and J. A. B. van Buitenen. Philadelphia, 1978.

IV. REFERENCE

1. Benjamin Walker. *Hindu World: An Encyclopedic Survey of Hinduism.* 2 vols. London, 1968.

C.
Buddhism and Christianity

Chronology

486 (corrected longer reckoning) or 368 B.C. (shorter reckoning) *Parinirvāna*
(death) of the Buddha at the age of eighty
268–233 B.C. King Ashoka; first reforms; Council of Pātaliputra; introduction
of Buddhism into Lanka (Ceylon)
89–77 B.C. King Vattagāmanī Abhaya of Ceylon; the Pāli canon written down
first to fifth centuries A.D. Formation of the scriptures of Mahāyāna Buddhism
A.D. 67 Introduction of Buddhism into China (traditional date)
ca. 200 Nāgārjuna
ca. 300 Maitreyanātha
ca. 470 Arrival of Bodhidharma in China
ca. 480–540 Dignāga
ca. 620–49 King Srong-tsen gam-po of Tibet introduces Buddhism
836–842 King Lang-dar-ma of Tibet suppresses Buddhism
845 Suppression of Buddhism in China by Emperor Wu-tsung
972 First printing of the Chinese Tripitaka
eleventh to thirteenth centuries Destruction of Indian Buddhism by Islamic
conquerors
1044–77 King Anuruddha of Burma makes Theravāda Buddhism the state
religion of his kingdom
1130–1212 Hōnen Shonin, founder of Jōdo
1173–1262 Shinran, founder of Jōdo Shinshū
1222–82 Nichiren
1290–1364 Bu-tön, editor of the Tibetan canon
1357–1419 Tsong-kha-pa, reformer of Tibetan Buddhism
1575 Second (final) conversion of the Mongols
1750 Reform of the sangha in Ceylon by Saranankara
1864–1933 David Hewavitarne (Anagārika Dharmapāla)
1871 Fifth Council, in Mandalay
1873 The Pānadurā Dispute
1891 Nyanatiloka ordained
1919 Founding of Reiyū-kai, the oldest "Lotus sect"
1950 Founding of the World Fellowship of Buddhists; public conversion of
B. R. Ambedkar (1893–1956) to Buddhism
1954–56 Sixth Council, in Rangoon
1959 Flight of the Dalai Lama to India

I.
The Historical Buddha: His Teaching as a Way to Redemption

1. *Heinz Bechert:* Buddhist Perspectives

LIFE AND SIGNIFICANCE OF THE HISTORICAL BUDDHA

After Islam and Hinduism, we now come to Buddhism. Treating the great world religions in this order makes sense, first of all, geographically. For the regions in Southeast, Central, and East Asia where Buddhism was disseminated form the eastern frontier of the homelands of Islam and Hinduism. But there is also a material reason for putting off discussion of Buddhism until now: Just as Christianity and Islam grew out of Judaism and would be unthinkable without this historical foundation, so Buddhism as a historical phenomenon must be seen against the background of the religious and philosophical thought patterns that were widespread in India at the time and that we can call the preliminary or early forms of Hinduism. There was, first of all, the doctrine of the transmigration of souls and the cycle of existences, which can be found as far back as the pre-Buddhist Upanishads. These ideas were bound up —likewise in the pre-Buddhist period—with the notion of karma, that is, the effect of good and evil deeds on the way reincarnation takes place. And above all, the question of the way to get out of this cycle had already been posed, and some of the methods later used for Buddhism's way of

As mentioned earlier, the author of the "Buddhist Perspectives" and the author of the "Christian Responses" were unable, on account of deadline pressures, to coordinate the Buddhism sections with the definitive and greatly expanded version of the "Christian Responses," and Licentiate Alois Payer has helpfully advised the author of the "Christian Responses" in this context.

salvation were already, in principle, familiar. There were many kinds of ascetic practices and yoga exercises. Another factor was that the claim of the Brahmanic-Vedic tradition to general recognition had been questioned by several religious groups even before the time of the Buddha.* The question of whether God (or the gods) existed had already been raised and been given altogether different answers. The meaning and authority of old and apparently sacrosanct traditions—sacrificial rites, the caste system, etc.—were no longer going unchallenged.

As we can gather from the sources, there was in northern India around the time of the Buddha an unusually large variety of teachers and teachings. It was one of those happy periods of almost boundless intellectual diversity such as humanity has seldom enjoyed. And it was in this setting that an ascetic named Siddhārtha Gautama became the Buddha, the "awakened" or "enlightened" One. Who was he, and how did he reach that state?

Leaving aside subsequent legendary additions, to historical career of the Buddha can be clearly reconstructed. The young Siddhārtha came from the noble Shākya clan, and for this reason was also known as Shākyamuni, the wise man from the Shākya family. His father, Shuddhodana, was the head of one of the families that jointly ruled the little aristocratic republic of the Shākyas, on what is now the Indian-Nepalese frontier. These families belonged to the caste of the Nobles *(kshatriya)*. The young Siddhārtha married Yashodharā, and they had a son named Rāhula. Despite the outwardly happy circumstances of his life, at the age of twenty-nine Siddhārtha decided to leave his home and family to become an ascetic and search for final redemption from suffering. He informed his relatives of his irrevocable decision—the story of his clandestine departure is only a legend—and attached himself to various teachers who claimed to know the way to redemption. When following their teachings brought him no closer to this goal, he subjected himself to the harshest asceticism, with strict fasting and dangerous breathing exercises. This led him to the edge of the grave, but even the severest asceticism proved to be in vain. After six years, Siddhārtha gave it up and was then abandoned by his disciples and admirers. On the bank of the river Nairañjanā he recovered from his long exertions. And now at last he succeeded: Sitting under a tree, in deep concentration, he gazed upon the truth, salvation, and the way to get there. Siddhārtha had become the Buddha and had reached nirvāna. He knew that he would not be reborn. This happened on the site of the modern Bodh Gaya, in the Indian state of Bihar, under the bodhi tree, the "tree of enlightenment."

* Ājīvikas and Jains challenged the value of the Vedas and thus deliberately put themselves outside the Vedic-Hindu tradition.

Only after long reflection—the legend says, on the urging of the god Brahmā—did the Buddha resolve to present to men the truth he had realized. For it was difficult to grasp; it could hardly be put into words. He wandered to Varanasi (Benares), where, tradition says, the first person to whom he tried to explain his teaching failed to understand and turned away. But then, in the grove of the gazelles at Sarnath, outside the gates of Varanasi, he met five wandering ascetics who recognized him from the days of his own extreme ascetical practices. He expounded to them his teaching of the "Four Noble Truths" in the so-called Sermon of Benares, and converted them. Thus was founded the sangha, the order of Buddhist monks and nuns. For about forty-five years he wandered about, teaching the people in what is today Uttar Pradesh and Bihar. At the age of eighty the Buddha died, in Kushinagara, from food poisoning. He thereupon entered parinirvāna, that is, he arrived at the state of complete extinction, in which there is no rebirth. Over the course of the years, the Buddha became so famous that a war almost broke out over the remnants of his ashes. But the fragments of his bones and ashes were peacefully divided, thereby inaugurating the Buddhist cult of relics.

We do not know exactly when to date all this. The moment of parinirvāna is calculated very differently by different authorities. According to ancient Indian tradition, the Buddha died in 368 B.C. Leading Japanese scholars prefer 386; Ceylonese tradition, 543. Since Ceylonese tradition makes other chronological errors, its date has been corrected to 486 or 480, which is what one finds today in almost all the history books. But that is evidently at least a hundred years too early.

Of course, this question has no significance for understanding the Buddha's teaching. The Buddha did not look upon himself as a unique historical phenomenon, and in no sense did he teach that humanity could be redeemed only through him. He was no one's envoy or agent, and he received a revelation from no one. He simply pointed the way to insights that he had achieved entirely on his own. He set no store by ritual or symbolic/magical ceremonies, such as we find in the Brahmanic sacrifices or in the traditional interpretation of the Christian Mass. As for the idea (widely held in India at the time) of a God who created and rules the world, he labeled it an illusion. In his view, there is no externally existing soul, and so there can be neither eternal bliss nor eternal damnation. Merely believing in the Buddha does not lead to redemption. Prayers and the hope for grace and forgiveness, which presuppose specific notions of God, have no place in his teaching.

Nevertheless, there is a definitive salvation from suffering, and only consistent following of the path shown by the Buddha can bring us to it. This way is absolute; it does not depend upon the Buddha or anyone else. One may be aware of it without ever having heard of the Buddha (the Buddhists speak of *pratyeka buddhas*, those "privately enlightened" all by themselves). There were other buddhas in the past, and there will be new buddhas in the future who will recognize the truth. One could go so far as to say that as far as the truth of Buddhist teaching is concerned, it does not even matter that much whether the Buddha as a historical personality ever existed, whereas Christianity would lose its meaning without the historical person of Jesus.

Hence if we are looking in the oldest form of Buddhism for many of the ideas and concepts centrally important to other religions, we shall never find them: The Buddha cast them aside as false or worthless. Most people, naturally, cannot in the long run get along without prayer, ritual, belief in miracles, and the like; and so, much of what was thrown out the front door of Buddhism, so to speak, came in through the back, as the historical evolution of Buddhism shows all too clearly.

MEANING AND AIM OF THE BUDDHA'S TEACHING

Buddhism has been accused of promoting spiritual egoism, of providing no comfort to the poor and weak, indeed of being nihilistic and pessimistic. Above all, the doctrine of each individual's total responsibility for his own fate strikes some critics as bleak and inhuman. Still, if the Buddha's description of reality is accurate, then the followers of other teachings have abandoned themselves to self-deception. The Buddha did not create the world, and he was not responsible for its flaws. Nor could he change it. He merely recognized its true nature, and thereby overcame it.

The assertion is often made that the teaching of the Buddha is actually not a religion, but a philosophy. This is wide of the mark: Philosophy is the attempt to explain this world, or a reflection on its explainability. But the Buddha declined to give an explanation of the world. He continually and unequivocally defined the purpose of his teaching as dealing only with what leads to salvation, to nirvāna. Once, when the Buddha was staying near Kosambī, he took some leaves from a simsapā tree in his hands and asked: "Which is more, these few simsapā leaves that I have taken up in my hand, or the other leaves over in the simsapā forest?" The monks answered, "The many leaves in the forest." "So too," said the Buddha, "what I have come to know and have not told you is much more than what I have told you. And why have I not told you that? Because it would do you no good, would not get you to turn away from earthly things, to overcome your desires, would not lead to nirvāna. And what have I told you? I have told you what suffering is, what the origin of suffering is, what the extinction of suffering is, and what the path leading to the extinction of suffering is, that is what I have told you." (*Samyutta Nikāya* V, 437–38)

"As the great ocean is saturated by only one taste, the taste of salt, so this teaching and system is also saturated with only one taste, the taste of salvation." *(Vinaya Pitaka* II, 238)

The Buddha is a doctor who cures his patients' illness by giving them the right medicine, so that they can become well. There is no room here for the questions of philosophers, which are asked only out of a thirst for knowledge. "A man," said the Buddha, "was struck by a poisoned arrow, and his friends called in a skillful doctor. Now, if the sick man said, 'I won't let my wound be treated until I know who the man is, which caste he belongs to, what his name is, etc.,' how would things end? The man would die from his wound." *(Majjhima Nikaya* I, 426) The Buddha is interested only in overcoming suffering; and hence he consistently limits himself to teaching the one essential, the way to cure one's sickness; for this sickness is none other than our existence itself.

The philosophers, who remain trapped by their greed for new knowledge, are like people born blind who have been allowed to touch an elephant. One has touched the head, another the trunk, a third the tail, and now they are arguing: "The elephant looks like this"; "No, he looks like this"—until the battle of opinions turns into a battle of fists. *(Udana* VI, 4) Isn't that the most telling account of the history of discussions about religious doctrines and world views?

The Buddha always appealed to man's rationality and his capacity for understanding. His method of teaching corresponds, in principle, to that of the Socratic dialogue. He proclaims nothing *ex cathedra;* he evokes knowledge from his conversation partner, convincing him through patient argument. But not everything in the world can be fathomed by mere reason or cogitation. The highest knowledge can be experienced only, as we shall see, by translating the Buddhist way of salvation into reality.

The Uselessness of Faith; Coexistence with Other Forms of Religion

The Buddha linked his teaching with the demand not simply to believe him, but to follow his advice and test the correctness of his ideas in practice. Believers are like a chain of blind men, none of whom sees anything. The Buddha saw how dangerous it is when human beings cling blindly and fanatically to any doctrine, even should it be the Buddha's. That is why he stressed the need for tolerance toward those who think differently. This tolerance is far more than merely putting up with such people: Once, after a long conversation, the Buddha converted the householder Upāli, formerly a follower of Mahāvīra, the founder of the religious community of the Jains. Now that he was converted, Upāli wished to close his house to the adherents of other teachings. The

Buddha disapproved of this and told him: "For a long time your house has been a source of gifts for the Jain monks. So you should continue to give them food when they come to you." *(Anguttara Nikāya* IV, 185)

It is true that Buddhist monks were given a mandate to announce the Buddha's teaching "out of compassion for the world and for the salvation of many." But they were not to preach unless explicitly invited to. Many centuries later, the monks were still supposed to write no books unless someone had approached them with this wish. And under no circumstances was the teaching of the Buddha to be imposed upon anyone.

Buddhism has often coexisted with other religions in the sense that one and the same person could profess both of them. Western observers, for the most part, have misunderstood this situation, but it becomes clear if one keeps in mind the meaning of Buddhism: The Buddha is not a god or a divine consoler who can help us, say, when the life of a relative hangs in the balance. In such cases it is often cold comfort to learn that all existence is suffering and that the dimensions of that suffering depend upon one's own earlier deeds. Perhaps we are too weak to bear this harsh truth. For that reason, Buddhism has always left the way open for its laity to the traditional gods and cults. As I have said, the teaching of the Buddha and its mechanisms are exclusively oriented to the goal of final salvation from suffering: nirvāna. Hence the invocation of gods and spirits from other cults may seem to make sense for religious needs of ordinary people in everyday life. This does not create a conflict with Buddhism, because such practices are defined not as a part of religion *(shāsana),* but as secular. There are some limitations, of course: Buddhist monks should not have anything to do with the cults of gods or spirits or join in their rituals, because they have renounced worldly life. Bloody sacrifices are likewise ruled out, because they violate the Buddhist commandment not to kill.

The Buddha also acknowledged that traditional piety has a social function. When asked what was required for a community to flourish, he named these: apart from regular council meetings, unanimity in carrying out its resolutions, adherence to the old laws, and respect for justice, the preservation of private and public sanctuaries and the giving of the traditional gifts and offerings—i.e., the rites for the ancient gods. These things were not in conflict with providing protection and security for the perfect, that is, Buddhist saints. That is why even today at the court of the King of Thailand, who is the protector of the Buddhist religion in his country, one sees resident Brahman priests. They are there to carry out the Hindu rites that, according to ancient custom, are performed at royal courts within the Indian cultural complex.

SUFFERING AND REINCARNATION

The foundations of Buddhist teaching are formulated in the "Four Noble Truths," which the Buddha disclosed in his first discourse, the "Sermon at Benares."

The first of these truths is, "Everything is suffering," or in other words: In the final analysis all forms of existence are by nature full of grief. That doesn't mean, of course, that existence is manifestly painful at every moment. If that were so, it would have long since self-destructed. In the textbooks, feelings are expressly characterized as being pleasant, unpleasant, or neutral. And yet, in the end, they are all sorrow-ful. Why? Because all the facts and conditions in this world of appearances are transitory. They are subject to the law of continuous change, the inescapable cycle of coming to be and passing away. All the parts of our personality are like the bubbly spray one sees constantly foaming up and disappearing on the surface of swift-flowing streams. Only out of ignorance and blindness do we keep searching for something permanent and imperishable in this life, an immortal soul, a self within us. The Buddha tells us that our existence is nothing but a process, the ongoing emergence and disappearance of elements of existence in a seeming continuum.

We can know with certainty that there is no eternal substance or soul in our person by analyzing the personality, which consists of five ephemeral "existence groups": bodily form, sensation, perception, psychic "structures," and consciousness. Since all these parts of the personality are subject to emergence and disappearance, it makes no sense to look for an immortal soul. The awareness of this is the most important special feature of Buddhism. It is expressed in the formula of the three "characteristics": Everything is sorrowful, everything is transient, and everything is "not the self."

If that is the case, we must naturally wonder: Then, how is reincarnation possible, how can anything exist at all? The answer to this question gives us the second of the Four Noble Truths. "This, monks," said the Buddha, "is the truth about the origin of suffering: It is desire that leads from reincarnation to reincarnation, that finds it joy here and there, the desire for enjoyment, for existence, and for annihilation." The Buddha used the symbol of thirst for this desire; it is the driving force that keeps the cycle of existence in motion. This cycle cannot be simply broken off, for example, by suicide, which would only have to lead to a new reincarnation. The desire for death and annihilation is just as much a form of this thirst as other desires are. Consequently, all forms of thirst lead to being caught in *samsara*, the cycle of existence. The sort of reincarnation one has is determined by the law of karma, which we are already familiar with. One is reincarnated in good forms of existence through good deeds, in evil forms through evil deeds (karma). The oldest texts speak of five places for reincarnation: hell, the animal world, the realm of ghosts, the human world, and the divine world. Gods are nothing more than creatures in the cycle of rebirths that have risen through good karma to an especially pleasant form of existence of limited duration.

Events in the world, therefore, are not arbitrary or random, but governed by unchangeable law. The laws of nature we are familiar with are only a small part of this regular pattern, which is, as a whole, inescapably complicated and only partly comprehensible to man. The underlying order of things is *dharma* (law). The same word is also used for the teaching of the Buddha, which discloses the portion of that infinite pattern which human beings must know in order to follow the way to salvation.

The connection between the individual factors in the cycle of existences is described in a famous phrase as "dependent origination" (*pratītya-samutpāda*). I will use this formula, often inaccurately translated as "causal nexus," as an example of the early Buddhist method of presenting doctrine in abbreviated form: As a function of (1) "ignorance," the (2) "psychic structures" arise; that is, impulses of the will directed at existing objects, and existence itself, arise in the person who lacks redeeming knowledge. As a function of these "structures" (3) consciousness arises after death as the bearer of a new existence; as a function of that, (4) "name and form" develop, i.e., psychic factors and the body, and further (5), the "six-fold realm," meaning the six organs of sense, or the five senses plus thought; from this follows (6) "contact" of the sense organs with their objects. From this (7) the "sensations" arise, which cause (8) greed (literally "thirst") for objects and existence. After death they bring about (9) the "seizing" of a new womb, to (10) "becoming," to the new (11) "birth," and therewith again to (12) "old age and death."

Can we ever escape this cycle of sorrowful existence? The Buddha answers that question with the third of the four Noble Truths: "This is the truth of the extinction of suffering: It is the complete turning away from desire, the extinguishing, rejecting, abandoning of desire." This total abandonment of desire is possible only for the person who has recognized that everything, including the pleasant and apparently constant things in this world, is fleeting, subject to suffering, and without a self, and who as a result of this realization can face everything with serenity. The end of desire is the definitive liberation, the undoing of all the foundations of existence, extinction, nirvāna.

The Way to Liberation

Now we must ask how this liberation can be attained. The answer gives us the fourth Noble Truth, which deals with the way to the abolition of sorrow, the "Eightfold Path," taught by the Buddha. The first step on this path, "right views," consists in the acknowledgement of the Four Noble Truths and in discerning that personality does not constitute an eternally existing "self" (ātman). The remaining steps on the path follow from this one; they relate to the moral conduct of the person seeking liberation and to the correct methods of meditation and concentration. With their help, the illusion of the "self," even in the deeper levels of the psyche, is removed, the greed for existence overcome, and liberation achieved. In this way, the three "harmful" basic causes, or "roots," namely greed, hatred, and delusion, are done away with.

Buddhist ethics, accordingly, is a part of the teaching on salvation, not an end in itself or "works righteousness," and certainly not the execution of a divine command, like, for instance, the ethics of the Old Testament. It is based on the counsels that the Buddha gave his followers. It is a purely mental ethics, concerned not with the action carried out but with the attitude of mind that underlies it and is expressed in it. Someone who mistakes a cord for a snake and strikes at it to kill it is already guilty of killing. The first fundamental principle of moral behavior is not to injure any living thing. The goal of moral behavior is at the same time mastery of the senses. Its foundation is the right inner attitude, as manifested in the four "divine lingerings": kindness, sympathy, the sharing of joy, and serenity. With these four spiritual stances, the meditating person radiates in all directions. An attitude of great kindness and great compassion defines the nature of Buddhas.

Ethical action in the Buddhist sense is also, in the long run, useful, and beneficial for the agent—who may not, however, steal a sidelong glance at any personal benefit. That would only strengthen his egoism, and then he wouldn't profit from his action at all. Thus his good conduct must be "unintentional." As already mentioned, this right conduct is determined by the world order in the sense that beneficial acts produce good karma, while mischievous acts produce bad karma. Hence action motivated by the key virtues of sympathy and kindness will have good consequences, while action motivated by the key evils of greed, hatred, and delusion will have bad ones.

As we can readily see, this regular pattern eludes direct recognition. And since all beings are different and are at different stages of the way to liberation, there is no code of laws that are equally valid for each one. Rather, as the Tübingen Indologist and professor of religious science Helmuth von Glasenapp (d. 1963) put it, Buddhist ethics is a "tiered ethics." We shall see in the next chapter that, for this reason, different rules of behavior hold for people who live in the world from those for the monks and nuns who have withdrawn from it. But, for all men and women who wish to follow his teaching, the Buddha laid down five rules as a sort of minimal guide for right conduct: Do not kill, do not steal, avoid sexual excess, do not lie, and abstain from intoxicants. These general recommendations for morally correct behavior do not amount to specific prescriptions for the legal and practical affairs of the world, since the Buddha consistently refused to see that as his responsibility. And so Buddhism set no new precedents, for example, on questions of sexual behavior and family law: Polyandry was allowed to continue in places where it had been customary, such as Tibet and in the highlands of Ceylon; and the same was true elsewhere for polygamy and monogamy. So long as one lives in the world, one should conform to the accepted standards, unless and until they violate the general principles of moral action.

The different forms of Buddhist meditation or "unfolding of the spirit" are of the greatest importance for making the Buddhist way of salvation a reality. The knowledge that leads to liberation is not the mere awareness of matters of fact, but consists in the total, radical transformation (which results from correct understanding) of the person striving for liberation. The methods of Buddhist meditation are manifold; and, according to the teaching of the Buddha, they are to be adapted to the psychic disposition of each individual. A distinction is drawn between "analytical" methods and kinds of "absorption." Among the analytical methods of meditation, the first that should be mentioned is the "awareness of mindfulness" (*smrityupasthāna*, Pāli *satipatthāna*), which concentrates on analyzing the personality of the one meditating and thus on the realization of the personality's fleetingness. At each moment, the person meditating experiences with full consciousness all the stirrings of his body and his psyche. Absorption is defined as directing the mind to a single object of meditation. By means of certain exercises, the individual reaches states of absorption (*dhyāna*), which range from the first level, marked by a feeling of happiness, to the fourth, where all is serene. Other texts say the scale extends to an eighth level, in the "Sphere of Neither-Perception-nor-Non-Perception."

NIRVĀNA

The Indic word for the final goal of the Buddhist way of salvation is nirvāna, which actually means "extinction." It is essentially defined by negative statements: It is the ceasing of pain, the drying up of greed, hatred, and delusion, the complete extinction of the existence-groups (life functions, both physical and mental). Critics of Buddhism have concluded from this that nirvāna is synonymous with absolute annihilation, and that the religion of the Buddha is essentially nihilistic, but they are wrong. It is true that, for the redeemed person, all the existence-groups are extinguished, but nirvāna appears to be annihilation only to the ignorant worldling. For the person with knowledge, it is the realm of absolute peace, wholly cut off from the world. A famous passage in the Pāli canon says:

"Monks, there is a domain where there is neither solid nor fluid, neither heat nor movement, neither this world nor that, neither sun nor moon. Monks, I call that neither a coming nor a going, nor a stopping, nor a being born nor a dying. It is without any foundation, without development, without foothold: That is what the end of suffering is."
(*Udāna* VIII, 3)

Nirvāna is therefore "the complete 'extinction' of the volitional drive that manifests itself in greed, hatred, and illusion, that says yes to life and desperately clutches it. And so it is the definitive, complete liberation from all future rebirth, aging and dying, suffering and misery," as the renowned Buddhist monk and scholar Nyanatiloka puts it. One has to avoid two misunderstandings here, the idea, on the one hand, that nirvāna is simply annihilation and, on the other, that it is something like eternal life. It is, rather, a state that can only be experienced, that defies our categories of thought and description.

Nor is nirvāna something that can be known only after death, like the paradise of Islam or the eternal life and resurrection of the body for Christians. Rather, nirvāna is experienced from the moment one attains holiness. The Buddhist saint has already reached the complete extinction of passion, absolute inner peace. "Bliss is nirvāna," says Sāriputta, one of the Buddha's two main disciples. And to the question of how there could be bliss where there is no sensation, he answers: "That is just where the bliss of nirvāna lies, in there being no sensation there."
(*Anguttara Nikāya* V, 414–15) The body and psyche of the liberated person go on functioning until the moment of physical disintegration arrives. But liberation from the clinging to existence, absolute inner freedom, has been achieved. Hermann Oldenberg summarizes what the texts tell us: "Off in the insubstantial distance lie hopes and fears. Willing, the clinging to the delusions of the self, has been overcome the way a man sheds the foolish wishes of childhood. What does it matter if fleeting existence, whose root is now destroyed, continues its indifferent semblance of life for a few more moments—or for aeons? If the saint wishes to put an end to this existence now, he may do so. But most hold on until nature has reached its goal. To such people apply the words that tradition places in the mouth of Sāriputta: 'I do not long for death, I do not long for life. I wait till the hour comes, conscious, with my mind awake.' " (Oldenberg, *Buddha*, p. 265)

We must now ask who exactly is reborn, who enters nirvāna and then is reborn no more. Nāgasena, who explained the Buddha's teaching to the Indo-Greek king Menandros (Milinda), uses the following image: "If someone lights a lamp, would it not burn the whole night through? Then, is the flame in the first night watch identical to the flame in the middle and the last night watch, or are they different?" The king has to say no to both questions. "In the same way," says Nāgasena, "the chain of all the circumstances in this life is joined together: one comes into being, another passes away. Without beginning, without end, it is all a unit. Thus whoever attains the last stage of awareness is neither the same being nor a different being." *(Milinda-pañha 40)*

Now we understand why the Buddha did not answer the question about the further existence of the liberated individual in nirvāna. He declines to answer questions about "whether the world is eternal or not eternal, whether the world is limited or infinite, whether living creatures are identical to their bodies or different from them, whether the perfect survive after their death or not, or whether they neither survive nor do not survive." *(Majjhima Nikāya I, 426)* These questions lead into the maze of conflicting opinions, to confusion, far from what is alone necessary and meaningful, namely the way to nirvāna.

But the questions about eternity and the existence or nonexistence of the liberated in nirvāna, and about the absolute, are so universally human that over the course of the history of Buddhism they kept being asked again in a new fashion. The Buddha did not refuse to answer them because he didn't know the answer. For Buddhists, a buddha is potentially "omniscient"; that is, he can know whatever he wants to know. Once he is enlightened, his consciousness is no longer subject to the restrictions that our normal consciousness must labor under. Modern Buddhists remind us that physics now makes statements about the nature of the subatomic world and of the universe that baffle our ordinary categories of thought (as happened with the theory of relativity), and that even these statements may be only quite provisional. But questions about the world's finitude or infinity, etc., carry us beyond the reach of our normal cognitive faculties. They are, therefore, false questions and cannot be answered correctly. If nirvāna is a state that no longer belongs to the domain of the *samskāras*, the "structures," no longer subject to the intuitive forms of time and space, then it would make no sense at all to label it as "eternal life," and we can speak of it as the "highest bliss" only figuratively, as a description of the indescribable, as in the passage cited earlier. And if Buddhist enlightenment opens up unlimited awareness, it also affords the insight that with our limited powers of cognition we cannot understand the universe, and it would be senseless to try.

BUDDHIST COSMOLOGY

Buddhism agrees with the other great religions on one point: on the special role that it assigns human beings. Of course, for the Buddhist, all forms of life are in principle of equal value. For him, as for most Hindus, this is a consequence of the doctrine of reincarnation. For that reason, it is a moral ideal and the first rule of Buddhist ethics not to injure any living creature. Schopenhauer, who was one of the first Europeans to understand the essential features of Buddhism, declared that Buddhist ethics was superior to that of Christianity, because the latter ignored animals. In our day, when we have begun to understand what a catastrophe the ruthless exploitation of other forms of life by humans has provoked, the correctness of this observation has become particularly clear.

Nevertheless, man enjoys a special prominence insofar as only he can recognize his own need for salvation; he alone has the capacity to follow the way to salvation. In the form of human existence, beings acquire the ability to reflect on themselves. The higher beings, the so-called gods, also have consciousness in our sense; but their existence, which is conditioned by earlier good deeds (although it, too, has an expiration date), is framed in such a way that suffering too rarely enters their consciousness. Thus the first stage of the way to liberation is trodden by humanity (perhaps too by beings with a similarly structured consciousness in different worlds), and human beings obtain enlightenment and become Buddhas.

Buddhist cosmology is characterized by its knowledge of the enormous dimensions of time and space. The first modern scholars to study Buddhist texts were amazed by the "huge numbers of the Buddhists." For Westerners, whose own religious tradition dated the creation only a few millennia back, this was still, 150 years ago, a source of astonishment. Buddhist cosmology starts out from the assumption that world history runs in cycles, from periods of origin, through repeated evolutions, to cosmic disasters, whereupon new worlds emerge. In principle this is the same thing, on the cosmic scale, as the pattern we perceive of emergence, persistence, and dissolution of the individual factors of existence in unimaginably brief time periods, and the sequence we observe in our world of the birth, life, and death of any creature.

An ancient text uses a rationalistic reading of a myth to explain the idea—familiar to many Indians around the time of the Buddha—of a divine ruler of the world: After the world has gone under, it unfolds anew. The creature that comes first into existence in the new world gets the idea: "I am Brahma, the great, almighty God, whose eye sees all things, the absolute Lord, the Creator, who governs all things by his will. I have fashioned these creatures, because earlier the idea came to me: 'Oh if only other creatures would come into existence. That was the wish of my mind, and now in fact all these creatures *have* come into existence.' And the creatures that came into existence after the first also think: 'That is Brahma, the almighty God, etc.' " (*Dīghā Nikāya* I, 17–19) This is in truth only an illusion, for all creatures are subject to the unchangeable laws of the world process. Even Brahmā became God only through his good karma. When the good karma is used up, he will die and be reborn in a different form.

For Buddhists, the question of God is not worth discussing at length. Some years ago, the Buddhists of Indonesia were suddenly compelled to give their views on the subject of God, because the country's constitution stipulates that citizens must believe in God. Pressed to define their position, they gave different answers. Some said, for us nirvāna, the totally Other, the Transcendent—is God. Others had recourse to the notion of the Adibuddha, the primal Buddha, from whom all other Buddhas have come forth. This teaching was known to the medieval Vajrayāna Buddhism of Java. They might also have named *shūnyatā,* the "void" (more on this in Chapter III) as God, as medieval Islamic mystics in Java did, when they gave Allah the Buddhist title *kesunyataan.* Finally, they could have identified dharma as their idea of God (some did). Actually, dharma designates the highest principle in Buddhism: It is the order, the pattern of regularity that marks the world process. It is the teaching of the Buddha, which is in keeping with this law. But it is also every individual element of existence that the world is composed of.

There is no room in Buddhism for the idea of God familiar to us from Christianity. Thus, according to an ancient text, the Buddha says: "There are ascetics and priests who claim that whatever good or evil befalls a person is brought about by God's creation. I sought these people out and asked them: 'Is it true that you advocate this teaching?' They said yes. Then I told them: 'In that case, honored sirs, God's creation would be the reason why human beings become murderers, thieves, violent, liars, talebearers, avaricious, and so on.' " (*Anguttara Nikāya* III, 174) In this regard, all the early Buddhist texts are consistent, even though Christian theologians have often found this hard to understand. Hence the opinion one frequently meets with, that the Buddha announced his "indifference" to the question of the world's creator and rejected the question of God, distorts the facts. The difficulties of understanding such a foreign conceptual world become further apparent when visitors to Buddhist temples see images of the gods and jump to the conclusion that this is "polytheism." As we learned in the discussion of the cycle of existence, the so-called world of the gods is nothing but a somewhat higher form of existence, which we, too, in principle, could reach. Since the Indian texts use altogether different words for our terms "God" and "gods," only the outsider would confuse the two.

If dharma, the strictly impersonal law regulating the world, and its expression in the Buddha's teaching are timeless, the form of its earthly appearance is as fleeting as everything else. The teaching of the Buddha will be forgotten, the order he founded will cease to be, until at some point in the distant future another being will receive enlightenment and thereby become the Buddha. The Buddha himself said his teaching would last five hundred years. Later Buddhists have reinterpreted this prediction in various ways, but a glance at the history of Buddhism shows how realistic it was. Around five hundred years after its founding, Buddhism was linked to nationalism in Sri Lanka, in opposition to its original principles. And around the same time in India the ancient teaching that one can arrive at salvation only through one's own efforts began to be overlaid by ideas of a possible "outside redemption," that is, a salvation with the help of supernatural beings, the purest form of which we shall later find in Japanese Amidism.

2. *Hans Küng:* A Christian Response

Professor Bechert has given us an impressive survey of Buddhism and pointed the way toward its heart. It is no secret that Buddhism takes a radical intellectual stance by comparison with Christianity. For almost two and a half millennia, hundreds of millions of Asians have accepted the message of the Buddha and shaped their lives with it. What, for Christian theology, is the center of things, appears in a very different light for Buddhism: "God," "soul," "salvation," "history." There is power in Buddhism's great concentration on the "Four Noble Truths," in its rejection of superfluous metaphysical "speculation," in its appeal to human reason and cognitive faculties. It is a religion without an "afterworld" in Nietzsche's sense; it demands no sacrifice of the intellect and imposes no moral casuistry—ideally designed, or so it would seem, for the critical Western intelligentsia.

In this first response, I cannot take a stand at once on all the issues that have been broached: the life and teaching of the historical Buddha, suffering and reincarnation, ethics, meditation, and cosmology. I will have to take a systematic approach and slowly work my way through the various questions. That is why I shall "set the mood"—as in my responses to Islam and Hinduism—with a sketch of the historical contacts between Christianity and Buddhism. I shall then focus on the person of the Buddha—vis-à-vis the figure of Jesus—and then make a brief statement on the question of nirvāna. It is precisely from what they have to say on these matters that Buddhism and Christianity acquire their unmistakable profiles.

THE FIRST CONTACTS

Today Christians and Buddhists are entering a new epoch in their relations: For the first time in history, they are taking up a serious dialogue. Until the nineteenth century, the Christian world did not even know the difference between Hinduism and Buddhism. And this despite the fact that, as we discovered in the discussion of Hinduism, in *antiquity* there had been cultural exchange between India and the West, starting with the time of Alexander the Great; and that through the art of Gandhāra the Greeks left their mark on the artistic representation of the Buddha throughout the East, as far afield as Japan and Indonesia. And another surprise: The first mention of the Buddha in Christian sources appears as early as around the year 200 in the *Miscellany (Stromateis)* of Clement of Alexandria, who wished to show that Christian gnosis was superior to every other kind: "And there are in India those who follow the commandments of the Buddha, whom they revere as a god because of his immense holiness." (1, 15)

To be sure, one hears scarcely anything from this period about the Buddha's teaching; and we can only conjecture, as we have seen, how far Indian influence extended in the valley of the Nile and the Hellenistic world as a whole. Still, whatever the exact historical connections may be, a comparison of Buddhist and Christian monasticism (which, we notice, got its start in Egypt) ought to help clarify the situation, as should a contrast of Buddhist and Christian speculative thought (which in Greece takes the form of a "negative theology" reminiscent of Buddhist tendencies).

We are also ill informed about relations between Christians and Buddhists in the *Middle Ages*. It is known that "heretical" Nestorian Christians from Asia Minor pressed as far East as India and beyond, into central Asia, and finally, already in the seventh century, had gotten as far as China. Evidently they lived together with Chinese Buddhists over the centuries, as attested to by the famous inscription on the commemorative stone of Hsianfu from 781. In addition, we know that in the thirteenth and fourteenth centuries, Franciscan missionaries arrived at the court of the Mongol emperor in Peking and reported back to Europe how impressed they were by the asceticism of mendicant Buddhist monks. But with the fall of the Yüan dynasty, in the second half of the fourteenth century, these good relations came to an abrupt halt.

Not until the beginning of the *modern period* in Europe, during the sixteenth century, did further encounters take place between Christians and Buddhists. We know of the friendship of the first Christian missionary in Japan, the Jesuit Francis Xavier, with a Buddhist abbot. We also have an account of the debate between another Jesuit missionary,

Cosme de Torres, and Japanese Zen Buddhists. But these amounted to little more than an exchange of Christian scholastic proofs of the existence of God, on the one hand, and mystical Buddhist arguments for the "void" and the unfathomable "nothing," which the Jesuits understood in the nihilistic sense.

Francis Xavier introduced the word "Deusu"—Latin *Deus* altered for Japanese ears—for "God." He then learned that Buddhist bonzes associated "Deusu" with the similar-sounding *dai-uso*, which in Japanese means, of all things, "great lie." Later, out of concern for orthodoxy, the Latin terms for the three persons of the Trinity were taken over whole into Japanese ("Deusu Patere," "Deusu Hiiryo," and "Deusu Supiritsu Santo"). Not only that, but key theological terms such as *persona* (person), susutanshija (substance), *garasa* (grace), and even *diidesu* (from *fides*, faith)—a grand total of about fifty—received the same treatment. No wonder the message about the Christian God must have seemed a wholly alien, Latin/European import to the Asians, even though, later, many Japanese terms *(kami-sama,* for God) were introduced.

This dogmatic quandary makes it clear why *conflict* was bound to arise a generation later. It was recent Japanese converts, in fact, who protested against the methods of the China missionary Matteo Ricci (born in 1552, the year Francis Xavier died), whom they considered too progressive. Ricci had dared to use traditional Chinese names for God in Christian liturgy and preaching. This was the source of the "rites controversy," which ended with Rome's condemning all use of "native" rites and names for God, and led to the catastrophic collapse of the Christian mission to China and Japan, as well as to a violent persecution of the Christians. Hindsight compels us to admit that even if the rites controversy had been settled happily, the Christian mission to China and Japan might have failed anyway on account of its dogmatism, biblicism, and exclusivism. Ultimately, political factors were decisive: Against the background of expanding European imperialism and colonialism, the peoples of Asia increasingly perceived Christian missionary activity as a threat. The upshot was that for a long time access to the souls of Asians and especially Buddhists was closed to Christianity. The countless travelogues by missionaries, even in modern times, tell us less about the doctrine of Buddhism than about its myths and cults.

THE TURNING POINT FOR SCHOLARSHIP AND THE CHURCH

One cannot speak of a serious attempt to understand Buddhism until the emergence of *scholarly research on Buddhism* in the nineteenth century (growing out of the requirements of European colonialism). The study of Buddhism had begun as a part of Indology and soon led to a clear distinction between Hinduism and Buddhism. Even the philosopher

Arthur Schopenhauer (1788–1860), who was a pioneer of Buddhism in Germany and whose ideas on Buddhism influenced Friedrich Nietzsche, Richard Wagner, and Paul Deussen, tended to confuse Vedānta and Buddhism, owing to the imperfect history then available of the spiritual world of India. "In addition to that, he was much too subjective a person not to have a predilection for finding in other systems material that suited his own" (H. von Glasenapp, *The Image of India in German Thought*, 1960, p. 77).

The whole situation was radically changed by the discovery, publication, and study of original *Buddhist texts* from Nepal, Tibet, Burma, Sri Lanka, and Thailand by European scholars. Particularly significant were the texts of the Theravāda canon, written in the Middle Indic language of Pāli (the Church Latin, as it were, of Theravāda Buddhism). The Frenchman Eugène Burnouf is considered to be the father of modern Buddhist studies, with his introduction to the history of Buddhism (1844), which is, however, still based on Sanskrit texts. A generation later, the study of Pāli, properly speaking, got under way in earnest. The year 1881 was epochal: It saw Hermann Oldenberg's classic biography of the Buddha, Thomas Rhys David's famed Hibbert Lectures, and the founding by Rhys David and Max Müller, the father of modern religious studies, of the Pāli Text Society, followed in 1892 by the Buddhist Text Society, in Calcutta.

Buddhist societies, periodicals, and important converts all over the world now led to a completely different attitude toward Buddhism and finally to a Buddhist mission (whether promoting classical Buddhism or some contemporary adaptation of Buddhism) in the Americas and Europe. In the twentieth century, both scholarly and popular literature on Buddhism in Europe and America, but also in India, Sri Lanka, and Japan, has swollen to such proportions that hardly anyone can still keep up with it. And Buddhism itself has received so many impulses for renewal from this research that nowadays the prejudices of the old missionaries (that the Buddhist scriptures are neither published nor read) have become totally obsolete. We shall hear more about this in a later presentation.

During this process of enlightenment—recently given powerful encouragement by the mass media, schools, and universities—*the situation within the major Christian churches has also undergone a fundamental change.* Ever since the Second Vatican Council accepted, at least in part, the Reformation and then the modern paradigm of theology and the Church, the Catholic attitude toward other religions has taken a positive turn. And so today the Christian view of Buddhism stresses information instead of denunciation, complementarity instead of antagonism, dialogue instead of proselytism, "speaking of Christ with people of different faiths" instead of "winning unbelievers for Christ."

Of course, the self-concept of the Christian churches vis-à-vis Buddhism still vacillates between an approach aimed at conquest and one aimed at adaptation. As far as one's own church is concerned, one may favor a theory of completion (the Church as a complete synopsis of *all* religious elements) or a sacramental theory (the Church as a sacrament, a sign of salvation among the nations). But there is no overlooking the fact that a shift has occurred. In various parts of the world, significant dialogue groups of Christians and Buddhists have been formed, and Christian research institutes for the study of Buddhism in Colombo, Hong Kong, Tokyo, Kyoto, and Nagoya have carried dialogue between Christians and Buddhists a great deal further than parallel efforts involving Christians and Muslims. The names of Christian scholars like M. Doi, H. Dumoulin, H. Enomiya-Lassalle, W. Johnston, K. Kadowaki, W. L. King, E. Lamotte, J. van Bragt, L. A. de Silva, J. Spae, and H. Waldenfels have also won the respect of many Buddhists.

Some of the forces behind this turnabout have been the World Conference on Religion and Peace, the World Congress of Faith, and the Interreligious Peace Colloquium; on the Christian side, the reorientation of the *World Council of Churches*, with its conferences in Ajaltoun, Lebanon (1970), and Colombo (1974), and the plenary assemblies in Nairobi (1975) and Vancouver (1983); but above all the statements, mentioned before, of the *Second Vatican Council* on the possible salvation of non-Christians, indeed of sincere atheists. Concerning Buddhism, in its truly historic declaration on the non-Christian religions (1965), Vatican II said:

> Buddhism, in it various forms, realizes the radical insufficiency of this changeable world; it teaches a way by which men, in a devout and confident spirit, may be able either to acquire the state of perfect liberation, or attain, by their own efforts or through higher help, supreme illumination. Likewise, other religions found everywhere try to counter the restlessness of the human heart, each in its own manner, by proposing "ways," comprising teachings, rules of life and sacred rites.—The Catholic Church rejects nothing that is true and holy in these religions. (Art. 2)

The Church has thus irrevocably committed itself to following the path of dialogue. And yet dialogue is a highly controversial business. What is it all about? Is it merely a comparison of doctrines and theories, of structures and practices? Or the exchange of "religious" experiences? But does not Buddhism in particular challenge every type of theorizing? The question is a fair one and must be rethought each time we attempt a dialogue.

Is Buddhism Purely Experiential?

What can one say "about" Buddhism? Here the theologian faces the same hermeneutical problems as the student of religion, who can describe the religion only as a product of historical evolution seen "from the outside." But one can hardly grasp the "essence" of a thing that way. Consequently, many Buddhists do not set much store by theoretical information "about" their religion. If you want to know what Buddhism is, you have to practice it. "Sit and meditate until your legs hurt," Japanese Zen masters tell us. Not information "about" Buddhism, but experience with it, enables one to penetrate its "essence." One reaches "salvation" not through philosophical discussion or theological speculation, but practical action.

Of course, much the same is also true of Christianity or any other religion. For the message of Christ, and not only the message of the Buddha, is something one grasps not in a purely cognitive manner, "from the outside," but through an act of commitment, "from within." The Christian way of salvation, as well as the Buddhist way, is not mere knowledge of matters of fact, a new theory, a systematic world view, a theology, but practice, experience, conversion, exercise, a way, *the* way that Christ took: ". . . he who does what is true comes to the light." (John 3:21)

Zen Buddhists in particular would argue that the crucial thing in encounters between Buddhists and Christians is to grasp the teaching of the Buddha through *joint experiences in the act of joint meditation.* Other schools of Buddhism, admittedly, consider doctrine more important. Now, there is no doubt that common experiences, silent meditation, and wordless communication can be very helpful for interreligious encounter (between, say, European or American Benedictines and Japanese Zen monks). Still, they can also simulate inner understanding and genuine communication. Even enemies can silently admire a sunset together —silence stops the argument. But as soon as the common experiences and unspoken emotions are put into words, the doctrinal distinctions (I —not-I, God—not-God, grace—karma) again come to mind. There is, after all, no religious practice without an implicit "theory"; no way of salvation that does not also claim to be true; no experience that needs no reflection. And it is precisely religious experiences, not merely those had while meditating, that are extremely hard to communicate.

Besides, the most recent hermeneutical discussion has shown that there is no "pure" experience, neither in Christianity nor in Buddhism. I have already mentioned, apropos of Hinduism and mysticism, that there is only *interpreted experience.* Anyone who reads the discourse of the Buddha "On the Foundation of Attentiveness" (Satipatthāna-Sutta), already mentioned by Professor Bechert and revered in all the Theravāda countries of Southeast Asia, will have discovered something that can also be easily demonstrated from the commentaries of the *great present-day masters of the Satipatthāna method,* such as Buddhādāsa Bhikkhu, in Thailand *(Ānāpānasati,* 1976), Mahasi Sayadaw, in Burma *(Vipassanā,* 1979), Nyanaponika Thera, in Sri Lanka *(Geistestraining durch Achoan keit,* 1979): From the simplest exercises in breathing and walking on up, instructions for Buddhist meditation are directed and stamped by a typically Buddhist interest: "The first strong impression one gets from methodical practice of pure observation will probably be the direct and constant confrontation with the ubiquitous transience of things, with incessant change. In the teaching of the Buddha, transitoriness *(anicca)* is the first of the three features of all existence . . . This experience of changeableness will become stronger and more emphatic as one acquires practice in meditation, and the other two features of existence, the lack of self or substance *(anattā),* as well as its sorrowfulness and inadequacy *(dukkha)* will likewise become facts of personal experience and cease to be mere abstract terms, as one stays with the same objects of meditation." *(Nyanaponika,* p. 33)

Of course, unbiased observation of breathing already reveals the ambiguity of the whole phenomenon. Because here, for all the transitoriness, one also experiences a uniform continuity; for all the sorrowfulness, also a deep relief; for all the absence of self, also a self that cannot be denied. Doubts arise about the correctness of the Buddhist theory that *all* life is suffering.

In any case, there is no disputing the fact that there is more to Buddhist meditation than pure observation: There is already interpretation and reduction, although involuntary, in this sort of observing. We have here not just a practical way, but a specific metaphysical vision.

Past relations between Christians and Buddhists have been weighed down by endless incomprehension and misunderstanding. Just as Catholics and Protestants long thought there was nothing to be gained from ecumenical dialogue, so did many Buddhists and Christians, biased by a fundamentalist belief in their infallible sacred scriptures. In the meantime, my experience has been that even members of Buddhist elites—precisely in the interests of world peace—increasingly understand how important it is to exchange not just religious experiences, but the religious teachings implied in them, to have a sense for the theory underlying the practice. Terribly difficult as this is, only through such interweaving of theory and practice, experience and reflection, will we be able to put the dialogue between Buddhists and Christians about the message of the Buddha and the message of Christ—a dialogue that is indispensable for humanity and its peace—on a solid foundation. Otherwise, the points of agreement will be obscured by all the differences, or the differences will be obscured by all the points of agreement.

"It would therefore appear," writes Maha Sthavira Sangharakshita, a practicing Buddhist (a native Englishman) and an authority on the three main forms of Buddhism, "that some more peripheral topic than 'religious experience,' or the experience of liberation from suffering is needed as the starting point for dialogue with Buddhism: that is, some point of doctrine, or religious practice, or liturgical observance, that is intelligible to, and within the imaginative grasp of both parties. Religion need not be identified exclusively with 'religious experience.' " (*Buddhism and Christianity,* eds. C. Geffré and M. Dhavamony, 1979, p. 63)

It should be the responsibility of the theologian to go beyond the comparison of *externals,* rites, ceremonies, and ways of acting, beyond, that is, all the similarities in such things as asceticism, celibacy, tonsure, the cult of relics, incense, and rosaries, and to sort out the *doctrinal convergences and differences* between Christianity and Buddhism. He is to do this in all objectivity, but also without denying his faith commitment or bracketing his personal spirituality, precisely so as to arrive at an *experience purified* by rational insight and a *theory supported* by experience. What would, say, Christian Zen meditation, as it is often practiced these days, contribute to Buddhist-Christian understanding if Christian liturgy (perhaps celebrated immediately following it) and Christian theology remain wholly untouched by it?

The task now is to elaborate the convergences and the divergences with regard to the figure on which Buddhism is based. The name of the Buddha was conspicuously absent from the Declaration of Vatican II, as was that of Muhammad from the corresponding section on Islam. Yet the unity of Buddhism, in all its various paradigmatic forms, rests on more than just certain basic notions and thematic motifs. It is based, first of all, on the historical personality of the Buddha. And needless to say, the rank and configuration of that personality is of great importance—precisely when it comes to a comparison with Jesus of Nazareth.

The Relation of Truth and History

"There is only one whom we might be inclined to compare with Jesus: Buddha. This man is a great mystery. He lived in an awful, almost superhuman freedom, yet his kindness was powerful as a cosmic force. Perhaps Buddha will be the last religious genius to be explained by Christianity. As yet no one has really uncovered his religious significance. Perhaps Christ had not only one precursor, John, last of the prophets, but three: John the Baptist for the Chosen People, Socrates from the heart of antiquity, and Buddha, who spoke the ultimate word in Eastern religious cognition." That was the Catholic theologian Romano

Guardini *(The Lord*, tr. Elinor Castendyk Briefs, 1954, p. 305), writing back in 1937.

But was the Buddha a "precursor of Christ"? Buddhists would likely find that idea unacceptable. But how would it be for Buddhists—remarkably, no one has hitherto suggested this—if Christ, too, was an "enlightened one," a buddha? Buddhism in no way excludes future buddhas. But Christians must first deal with the question, Who is this Buddha Gautama for Buddhists, who is he for Christians?

Like "the Christ," "the Anointed One," so also "the Buddha," "the Enlightened One" (literally "the Awakened One" or "the one who has come to knowledge") is an honorific name, a sublime title. On the other hand, Buddha Gautama no more called himself "God" than did Jesus of Nazareth. Later generations, of course, saw in Buddha not only the sage but the savior, whom they invoked as a helper in time of need, one greater than all the gods, to whom the believer owes veneration *(pūja)*, expressed through symbolic actions, e.g., donations at the altar. This means that just as the Jesus of history is not simply identical to the Christologies of later Christian theology, so *the Gautama of history is not simply identical to the Buddha images of later Buddhist schools.* For this reason, Heinz Bechert has rightly omitted from his portrait of the Buddha the material added by later legends.

Hence it would be superficial thinking to argue that history and historical research pose no serious problems for Buddhism. Its teaching, to be sure, is understood as "eternal truth," as the "universal norm," accessible to human reason and valid for all men and women. It is identical to the "world law" that founds the entire natural and moral order. As we have heard, this "dharma," this cosmic law, this eternal truth, this teaching of the Buddha, is more important than his person, whence the Buddha's saying "Follow the teaching [the dharma], not the person [the Buddha]."

But does that settle the historical question? Hasn't a similar approach to history and truth also been advanced in Christianity? Wasn't the first reaction to the historical criticism of the Enlightenment (as seen in Lessing's response to Reimarus) a desire to protect the truth of Christianity by declaring it an "eternal truth," truth of reason, independent of random facts of history? Christian teaching, it was said, is not true because Christ proclaimed it, but Christ proclaimed it because it is true.

Naturally, this sort of appeal to "eternal validity" could not put a stop to historical research. At first the concern of a few specialized scholars, it ultimately reached the believing masses. Won't this also happen to Buddhism one day? The distinction between "teaching" and "person" is in itself an abstract, unhistorical distinction: Buddhism as it actually is, lives on its *de facto identity. Eternal* truth exists for us only in *history.* Viewed from a concrete, historical standpoint, the "eternal truth" of

Buddhism was just the truth "discovered," experienced, lived, proclaimed, and finally embodied by Gautama Buddha. In all this, his silence was just as important as his speech, his smiles as his deeds. Whatever may be said about individual buddhas who have become enlightened on their own *(pratyeka-buddhas)*, for the general population, "eternal truth" is not simply discovered on the highways and byways of the world, nor can it be summoned at will by rational means (assuming a little practice). Anyone who is no buddha will find it only when prodded by the Buddha.

Needless to say, accenting the significance of the Buddha Gautama in this way is not to tie the truth of a religion to its origin and to that alone, as if fresh truth could not be found later on. The truth of a doctrine is also not unconditionally dependent upon the historicity of its author. Something can be doctrinally true though historically unreal. Thus the discourses by Christ in the Gospel according to John or the discourses by the Buddha in the Mahāyāna Sutras contain deep Christian or Buddhist truth, even though they demonstrably do not come from the historical Jesus or the historical Gautama.

And yet, just as the late date assigned to John's Gospel and the historical understanding of the New Testament scriptures in general have profoundly modified our understanding of Christianity, so assigning a later date to the Mahāyāna Sutras and a historical understanding of the Buddhist scriptures will—with time—also profoundly modify the self-understanding of Buddhism. Or can one invoke the "eternal truth" to wipe out the finding of Senshō Murakami (d. 1929), which is now an established fact of Buddhist history, that the Mahāyāna Sutras evidently were not spoken by the historical Buddha, as had always been supposed, but were composed many centuries later by unknown authors?

Unlike most of the Hindu religions, Buddhism can be traced back to a concrete personality who was its founder. For this reason it is properly considered a "founder-religion." This Buddha Gautama is the one who, roughly half a millennium before the birth of Christ, discovered, experienced, lived, and proclaimed the "eternal truth" for hundreds of millions of people from the Indus and the Hindu Kush to Java and Kyoto, and who for that reason is often revered in the real Buddhist world almost as much as the Christ Jesus is in the real Christian world.

That is why in Buddhism, as well, it is not simply a matter of indifference whether a truth has the authority of the founder for it or against it. Continuity with the "founder" was highly important not only for all Christian groups and denominations, but also for all Buddhist schools and movements (including Zen). Accordingly, even Buddhist scholars who have spoken decisively in favor of a late date for the Mahāyāna Sutras have tried to show, almost in the style of "organic" Roman

Catholic interpretations of dogma, that the later teachings are contained at least implicitly in the original teaching of the Buddha and reflect its "spirit." And in fact, all the emulators of the Buddha may have more in common with him than just a certain teaching—namely a certain spirit, a certain mentality.

Obviously, no one contests the fact that the figure of Jesus has, theologically speaking, a different degree of significance in Christianity than that of the Buddha Gautama in Buddhism. For *Buddhism,* first of all: much as the Buddha can point away from himself to his teaching, it remains the teaching of the *Buddha.* As the "Enlightened One," he guarantees the reliability, the truth, of his teaching. All the various Buddhist schools, in the final analysis, wish to be disciples of the Buddha Gautama. Otherwise, taking one's refuge first in the Buddha, then in his teaching, would be unintelligible, as would the reason why the question, What did the Buddha himself want? has, though often concealed, never fallen completely silent in Buddhism. Again and again there have been individual reformers and reform movements demanding a return to the canonical scriptures, to early Buddhism, to the teachings of the founder, even—in the language of historical criticism—to the historical Buddha. The aim is to transpose the original dharma, now purified of myth, magic, and superstition, into a changed, increasingly secularized society shaped by modern science, technology, and social reforms. For, whatever may have been said about all the potential buddhas arriving at enlightenment through their own intelligence and perhaps even preaching their insights to others, there is no nonobligatory multiplicity of roads to salvation. In the end, even for the Buddha, though there are many different approaches to it, there is only a *single* Truth.

And a parallel situation obtains for *Christianity:* Just as the Buddha pointed away from himself to his teaching, and his disciples experience their own enlightenment (in the Mahāyāna they are supposed to discover the Buddha in themselves), so the Christ, too, pointed away from himself, away from those who say, "Lord, Lord," to active love. Paul writes that the Christ is to take shape in the believer so that not he but Christ lives in him. Just as the Buddha's "teaching" is a raft that has no purpose in itself, but is left behind as soon as one gets to the other shore, so, too, the "gospel" of Jesus Christ is a message that is entirely oriented to the Kingdom of God, an instrument that announces the future God will bring. Furthermore, just as later Buddhists—despite all the theories about an endless multiplicity of buddha figures in all worlds and at all times—continually thought of the very earthly wandering preacher Gautama, the Buddha, so, too, Christianity—despite all the speculation about the cosmic dimensions of the Christ-event, about the cosmic Christ's playing the role of mediator in creation—Christianity has always remembered the wandering preacher from Galilee, the friend of the poor and of sinners, of those who labor and are heavily burdened. And just as Buddhists early on were plunged into controversies about the interpretation of the message, had to hold councils and write learned commentaries (of which the Buddha would presumably have understood nothing and would probably have disapproved) and yet, despite all the antagonistic schools of thought and contradictory doctrines, continually rediscovered unity in the acknowledgment of the one "Lord" Buddha, so, too, Christians, with their disputes over the interpretation of the gospel, their schisms, their councils, their learned summas, despite all the differences and contradictions, kept finding common ground in the confession of faith in the one "Lord" Jesus Christ.

For all its liberality and tolerance, Buddhism, like Hinduism, faces the *criteriological question*, Is everything that passes for Buddhist teaching (dharma) automatically Buddhist? The same question, of course, applies to Christianity. What is really Christian, what is really Buddhist, cannot be decided either in an abstract, theoretical fashion or in a purely empirical, experimental one, but only in the context of historical reflection on the early scriptures, on the original teaching, on the figure of the founder himself. Only from this standpoint can one demonstrate concretely what it is that binds the very different Buddhist "sects" together and separates them, despite everything, from Hindu, Islamic, or Christian schools and movements: not a doctrinal "principle" or an abstract "core," but a *common basis* for their ever so variously interpreted experiences and characteristic features.

In other words, the common ground of the different Buddhist schools and movements can hardly be made clear—for the purpose, among others, of spreading the religion—without some reflection on specific, generally recognized, classic Buddhist texts, which may not literally mirror the teaching of the historical Buddha, but which most likely reproduce its essential themes with real fidelity.

THE NECESSITY OF REFLECTING ON THE HISTORICAL BUDDHA

However much the Buddha Gautama is seen, even back in Theravāda Buddhism, as one of several buddhas, and however much his teaching is the eternal truth of all present, past, and future buddhas, the Buddha was originally and without any doubt no myth but a *historical personality*. Though some critics had denied it, his historical existence was proved around the end of the nineteenth century by E. Senart and H. Kern, just as the historical existence of Jesus of Nazareth has been proved, though some, like A. Drews denied it in the early-twentieth century. But the hard, controversial question is, What can we know about the historical Buddha?

In principle, only the words of the Buddha should qualify as binding,

or "canonical," for the various Buddhist schools and movements. But of
the many ancient versions of the canon, only the one in Pāli, first written
down in Sri Lanka around the first century B.C., has been transmitted
completely in its original language. So at least for the Pāli tradition of
southern Buddhism or Theravāda (in Sri Lanka and Southeast Asia), the
dividing line between canonical and noncanonical literature can be
drawn with some precision. But the later Mahāyāna Buddhism and
Tantric Buddhism, which have accepted other texts besides the Pāli
canon into their own canon, also justify themselves by appealing to an
ostensible rediscovery or unveiling of teachings by the Buddha, which
had been hidden until then.

With greater understanding of the historical problems, determining
what were really the Buddha's words naturally proved to be just as hard
as it was in the case of the *historical Jesus.* Only in recent decades have we
witnessed the dissolution of the skepticism (which had been shared in
the first half of this century by theologians as different as Karl Barth,
Rudolf Bultmann, and Paul Tillich) concerning a historically verified
image of Jesus. This shift came about particularly because of developments in the Bultmann school itself (the work of Ernst Käsemann).
Today Christian scholars have largely agreed that because of the nature
of the sources available, it is impossible to write a biography of Jesus.
But it is altogether possible to describe the unmistakable key features of
his message, his conduct, and his fate. And anyone who still speaks
nowadays of the "end" of research on the Jesus of history has neither
finished Albert Schweitzer's *Quest of the Historical Jesus* nor looked at the
studies done since Barth, Bultmann, and Tillich.

There is at the moment no consensus among Eastern or Western
scholars on *the historical Buddha.* On the one hand, such historical research is often labeled unnecessary or even impossible (thanks to uncritical fundamentalism in the East and hypercritical skepticism in the
West): and, because of dogmatic bias, scarcely anyone still dares to raise
the question of "original Buddhism." On the other hand, scholars such
as E. Lamotte, E. Waldschmidt, and others have pushed the quest for the
historical Buddha back beyond the time of the Emperor Ashoka. In so
doing they have tried to avoid the mistakes of the "liberals," who approached the material with a ready-made notion of the "rational, kind-
hearted Buddha," and so reconstructed an image of the Buddha (analogous to the "liberal" image of Jesus) that often said more about the
scholars than about the Buddha.

As we have seen, historical reflection is necessary and has practical
relevance: It is a different sort of Buddhist "preaching" that begins with
the historical figure of the Buddha Gautama and his human experience
(of the instability and sorrowfulness of life) rather than with an other-

worldly/transhistorical Buddha, his preexistence, and his legendary miraculous birth, as reported by what are evidently later texts. We need to work back through all the mythologies and later transformations and recover (not reconstruct) the historical Buddha. Although Buddhists value history differently from Christians, Buddhist faith, like Christianity, is ultimately based not on a legend, a novel, or a myth, but on a historical personality.

There are ancient biographies of the Buddha, such as the (noncanonical) *Nidānakathā*, from the Theravāda tradition, or the *Lalitavistara* ("Detailed [Presentation] of the [superterrestrial] Game" of early Mahāyāna Buddhism); but naturally they do not tally with the Buddha's historical career. Thus if we want to be on solid historical ground in speaking about the Buddha, we cannot start off with the legendary accretions of later tradition or with the Mahāyāna's new understanding of the Buddha as a celestial being. Rather, we have to work our way back critically, as historical criticism has done for the New Testament, and distinguish, in the various traditions of canonical texts, between what is reported by the earlier and the later strata of the text. We must determine what in the Buddhist tradition is redaction, interpretation, explanation, and even, under certain circumstances, reduction.

In this situation, *historical scrutiny* is not only *necessary*, but also *possible*, so long as one does not make impossible demands. Here, too, we can find a "middle way" between uncritical acceptance and hypercritical rejection. Admittedly, this is considerably *harder in the case of the Buddha than for Jesus*. Not only have the discourses of the Buddha (as have those of Jesus) been adapted to new situations, altered, and edited; but in the case of the Buddha, the texts were written down not two decades after the events (as with Jesus) but around two centuries later. They are anonymous and can scarcely be dated with any accuracy. Given the amazing achievements of oral tradition in ancient India, this gap is doubtless not as wide as it seems. Still, by comparison with the New Testament, the sheer extent of the canonical scriptures in Buddhism (e.g., the Pāli canon) is enormous. It encompasses a great variety of texts and tens of thousands of pages, a breadth that does not make the job of the critical historian any easier. In addition, we know a great deal less about the India of Gautama's day than we know about the Palestine of Jesus' day.

Nevertheless, in the pre-Mahāyāna scriptures, we find various important texts (concerning, say, the Buddha's leaving home, his enlightenment, his end, and some of the rules for monks) whose content (though not necessarily their exact wording) goes back to the historical Buddha. Here, as so often in historical research, we hardly have absolute certainty, but the probability is high enough. And whether we use this set of texts or that, the idea of describing the message, conduct, and fate of the

Buddha Gautama, in its basic outlines, is not a hopeless dream—as it was not with Jesus. No doubt we can never reconstruct his biography exactly, we cannot establish his chronology or plumb his psyche by means of verbatim statements guaranteed to be his—a biography like the one Hans Wolfgang Schumann has optimistically provided *(Der historische Buddha,* 1982). But we can, as Professor Bechert's presentation has made clear, trace the key tendencies, the peculiar patterns of behavior, the typical outlines of the Buddha's message, the contours and leading themes of his "preaching," the resounding dominant chords of his life as registered by the various old traditions. Thus we have a general picture of the Buddha—which should not be twisted to fit some preconceived system, and which is open around the margins to legend— who set the "wheel of doctrine" in motion and who stands in sharp contrast to other great religious "founders."

LEGEND FORMATION

As opposed to the mythological Hindu folk religion, with the Buddha things begin not in myth but in history that leads to myth: the story of the prince and then ascetic Siddhartha Gautama, who after long practice in profound concentration became the Enlightened One, the one who points the way out of this sorrowful life to a state of final rest beyond pain and transcience.

Early on, Buddhist piety endowed this story with a series of *miraculous events.* As with Jesus, the Buddha was not born in the ordinary human way (the motif of sex as pollution). As with the boy Jesus, miracles are reported from the childhood of Prince Siddhartha. Like Jesus, Gautama is tempted by the evil spirit. And, following later tradition, not only Christ, but also the Buddha performs a number of miracles, just as both deaths are accompanied by earthquakes.

But are not the miracles of Jesus of Nazareth historically authenticated? Even critical exegetes agree that Jesus' appearance was associated with *cures* of various sick and "possessed" people (mentally ill individuals with particularly striking symptoms such as epilepsy). For the men and women of that time, these were astonishing, miraculous victories over the demon of sickness. Meanwhile modern medicine has long since recognized the psychosomatic nature of many diseases, and knows of astonishing cures based on extraordinary psychic influences, on boundless trust, on "faith." (The oldest gospel tradition still knows of cases where Jesus could not work miracles, as in his home town of Nazareth, because faith and trust were lacking.) So it is historically certain that, unlike the historical Buddha, Jesus of Nazareth was not just a preacher and adviser, but also a charismatic healer and helper. Yet there is no proof that either the Buddha or Jesus performed *miracles in the strict modern sense* of a "supernatural" suspension of natural laws. Their "miracles"—such as walking on water, which both Jesus and the Buddha are reported to have done—are to be regarded as legendary additions and retouchings.

Extraordinary events have been reported, we know, of many great figures in religious history. They give such persons and their actions transhistorical authority, "divine" legitimation. The important point for us is that, in the light of today's understanding of religion, these miracle stories, which have often been considered the crucial element in the life of Jesus, tell us nothing about the uniqueness of the Nazarene. We find this sort of thing with Shākyamuni, with Muhammad and Confucius as well, in practically all religions. If what is commonly called Jesus' "divine sonship" were reduced to such extraordinary events at birth and miraculous deeds in life or death, he would not be essentially different from the founders of non-Christian religions—not to mention the demigods, sons of gods, heroes, and thaumaturges of antiquity.

But what, then, does mark Jesus off from the other great figures of religious history, particularly from the Buddha? Let us now attempt carefully to touch upon this difficult question, always conscious that the boundary between history and legend is more fluid with the Buddha than with Christ, because the sources are more complicated. We can begin with certain rather surprising outer similarities (but inner ones too) between Gautama and Jesus. Instead of going into all kinds of detail, I shall concentrate on significant basic structures.

What Unites Jesus and Gautama

A number of *broad ethical directives* are *common* to Buddhism and the entire Jewish-Christian-Islamic tradition: Do not kill, do not steal, do not lie, do not indulge in sexual vice. Jesus fails to mention the use of intoxicants, and that, as we shall see, is no accident; for he is said to have frequently taken part in banquets. Still, in his *behavior* as a whole, Jesus shows a greater similarity to Gautama than, say, to Muhammad, the warrior and statesman who had a hearty lust for living till the very end.

Like Gautama, Jesus was a wandering preacher, poor, homeless, unpretentious, who experienced a crucial turning point in his life that moved him to go out and proclaim his message.

Like Gautama, in preaching that message Jesus did not use a sacred language that had become unintelligible (Sanskrit/Hebrew), but the colloquial language (a Middle Indic dialect / the Aramaic vernacular); and he ordered no one to codify or even write down his teaching.

Like Gautama, Jesus appealed to the reason and cognitive faculties of men and women, although not in systematic, deliberately composed lectures and discourses, but with readily graspable proverbs, short stories, and parables, taken from the unadorned, accessible, everyday world, and without committing himself to formulas, dogmas, or mysteries.

As for Gautama, so for Jesus, greed, power, and delusion constitute the great temptation, which, the New Testament says, stood in the way of the great task to be done.

Like Gautama, Jesus was legitimated through no formal office. He stood in opposition to the religious tradition and its guardians, to the formalistic and ritualistic caste of the priests and scribes, who were so insensitive to the sufferings of the people.

Like Gautama, Jesus soon gathered around him a group of his closest friends, the circle of his disciples, and a broader following.

But we can see a fundamental similarity not only in their conduct, but also in their message:

- Like Gautama, Jesus essentially played the part of the teacher. Their authority lay not so much in their educational training as in their extraordinary experience of an ultimate reality.
- Like Gautama, Jesus had an urgent message, glad tidings (the "dharma," the Gospel) to deliver, which demanded of people a change of mind ("stepping down into the stream," *metánoia*) and trust *(shraddhā,* "faith"), not orthodoxy, but orthopraxy.
- Like Gautama, Jesus had no intention of giving an explanation of the world. He did not engage in profound philosophical speculation or learned legal casuistry. His teachings are no secret revelations about the nature of the Kingdom of God. They do not aim at any specific ordering of legal and practical matters in the world.
- Like Gautama, Jesus works from the assumption that the world is transient and temporary, that all things are inconstant, and that man is unredeemed, as shown by his blindness and foolishness, his entanglement in the world, and his lovelessness toward his fellow human beings.
- Like Gautama, Jesus sees the root of this unredeemed state in man's desires and cravings, in his egoism, self-seeking, and self-centeredness.
- Like Gautama, Jesus points out a way of redemption from self-seeking, "fallenness," blindness. This liberation is achieved not through theoretical speculation and philosophical ratiocination, but through religious experience and inner transformation: a thoroughly practical way to salvation.
- As with Gautama so with Jesus, there are no special intellectual, attitudinal, or moral prerequisites for taking this way to salvation: The individual is supposed to listen, understand, and draw conclusions. No one is asked about the true faith or the orthodox creed.

● Like Gautama's way, Jesus' way is a *via media* between the extremes of sensuality and self-torture, between hedonism and asceticism, a way that makes possible a new selfless concern with one's fellow man. Not only do the general moral rules coincide for the Buddha and Jesus; so, in principal, do their "mental ethics" and the basic demands of kindness and sharing in another's joy, of loving compassion (the Buddha) and compassionate love (Jesus).

But, though there are major similarities in their conduct as a whole and in the broad features of their attitudes and teachings, there are equally important dissimilarities in their particular background, in their concrete development, and in the ways they translated their message into reality.

How Jesus and Gautama Differ

The New Testament says that Jesus did not come from a family of rich, noble landowners; he did not grow up spoiled, as tradition has Gautama confessing he did, utterly spoiled by feasts and all sorts of enjoyment. Jesus evidently came from a family of artisans who could hardly allow themselves the superfluities that left so many rich sons like Gautama disgusted with life and then drove them from their parents' homes.

Unlike Gautama, Jesus did not turn primarily to his surfeited contemporaries who were trying to escape their affluent society. Unsupported by any party or human authority, without claiming any titles of honor or making his own role or position the theme of his message, he turned to those who labored and were heavily burdened, the poor, whom he called blessed, not because poverty was a desirable ideal, but because they had kept an openness to that other reality which truly mattered to him.

Jesus was no solitary among solitaries (the literal meaning of *monachus*, or monk), wrestling with the One. He was the master in a community of disciples for whom he had founded no order, laid down no rules, vows, or ascetical commandments, had stipulated no special clothing or traditions.

The world, for Jesus, was not something futile and empty you withdrew from, seeing through its nothingness in the act of concentration. Still less was it to be identified with the Absolute. It was, instead, creation, good in itself, although continuously spoiled by human beings.

The turning point in Jesus' life did not mean giving up a false way and seeking his own salvation. He never referred to an actual enlightenment or conversion experience. The turning point meant coming forth from obscurity into the public eye; not a turning away from the world and a pantheon of gods, together with a turn inward, but a turning *to* the world out of a peculiarly immediate relation to the one God of Israel, whom he called—with scandalous familiarity—*abba,* "dear father," a name expressing at once nearness and distance, power and security. The goal, then, was not to get out of the cycle of rebirth through one's own effort, but to enter into completion through God's mercifully completing judgment.

After the presentations on the religions of India, I need call the reader's attention only for a moment to the fact that the religious–philosophical backgrounds of the Buddha and Christ were extremely *different.* Jesus had no notion of an automatic law of retribution for all morally significant acts, good or bad (karma). Though he recognized human guilt and sin, he put the accent on God's continuously forgiving grace. Jesus never thought of reincarnation in another earthly life. Human life came once and only once, and it was oriented to a final, eternal life. All things considered, therefore, Jesus' thinking had nothing to do with cycles, it was goal-oriented and historical, with respect to both the individual and all of humanity. Thus, although he bears witness to God's "eternal truth," Jesus does not deliver a message for all times. He announces the beginning of the end time, the breaking in of God's eternity upon worldly time. For the in-between time, Jesus demands not only imperturbable freedom from hatred and the restful sense of genial concord, but loving concern and active interest.

We can get the clearest picture of the difference between Gautama and Jesus by returning to the distinction between *mystical* and *prophetic* piety as developed by Friedrich Heiler and others and recently applied by Gustav Mensching in his *Buddha und Christus—Vergleich* (1978). From this standpoint, we can see the specific greatness of both the Buddha and the Christ:

● The Buddha Gautama is a harmoniously self-contained, peaceful, *enlightened guide, inspired by the mystical spirit.* Sent by no one, he demands renunciation of the will to life for the sake of redemption from suffering in nirvāna. He calls for turning away from the world and turning inward, for methodical meditation through the stages of absorption, and so finally to enlightenment. Thus he shows calm fellow feeling, with no personal involvement, for every sentient creature, man or animal: a universal *sympathy* and peaceful *benevolence.*

● Jesus Christ, however, is a passionately involved *emissary and guide, inspired by the prophetic spirit* and, for many, even in his own lifetime, the Anointed One ("Messiah," "Christ"). He calls men and women to conversion for the sake of redemption from guilt and all evil in the Kingdom of God. Instead of demanding a renunciation of the will, he appeals directly to the will of man, which he bids orient itself to God's will, itself aimed entirely at the comprehensive welfare, the salvation, of man. Thus he proclaims a personally concerned love, which includes all the suffering, the oppressed, the sick, the guilty, and even opponents and enemies: a universal *love* and active *charity*.

THE ENLIGHTENED ONE AND THE CRUCIFIED

But if we stick to a historical viewpoint, where is the basic difference between Jesus and the Buddha to be found? We can bring it into sharpest focus by holding side by side the figure of the smiling Buddha, seated on a lotus blossom, and that of the suffering Jesus, nailed to the cross. Only from this perspective can the far more comprehensive significance of the Buddha for Buddhists and of Christ for Christians be correctly understood.

By means of his enlightenment, Gautama entered nirvāna (which can be reached in this life), but lived on for decades afterward as the Enlightened One, until he finally entered the definitive nirvāna, parinirvāna, through his death, which came from a trivial cause. He lived, though not without pain and suffering, in a cheerful-serious spirit, harmoniously and successfully, and ultimately highly respected by the powerful. His teaching spread, and the number of his disciples grew past counting. He died an old man, aged eighty, from food poisoning, but peacefully, surrounded by his disciples. Everywhere in the world, the statues of this Buddha still remind us of his tranquillity, his detachment, his peace, his deep harmony, indeed his good humor.

The man from Nazareth is altogether different: His public life lasted not decades but, at most, three years, perhaps only a few dramatic months, before it ended in violence. It is a story bristling with tension from beginning to end, shaped by a perilous conflict with the religious institution and its hierarchy. His whole story is ultimately a story of suffering that ends with arrest, flogging, and execution. This life has no suggestion of mellowness or completion; it remained a fragment, a torso. There was, in any event, not a trace of success in his lifetime. The accounts we have tell us that this man died cursed and despised, as a heretic, a false prophet, a blasphemer and seducer of the people. His end came in loneliness amid the greatest agony: avoided by his family, abandoned by his disciples, obviously forgotten by his God. The very last thing they heard from him was his cry on the cross. From that time till today—and for many centuries no one dared to represent this in art—Jesus was the image of *the sufferer pure and simple:* a suffering, to be sure, that from the outset the first Christian communities understood not as the sheer despair of a man come to grief, but as an act of supreme self-sacrifice, of ultimate love for God and men.

Jesus is a sufferer who does not exude compassion, but demands it himself, who does not rest within himself, but totally gives himself. In this way, then, as *the sufferer in devotion and love,* this Jesus, as Christians

see him, differs from the Buddha, the Compassionate One, differs unmistakably from all the many gods and divinized founders of religion,
differs from all the religious geniuses, heroes, and caesars of world
history—as the sufferer, as the slain one, as the *Crucified*. Still, Christian
faith is convinced, this Crucified One did not fall into nothingness, but
was taken up out of this temporary, fleeting, inconstant reality into the
true, eternal life. This was no "supernatural" intervention by a *Deus ex
machina*, but the "natural" dying into the actual, true reality: a final
condition, in any case, without any suffering. But, one wonders: Does
not Buddhism also accept such a painless final state on "the other
shore"—nirvāna?

NIRVĀNA OR ETERNAL LIFE?

Neither the endless discussions in the East nor the countless studies
in the West have thus far resulted in any agreement on what nirvāna
really means. The basic sense of nirvāna, as we have heard, is "extinction": a final state without suffering, without greed, hatred, and delusion
—that much is uncontested. The quarrel is over whether, with the extinction of suffering, the person himself is extinguished; in a word,
whether this final state should be thought of negatively as the total
annihilation of the individual or positively as the *preservation* (however we
should interpret this, in the concrete sense) of the individual. We can
scarcely find our way back now to a clear picture of what the Buddha
himself and his first disciples thought about it. Since he was in general
ill-disposed toward such metaphysical questions, he was presumably not
at all interested in giving an unequivocal clarification.

But does not the image of a flame going out, which the Buddha used
to illustrate nirvāna, express the idea of total annihilation? In Professor
Bechert's presentation, we heard that nirvāna should not be understood
nihilistically. And L. Schmithausen has recently informed us: "An old
Brahmanic text [proves] ancient Indians thought that the fire is not
destroyed when it is extinguished but merely becomes impalpable by
entering space-aether. Actually there are also some passages in the old
Buddhist canon (although for the time being we cannot say whether
they belong to the oldest textual corpus, which goes all the way back to
the Buddha himself, because so far we are still at a very early stage of
stratifying the material) where the image of the flame going out is
emphatically used to express the idea that the mode of being of the
redeemed person is an unfathomable, incomprehensible state, which is
sometimes even characterized as joyful." (*Historisches Wörterbuch der
Philosophie*, 1984, p. 855)

Long before this, authors both Western (e.g., E. Conze) and Eastern
(H. Nakamura) have likewise put together entire lists of positive state-

ments about nirvāna (on the basis of the canonical scriptures). These contain all sorts of poetic expressions, which should, of course, be taken just as seriously (if we can drop our Western bias) as the philosophical reflections that take a negative view of the question. Thus Schmithausen says (with reference to *Udāna* VIII, 3): "Finally, some passages even speak of nirvāna as a transcendent 'metaphysical' state or essence, removed from all the conditions of phenomenal existence, as the deathless place *(amritam padam)*, the unoriginated, unbecome, uncaused *(asamskrita)*. According to these passages there is a metaphysical reality, an 'eschatological absolute' (L. de la Vallée Poussin), which is also called nirvāna and preexists the nirvāna that is a spiritual event." And even if in Theravāda Buddhism some movements have understood the extinction to be total and complete destruction, still "most of the Hīnayāna schools" have thought of nirvāna "as a positive metaphysical entity." "They take the spiritual event of nirvāna to be participation in this metaphysical entity." (ibid.)

This differentiation in the understanding of nirvāna, derived from historical reflection, might be very helpful in Buddhist-Christian dialogue, which is rife with difficulties. For, it seems to me, there *need not be any contradiction* between the *Christian* notion of a positive final state ("eternal life") and the notion, supported by most *Buddhist* schools, of a positive final state (nirvāna). Whatever points of difference will have to be discussed about the way there, whatever the "conditions of entry," in both cases we are dealing with an—ultimately indescribable—"other shore," another dimension, the transcendent, the true reality. "Eternal life" is also a condition that cannot be grasped by our intellectual and descriptive categories, a condition that can only be experienced: "What no eye has seen, nor ear heard, / nor the heart of man conceived." (1 Cor 2:9) "Eternal life" also is where the drives of the will, desire, and sensation are extinguished, insofar as all this implies inconstancy, imperfection, sorrow. "Eternal life" also can be experienced now, as the Jesus discourses in the Gospel of John repeatedly stress.

I shall have more to say about nirvāna in the context of Mahāyāna, but some convergence can already be seen from here:

Even though *Buddhists* in general are careful not to speak about the survival of the individual in nirvāna, they make so many positive statements about the painless final state that we cannot exclude in advance some agreement with the Christian idea of "eternal life."

Even though *Christians*, for their part, emphasize that the idea of "eternal life" includes the survival of the human person, they remain thoroughly aware that their statements about "eternal life" are only images of the unimaginable and that finite personhood in the dimension of the infinite beyond space and time escapes all the restrictions of finitude.

The familiar symbol of the drop of water dissolving in the ocean does not capture what I mean here. Even in the Buddhist vision, man is more than a drop of water. I prefer the image of the escape, the liberation, the redemption of the caterpillar out of the cocoon as it becomes the butterfly, no longer bound to "earthly" dimensions, but released in "heavenly" dimensions. Christians, in any event, will always stress both points: the individual and the supraindividual character of the painless final state. Because where God is not only "in everything," but *"everything to everything"* (1 Cor 15:28), then it will be manifest that human beings, who are never everything, still have a share in that everything that God is for Christians.

II.
The Buddhist Community and Its Earlier History

1. *Heinz Bechert:* Buddhist Perspectives

THE SANGHA

Early Buddhism was a teaching about salvation for the individual in a pluralistic society. Anyone who wished to follow this way of liberation in a consistent fashion could join the *sangha,* the monastic community of monks and nuns founded by the Buddha. The Buddha himself describes the purpose of his order as follows: "Here a father of a family, a son, or someone reborn in another family hears the teaching. After he has heard it, he comes to trust the Perfect One, and he says to himself: 'Domestic life is full of obstacles, a place of uncleanness. But having no house is like the open sky. It is not easy to lead a stainless, holy life within one's house. Suppose I cut off my hair and beard, put on the yellow robe, and went off into homelessness.' So he gives up his wealth and his relatives, cuts his hair and beard, and goes off into homelessness.

"Having done all this, he complies with the rules for monks: He avoids harming living creatures, he is full of sympathy and compassion for all beings. He avoids stealing, takes only what he is given, and is pure of heart. He avoids unchastity, lives purely, and abstains from sexual intercourse. He avoids lies, tells only the truth, and deceives no one. He avoids talebearing, harsh words, and empty chatter. He avoids destroying shoots and plant life. He eats only once a day; attends no dance performances, events with singing and music, and the like; does not adorn himself with garlands, perfumes, or ointments; does not sleep in high and wide beds; accepts no gold or silver, no red grain or red meat, no men servants or women servants; possesses no domestic animals, etc.

He is content with the garment that protects his body, and with the donated food that fills his belly." (abbreviated from the *Majjhima Nikāya* I, 179–80)

The reason for founding the order is to provide an opportunity for realizing this ideal of monastic life. Buddhism, properly understood, is never works-righteousness, for the rules serve only practical purposes. They are only a help, not an end in themselves. The way to salvation itself can be realized only through the right mental attitude in meditation and awareness. In the end it makes no difference how exactly one observes the rules. According to a famous comparison, the rules are like a raft that helps one to get to the other shore of a river. Once the raft has done its job, one leaves it behind and carries it no farther on one's shoulder. Then it would only become a burden. (*Majjhima Nikāya* I, 134–35)

Nevertheless, for practical reasons distinctive outward signs *were* used so that lay people could tell whether someone had dedicated himself to the goal of salvation and so was worthy to receive donations. For that reason, the Buddha also issued formal instructions regulating the behavior of the members of the sangha both within the community and toward lay people. They prescribe, for example, that the monks' robe is to be of certain colors and to be worn in a certain way. The collection of these rules breaks down into two main parts, the prohibitions and the procedural regulations.

The prohibitions include about 220 items, which constitute a binding code of behavior. They range from the fundamental rules of ethical conduct, such as the prohibition against killing a human being, to the purely external rules of behavior, such as the ban against holding water games. These rules are divided into several groups, corresponding to the penalties provided for transgressing them. Violation of the rules in the first group ipso facto leads to permanent and irrevocable exclusion from the sangha. Other serious offenses against the rules of the order have as a consequence the temporary loss of rights in the sangha, while the Buddha left it up to his community's discretion if they wished to repeal the so-called "lesser rules." These rules, which govern external conduct, are supposed to ensure that the monks always behave with decency and propriety toward the world around them. Tradition says that the Buddha himself framed all the rules. The so-called confession formula, which is the text of these prohibitions, was read aloud at the regular confession ceremonies. In the old community, one had to confess one's offenses before the assembled sangha. This was later replaced by a sort of private confession with a monk who was one's senior by ordination.

The procedural rules specify precisely how monks are to be received into the order and how all other legally binding actions of the community are to be carried out. The rules stipulate, for example, what sort of monk's robes, and how many, one may own, what special regulations apply to invalid monks, etc.

In the community of monks and nuns, there was at first no hierarchy. All monks were equal; their position in the sangha was determined solely by the time that had passed since their ordination. And the Buddha never installed a successor as head of his community. After his death, his teaching and the rule of his order were supposed to serve as a guide all by themselves. The teaching was to be accessible to everyone who could grasp it. The Buddha never wanted to found a secret tradition reserved to an elite. Thus there were no elements of domination over others, and the constitution of the sangha could stand as the paragon of a constitution for communities where everyone is equal.

The oldest order was made up of wandering mendicant monks (*bhikshu*) and nuns (*bhikshuni*). But, early on, lay people gave the order property that was used for the construction of huts and later of other permanent residences for the monks and nuns. Thus, over the course of time, the sangha became sedentary and thereby changed its peculiar character and functions, as well as its relationship to the lay community, as the monks took over certain responsibilities (comparable to Christian pastoral care) for the benefit of the laity.

One could leave the order at any time and reenter it again later, so that there was at first no sharply defined "professional" monastic class. In some countries, Thailand and Burma for example, it has remained this way. There the custom has grown up that every young man spends a certain period of time as a member of the order. This may be akin to the retreats that Catholics go on. The custom has also further strengthened the ties between lay people and the monasteries. In other Buddhist countries, however, such as Sri Lanka, the sangha has evolved into a sort of Buddhist clergy—with the usual problematic concomitants of such a condition.

In traditional Buddhist societies, the monasteries have also taken over the job of teaching the three R's to the masses. With the modernization of education, this task has been largely transferred to state schools, but it is to the enduring credit of the monastic schools in Buddhist countries that they raised the level of general education among the people to a high level, on which the modern educational system could build. That is why the percentage of illiterates in Buddhist countries has always been small. Even 150 years ago it was less than in Western and Central Europe at the time.

THE BUDDHIST LAITY

The external profession of "faith" as a Buddhist is made with no more formalities than the formula: "I take my refuge in the Buddha; I take my refuge in the teaching [dharma]; I take my refuge in the sangha." This, of course, is not a definition of a Buddhist, or an answer to the question of who a Buddhist is. Only when these phrases reflect an inner attitude can they qualify as an outward sign that one has made the message of the Buddha one's own. But while the sangha of monks and nuns has a specific constitution, the lay community is not formally organized. But it is no less important than the sangha for the existence of Buddhism as a religious body. It would be a mistake to view Buddhism only as a religion for monks and nuns.

The monks' daily round of soliciting alms, going through the villages with their begging bowls, is still a living custom today in such countries as Thailand and Burma. In this way, the sangha was dependent for its existence on the laity. If they had to, the monks could always sew robes together from rags found by the wayside or on places where corpses are left to rot. Especially strict groups of monks wore nothing but clothes of this sort. Still, the monks were allowed to receive as gifts both cloth and other things needed for their ascetical life. Although there is textual evidence that in ancient India it was customary to offer food and other donations to wandering mendicant monks and nuns of any denomination, the permanent existence of the sangha was always dependent on the existence of a lay Buddhist community.

The Buddha and his disciples, we know, expounded their teaching to everyone who asked them about it. If anyone was convinced by their words but would not or could not leave worldly life and enter the order, he might support the sangha as a layman through his gifts and thereby acquire religious merit, that is, good karma. But the lay member can also, depending upon the circumstances of his life and his abilities, go beyond the mere accumulation of good karma and aim at striding far ahead on the way to liberation. Thus we see from the early texts that some lay people even reached nirvāna. Later, admittedly, the view prevailed that only monks could fully attain this goal. But we often hear of both lay men and women zealously devoting themselves to the practice of meditation. Thus it says in the commentary on the "Discourse on the Awareness of Mindfulness" that women at bathing places and the loom discussed at length this most important of the Buddhist methods of meditation. Even that part of Buddhist life was never reserved to the monks.

Even today, pious lay people, aside from keeping the five basic commandments of moral conduct, also follow three additional rules, especially on Buddhist holy days: They eat nothing after noon, and they avoid amusements and luxuries. Many lay people also take upon themselves, like novices, the stricter custom of observing ten rules.

TRANSMISSION OF DOCTRINE AND SACRED TEXTS

Like many other founders of religions, the Buddha delivered his teachings in the form of sermons and discourses, but he never asked that his teachings should be codified or even written down. Buddhist tradition reports that immediately after the Buddha's death, an assembly of leading monks collected and organized his teachings. The result of this effort is said to be the Tripitaka (Pāli Tipitaka), that is, the "triple basket," the three-part Buddhist canon. In this earliest period, though, only the most important parts of the monastic rule were actually codified. Deviating from the Vedic-Brahmanic tradition, the Buddha did not make use of Sanskrit, the sacred language of ancient Indian tradition. Instead he taught in the colloquial language of his time, that is, in a Middle Indic dialect. He also wanted his followers to use their respective mother tongue to pass on his teachings. It is true that, later, during the "Sanskrit Renaissance," several schools of Indian Buddhism proceeded to translate the texts into Sanskrit. In the domain of so-called southern Buddhism, the role of a sacred language was assigned to a Middle Indic language, Pāli, which is relatively close to the language used by the Buddha himself. Incidentally, the majority of the texts were transmitted orally—as the traditions of the Vedic-Brahmanic religion had been for centuries—until the first century B.C. Preserving the tradition of the sacred texts for posterity was one of the responsibilities of the sangha.

The oldest collection of sacred texts consisted of only two parts: Vinaya, meaning texts on monastic discipline, and Sūtra (Sutta, in Pāli), meaning doctrinal texts. Out of this grew, through the addition of the Abhidharma (Abhidamma, in Pāli), a sort of systematic compilation of doctrinal terms and themes, the tripartite canon, or Tripitaka. The Pāli version of the canon is preserved intact in the ancient original text. Large parts of the parallel versions in Sanskrit and other Middle Indic languages have been rediscovered and published. Several recensions of the monastic rules and the old doctrinal texts have been handed down in what are at times very exact Tibetan and Chinese translations. The parallel recensions do not differ significantly, as far as content goes, so that we can infer with considerable precision what the oldest version must have been by a comparison of the texts that we still have. The oldest text of the whole codex of monastic discipline (Vinaya), as reconstructed from the extant versions of the tradition, must have already been in existence a hundred years after the death of the Buddha. The tradition of the discourses (Sūtra) was at first dealt with more freely.

Somewhat later, they were joined together, on formal grounds, in four collections. Still later, a fifth collection of various works, mostly more recent, was added on. Even the somewhat more recent Abhidharma still represents the doctrinal development of early Buddhism.

Owing to the growth of Mahāyāna (to be discussed in the next chapter), the importance of the early doctrinal texts was relativized for the adherents of this new form of Buddhism. For this reason, the early texts form only a relatively small part of the gigantic collections of texts made by Tibetan and East Asian Buddhists.

Not surprisingly, over the course of time, the early tradition about the life of the Buddha was increasingly overgrown with legends. The teaching originally held such a prominent position that at first no need was felt for a supplement describing the life of the Buddha. And so such works were, for the most part, relatively late in appearing; and the historian has to extract the life story of the Buddha from passing references in discourses and in the accounts of the origin of the sangha in the texts on monastic discipline. In addition, there are coherent texts about the beginning of the Buddha's teaching activity and about the end of his life.

ASHOKA AND THE BEGINNINGS OF THE BUDDHIST WORLD MISSION

One of the most important personalities in the early history of Buddhism was King Ashoka. He was a grandson of the conqueror Chandragupta Maurya, who had founded the first Indian Empire shortly after the Indian campaign of Alexander the Great. Ashoka ruled from 268 B.C. until his death, in 233. The most important source for understanding the man are the stone inscriptions he left behind. Ashoka waged a successful but bloody war of conquest against the Kalingas and thus became the lord of almost the entire subcontinent. Then he converted to Buddhism. As he confesses in one of his great inscriptions, he was seized by deep regret over the bloodshed caused by the war he had waged. The king wished to change the world, no longer by means of the sword but through the power of the moral law, through dharma. In some of his inscriptions he also expresses his personal belief in the religion of the Buddha. He is not concerned here with propagating his own religion, but with the principles of a universal, "ecumenical" moral doctrine. Reverence for life and the uniform encouragement of all kinds of religion are strongly in evidence. Granted, there cannot be anything like a Buddhist form of government, from the very nature of the goal of Buddhism. Nevertheless Ashoka may be considered the founder of political thought based on the principles of Buddhism. In his view, the state has the responsibility of looking after the social welfare of all men and women, indeed of all creatures. Hence, for example, he ordered hospitals built not only for human beings but also for sick animals. To this day, the Buddhists of Burma still run animal hospitals. Ashoka was enough of a realist to see the limits to the realization of this ideal. Thus it was practically impossible to do away completely with hunting and the slaughter of animals. Instead of this, we read that certain species were declared sacred, while for other animals closed seasons were established.

Ashoka was the first person to formulate the goal of deliberately changing the world in accordance with Buddhist ideals as a task for political thought and action. One may question whether this effort can really be justified by the teaching of the Buddha. Still, this development shows us that we cannot simply label the Buddhists as a community of refugees from the world, or "dropouts."

King Ashoka was also concerned with reforming the Buddhist order. The sangha made heavy demands on individual behavior, which were hard to meet. This had already become clear in the period between the Buddha's death and the time of Ashoka. Thus the king made arrangements so that unworthy monks, already excluded from the sangha by the spiritual authorities, would not in fact continue to pose as monks.

In addition, Ashoka was the founder of the Buddhist world mission. He sent religious emissaries to the countries adjoining his kingdom to proclaim the teaching of the Buddha. In this way, Buddhism was brought by Ashoka's son Mahinda to the island of Ceylon (Sri Lanka), where it became the national religion of the Sinhalese. Around the same time, the first Buddhists arrived in the "Gold Land" (Suvarnabhumi), meaning the coastal regions of present-day Burma. Other missionaries were sent to the Western countries, and Ashoka ordered some of his inscriptions to be engraved in Aramaic and in Greek.

And so, around 150 years after the death of its founder, Buddhism had already become a world religion.

THERAVĀDA BUDDHISM

The form of Buddhism carried by Ashoka's missionaries from India to the island of Ceylon and the coastlands of lower India was called by its adherents "Theravāda" ("teaching of the elders"). Since it was disseminated throughout the countries of Southeast Asia, it is also called "southern Buddhism." The southern Buddhists handed down the Tipitaka, or canon, in Pāli, and they took pains to see that it was handed down with extreme accuracy. They held a number of "councils," or gatherings where the sacred texts were read aloud and carefully scrutinized for their fidelity to tradition. The most recent great gathering of this kind was the Sixth Council, which took place in Rangoon from 1954 to 1956, on the occasion of the twenty-five-hundredth anniversary of parinirvāna, or the Buddha's death (according to traditional Theravāda chronology).

Ashoka's political ideals, which have been mentioned above, brought a new, dynamic element into a tradition that was in principle very conservative. The ruler was supposed to build up a welfare state in which so much material abundance was produced that, on the one hand, the fulfillment of social obligations toward the poor and sick would be guaranteed and, on the other, as many people as possible would be enabled to make spiritual progress on the way to nirvāna. In connection with the state's obligation to protect the sangha from internal decay, this development turned the state into an institution with sweeping, indeed religious, objectives. The state, as Manuel Sarkisyanz put it, was seeking "to be transfigured into an instrument of salvation, to symbolize a church in itself."

In this way, Buddhism, once a doctrine of salvation for a relatively small elite, became a determining factor in the self-concept of governments. But Buddhist ideals naturally do not describe the reality of life in Buddhist countries, and they never have. Instead they served to legitimate existing structures of authority. But they could also serve to legitimate resistance to this authority and even support political revolution when the gap between ideal and reality became too great.

Theravāda Buddhism is still the religion of the majority of the Sinhalese in Sri Lanka, and of the Burmese, the Thai, the Laotians, and the Khmer. In Thailand and in Burma, ancient methods of meditation have survived as well. Theoretically, Buddhists in these countries also consider the old monastic rules binding, although in practice they have accepted many adaptations to changing circumstances. For Theravāda Buddhists the formal tradition of the ordination of nuns has ceased to exist ever since A.D. 456, so that their sangha is now made up only of monks. But lay women adherents who observe the ten rules of moral conduct and wear yellow or white robes are generally known in Theravāda countries as "Buddhist nuns."

In Thailand, Buddhism has remained to this day the state religion. The relation of the king to the sangha is defined as that of a protector of religious institutions. This derives from a tradition going back to King Ashoka, by which the king helps all religious communities but feels a special obligation toward the sangha. The king—and in his name the institutions of the state—continually supervises the sangha, in order to ensure the preservation of Buddhist doctrinal tradition and compliance with the rules. The king, then, can exercise authority over the sangha, but only within, and in the spirit of, limits prescribed by Buddhist ecclesiastical law.

At this point let me mention a widespread misunderstanding one finds flitting through some recent surveys of religion, namely the idea that in traditional Theravāda there are really two kinds of Buddhism, "nirvanic" and "karmic." The first is supposed to be the Buddhism of the canonical texts, in which liberation in nirvāna is acknowledged and pursued as the goal. "Karmic" Buddhism, on the other hand, would be the religion of all those who wish merely to win a better rebirth. This division completely misses the facts of the matter. The Buddha's message is for everyone. But because people are different, all individuals will receive it with varying degrees of comprehension. Only a few will understand it totally, but even grasping a little is helpful. There is no dividing line between good works and the endeavor to follow the way of salvation: The former are only a step in the right direction.

EARLY HISTORY OF BUDDHISM IN INDIA

By contrast to its success in the Theravāda countries, just mentioned, in its Indian homeland Buddhism always remained one of a group of competing religions. It was never the determining factor in any social order for any great length of time, and finally, in the twelfth and thirteenth centuries, it was almost entirely overwhelmed by the onslaught of the victorious Muslims.

From an early date, various schools of thought grew up within Indian Buddhism. These have been labeled "sects," but in reality the areas of disagreement were quite limited, the issues involved of lesser importance, and lay people, even as they do today, scarcely paid attention to them. Even later, when so-called Mahāyāna Buddhism came into being, this in no way led to a universal, radical division between conservatives and the new line. In many places, as we know, the followers of both parties lived peacefully together in one and the same monastery.

The schools of early Buddhism can be grouped together under the heading of Shrāvakayāna ("vehicle of the hearers," i.e., of the Buddha's disciples), since Buddhists agreed, about thirty years ago, to abandon the disparaging term Hīnayāna ("lesser vehicle"). The term covers all the forms of Buddhism that are based exclusively on the teachings of the old canonical scriptures and so do not accept the additional teachings advocated by the Mahāyāna (or "great vehicle"). From the fragmentary reports we have about the early schisms in the sangha, one gathers that the differences of opinion concentrated on conflicting interpretations and applications of the rules of monastic discipline. The first great schism split the community into the more liberal majority of the Mahāsānghika and the stricter minority of the Sthavirādin, or Theravādin, whom we have already seen. The split is to be dated in the period before Ashoka. The quarrel over particulars in the application of the monastic rule focused more on the letter than the spirit of the Buddha's teaching. Later on, however, disputes arose over questions of interpretation, although at this stage they were not concerned with crucial issues of Buddhist doctrine. One exception to this were the Vātsīputrīya, with the great subordinate school of the Sammatīya, who modified the old teaching of the nonexistence of the "self" and postulated the existence of an "undefinable individual." Although this approach made broad advances in India from the fourth to the seventh centuries A.D., few of their writings have come down to us.

One area that gave rise early on to extensive reflection and speculation was the issue of the different kinds of saints and their qualities. The early teaching says that there are three types of Buddhist saints who have reached the final goal of enlightenment, namely the *arhat*, the *pratyeka-buddha*, and the *samyaksambuddha*. An *arhat* attains nirvāna by following the teaching of a Buddha, and thus is a disciple of a Buddha. A *pratyeka-buddha* ("enlightened-for-himself") has reached liberation by his own efforts, without having learnt about the teaching of a Buddha. But he is not able to formulate the way to nirvāna for others and to announce it to them. Finally, a *samyaksambuddha* ("perfectly enlightened") has not only reached nirvāna through his own efforts, but can also disclose this knowledge to others. When one speaks of a Buddha, this generally means a *samyaksambuddha*. Only such a Buddha can found an order, or sangha. Before his enlightenment, a future Buddha is called a *Bodhisattva* ("enlightenment being"). Buddhist literature contains a great number of stories about the good deeds of the *Bodhisattvas* in the course of many existences—the so-called "Buddhist birth stories," or *jātakas*, which embodied many lively folkloric narratives, fairy tales, etc.

In the period when dogmatic speculation flourished, various opinions developed about the qualities of the *arhats,* Buddhas, etc. In the further development of Buddhism the most important schools were those that expanded into Central and East Asia. The first phase of the spread of Buddhism to Central Asia, above all to Turkestan, was the work of the Dharmagupta school. The starting point of this mission lay in the northwest Indian district of Gandhāra. Later the Sarvāstivādin prevailed in northern East Turkestan. Their old center lay in Kashmir.

The Sarvāstivādin became the most important school of Indian Shrāvakayāna. While the Buddha had commented on philosophical questions only insofar as this was necessary to explain his doctrine about the way to nirvāna, the second century B.C. saw the beginnings of a "scholasticism of salvation." This started out by listing all the important terms in the doctrine of salvation and later grew into a highly developed philosophical literature. Building on the foundation of older efforts, the Sarvāstivādin created the so-called dharma theory, according to which the world of appearances exists only as a result of a combination of "factors of existence" termed "dharma." Though these dharmas exist, they are to be described as impermanent, insubstantial and momentary, that is, existing only for the duration of an atom of time. Using texts from this school (which were codified around the first century at a council under the aegis of King Kanishka), some four centuries later the philosopher Vasubandhu the younger composed his great work *Abhidharmakosha*, that is, *The Treasury of Dogmatics*. This is still considered the classic summary of the teachings of this school and of Indian Shrāvakayāna as a whole.

2. *Hans Küng:* A Christian Response

In my first response to the problems raised by Buddhism, I tried to base my position on a comparison between the historical Gautama and the historical Jesus. I focused on the key problem facing both religions, suffering and the way to overcome it, by contrasting the smiling Buddha, who has already reached nirvāna through enlightenment, and the crucified Christ, who is taken up into the consummation of eternal life only through suffering and death. All this will be further clarified when I address the central problem of this chapter and deal with the questions concerning the "community," monasticism, and the sangha.

THE IDEAL BUDDHIST

The Buddhist formula "I take refuge in the Buddha . . . the dharma . . . the sangha" is, of course, not a definition of a Buddhist, but, as we read in the last presentation, a confession of faith, an outward sign of inner readiness to make the Buddha's message one's own. This formula has a close Christian analogue. If a Buddhist is someone who in a thoroughly practical sense takes refuge in (1) the Buddha, (2) the teaching (dharma), and (3) the community of monks (sangha), a Christian is someone who (1) believes in Christ, (2) affirms Christ's message (Gospel) in practice, and (3) is ready to do this within the community of believers (the Church).

But this means that *monks* (and nuns) are not the only Buddhists, because, among other reasons, the sangha, the monastic community that does no physical work, is constantly dependent on the labor and charity of Buddhist *lay people*. The laity is thus no less important than the monks for the continued existence of Buddhism. The message of the Buddha has no intention of being esoteric or elitist, it is fundamentally *meant for everyone*. Everyone is supposed to give alms (especially to monks and nuns). Everyone is supposed to do good deeds and observe the five moral commandments (proscription of killing, stealing, lying, illicit sex, and consumption of alcohol). Everyone is invited to keep the additional commandments of the ascetical monastic rule. Everyone is promised the reward of a good rebirth for a good life. And thus, at least according to certain early texts, some lay people can even attain enlightenment: nirvāna.

To be sure, there was a widespread notion from the beginning that lay people—with a few exceptions—were simply to perform the works of "lesser righteousness," which, in keeping with the law of karma, gain for them worldly goods (wealth, children) and a better rebirth. Every person has several lives at his disposition, so as finally to come to enlightenment without all sorts of tension and struggle. Conversely this means that under normal circumstances only the monk succeeds in escaping the cycle of rebirth for good (and thereby entering nirvāna). Only the monk, as we have heard, consistently follows the Buddhist way of salvation: He retreats from the world in order to join the monastic community founded by the Buddha.

Anyone prepared to follow the Buddha's teaching in a radical way must also withdraw from the world, give up wife, family, friends, and home to reach salvation as a homeless wanderer. How else can a person really abandon all desire and attachment? How else can one blot out the effects of evil deeds (bad karma) or—what is just as important for obtaining extinction in nirvāna—cease to accumulate any more good karma? Only the nonacquisition of karma (bad or good) brings an end to the process of rebirth.

And yet how is one supposed to be able to renounce all desire and attachment in everyday life? What would happen to the state, the economy, the family, all of society, indeed, what would happen to the Buddhist monastic order, if everyone followed the ascetical ideal and renounced all striving and clinging, marriage and physical work? The radical way to redemption is basically reserved for the few, for a religious *elite* willing and intellectually able to lead a contemplative life. And it is to this elite that the threefold canon, the "three baskets," of the Tripitaka is addressed. As in the monastic rules (Vinaya), so the discourses (sūtra) are, with few exceptions, addressed only to the monks. Nor were the speculations of Abhidharma written for the people. Only a few will understand the message completely, only a few will consistently follow the Buddhist way of salvation to the end by bidding the world farewell.

No doubt the layperson is a Buddhist too. But lay people (in their own minds and still more in the minds of the monks) are on a lower level, while in the final analysis only the monks can reach nirvāna. In other words, the model or *ideal* Buddhist for all the laity is . . . the *monk!* Only the monks are "sons of the Buddha!" Is the same thing true of Christianity? How does the Christian message relate to the monastic way of life?

SONS OF BUDDHA—SONS OF CHRIST?

Monasticism, although the heart of Buddhism, was not invented by the Buddha, but is an *ancient Indian institution.* Its theoretical rationale can be found as far back as the Upanishads, with their stress on renunciation as the highest virtue. *Buddhist* monks differed from other Indian monks in the fact that they followed the Buddha and accepted his teaching as normative. They lived first as eremites and wanderers, then as cenobites in monasteries.

If we now turn from Indian Buddhist monasticism to the history of Christian monasticism (both the Greek/Eastern and the Latin/Western varieties), we can see, despite their very different backgrounds, striking *similarities between Buddhist and Christian spirituality.* Still we must ask whether this amazing similarity also implies a similarity with Jesus Christ. The monks, as the "Buddha's sons," are the true Buddhists. Are Christian monks, as "the sons of the Christ," perhaps also the true Christians?

Christian monks have often thought of themselves in this way, but were they right? The question must be put to both the Eastern Orthodox and the Roman Catholic Churches: Christian monasticism is old— but is it *originally Christian?* There is no doubt that the apolitical (though only seemingly unpolitical) radicalism of the monks, the "ones who live alone" (Greek *mónachos* = alone) or the "anchorites," the "ones who have withdrawn" (from the world into the wilderness), that this tradition of critical distancing oneself from the world in the name of Christ goes back to the first centuries of the Christian Era. I have already referred to the possible but not provable Indian influences on Alexandria and the valley of the Nile. There one finds at first individual *ascetics* or *hermits* (their classical model is the third-century Egyptian desert father Anthony). Then came organized monastic communities (later encouraged by the Church), leading a common life ("cenobitism"), originated by Pachomius in the fourth century.

There are obvious parallels between Christian and Buddhist monasticism, not only in their common motives and formal elements, but above all in their common ascetical frame of mind. They reflect an altered consciousness that at the time gripped a broad cross section of civilized humanity, rose to a high point, but then—though only after a long lag—subsided. Buddhist monks could always invoke the example of the Buddha, but what about Christian ones? What sort of parallels are there between both varieties of monasticism and Jesus himself? I would like to call attention to three aspects of this question:

Is Monasticism Originally Christian?

1. Buddhist and Christian monasticism are united in the demand for *separation*, departure, exodus from the world. The watchword is emigration, by the individual or the group, in the outward, local sense and the inward, spiritual sense, isolation through removal or resettlement. On this point the anchoritic-monastic tradition of Christianity is in full agreement with Buddhism, whose Eightfold Path was originally meant for people who were expected to take such a radical option for monastic life. *Gautama* himself had withdrawn, as he said, from "domestic life," a "place of uncleanness," and had sought salvation apart from common people. *In Christianity*, too, monasticism, whether lived by men or women, has always justified its existence with the categories of purity and perfection, with a "tiered ethics" of moral improvement. Even Judaism had monastic communities, like the one at Qumran, on the Dead Sea.

But *Jesus* the Jew was different: "Why do you call me good? No one is good but God alone." (Mk 10:18) Asked what one must do to be perfect, he did not, as we know, send the rich young man to the monastery of Qumran (see Mk 10:17–31, Mt 19:16–22). If they wish to enter eternal life, he demands of his followers only that they keep the basic commandments (honor father and mother; do not kill, commit adultery, steal, or give false witness) and above all to "love thy neighbor as thyself." Only in certain cases did Jesus ask anyone to give up everything and follow him—for the sake of preaching the gospel. Following Christ, being his disciple, can, as a matter of principle, be done in many ways. In any event, unlike the Buddha, Jesus founded neither an order nor a monastery. His company of apostles was neither eremitic nor cenobitic in style. His message called for neither outward nor inward emigration, neither turning away from the hustle and bustle of the world nor bidding farewell to society. The salvation he announced was not to be achieved through dismantling the self and breaking its ties to the world, but through loving commitment amid the everyday worldly routine. Teachings on the art of mental concentration, as developed in the East and later in the West (invoking his authority), are foreign to Jesus.

2. Buddhist and Christian monasticism are united in their zeal for

fulfilling the rule. According to tradition, the *Buddha* himself (despite the criticism he voiced of the Brahmanic rules and rites, such as animal sacrifices or bathing in the Ganges to wash away one's sins) is supposed to have established all the many hundred rules, all the stipulations of the penal and procedural code governing the monastic community. But even if only the basic elements of all the regulations for the monks should be traced back to the Buddha, a clearly regulated life remains characteristic of all monasticism, particularly in its cenobitic form (whether Buddhist, Christian, or Jewish). The Vinaya (monastic rule) proved from the very beginning to be a far more stabile and uniform feature of the Buddha's message than the dharma (doctrinal law).

It goes without saying that the rules are not an end in themselves. Buddhism does not support works righteousness, as though redemption could be won through external observance. Still they are the help, the raft that the monk needs if he is not to be drowned in desires but reach the other shore: enlightenment, salvation. For this reason, observance of the rules is strictly required. The other side of this coin is a regulated penal procedure, which safeguards the commandments, imposes sanctions on offenses, and so preserves the monastic community from decay and the loss of its credibility within and without. Thus we find a parallel to the Christian practice of confession and penance in the Buddhist confession, which was originally made in the presence of everyone in the monastery, but later in private. In both cases, we see special formulae and ceremonies for confessing one's offenses.

It is perhaps interesting to note that in monastic communities the habit and its color play a significant role, whether it be the ocher-colored robe of the Buddhist monks or the white one of the Jewish Qumran monks, or the Catholic spectrum from the black and brown Franciscans to the blue Little Sisters of Charles de Foucauld to the White Fathers or the Trappists. The many regulations as to the number, cut, color, and way of wearing the Buddhist monk's robe are only one example of how observance of the law generally entails a proliferation of laws (one of the main differences separating two branches of Buddhist monasticism was whether the robe should be worn over one shoulder or over both).

Jesus, once again, was different. All through the Gospels, he displays an astonishing freedom toward the law. He imposed no specific formal rules on those who wished to follow him: no novitiate, no vows, no regular exercises, no long meditations, no liturgical directions. And no distinctive garments, no dietary prescriptions, no ritual ablutions, no penal or procedural law. In comparison with both Buddhist and Christian monasticism, there was in his company an inexcusable disorderliness, casualness, spontaneity, and freedom. Instead of demanding rules to govern the meal times or the long-standing dependency of the disciple on his personal teacher (guru), he told parables about God's rule for man's benefit. And so he dispensed with any kind of catalogue of penalties. He insisted on obedience to the will of God, and to that extent obedience consisted in breaking free from all other attachments. He cared little for "elites"; he took pity on the people. He condemned the struggle to get better positions or places of honor. He did not even recognize seniority in religious life. He turned the usual hierarchical order upside down: The lowest are to be the highest, and the highest are to be the servants of all. Subordination has to be reciprocal, in common service.

3. Buddhist and Christian monasticism are united in their demand for *abstinence and asceticism.* The basis for this demand is in many cases the quest for purity, especially by renouncing marriage. With his "middle way," the *Buddha* himself rejected active self-torture and deliberate undernourishment (which were widespread in India at the time). Still he was unequivocal in demanding ascesis (in the passive sense) from his elite, the monks. Concretely and most especially, he demanded sexual continence (because the body and bodily desire are the main obstacle to liberation). At the same time, he wanted all meals to be eaten before midday, with food that had been begged, not worked for. He wanted monks to renounce most forms of property, musical performances, domestic animals, elaborate coiffures . . .

Among Christians and Jews, some have viewed such forms of asceticism (which, in the Christian world, often went so far as downright self-torment) as the essence of monasticism. Celibacy ("chastity"), the handing over of one's property to the community ("poverty"), and absolute submission to superiors ("obedience") are widely known as the three "evangelical counsels," even though they were already being practiced in Qumran, and the third has no basis in the gospel. To be sure, Buddhist and Christian monasticism have, in certain areas, different customs, both sorts of which can be justified on ascetical grounds: on the one hand, closely cropped heads and shaven beards (among Buddhist monks and some Christian mendicant orders), on the other, long hair and full beards (among Hindu sadhus, Orthodox monks, and the Capuchins); on the one hand a refusal to wash (many ascetics in India), on the other prolonged baths (Qumran had sophisticated plumbing, with eleven different water basins). At all times, whatever the form taken, there was a concern for purity, ascesis, and perfection, but also with extinguishing sexuality. This impulse often turned into a phobia; it was bound up with a disparagement of the body and, above all, of woman, the greatest temptation for an ascetic.

Here, too, *Jesus* was different. Even by comparison with Muhammad, the man from Nazareth did not give the impression of being an ascetic. Extra ethical demands and extraordinary ascetical achievements with an eye to perfection were not in his line. The "baptism of repentance" and fasting were less typical of his career than meals in common (even attended by "sinners"). Compared with ascetics like John the Baptist, he had to put up with being called a glutton and winebibber (a reproach so embarrassing that it must be authentic). Jesus demonized neither the body nor sexuality nor women. Tradition records no harsh words from him about sexual intercourse. He was solicitously cared for by women. Marriage in his view had nothing impure about it; rather, it was the will of the Creator. That is why, although unmarried, he required celibacy of no one. Giving up marriage was voluntary, a charismatic exception and not a rule for his disciples. Peter and the apostles were married (Paul was the exception), and they took their wives with them on missionary journeys. Even the renunciation of material possessions was not always necessary for those who wished to follow him. Over against the somber teaching of Qumran and the Baptist's harsh call to repentance, Jesus' message appeared in many ways a happy, liberating one. Characteristic for him was not the penitent baptism for the sinners but, rather, the festive meal with sinners.

What conclusions does my deliberately sharp contrast leave us with? Essential elements of Christian cenobitic life, as founded by Pachomius, theologically bolstered by Basil the Great, passed on to the Latin West by John Cassian, and exemplified for all of Western monasticism by Benedict of Nursia and the Benedictine Rule, can also be found in Buddhism (and in Qumran). They are: "1) Common quarters for living, working, and praying; 2) uniformity in dress, diet, and ascetical bearing; 3) safeguarding of the community by means of a written rule based on obedience." (K. Baus, article on "Kionobitenum," in *Lexikon für Theologie und Kirche,* VI, 368) Despite differences in background and many modifications (no vow of obedience), this pattern is also characteristic of the Buddha—but not of Jesus, the Christ of Christians.

THE PARADIGM CHANGE FROM ELITE RELIGION TO MASS RELIGION

It was a pregnant moment for Buddhism when it went from being a doctrine of salvation for a few radicals, most of whom came from the privileged class of worldly notables, to being a doctrine of salvation for the many, for the masses. This dissemination across all of India, Sri Lanka, and the coastlands of Southeast Asia in the centuries before Christ led to the creation of Theravāda Buddhism. Many years ago, Max Weber called attention to this "transformation" of a uniquely radical "aristocratic, intellectual soteriology," whose "driving factor . . . ," alongside the unavoidable accommodation to the actual conditions of the world, was the interest of the laity." "The petty bourgeois and the peasant could make nothing of the products of the soteriology of educated gentility. Least of all could they find satisfaction from early Buddhistic soteriology. The petty bourgeois or peasant could as little think of yearning for *nirvāna* as he could of uniting with the Brahman. Above all, he did not have the means at hand to attain these holy objects; it required leisure for the meditation necessary to achieve the gnosis. He had no such leisure and, as a rule, saw no reason for gaining such leisure by living as a penitent in the woods." (*The Religion of India,* trans. and ed. Hans H. Gerth and Don Martindale, 1958, pp. 234, 236) Or, putting it positively: "The kind of salvation which was promised to the mendicant and was not to the taste of the socially oppressed strata which would have rather demanded compensation in the hereafter or this-worldly hopes for the future." (p. 228) Instead of concentrating on a speedy entrance into nirvāna (except insofar as this was understood in a positive sense as "bliss"), common people were primarily interested in a better rebirth this side of eternity.

All this makes it clear that monasticism is indeed common to Buddhism and Christianity, but that it has an unmistakably different value for each. It is altogether more central and essential to Buddhism than to Christianity: The Buddha's message denied the world so radically that only the monastic lifestyle of his "sons" could match it. Things were different with Jesus: To belong to his community, one had to be his "brother" or "sister," one did not have to change one's condition in life. His message can in principle be lived in different ways, and from the beginning *was* lived in different ways. One could be for Jesus without traveling around with him, without literally following him. From the first, one could be a Christian in the full sense without giving up marriage, property, and home. And neither Jesus nor any Christian monk ever claimed that only on *his* way of "perfection" could one attain the definitive redemption, eternal life. In a word, *monasticism is the foundation of Buddhism, not of Christianity.* Where monastic life was destroyed (as in India, by Islam), Buddhism was struck to the heart.

This is a crucial difference, which also has far-reaching implications for the understanding and practice of present-day Buddhism. For if monastic existence is the actual existential equivalent of Buddhist teaching, then, unlike Christianity, Buddhism has a built-in conflict that over the course of history necessarily and continually occasioned great changes—a *basic tension between "authentic," monastic existence, and "inauthentic," lay existence.* To be sure, the immanent conflict between message and practice, claim and reality, has pervaded the history of Christianity, as of every religion. But in Buddhism this conflict reaches a still more intense level: It is between being a Buddhist and being a monk, and arises from the fact that, originally, being a monk was the only genuine way to be a Buddhist.

What happened to Buddhism was a metamorphosis on the grand scale. Just as Christianity could never have become a world religion without changing from the Jewish-Christian/apocalyptic paradigm to the Hellenistic/ecumenical paradigm, and just as in Islam (because of armed expansion and the scattering of the Prophet's companions) the paradigm of the original community was replaced by a new one, so too —according to Weber—Buddhism only became a "world religion" "when it deeply transformed its own inner structure." (p. 234) It is true that the old Buddhist message, the constants (Buddha-dharma-sangha), remained the same, but now they were interpreted with other variables, in the context of another entire constellation of beliefs, values, and techniques and so on—of another "paradigm." (Thomas S. Kuhn) In other words, certain basic elements of Buddhism were retained, but were now lived out in a new paradigm, where familiar concepts changed, criteria that determine the admissibility of individual problems and solutions shifted, and where "much of what was thrown out the front door of Buddhism, so to speak, came in again through the back." (H. Bechert)

How the structures of this altered paradigm have been preserved in Theravāda countries right up to the present (one finds a similar pattern of survival with the Hellenistic/Byzantine paradigm in the Eastern Orthodox churches) can be seen in Heinz Bechert's detailed three-volume study *Buddhism, State, and Society in the Theravāda Buddhist Countries* (1966–73). Professor Bechert rightly points to the fact that "even Theravāda . . . , despite its theoretically conservative stance, has not been spared a whole series of changes": "Vital transformations in the articulation of Buddhism had to take place above all because in the course of its dissemination it became the religion of the masses in the nations of Southeast Asia. Although the Buddha had viewed belief in the effectiveness of rites and ceremonies as one of the ten "fetters," at a very early date forms of Buddhist worship developed, starting with the veneration of relics, which began immediately after the Buddha's death. Of course, cultic actions were originally supposed to do no more than serve as a lively illustration of the Buddha's teaching and thereby effect an inner purification of the worshipper. But these ritual performances soon came to be treated as a source of boundless merit and the guarantee of a good rebirth . . . While the quest for nirvāna and the effort to understand the deeper meaning of Buddhist teaching naturally had to remain the concern of a small minority, for the mass of the Buddhist population the substance of piety could only be the moral commandments, knowledge of the life story of the Buddha and the saints, and, finally, gathering religious merit. In this process of change, magical thinking, which was alien to the Buddha's original teaching, gained considerable influence." (I, 19–20)

Recent anthropological studies such as Melford E. Spiro's *Buddhism and Society: A Great Tradition and its Burmese Vicissitudes* (1970), S. J.

Tambiah's *Buddhism and the Spirit Cults in Northeast Thailand* (1970) and *World Conqueror and World Renouncer: A Study of Buddhism and Polity in Thailand Against a Historical Background* (1976), and Richard F. Gombrich's *Precept and Practice: Traditional Buddhism in the Rural Highlands of Ceylon* (1971) point in the same direction. In Spiro's view, these changes do not consist

> so much in an incorporation of foreign elements into the normative ideology —although that has occurred to some extent—as in a selective emphasis and reorganization of the original elements. (p. 68)

What concrete changes are we talking about? Following the line of Max Weber, Spiro summarizes his case, which is based on his (actually very limited) field work in Burma, and which, he believes, holds true for other Theravāda countries as well:

> Typically, instead of renouncing desire (and the world), Buddhists rather aspire to a future worldly existence in which their desires may find satisfaction; contrary to nibbanic Buddhism, which teaches that frustration is an inevitable characteristic of samsaric existence, they view their suffering as a temporary state, the result of their present position in *samsara*. But there are, and they aspire to achieve, other forms of samsaric experience which yield great pleasure. These range from the earthly existence of a wealthy human being to the heavenly existence of a blissful *deva*. Frustrated in their striving for greater pleasure in their present lives, the Burmese—to particularize this generalized discussion—hope to find it in a future life. Their aim is not to transcend the samsaric world, but to alter their fate (in a future life) within it.
>
> Contrary, then, to the ideology of nibbanic Buddhism, Buddhism for most Buddhists is a means not so much for the extinction of desire as for its satisfaction; not so much for the cessation of rebirth as for a better rebirth; not so much for some kind of absolute Deliverance—whether this be conceived as the extinction of being or, less extremely, of an individualized ego —as for the persistence of the individuated ego in a state of sensate happiness. Hence, even when the soteriological aim is expressed in nibbanic rhetoric—"May I attain nirvana"—the content of the aspiration is samsaric rather than nibbanic. (p. 67)

A small elite, as we have seen, has no doubt always been capable of making positive efforts to reach a negatively framed nirvāna. But, for most Buddhists, this was asking too much. For the great majority, there were two possibilities:

- Either one understood nirvāna negatively as the total extinction of the individual, and then it was, for the mass of Buddhists, not an attainable goal. People preferred (by accumulating as many merits as possible) to aim for a better rebirth in one life or several. In this approach nirvāna was not, of course, denied outright, but largely displaced from consciousness.

- Or one understood nirvāna positively, as a happy final goal of imperturbable rest, of definitive peace, and inexpressible bliss *(sukha* instead of *dukkha),* which, naturally enough, could be directly striven for. Nirvāna in this sense largely corresponded to the Christian idea of "eternal life."

SANGHA AND CHURCH

In their earliest days, Buddhism and Christianity faced a number of analogous problems, for which they found analogous solutions: Just as the Buddha, for example, would not or could not do away with the Indian caste system, but in fact relativized it by accepting men (and women, too) from all castes into his sangha, so (after Jesus died the death of a slave) Paul did not combat the Greco-Roman system of slavery, but radically relativized it in the spirit of Jesus Christ by accepting masters *and* slaves, men *and* women, into the Christian community, and by stressing the equal rights of all human beings before God. We may say that although they were no social revolutionaries, the Buddha and the Christ changed humanity in a more revolutionary fashion than any revolutionaries, so that after them (and Muhammad should be included here) time began to be calculated anew.

The paradigm change from a religion for an elite to one for the masses inevitably affected not just the individual, but also the religious community, whether sangha or Church. Over the course of time, unfortunately, both religions (in Christianity, at least, contrary to its "founder's" intentions) encouraged the formation of a *new two-class society.* They created a religious and social dualism of elite and masses, hierarchy and people, "clergy" and "laity." And the influence of these religious power elites on state and society has remained especially strong in countries where their religion has de facto or de jure become the established creed of the state.

As far as the role of the *laity* is concerned, for all the differences, we can note two parallels. In both religions, lay people have *two primary functions:* 1) to defray the living expenses of the monastic or clerical hierarchy, 2) to accumulate "merits" with a view to rebirth or eternal life. Or, putting it negatively, ordinary lay people (in contrast, of course, to the rulers of the respective countries) had scarcely any rights vis-à-vis the sangha or the Church. Thus there is clericalism or "bonzeism," or whatever one wishes to call it, on both sides. The sangha, though, never had anything like the elaborate hierarchy, the feudal arrangements, or the vast bureaucracy that developed in the Christian (Roman Catholic) Church, which for a long time set itself over against the state as a "perfect society" ("societas perfecta"). This did not happen, because the sangha never "organized" lay people, hardly troubled itself about them, and left them in an unstructured condition prone to sectarianism. There was no lay "community." Yet the sangha largely depended for its survival not only on the voluntary, sporadic "kind gifts of believers," but also on the ruler, who supported the monasteries with state funds. The loss of this support after the Muslim conquest was a major factor in the downfall of Buddhism in India, whereas Jainism, for example, was supported by rich merchants and managed to survive.

Another fact of Buddhist and Christian life that we still see today is the discrimination against women. I shall mention only two characteristic symptoms of this: Although the Buddha finally permitted the ordination of nuns, it has not been practiced among the Theravāda Buddhists of Southeast Asia since A.D. 456, for not very convincing reasons. In the Christian world, as everyone knows, only some Protestant denominations (and, in part, the Anglican Church) ordain women, while Catholicism and Orthodoxy continue to refuse to do so. Behind this intransigence, on both sides, we find dogmatically hardened patriarchal notions of the inferiority of women. In Christianity, there is the idea of the intrinsic masculinity of the Redeemer (and preexistent "Son" of God) and his priesthood, in Buddhism the idea that a being can become a Buddha only when it has been born, or reborn, in "the form of a man." It was not until much later that the Mahāyāna school accepted female Bodhisattvas and even came to venerate the male Bodhisattva Avalokiteshvara as a female figure too, a "Madonna" (Chinese Kuan-yin, Japanese Kannon).

Thus the paradigm change from the Buddha to the "earlier community" had consequences not only for purely private piety but also for the religious community. Finally, it also had significant effects on political theory and practice.

RENOUNCING THE WORLD AND RESHAPING IT

Renouncing the world remained the business of the monk. But, with new political developments, the question of how to shape the world loomed increasingly larger for the Buddha's successors. As far back as the Pāli canon, we find exhortations to moral, just conduct on the part of the king. But the first Buddhist to develop an actual political theory and strategy was, as we have learned, *Emperor Ashoka,* the great representative of Buddhist humanity and tolerance—but also of state centralization and of the leveling of Indian society. He succeeded in uniting all of India under the sign of Buddhism: The dharma was now understood as a principle of religious and sociopolitical order. In this way, Ashoka fashioned the "model that both generated and legitimated political action," the tension-filled and ambivalent "realization of a paradigmatic Buddhist politics," the "great precursor and model for the rising political systems of South and Southeast Asia," in short the religiopolitical "paradigm" still operative in the Theravāda countries of Southeast Asia. (S. J. Tambiah, *World Conqueror and World Renouncer*, pp. 54, 55)

Buddhism, too, had to go through a sort of "Age of Constantine," with all its dubious consequences. The Buddhist "Middle Ages" were in the making. It was chiefly in this period that people began to build innumerable stupas over the Buddha's relics as works of merit. These shrines offer architectural evidence for the great shift from ceasing to accumulate any karma (and so entering nirvāna) to accumulating good karma, to accumulating merits for a better rebirth. Starting with Ashoka, a religion for world-renouncing monks turned into a power for changing and reshaping the world, first in India (where monasteries became great landowners, feudal institutions, which, contrary to the Rule, had many servants, and became ever more worldly, so that by the time of the Muslim conquest they no longer had the support of the people), then in Sri Lanka and all of Southeast Asia. Christianity, too, needless to say, began as a persecuted sect, only to become the official (and very worldly) state religion of the Roman/Byzantine Empire. In both cases, in spite of fundamental differences, we find a state with religious objectives, a religion with political ambitions. And as in Christian Byzantium, so too in Buddhism—despite all the differences between sangha and Church—the secular ruler became the patron of the religious community: a perfect unity—consider the Theravāda countries of the premodern period—of state, culture, and religion.

In point of fact, given the possible choices in the real world, both Buddhism and Christianity have associated themselves down through the ages with a great variety of political philosophies and sociopolitical systems. One can no more speak of *the* Buddhist form of government than of *the* Christian form. From the days of Christian Rome, East and West, through the "Holy Roman Empire of the German Nation" to the modern democracies and Christian Democratic parties, practically every conceivable kind of symbiosis between Church and state, and occasionally antagonism (Christianity as a social utopia) has seen the light of day. Many of these social realizations of Christianity have some sort of parallel in Buddhism; and in any case, it must be repeated, they are not specifically Christian.

We should not overlook the fact, however, that *parliamentary democracy* has not developed independently in any Buddhist country of Southeast Asia. Although the Buddha himself was rather a republican by tradition and conviction, Buddhism showed a preference early on for monarchical government. Together with the monk as the supreme religious ideal, the "just king" was a guiding figure for Buddhist society. And not only in the early centuries, but also in the past few decades, prime ministers of Thailand, Burma, and Sri Lanka have tried to gain support and legitimacy through the sangha. Still, in countries where parliamentary democracy was introduced from outside (Sri Lanka, Thailand) it was important, as Heinz Bechert reminds us, "that it was given legitimacy from the native cultural tradition. Hence the survival of democracies in these countries is surely not an accident. This integration took place by viewing the structure of the Buddhist sangha as a model to be applied to human society in general. For in the sangha all monks are in principle equal, and wherever possible all decisions should be unanimous. Where this cannot be done, certain resolutions are not allowed to pass. Others can be passed by majority decision. In this way it proved possible to claim the basic rules of democratic self-government as a part of Buddhist tradition." (*Weltflucht oder Weltveränderung: Antworten des Buddhistischen modernismus auf Fragen unserer Zeit,* 1976, pp. 29–30)

TOLERANCE?

An important question connected to the political dimension of Buddhism is the *tolerance* that Buddhism has practiced toward people with different ideas. Has not in fact Buddhism, quite unlike Christianity, managed to keep presenting its teaching and its truth in a decisive fashion without having to suppress or even violently eradicate other forms of faith and life? There is no room in Buddhism for religious persecutions, crusades, or an Inquisition. Throughout Asia, Buddhism has had a humanizing impact, and the Buddhist centuries in India, China, Japan, and Sri Lanka belong to the most brilliant in the history of those nations. On the whole, mystical religions seem to have an easier time with tolerance than do religions in which God's prophetic word demands a decision, provokes a "crisis," and so virtually creates a division between those who listen and those who do not, between the chosen and the not-chosen, and finally between the saved and the damned.

But does this picture of tolerant Buddhism and largely intolerant Christianity fit the historical facts? Alongside all the horror stories of dogmatic, ecclesiastical, and political domination, alongside all the outrages of "Christian" imperialism and colonialism, is there not *also* a *history of tolerance,* of freedom of conscience, that made an epochal breakthrough, from the Church's standpoint, in the Reformation "freedom of a Christian man" and, for society as a whole, in the religious freedom of the Enlightenment (though the decisive impulses for this came from outside the Church)?

Buddhists, too, have been involved in wars, disputes, and acts of violence; and Buddhism has not always been spread peacefully by Buddhist kings. Buddhist monks have often enough had recourse to violence in Tibet and Burma, China and Japan; and recent setbacks for

Buddhism in Burma and Sri Lanka can be traced to the exaggerated influence of the sangha. Edward Conze, a scholar who always presents Buddhism in a sympathetic light, points to various examples of the use of violence by Buddhists (the role of the Buddhist monks in the Vietnam War, and the suppression of the Hindu Tamil minority by the Buddhist Sinhalese majority in Sri Lanka ought to be looked into), and observes:

> In their desire to express disapproval of Christianity, many authors have painted the record of Buddhism too white, and it will be necessary to admit that on occasion the Buddhists were capable of behavior which we usually regard as Christian. [*Buddhism: Its Essence and Development*, 1959, p. 65]

No religion is innocent; each religion has its saints and its scoundrels. Yet, rather than totting up the guilt incurred by both sides, rather than engaging in mutual self-righteous recrimination for (possibly accidental) failure to live up to one's religious and ethical principles, I would propose a discussion of the related *problem of an easy, cheap tolerance* in Buddhism, an issue that should not be dodged, least of all in interreligious dialogue. There is a danger of uncritical assimilation, of an opportunistic attitude of compromise, of a dangerous lack of discrimination and insufficient resistance to some highly dubious Western "achievements," and this danger can be seen with special clarity in the most technologically advanced country in Asia: Japan.

A *critical tolerance* need not be opposed to the ideal of Buddhist ethics, its first commandment: *Do not harm living things.* This rule of nonviolence, which Buddhism shared from the first with Jainism, was aimed both against the use of force between tribes and individuals and against the extensive slaughter of animals in Vedic sacrifices. Even though the sacredness of *all* life (meaning complete vegetarianism) cannot be practiced by Buddhists with perfect consistency, it would be worthwhile for Christians to consider how they might better live up to the ideal of reverence for life—including the life of animals and plants (in this connection, Schopenhauer called attention to parallels between the Buddha and Francis of Assisi). Christians have been only too one-sided in their readiness to quote—and carry out—that one verse of Genesis to "subdue the earth."

THE QUEST FOR SALVATION AND THE ECONOMY

Though Buddhism may have monastic origins and a monastic flavor, we have seen that it can in no way be understood today as a religion whose principal concern is to deny the world. Mystical religion is simply not always world-denying and passive, nor is prophetic religion always active and world-affirming. Still, we cannot overlook the fact that it is easier to justify the social status quo with the Buddhist doctrine of karma (and, in connection with it, the doctrine of reincarnation), since all differences in power, prestige, and wealth are explained as the result of karma. One thinks of the Christian Middle Ages when one visits Burma's oldest capital, Pagan (now a village), and observes that despite all the destruction by the Mongols there are still over eight hundred temples and pagodas (once, there were roughly nine thousand), some in a fairly good state of preservation. Over many square kilometers, one keeps encountering the same symbol of *economic profit being used to acquire religious merit.* Is not this system of "dāna," with all its pious donations—beginning with flowers and incense, moving on through clothes, watches, and shrines for monks, all the way to the founding of temples and pagodas—a classic case of the problem in which Max Weber had such a burning interest: that of the relation between the quest for salvation and economic activity?

Melford E. Spiro takes issue with Weber, and notes some important differences between this situation and the one addressed by the Weber thesis:

> For the Buddhist—i.e., the *kammatic* Buddhist—no less than for the Puritan, the pursuit of salvation provides a powerful motive for economic action. If, then, Buddhism and Puritanism have had opposite consequences for economic development and growth, it is not because the soteriology of the one (as Weber has argued) provides a motive for worldly action while that of the other provides no such motivation. It is rather—so far as the role of religion (rather than social structure, culture, or character) is concerned—that their soteriologies lead to different motivations with respect to savings. For the Puritan, who has already been predestined for salvation or damnation, successful economic action—if Weber (1930: Ch. 5) is correct—provides him with proof that he is one of the elect, and savings are to be reinvested to create further wealth—for the greater glory of God. For the Buddhist, whose salvation is problematic, successful economic action is a prerequisite to enhancing his chances of salvation, and savings are to be spent on *dāna*—for the greater increase of his own store of merit. For the Buddhist, the proof of salvation is to be found, not in accumulating and creating new wealth, but in giving it away in the form of *dāna.* (p. 460)

The consequences of this dāna system for the social situation of the country are far-reaching, and Spiro bluntly names them:

> It should be evident, then, that just as Burma might have achieved more rapid economic development if such a large percentage of its wealth had not been spent on *dāna,* so too its standard of education, the level of its social services, the quality of its medical facilities, etc., might have been markedly improved if the Burmese were not so deeply absorbed in acquiring merit through *dāna,* or if contributions to secular institutions were also interpreted as *dāna.* Indeed, if the funds spent only on superfluous gifts for monks—the second monastery which remains unoccupied, the fourth grandfather clock,

the extra food which is eaten by the pi-dogs, etc.—were allocated to education, the effects on Burmese society would not be inconsiderable. This is all too well recognized by some of the Burmese themselves, although they are too few to change the system. (p. 466)

On the other hand, there are hopeful signs: Within the sangha we find strong trends toward change, especially among the younger monks, who no longer wish to be bound to their traditionally limited role, who sharply criticize traditional religious practice, who demand the abolition of outdated rules (fasting after midday, the prohibition against private conversations with women, the separation of monks and lay people) and are ready to commit themselves socially and, under certain circumstance, politically, too. A new sense of social responsibility and the providing of concrete social services are indications of an authentic Buddhist renewal. Efforts such as those of the monk Rajavaramuni to establish a Buddhist social ethics in Thailand (*Social Dimensions of Buddhism in Contemporary Thailand,* 1983) are just as important as those of the layman Sulak Sivaraksa and his Asian Cultural Forum on Development, which is trying to set in motion social and political improvements on the basis of authentic Buddhism. Here prophetic Christianity meets social reform-minded Buddhism. In some places, practical cooperation is already going on between Buddhists and Christians.

IMMANENT TENSION BETWEEN MONASTIC AND LAY EXISTENCE

At this point we interrupt the historical-systematical analysis and ask what consequences the internal Buddhist paradigm change sketched out here might have for interreligious dialogue with Christianity. With the first half of the Buddhism section behind us, I shall now attempt a methodological résumé of what I have done so far and then try to formulate, without going into detail, some considerations for dialogue with Theravāda Buddhism.

1. We began by trying to understand Buddhism from the standpoint of its *origin.* Following the order of Heinz Bechert's presentation we went back to the figure of Siddhārtha Gautama in the certainty that we would sense in its origin all the power and radical uniqueness of Buddhism; and, at the same time, in the hope that, by going back to the Gautama of history, we would find that it was possible to distinguish historical events from their reverberation in history, the specific from the nonspecific, and thus—after a bewilderingly complex historical process—to frame a clear picture of Buddhist identity and authenticity for the Christian observer. Even though the figure of the Buddha is historically less palpable, and has a different theological importance, for Buddhists, and though his person fades into the background of the teaching

more so than the figure of Christ does for Christians, any religion, insofar as it harks back to a "founder," a guiding figure and life model, can avoid the criteriological question about the authenticity of its origins only under penalty of diffusing its sense of identity.

2. In principle, the parallel holds: just as for actually existing, *de facto* lived Christianity a radical critique must always mean a confrontation with the concrete Jesus of Nazareth, with his life and teaching, so the confrontation of actually existing, *de facto* lived Buddhism in the Theravāda countries with the Gautama of history, with his doctrines and practices, had to be nothing less than a radical critique that could be an occasion for self-reflection and a radical change in one's life.

3. The peculiar problem of Buddhism, however, lies in the fact that the Buddha was a monk. Our analysis has clearly shown that from the earliest days of Buddhism onward an *immanent tension between monastic and lay existence* has run through older Buddhism, one that goes deeper than the "classical" ethical tension between claim and reality that every religion must endure, because the radicality of the Buddha and his teaching demands a radical life-style whose conditions can in general be met only by monastic existence. But since the overwhelming majority of men and women cannot, or do not want to, become monks, and indeed, since the monks are necessarily dependent upon lay people, dependent, that is, on a majority of the Buddha's followers' not wanting or not being able to be radical Buddhists (even though they would perhaps like to), Buddhism has to undertake some fundamental reinterpretations of its doctrine and practice.

4. For this reason we argued one step further in discussing recent research findings, in an effort to make it clear that in the Buddhism of the Theravāda countries, as it is actually lived outside the Order, we find few traces of the Buddha's radicality. The paradigm change from an elite religion to a mass religion seems to indicate that the Buddha's message of denying the world and dissolving the self is meant to be led in the monastery, but not in concrete private or public life. Only the, so to speak, nonmonastic side of Buddhism is to be lived here. But what is the case with Christianity? Do the "Christian" countries show us much of the radicality of the Sermon on the Mount? Hardly. But what is at stake here is *not* the undeniable *ethical* conflict between theory and practice, between a lofty ethos and its miserable realization, but the *life-style that in the final analysis is demanded* in order to translate a teaching into reality. Jesus' radical message (the Sermon on the Mount) can in principle— because it was not designed for monks—be lived by anyone in everyday life and, for all the visibly unchristian behavior going on in Christian countries, it *is* being so lived, unobtrusively, by innumerable men and women in the West and the East, people who strive day after day to love and sympathize with their neighbors, to serve others regardless of their

status, to forgive without limits, to renounce power or rights without getting anything in return, to put love into practice, indeed to love their enemies. The ideal Christian is simply not the monk.

However, the Buddha's radical message about completely following the way to redemption can be lived in practice (apart from exceptions) only by monks. As a layperson one can, under normal circumstances, do no more than try to better one's karma and thus create better preconditions for entrance into salvation. This fact presents no problem for most lay people (and monks): the majority of people (and nowadays even of the monks) either feel no need for salvation (a new life under better or "paradisiacal" circumstances seems a much more worthwhile goal) or consider themselves too spiritually backward—and so have enough of the sort of patience with themselves that is the opposite of "prophetic impatience." This can become problematic, even tragic, in cases where a person has the clear wish for redemption in the Buddhist sense, yet cannot maintain the monastic life-style to which the Buddhist doctrine of definitive salvation is *de facto* linked; or, alternatively, in spite of scrupulous adherence to this life-style, fails and so cannot summon up that Buddhist patience with oneself which reckons with thousands of rebirths. Here we can see just how harsh the total self-reliance of a Shrāvakayāna Buddhist can be. And here, of course, would be an opening for Buddhist-Christian dialogue. Christians would introduce the theme of "grace alone" (properly understood), while the Buddhists would have to ask critically to what extent the Christians were not succumbing to illusions about "hard" reality.

5. The question at hand, then, is the identity of *de facto* Buddhism as the teaching of the *Buddha*. In other words, in Buddhism, unlike other religions, *general doctrinal content* coincides with a *specific pattern of life*. Life and teaching, form and content are so fused together in the case of the Buddha that Buddhism threatens to lose its original power when they are sundered—whether in the form of a rarefied, intellectual philosophy of religion in the Western style, which has little use for monasticism, or in the form of an ordinary, everyday popular Buddhism, lived pragmatically on an altogether different level, which only venerates and nourishes monasticism—and sometimes lets it perish, and for itself, at least, follows completely different paths. To be sure, the doctrine of karma and reincarnation, i.e., the conviction that one day the layman will have accumulated enough good karma to be reborn as a monk, makes it easier for the Buddhist lay person to reconcile himself with his inferior form of Buddhist existence. But if one seeks not nirvāna, but only repeatedly a better life in this world, is one not perhaps forfeiting the radical seriousness of the Buddha's message? The result in any event is that the Buddha's key teachings—the transitoriness of samsaric existence, the doctrine of the no-self, the extinction of desire as a prerequi-

site for entrance into nirvāna, and the striving for nirvāna through the strictest self-discipline—are at best commemorated by the masses, but as a matter of fact they have been and still are ignored.

IMPLICATIONS FOR DIALOGUE WITH THERAVĀDA BUDDHISM

What should dialogue with Buddhism concentrate on? The figure of the *monk Gautama*? Should we measure Buddhism by what the Buddha sought, lived, and achieved, and what countless monks following the Buddha have taken upon thems··lves? That would be a possibility. Then we would have to start out from the fundamental *difference* between Gautama the monk and Jesus the nonmonk. This, of course, would virtually tie Buddhism down to monasticism and would, to a large extent, reduce dialogue between Buddhists and Christians to a dialogue between actual and potential monks on both sides.

The other possibility is to go beyond monasticism to that *deeper level of agreement* between Jesus the Christ and Gautama the Buddha, which holds up even when we look at the differences in their life-styles and religious/metaphysical frameworks. Here we must give no less attention to religious practice, on both sides, than to theory. In point of fact, many *Christians* in Asia are already unconsciously incorporating certain key Buddhist ideals into their lives (without thereby becoming "anonymous Buddhists"): beyond the basic moral commandments, an ultimate selflessness, a striving to overcome contradictory, sorrowful, inconstant earthly existence, an openness to definitive redemption (however understood). Whatever points of agreement we have managed to elaborate between Jesus and Gautama with regard to fundamental morality, their personal lives and the message they preached are as valid here as ever. In these matters, dialogue between Christianity and Buddhism can and must be continued and deepened across the whole religious spectrum.

By the same token, it is important for Buddhist-Christian dialogue that many *Buddhists* in the Theravāda countries are (unconsciously) incorporating so many ideals into their lives that have strong affinities with the way Christianity understands the world and existence. This is not, in any sense, to co-opt such Buddhists as some kind of "anonymous Christians," but to realize that in the practice of religion, despite all the divergences, there are often more convergences than defenders of official doctrine and authors of textbooks would admit.

But if the religious practice of the people steadily ignores certain doctrines (because they cannot be put into practice), would that not have to have consequences for the rethinking of the doctrine? Surely it cannot be a matter of indifference that the way of monastic perfection through radical denial of the world and self can be lived by, at best, a tiny minority, but evidently not by the Buddhist masses in their hundreds of millions. And so a form of religious behavior, with a theory to match, has been developed that must strike Christians as not so strange at all. Would this not mean that Christian and Buddhist practice are bound together by common religious needs and structures, which Christianity (and along with it all prophetic religions) has, perhaps, perceived more clearly and interpreted more adequately (from its standpoint of a *via media* between denying and affirming the world) than radical, monastic Buddhism?

When Christians come to know the *Buddha,* whose thinking ran along *elitist* lines, they will feel impelled radically to question their lives, which may well be too bent on success and achievement, and to shape them anew. Conversely, when Buddhists decide to encounter Jesus of Nazareth, the *Christ,* who had compassion on the people and took the part of *those who had come to grief,* they will sense an invitation to overcome the division of believers into two classes, for the well-being of *all* men and women, to give the layperson, the supposed inferior, something more than second-class status: a direct access to salvation, his own rights and his own dignity; and to come to the aid of the weak, the failures, the defeated and exploited, so as to change the world here and now in compassion and love for the well-being of everyone.

In any event, the figure of the Buddha, his teaching and his life, stands in the way of Christianity and Buddhism like a great boulder. In a fashion altogether different from Christianity's problems with Jesus, Buddhism has been placed by the Buddha in a dilemma of relevance and identity that has made it hard, except for a small elite, to achieve the sort of authenticity that the Buddha himself would have wanted. The paradigm change from early Buddhism to Theravāda Buddhism was no accident, nor was it by chance that Buddhism has been shaken by further profound changes again related to the position of the laity. Mahāyāna Buddhism, which we shall hear about in the next presentation, is the second great, totally transforming paradigm change within Buddhism. It leads to a much freer interpretation of monasticism, indeed to what is in many ways an emphatically lay religion.

III.
From Theravāda to Pure Land: Forms of Buddhist Thought and Life

1. *Heinz Bechert:* Buddhist Perspectives

Shrāvakayāna (Hīnayāna) and Mahāyāna

Buddhism has not managed to escape the law that all existing things are mutable. Thus, a bewildering variety of religious forms has grown out of the Buddha's teaching, such a variety in fact that at times their common root is barely visible. In some cases, however, one is surprised to see how much of the spirit of the old teaching survives or spontaneously returns to life even at the furthest remove from the parent stock.

The original teaching of the Buddha had no ritual, an arrangement that failed to meet the needs of most of his followers. Starting out with the cult of relics and belief in miracles, all sorts of ritual soon developed, even though the doctrinal tradition long maintained that cultic activities were of no value for liberation and could, at best, serve to spread the teaching and memory of the Buddha. Nevertheless, the cult of relics was already in full swing when Theravāda Buddhism came to Ceylon, in the time of Ashoka, and afterward expanded into Father India. This school, generally speaking, did a good job of handing down the early texts, and it largely kept the old doctrinal interpretation. Still, it altered its character by transforming Buddhism from a way to enlightenment for the individual into a religion for entire nations, with its consequent interweaving of religion and government.

In the motherland, India, different forms of Shrāvakayāna, or Hīnayāna (i.e., the old Buddhist schools, including Theravāda), survived for a long time. But they were more and more thrust into the background by Mahāyāna (the "great vehicle"), which had been developing since about the first century B.C. Mahāyāna Buddhism was not a uniform, self-enclosed doctrinal system, as ancient Buddhism was. It comprised a multiplicity of religious forms with some common principles. Thus all the adherents of all the versions of Mahāyāna were agreed, for example, that the teachings held by the traditional monastic communities were incomplete. They argued that the historical Buddha and other Buddhas had taught, above and beyond the already known doctrines, a number of additional teachings which earlier generations had not been mature enough to understand. But now the time had come to proclaim those more profound teachings, which revealed the true nature of the world and led to the "perfection of knowledge" (*prajñāpāramitā*). These are laid down in doctrinal texts of Mahāyāna, which must have acquired their present form, for the most part, between the first and the fifth centuries A.D.

The followers of Mahāyāna in no way disputed the authority of the old canonical scriptures. Instead they merely relativized their validity by applying the doctrine of double truth, with which the Buddha had accommodated himself to the mental capacities of his listeners by making statements now formulated in line with conventional truth, now truth in the highest sense. Their ideas on the relation of the Hīnayāna canon and the Mahāyāna-Sūtras can be compared in some ways to Christian thinking on the Old and New Testaments. Above all, the Mahāyāna monks insisted on the binding force of the traditional rules of monastic discipline. They adopted the Vinaya of the monastic community, from which their own tradition of ordination derived. Since the structure of a monastic community was not primarily determined by common dogmatic views, adherents of both religions sometimes lived peacefully together in one and the same monastery.

Whereas the meaning of ancient Buddhism lay entirely in the individual effort to obtain salvation, the followers of Mahāyāna proposed the new goal of becoming Buddhas themselves, preachers of the way to nirvāna. With this in mind, they were to undertake the long and wearisome path laid out for a bodhisattva, that is, a future Buddha. Mahāyāna also sets forth a great promise. Salvation is no longer available for only a few ascetics, but for the mass of human beings. The presence of countless Buddhas and bodhisattvas gives everyone the possibility of cooperating in the process of salvation or of sharing in the rich store of merits gained by those world-redeemers.

SHŪNYAVĀDA AND YOGĀCĀRA

Indian Mahāyāna Buddhism produced two great philosophical schools whose teachings have decisively influenced the later forms of

Buddhism in East Asia and Tibet. The older of these schools is Shūnya-vāda ("doctrine of the void"), also known as the doctrine of the Mād-hyamikas, the followers of the "middle" teaching. Its prototypes can be found in older Prajñāpāramitā-Sūtras ("Doctrinal texts on the Perfection of Knowledge"). The most famous master of early Shūnyavāda is the philosopher Nāgārjuna (ca. A.D. 200), who explained the school's doctrine with a highly elaborated dialectic. At its center stands the teaching of "emptiness" *(shūnyatā)*.

Let us recall once again what was to be said about the question of the existence of the liberated in nirvāna—a question to which no answer could be given. Where the ways of imagination and thought that characterize our impermanent existence as well as the alternatives existence and nonexistence are no longer relevant, the concept of "the void" is introduced. It constitutes the midpoint (hence the "middle" teaching) between two contraries. The doctrine of the "twofold emptiness of beings and things" in the philosophy of Shūnyavāda is, accordingly, a consistent continuation of the old Buddhist thesis of the "emptiness of beings," that is, the nonexistence of the "self."

Shūnyavāda occupies a specific place in the historical evolution of philosophy. It opposes the "realism" of the Hīnayāna school of the Sarvāstivādin, which was highly influential in India at the time. As we have noted, the Sarvāstivādin claimed that the "factors of existence" (dharma) exist, that is, there is a certain reality in them. They agreed, however, with all other Buddhists, that these dharmas neither contained nor constituted a "self" or an immortal soul. The Mādhyamikas objected that the dharmas could have no "being of their own," because they were caused and conditioned and subject to decay. One could not say of them either that they existed or that they did not exist. In truth they were "empty" *(shūnya)*. It is exactly because they do not possess an essential nature of their own, and thus are impermanent, that they arrive in and vanish from the world of appearances in keeping with the law of "dependent origination." In this way they could be considered existent in the sense of conventional truth. In the sense of the highest truth, though, all the appearances in this world, including the Buddhas, their teaching, and their communities, are "empty." This implies, say the Mādhyamikas, that no definite statement can be made about them—not even about their nonexistence. That is why from the standpoint of the highest truth there is no difference between samsāra (the world of appearances) and nirvāna. Both of them have the same nature; they are "empty."

Some authors are inclined to view "emptiness" as a description of the Absolute, even as a sort of term for God. But such a judgment on the nature of the "void" is misleading, because it would oppose the "absolute" to the "relative." Liberation, however, consists in the overcoming of all opposites. On this issue I would like to quote a few sentences from the last article of the late Étienne Lamotte, probably the most eminent expert on this form of Buddhism. He is answering the question of how Shūnyavāda appears in the light of an unbiased interpretation of the texts:

> Some Western interpreters have tried to see a sort of negative absolute in Emptiness, but when the Mahāyānists say that beings and things are empty, they are not attributing any characteristic to them. They refuse to hypostatize an Emptiness which is nothing at all *(akiṃcid)*, "mere non-existence" *(abhāva-mātra)*. It is not that by virtue of Emptiness beings and things are empty: they are empty because they do not exist. The very notion of Emptiness is only of provisional value: it is a raft which is abandoned after crossing the river, a medicine which is thrown away after the cure. That is why the Mahāyānists are not nihilists: nihilists deny what they see but the Mahāyānists do not see anything and, consequently, neither affirm nor deny anything. (E. Lamotte, "Mahāyāna," in *The World of Buddhism*, p. 93)

The question of the Absolute, as it is continually being raised, even in this dialogue, is, in the view of Shūnyavāda, a false one. It is a useless question, which only ties us down to a misconception, distracts us from the way to liberation, and leads us astray.

On the other hand, the second great school of Mahāyāna, Yogācāra (also known as Vijñānavāda, "the doctrine of consciousness"), gives a different answer to the question of the Absolute, one that seems easier to grasp and more plausible to our ordinary way of thinking. This new approach finds expression in a work formally ascribed (in the broad sense) to Mādhyamika, the Ratnagotravibhāga (also known under the title of Mahāyāna-Uttaratantra). This text was composed by a philosopher named Sāramati around A.D. 250. The actual founders of the Yogācāra doctrine are Maitreyanātha (ca. A.D. 300) and Asanga (fourth century A.D.).

At the center of Sāramati's vision is the Supreme Being, "spotless," "luminous spirit." Some terms often used to characterize the Absolute are "thusness" *(tathatā)*, "element of dharma" *(dharmadhātu)*, "element of the buddhas" *(buddhadhātu)*. The word "emptiness" *(shūnyata)* is also used in this new sense. Whereas according to Sāramati the Highest Being even has specific qualities, classic Yogācāra doctrine says that it is "inexpressible" and "without multiplicity." All the same, it underlies the deceit of the world of appearances. The phenomenal world itself is now conceived as an idea of the Mind that inhabits all living creatures as an "element" *(dhātu)*. This idea is unreal, meaning there are no really existing things that correspond to it. Strictly speaking, there is no reality either within or without "consciousness." The contrast between (or the "twoness" of) subject and object is only something this idea deludes us into believing. The perfection that the meditating person finally reaches is the complete liberation of the mind, now free of all representations, the realization of the true Buddha nature.

In this way, the Yogācāra doctrine resulted in a new kind of "Buddhology," i.e., a new understanding of the true nature of the Buddhas. Their real nature is identical to the Absolute. They have, apart from their "changing body" *(nirmānakāya)*, i.e., the form of their earthly appearance, a heavenly mode, the "pleasure body" *(sambhogakāya)*, and finally the "doctrinal body" *(dharmakāya)*, which is their true essence, identical with the Highest Being.

Even while the Yogācāra school was flourishing in India, the Shūnyavāda and Yogācāra traditions began to fuse. In the process, the new buddhology and the new approach to the Absolute largely prevailed. I cannot address here the further details of their evolution or the later history of Buddhist philosophy in India, which reached its apex with the logical and epistemological school of Dignāga (ca. 480–540) and Dharmakīrti (seventh century).

The Yogācāra school was a crucial factor in shaping East Asian (and Tibetan) Buddhism. And thus even today it governs the Japanese interpretation, not only of the sources of Indian Mahāyāna, but, not surprisingly, the Japanese "theological" concept of the doctrines of original Buddhism, to which the old Yogācāra teachers had given an equivalent reading. In this way, even the Japanese notion of nirvāna was strongly influenced by the teachings of Yogācāra.

VAJRAYĀNA BUDDHISM

Sometime around the middle of the first Christian millennium, so-called Tantric Buddhism came into being. "Tantra" ("the warp of a fabric") is used as a label for certain systems of religious practices, mostly occult doctrines. Their adherents were initiated into the community by means of special rites. Tantrism probably first developed in Hinduism, and Buddhist Tantrism brought with it an affinity for Hindu ways of thinking. It characterized itself as Vajrayāna ("diamond vehicle") or Mantrayāna ("vehicle of the sacred formulas").

Ancient Buddhism taught that belief in the effectiveness of rituals and magic formulas was an obstacle for the person seeking liberation. Nonetheless such practices made their way, early on, into the exercise of popular religion. Older Mahāyāna texts already contain *dhāranīs*, spells to control good and evil forces. In Theravāda Buddhism, it became customary to recite sacred texts at the so-called Paritta ceremony in order to ward off evil. What had thitherto been a marginal phenomenon was changed by Tantrism into a central means of enlightenment. Ritual and sacred formulas were to open a shortcut to nirvāna.

In each tantra, one distinguishes four systems. The first stage, *kriyā* ("action"), consists in public ritual, in which everyone can take part. It is the outer aspect of the Tantric community of worship, its link with the uninitiated. The second stage is *caryā,* the "conduct" of the tantra student, and is reserved for initiates. The adept must have demonstrated his capacity for self-mastery; he is admitted to the first "consecration" *(abhisheka)* and, beyond that, to the other rituals, only after being carefully tested by his teacher. A deity or bodhisattva will be his personal protector.

At the center of Tantric symbolism, one always finds a mandala ("circle"). This is a device in which symbols for lofty insights, supernatural powers, and spiritual connections have been inscribed to serve as an object for ritual and meditation. Each tantra has certain mandalas assigned to it. They are either drawn on the ground or produced in a permanent form, e.g., as a picture or even a building. The Borobudur, in Java, the largest Buddhist temple in Southeast Asia, is considered to be a most powerful mandala. Numerous temple statues with mandalas have come to our museums from Nepal and Tibet.

Even at the stage of "conduct," the adept should never lose sight of the goal, which is to find the Buddha, who is at the same time the Absolute, in his own "enlightenment thinking" *(bodhicitta).* The next stage is yoga. Here the adept advances from ritual as an external form to meditation, which brings him closer to union with the Absolute. At the highest stage, the *anuttarayoga* ("unsurpassable yoga"), he comes to see the Buddha, with whom he achieves unity. The Buddha appears, surrounded by other supernatural beings, again in the form of a mandala. But this mandala is not drawn; it originates within the person meditating as an image of the highest reality. The ultimate, highest knowledge consists in the realization of "nonduality." All distinctions prove to be an illusion. The Absolute is symbolized by the *vajra* ("diamond")— originally, Indra's thunderbolt. It is often called *vajrasattva* ("diamond being"). Thus the tantra is the "vehicle to the *vajra" (vajrayāna).*

Shaktist Tantrism

There are two main forms of Vajrayāna, namely non-Shaktist and Shaktist tantra. Most forms of Tantrism belong to the first group. The second form, Shaktist Tantrism, is not accepted by the majority of Buddhists, but it has nevertheless received a great deal of publicity, so I shall say a few things here about this peculiar offshoot of Buddhism. The word and concept *shakti* ("force") have already been mentioned in the context of Hinduism. Divine forces were personified as female divinities, and the development of the Absolute into the world of appearances was explained as the result of the seeming self-division of the Highest Being through its own "force" *(shakti),* viewed as feminine. In the ritual of Shaktist Tantrists, the so-called five *ma-kāras* are used, that is, five things whose Sanskrit names began with the sound of "m": *mada* (alcoholic spirits), *matsya* (fish), *māmsa* (meat), *mudrā* (seeds of grain), and *maithuna* (sexual intercourse). The goal of the Tantrist is to liberate the animal manifestations of life from the domain of human passions in the knowledge of the ultimate unity of the world, and to make these manifestations the basis of religious experience and lofty insights.

Since the goal of Tantric yoga is the attainment of perfect happiness (*mahāsukha*), in which the "self" and the world coincide in the unity of the Absolute, the boundless sensation of the bliss of self-realization must take the place here of our sensuous feeling of happiness through a process of "mystical realization" (*sādhanā*). This transformation occurs through the correct linkage of cult and yoga. Now, sexual experience offers one of the most intense feelings of happiness in our normal life. Sexuality and the supreme bliss of nirvāna are, for earlier Buddhism, opposite poles of reality, so that the monk is forbidden to engage in sex. In Shaktist Tantrism, all that is radically altered. Here methods have been developed so as to use sex for the realization of *mahāsukha*. The unity of the opposite means the coinciding of all contraries, which is, in the spiritual sense, the unity of *prajñā* ("awareness") and *upāya* ("means of liberation"), symbolized through the union of the female and the male. This is the key to the sexual symbolism of the Shaktist tantras, as found in the texts and in Tantric art.

Tantric yoga theory grows out of some peculiar ideas about the movement of the vital forces in the body and about the nervous system, which has nothing to do with modern medical science. The Tantrists speak of three, four, or five *chakras* ("wheels") in the human body, which are considered centers of the life system. They are the seat of specific psychic forces, and by unifying the macrocosm and the microcosm they become the locus of certain deities and principles, as well as the object of identification with religious values. The main arteries of the nervous system are connected to the key concepts of the teaching on liberation: The left-side nerve cord (*lalanā*) has the nature of *prajñā* ("awareness") and the feminine principle, the right-side nerve cord (*rasanā*) has the nature of *upāya* ("means of salvation") and the masculine principle. In the middle, leading through the *chakra* situated in the heart, lies the *avadhūti*, through which flows *bodhicitta*, "thinking about enlightenment." Through the union of the left and right nerve cords with the central one, the great happiness of *prajñopāya*, the union of *prajñā* and *upāya*, comes to fruition.

Consequently the term yoga refers to something different in the Tantric systems from what we are familiar with from the classic yoga exercises. Tantric yoga is also basically different from the meditation and concentration of early Buddhism, even though these same words may be used. While the early Buddhist exercises of *samādhi* ("absorption") and *vipashyanā* ("clear view") are wholly oriented toward spiritual concentration and surveillance of one's physical and mental functions, Tantric yoga is directed toward one's own body. While, in early Buddhism, reflection on the transiency of everything physical occupies the foreground of meditations focused on the body, in Tantrism the body is seen as the abode of all higher knowledge. The Tantrists look upon the feeling of happiness and the essence of the Absolute as belonging together. When we realize perfect happiness, we reach the Absolute, nirvāna. This is not, of course, something produced by mental activities, since it consists in the overcoming of all our thought processes. Nirvāna can be realized therefore only in a state of total freedom from thoughts and sensations. Even the sensation of freedom must itself be overcome.

The texts of Shaktist yoga disclose under what special conditions and in what form enlightenment-thinking can be brought about, through the union of the yogi and the yogini, who is also called his prajñā, as well as how to realize the unity of the self and the world of appearances. Later commentators, along with the Tibetan tradition of "exegesis," tend to a metaphorical explanation of these texts. They would say that this union takes place only in the yogi's sphere of meditation. But the practices described in the texts were in fact performed during the heyday of Tantric Buddhism in India.

The authors of the oldest forms of Shaktist tantra were religious loners, who deliberately broke out of the well-ordered traditions of monastic life and went about the country as wandering monks. Equipped with magical powers, known to be experts in secret spells and mystical practices, they provoked scandal, sensational interest, and admiration. Apparently scorning all traditions, they antagonized people by deliberately flouting convention. They often came from the disadvantaged classes, and yet the social establishment was ready to show them respect, compounded of fear and curiosity. Later, however, the scholars took up the traditions of Tantrism. Its teachings, which had previously been passed on in no particular shape or form, were written down in an extensive literary corpus, systematized, and finally served up with supplementary astrological lore.

The last of the great systems of late Indian Buddhism, Kālacakra ("time wheel"), which arose around A.D. 1000 in Bengal and was deeply influenced by astrology, held the doctrine of the Ādi-Buddha ("primal Buddha"), from whom all other buddhas, bodhisattvas, gods, et al., and finally the whole world, came forth. In this way, Tantric Buddhism developed its concept of the Absolute until it ultimately arrived at a notion of faith quite close to the Christian and Islamic concept of God.

The following abbreviated version of the tradition concerning the career of the Tantrist Tsi-lu-pa or Mahākālacakrapāda (from H. Hoffmann, *The Religions of Tibet,* pp. 122–23) may exemplify the development of a Tantric system: One day, a yogi in the blue robe, who had a third eye on his forehead, came to a yogini selling brandy in Bengal. He had a *vajra* (thunderbolt) of acacia wood in his hand. This yogi bought some brandy and spent the night with the yogini. In the morning he had disappeared, but the *vajra* was still there. When the yogini picked up this *vajra,* it emitted a blue light that entered her arm. The yogi was the Bodhisattva Vajrapāni. A year later, as a result of this mystic union, the yogini gave birth to a son. When he was seven years old, a monk, who was identified as the Bodhisattva Avalokiteshvara, accepted him as a novice and taught him the tantras. He carried him through the air to the land of Shambhala, where he listened to the sermon of the master Kulika. The monk bade the novice, who now bore the monastic name Tsi-lu-pa, go and spread the contents of this sermon, the Kālacakra, in Bengal. Tsi-lu-pa later went to southern India and wrote down the teaching of the Kālacakra, which had thitherto been passed on only by word of mouth. Finally, he made his way to the monastic university of Nālandā, where he vanquished the abbot of the monastery, Nādapāda, in a disputation and converted him to Kālacakra. Nādapāda, whom the Tibetans call Naropa, became the most eminent interpreter of Kālacakra in his time.

Thus the way of Kālacakra began with a wandering nun, who, contrary to all the conventions, sold spirits, and who, by scorning the traditional forms of ascetical life, illustrates the insight that all contraries—including good and evil—are identical. At the end of this path, however, lies scholarly work in the famous Nālandā, the incorporation of the tantra into established tradition, in which it is no longer permitted to violate the conventions—and the metaphorical interpretation of the text is complete.

THE DOWNFALL OF INDIAN BUDDHISM

While Buddhism in southern India had been displaced much earlier by the renaissance of Hinduism, as late as A.D. 1000, there were still many Buddhist monasteries and temples in northern India. But they fell victim to the destruction unleashed by the Islamic conquerors, who in the eleventh and twelfth centuries overran the northern Indian plains. Muslim historians proudly report how thoroughly the sanctuaries of the "heathen" religions were wiped out. The Buddhist culture of India, which unlike Hinduism was bound up with the tradition of the monasteries and the academies, sank without a trace beneath the waves of this onslaught. The last of the great monastic institutes, Vikramashīla, was destroyed in 1207. Even the foundation stone was dug out and pushed into the Ganges. The site of Vikramashīla has vanished forever.

Only in the high plain of the Nepal Valley, surrounded by mountains, beyond the reach of the conquerors, was it possible for remnants of Buddhism to survive on the Indian subcontinent to this day. The Vajrayāna Buddhism cultivated there was, however, saturated with elements of Hinduism. Under the rule of Hindu kings, the Buddhist monastic system was suppressed, so that in the traditional Buddhist sanctuaries of Nepal one finds only a lay community.

In other parts of the subcontinent, groups of Buddhists that had survived the Muslim conquest increasingly conformed to Hinduism. Thus the personification of Buddhist teaching, Dharma, became a folk god in Bengal. Sahajavāda, which had grown out of Buddhist Tantrism, was transformed over the centuries into a form of Vishnuism. Although Buddhism had died out in most regions of India as an independent religion by the fourteenth century, it nonetheless influenced the evolution of Hinduism in many ways.

THE DISSEMINATION OF BUDDHISM IN ASIA

Within the space available to me here, I can give only a very rough sketch of the further history of Buddhism. In its first wave of expansion, the religion of Buddha got as far as modern-day Afghanistan, as well as West Turkestan (Soviet Central Asia) and East Turkestan (Sinkiang). Numerous monuments of art and ruins still bear witness to this epoch, which ended with the Islamic conquest of these countries.

Tibet, on the other hand, was permanently won over to the Buddhist religion. It was first introduced under King Srong-tsen-gam-po (620–49). Soon thereafter, a great number of Buddhist texts were translated into Tibetan. Translation committees unified Buddhist terminology. It is true that under King Lang-dar-ma (836–42) Buddhism was suppressed and the native Bon religion brought back, but Buddhism in Tibet had a renewal in the eleventh century, again under strong Indian influence. The ancient Buddhist texts taken over from the Mahāyāna and Vajrayāna traditions in India were grouped together in the Kanjur, a collection of sacred scriptures totaling 108 volumes. Added to this was the Tanjur, with its 225 volumes (commentaries, doctrinal texts, etc.). Over the centuries, the Bon religion, at first the rival of Buddhism, became so thoroughly assimilated that it may now be labeled a Buddhist sect. By way of Tibet, Buddhism came to the Mongols, who were finally converted around 1575, and to other central and northern Asian peoples.

Tibetan Buddhism has preserved for us the doctrinal traditions from every epoch of Indian Buddhism, including Vajrayāna; but it has carried on their development in a peculiar fashion. For centuries, Tibet was isolated from the outside world. Now its religion has become better known to us, ever since many Tibetans were forced to leave their home-land as a consequence of the invasion and oppression by the Chinese.

Southeast Asia felt several waves of cultural influence from India. With this impetus, both great Indian religions expanded their range. In several countries of Indochina, as we have seen, Theravāda Buddhism prevailed. In the Indonesian archipelago, at first Vajrayāna Buddhism and Hinduism existed side by side, but eventually joined together to form a new, syncretistic religion, known as "Shiva-Buddhism." This was almost entirely supplanted by Islam, although it still survives on the little island of Bali. On Java, Buddhist modes of thought had a pronounced effect on Islamic mysticism.

EAST ASIAN BUDDHISM

The Buddhist religion arrived in China as early as the first century. The year A.D. 67 is traditionally considered the beginning of Buddhist history in the "Middle Kingdom." There, too, many texts from all three "vehicles" (Hīnayāna, Mahāyāna, and Vajrayāna) were translated from the original sources in Indian languages. In addition, a large number of works from Chinese sources were included in the Chinese collections of Buddhist scriptures. These great collections do not make up a "canon" in the usual sense, but, rather, an encyclopedia of all available older Buddhist literature. In the course of the history of Chinese Buddhism, two main schools took shape, namely meditation Buddhism and "Pure Land" Buddhism. The first is known as Ch'an (Zen in Japanese), and was brought to China, it is said, by the Indian monk Bodhidharma around the year 470. His philosophy is based essentially on Yogācāra and Shūnyavāda traditions. "Pure Land" Buddhism rests on the belief that Amitābha, the Buddha of "immeasurable light," will lead to liberation all those who trust in him. With this turnabout, the doctrine of "self-salvation" announced by the Buddha was transformed into its opposite, a doctrine of "outside salvation," in which the individual looks for liberation through the help of a supernatural being. This form of Buddhism has also been called a "Buddhism of faith," and its Japanese variants in particular have been compared to Protestant Christianity. Amida Buddhism has won a broad following through all of East Asia, primarily as a folk religion.

The Buddhism of Japan, like that of Korea and Vietnam, originated in China and has undergone further development in a great variety of forms. Some movements are based on the traditions of non-Shaktist Tantrism. The important forms of Japanese Buddhism, however, are Zen and Amidism.

Zen is the Japanese form of the Chinese Ch'an, or meditation Buddhism. The term *ch'an* is derived from the Sanskrit word *dhyāna*, "meditative absorption." In most kinds of Zen, which has deeply influenced Japanese painting and poetry, one postulates the possibility of a lightning-like illumination, which may come after many years of preparation. The Zen master makes use of a *koan,* which he gives his disciple as a task to work on and a basis for meditation. It is generally a riddle or other statement appropriate for this purpose. Let me quote one such koan and sketch out its prehistory, which we now know thanks to a recently published study by Professor Toshio Kazama:

> The follower of another teaching once asked the Buddha: "One asks neither for instruction through words nor for instruction without words." The Buddha sat there in silence. Full of amazement, the follower of another teaching said: "The great kindness and the great compassion of the exalted one have broken through the clouds of my errors and brought me into the way to liberation." He bowed and left.
>
> Then Ānanda asked the Buddha: "What enlightenment did the follower of another teaching obtain, that he praised you so and then went away?"
>
> The Buddha answered: "It is that way whenever a good horse sees even the shadow of a whip: he runs." (translation after H. Dumoulin)

The philosophically important part of the koan is the beginning: "One asks neither for instruction through words nor for instruction without words." This passage can be traced back to a text that belongs to the canon of early Buddhism. In the oldest version of this doctrinal text, a non-Buddhist pilgrim named Dīghanakha, who is also called Aggivessana, visits the Buddha. He is an absolute skeptic, who will not admit any doctrinal statements, including the Buddha's. The Buddha explains to him that in principle he is right. One may not cling to anything if one wishes to attain liberation, not even to a teaching, because liberation consists precisely in the freedom from all attachments. The Buddha then explains the frailty of the bodily form and the feelings. The pilgrim Aggivessana now arrives immediately at the final liberation—very much in the sense of Zen *satori.*

Our koan reflects the first part of the dialogue, in which Aggivessana voices his skepticism and the Buddha answers him. The dialogue goes as follows:

> Aggivessana: "Lord Gautama, I speak in the following manner, this is my opinion: 'I do not accept any opinions.'"
>
> The Buddha: "What about this opinion, Aggivessana: 'I do not accept any opinions'? Don't you accept that one either?"
>
> Aggivessana: "Lord Buddha, if I were to accept that opinion, that would be, on the one hand, something like the nonacceptance of all opinions and, on the other hand, something like the acceptance of the opinion that I accept no opinions."
>
> The Buddha: "That is why, Aggivessana, there are more than many people in the world who speak as follows: 'That would be, on the one hand, some-

thing like the nonacceptance of all opinions and, on the other hand, some-thing like the acceptance of the opinion that I accept no opinions.' On the one hand, they do not give up this opinion and, on the other, they accept a different opinion. That is why, Aggivessana, there are fewer than a few people in the world who speak in this way: 'That would be, on the one hand, something like the nonacceptance of all opinions and, on the other, some-thing like the acceptance of the opinion that I accept no opinions.' On the one hand, they give up this opinion and, on the other, they do not accept a different one." (translation after Toshio Kazama)

Thus Aggivessana does not back off from his skepticism. But he shows that he has spotted the contradiction in his statement. He is unwilling to give his proposition the universal scope it deserves. The Buddha then explains that Aggivessana's words can be understood differently. Most listeners fall into an unsolvable paradox. Only a few are capable of going beyond the intellectual contradiction and deducing from the meditation an immediate mystical insight that wholly defies linguistic formulation. That is the reason why the text is used as a koan.

Aggivessana goes away. This doesn't mean that he has become a Buddhist. And why should he? That is not the point. Only one thing matters: Aggivessana has succeeded in making a breakthrough to see the truth. He is on the way to escape from the world of contradictions once and for all.

While Zen Buddhism, as this example shows, has preserved and con-tinually renewed essential elements of the spirit of the old teaching and of the traditional meditative practices, Amidism is a "Buddhism of faith." It takes the ideas of the Buddha and, in a way, twists them into their opposite. The most radical spokesman for this approach is Shinran-Shōnin (1173–1262), the founder of Jōdo Shinshū, which main-tains that we attain salvation purely and simply through the grace of Amitābha. This doctrine, incidentally, is based on a passage in the Sukhāvatīvyūha (a Mahāyāna work from roughly second-century India) that textual scholarship has proved to be a later interpolation. And so we have the emergence in medieval Japanese Buddhism of a form of reli-gion with an obvious similarity, as I have said, to Protestantism.

With the school of Nichiren (1222–82), which is based on a highly arbitrary interpretation of the Lotus Sūtra (*Saddharmapundarīkasūtra*, a scripture of early Indian Mahāyāna), Japan produced an aggressively political Buddhist movement that, especially in its initial period, stood in harsh contrast to the other forms of Japanese Buddhism, most of which are inclined toward peaceful coexistence.

2. *Hans Küng:* A Christian Response

The Buddha Gautama and the Christ Jesus, being a Buddhist and being a Christian—these two comparisons have stood in the foreground of my previous responses. I have noted divergences and convergences, but in the meantime I have deliberately bracketed one question, the difficult but unavoidable question of an "ultimate reality," an "Absolute," "God." With the further development of Buddhism from Theravāda to Pure Land, with the very diverse forms of Buddhist thought and life, and with regard to Buddhist-Christian dialogue, this question must now become the focus of my reflections. There is no gainsaying the fact that the backgrounds and substrates of both religions are utterly different: On the one side, Christianity, with its belief in God; on the other, Buddhism with its decisive rejection of a personal God. Will a theistic and an a–theistic religion ever really be able to understand or even communicate with one another? This question has a special significance in the light of the shift from Theravāda to Mahāyāna Buddhism, that further "turning of the wheel of doctrine."

THE PARADIGM CHANGE FROM THE LESSER TO THE GREAT VEHICLE

Mahāyāna Buddhism was the product neither of a sudden *creatio ex nihilo* nor of an innocuous continual evolution. Neither a "big bang theory" nor an organic theory of development would do justice to the historical reality of Mahāyāna. It took a slow, far-flung, many-layered process of transformation, first unsystematic, then systematic and philosophical, which, for all its continuity, displays a crucial discontinuity. In a word—without necessitating an overly schematic picture of the historical process—what we have here is a *paradigm change,* implying progress, but not just progress: Much is won, but many good and true features of the earlier paradigm are lost, forgotten, repressed. To that extent the genuinely dialectical theory of the history of paradigm changes—situated between historical-philosophical melancholy and triumphalism—implies an *Aufheben,* or sublation (in the threefold Hegelian sense) both of all theories of progress (continual ascent to greater truth) and of all similarly monochromatic theories of decadence (increasingly sharp decline from the Golden Age of the origins).

This *paradigm change* also presupposes the *crisis endured by the earlier paradigm* of Hīnayāna, or the lesser vehicle, as tersely described by Edward Conze:

> [Mahāyāna] was prepared by the exhaustion of the old impulse which produced fewer and fewer Arhats, by the tensions within the doctrines as they had developed by then, and by the demands of the laity for more equal rights with the monks. Foreign influences also had a great deal to do with it. *[A Short History of Buddhism,* 1982, p. 44]

In this way, the *fundamental built-in tension between monastic and lay existence,* which was already immanent in early Buddhism and which became visible across a broad front in Theravāda, and although relieved by dāna piety, finally made itself felt in Mahāyāna. As Heinz Bechert said, "Salvation is no longer limited to a few ascetics, but to the mass of human beings." To that extent, the term "great vehicle" (carrying the believer across the wide river of suffering to the other shore, or salvation) is justified, although the earlier paradigm should not be given the disparaging name "lesser [faulty] vehicle," but "Shrāvakayāna" ("vehicle of the hearers"), whose most important branch is Theravāda.

The shifts that occur here are considerable: We have the same fundamental data of Buddhism fitted now into a different frame of reference, the same constants realized now in a *new constellation of variables:*

- Instead of the way to definitive salvation being limited to a few monks, it is now to be opened up to many men and women. Instead of the monastic ideal of the arhat, the saint turned away from the world, we now have the ideal of the humanitarian saint, the bodhisattva: a religion for monks is increasingly becoming a religion for lay people.

- Instead of seeing the essence of all existence in its instability, sorrowfulness, and insubstantiality, all that is to be understood now in a radical sense as emptiness: lack of essence as the true essence of the universe or—to take a more positive, Taoist view—as the cosmic Buddha-nature, common to nature and man.

● Instead of salvation through renunciation and turning away from the
  world, we have the possibility of enlightenment, liberation, and wisdom in the middle of this life: nirvāna in samsāra.

The dissemination of Mahāyāna in India, China, Tibet, Korea, and
Japan was helped by the fact that people there were far less interested in
sticking to the letter of canonical texts and were capable of interpreting
flexibly and adapting both the monastic rule and the doctrinal discourses. In this way the spirit of the Buddha was preserved, even revitalized in a new manner. But the codified wisdom for an elite now became a
devotional movement for the masses, with the assimilation, in many
cases, of Hindu, Taoist, or Shintoist ideas and cultic practices featuring
a great many buddhas and bodhisattvas as dispensers of grace. Buddhism was turning into something like a universal church.

Even though Shrāvakayāna and Mahāyāna monks, united, at least in
the beginning, by the same rule, often lived peacefully together in the
same monasteries, in the long run such a *revolutionary change* could not be
ignored:

> It has never been fully realised what a radical revolution had transformed
> the Buddhist church when the new spirit which however was for a long time
> lurking in it arrived at a full eclosion in the first centuries A.D. When we see an
> atheistic, soul-denying philosophic teaching of a path to personal Final Deliv-
> erance, consisting in an absolute extinction of life, and a simple worship of
> the memory of its human founder—when we see it superseded by a magnifi-
> cent High Church with a Supreme God, surrounded by a numerous pantheon
> and a host of Saints, a religion highly devotional, highly ceremonious and
> clerical, with an ideal of Universal Salvation of all living creatures, a Salvation
> by the divine grace of Buddhas and Bodhisattvas, a Salvation not in annihila-
> tion, but in eternal life, —we are fully justified in maintaining that the history
> of religions has scarcely witnessed such a break between new and old within
> the pale of what nevertheless continues to claim common descent from the
> same religious founder. [T. Stcherbatsky, *The Conception of Buddhist Nirvana*,
> 1927, p. 36]

Thus even for the Mahāyānists there was only one method of reaching
salvation: the great vehicle, for which the lesser vehicle and the *pratyeka-
buddhists* (who have found the truth themselves, but did not preach it)
have only a preparatory value. Despite all the critical differences between the two sides, it proved possible in a number of ways to compare
the changeover from the early Buddhist to the Theravāda paradigm with
the transition from the early-Christian to the Hellenistic/Byzantine paradigm. Similarly, and again despite indisputable essential differences,
we can now compare in various ways the change from Shrāvakayāna
("orthodoxy") to Mahāyāna with the change from the Byzantine/Helle-
nistic to the medieval Catholic paradigm.

> . . . a magnificent High Church with a Supreme God, surrounded by a numerous pantheon and a host of Saints, a religion highly devotional, highly ceremonious and clerical . . .

Parallels to the practice of medieval Christianity readily suggest themselves. And anyone who compares medieval Roman Catholic Christendom with early Christianity will presumably be unable to agree with Stcherbatsky when he says,

> . . . the history of religions has scarcely witnessed such a break between new and old within the pale of what nevertheless continues to claim common descent from the same religious founder.

We cannot overlook the fact that an analogous upheaval took place in the history of Christianity.

It is nonetheless true that Mahāyāna remained, quite obviously, Buddhist. The sun and stars were still in the sky; only their constellation had radically changed. The old message of the Buddha, the basic ideas, attitudes, and practices that had been seen as important from the very start, were still the major focus. For all the new variables, *the old constants of Buddhist teaching, practice, and institutions remained in place.*

- There were still the same pre-Buddhist Indian concepts such as reincarnation, karma, and methods of meditation, as well as many originally Brahmanic religious practices.
- There was still the "refuge in the Buddha," the great, predominant teacher and pioneer of redemption, to whom were ascribed (though in mythological fiction) even the doctrinal texts composed from the first to the fifth centuries A.D., in a way that remained characteristic of later Buddhism.
- There was still the "refuge in the dharma," in the teaching of the "Four Noble Truths," concerning suffering and the overcoming of suffering, the fleetingness and insubstantialness of the world and the self, and the extermination of ignorance, greed, and hatred through enlightenment and wisdom—a teaching, however, that had to be not simply repeated, but reformulated in the face of new needs and capacities of people, that was "imperfect" and had to be brought to the "perfection of knowledge."
- There was still the "refuge in the sangha," in the community of monks, whose traditional Rule, however, could also be lived in a variety of different teachings with a much greater freedom in matters of form, thus leveling the distinction between monks and lay people.

The Buddhist Concept of Reality

It was reserved to Mahāyāna to work out a comprehensive Buddhist understanding of reality, based on such ancient concepts as "dependent origination" (Sanskrit: Pratityasamutpāda) and the nonexistence of the self. The individual "void" appears here (under Taoist influence) as sublated into the unity and totality of a "fullness" encompassing man and nature. This is called the cosmic (transpersonal) Buddha nature, or dharmakāya (like the Tao). But, rather than simply transcending the human, it brings to fulfillment the depths within humanity. Before we turn to the question of the Absolute, we must first, for the purposes of dialogue, settle the question of Buddhist and Christian concepts of reality in general and man in particular.

In the process I can assume the reader is familiar with Heinz Bechert's treatment of the problem of "origin in dependence" and turn immediately to the question, so important for this dialogue, of whether the teaching of "conditioned origination" need be unchristian.

The only *reality* proper to man and the world is *conditioned in every way:* This general formula is one that Christian theology, too, could accept as a basic conviction. Christian theology likewise affirms—following the lead of the Bible and Greek philosophy—that everything in this world is conditioned, relative, coming into existence and passing away, nothing existing eternally in itself. Things are not unreal, of course, but they exist only relatively, in reciprocal dependency, however this may be ultimately explained. Non-necessity, contingency, inconstancy, transiency all mark the world as it appears to us, the world of "appearances," or "phenomena."

Hence, Christian theology is familiar with the idea that all the physical and mental phenomena which make up individual existence are conditioned, an idea that has also been confirmed by modern science (the law of causality). Twentieth-century physics especially, but psychology, too, have shown that man can be adequately understood only as the *creature of a fleeting instant,* both on the level of subatomic elementary particles and on the level of complex brain processes. Indeed, the unimaginable orders of magnitude with which these sciences deal (ca. 13 billion years since the beginning of the world, ca. 10 billion nerve cells in the human brain) seem to corroborate the stupendous mythical numbers of Buddhistic scriptures, rather than the Bible's very brief chronology. So we can easily understand the skeptic's question: Is there really any *"matter"* at all? That is, is there something we must conceive as the hidden reality behind the appearances of this world, as a substrate or thing in itself? Or are there really only indescribable subatomic structures and processes? Is there really an *"I,"* that ongoing, lasting subject of all perceptions, imaginations, thoughts, feelings, and actions? Or is there only a sum or nexus of perceptions and ideas (the ego as the longest of all memory chains)?

Theology must keep going back to Immanuel Kant. It was he who disclosed in his critique of knowledge that our theoretical reason knows only this world of "appearances," or "phenomena," not the world as it is in itself. The "world," the "self," and even "God" are ideas that guide and govern our knowledge, but their reality is a matter of faith—or, to use less misleading language, of reasonable trust. *The world as it "appears" to us*—depending upon the standpoint of the observer: Modern atomic physics, which despite all its enormous progress does not claim to know the innermost essence of matter, has confirmed this philosophical insight of Kant. And so has experimental psychology, which, despite all the data it has amassed on mental processes in man, does not pretend it can know the innermost essence of the person. The cosmos, the atom, and human beings remain in their inmost core *terra incognita.* We have no recourse but to grope our way toward reality with interpretive concepts, with symbols, formulas, and models, always with the proviso that these things have by no means taken us to the bottom of phenomena. This is true for the natural and the social sciences, but also for philosophy and theology—and for Buddhism and Christianity.

For that reason, the recent studies by the American physicist Fritjof Capra are of invaluable assistance, even though they take an all too exclusive interest in the convergence between Western physics and Eastern wisdom (Hinduism, Buddhism, Taoism). In his pathbreaking books (*The Tao of Physics,* 1975, and *The Turning Point,* 1982) Capra follows the lead of Max Planck, Albert Einstein, and Werner Heisenberg as he argues impressively for the *complementarity* of analysis and synthesis, rational knowledge and intuitive wisdom, research and morality, *science and religion*—and thus for a *postmodern paradigm.* But the *complementarity* he talks about is an attainable goal also, from a Western Christian standpoint, as physical biochemist and theologian A. R. Peacocke, among others, has shown (*Creation and the World of Science,* 1979), on the basis of the latest scientific data. But one is not necessarily easier to work with than the other. For, in order to demonstrate the convergence from the point of view of Eastern wisdom, Capra has to abstract from the whole bizarre, mythic cosmology of the East (so unlike the historically oriented Judeo-Christian tradition). He has to concentrate, in a vague, eclectic manner, on certain selected philosophical aspects of Eastern mystical thought without always paying sufficient heed to their complexity and even contradictoriness.

There is no ignoring the fact, however, that Capra does point up some amazing parallels: Unlike the static, substance-oriented thinking of Greek philosophy in the Middle Ages and Cartesian philosophy in the modern period, *Eastern thought* intrinsically has a very sharp sense for *the fundamental unity and inner dynamism of nature both in the macrocosm and the microcosm,* for the universal interdependence and interaction of all things, events, phenomena, as present-day physics is discovering in the subatomic realm. Elementary-particle physics especially (which has become increasingly important for molecular biology as well) no longer understands reality as a collection of physical objects made essentially of the same "stuff," but as an infinite, indivisible, complex network of relations, a highly dynamic system that already in the subatomic domain encompasses every possible kind of difference, contrast, and opposition in a complementary unity, that cannot be known through objective observation but only through objective/subjective participation. It is described with concepts that are not copies of reality, but creations of our mind, part of the map of the country, not the country itself. Does that not make "mystical" Eastern thought and especially the teaching of the dharmas, or "facts," seem brilliantly rational? Doesn't it point up an obvious affinity to modern science's concept of nature? Isn't it truly capable of taking the unity of humanity with the cosmos seriously, without metaphysical presuppositions, without religious assumptions that lie beyond the scrutiny of reason?

By the same token, *Christianity* is by no means tied down in advance to any specific physical or philosophical explanation of the world. As we know, medieval Scholasticism, following Plato and Aristotle, developed an extremely complex doctrine of potency and act, matter and form, to explain this fleeting, contingent world of change. But Buddhist scholasticism elaborated a no less complicated speculative view, taught by the Buddha, of the twelve-part chain of conditioned dependent origination. From the standpoint of present-day science, both explanations are outdated, but in any case they need not be an obstacle to understanding between the two religions. For, however one wishes to explain the origin and structures of the world, physically, psychologically, philosophically, or all three together, such explanatory models will not ultimately divide Christians and Buddhists unless they are presented as universal truth. For one thing, this sort of speculation meant little to the Masters themselves, the Buddha and the Christ, both of whom approached the world not in a theoretical/philosophical, but in an existential/practical, fashion. And so, just as one can be a Christian in the context of an Indian / East Asian philosophy, so one can presumably be a Buddhist even in the context of European-American philosophy.

Nevertheless, even allowing every possible convergence and complementarity between Buddhism and philosophical/scientific theories of reality, the Buddhist concept of reality has consequences for the understanding of the human *person* that will pose serious problems for Christian thinkers.

For, as we have already seen in the context of Hinduism, Western

Christian thought can perhaps, by taking a different approach to history, develop a deeper understanding of the uniqueness of the human person within the universe. Can we—and I ask this as a Christian theologian— take human dignity seriously if we deny man a self?

THE DIGNITY OF THE HUMAN PERSON

In the context of the doctrine of the mutual dependency of all things (phenomena), Buddhists disagree how the complementary doctrine of selflessness, the no-self *(anātman)*, is to be understood. Even if this was part of the historical Buddha's teaching, here, at least, it was not yet a metaphysical doctrine (which the Buddha rejected in principle), but an ethical/practical invitation to an experience—a call to turn away in *"selflessness"* from "self-centeredness" in this sorrowful, transitory world of appearances, to free oneself from the egocentricity of the empirical self, which does not last and is at bottom "empty" and "futile," and to attain salvation by means of insight into the nothingness of all things (passing through the "great death," as it was later called).

From this ethical perspective, it is evident such ideas are by no means alien to Christianity. Is not Christianity's original concern with the conversion *(metánoia)* of the *whole* person (minus the Greek body-soul dualism) from the egocentricity of his ego (however understood) to true selfhood? Is not the point to undergo a radical change of consciousness ("heart") and press forward to a new existence? Must not the phenomenal, empirical ego die—in a Christian sense—in order to come to the real life of the true self? ". . . whoever loses his life will preserve it" (Lk 17:33)—a key principle, which some Buddhists like to quote in dialogue with Christians.

Christian thinkers, who have long understood "person" in an individualistic sense as a self-contained *individuum*, are trying nowadays to work out a deeper, *relational understanding of the person*, that is, an understanding of the human person as a being that relates. They are reacting to that fatal Western individualism that by invoking the self and self-fulfillment (of the individual, the nation, or the Church) has had a highly destructive impact on communal life, on Western economies, politics, and culture, even on philosophy and theology. In his excellent report "Horizons of Christianity's New Dialogue with Buddhism" (in *Horizons* 8/1, 1981, 49), Paul F. Knitter cites leading Christian proponents of this dialogue (e.g., R. H. Drummond, C. Dunne, W. Johnston, P. Kreeft, T. Merton, L. A. de Silva, and D. K. Swearer) and calls attention to a surprising agreement—after all the misunderstandings—by Christians with the Buddhist doctrine of nonself:

They recognize that Buddhism provides Christians with an opportunity to know and experience that the true reality of the person does not consist in being and *individuum*, a given entity; rather, the true self is radically, essentially, constantly in relation to other selves and to all reality; its "being" is constantly one of ongoing "dependent co-origination"; its being is relating. Therefore, the true self is a selfless self, constantly losing-finding its self in its relations with others.

The task at hand, then, is to break out of ego consciousness and to experience a nonegoistic, Buddhist awareness of unity, which is expressed in the universal "Buddha nature" of Mahāyāna, but which can also be understood in a new way through biblical symbols and statements ("to be in Christ," "I live, not I, but Christ lives in me," "to be united with God"). Whether Christian theologians, so as to come to an understanding (a dubious one, in this case) with Buddhism, should get involved with risky formulations of Christian mystics (such as "the soul *is* God" or "God is my true identity") is, of course, another question. In any event, I think we must pose frankly *critical counterquestions* about the Buddhist position, so that not only the Christian concept of man will be altered in the light of Buddhism, but the Buddhist concept of man will also be altered in the light of Christianity.

In a process of "reciprocal transformation" (John Cobb), Christians will have to keep showing why they are not simply prepared to dismiss the familiar experiential reality of man's psychosomatic unity and of the individual self as a mere "conventional truth," indeed as a mere illusion, and thus to grant it no more than a borrowed, illusory existence. The ego is certainly not something solid, palpable, static, or substantial. But does that mean that it is not real?

Luis O. Gómez remarks from a Buddhist perspective:

> A self that does not change, a self that can have what it wants and has what it can keep, a self that actually possesses things, thoughts, and feelings, such a self patently does not exist according to Buddhism. On the other hand, a self that is in constant flux, that is a composite of factors (mental, physical, emotional), a conglomerate of factors that is amenable to moral direction and transformation—both good and bad—that self does exist. But, when properly understood, this self is so different from our conception of the "self," that it is more accurate to speak of "no-self." Because normally—that is, in the context of our expectations and behavioral pattern—the word "self" implies an unchanging core "inside" the person . . . ["Original Buddhism: A Pedagogical Model," in *Udumbara* 1.4, 1982, 42]

But, I wonder, is such talk about the no-self not needlessly radical? In my response to Heinz Bechert's first presentation, I referred to the fact that there are experiences in classic Theravāda meditation, following the *satipatthāna* method, that can be interpreted differently—and less negatively. And Winston King, who has been dialoguing with Theravāda

Buddhists for decades, observed in a paper on "Paradigm Change in Buddhism and Christianity" (delivered at the East-West Encounter Conference, held at the University of Hawaii in January 1984): "There is in fact an unacknowledged but functionally real 'implicit self,' of decidedly significant proportions right in the center of the Theravāda not-self, which gives this doctrine its redeeming and enlightening meaning . . . Whether this is called a 'self' or not is essentially unimportant. Theravāda Buddhists would certainly not call it that. But an ability to look upon the ordinary self as a no-self, as a mere series of events, *sub specie aeternitatis* or should we say here *sub specie nibbanis,* is absolutely necessary and in fact functionally recognized even in Theravāda. And a very important fact here is that this ability to raise oneself above the flux of one's own specific selfhood and to contemplate it as such is the essence of all enlightenment." In view of such a "combination of the uncombinable" ("the doctrine of the 'not-self' and the almost instinctive belief in a self"), some reflections suggest themselves that might be the occasion for Buddhists to raise self-critical questions:

1. Japanese scholars like Yoshinori Takeuchi have pointed out *(The Heart of Buddhism,* 1983) that the individual ego was not thought to be entirely reducible to psychosomatic facts or elements of existence (dharmas) until a later phase of Buddhist doctrinal development, at which point Buddhists no longer wished to speak of a "subject" at all.

2. Still, from the Pudgalavādins in the third century B.C. till today, there have always been Buddhist interpretations that resisted the extreme formulations of the not-self dogma and tried to satisfy "sound common sense." Along with the impersonal dharmas, such Buddhist interpreters have accepted something like personality and have been able to prove conclusively from the sacred texts that there is a basis for the different processes that occur in a self-identical person.

3. The ancient Indian teaching on reincarnation and karma—this has always been a thorn in the side of Buddhism—seems to require a continuous subject. How can identity be preserved without an ego? Can karma —even in its philosophical interpretations (as karma bundle, the formation of basic dispositions, factors, inner structures)—replace personal existence?

4. From the standpoint of the Kantian critique, it is altogether possible not only to deny but also to affirm the existence of a self. Indeed on ethical (not to mention psychoanalytical) grounds, such an affirmation is imperative.

The counterquestion boils down to this: Should not Buddhist thinkers, as they critically assess their own and alien traditions, make a more direct effort to establish an anthropology centered around *human dignity* (which the Buddha himself deeply respected)? Buddhists are fully aware that man can be adequately understood only as conditioned in every way, as a relational being within the totality of life and the cosmos. But should not they reflect more earnestly, especially in an ethical vein, on the problems of the unique, inviolable, noninterchangeable human self, with its roots in the past and its future destiny? Has it not become clear in our century, in a dechristianized Europe (but in China and Japan as well) how easily a totalitarian system (whether feudal–militaristic or proletarian–communistic) can put its own power in the place of the ignored, denied, repressed ego; how easily human identity and dignity can be sacrificed to the interests of absolutist power politics? Hasn't it become equally clear how easily, even in democratic systems, ego–weakness or even ego–negation bring in their wake uncritical assimilation to prevailing trends, an attitude of opportunistic compromise, a tolerance of everything, and a lack of resistance to injustice and oppression?

Christianity was unable to prevent such dehumanizing uses of power in its own sphere of influence (state *and* church), and totalitarian systems triumphed under the banner of dechristianization. Despite this failure, Christians can perhaps more easily draw upon their own tradition in order to develop criteria for a qualitatively different image of man. On the basis of its own presuppositions, Christianity can rise up in the name of the one true Absolute against all absolutizing of the relative, can protest in the name of God, who founds the personal dignity of human beings, against every kind of depersonalization, every false self-denial, every surrender of the ego in state *and* church. For a critically reflective biblical concept of God allows a concept of man that, I believe, deserves respect even from Buddhists. The individual's new self is truly constituted by the fact that he lets his empirical ego be grounded in the Absolute. This means that he will no longer be trapped within self, and so misunderstand (ignorance) and misuse (greed) his true self, but will find his true identity in freedom from self-seeking, in the Absolute. In the biblical vision, encountering the Absolute does not extinguish man's self, but lifts it up.

But—there is no stifling the critical question—what is a Buddhist supposed to make of talk about an Absolute, let alone God, when each and every thing is "empty" anyway? There is now no way to dodge this issue, and in preparation for dialogue let us review Buddhism's utterly radical answer to that question—taking and building on what we have already heard in Heinz Bechert's presentation. And so we come to what is likely the most difficult point in Buddhist-Christian dialogue, which some see as an unbridged abyss. I hope the reader will appreciate the fact that the problem, which I aim to address as carefully as possible, demands a considerable mental effort from anyone who tackles it. We are confronting here the most troublesome and most radical of all Buddhist thinkers, a man who left his mark on all later ages.

SELF-IMMOLATION OF THINKING THROUGH THOUGHT ITSELF

All things are empty, without being and substance, only a dream, a delusion, *Māya:* This was the teaching of the bold, legendary Indian sage *Nāgārjuna* in the second century A.D. His ideas also belong to the paradigm change from Shrāvakayāna to Mahāyāna: The term "shūnyatā" ("void," "emptiness"), which appears in only a few passages of the Pāli canon, became the central concept for Shūnyavāda, the school or "teaching of the void." Of course, this first developed Mahāyāna system in no way understands the term "emptiness" in a purely negative or nihilistic sense. The only correct way to conceive it is dialectically, as the key concept in philosophy not of pure nothingness, but of becoming—suspended between being and nothingness. Nāgārjuna—whom Karl Jaspers includes among *The Great Philosophers* (1966)—consciously follows the Buddha in proposing a *"middle way"* (= *Māhyamika*) not only between the extremes of hedonism and asceticism, but also of affirmation and negation, of being and nonbeing. Man comes to nirvāna only through knowledge of the emptiness of all things, only by giving up all specific intents, standpoints, and categories.

Nāgārjuna, who thought of himself as the Buddha's most consistent disciple, "compels" this abandonment with the help of a highly refined dialectic, overcoming opposition and contradiction with frequently dizzying flights of thought, with the help of a method of refutation that constantly bends over backward. His goal is to show that all statements and theories about reality are contradictory and can be reduced *ad absurdum,* something which makes his arguments seem at once profound and incomprehensible. Classical Greek *two-step dialectic* makes it clear to a person that, in reality, it is not so, but otherwise. Someone familiar with this may be confused by Hegel's *three-step dialectic,* which will explain to him that it is so in reality but also otherwise, and therefore so *and* otherwise (Hegel begins his *Logic* with the dialectic of being, nonbeing, and becoming). But even someone trained in Hegelian dialectic may be perplexed by Nāgārjuna's *four-step dialectic,* which denies all four possibilities: that something really is so, that it is otherwise, that it is so *and* otherwise, and that it is *neither* so *nor* otherwise. In this way, all the exits are blocked for logical thinking, so that it finally chokes and gives up.

What interest is Nāgārjuna (and the many Mahāyāna thinkers he influenced, including Japanese Zen Buddhists) pursuing with this consciously provocative logic, as rich in variations as it is in hairsplitting subtlety? Why this "self-immolation process" of the mind (Jaspers), in which logical thinking consumes itself? There is only one reason: The individual is supposed to be free from the *conventional, limited, veiled truth of the world of appearances,* whose essence is *"emptiness."* As Frederick J. Streng has demonstrated in his penetrating study *Emptiness* (1967), what Nāgārjuna understands by "emptiness" is the "means to achieve a final transformation," not an ultimate reality (God), but, epistemologically speaking 'enlightenment,' psychologically 'freedom,' and cosmologically 'relatedness' to all things, which excludes any absolutizing." The individual is to be free for the *highest, religio-mystical truth,* which goes beyond both mythical thought and metaphysical speculation, but which can dawn upon him only in the act of absorption. In this way, conceptual intelligence overcomes itself through itself: The individual becomes open to the final truth, beyond all speech and thought, attainable only in the act of silence.

On this "middle way" of "dependent origination" (and passing away) and of the "void" (between being and nonexistence), the *Four Noble Truths* of the Buddha can be understood in all their depth: the coming to be and passing away of all things, suffering, which points to the "void" of all things. Only by seeing through the "void" is it possible to overcome suffering. In fact, the Buddha and his teaching exist, to begin with, only because things are "empty." And even the Buddha, his teaching, and his sangha should not be absolutized. In the end, when man no longer perceives the deception of the multifarious world of appearances and comes to rest in nirvāna, they, too, will be as superfluous as the raft on the shore of salvation. "All perception ceases, multiplicity comes to rest, and peace prevails. Nowhere has any teaching of the Buddha been preached to anyone." This is Nāgārjuna's treatment of nirvāna in his *Mnemonic Verses on the Middle Doctrine.* (Chapter 25, 24)

THE "EMPTINESS"—NEGATIVE OR POSITIVE?

It would make little sense here to join other critics in a detailed argument against Nāgārjuna's logic-chopping that explains away all relational concepts, such as cause and effect, as "impossible" contradictions. Even the most competent and best-intentioned Western interpreters speak of "obvious logical flaws" (K. Jaspers, I, 424) and of "Nāgārjuna's conclusions, which for the most part proved to be debatable fallacies" (E. Frauwallner, *Die Philosophie des Buddhismus,* 1956, p. 221). But, on the other hand, we should not overlook the fact that in his sublating trains of thought he is dealing with "[the] logically necessary, resulting from an attempt to do the impossible—namely—to express absolute truth." (K. Jaspers, ibid.)

But was Nāgārjuna really interested in absolute truth? One of the main difficulties posed again and again by dialogue about the central concepts of Buddhism is that they are interpreted by Buddhists themselves in quite different, indeed diametrically opposite, ways. We first saw this with nirvāna, and now with the concept of emptiness, which is understood very differently, as Heinz Bechert has shown, by the first two great philosophical schools of Mahāyāna Buddhism. We have *two* options to consider:

Anyone who wishes to can understand "emptiness" with Nāgārjuna and the Mādhyamikas as completely *negative*. In that case, all the beings and facts of everyday life, seen from a distance, are "empty," because they come into being and pass away, neither exist nor do not exist, and in any case "are" not. Thus all positive statements are impossible, the question of the Absolute is false and perfectly useless, a projection, a fiction, an illusion. Where does that leave us?

No one will ever be able to force an advocate of this sort of "mysticism" (etymologically, "to close" the lips) to open his mouth and make a positive statement—except, of course, for one, that there are no positive statements. Is Nāgārjuna perhaps like Pyrrho, the first Greek skeptic (and Alexander's companion on the campaign in India)? Contrary to Greek tradition, he pleaded for "abstention from voting" *(epoché)* on all theoretical questions and for "imperturbability" *(ataraxía)*, the only way, he thought, to happiness. As with Pyrrho, might we not be dealing here with a dogmatic standpoint that ultimately (for all its subtle dialectic) makes dialogue impossible? Is this a "middle way" that, in the dialectic of affirmation and negation, ultimately gives up on affirmation (unlike the Buddha himself with his metaphysical abstinence) and rivets itself one-sidedly and apophantically to the extreme of negation? As if the very "emptiness" of facts and beings, the very suspension between being and nonbeing did not raise questions about where the suspension comes from. If the "emptiness" may not be understood nihilistically as Nothing, then why is there anything at all, rather than nothing? In other words, are these beings and facts possibly empty, do they possibly have no being, precisely because they are altogether not their own source but are identical, in varying ways, to the one Absolute? This is the teaching of the second (later) great Māhāyana school, of Yogācāra. "Naturally, in all mysticism it is easy to cross from nonbeing to super-being," as Max Weber noted in *The Religion of India* (trans. and ed. by Hans H. Gerth and Don Martindale, 1958).

For anyone who wishes can also interpret "emptiness" *positively* with the Yogācāra school. In that case, all beings and facts are forms of expression of the one ineffable Highest Being, which also is real. Now, of course, the question of the Absolute—the spotless, luminous, pure spirit, which constitutes the facts and even the buddhas as their "element"—stands at the center of attention.

Here too, analogously, no one will ever get an advocate of Yogācāra to call this question useless or even as falsely put. No wonder the fusion of

the Mādhyamika and Yogācāra traditions was already under way during
the heyday of Yogācāra in India, and the "new" (but from the Indian
standpoint most ancient) notion of the Absolute prevailed. Because,
insofar as they did not fall victim to total skepticism, Nāgārjuna's successors made one thing clear: All these negations include an *affirmation*.
Denial is not the end but the means of discovering the hidden reality,
the transcendent ground of everything and at the same time the true
nature of things as the norm for true and false. Nāgārjuna's great critic,
the Vedānta philosopher Shankara (eighth century), who learned so
much from him that he has been called a "crypto-Buddhist," thought it
consistent to proceed from the "emptiness" of the world of appearances
to the true being of Brahmā. Shankara in turn was corrected, as we
know, by Rāmānuja, who defended a modified nondualism, a differentiated unity of the Absolute and the world. And even though the Buddhists themselves rejected a "Brahmā," or "God," the majority in no
way flatly objected to transcendence or the Unconditioned.

The Yogācāra school, as we heard, made a vital contribution to East
Asian Buddhism and in particular shaped the Japanese concept of
"emptiness" and the Absolute. We wonder, is this still Buddhism as it
originally was? The answer is obvious, and it also holds, in its way, for
the school of the Mādhyamikas: We have, in any event, a new paradigm
of Buddhism.

ABSOLUTE BEING?

Westerners might have avoided many misunderstandings of Buddhist
doctrine, had they borne in mind that words like "emptiness" (or the
"nothing" or "absolute nothing" favored by the modern Kyoto school
of Kitaro Nishida and Keito Nishitani), which have a purely negative
meaning in our modern languages, can have thoroughly positive meanings in Eastern languages. One analogy might be the German word
Schein, which has both the negative sense of "illusion," "deceptive appearance," and the positive sense "shine" or "gleam." And as negative
expressions (such as the "incomprehensible," the "unutterable," or the
"ineffable") are applied to the reality of God, so "emptiness" (or "nothingness") can likewise take on a quite positive meaning. Thus the nega-
tive-sounding word "emptiness" (or "nothingness")—applied to statements about the reality of the Absolute—is altogether compatible with
"ineffability," another negatively formulated but positively meant descriptive term. Both words would then mean, not the contesting or
denying of this reality, but the relativizing of all thoughts, images, and
statements that limit it.

And so, if the Absolute is identical to "emptiness" ("nothingness")
and yet not nothing, then a *further question* suggests itself concerning the

definition of this final reality, this Absolute. *Christian theology* also maintains that the Absolute is not a mere existent being, not even the highest existent being. But why should we not at least be allowed to add that the Absolute is absolute *being* or *Being* Itself? That would not be to say—as Nāgārjuna, with his constricted notion of being, did—that the Absolute arises and passes away, but to ascribe to it pure, constant, eternal being.

In the spirit of Nāgārjuna and the Kyoto school, the Japanese Buddhist Masao Abe has argued against Paul Tillich that God must be viewed as not only beyond essence and existence, personal and impersonal, but even beyond being and nonbeing. One can say this only if one understands being in a narrow sense (as transitory being). But if we understand the terms in the broad sense, what, then, is beyond being and nonbeing? Beyond being, understood in a broad sense, is only nonbeing, beyond nonbeing only being. And Abe himself says that absolute nothingness (nirvāna as the absolute *mu)* is "absolute negation," thus also "negation of negation," and therefóre "absolute affirmation" (according to Hegel, from whom these terms have been borrowed, the negation of the negation is actually the power of life).

It is precisely at this point that in the interest of an authentic dialogue, I must be allowed a counterquestion: Why should the absolute affirmation be characterized exclusively as "nothingness," when it does *not* mean nothing? Would it not be less misleading to say that the Absolute is *also* absolute being or Being Itself, that "emptiness" is *also* "fullness," "shūnyatā" is *also* "pléroma"? Or will Buddhist traditionalism not permit any such alternative, although—on this particular line of tradition— "nothingness" and "emptiness" have actually long since ceased to be meant in a purely negative way as painless and desire-less extinction, but in the most positive sense as the real truth and highest reality, the good and the sole fulfillment of our life? But the Buddhist will have problems here because of his basic assumptions: Such statements seem to imply the concept of God. And this above all, it seems, is what the Buddhist cannot accept. With good reason, Buddhism has often been called an atheistic religion.

Is Buddhism Atheistic?

Nothing about Buddhism seems more alienating to Christians than the information that it is a religion without God. How could that be? Can a religion without God still be a religion? But does Buddhism really not have a "God"? We must take a closer look and learn to make some distinctions.

Philosophically oriented introductions to Buddhism sometimes pass over the fact that Buddhism, as it is *concretely* lived, is quite familiar with "God"; in fact it knows, about a whole *variety of gods*, taken from popular religion (Indian and otherwise): those personified natural forces or divinized kings and saints, whom Buddhists implore for help and protection. The Buddha considered the gods *(devas)* real, although subject to birth and rebirth. But since they have a form of existence far above man, it is completely consistent for the Buddha to obtain the help of the gods for worldly matters not related to salvation (such as prayers for rain or children). The gods, too, come and go, depending on their respective karma. And according to many passages in the Pāli canon, they should be venerated. From this angle we encounter within the domain of Buddhism something that is quite the opposite of atheism: *polytheism,* often imbued with magical practices.

But what if "God" means the one *supreme personal God, the creator and ruler of the world,* who, like the god Brahman, is proudly enthroned atop the pyramid of the gods and is likewise subject to becoming and passing away? Here the Buddha admits his *indifference:* In his total concentration on the redemption of man from suffering, he refuses to answer speculative questions about, say, God or the origin of the world. In this sense, on this level, Buddhism, if not atheistic, is nonetheless decidedly *agnostic.*

Christians who, in conversation with Buddhists, refer to acknowledging a personal "God," often do not realize how changed the concept of "God" (mostly used by Christians all too anthropomorphically) is to the Buddhist (and not just the Buddhist) way of thinking: often a potent projection by human beings and an illusion, only the highest being among other beings. Christians have been all too hasty to fill up the Buddhist silence before the Absolute with their own words. It is clear that such a concept of God, this sort of belief in God, stifles any conversation with Buddhism before it is scarcely begun.

But will we get any further in this dialogue with a purified, deepened understanding of God, far enough, at least, that the theological affirmations made by the Christian cannot be dismissed in advance by the Buddhist as inadequate? Despite the affirmations, if we cannot have "more" depth, complexity, and moderation, can we, in any case, not have less?

Dialogue with Buddhism should determine whether what Christians, on the deepest level, call "God" may not also be present in Buddhism *under different names.* Our previous reflections on basic terms such as nirvāna, emptiness, and dharma (about which I shall soon have more to say) have already given us some leads that can easily be followed up with an eye to our question.

A. "Emptiness": I have already shown how this term took an increasingly positive turn in Mahāyāna Buddhism. Hans Wolfgang Schumann has ably summarized its development: "Emptiness—originally an expression for the absence of a soul—becomes in Mahāyāna a positive term of value, a name for the Absolute that has no attributes . . . The Absolute is inherent in all appearances; samsāra and nirvāna are at bottom the same. As appearances, i.e., on the level of mere semblance, beings are different and separate; in their emptiness they are identical to the Absolute. And since the Absolute is also salvation, they are in essence already redeemed, only most people are not aware of this. All it takes for liberation is a change in mental attitude. Anyone who recognizes the illusoriness of suffering and his own essential emptiness (= identity with the Absolute = redeemedness) can no longer be touched by the chattels of existence. Lifted above the world, he lives as a sage in inner freedom and cheerfulness on his way to Perfect Extinction." (*Buddhismus*, 1976, p. 209)

The individual comes to know what is hidden in this "emptiness" not through strenuous reflection or rational argument, but only through meditation (yoga), experience, encounter. The way of speculation (Hegel's "thought thinking itself") is not the highest thing, rather the way of meditation leads to the Ultimate—right now. For, on the highest level of mystical experience, the individual realizes that "emptiness"—beyond all words and concepts—expresses the deepest reality, the Absolute, what Christian theology calls "God."

B. "Nirvāna": It has already been made clear, in the context of Theravāda, how nirvāna was understood by most schools as a positive reality. In Mahāyāna, nirvāna is no longer understood as just that otherworldly/future reality, but as a unitary true essence that even now penetrates the entire universe: nirvāna is nothing else than "emptiness." "The true essence of all existence is thus a lack of essence, its having-come-to-rest-from-time-immemorial, its being-by-its-very-nature-already-extinguished, that is, nirvāna. While the *Mādhyamikas* limit themselves to this negative determination of the ontological aspect of nirvāna, other Mahāyāna schools give it a positive character and describe it as a highest being, which pervades all appearances as their actual essence, or even as a metaphysical aspect of the Buddha hidden in all living creatures and endowed with countless advantages and effective powers." (L. Schmithausen, *Historisches Wörterbuch der Philosophie*, 1984, p. 855)

C. "Dharma": Even as far back as Theravāda, dharma is a central religious concept, encompassing authoritative teaching and practice: the eternal truth of salvation, which can save humanity in this fleeting, sorrowful world—that is the position taken by J. Ross Carter in *Dhamma*, 1978, following the lead of his teacher W. C. Smith. Nevertheless, it strikes me as doubtful that, as early as Theravāda, dharma, like nirvāna, referred to a truly transcendent reality. It is certain, though, that in Mahāyāna the idea of *dharmakāya*—"body" (*kāya*) of the "doctrines" (*dharma*)—is a symbol for the ultimate transcendent reality, a term at least as central as "emptiness," because it characterizes both the substance of the Buddha's teachings and the content of his enlightenment, as well as the reality that he experienced. Citing Indian, Tibetan, and in particular Chinese texts, David L. Chappell (discussing John Cobb's concept of emptiness) clearly shows that

> Buddhists developed the doctrine of Dharmakāya, and have placed it—as the fullest expression of the truth—above the "void." They believed that dharmakāya could become present and did become present and manifest, to the advantage of all living things in different forms. For this reason they found that the appropriate response to it was one of "respect, veneration, and worship," even petition and prayer. [in *Spirit Within Structure*, ed. E. J. Furcha, 1983, p. 189]

Nonetheless, at the same time, Chappell has rightly called attention to the fact that the use of *dharmakāya* in very different senses

> has sometimes made it an elusive and dispensable symbol, unlike the powerful monotheistic association of "God" with the God of the Bible, who commands and forgives. (ibid.)

But Mahāyāna Buddhists have also

> a) used a multiplicity of symbols for the ultimate reality, b) criticized all symbols of the ultimate reality as only partially adequate, and c) emphasized personal praxis . . . as the main prerequisite for truly seeing reality." (ibid.)

Nirvāna, emptiness, dharmakāya do, in fact, manifest divine qualities: a different dimension beyond or within phenomena, true reality. Nirvāna, emptiness, dharmakāya have, in fact, brought about a twilight of the gods: They have supplanted the Hindu gods as the supreme authority, yet they have not put any other gods—not even the Buddha—in their place. Nirvāna, emptiness, and dharmakāya appear in this sense as parallel terms for the Ultimate Reality. Their function is analogous to that of the term "God." Would it, then, be wholly impermissible to conclude that what Christians call "God" is present, under very different names, in Buddhism, insofar as Buddhists do not refuse, on principle, to admit any positive statements?

What, in Christianity, is the one infinite reality at the beginning, in the middle, and at the end of the world and man appears in Buddhism under various facets and appellations, distinguished with respect to different aspects and functions. Perhaps, then, we can risk an answer to the question asked of those Indonesian Buddhists who did not know what God meant to them, whether nirvāna or the void, the dharma or the primal Buddha. Based on what I have developed thus far, I would like to attempt to answer in a single complex proposition:

If God is truly the Absolute, then he is *all these things in one:* nirvāna, insofar as he is the goal of the way of salvation; dharma, insofar as he is the law that shapes the cosmos and humanity; emptiness, insofar as he forever eludes all affirmative determinations; and the primal Buddha, insofar as he is the origin of everything that exists.

Could it be that—after all that has been said about emptiness, nirvāna, and dharmakāya in comparison with the Christian idea of the Absolute —despite all the divergences, some *convergences* are taking shape *between Christianity and Buddhism?* Unfortunately, I do not have the space here to discuss the various reinterpretations by Buddhists themselves that highlight these convergences. I should mention, along with the voices from Japanese Mahāyāna, especially the Kyoto school, a figure from Theravāda, the Thai monk Buddhadāsa. In his highly respected lectures on *Christianity and Buddhism* (1967), he analyzes the parallel meaning and function of the eternal, universal, absolute dharma in Buddhism and of God (who must be thought of as beyond time and space and all concepts and images) in Christianity, always presupposing that this Christian God is not understood in a personal–anthropomorphic manner. That, says Buddhadāsa, is something a Buddhist would never do.

It is now imperative to turn again to the problem of the personality or impersonality of the ultimate, absolute reality. Once again, we cannot avoid some strenuous conceptual effort. For if no agreement can be reached on this issue, any agreement on the reality of the Absolute between Christians and Buddhists will always remain highly superficial. Hence the direct question:

IS THE ABSOLUTE PERSONAL OR IMPERSONAL?

In order to make clear how complex the matter is, let us attempt a sort of negative thought experiment to see the effects of Nāgārjuna's four dialectical steps (affirmation—negation—affirmation and negation— neither affirmation nor negation) on our problem.

Here it must be freely admitted in advance that our attempt at an interpretation—unlike the teaching of Nāgārjuna, which in the final analysis fixates dogmatically and apophantically on negation—tries to take the truly "middle" way between naïve conventional affirmation and skeptically oscillating negation: between an "eternalism," rightly rejected by the Mādhyamikas, that would understand the Absolute as a separate, immovable, eternal substance, and a "nihilism" (which they reject in principle while showing a strong bias in its favor) that would dissolve the Absolute—as essentially a "fiction"—into the "absolute" experience of redemption of "things as they are," thereby making it difficult to establish any positive ethics. How, then, are we to think of the Absolute if we find ourselves between affirmation and negation, unwilling to abandon either immanence or transcendence?

First, we deny that the Absolute is *personal.* Why? It would be just too superficial to make the Infinite One shrivel up into one finite thing, into a kind of metaphysical "personality." As if the Absolute could be grasped with the help of a clearly outlined anthropomorphic concept, as if it were a person in the sense that a human being is a person for Western thought. That way, the all-encompassing and all-penetrating One would become an object, which man would have "at his disposal," which he could "put into words." No, the Absolute, which for Christian and Buddhist thought is the primal goal of all reality (salvation) and which hence already defines and determines every individual existence in a hidden manner, cannot be an individual person among other persons, someone we would have to imagine as a "super-man or "super-ego." The Absolute is simply not something infinite (or even finite) *alongside* or *over* finite things.

However, if we deny that the Absolute has personality, are we not *ipso facto* asserting its impersonality? No, we deny, *in the second place,* that the Absolute is *impersonal.* Why? It would be degrading to explain the Absolute as a neutral "principle," as if the Absolute were merely something like an abstract "world formula," an unfeeling world law or natural force. That would even run counter, perhaps, to the many (and often quoted) poetic expressions for the final reality in Buddhist scriptures. If human beings try to think of the Absolute, they must positively not imagine it as below the human level, as subpersonal or nonpersonal. An Absolute without mind, without freedom, joy, bliss, and love would not be a true Absolute.

But if we deny both that the Absolute is personal and that it is impersonal, are we then claiming that it is both personal and impersonal? No, we deny, *in the third place,* that the Absolute is *both personal and impersonal.* Why? Because the Absolute is not a compound, but utterly and completely simple, not a *mixtum compositum* of personal and impersonal elements. Nothing meaningful can come out of personality-and-impersonality, as if, in the Absolute, form and formlessness were, to speak, quantifiable or addable. No, if we try to think of the Absolute, this must not be in a contradictory fashion, as if the impersonal could be simply defined as personal, and the personal as impersonal.

But if we deny that the Absolute is both personal and impersonal, are we not then affirming that the Absolute is neither personal nor impersonal? No, we deny, *in the fourth place,* that the Absolute is *neither personal nor impersonal.* Why? Because the Absolute is utterly and completely simple, but not without content. As if the Absolute could be imagined in the nihilistic sense as "nothingness" or the "void." No, if human beings try to think of the Absolute, this cannot be done by leaving personality and impersonality out of account. The Absolute encompasses and bursts through both at once. Where does this leave us, then?

No one could miss the fact that such a four-tiered negative dialectic drives language to its limits and forces it into paradoxes. I have tried to suggest a dangerous tightrope walk on the borderline separating what is imaginable and unimaginable, sayable and unsayable, comprehensible and incomprehensible. Discourse about the Ultimate Reality that is not at the same time discourse about the ineffability of the Ultimate Reality easily turns into idle talk. Discourse about the Absolute is adequate only so long as it is conducted in the awareness of the dialectic of gripping and releasing, speech and speechlessness, language and silence, with utmost discretion in the face of what is not determined by the factitious "mysteries" of the theologians, but *is simply the secret heart of this reality*. And actually, would not silence before this hidden reality be the far more appropriate demeanor, a silence which comes from the negation that the East so urgently insists on and that is not continually being drowned out by the affirmations to which the West is undoubtedly inclined?

Language, to be sure, is a barrier. Yet language can break down barriers. Language limits, but it can also remove limits and open the way to the ever greater mystery. And if our terms "personal" and "impersonal" are not sufficient to describe the mystery of the Ultimate Reality, they are at least not wholly alien to their subject, not meaningless. For Christian theology, they serve to designate indispensable dimensions that we ought to, but barely can, think of as bound up together. This is an ideal example of what Nicholas of Cusa called the *coincidentia oppositorum*, the "synthesis of opposites," the distinctive mark, as it were, of the Ultimate. Could it be that from this point we can make out a structural similarity between that "emptiness" which, for Buddhists, transcends all opposites, and that "pléroma," that infinite "fullness" which embraces all opposites?

THE SYNTHESIS OF OPPOSITES

It is with good reason that Japanese Buddhists frequently quote *Nicholas of Cusa*. Nicolaus Cusanus was a great humanist who in 1437, as a cardinal legate in Constantinople, became acquainted with both Islam and the negative ("apophantic") theology of the Greeks, especially of Pseudo-Dionysius. He believed that it required "learned ignorance" (*docta ignorantia*) to come to know God. Purely affirmative theology without negative theology makes of God a creature of our intellect, a projection of our imagination; indeed it turns the worship of God into idolatry.

In God, the origin without an origin, all opposites fall together. He is the *coincidentia oppositorum;* he is, as the maximum, also the minimum, and thus transcends minimum and maximum. "From the standpoint of negative theology," says Nicholas of Cusa, "there is nothing in God but

infinitude. Accordingly, he is knowable neither in this world nor in the
world to come, since all creatures, which cannot comprehend the infinite light, are darkness in comparison with him. Rather he is known only
to himself." *(De docta ignorantia,* I, Chapter 26, pp. 112–13) As Cusanus
sees it, this has the implication, for discourse about God, "that in theological statements negations are true and positive statements are insufficient. Likewise, negative statements are all the truer, the more they
guard the simply Perfect One from imperfections." (ibid.) Nicholas
continually rethought and varied the ideas of his early and principal
work, *On Learned Ignorance,* till his late work, where in a highly dialectical
manner God is defined in identity with and difference from all other
beings as the "not other," the *non aliud,* and precisely because of that as
the "center of the center, goal of the goal, name of the name, being of
being, and nonbeing of nonbeing." *(Tetralogus de non aliud,* p. 87, thesis
5)

We cannot go any further here into Cusanus' metaphysics, which set a
standard for intellectual creativity still valid today. Let me take a brief
melancholy sidelong glance at the course of history since Nicholas of
Cusa died, in 1464. It is strange to think what might have happened if
Christian theologians had not always buried their own tradition of negative theology beneath their prolix tomes, but had taken it more seriously. How many controversies over doctrines, dogmas, and definitions
might have been spared over the centuries! How much more deepened
understanding might have been applied to foreign religions just when
new continents and peoples were beginning to be discovered! And how
might the conversations with Japanese Buddhists have gone, if the first
Jesuit missionaries had cited, not Scholastic proofs for the existence of
God, but the penetrating analysis of the experience of God as detailed
by Cusanus, whose writings they could have been familiar with?

Our thought experiment in connection with Nāgārjuna has set up
fence posts and warning signs with the help of negations. If we wish to
say more, to define more exactly what *coincidentia oppositorum* means with
regard to the problem of the personality and impersonality of the Absolute, we can (still walking the razor's edge between speech and silence)
work only with limit concepts, which aim neither to restrict the Absolute
nor, of course, to leave it in total silence. One such limit concept might
be *"transpersonal,"* a determination that embraces the concepts of personal and impersonal but bursts through them and so "sublates" them
in the infinite.

That would give us an intellectual, hermeneutic basic structure, enabling Eastern and Western, Buddhist and Christian, theistic and atheistic schools of thought about the Absolute, about God, to commingle in a
dialogue. Thinking transpersonally about the Absolute: This would be
the permanent challenge to the Christian Western concept of God—but

at the same time to the Buddhist Eastern concept of the Absolute. Here is a rough outline of this sort of thinking:

AN EASTERN-WESTERN UNDERSTANDING OF GOD

If the West takes the *challenge of the East* seriously, this will decisively frame its basic attitude toward the Ultimate Reality: more respect in the face of the Ineffable, more reverence before the Mystery, in brief more awe in the presence of that Absolute that Jews, Christians, and Muslims call the one true God. The concept of the "void" could then be adopted in a Christian sense, as an expression for the ineffability of God. Thus, the West will always begin its theological reflections here: God, as the Ultimate, is and remains the incomprehensible, the one who is by definition undefinable, the mystery pure and simple of all reality. His essence cannot even be fully disclosed from the standpoint of *being:* God is nothing of what is. He is no being, he transcends all beings. This has consequences for what we say about him. Human thought here enters a realm where all positive statements (e.g., "God is good") prove inadequate. In order to be true, they must be immediately negated ("God is not good"—in a finite, human way) so as finally to be translated into the infinite: "God is ineffably, immeasurably, infinitely good, absolute goodness."

By the same token, if the East should wish to take the *challenge of the West* seriously, it would have to consider this: The Absolute does transcend all concepts, statements, and definitions, yet it is not separate from the world and humanity, nor is it—as the East itself conceives it— outside all existing things: Dwelling in the world and humanity, *it determines their being from within.* And hence the Buddhist, too, might be able to accept the idea that the Ultimate, that God, as Christians understand him, must be conceived out of the ontological difference between being as such *(Sein)* and existent beings *(das Seiende).* This means, God is, but he is not just a being. Rather, he is the hidden mystery of being: not an overbeing, but the mysterious unifying factor *in* all existing beings, Being Itself as the ground, center, and goal of all existents and all being, at once immanent and transcendent. This implies for our discourse about God that negative statements ("God is not finite") can say something eminently positive ("God is infinite").

How, then, can we try to think adequately about the Ultimate? In such a way, at all events, that it simultaneously transcends and permeates the world and man: infinitely far and yet closer to us than we are to ourselves, intangible even though we experience its presence, present even when we experience its absence, affirmative through all negations. An Ultimate that pervades the world and still does not merge with it, that encompasses it round but is not identical to it: transcendence in immanence. Every statement about God would, in this approach, have to pass through the dialectic of negation and affirmation. Every experience of God would have to survive the ambivalence of nonbeing and being, dark night and bright day.

Christian tradition has never denied that we can speak about God or the Absolute only with analogous terms, images, and ideas, in metaphors, codes, and symbols. Even the expression "God's *transpersonality*" is aimed at something that transcends all thought. And yet we must confront the reality that this phrase means. For many Buddhists would agree that the Ultimate is not something indifferent to us or that we can be indifferent to: Rather, it lays a liberating and challenging claim on us. At this point, however, prophetic religions take a crucial further step. According to Jewish, Christian, and Islamic witness—and this claim can be accepted after subjecting it to every kind of critical reflection, in "second naïveté" (P. Ricoeur), so to speak—God is not neuter, not an anonymous "it," but *spirit in creative freedom,* the synthesis of all opposites, the primeval identity of justice and love, and thus a partner who grounds and embraces *human interpersonality.* By "God," the Bible means an authentic partner, not a transcendental crutch for insecure humanity, a force forever controlling humanity and keeping it in leading strings (a narrow distortion of the Christian idea of God and rightly criticized by Buddhists), but an "opposite number" who is benevolent, liberating, and unconditionally reliable. This God is at once the origin, support, and completion of the human race.

Where others only heard an endless silence, the Jewish, Christian, and Islamic scriptures tell of a people being addressed and claimed by its God. Where others experienced unechoing space and the void, this people was allowed to discover for itself and others that the Absolute can be heard and spoken to, that it is a mysteriously communicative and responsive *Thou.* This idea, indeed this promise, has ever since been an ineradicable part of all the Semitic religions, even though it was often forgotten and betrayed in the secular West. In being addressed by this Thou, human beings can experience their own "I" as raised to a dignity that is hardly ever seen in the East and that no Western secular humanism, no technological progress, and no cosmic piety can guarantee.

That is what Christians mean when they argue for a *God* who has chosen humanity as his partner, and made us into a "Thou" by speaking to us, who has through his word challenged human beings to respond, so as to make them responsible to himself. That is what they mean when they argue for *men and women* whose dignity will not permit them to be misused as cannon fodder or guinea pigs or as fertilizer for evolution.

It was not possible here to delve into the questions raised by such Buddhist movements as Tantrism, Zen, and Amidism. I shall turn to these issues in my response to Heinz Bechert's fourth presentation on Buddhism.

IV.
Buddhism and Society: Buddhism in Our Time

1. *Heinz Bechert:* Buddhist Perspectives

Downfall and Renewal

As we have already learned, the Muslim invasion largely destroyed Buddhism in India. Faced with such a violent onslaught of intolerance, the Buddhists were defenseless. In the fifteenth and sixteenth centuries, the Indonesian Archipelago—with the exception of Bali—was also Islamized. Only in parts of Central Asia was the teaching of the Enlightened One able to gain ground for a few more hundred years. Then, with the sixteenth century, a new threat appeared on the stage of world history, namely Christianity. The Church, as everyone knows, had entered an unholy alliance with the exploitative colonial powers. There were forced conversions on the grand scale in the coastal regions of the island of Ceylon, which had been conquered by the Portuguese. When the Dutch Government restored freedom of religion during the Enlightenment (1785), the majority of the Sinhalese returned to the religion of their forefathers. On the whole, the success of Christian missions in Buddhist countries was and remained minimal. Since the beginning of our century, Buddhism has found followers in Europe and North America. In the most recent past, it has been communism that aimed at doing away with Buddhism. In the Stalin era, this was especially true in the Asiatic republics of the Soviet Union and in Mongolia; a similar pattern occurred later during the Cultural Revolution in China and neighboring countries and, with particular virulence, in Cambodia. So far as one can judge today, it may be said that, while Buddhism has lost a good deal of its influence in these countries, it has nonetheless, contrary to what happened with Islam, weathered the storm of persecution.

Buddhist renewal movements have been active at all times. Thus, around the middle of the eighteenth century, the monk Saranankara launched a thoroughgoing reform of the sangha in the then still independent Sinhalese kingdom in the interior of Ceylon. Around the middle of the nineteenth century, King Mongkut of Thailand, who had been a monk for many years before ascending the throne, saw to the reform and modernization of the sangha in his country. In 1871, King Mindon Min of Burma (reigned 1853–78) convened the Fifth Buddhist Council, in his capital city of Mandalay, and ordered the sacred texts engraved on stone plates. All this took place in traditional fashion, without any real contact with modern ways of thinking of Western origin.

That sort of encounter began shortly after the middle of the nineteenth century, first of all in Ceylon. Starting in 1865, public disputes were held between Buddhist monks and Christian clergymen over the advantages of both religions. The most famous of these debates was the "Great Dispute of Pānadurā," in 1873, between Mahottivattē Gunānanda, on the Buddhist side, and David de Silva and F. S. Sirimanne, speaking for the Christians. This is considered a turning point in the relations between the two religions, because, as a result of the debate, the Buddhists recovered their sense of being in possession of the better view. An English translation of the text of the dispute was published in the same year in Battle Creek, Michigan, by an American named James Martin Peebles. This book, in turn, convinced the Theosophist Henry Steel Olcott that Buddhism was spiritually superior to Christianity. Olcott was a cofounder of the Theosophical Society in America, and this group now took up elements of Indian thinking into its doctrine. The "Buddhist Theosophical Society," founded during Olcott's visit to Ceylon in 1880, was, despite its name, purely Buddhist and not theosophical at all. The crucial experience for the Buddhists of those days was that a representative of Western culture had come not only to study their religion and culture, but to learn from it.

Among the leading personalities of that early phase of the Buddhist renewal belongs the Sinhalese David Hewavitarne (1864–1933), who took the religious name of Anagārika Dharmapāla. In 1891 he founded the Mahabodhi Society, the first international and interconfessional Buddhist organization. From 1892 on, its headquarters were in Calcutta, then the capital of India.

BUDDHISM IN THE WEST

Around the same time, came the beginnings of the dissemination of Buddhism in the West. The work of Arthur Schopenhauer (1788–1860) contributed a great deal to the awakening of interest in Buddhist thought. For Schopenhauer, Buddhism was the best of all imaginable religions; and he pointed to similarities between his own philosophy and teachings of the Buddha, stressing the fact that he had come to his findings quite independently. Schopenhauer's teaching is admittedly not identical to the Buddha's, but much of it strikes us as a sort of incompletely thought-out Buddhism.

In England, Sir Edwin Arnold's long poem *The Light of Asia*, published in 1879, opened the way for the acceptance of Buddhism. In the U.S.A., the participation of two Buddhists at the "World Parliament of Religions," in 1893, marked the beginning of a Buddhist movement there. They were Anagārika Dharmapāla, from Ceylon, and the Zen master Sōen Shaku. Daisetsu T. Suzuki came to America at the invitation of the publisher Paul Carus. It is to Suzuki that the West owes much of what is known here about Zen Buddhism.

We should also not forget the importance of scholarly study of Buddhism. Buddhism did not come to the West by means of active missionary work, but only by way of books that were written about its teachings —and by which readers were convinced. The actual founders of modern research on Buddhism were Thomas William Rhys Davids (1843–1922) and Hermann Oldenberg (1854–1920). Hermann Oldenberg thought of himself exclusively as a scholar, not a believer, and yet many people came to understand the nature of the Buddha's teaching thanks to his book *Buddha: His Life, His Doctrine, His Order* (1st ed., 1881, English translation, 1882). Thus I was told not long ago by a Buddhist journalist in Chiang Mai, in northern Thailand, that the reading of Oldenberg's book had first opened his eyes to the true meaning of the Buddha's teaching. Rhys Davids went one step further than Oldenberg and professed himself a follower of the Buddha.

The first European to enter the Buddhist monastic order was Allan Bennett McGregor, who was ordained in Akyab, Burma, in 1902, and given the name Ānanda Maitreya. In 1904 the German violin virtuoso Anton Gueth received ordination in Rangoon; his spiritual name was Nyanatiloka. He lived more than half his life on Ceylon, and through his many publications was an important agent in informing the Western world about the teachings of Buddhism.

The introduction of Buddhism into America began with Japanese immigrants. Most of them were followers of Jōdo Shinshū, the most popular form of Japanese Buddhism, which I have already mentioned as the "Buddhism of faith." Zen Buddhism has also spread in the New World, and since the Chinese occupation drove many Tibetans into exile from their country, some of them have come to America, where several forms of Tibetan Buddhism have won adherents.

Many Western Buddhists feel that Buddhists should bridge over the differences among the numerous varieties of their religion. They see in these differing forms not mutually exclusive positions but only different aspects of the same ultimate truth. This "ecumenical Buddhism" has come to play a special role particularly in England, the U.S.A., and recently Indonesia as well. "Why," asks Christmas Humphreys, president of the Buddhist Society of Great Britain, "should there not be in time a Western Buddhism, a Nava-yana or 'new vehicle' as Captain Ellam called it, not deliberately formed as such but a natural growth from the same roots of Buddhism as all others, that is, the record of the Buddha's Enlightenment?"

WESTERN AND ASIAN REACTIONS

Modern Christian theology has probably never had to struggle before with such great intellectual difficulties in encountering a non-Christian religion as it has had in the case of Buddhism. It has also probably never viewed the inroads made by a "foreign" school of thought as so great a challenge to its own ancestral rights as the only alternative to no religion at all. Thus Joseph Dahlmann, S.J. (who did important scholarly work on the "more neutral" ground of Indian literary history), issued the following judgment on Buddhism in his *Buddha: A Cultural Picture of the East* (Berlin, 1898, p. 121), a book quite famous in its day: "A system that expresses such views unites only the very crudest elements of materialism and nihilism. Such a philosophy is simply a confluence of demoralizing elements . . ."

In Germany this theme turned political when Emperor Wilhelm II had his court painter, Knackfuss, do the famous painting supposed to symbolize the "yellow peril." Here let me quote from a lecture on "Christianity and Buddhism," delivered in Berlin in 1898 by Pastor Robert Falke: "Some years ago our Emperor sketched out a well-known drawing with the inscription 'Peoples of Europe, guard your most sacred possessions.' On this picture stood the allegorical figures of the civilized nations of Europe, ready to battle the onrushing hordes of the Antichrist, who was enveloped by dark clouds and the smoke of burning cities, and who bore the features of Buddha. In the face of the onrushing political dangers in the awakening East that still threaten our culture, and above all in the face of Buddhism, which is now leading a powerful charge against Christianity, anyone who failed to understand the picture three years ago, will now have to appreciate the warning of our sovereign, who saw so clearly and so far into the future. Buddhism has become a force in Europe and America, and ever since entering upon its campaign of conquest in the West about fifty years ago, it has won enormous success."

Since Falke's day a veritable flood of apologetic literature against this "danger" has been unleashed. Its authors share both extravagantly exaggerated data about the success of the Buddhist mission and more or less the same apologetic scheme. None of them miss the opportunity to condemn Schopenhauer's philosophy, through which the "pessimistic Buddhist spirit" has penetrated our consciousness. None of their pamphlets omits a flowery section depicting the fundamental difference in the biographies of both religious founders: There the Buddha, the "aristocrat," who had "no sensitive heart in his breast," who is said to have become "a reformer out of loathing for life," who chose his disciples from the "upper classes," who set up a complicated system of rules, whose life story, in the "mysterious, stilted account of Lalitavistara," is miles apart from the "simple, sober style of the Evangelists," etc. (Falke) Here Jesus, whose life and teaching are then contrasted as forcefully as possible with those of the Buddha. It is a whole bundle of emotional judgments and prejudices that have not, I think, been completely overcome even today.

This sort of polemics, centered, as ever, on the charge of Buddhist atheism, was immediately picked up and turned around, as it were, by Buddhist apologists. They showed that high moral ideals (which even Christian critics could not deny that Buddhism had) could be justified without thinking about God and the soul as Christians did. And what did Christianity really have to offer? Constant wars, the Inquisition, burning of witches, and exploitation of the poor by the powerful. Buddhist apologetics in those days were hardly different in tone from Christian apologetics, and they displayed more righteous indignation than serenity.

But, for that very reason, this confrontation proved to be intellectually fruitful. Without it, the modernization of Buddhist thought would have been longer in coming. Over the centuries, traditional Buddhism had become increasingly involved with obsolete cosmologies and other outdated ideas. By the turn of the century, on the other hand, Christian theology had long since said good-bye to the geocentric world picture and the condemnation of the scientific mentality. The Buddhists now made up for lost time, helped in the process by the rediscovery of the Buddha's original teaching. This was the crucial contribution of Western Indology, which, as mentioned before, succeeded, from around 1880 onward, in unearthing the earliest layers of Buddhist tradition and in extricating the life and the teaching of the historical Buddha ever more clearly from the mass of traditional texts. In this way, Western experts on Buddhism and modern Buddhists, working together, managed to effect a "demythologizing" of traditional Buddhism. Belief in miracles and other elements of irrational thinking were eliminated as secondary, insignificant additions to the original teaching. Buddhism was described as a rational system, a "religion of reason," in sharp contrast to the religions of faith: Christianity and Islam. It does not demand blind faith, but invites people to test the truth for themselves through religious practice and meditation. Modern Buddhists have always shown a special interest in the progress of science, from whose findings they expect further support for their convictions. "Buddhism and Science" is a recurrent theme in the writings of the Buddhist modernists. They know, of course, that science cannot show the way to liberation. But they believe that they can draw an important argument for the correctness of their view from the congruence of the Buddhist and the scientific worldviews.

Another important element in the Buddhist renewal is the increased popularity of meditation. In traditional monasteries, instructions for meditative exercises were passed along by teachers to their carefully chosen disciples. The number of monasteries where such exercises were conducted has, over the past hundred years, ceased to be very large; and so, in order to revive the practice of meditation, students of Buddhism referred back to texts. Thus it happened that, around 1890, Anagārika Dharmapāla discovered an old meditation handbook and developed his own exercises after studying this work. Around the same time, in Burma, a monk named Nārada likewise began with textual studies in his renewal of the meditative practice known as the "awareness of mindfulness" (*satipatthāna*). He became the founder of the so-called Burmese school of *satipatthāna* meditation. One of those who belong to this tradition was the world-famous Mahasi Sayadaw, in Rangoon. Many people have come to him to study meditation, including those who did not convert to Buddhism but kept the religion they were born into. The same is true of other schools of meditation and masters in Burma and Thailand, such as Sunlun Sayadaw, Monhyin Sayadaw, Acharn Dhammadharo, Acharn Buddhadāsa, et al. The methods of meditation taught by these masters are open to everyone. In Thailand especially, old, traditional monasteries where, earlier, only monks had studied were now opened to lay people as well.

The Buddhist Ecumene

We have come to know from various examples the major differences between the various forms of Buddhist religiosity. The goal of spanning these differences, uniting the adherents of the different forms of Buddhism and getting them to work together, is one Buddhists have striven for ever since the early days of the renewal movement. In 1891, the First International Buddhist Conference, at Adyar, near Madras, elaborated the "Fourteen Fundamental Beliefs of Buddhism." Participants in the meeting included followers of Theravāda from Ceylon, Burma, and East Bengal, as well as Buddhists from China and Japan. The World Fellowship of Buddhists gave a permanent external form to the idea of a Buddhist ecumene. This association was created in 1950 at the instigation of the Sinhalese Buddhist Dr. Gunapala Piyasena and has since then held regular conferences; Buddhist communities in practically every country of the world have joined the Fellowship. Adherents of the most varied forms of Buddhism have also joined together on the national level, for example in the German Buddhist Union. Such associations have served to promote cooperation, not to blur the differences between the several doctrinal traditions, because modern Buddhists see that diversity as one of the advantages of their religion, allowing the individual to choose the way most suitable to his or her spiritual progress.

AMBEDKAR AND INDIAN NEO-BUDDHISM

Speaking of recent developments in Buddhism, we should not fail to mention the revival of Buddhism in the country of its origin. When India became independent, in 1947, there were only a few Buddhists there. We have already spoken of the downfall of Indian Buddhism in the Middle Ages. Hindus considered the Buddha's teaching a dangerous heresy. It is true, they declared, that the Buddha was one of the ten incarnations of the god Vishnu, but he was assigned the negative task of tricking the demons by proclaiming false doctrine. In the early-nineteenth century, the European view of Buddhism was still influenced by this negative image from Hindu sources.

The Mahabodi Society (1891) made it possible for a few educated Indians to develop an interest in Buddhism, but it could not reach the masses of the subcontinent. The first one to come closer to this goal was Dr. Bhimrao Ramji Ambedkar, who was born in 1893 in a village in the present-day Indian state of Maharashtra. He came from the Mahars, a group of endogamous castes belonging to the Untouchables. The Mahars had to clean streets, cemeteries, etc., and haul away dead cattle. The young Ambedkar was one of the very few members of his caste at the time who had a secondary education and was able to attend a university. A progressive Indian prince, the Maharaja Sayajirao, Gaekwar (ruler) of Baroda, gave the talented young man this chance, and in 1916 he gained his first doctorate, at Columbia University, in New York. In 1922 he began to work in his native country at improving the lot of the Untouchables and at doing away with the social discrimination against them, which is surely the most shameful feature of traditional Hindu society.

Ambedkar's great antagonist was Mahatma Gandhi. Gandhi, who remained a convinced Hindu all his life, also viewed the abolition of untouchability as one of his great goals. But while they agreed on the end, they were irreconcilably opposed on the means. Gandhi looked upon the caste system as a positive factor in a stable social order; he wanted simply to remove its abuses. By contrast, Ambedkar thought the caste system was itself the basic evil. Untouchability, he argued, was not a corruption, but a necessary consequence of the nature of that system. He felt that the liberation of the Untouchables could be achieved only by destroying the caste system.

As the Minister of Justice in the first government of independent India, Ambedkar played a vital role in the formulation of its constitution. He also saw to it that the Buddhist symbol of the wheel was put on India's national flag. He failed, however, to realize his plans for a comprehensive reform of Indian civil law and a radical improvement of existing conditions along the lines of democratic socialism. In 1951 he resigned his position as Minister. Nevertheless, anyone familiar with the development of modern India will marvel at how many reforms he managed to get passed.

For his followers, Ambedkar's conversion was the critical event of his life. Even today it is hard to separate history and legend in the reports about it. According to legend, he was predestined to take this step from his childhood days. He is held to be a bodhisattva, that is, an "enlightenment being," or future Buddha. His followers go so far as to add a fourth sentence to the traditional Buddhist profession of faith: "I take my refuge in Ambedkar." In point of fact, we can trace his interest in Buddhism back to 1927. In 1935, Ambedkar, who was already a recognized political leader of the Untouchables, publicly announced that he would break completely with Hinduism and go over to another religion. He was courted by religious leaders of Indian Christians, Muslims, and Sikhs. In 1950 he made known his decision to become a Buddhist, and appealed to the masses of the Untouchables to follow his example. His symbolic reception into the Buddhist community took place on October 14, 1956, in Nagpur. He died on December 6 of the same year. Since then, the "Neo-Buddhist" movement he founded has won many followers and has once again made Buddhism a living force in India.

Ambedkar's Buddhism is essentially a philosophy of ethical and social values. Dharma, for him, is simply the principle of morality, nirvāna the definitive realization of moral order. This order must be created in each one of us; it can never come into being through violence. For this reason, Ambedkar rejected communism, which he saw as a philosophy of violence.

The doctrinal tradition embraced by Ambedkar and his followers is Theravāda. But he thought it necessary and timely to place the social tasks of the Buddhist community in the foreground without denying its other aspects. Thus he saw in the sangha a model for a better society of the future, because the sangha is a community of equals, to which everyone has access so long as he submits voluntarily to the spiritual discipline of meditation and ascetical living.

I have described Ambedkar's "Neo-Buddhism" here as one particular example of movements that are aimed at changing the world and therefore have redefined the relation between Buddhist religious and political thought. There have been other models with similar aims, for example the Burmese attempt to integrate Buddhism and socialism into a larger system of thought. These approaches by modern Theravāda Buddhists are based on the old ideal, going back to Ashoka, of a Buddhist welfare state. Novel forms of Buddhism have also arisen in Japan, including the modern so-called Lotus sects, whose doctrines are founded on Nichiren's radical interpretation of the Indian Mahāyāna text Saddharmapundarīka-Sūtra ("Lotus sutra"). The oldest of these "new religions" of Japan is the Spiritual Friendship Society, Reiyū-kai. It was established in 1925 and takes a tolerant stance toward other forms of Buddhism. Altogether different from Reiyū-kai is the much more influential Sōka-gakkai, which must be rated as one of the most active and aggressive of these groups and which has proselytized successfully in the U.S.A. All Lotus sects are messianic. They hope ultimately to convert all men and women to their teaching and thereby to change the world radically for the better. They have been criticized by traditional-minded Buddhists as out of touch with reality: How could we hope to escape the consequences of our karma and the sorrowful nature of all existing things merely by creating new social structures?

RETROSPECT AND PROSPECT

In my historical survey I have tried to sketch some of the many religious forms that think of themselves as Buddhist, from ancient Buddhism to Jōdo Shinshū and Sōka-gakkai. In the process, it has become clear that, although they all claim to have historical roots, one way or another, in the same tradition (and this is in many ways visible from their appearance), they are much more profoundly different from one another than it seems at first. Still, I would like to recall one common feature of all forms of Buddhism, especially important for our purpose of comparing Buddhism and Christianity:

For Buddhists, the idea of a "God" who created the world and, despite his omnipotence, permitted suffering and evil to come into being, makes no sense. We have discussed which forms of Buddhism recognize an "Absolute" as the primal foundation of the world. Professor Küng has also suggested that these forms might be comparable, in some degree, to the "negative theology" of Nicholas of Cusa. However, there is no bridge leading from the Buddhist concept of liberation from this intrinsically sorrowful world to the biblical notion of God. This holds true both for the old Buddhist doctrine of "self-salvation" and for the more recent versions of "outside salvation." The idea of a "dictatorship by God," as a modern Burmese Buddhist once phrased it, remains unacceptable to Buddhists as a matter of principle, because they find the idea of God's omnipotence incompatible with the pain-ridden nature of the world.

Measured against the original teachings of Buddhism, the idea of vicarious redemption is likewise unacceptable in principle. Each person is responsible for his or her own way. On this point, admittedly, historical evolution has led to similarities with Christianity, because, as Richard Gombrich puts it, the doctrine of total individual responsibility has proved, in the long run, to be too heavy a burden. Later Buddhists have developed the idea, not found in the original teaching, of the possibility of transferring merit. In Japanese Amidism, reliance on the merit that the Buddha Amitābha has accumulated ultimately becomes the sole means of salvation at our disposal in this period of the world. For the Christian, naturally, "salvation from the outside" is the only way to salvation. But even here there is an obvious difference; Amitābha is not God; the world is sorrowful, not a divine creation. Amitābha merely helps us to get to the end of suffering, to nirvāna, by a detour through the paradise of the "Pure Land." Despite external similarities, both the point of departure and the way of thinking remain utterly foreign to those of Christianity.

Wherever Buddhism existed on a level of equality alongside other religions—together with Shinto in Japan or in pre-Maoist China with Confucianism and Taoism—the Buddhist element in these systems of thought was always assigned the responsibility of giving an answer to people about the question of their existence beyond death, to prepare them for it, and to help them when the time came. Thus Buddhist temples are primarily used for funeral rites. The Buddhists do not think that the world has any meaning (outside itself), but they believe that an order prevails in it that is valid above and beyond the existence of the individual. This conviction has, it seems to me, given them the strength to endure suffering in this world. After all, they always have the hope of arriving, on some distant day, at the end of suffering in a future existence. Victories over pain and death, like those won by modern medicine, remain, in the final analysis, illusory. Staring them in the face is the threat of new and perhaps still more terrible kinds of death. No outside force can help us on the way to overcome suffering. We can only overcome it in ourselves, as the Buddha teaches, by withdrawing from it. We must withdraw not only from evil and suffering, but likewise from the good, from everything "that makes life worthwhile." Because, for the one who knows the truth, they are both the same, they are no longer contraries.

But the truth is to be fathomed not through reflection or science, but only through immediate mystical experience. Perhaps the famous Buddhist logicians and epistemologists "saw" less of the truth than the solitary, meditating monk I noticed a few years ago sitting in front of the Shwe Dagon pagoda in such a state of absolute repose that I at first mistook him for a statue.

If it ultimately does not matter so much about opinions and creeds, then it is only logical that the Buddhists should have exerted themselves more, from the very beginning, on behalf of tolerance than the followers of other great religions—although, in our imperfect world, Buddhists, too, have occasionally sinned on this score. But there is scarcely another great religious community that has gone through so many persecutions and, thus far, survived them.

Only a few people can completely understand the Buddha's teaching, but all beings will be helped even if they grasp only a little of it. That, we might say, is the Buddha's "Gospel."

Some Thoughts on Buddhist-Christian Dialogue

Readers will not have failed to see the problems of mutual misunderstanding that still block the way to Buddhist-Christian dialogue today. We should, I think, look for the causes of this. I have taken it as my responsibility to present the "Buddhist position" in the light of modern scholarship and in such a way that adherents of Buddhism may also identify with it.

We are caught up in difficulties, however, whenever we try to agree on what Buddhism actually is. My initial idea was to limit the dialogue to ancient Buddhism, so that we could deal with a self-contained system, but this was not practicable, so I have presented a survey of various forms of Buddhist religiosity. But Professor Küng is working from a quite specific, clearly defined Christian theological position when he addresses a variety of counterpositions. Thus in his responses he has by no means consistently chosen the teaching of the Buddha as his counterposition. Instead he has repeatedly selected from the diverse historical forms of Buddhism whichever one best suited the question at hand. I believe, though, that a self-contained system should also be presented and understood as such. And I am afraid that an approach so bent on assimilation does not always facilitate understanding. If the dialogue is to be carried on, I think the Christian side should stick to a definite form of Buddhism (the best, in our case, it seems to me, would be the original one). Only then would we have one coherent position facing another.

Needless to say, the individual elements, mentalities, and concepts of every existing form of Buddhist piety can be traced back, one way or another, to older forms of doctrine, but Shaktist Tantrism, for example, or Amidism or Sōka-gakkai have, on the whole, turned into something radically different from the old Buddhist teaching. Some "Buddhist theologians," who advocate a specific kind of Buddhism that they have drawn from, or read into, ancient texts, will perhaps have an easier time communicating with their Christian dialogue partners than would philologists and historians, who try to understand the development of Buddhism objectively—i.e., they always have to keep the original meaning separate from later interpretations and cannot make any concessions, so to speak, at the expense of a third party.

I have already spoken, apropos of the emergence of Buddhist modernism, about the difficulty many spokesmen for Christian theology have had—and still have—to struggle with in dialogue with Buddhism. We need to eliminate from religious encounters those emotional factors that work on people because they are rooted in a specific tradition of thought and feeling. Here, too, we must look at the individual doctrines and peculiar features of the alien religion in their own internal context, which makes them meaningful to begin with. Similarly, it would not be fair to spotlight contradictions between theory and practice in making one's case—that would be hypocritical. The Buddha's teaching, of course, was not always rightly understood or consistently followed—no more than Jesus' teaching was. As I have already mentioned, the Buddha himself predicted the downfall of his teaching.

We must bid farewell, then, to many old apologetic stereotypes (the indifferent Buddha versus the compassionate Jesus, or however such commonplaces should be labeled) and think our way into a context appropriate to the matters at hand. Just how far Professor Küng has managed to do this in his "Christian Responses" and where one would have to carry the thinking one step further is something readers will have to judge for themselves. When I was putting the final touches to my presentations, I had not yet seen the greatly revised and expanded version of the "Christian Responses" and so could not take them into consideration. My own replies to Professor Küng's positions are based on an earlier stage of our exchange. As far as my own presentations are concerned, they have been primarily designed to provide the reader with factual information. The length of the presentations, which was stipulated in advance, as well as the necessity of covering the whole historical development of Buddhism, have inevitably led to a highly oversimplified picture of Buddhism and surely, too, to a subjective choice of facts and examples. Nonetheless, I hope that I have at least succeeded in outlining the teaching of the historical Buddha, as well as the essential aspects of its later development. And this, I hope, may make it a little easier to understand a world that many people still find strange. Understanding is the sine qua non for mutual appreciation and thus for the ecumenical dialogue we all want to see.

2. *Hans Küng:* A Christian Response

We have traversed together the path laid out in Heinz Bechert's presentations from primitive Buddhism through Shrāvakayāna to Mahāyāna, while—as in the responses to Islam and Hinduism—interweaving historical and systematical methods, because only in this way could the prerequisites for a fruitful dialogue be met.

ONCE AGAIN, ON THE METHOD OF DIALOGUE

Our encounter with Buddhist thought, as presented by Heinz Bechert, has shown how complex the whole discussion is. The previously described change in Christian theology and church is witness to the fact that the days are finally gone when Westerners could keep Buddhism at a distance by invoking the "yellow peril" and similar specters conjured up by anxious bigotry. Gone, too, are the days when one could say one's piece only by putting down the other side, setting a positive image of Jesus in opposition to a negative one of the Buddha.

Serious Christian study of Buddhism, to which I have been able to refer again and again, has by now freed itself as far as possible from "hypocrisy," from emotional judgments and prejudices. Even official Catholic Church doctrine, as we have seen, no longer denies that non-Christians can have high moral ideals and that Buddhists can have authentic religion. Unless each side takes the other seriously, there is no sense in talking about authentic dialogue. My responses, too, were aimed at overcoming "old apologetic stereotypes," such as the "indifferent Buddha" and the "compassionate Jesus." That is why, after an extensive analysis of their common features, I pointed up, without any bias, the difference between the "sympathetic Buddha" and the sacrificially "suffering Jesus."

Gone as well, of course, are the days when, for their part, Buddhists could dismiss in advance any discussion of the Absolute with a reference to distorted Christian images of God ("omnipotence," "divine dictatorship"). And the days are gone when the Buddhists could proclaim their superiority to Christianity with a reference to their "more rational," "more scientific," philosophical system.

My responses endeavored to show that in Buddhism, too, from the time when it first appeared in India, the question of the Absolute has remained passionately alive and has been taken quite seriously by influential schools and representatives of Buddhist thought. This is a fact that numerous competent Western authorities on Buddhism today have fully recognized. I myself, in the difficult process of thinking my way into the religious world of Buddhism, have been able to experience that even at the most difficult point of the question about the Absolute and salvation, apparently immovable boundary stones can turn into the bridge piers of expanding communication—so long as one does not, like the apologists on both sides—simply plant oneself down on them.

As a Christian theologian, I necessarily—and willingly—set out from a "quite specific, clearly defined Christian theological position." This is not, of course, a random stance, but a historically and critically responsible one, supported by modern exegesis and the history of dogma. Despite my sense of religious identity—something one naturally expects from one's Buddhist dialogue partner as well—my responses were as self-critical as I could make them, open-minded, inclusively oriented, and not in favor of any sort of false "assimilation."

In the face of the "diverse historical forms of Buddhism," it was characteristic of the method I used that

1. In my very first response I went back to the origins—to both the historical Gautama and the historical Jesus—and critically measured every new form of Buddhism (and Christianity) against those origins; while at the same time

2. I did not dismiss any of the great historical forms of Buddhism (such as the "Buddhism of faith") in advance, but tried to understand them all in "their own internal context," to acknowledge, within the framework of a theory of paradigms, their inner logic and therefore their right to exist as Buddhism; in such a way, however, that

3. I could avoid playing the different forms of Buddhism off against one another and grinding an apologetical ax by using "whichever one best suited the question at hand"; so that, on the contrary

4. I might conduct a dialogue with every important form of Buddhism, from early Buddhism to the three vehicles all the way to Zen and Shin (Jōdo Shinshū), referring along the way to the various Christian paradigms.

In the process, I have taken Heinz Bechert's picture of Buddhism very seriously indeed and compared it with Christian positions. But a dialogue that thought of Buddhism exclusively in a Western intellectual fashion as a "religion of reason" would surely miss the reality and dynamism of concretely lived Buddhism as Heinz Bechert himself has described it. We have already heard, in his third presentation, about a further "turning of the wheel of doctrine," and I mentioned that I would return to the problems posed not only by Tantrism but also by Zen and Amida Buddhism. This will give us an opportunity to go into the questions of the way to salvation, its means and mediator, of Buddhology and Christology of redemption through one's own or another's power, and—first of all—of the meaning of sexuality and meditation in religion.

THE PARADIGM CHANGE FROM THE GREAT VEHICLE TO THE DIAMOND VEHICLE

We have heard a good deal about those forms of Buddhism found today particularly in Nepal, Tibet, and (in a nonerotic variety) Japan that can be called *Vajrayāna, the Diamond Vehicle:* an esoteric, occult Buddhism, in which magic of all sorts, veiled language, and, in its Shaktist manifestations, sexual practices, play a major role. Is this a "third turning of the wheel of doctrine"? This question would seem to have not yet been satisfactorily answered, from a historical and systematic standpoint. But there is no gainsaying the fact that five hundred years after the turn to Mahāyāna, about the middle of the first Christian millennium, a new major paradigm change occurred. Was it still Buddhism? Yes, but "mounted" in a new "fabric" *(tantra)* of religious practices and doctrines. Because with this Vajrayāna paradigm, which as always had been prepared for in many ways in the preceding paradigm of Mahāyāna, what happened was that:

- Pre-Buddhist Indian notions such as reincarnation and karma, and practices such as meditation, were kept.
  But the sharp distinction from a now resurgent Hinduism was blurred (probably also as a defensive measure) in favor of a rapprochement that has often been called the "re-Hinduization" of Buddhism. Instead of being entirely oriented to mental concentration, absorption, and clear-sightedness, yoga in its Tantric phase became oriented to the body of the individual—not a piece of transient flesh, but the place for higher knowledge.

- The "refuge in the Buddha" was still kept. But: the connection between the sacred scriptures and the historical Buddha Gautama, essential even in Mahāyāna (although often feigned), is abandoned and one's own conception is boldly connected to the figure of a mythological Buddha.
- The "refuge in the Dharma" was still kept.
  But ritual, magic, the occult, and miracles—previously tolerated, at most, on the fringes—now moved into the center. Magical sacred formulas (mantras), shapes (mandalas), gestures (mudrās), and rituals (including dances) became key means of salvation, designed as a shorter way to achieving union with the Buddha, who is the Absolute.
- The "refuge in the sangha" was still kept.
  But the order was broken up into smaller, esoteric groups of initiates (yogis) that were unconditionally subordinated to a spiritual leader (guru), that worshipped a deity or bodhisattva as their patron and formed the core of public cultic communities. Their ideal was no longer the monk-saint (arhat) of Shrāvakayāna, who seeks salvation for himself, nor even the saint turned toward the world (bodhisattva) of Mahāyāna, who seeks above all to save his fellow men and women, but the saint magician *(siddha)* equipped with supernatural powers, who attains his goal often in a miraculous manner. Here trance experiences had more reality than historical facts, persons, places, and actions.

The fundamental tension built into Buddhism from the very beginning, between monastic and lay piety, which had already had a powerful impact on Mahāyāna, proved in this case to be a factor of disintegration. No doubt, the criticism voiced by Tantrists (such as the wandering Tantric monk Tsi-lu-pa) against traditional Buddhist monasticism and organized religion was justified. There was something to be said against pious posturing, self-righteous virtuousness, prudery, academic hairsplitting, and empty rituals. Nevertheless, the critical observer may well wonder whether the message of the Buddha has merely been translated into another framework, or paradigm, here, or whether vital parts of it have not been abandoned. It is especially hard for the Christian theologian to discuss the second main form of the diamond vehicle, Shaktist Tantrism with its orientation toward female power or divinity, when European scholars are divided in their judgment of it between moral indignation and amoral justification.

RELIGION AND SEXUALITY

No one could fail to see that all the Tantric systems, and the Shaktist practices especially, are extraordinarily alien to Christians, more alien than anything we have met thus far in Buddhism or Hinduism. The following brief comments will have to suffice here.

1. A Christian evaluation of this Eastern "occult doctrine" should *not* have its source in *prejudice against the body and sex.* Sexuality belongs to man's creaturely character, and must be interpreted, not depreciated, by theologians. Bourgeois Western Christianity was and is vulnerable to a kind of Stoic-Gnostic-Manichaean hostility toward the body, sex, and women. This antagonism was passed along to Western Christianity above all by the older Augustine (sexual pleasure allowed only for the purpose of procreation) and medieval and modern popes (like Innocent III: "Who does not know that even the consummation of marriage never takes place without the lasciviousness of the flesh, the flames of lewdness, and the loathsomeness of lust?") *(De contemptu mundi,* Chapter IV). Down through the centuries, both celibate Catholic and puritanical Protestant clergymen have tried to this day (see the campaign against contraception) to impose a rigorous/prudish sexual morality in Europe and America, not to mention the "missionary regions" of Asia, Africa, and the Pacific. As far as possible, this ethic repressed and suppressed all unselfconscious joy in the sensual, the corporeal, the sexual.

Yet, in their original religious tradition, Christians have points of departure from which interpersonal and even sexual experience need not be religiously tabooed, and from which the language of the human body can be interpreted in the symbolic language of religion. Man *and* woman are made in God's image. Erotic love between man and wife in the Old Testament is not only taken for granted but poetically glorified in the Song of Songs. For Jesus, the fact that man and woman become one flesh is not at all demonic, but the will of the Creator; in the Letter to the Ephesians it even becomes a symbol of the relation between Christ and the Church. Dealing with Shaktism can, in any event, make Christians freshly aware that there is no need for human sexuality to be screened off by a barrier of archaic fear, but, rather, that—particularly when it makes possible a deep interpersonal encounter—it bears the character of a sign, pointing to the experience of something absolute. The basic Christian attitude toward sex will move between two extreme poles: that of the Buddhist monk, who radically separates sex and the supreme happiness of nirvāna, and thus forgoes all sexual activity, and that of the Tantrist, for whom, in the act of sexual consummation, "self and world coincide in the unity of the Absolute." The Christian will neither disavow sexuality nor absolutize it, but interpret its peculiar felicity as an intimation of a more encompassing and permanent happiness.

2. The highly positive meaning of the *female principle* in Shaktist Tantrism—we see here the emergence, as in Marian piety, of a primal need

for the female archetype—can make Christians aware how much the feminine has been repressed and suppressed in Christian teaching and ecclesiastical practice, how thoroughly Christianity has become a patriarchal religion. This will challenge Christians to "reread" their own traditions, their rigid linguistic codes, their ground-in prejudices and practices. This should not lead us into speaking of a "self-division of the Absolute" into masculine and feminine forces. The starting point of all Christian theology today, in an age of feminist theology, must be that "God" is not subsumed under a sort of *principle of masculinity*, but that "he" at once embraces and transcends, "sublates" masculinity and femininity in a kind of *coincidentia oppositorum*. More concretely, if Christians continue to use the name "Father" for God, then they must become conscious of the one-sidedness of such symbolic language. If we use such symbols in "second naïveté," then we shall be aware that "Father" can no longer be understood as an expression for God's masculinity, but must be metaphorically decoded as meaning helpful strength and intimate security, in a sense that includes motherliness. According to the New Testament, the man Jesus of Nazareth reveals not God's masculinity but his humanity, his love of human beings, *philanthropia*. It is theologically relevant that God became man (not male).

The American theologian Rosemary Radford Ruether is right to stress that:

> God is both male and female and neither male nor female. One needs inclusive language for God that draws on the images and experiences of both genders. This inclusiveness should not become more abstract. Abstractions often conceal androcentric assumptions and prevent the shattering of the male monopoly on God-language, as in "God is not male. He is Spirit." Inclusiveness can happen only by naming God/dess in female as well as in male metaphors. (pg. 67)

3. *Hence all of Shaktist Tantrism may not simply be written off as a sexual cult* or even as sexual dissipation. In many cases, these are profound religious systems and practices, which affirm sexuality as a creative force of human life and attempt to incorporate sexual communication, as the deepest form of human communication, into religion. As we learn from the important studies by Mircea Eliade (*Le Yoga*, 1960) and Agehananda Bharati (*The Tantric Tradition*, 1965), the linking of yoga and sexuality in (originally Hindu) Tantrism aims not at the mere satisfaction of temporary "needs," but at the sublimation of sexuality: at salvation and union with the Absolute. Furthermore, we should not forget that these cults come from the socially disadvantaged classes and thus seek to give religious expression not just to lay piety generally, but to the often suppressed strata and dimensions of humanity. In all this, the equal status of women, like the irrelevance of caste, plays a role, and a socially significant one at that. Hence we should not deny that *authentic religion* can be found in these cults that are so alien to Christianity.

4. Historians remind us that the spread of Tantrism in the sixth and seventh centuries coincides with the decline of Indian Buddhism. The connection between these two developments will have to be examined more carefully. It was undoubtedly external persecution through a deliberate policy of extermination by the Huns in the sixth century, by the Shivaite kings in the seventh, and by the Muslims from the eighth century onward that gravely weakened the Buddha's teaching in the country of its origin in the eleventh century and finally stamped it out in the thirteenth. But it was also the increasing signs of decadence in the Buddhist monasteries, which kept getting richer in lands and servants. And it would be interesting to investigate the *negative effects of Tantrism,* as noted, for example, in the careful, critical study by R. C. Mitra, *The Decline of Buddhism in India* (1954). The key question here is, Was there a

CONTRADICTION TO THE BUDDHA'S TEACHING?

In his presentation, Heinz Bechert emphasizes that Shaktism, by using magic and alcohol and activating the forces of sex, was not merely an adaptation of one and the same Buddhism to altered cultural conditions, but *contradicted the teaching of the Buddha himself,* who had demanded abstinence of the monks, especially in the realm of sex. The facts that Mahāyāna had in many ways replaced the historical Buddha with a timeless Buddha-principle and that there was no touchstone for new developments may have had an especially powerful impact on Tantrism. In any event, we can only agree with the judgment of Helmuth von Glasenapp: "It is clear that in this case ideas and rites came to the fore that by their nature are altogether foreign to ancient Buddhism, that, indeed, turned its views upside down. For according to the Pāli canon Buddha opposed all esoteric doctrines and preached an ascetical path to salvation. For this reason, Vajrayāna has never lacked opponents from the traditional Buddhist camp." *(Pfad zur Erleuchtung,* 1956, p. 14)

How do things stand with a Buddhism (Christianity) in which the Buddha (Christ) and *his* teaching are no longer the key authority? What does it mean when Shaktist Tantrism "turned into something radically different" from the teaching of the Buddha? Because it *does* contradict essential features of monastic life that the Buddha says should be striven for. It reinterprets the Buddha's highly intellectual enlightenment into an orgiastic sexual act of liberation from servitude to religious institutions as well as to moral and ritual conventions. All this can be seen in the hagiography (long kept secret and translated into English only in 1980) of the most famous Tibetan saint and Tantric master, Drupka Künleg, from the sixteenth century. Can "the dissolute life and blasphemous songs" of this "Holy Fool" (to quote the title of the 1982 German edition) really be, as the editor, Keith Dowman, boasts, "an excellent means" of passing on "the tradition of Tibetan Buddhism"? (pp. 11–12)

The question of a criterion for discriminating fresh developments arises here with respect to both abuses *and* uses. To what extent is all this still Buddhist? Or, if it came from popular cults, to what extent was it ever Buddhist? One does not have to be a victim of Western-Christian prejudice to wonder: Is the way not being paved for sexual libertinism, promiscuity, and amoral egoism that makes one's partner an object (all of which are welcome to many secular Westerners), if "marginal phenomena" such as every sort of sexual practice and magical sleight of hand can become the "central way of salvation"? If they can appear to be so totally disjoined from what originally stood at the center of the Buddhist way: moral living, ascesis, knowledge, meditation? However much women may justifiably be getting equal rights as partners, is one supposed to experience the bliss of the Absolute and the highest salvation in the sacred sexual union (with no ethical corrective), as some gurus in the West proclaim?

For all the talk about initiation and preparation, about sublimation of sexuality, the necessary degree of perfection, and the supposedly already realized Buddha nature, can we stifle the critical questions that arise? At this point, Buddhist critics raise their voices too. Christians and the immense majority of Buddhists agree that an ethical order is needed to regulate biological drives, that sex in principle belongs in marriage (which should be entered into and lived as a partnership) and not in cultic practice, especially not in cultic practice with interchangeable partners, in which the misuse of religion for sexual purposes and the misuse of sex for religious purposes is almost unavoidable, as is clear from the widespread phenomenon of sacred prostitution.

While we reflect on the misuse of religion and sexuality, which was and is possible in all religions, the basic question poses itself once more for all religions: Can the religious end justify any means? Is everything permitted in the service of religious devotion? May a religion command something that debases, harms, or even destroys human beings?

No form of Buddhism would seem to be so problematic as this esoteric-erotic Buddhism, and not just from the standpoint of Christianity and the origins of Buddhism, but also from the perspective of the function of religion for the overall welfare of man. To what extent Shaktist Buddhism is in need of demythologizing, demystification, and humanization is at any rate an open question. As emphatically as possible, I would like to raise here the question of the *criteria for mutual criticism* in dialogue between religions.

But this criticism should not be exaggerated: Shaktism is only a marginal phenomenon in Buddhism. It would be completely misguided to identify Tibetan Buddhism simply with its Shaktist form. Alongside the "left hands" (Shaktists), there are also the "right hands"; alongside the Red Sect, the official Yellow Sect. And one need only look into *The Practice and Theory of Tibetan Buddhism* (eds. L. Söpa and J. Hopkins, 1976) and *Tantra in Tibet* (ed. J. Hopkins, 1977), both with introductions by the fourteenth Dalai Lama, to find how thoroughly "right-handed" Buddhism is oriented toward meditation.

We must now turn to "meditation Buddhism," which is of the greatest theoretical and practical significance, and which Heinz Bechert treated only briefly.

MEDITATION BUDDHISM

Unlike the world of the sciences, where mathematics and experimentation can with time compel us to replace an old paradigm, in the domain of religion old paradigms do not necessarily disappear. Often they survive for centuries, side by side with the newer ones, in their traditionalist forms, although after submitting to all sorts of adjustments. Every treatment of history takes more or less for granted the continuance of the old (which lives on unobtrusively) and concentrates, of necessity, on more recent developments.

Tantrism represents a new evolutionary form of Buddhism on Indian and Nepalese-Tibetan soil. But outside of India, in China, at about roughly the same time, there were two new developments, two paradigms, that would eventually carry the day in Southeast Asia: the Buddhism of faith (Amida Buddhism), which I shall discuss later, and meditation Buddhism—Chinese *Ch'an*, Japanese *Zen*—which began to take shape, along with Tantra, in the second half of the first millennium A.D., flourished in China from the eighth to the thirteenth centuries, and in the early-thirteenth century made its way into Japan.

From the very first, Buddhism has been characterized not so much by specific liturgical practices or a specific philosophical system, as by the *exercise of meditation*. Meditation was supposed to lead the individual, mired in delusion, hatred, and greed—in a word, self-seeking—to attentiveness, recollection, and liberation of the spirit, to the four levels of absorption, and so to the redeeming wisdom that all things—including the person meditating—are conditioned in their coming to be and passing away, insubstantial and thus sorrowful, and that freedom from all desire and attachment will also bring about the end of suffering. There can be no wisdom without mental concentration. This sort of concentration, however, was not to enrich the mind with ideas, but to empty it of all ideas. The best meditation is the meditation with no object.

From the beginning, meditation belonged to the Buddha's "Eightfold Path" as a means for intellectual self-discipline. Nevertheless, even in

Theravāda countries, such as Sri Lanka, meditation has faded into the background, with Buddhist teachings, rites, and merits holding center stage. Likewise in Thailand and Burma, though meditation is still as highly praised as ever, the majority of the monks hardly ever practice it.

That meditation returns to the center in Zen is revealed by this word itself. As we heard in the exposition, the word "Zen" means nothing else than "meditation." Unlike Amidism, the second main current in Chinese-Japanese Buddhism, Zen stresses the direct, immediate experience and enlightenment of the individual person, and in so doing it goes back to a primal aspect of Buddhism.

Actually there are definite parallels between Chinese Zen and its contemporary, Indian Tantra, insofar as both are directed against traditional Buddhism. But whereas Tantrism can be thought of as a new, *syncretistic paradigm*, that has assimilated every conceivable feature of Hinduism and various popular cults, we can consider Zen a reformative paradigm, intent on *concentration, simplification, and interiorization*. Of course, given Buddhism's faint historical consciousness, we should not expect anything like the Protestant Reformers' solemn cry "Back to the origins." Instead, the individual is to become conscious of his Buddha-nature here and now. But there is no mistaking the presence of the following tendencies in Zen:

● Against all exaggerated traditional reverence for the Buddha and the usual misunderstanding of his role ("If you meet the Buddha, kill him"); a new *effort to take the original Buddha seriously* as a guide, explicitly looking to him past the legendary figure of the Indian monk Bodhidharma (beginning of the sixth century?) and the other Zen patriarchs.

● Against all overrating of philosophical abstractions and subtleties, rites and images, against all intellectualization and systematization in countless commentaries and glosses, against all complicated yet useless cosmological and psychological theories, a return to the *simple, spiritual teaching* that aims to point out a practical way of experience, of meditation practice and toward enlightenment. The individual reaches enlightenment after gradual quiet preparation (as in the Sōtō Zen school) or quite suddenly (as in the Rinzai school).

● Against all the "ecclesiastical" petrifaction and all the "bonzist" clericalism of traditional Buddhism, which could no longer produce any arhats (Theravāda) or bodhisattvas (Mahāyāna), *an opening up of the Buddhist community:* Enlightenment can be, and often is, reached in this life by lay people, sometimes in unexpected moments and amid the ordinary doings of everyday life. Everyone can become conscious of the Buddha-nature dwelling in the depths of each person. The ideal here is not, as in Tantra, the magician *(siddha)*, but the *rōshi*, who leads a life no different from the common man and who has nonetheless experienced enlightenment, the "emptiness" of all things: in the world and yet distanced from the world, at once passive and active.

In this paradigm, then, the basic tension between monastic and lay piety has also shifted in favor of the layman, even though Zen, to a certain extent, did not abandon its elitism until after World War II. The novelty of Zen lay in the fact that the monks were no longer supposed to beg, but to work. Especially new was the hard physical discipline that everyone had to submit to in Zen meditation: not only sitting *(zazen)* in the lotus position, deep breathing, turning off all thoughts, but also the harsh supervision of the Zen master, beatings with a stick, and then the astonishing stories, obscure sayings and puzzles (Japanese *kōan*) that one might meditate on for years, such as the one cited by Heinz Bechert.

Another of these kōans says: "Where do you see nothingness? When do you see nothingness? How old is nothingness? . . ." But, especially in Japanese Zen, "nothingness" or "emptiness" should not be understood nihilistically, but, rather, as a description of an indeterminable ultimate reality. Zen trains the individual so that he or she can overcome the dualism of the ego and the Absolute and so attain emptiness, the Absolute, as the Kyoto school has made clear once more in our time. Buddhism teaches that the excited, anxious, alienated human mind is a storm-tossed sea in whose waves the moon and stars can leave no reflection. The mind needs to calm down through exercises in which compulsive activity, and in particular discursive thought, winds down. It needs intense concentration (Sanskrit *samādhi*), so that it can finally come to enlightenment (Sanskrit *bodhi*, Japanese *satori*). In all this, the danger of hallucinations (Japanese *makyō* = illusion) and nervous breakdowns (Zen madness) cannot be ruled out. Those who practice Zen know that enlightenment may well surprise them amid the daily routine, but that one often has to wait in vain for it year after year. In keeping with original Buddhism, therefore, Zen puts all its trust in individual experience, in *"one's own power"* (*jiriki*). And yet enlightenment is not something that can be produced simply and methodically. Zen maintains that anyone who tries to force enlightenment will miss it. Only the person without self-will, someone not imprisoned in ego, will finally reach it.

In a critical evaluation it should not be overlooked that Zen's talk about the sublation of all contraries in "emptiness" often promotes a sort of immunization against any kind of criticism by refusing to supply precise information about its own teaching and activity (someone who says "nothing" can't be criticized). This can have disastrous effects, especially in ethics. As impressive as Zen discipline (and the ideal of imperturbability) may be, it can, if the ethical dimension is neglected, be used for every conceivable purpose, not least of all for military ones (reckless heroism, moral indifference, and docility). What, then, is the basic attitude of the Christian toward the "essence" of Zen, to meditation, which is so frequently contrasted with Christian prayer?

MEDITATION OR PRAYER?

There is, of course, in the concrete religious life of humanity, a broad spectrum of religious postures and activities. Still, we can distinguish *two basic forms of "prayer"* (in the broadest sense), corresponding to the two basic forms of piety: prophetic prayer, and mystical prayer (meditation). Relying upon Friedrich Heiler's classical work *Prayer,* we shall now distinguish sharply between prophetic prayer in its biblical form and mystical prayer, or better, meditation, confronting them with each other. We have already become acquainted with this in the context of Hinduism, but we were not able to deal with it there.

How does *prayer* occur in the *Bible?* In the Bible, the prayer of the pious (and the not so pious) occurs in an amazingly uncomplicated, straightforward fashion: in the middle of life and from its depths—a naive "outpouring of the heart" in unpretentious, unbroken realism. Everything is wholly and completely oriented to God: requests to be heard, for help, compassion, grace, salvation for oneself, for others, for the people. A freely unfolding act of petition, thanks, and praise.

But however much, in the course of history, biblical prayer has been fixed in verbal formulas, liturgically stylized, and sometimes even coupled with the performance of ascetical acts:

> The Bible never speaks of methods, systems, or the psychological techniques of prayer;
> it has no stages of prayer worth mentioning,
> no uniform treatment of religious experience;
> no psychological reflections on prayer, despite all the prophetic criticism of prayer and sacrifice,
> no self-analyses or ascetical exertions to attain certain states of soul.
> Instead of this, there is a naive, unreflecting "conversation with God": expressions of faith, hope, and love, of thanksgiving, praise, and petition—with great individual variety and diversity.

How does *mystical prayer, or meditation,* differ? The meditation of the mystical person takes place in detachment from the world and one's own passion, in turning inward. It is supposed to lead the individual methodically and systematically to ultimate reality—whether understood as "fullness" (in Hinduism) or "emptiness" (in Buddhism): from the outer/sensory to the inner/mental universe, a sinking of the self into the Absolute or entering into nirvāna, a fulfillment or an extinction. All this happens in an ordered progress, or, as we would say in traditional Western categories:

> first, voluntary *concentration*, often strained and brought about with various physical and psychic means;
>
> next, relaxed, passively moved, self-forgetting *contemplation;*
>
> finally, rapturous or oblivious *ecstasy*, in which the individual loses himself in the immeasurable abundance of the Absolute or in the eternal rest of nirvāna.

But, needless to say, as has already been suggested, these two types of prayer have not been handed down in a state of genetic purity. Through *crossbreeding* of mystical piety with either primitive folk religions or creedal piety, numerous *different modes of mystical religion* have come into existence in the East and in the West: warmly affective or coolly unemotional, erotic or detached and intellectual, cultic or noncultic, imaginative and poetic or rationally reflective, impersonal/monistic or personal/theistic, and so forth. The common ground of the various mystical modes (despite the often personalistic vocabulary) is nevertheless unmistakable. Many elements of this Eastern piety recur in the Christian world: in German, Dutch, French, and Spanish mysticism.

For all the crossbreeding and mixed forms, though, the basic difference separating biblical and mystical prayer should not be smoothed over. If we look in particular at the way the *New Testament* speaks of prayer and at the way it is practiced here, we can come to only one conclusion: The attitudes implicit in mystical prayer can be important for the Christian, but they can never claim to be normative. No doubt, the *"ladder of prayer,"* with its various rungs (highly prized in Christian monasticism, recommended, taught, and practiced in traditional seminary education and retreats) will always have a useful psychological and pedogogical function: By describing and analyzing the individual phases of prayer, people praying can continually sharpen the vision of themselves and others, can practice self-criticism, can orient themselves entirely to the Absolute. But if we take the New Testament as our critical standard, such a scheme of prayer will never have any sort of definitive validity for Christians. And however much we may admire the great Teresa of Ávila, a brilliant woman who belongs with the most important mystics in the history of religion, neither in the Old nor the New Testament is there any ideal of inner prayer or "prayer of the heart." We find in the Bible no summons to observe, describe, and analyze mystical states and experiences, no ladder of mystical prayer leading up to ecstasy, no stress on any prayer that presupposes special religious gifts.

All too often, religious educators with mystical spiritual ideals (but without the Zen Buddhist sense for beauty—in flower arrangement, say, or gardening, calligraphy, painting, dance, and poetry) have done spiritual violence to people of good will who were neither talented nor interested in such prayer. All too often, they have inoculated their charges with guilt feelings and made praying difficult or driven them away from prayer altogether. Some fundamental rules: Christians can concern themselves with the more demanding forms of prayer, but they *do not have to.* Under no circumstances ought such prayer be made the distinguishing mark of Christianity or even the esoteric specialty of a spiritual elite wishing to elevate itself above "run of the mill" prayers. Most people would be helped more by the recommendation of a few words of thanks and petition before meals or going to sleep, in the spirit of Jesus (". . . do not heap up empty phrases as the Gentiles do . . . ," Mt 6:7), than by impossible demands for profound meditation. Mystical prayer is *a* charism—only one among many and not the highest. It can contribute to the following of Christ, which culminates in love, but it can also become an end in itself and lead away from it.

CHRISTIAN MEDITATION AND BUDDHIST PRAYER

And yet we should not heighten the opposition between the prophetic and the mystical so that they radically exclude each other. We have seen, in connection with Hinduism, that a mutual exchange and enrichment is altogether possible and has been prepared by the varied intercourse between prophetical and mystical piety in the religious history of mankind. From a more profound Christian perspective, one attains fullness only through an emptying, life only through dying, new being only through self-sacrifice. And so *convergence* is very much possible in personal piety as well, for Christians practice Eastern meditation techniques, and Buddhists engage in forms of prayer that Christians find quite familiar. This means:

1. There is not only Buddhist meditation, there is *Christian meditation* too. Eastern meditation, unless it degenerates, as yoga has in the West nowadays, into a kind of therapeutic technique for unburdening oneself psychically or socially, can be a critical catalyst for Westerners and Christians, too. It can help them recognize their own one-sidedness and, as many Christian authors, from Thomas Merton *(Zen and the Birds of Appetite,* 1968) to Hans Waldenfels *(Meditation—Ost und West,* 1975), have stressed, rediscover forgotten or buried elements of their own Christian tradition (Christian religious communities especially will find plenty of work in that area for themselves and others):

- As opposed to falsely understood self-renunciation and self-denial (a misreading of the Cross), a new *effort for human wholeness and wellness* (openness, naturalness, simplicity, human warmth).
- As opposed to making piety too intellectual and theoretical (separation of theology and piety since the time of High Scholasticism), a

new practical training (orthopraxy) in the spiritual life (not by teachers, but "masters," i.e., practitioners, of that life).

● As opposed to an all too rarefied "spirituality" and a "cure of souls" that does not care for bodies, the awareness of the connection of all existing things and a new stress on *corporality*, by paying attention to bodily posture (the lotus position as an expression of repose and intense recollection), as well as through an effort to control and regulate breathing.

● As opposed to the Western (and modern Japanese) diffusion of the spirit in the superficiality, hustle-and-bustle, hectic busywork, and inner dismemberment of everyday life, a quieting of the mind and a new concentration through an *intuitive descent into the depths of one's own spirit* (no more rationally solvable "Puzzles"), an illuminating and expanding of consciousness.

● As opposed to all the constant talk and action entangled in the web of things, a new practice of *silence* and *waiting* that is free from thoughts, feelings, and wishes, that learns to dispense even with words and images, so as to be free from everything, to reach oneself within the silence, to attain the happy void, selflessness, and so the Absolute, to which man must be awakened through enlightenment.

Thus Eastern meditation in general and Zen in particular can be summed in one great programmatic word: *freedom*. Freedom from oneself in self-forgetfulness. Freedom from every physical and mental compulsion, from every authority that wants to interpose itself between the individual and his immediate experience and enlightenment. Freedom, too, from the Buddha, from the sacred scriptures, freedom—to be totally consistent—also from Zen, which is and remains the way, not the goal. Only in complete inner freedom can man come to enlightenment in this life or afterward.

After all this, it should come as no surprise that Christians, who feel regimented, even in their prayer life, by church dogma, inflexible rules, and the aftereffects of religious "obedience school," have come to see such content-free thinking, such objectless meditation, such blissfully experienced emptiness, as true liberation. Here they find inner rest, greater tranquillity, better self-understanding, and a finer sensibility for all of reality. But the converse is also true:

2. There is not only Christian prayer, but *Buddhist prayer* as well. This is where concretely lived Buddhism differs from pure Buddhist doctrine. The forms of Buddhist piety are far richer than the guides to Buddhist meditation would lead us to believe. Hans Waldenfels, a Catholic theologian and expert on Buddhism, has convincingly shown how much variety there is in Buddhist forms of prayer: "1. There are forms of petitionary prayer that Buddhists themselves rightly feel are in need of purification. 2. There are forms of praise, thanksgiving, and attention that betray a sense of mystery. This mystery can be present in the manner of the ineffable and the nameless or else in the manner of the 'messengers,' specific buddha and bodhisattva figures, including the historical figure of Nichiren. 3. There are cries of distress, of joy, and of happiness, which are signs of relief that one hopes for against all hope or of the happiness one has experienced, and that can perhaps be divined as 'sites' of divine activity. 4. This would lead to the conclusion that true prayer, in the sense of praise, thanks, and petition, should not be ruled out, so long as the mystery itself has not been arbitrarily thrust aside, thereby closing off access to God, who comes to meet human beings wherever they make a radical breakaway." *(Faszination des Buddhismus. Zum christlich-buddhistischen Dialog*, 1982, p. 111) All this will become much more intelligible as we now turn to the second main form of Chinese-Japanese Buddhism, which was likewise given only brief treatment in Heinz Bechert's exposition.

THE ONE BUDDHA AND THE MANY BUDDHAS

In the second half of the first millennium A.D., when the *paradigm change* to Tantrism occurred in India, Nepal, and Tibet, while in China the changeover to Zen was taking place, China also witnessed the emergence of *Pure Land*, or *Amitābha, Buddhism.* But where did this idea arise of the Buddha Amitābha, who promises to remove all the obstacles on the way to salvation through rebirth in a Pure Land—for the masses, who cannot, like the elite of religious aristocrats, withdraw from the world and devote themselves to meditation? What is this Pure Land, where even the ordinary person can prepare himself in peace for enlightenment? What is the source of this astonishingly democratic and (understandably) still highly popular religion, which resolves the ever-present tension between monastic and lay piety in Buddhist life?

We know from India of the *legend* of a king, and later monk, who took the name *Dharmākara* and made a *vow*, in the face of human suffering, to become a Buddha—but not to assume this title and enter nirvāna until he had the power to call into being a supernatural Pure Land, a Buddha-land of peace and happiness without suffering and passion, where believers, unhindered and unburdened by any karma, could ripen toward enlightenment and nirvāna. And so it allegedly happened. The monk reached the highest level of enlightenment, worked as a bodhisattva in boundless compassion, and collected an infinite supply of merit to make good on his promise.

In this way, the bodhisattva finally became one of the buddhas of the four compass points, who now presides over the Pure Land, that Western paradise of bliss a million billion Buddha-lands away, and who bears the name *Amitābha* (Sanskrit) or *Amida* (Japanese), which means a cosmic buddha of "immeasurable light," or *Amitāyus*, which means the buddha of "eternal life." In Mahāyāna, a cult grew up around this buddha, with an infinite number of statues and pictures. By the fifth century, it had its own school in China; by the ninth century, it was a pervasive current in all forms of Buddhism. In Mahāyāna, *not only as taught but as lived*—in the religion of rites, ceremonies, invocations, and customs, the Buddha often appears as a redeemer figure, as an object of all sorts of sensations, of worship, and of artistic representation, something, therefore, like a manifestation of the eternal dharma in the worldly sphere, a projection or manifestation of the Absolute on the lower level of the empirical and human. In popular religion, the trend naturally persists to look upon the Buddha, although he has entered nirvāna, as the highest of all the gods, and to view nirvāna itself as heaven.

Thus it is clear that, just as studying the philosophical works of Nicholas of Cusa would never suffice to get a grasp of Catholic Christianity, so our grasp of Mahāyāna Buddhism would be equally limited if we took Nāgārjuna's profound philosophical aphorisms as the only standard. It is certainly characteristic of Buddhism that it tries to find salvation for man through independently obtained enlightenment and thus through a new vision of man and the world, particularly by self-discipline and the practice of meditation. But there is more to Buddhism than meditation and ethos, more than philosophy and theology. There are also, though Western studies often neglect them, *liturgy, ritual, and cult*.

It is true that, given the *enormous evolutionary distance traveled from the historical Buddha to Amitābha Buddhism*, some questions quite spontaneously arise. How are we to explain

1. that creed and cult—originally more of a concession in Buddhism—now move right into the center with the believer's invocation and recitation of the name of the Amida buddha?

2. that "self-redemption"—as we saw at the end of the previous exposition—turned into "redemption from the outside," where the individual does not find salvation in himself but looks for it from a supernatural being?

3. that the historical Buddha is so overshadowed by another buddha, the buddha of immeasurable light (Amitābha, Amida) or eternal life (Amitāyus)—an evidently unhistorical, mythological figure (presumably from the Indo-Iranian frontier region)?

Are we really talking here about a new paradigm change, or has "Amidism," as Heinz Bechert insinuates, perhaps just ceased to be Buddhism? Can there be any sort of meaningful development from the historical Buddha Gautama to the supernatural-ideal Buddha Amida? Has not the Great Vehicle perhaps overturned? No, we see here, as we did not in Shaktist Tantrism, an essential continuity, so that perhaps there is no need to speak of "something radically different." "From Sakyamuni to Amitābha," Chinese Buddhologist Whalen Lai argues convincingly there is "a logic behind the Pure Land devotion." (Ching Feng 24:3, 156–74) What is this inner logic?

From the beginning, Shākyamuni, the historical Buddha Gautama, was more than an "arhat," a "saint," in relation to other "enlightened ones." As their teacher, he stood over them, his disciples and listeners— he was *the* Buddha. Originally, of course, there was only *one* Buddha in this one world of time and space. But it was part of the *logic of karma* that this one great Buddha life must have had many important *preexistences* (some counted 550). Thus, at an early date, the victorious present was projected back into the past, with the help of a whole series of life stories (*jātakas*), which were placed in the mouth of the Enlightened One himself.

Furthermore, in *Theravāda*, one came to be convinced that there must have been *other Buddhas before* the Buddha Gautama. Thus the idea developed of the six buddhas for the six epochs *before* Buddha Gautama. But Gautama, in the form of the young Brahman Sumedha, appears already as a pupil of the first buddha (Dīpankara = lamplighter = initiator of enlightenment). Here he makes his first vow to become a Buddha, and receives from Dīpankara the promise of his own future as a Buddha. From this "prehistoric" time forward he was on the way, a Bodhisattva until his enlightenment under the bodhi tree. He was an ideal that now took on increasing importance precisely because Gautama as *Bodhisattva* had collected so much positive karma, so many merits, that he could in the end fulfill his enormous responsibility as the *Buddha*.

In *Mahāyāna*, which in general turned more decisively toward the world and nature, humanity and secular life, Buddhist piety becomes still more oriented toward the bodhisattvas. Rather than enter nirvāna immediately, it is nobler to imitate the Buddha himself, who in his preexistences voluntarily stayed behind in samsāra to serve living creatures out of his great compassion. In this way, the wisdom-seekers of Shrāvkayāna became in Mahāyāna wise *and* compassionate. The bodhisattva who wishes to help all creatures in this world (man, animals, gods) becomes the great Mahāyāna ideal, which lay people can also follow: doing good *for another's sake*, accumulating merits that can be passed on to others. Even the Buddha, who had been worshipped from the earliest time in stupas (with relics), was thought not to have simply disappeared in parinirvāna, but to continue to live in a formless and sorrowless (because removed from samsāra) spirit-body. He is now above the law of karma, and from the abundance of his merits he can apply them for the benefit of others.

This notion of the transferability of merit is not as unfamiliar to

Christians as it first sounds, because Christian theological tradition includes the doctrine that believers can draw upon the "treasury of grace" accumulated through the deeds of Christ. We might also find a number of (somewhat simplified) *parallels between Christianity* and the teaching of the *three bodies of the Buddha* (earthly body, spiritual body, and dharma body), which came into existence in the context of the development I've just sketched. These parallels do not relate, as was often supposed, to the Trinity, but to Christology:

1. between the earthly/mortal Buddha (the coarse terrestrial body = nirmānakāya) and the earthly Jesus, who is likewise a teacher and a guide to salvation;

2. between the invisible/transcendent Buddha (the supernatural/rarefied body = sambhogakāya, or "body of bliss") and the exalted Christ, who according to Paul exists in a "spirit-body";

3. between the Buddha present in all things (the dharma principle or the Absolute itself = dharmakāya) and the eternal "Logos," which is "God" and was "made flesh" in Jesus of Nazareth.

The Christian-Buddhist parallel, I would venture, might be expressed as follows: The man Jesus (nirmānakāya) is at the same time the exalted Christ (sambhogakāya) and, as such, the manifestation or revelation of the Absolute, God himself (dharmakāya). It would naturally be of little use for Christian-Buddhist dialogue simply to note structural convergences only with respect to ideas (and to cite them only where they support one's own position). These ideas are, after all, the project of a long, complex tradition, with all its social and cultural conditions, and for all their continuity they have come a long way from their origin. Here, too, one would have to ask the hard but unavoidable question about the original criterion.

Whatever one thinks of these parallels, the convergences between Christian theology and the basic concepts of Japanese Amidism are still more astonishing. Even in China the Amitābha Amida Buddha was considered by many the chief Buddha. Some Japanese looked upon him as the higher and ultimately the highest Buddha, who—and here is food for thought—becomes identified with the highest reality. It is amazing how this form of Japanese Buddhism, in traveling the way to salvation, affirms the principle of "by faith alone." The Indian religion of grace, discussed earlier in the context of Hinduism, now finds a parallel or even a continuation in the Far Eastern "religion of faith."

THE BUDDHISM OF FAITH

Chinese Pure Land Buddhism took on an extra depth dimension and achieved its definitive elaboration as a new Buddhist paradigm in Japanese Shin or Pure Land Buddhism, especially through the *"Pure Land True School"* (Japanese: Jōdo Shinshū). This school, which, beside Zen Buddhism, is often overlooked in Europe, has today the greatest number of followers among the Buddhists of Japan. It originated in a time of social and religious crisis during the Japanese Middle Ages, in the militaristic Kamakura period. The actual founder of this radical school is considered to be Shōnin (= the saint) *Shinran* (1173–1262), a contemporary of Thomas Aquinas, who was introduced by his teacher, Hōnen (1133–1212), to belief in Amida Buddha and to the practice of reciting the Buddha's name as the sole means of salvation.

Shinran gave theological expression to the new paradigm of Buddhism and initiated its practice. It included not only a fresh interpretation of the whole Buddhist perspective and of its central concepts, but also a reshaping of popular piety and the lifestyle of the Buddhist clergy (abolition of celibacy and vegetarianism). "Total individual responsibility" (R. Gombrich) for salvation proved in the long run too hard to bear. As the Christian monk Martin Luther would learn centuries later, the monk Shinran found through painful experience that performing many works of traditional piety did not provide him the certainty of salvation, and he broke with monastic tradition. In despair over his incapacity and fearing for his salvation, Shinran left the monastery on Mount Hiei, near Kyoto, after twenty years. He was persecuted by the order; he married, founded a family, and propagated the teaching of the Pure Land, first among the peasants in eastern Japan, but ultimately he made his base in Kyoto once more. What were his main concerns?

The "Four Noble Truths" of the Buddha Gautama are valid for Shin Buddhism, too; but their total configuration, the paradigm, is very different. There are surprising *parallels* between Shinran's teaching and the *Protestant* (often enough Catholic, too, nowadays) *attitude of faith*—surprising not least of all for theologians who think in exclusively Christian terms, such as Karl Barth *(Church Dogmatics,* 1948, I/2, 370 ff.). One should not, however, immediately reach for such Christian theological categories as "sin" and "grace." In contrast to the classical Buddhist doctrine that the individual can effect salvation on his *own power (jiriki)*—without a merciful God, without a saint to intercede or a priest to sacrifice—Shinran is convinced, on the basis of one existential experience

- that man is a weak, imperfect creature, forever doubting, ensnared in his passions, and subject to karma;
- that he is incapable of redeeming himself and overcoming his suffering on his own;
- that he—whether man or woman, priest or lay person, educated or illiterate—can attain salvation through *the power of another* (Japanese *tariki),* only on the strength of *faith.*

Given this situation, how does the Amida Buddha help men and women to salvation? If the average person is in fact too weak and his own strength inadequate, there remains one possibility: *to trust the promises of Amida Buddha* completely and thus rely on *"the power of another,"* believing that the Amida Buddha can save even the most insignificant creature, if it only trusts and believes in him. For Amida's promise applies to everyone, without regard to person, to the extent that they believe in the power of this promise, in the "power of another." And in fact, this offers hope precisely for those people who had previously shown no gift or had no opportunity for enlightenment in a monastic context, the ordinary people, indeed for people with the wrong frame of mind and false ideas, the misled and the hopeless. By believing in the power of this promise and of Buddha's graciousness, man has become certain of redemption. Thus, certainty of salvation comes not through pious achievements but is unconditioned, and based on faith, so that one has every right to say: *by faith alone.*

This faith finds its outer expression in pronouncing *the name of Amida Buddha:* in *nembutsu,* as it is solemnly sung in the Shin liturgy. Shinran was convinced that Amida Buddha revealed his name in his promise, and that one need only pronounce this name in faith to be reborn in the Pure Land. Needless to say, a mechanical or mantra-like recitation of the name (as Shinran sometimes did up to sixty thousand times a day for himself and others) is not enough. (Shinran helped to stamp out magic and superstition in Buddhism.) What is required is that one pronounce the name in deep trust and great thankfulness: "Namu [worship] Amida butsu [buddha]!" By expressing one's faith (perhaps only a single time), a person can arrive at the Pure Land and there finally obtain enlightenment. Popular Amidism, in this case, thinks less of nirvāna and more in terms of a kind of eternal life.

Yet the reader will have already noticed that *faith* in this teaching is not directed toward the objectified person of the Buddha or to specific doctrinal principles. Faith is not an achievement by the individual but freedom from one's own power and unconditioned trust of the believing heart in the other power which is the promise of Amida Buddha. The Amida Buddha himself effects faith in man by embracing everyone, worthy or unworthy, with the light of his compassion. No one is excluded or rejected.

When Buddha turns toward man, the result is a conversion, *a turning of the heart.* One can feel it; it is entirely spontaneous, "natural," "instantaneous." This means that even in this world of suffering the believer can be sure of his salvation. He no longer falls back into the fleeting illusion of this world, since he has been accepted by the Amida—and is born in the Pure Land. For Shinran, this *birth in the Pure Land* is no longer, as it was for Hōnen, a mere future event beyond the grave. Rather, it occurs in a moment of tension like that between the "already" and the "not yet" of the New Testament's proclamation of the Kingdom of God—*in the moment of coming-to-faith.* The Pure Land is realized where the individual believes, dismisses his own strength, and recognizes that on his own he can do nothing. Where there is no longer any egoism, any suffering, any fear, where the false ego is overcome, there the Pure Land will already have become a reality. There are some possible cross connections here between Zen (using *nembutsu* for meditation) and Shin (using "emptiness" to interpret the Amida).

Without long explication, the convergence between all this and Christian faith is evidently great. The New Testament agrees that man is not saved by his pious achievements, not by asceticism and not by meditation, but on the strength of Christ's promises, by unconditional trust in the power of another, the "power" of God, by faith alone.

And yet with this sort of faith, the question arises on both sides about the historical foundations of religion. One reason for asking it here is the fact that Shinran's contemporary the nationalistic, belligerent, and intolerant Nichiren (whose name is invoked by the millions of Japanese adherents of lay religions such as Sōka-gakkai [founded in 1930], Reiyū-kai [1925], and Risshō-Kōseīkai [1938]) abruptly replaced the *nembutsu* with the invocation of the Lotus Sūtra. Faith in Christ has historical foundations, though these are more modest than Christian dogmatics often high-handedly but uncritically assumes. Does faith in Amida rest on solid ground?

BUDDHOLOGY AND CHRISTOLOGY

Clearly, Buddhology has in many ways evolved as far away from the historical Gautama as Christology has from the historical Jesus of Nazareth. In both cases, the preacher became the subject of preaching, and the one who pointed the way became for his own group of followers the supernatural bringer of salvation and universal savior of mankind. Beyond that, in both cases events took on a cosmic dimension, history was extended in thought to infinity: into the "protological" (Ādi-Buddha, or Primal Buddha, the origin of all Buddhas and higher beings) above time and into the eschatological (the future Buddha Maitreya) at the end of time. In both cases, dogmatic thinkers take endless pains to define precisely the nature and qualities of the savior.

Nonetheless, the very use of the plural, *"the Buddhas,"* calls attention to the crucial *difference* here: The Christ-event is bound up with *concrete history* in a way quite different from the Buddha-event. The earthly Jesus could never have been turned into a figure of such indifference as the earthly Gautama was. Never were Christ's earthly life and its completion presented as a sort of pedagogical game. In the Mahāyāna Lotus Sūtra, for example, a timeless, transcendent Buddha, out of compassion for living creatures, through meditation projects his own life (almost "docetically") onto earth, in order to show a perfectly virtuous human being as an example for the way to salvation. And, above all, given the historical rootedness of Christianity, the idea of multiplying Christ over and over is unthinkable. Theravāda, as we have seen, knew six predecessors of the Buddha by name; later it spoke of twenty-eight Buddhas. Still later on in Mahāyāna there would be thousands, indeed an infinite number of Buddhas in every region of the world and in every period, as many Buddhas as the grains of sand on the banks of the Ganges. And Amitābha, or Amida, is only one of these innumerable, transcendent Buddhas (Sambhogakāya)—though easily the most beloved. Once again, the multiplicity of world periods and buddha figures illustrates the gap between prophetic-historic and mystical-cyclical religion.

Educated Buddhists have often objected heatedly to the sort of historical questions I have posed. To ask them, they say, is to indulge in a typically Western inclination and mount history on top of myth. We cannot, of course, simply make history the universal religious criterion. But our historical reflections and the distinctions they have pointed up might have demonstrated even to a Buddhist the importance of asking questions about the Buddha of history as well as the importance of analyzing the epochal paradigm change from primitive Buddhism to Shrāvakayāna and from Shrāvakayāna to Mahāyāna or Vajrayāna. In other words, like Christianity, traditional Buddhism will not be spared a process of "demythologizing," something that Western Buddhism scholarship in the person of Heinz Bechert and modern Buddhists as well have already taken into account today. And that means critical analysis of "obsolete cosmologies and other outdated ideas," of "belief in miracles and other elements of irrational thinking"—not excluding the problems of Buddhology.

This sort of historicocritical reflection is something that must also be applied to this Mahāyāna paradigm, which might be called the *devotional paradigm* of Shin Buddhism, to distinguish it from the syncretistic paradigm of Tantra and the reformist paradigm of Zen. In opposition to the ceremonial-clerical, "medieval" Mahāyāna, this paradigm urgently promotes simplification, greater democratization, and concentration on believing submission to Amida Buddha, and thus, in its own independent fashion, sweeps away the fundamental conflict, which had been present from the first, between monastic and lay piety. If we could compare the paradigm change of Zen vis-à-vis the "medieval" Mahāyāna to the Enlightenment (in an overly rational sense), then the paradigm of Shin would be most comparable to that of the Reformation: from the standpoint of content it is a paradigm of faith.

For the past two hundred years, Christians have subjected their faith to an exhausting, crisis-racked process of enlightenment, and have learned to distinguish between history and myth, authentic and in-authentic, original and derivative material in their biblical traditions—without ceasing to be Christians. It proved possible critically to work out a *new correlation of historical events and transhistorical reality,* so that they could echo the words of the New Testament: ". . . we did not follow cleverly devised myths when we made known to you the power and coming of our Lord Jesus Christ . . ." (2 Pet 1:16)

Shin Buddhism, too, for all the differences of accent, emphasizes this correlation: Faith in the great, gracious, compassionate power of the Amida Buddha is firmly bound up with the history of the monk Dharmākara (which is presumed to be a historical event). But must not this faith crumble if Dharmākara can no longer be viewed (even by scholars who are Buddhists themselves) as a historical figure and has to be acknowledged as only mythological?

Critical-minded Buddhists, especially from Japan, are now beginning to face the problems of *historical research,* from which they have various solutions ready, as American theologian John Cobb reports in his *Beyond Dialogue: Toward a Mutual Transformation of Christianity and Buddhism* (1982). What this leading representative of Buddhist-Christian dialogue has to say should give us pause:

> Jōdoshinshū has not yet worked through the crisis of the relation of history to faith. If this crisis must be faced, then in some respects its problems are more acute even than those faced by Christianity, for its basis is still further removed from the actual course of history. It can indeed find in Gautama himself and in the history of Buddhism much to support it, but its most distinctive teaching is the one that is least adequately supported in this tradition prior to Shinran himself. (p. 139)

Then Cobb takes a long step that only a few Buddhists, I would think, will be ready to take with him:

> However, there is nothing about Buddhist self-understanding that leads to the necessity of finding the requisite history solely in India and East Asia. On the contrary, Buddhism intends universality. It, too, needs an inclusive view of all things, and today such a view must include world history. World history includes the history of Israel and the event of Jesus. The history that supports the Christian understanding of the graciousness of God supports equally the Jōdoshinshū understanding of the wisdom and compassion that characterize ultimate reality. It provides also the grounds for a desirable expansion of the Pure Land Buddhist understanding of Amida. (pp. 139–40)

John Cobb is obviously under no illusions. Yet he claims we can imagine that once the still ongoing phase of "mutual suspicion and defensiveness" is past, Shin Buddhism may look to Christian history for support. ". . . once that attitude is truly superseded, there is no reason in principle why Buddhists cannot internalize the Palestinian as well as the Indian past. It is in Palestine, rather than in India, that history, when it is read as centering in Jesus, provides the strongest basis for believing that we are saved by grace through faith." (p. 140) Is this an all too bold vision for Buddhist-Christian dialogue, which is still in its infancy?

I would like to extend this train of thought a bit and to conclude this difficult dialogue by returning to that key Buddhist difficulty with Christianity that came up when I spoke of the difference between the smiling Buddha and the suffering Christ.

SUFFERING AND FULFILLMENT

Gautama, too, was a person who could suffer, and in that he was not essentially different from Jesus. For, on the way to enlightenment, Gautama was a bodhisattva who was not exempt from suffering. Might not the Nazarene likewise be understood by Buddhists as a bodhisattva?

Admittedly, Buddhists say that the bodhisattva Gautama succeeded, even during this earthly existence, in attaining enlightenment and becoming a Buddha. And the "bodhisattva" Jesus? Buddhists have always had their doubts. For them it is simply unthinkable that a truly Enlightened, Redeemed One should have to suffer so unfathomably, as the scenes of the Via Dolorosa, from the Mount of Olives to Calvary, show them with such drastic realism. The Buddha Gautama was completely different here. As an Enlightened One, the Buddha stood *above* suffering, for whoever has recognized through meditation the nature of suffering, its causes, and the way to overcome it, and has given up all ambitions and attachments, may still register suffering, but it can no longer touch his self, because it is no longer a true self. This is what Buddhist art has always portrayed, accentuating the smiling composure and peaceful detachment of the Enlightened One.

To be sure, the Buddha could and had to suffer, even bleed, after his enlightenment. We hear of his being sick and being wounded by an enemy (since then, "making the Buddha bleed" has been called one of the five gravest sins in Buddhism); and finally, the Buddha had to die, from the most trivial of causes. But as the one who had been enlightened beyond suffering, the Buddha transcended it—even here and now in this life.

This must be the reason why Buddhist art shied away from showing the Buddha's suffering pictorially. Buddhology, in fact, early on developed a tendency to repress it completely. In Mahāyāna there are tendencies, such as the Lotus Sūtra, that maintain that the Buddha suffered in his preexistence as a bodhisattva, but not in his life as the Buddha. The figure of the Buddha gets exalted to such an extent that he is said to have had only the semblance of birth, suffering, and death.

Christian theology too has always been tempted to play down or repress Jesus' suffering, or to see it literally as a problem of mere semblance. The Christian world quickly rejected such Hellenistically inspired Docetism, at least in its radical form, as totally contrary to the New Testament image of Jesus. Jesus' humanness—which means suffering, dying, and death—was therefore never concealed, but taken with radical seriousness.

But how could this man, who died in such an ignominiously human fashion, be an Awakened, an Enlightened One? For Christians, too, this shameful death on the cross was at first a sign of failure and not of salvation. Only because, as the community bore witness, this suffering and dying person did not remain in death, but died into an ultimate reality that Christians call God, does the cross receive another, positive meaning, a different key signature. In other words, only through the "resuscitation" to new, eternal life did Jesus become the truly "Awakened One," the definitively "Enlightened One." Only now was he proclaimed, in Christian language, as the "Lord," "Messiah," "Christ," as the "Image, Word, Son of God," "the Light of the World," "the way, the truth, and the life." Only now, therefore, did his suffering come to an end, and did faith see his continued effective presence in the community as a spiritual reality: ". . . the Lord is the Spirit . . ," says Paul. (2 Cor 3:17)

Only now did Christians dare to understand the Absolute itself in a new way: In the light of Jesus' cross and resurrection, it was possible to speak of *God's com–passion,* of a unique "solidarity" on the part of God, precisely with the suffering, the humiliated, the exploited, those who had been abandoned unto death. In this way, everything negative in the world was taken seriously in all its reality, but finally sublated positively into infinity.

And "where" did the Buddha go, if nirvāna is not to be understood nihilistically, as pure nothingness? Early on in Buddhism there were already difficulties with the idea that the Buddha Gautama was simply no more. A spirit-body was attributed to him; in fact he was identified with the dharma-body, with the Absolute itself. For Amida Buddhism, the Buddha is ultimately an *eternal* Buddha, the Buddha of *eternal life,* the direct representation of the highest reality. As such, he manifested himself in the Buddha Gautama.

Does this not make it clear that the ways to liberation from all suffering for Buddhists and Christians, who take the Buddha or the Christ as their standard, were originally different, but not simply divergent? In Buddhism as it originally was, we find the trust that one can reach the exit from this prison of sorrow and the entrance to the Absolute, through one's own efforts and even in this life; in Christianity we find the trust that redemption from all suffering can be attained through the power of Another only at the end of life through entrance into the

Absolute. The very fact that certain forms of Buddhism view salvation in a similar way ought to guard us from exaggerating this contrast.

The decisive point here is that Christianity and Buddhism stand or fall with the hope that the ultimate, *the definitive reality is without suffering*. The Christian stresses that this definitive reality is a *life* without suffering, a life that man himself can never produce either through his own individual or collective/social exertions, but that he may look forward to from the ultimate and original reality, to whom he has committed himself in rational trust—as he waits for the definitive abolition of all suffering in the fulfillment of *eternal life.*

This promise of a future without suffering is not a prophecy designed to gratify our curiosity, and certainly not a demand that we resign ourselves to the status quo. On the contrary, for those who have taken their "refuge" in Christ, who have committed themselves to his way, those in whom Christ lives, for them the old person with his egoism *has* already been "crucified," the new person *has* already become a living reality: the old has passed away, the new has come into being. To that extent, Christians, too, have received from Christ, *even now,* amid this life, liberation, redemption, enlightenment: ". . . he who follows me will not walk in darkness, but will have the light of life." (John 8:12) "Enlightenment" amid this life: Are the ways of Buddhism and Christianity really as contrary as the different traditional schools of thought insist?

Suffering still not overcome and the threat of death are and remain signs, at least for the Christian, that the fulfillment of humanity has yet to come, that man is to trust not in himself, but in the ultimate, true reality. Here he has been shown a path between *superbia* and *desperatio,* between presumption and despair. The Christian promise is that "another force" is at work precisely in our weakness, that "another power" has revealed itself just where we are powerless. And that is just what makes possible a *freedom from suffering* that can already be experienced amid our suffering.

In other words, Christians hold to the promise, inseparably bound up with Christ, that suffering is not a simply meaningless fact, not just the consequence of an all-encompassing world order, of the thirst for life and of earlier actions, but that suffering, even when it seems meaningless, is wrapped around by a comprehensive meaning. A meaning, though, that will shine forth for all to see only in the future consummation, that is, when all suffering, all evil, all death will be wiped away in what will then be revealed as the heart of the world, that depth and center of man, that mystery of reality, in which we already now "live and move and have our being." (Acts 17:28)

Basic Readings on Buddhism

GENERAL
1. *The World of Buddhism*. Eds. Heinz Bechert and Richard Gombrich. London, 1984.
2. Edward Conze. *A Short History of Buddhism*. London, 1966.
3. Helmuth von Glasenapp. *Buddhism, A Non-Theistic Religion*. London, 1966.
4. Christmas Humphreys. *Popular Dictionary of Buddhism*. 2nd ed. London, 1976.
5. Nyanatiloka. *Buddhist Dictionary*. 3rd ed. Colombo, 1972. Repr., 1983.
6. Richard H. Robinson. *The Buddhist Religion, A Historical Introduction*. Belmont, Calif., 1970.
7. Hans Wolfgang Schumann. *Buddhism: An Outline of Its Teachings and Schools*. Wheaton, Ill., 1974.

FOR PARTS I AND II
1. Hermann Oldenberg. *Buddha, His Life, His Doctrine, His Order*. London, 1882. Repr., Delhi, 1971.
2. Étienne Lamotte. *Histoire du bouddhisme indien. Des origines à l'ère sáka*. Louvain, 1958. Repr., 1976.
3. A. K. Warder. *Indian Buddhism*, 2nd. ed. Delhi, 1980.
4. Walpola Rahula. *What the Buddha Taught*. 2nd ed. New York, 1974. Repr., 1982.
5. Nyanaponika. *The Heart of Buddhist Meditation*. 5th ed London, 1975.
6. Winston L. King. *Theravāda-Meditation: The Buddhist Transformation of Yoga*. University Park, Penna., 1980.
7. Kanai Lal Hazra. *History of Theravāda Buddhism in South-East Asia*. New Delhi, 1982.

FOR PART III
1. Helmut Hoffmann. *The Religions of Tibet*. London, 1961. Repr., 1979.
2. Giuseppe Tucci. *The Religions of Tibet*. London, 1980.
3. K. K. S. Ch'en. *Buddhism in China: A Historical Study*. Princeton, 1964. Repr., 1972.
4. John Blofeld. *The Way of Power: A Practical Guide to the Tantric Mysticism of Tibet*. London, 1970.
5. Joseph Kitagawa. *Religion in Japanese History*. New York and London, 1966.
6. Heinrich Dumoulin. *A History of Zen Buddhism*. New York and Boston, 1963.

FOR PART IV

1. *Buddhism in the Modern World.* Eds. Heinrich Dumoulin and John C. Maraldo. New York/London, 1976.
2. Heinz Bechert. *Buddhismus, Staat und Gesellschaft in den Ländern des Theravāda-Buddhismus.* 3 vols. Frankfurt/Wiesbaden, 1966–73.
3. Trevor Ling. *Buddhist Revival in India: Aspects of the Sociology of Buddhism.* London, 1980.

SELECTED TEXTS

1. Steven Beyer. *The Buddhist Experience: Sources and Interpretations.* Encino Belmont, Calif., 1974.
2. Edward Conze. *Buddhist Scriptures.* 6th ed. Harmondsworth, 1959. Repr., 1971.
3. Henry Clark Warren. *Buddhism in Translations.* 11th ed. New York, 1982.
4. Nyanatiloka. *The Word of the Buddha, An Outline of the Teaching of the Buddha in the Words of the Pali Canon.* 14th ed. Kandy, 1967.
5. *The Teaching of Buddha.* Ed. Bukkyo Dendo Kyokai (Buddhist Promoting Foundation). 235th ed. Tokyo, 1982.

Hans Küng: No World Peace Without Religious Peace

Concluding Word

This dialogue was not supposed to be anything more than an interim report. It was, as explained, an attempt, a risky experiment, and it is not for me to say whether it succeeded.

In its course, certain convergences and divergences between the religions have become clear. And if we have managed to clarify the one question of what religious dialogue no longer has to argue over and what it does, we will have achieved a great deal.

The Christian Responses in particular will be criticized—presumably from both sides. For some they will be too "Christian"; for others, not "Christian" enough; for some, too open, too yielding, too pluralistic; for others, too narrow, too limiting, too self-conscious.

I have aimed at offering responses, above and beyond the structure of this book, that could meet the criteria not of every official manual of Christian dogmatics, but of historicocritical exegesis and religious history within the framework of a contemporary paradigm of theology. And at the same time, these responses were designed to be given in a coherent fashion to religions as utterly different as Islam, Hinduism, and Buddhism, so that some points would not be conceded to one of them and then have to be retracted when dealing with the others.

Why must dialogue go on? First of all, in order to get an increasingly better understanding of our contemporaries, the men and women with whom our lives are becoming ever more closely linked. But also to understand ourselves better, which we can do only through comparison and encounter. "If you only know England, you don't know England." And thirdly, because interreligious dialogue is anything but a private, personal, local, or regional matter. Its global dimensions are obvious, and so are its repercussions on the communal life of the nation and the world. These days, nobody would seriously dispute the fact that peace in the world very much depends on peace among the various religions. And in an age when the technology for an atomic holocaust is already in place, this aspect of religious dialogue is more important than all the meticulous academic precision, theological subtlety, and intellectual sophistry.

There is, then, a significant connection between ecumenism and world peace. Anyone who feels a sense of obligation toward the world community and who takes seriously the fragility of all human arrangements, who has glimpsed all the possibilities of technical and human error, must know what is at stake here. He must know that the threats to peace and the need to regulate it have long since burst through the dimension of specific, regional conflict, and have become global political problems, on which the survival of us all depends. The *alternative today is peace in the ecumene (inhabited world) or destruction of the ecumene itself.*

What can an ecumenical theology contribute to the pacification of our warlike world? Surely no direct solutions for all the complex questions of strategy, military-industrial technology, and disarmament. That is not its original and primary responsibility, anyway.

Its very own domain of reflection and action—and even scientists and politicians are beginning once again to pay more attention to this ethical-religious dimension—is behavior, morality, religion. And *here* ecumenical theology can help to discover and work through the conflicts caused by the religions, confessions, and denominations themselves. And there are a great many structures of conflict that will have to be dismantled.

Everyone knows how much disaster has been occasioned in politics by *religious strife among Christians.* One need only recall Northern Ireland to realize what I mean. And Catholic-Protestant antagonism was likely a contributing factor, at least subliminally, to the insane war over the Falkland Islands; just as the feelings of superiority and efforts to win hegemony by Protestant Yankees in Catholic Central and South America —and the reactions to them—have always borne the stamp of culture and religion.

What have the churches done to oppose this? True, they have *spoken* for peace and not for war, at least in recent days, and that is a good deal.

Generally they have done this speaking, to be sure, only where they could do so without any risk. But have they *done* enough for peace: in Vietnam, in Lebanon, in Argentina, in Great Britain, in Germany, in Europe and America, Africa and Asia? Let me say it once more, unmistakably: Religions, Christianity, the Church, cannot solve or prevent all the world's conflicts, but they can lessen the amount of hostility, hatred, and intransigence. They can, first, intervene concretely for the sake of understanding and reconciliation between estranged peoples. And second, they can begin to do away with at least the conflicts of which they themselves are the cause and for whose explosiveness they are partly to blame: They can settle the doctrinal (and ensuing practical) differences that have divided the Church.

This is not demanding the impossible of religions and the churches, it is merely asking them to live up to their own programs and basic intentions, asking them to direct their appeals for peace not only toward the outside (important as that is), but to the inside as well, and thus to do deeds of reconciliation and set up signs of peace in their own backyards. We can be sure that these deeds of reconciliation, that these signs of peace, will not fail to radiate powerful signals onto the fields of conflict "out there."

Furthermore, there is no denying that the great world *religions themselves* (and not just Christian denominations or ideologies that have swollen into quasi religions) share the responsibility for some of the most *notorious powder kegs in the world*. Looking from the Far East to the Near East, no one could fail to see that in the Vietnam War there were religious factors at work (antagonism between Buddhist monks and the Catholic regime); that the conflict between India and Pakistan, the territorial split that occurred against the will of Mahatma Gandhi, has to this day fed on the irreconcilable hostility between Hindus and Muslims, continually leading to new massacres (not to mention the blood shed by Indians and Sikhs); that the war between Iraq and Iran has roots in the centuries-old inner-Muslim rivalry and enmity between Sunnites and Shiites?

This is to pass over the Middle Eastern conflict, where, as everyone knows, Muslims, Jews, and Christians confront each other, armed to the teeth, and where they have already lacerated one another in the fifth war within the past few decades.

The most fanatical, the cruelest political struggles are those that have been colored, inspired, and legitimized by religion. To say this is not to reduce all political conflicts to religious ones, but to take seriously the fact that religions *share* in the responsibility for bringing peace to our torn and warring world. Christians, Jews, and Muslims, Hindus and Buddhists, are facing the same challenge. The peoples in question and the rest of the world would have been spared tremendous grief if the world religions had recognized sooner their responsibility for peace, love of neighbor, and nonviolence, for reconciliation and forgiveness—as exemplified by the Hindu Mahatma Gandhi, the Christian Dag Hammarskjöld, the Muslim Anwar el-Sadat, and the Buddhist U Thant, all of whom promoted the politics of peace out of religious conviction.

To sum up, ecumenical dialogue is today anything but the specialty of a few starry-eyed religious peaceniks. For the first time in history, it has now taken on the character of an urgent desideratum for world politics. It can help to make our earth more livable, by making it more peaceful and more reconciled.

There will be no peace among the peoples of this world without peace among the world religions.

There will be no peace among the world religions without peace among the Christian churches.

The community of the Church is an integral part of the world community.

Ecumenism *ad intra,* concentrated on the Christian world, and ecumenism *ad extra,* oriented toward the whole inhabited earth, are interdependent.

Peace is indivisible: it begins within us.

A Word of Thanks

The publication of such a thematically wide-ranging book at such an early date was possible for me only because I could count on two things: the division of labor and studies "on location."

1. This relieved me, the Christian theologian, of the burden of having to present the world religions in their complex history and themes. I was able instead to rely on the interdisciplinary division of labor between religious studies and theology. I am heartily grateful to my colleagues at Tübingen, Professors Josef van Ess and Heinrich von Stietencron, as well as to Professor Heinz Bechert of Göttingen (who was helped in the last phase of preparing the manuscript on Buddhism by Licentiate Alois Payer, research assistant to the Tübingen Chair for Indology), for joining with me in this unusual venture in dialogue and for advising me on difficult problems in their respective disciplines.

2. But my "Christian Responses" would never have been possible without the manifold support and encouragement that I have received since my first trip to Asia, twenty years ago, from numerous colleagues all over the world. I have learned a great deal, especially during the guest seminars I gave at the University of Chicago; at the University of Michigan, Ann Arbor; and at scholarly symposiums in Bombay, Peking, Tokyo, Honolulu, and Toronto. If I were to list the names of all the people from whose conversations and publications I have been able to learn, I would never come to an end. On behalf of all the others, let me name just a few of those who were of particular importance in preparing this manuscript: in North America, Julia Ching, Professor of Sinology, and her husband, Willard Oxtoby, Professor of Religious Studies (both now at the University of Toronto); Professor Mircea Eliade, Professor of Religion at the University of Chicago; Luis Gómez, a Professor of Buddhist Studies at the University of Michigan, Ann Arbor; finally the eminent Christian students of Buddhism Professor John Cobb (School of Theology of the Claremont Colleges) and Professor David Chappell (University of Hawaii), who performed an invaluable service by organizing the East-West Religions Encounter Conference at the University of Hawaii, which I was able to attend, in January 1984. For my friends in Tokyo, Nagoya, and Kyoto, let me mention Professor Hajime Nakamura of Tokyo University and Professor Heinrich Dumoulin of Sophia University; I am grateful both for the help provided by their important printed work and for their stimulating personal suggestions. Many valuable contacts were arranged for me in Thailand by Professor Seri Phongphit (Bangkok), in Burma by Dr. Kyaw Than (Rangoon); in Nepal by the German Consul, Annemarie Spahr; finally in Pakistan by Professor Riffat Hassan, Professor of Islamic Studies at the University of Louisville, who also organized for me some private conversations and public dialogues with Muslims, which I found most helpful, in her native country. I am grateful to Professor Joseph Neuner, S.J. (Poona) for my first invitation to India, in 1964, and to the American University in Beirut for my first invitation to visit the Middle East, in 1967.

In Tübingen I was able once again to rely on the trustworthy staff of the Institute for Ecumenical Research for the technical execution of this study. Among the readers at Piper Verlag I could always count on the work of Mrs. Renate Böhme and Mr. Uwe Steffen, who also had the difficult job of putting together the register of names. I am particularly grateful to my secretaries, Mrs. Eleonore Henn and Mrs. Hannelore Türke, for their endless patience with the continual revisions of the manuscript, to theologian Karl-Heinz Rauch for all his trouble in checking quotations, obtaining books, and correcting galleys, a labor shared by Dr. Anne Jensen. Mrs. Marianne Saur read this manuscript over and over again and gave me many valuable suggestions with an eye to making it more intelligible and readable. Most of all, however, I would like to repay my debt of gratitude for this book to Dr. Karl-Joseph Kuschel, Academic Advisor to our Institute, who has been in constant close collaboration with me on it and who contributed countless improvements, in form and content, to the manuscript.

It has been five years now since we were forced to change the status of our Institute at the University of Tübingen. This involved some nerve-racking confrontations, but I am grateful that we have found the strength to set off, theologically, toward new shores. In this regard I would also like publicly to thank all our friends in Tübingen and else-

where whose support we could feel all along. This is particularly important to me now that the Institute is celebrating its twentieth anniversary.

Tübingen, July 1984

HANS KÜNG

Indexes

INDEX OF SUBJECTS